Principles of Management

ISBN: 978-0-9986257-6-8

OpenStax
Rice University
6100 Main Street MS-375
Houston, Texas 77005

To learn more about OpenStax, visit https://openstax.org.
Individual print copies and bulk orders can be purchased through our website.

HARDCOVER BOOK ISBN-13	**978-0-9986257-6-8**
PAPERBACK BOOK ISBN-13	**978-1-947172-94-4**
B&W PAPERBACK BOOK ISBN-13	**978-1-59399-876-9**
DIGITAL VERSION ISBN-13	**978-0-9986257-7-5**
ORIGINAL PUBLICATION YEAR	**2019**

10 9 8 7 6 5 4 3 2 1

Printed by

XanEdu

4750 Venture Drive, Suite 400
Ann Arbor, MI 48108
800-562-2147
www.xanedu.com

OpenStax

OpenStax provides free, peer-reviewed, openly licensed textbooks for introductory college and Advanced Placement® courses and low-cost, personalized courseware that helps students learn. A nonprofit ed tech initiative based at Rice University, we're committed to helping students access the tools they need to complete their courses and meet their educational goals.

Rice University

OpenStax, OpenStax CNX, and OpenStax Tutor are initiatives of Rice University. As a leading research university with a distinctive commitment to undergraduate education, Rice University aspires to path-breaking research, unsurpassed teaching, and contributions to the betterment of our world. It seeks to fulfill this mission by cultivating a diverse community of learning and discovery that produces leaders across the spectrum of human endeavor.

Philanthropic Support

OpenStax is grateful for our generous philanthropic partners, who support our vision to improve educational opportunities for all learners.

Laura and John Arnold Foundation	The Maxfield Foundation
Arthur and Carlyse Ciocca Charitable Foundation	Burt and Deedee McMurtry
Ann and John Doerr	Michelson 20MM Foundation
Bill & Melinda Gates Foundation	National Science Foundation
Girard Foundation	The Open Society Foundations
Google Inc.	Jumee Yhu and David E. Park III
The William and Flora Hewlett Foundation	Brian D. Patterson USA-International Foundation
Rusty and John Jaggers	The Bill and Stephanie Sick Fund
The Calvin K. Kazanjian Economics Foundation	Robin and Sandy Stuart Foundation
Charles Koch Foundation	The Stuart Family Foundation
Leon Lowenstein Foundation, Inc.	Tammy and Guillermo Treviño

TABLE OF CONTENTS

Preface

Welcome to *Principles of Management*, an OpenStax resource. This textbook was written to increase student access to high-quality learning materials, maintaining the highest standards of academic rigor at little to no cost.

About OpenStax

OpenStax is a nonprofit based at Rice University, and it's our mission to improve student access to education. Our first openly licensed college textbook was published in 2012, and our library has since scaled to over 30 books for college and AP® courses used by hundreds of thousands of students. OpenStax Tutor, our low-cost personalized learning tool, is being used in college courses throughout the country. Through our partnerships with philanthropic foundations and our alliance with other educational resource organizations, OpenStax is breaking down the most common barriers to learning and empowering students and instructors to succeed.

About OpenStax Resources

Customization

Principles of Management is licensed under a Creative Commons Attribution 4.0 International (CC BY) license, which means that you can distribute, remix, and build upon the content, as long as you provide attribution to OpenStax and its content contributors.

Because our books are openly licensed, you are free to use the entire book or pick and choose the sections that are most relevant to the needs of your course. Feel free to remix the content by assigning your students certain chapters and sections in your syllabus, in the order that you prefer. You can even provide a direct link in your syllabus to the sections in the web view of your book.

Instructors also have the option of creating a customized version of their OpenStax book. The custom version can be made available to students in low-cost print or digital form through their campus bookstore. Visit the Instructor Resources section of your book page on openstax.org for more information.

Art Attribution

In *Principles of Management,* most art contains attribution to its title, creator, or rights holder, host platform, and license within the caption. Because the art is openly licensed, anyone may reuse the art as long as they provide the same attribution to its original source.

Errata

All OpenStax textbooks undergo a rigorous review process. However, like any professional-grade textbook, errors sometimes occur. Since our books are web based, we can make updates periodically when deemed pedagogically necessary. If you have a correction to suggest, submit it through the link on your book page on openstax.org. Subject matter experts review all errata suggestions. OpenStax is committed to remaining transparent about all updates, so you will also find a list of past errata changes on your book page on openstax.org.

Format

You can access this textbook for free in web view or PDF through openstax.org, and for a low cost in print.

About *Principles of Management*

Principles of Management is designed to meet the scope and sequence requirements of the introductory course on management. This is a traditional approach to management using the leading, planning, organizing, and controlling approach. The table of contents of this book was designed to address two main themes. What are the variables that affect how, when, where, and why managers perform their jobs? What theories and techniques are used by successful managers at a variety of organizational levels to achieve and exceed objectives effectively and efficiently throughout their careers? Management is a broad business discipline, and the Principles of Management course covers many management areas such as human resource management and strategic management, as well behavioral areas such as motivation. No one individual can be an expert in all areas of management, so an additional benefit of this text is that specialists in a variety of areas have authored individual chapters. Finally, we all made an effort to present a balanced approach to gender and diversity throughout the text in the examples used, the photographs selected, and the use of both male (odd-numbered chapters) and female (even-numbered chapters) when referring to generic managers or employees.

Pedagogical Foundation

We have taken a structured approach in the writing of the chapters that reduces inconsistencies throughout and makes selecting topics to match the course syllabus easier for faculty.

Exploring Managerial Careers. Each chapter starts with a profile that describes a manager and illustrates how the content of the chapter is vital for a successful managerial career.

Consistent, integrated learning. Targeted learning outcomes are listed at the beginning of each chapter and then repeated throughout the chapter. The learning outcomes connect to the text and the additional resources that accompany *Principles of Management*. After reading each section, students can test their retention by answering the questions in the Concept Checks. Every learning goal is further reinforced by a summary at the end of the chapter.

Hundreds of business examples to bring concepts to life. This book is designed to speak to the typical student. We have done a lot of research about student needs, abilities, experiences, and interests, and then we have shaped the text around them. We have used experiences both inside and outside the classroom to create a book that is both readable and enjoyable. We believe that the real applications found throughout every chapter set the standard for readability and understanding of key concepts.

Learning business terminology, made easy. As students begin to study management, they will explore new words and concepts. To help them learn this language, we define each new term in the chapter, display the terms in bold, and offer a complete glossary at the end of the book.

Applied Features

Rather than provide a dry recitation of facts, we illustrate concepts with contemporary examples. In addition to the in-text examples, we have several boxed features that provide more extensive examples in areas of importance in today's business environment. Each of the boxed features described below includes a series of critical thinking questions to prompt the student to consider the implications of each business strategy.

Ethics in Practice. Ethics in Practice features demonstrate how businesses are responsible not only to the bottom line, but to providing goods and services in a responsible manner.

Managing Change. The turbulent business climate requires companies to adapt their business strategies in response to a variety of economic, social, competitive, and technological forces. The Managing Change feature highlights how businesses have altered their business strategies in response to these forces.

Catching the Entrepreneurial Spirit. This feature highlights the challenges and opportunities available in small businesses and other entrepreneurial ventures.

Managerial Leadership. It is generally agreed that in a turbulent business climate leadership is an important function of management that helps to maximize efficiency and to achieve organizational goals. Leaders initiate action, motivate organizations, provide guidance, build morale, and create a sense of confidence within the organization and to outside stakeholders.

Sustainability and Responsible Management. This feature highlights the knowledge, skills, tools, and self-awareness that are needed to become responsible managers. While the area of corporate social responsibility and sustainability has gained wide general support and commentary, these featured boxed items should provide the reader with insights of how managers can embed responsible practices in their careers.

Activities and Cases That Put Knowledge to Work

Principles of Management helps students develop a solid grounding in the skills that they can apply throughout their managerial careers. These skill-building activities and resources help build and polish competencies that future employers will value.

Chapter Review Questions. These questions provide a broad set of challenging questions that students can use to assure themselves that they have mastered the chapter concepts.

Management Skills Application Exercises. These activities at the end of each chapter present real-world challenges and provide assignment material for students to hone their business skills.

Managerial Decision Exercises. These activities provide assignment material that challenge students' decision-making processes. There are a variety of exercises for individual or team assignments.

Critical Thinking Case. The Critical Thinking case in each chapter invites students to explore business strategies of various companies, analyze business decisions, and prepare comments.

Additional Resources

Student and Instructor Resources

We've compiled additional resources for both students and instructors, including Getting Started Guides. Instructor resources require a verified instructor account, which you can apply for when you log in or create your account on openstax.org.

Instructor and student resources are typically available within a few months after the book's initial publication. Take advantage of these resources to supplement your OpenStax book.

Comprehensive instructor's manual. Each component of the instructor's manual is designed to provide maximum guidance for delivering the content in an interesting and dynamic manner. The instructor's manual includes an in-depth lecture outline, which is interspersed with lecture "tidbits" that allow instructors to add timely and interesting enhancements to their lectures.

Test bank. With nearly 2,000 true/false, multiple-choice, fill-in-the-blank, and short-answer questions in our test bank, instructors can customize tests to support a variety of course objectives. The test bank is available in Word format.

PowerPoint lecture slides. The PowerPoint slides provide images and descriptions as a starting place for instructors to build their lectures.

Community Hubs

OpenStax partners with the Institute for the Study of Knowledge Management in Education (ISKME) to offer Community Hubs on OER Commons—a platform for instructors to share community-created resources that support OpenStax books, free of charge. Through our Community Hubs, instructors can upload their own materials or download resources to use in their own courses, including additional ancillaries, teaching material, multimedia, and relevant course content. We encourage instructors to join the hubs for the subjects most relevant to your teaching and research as an opportunity both to enrich your courses and to engage with other faculty.

To reach the Community Hubs, visit **www.oercommons.org/hubs/OpenStax**.

Technology Partners

As allies in making high-quality learning materials accessible, our technology partners offer optional low-cost tools that are integrated with OpenStax books. To access the technology options for your text, visit your book page on openstax.org.

Contributing Authors

David S. Bright, Wright State University

Anastasia H. Cortes, Virginia Tech University

Donald G. Gardner, University of Colorado-Colorado Springs

Eva Hartmann, University of Richmond

Jason Lambert, Texas Woman's University

Laura M. Leduc, James Madison University

Joy Leopold, Webster University

Jeffrey Muldoon, Emporia State University

James S. O'Rourke, University of Notre Dame

K. Praveen Parboteeah, University of Wisconsin-Whitewater

Jon L. Pierce, University of Minnesota-Duluth

Monique Reece

Amit Shah, Frostburg State University

Siri Terjesen, American University

Joseph Weiss, Bentley University

Margaret A. White, Oklahoma State University

Reviewers

Susan Adams, Bentley University

Shane Bowyer, Minnesota State University

Kim S. Cameron, University of Michigan

Linda Davenport, Klamath Community College

Allyson Foster

John Goldberg, University of California-Davis

Regina Greenwood, Nova University

Gina Hagler

Nai H. Lamb, University of Tennessee at Chattanooga

Kristie J. Loescher, University of Texas

Marcia Marriott, Monroe Community College

Therese Madden, Notre Dame de Namur University

Eleonor Moore, Kirtland Community College

Robert McNulty, Bentley University

Jeffrey Muldoon, Emporia State University

John Parnell, University of North Carolina-Pembroke

Jim Pennypacker

Karli Peterson, Colorado State University

Raymond Pfang, Tarrant Community College

Jodell Raymond, Monroe Community College

Richard Savior, SUNY Empire State

Carolyn Stevenson, Kaplan University

Amit Shah, Frostburg State University

Linda Tancs

Maria Vitale, Chaffey College

Valerie Wallingford, Bemidji State University

Exhibit 1.1 (Credit: Steve Bowbrick/ flickr/ Attribution 2.0 Generic (CC BY 2.0))

Introduction

Learning Outcomes

After reading this chapter, you should be able to answer these questions:

1. What do managers do to help organizations achieve top performance?
2. What are the roles that managers play in organizations?
3. What are the characteristics that effective managers display?

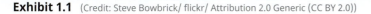

EXPLORING MANAGERIAL CAREERS

You

So, you're in this course and you may have pondered, or discussed with others, what this course will be about. You probably have some preconceptions of what management is all about. You must manage your time, deciding on how much study time you will devote to your management and accounting classes, for instance. You may have had a summer or part-time job where you had a manager whom you had to report to. You may have followed news reports on successful managers like Jeff Bezos of Amazon or Sheryl Sandberg of Facebook and want to learn what made them successful so you can emulate their practices in your business career. You may have the impression (not an accurate one) that management is basically just common sense and that you really don't need to take this course except that you must meet your degree requirement.

You may be an accounting or marketing major who is taking this class because it is required for completion of your degree requirements, but you don't think that you will ever require what you learn in this class during your career since you don't plan on applying for HR jobs upon graduation. If you're believing this, you could not be more mistaken. Regardless of where you are in your career, be it as an individual contributor, project leader, or middle or senior manager, what you will get out of this course will be valuable. If your first job out of college is as an accountant, sales representative, or another entry-level position, you will appreciate the roles that your managers, both direct and senior level, play in an organization and the behaviors and actions that will get you recognized and appreciated. Best of luck!

Most management textbooks would say, as does this one, that managers spend their time engaged in planning, organizing, staffing, directing, coordinating, reporting, and controlling. These activities, as Hannaway found in her study of managers at work, "do not, in fact, describe what managers do."[1] At best they seem to describe vague objectives that managers are continually trying to accomplish. The real world, however, is far from being that simple. The world in which most managers work is a "messy and hectic stream of ongoing activity."[2].

1.1 | What Do Managers Do?

1. What do managers do to help organizations achieve top performance?

Managers are in constant action. Virtually every study of managers in action has found that they "switch frequently from task to task, changing their focus of attention to respond to issues as they arise, and engaging in a large volume of tasks of short duration."[3] Mintzberg observed CEOs on the job to get some idea of what they do and how they spend their time. He found, for instance, that they averaged 36 written and 16 verbal contacts per day, almost every one of them dealing with a distinct or different issue. Most of these activities were brief, lasting less than nine minutes.[4]

Kotter studied a number of successful general managers over a five-year period and found that they spend most of their time with others, including subordinates, their bosses, and numerous people from outside the organization. Kotter's study found that the average manager spent just 25% of his time working alone, and that time was spent largely at home, on airplanes, or commuting. Few of them spent less than 70% of their time with others, and some spent up to 90% of their working time this way.[5]

Kotter also found that the breadth of topics in their discussions with others was extremely wide, with unimportant issues taking time alongside important business matters. His study revealed that managers rarely make "big decisions" during these conversations and rarely give orders in a traditional sense. They often react to others' initiatives and spend substantial amounts of time in unplanned activities that aren't on their calendars. He found that managers will spend most of their time with others in short, disjointed conversations. "Discussions of a single question or issue rarely last more than ten minutes," he notes. "It is not at all unusual for a general manager to cover ten unrelated topics in a five-minute conversation."[6] More recently, managers studied by Sproull showed similar patterns. During the course of a day, they engaged in 58 different activities with an average duration of just nine minutes.[7]

Interruptions also appear to be a natural part of the job. Stewart found that the managers she studied could work uninterrupted for half an hour only nine times during the four weeks she studied them.[8] Managers, in fact, spend very little time by themselves. Contrary to the image offered by management textbooks, they are rarely alone drawing up plans or worrying about important decisions. Instead, they spend most of their time interacting with others—both inside and outside the organization. If casual interactions in hallways, phone conversations, one-on-one meetings, and larger group meetings are included, managers spend about two-thirds of their time with other people.[9] As Mintzberg has pointed out, "Unlike other workers, the manager does not leave the telephone or the meeting to get back to work. Rather, these contacts are his work."[10]

The interactive nature of management means that most management work is conversational.[11] When managers are in action, they are talking and listening. Studies on the nature of managerial work indicate that managers spend about two-thirds to three-quarters of their time in verbal activity.[12] These verbal conversations, according to Eccles and Nohria, are the means by which managers gather information, stay on top of things, identify problems, negotiate shared meanings, develop plans, put things in motion, give orders, assert authority, develop relationships, and spread gossip. In short, they are what the manager's daily practice is all about. "Through other forms of talk, such as speeches and presentations," they write, "managers establish definitions and meanings for their own actions and give others a sense of what the organization is about, where it is at, and what it is up to."[13]

CONCEPT CHECK

1. What do managers do to help organizations achieve top performance?

1.2 The Roles Managers Play

2. What are the roles that managers play in organizations?

In Mintzberg's seminal study of managers and their jobs, he found the majority of them clustered around three core management roles.

Interpersonal roles. Managers are required to interact with a substantial number of people in the course of a workweek. They host receptions; take clients and customers to dinner; meet with business prospects and partners; conduct hiring and performance interviews; and form alliances, friendships, and personal relationships with many others. Numerous studies have shown that such relationships are the richest source of information for managers because of their immediate and personal nature.[14]

Three of a manager's roles arise directly from formal authority and involve basic interpersonal relationships. First is the *figurehead role*. As the head of an organizational unit, every manager must perform some ceremonial duties. In Mintzberg's study, chief executives spent 12% of their contact time on ceremonial duties; 17% of their incoming mail dealt with acknowledgments and requests related to their status. One example is a company president who requested free merchandise for a handicapped schoolchild.[15]

Managers are also responsible for the work of the people in their unit, and their actions in this regard are directly related to their role as a leader. The influence of managers is most clearly seen, according to Mintzberg, in the leader role. Formal authority vests them with great potential power. Leadership determines, in large part, how much power they will realize.[16]

Does the leader's role matter? Ask the employees of Chrysler Corporation (now DaimlerChrysler). When Lee Iacocca took over the company in the 1980s, the once-great auto manufacturer was in bankruptcy, teetering on the verge of extinction. He formed new relationships with the United Auto Workers, reorganized the senior management of the company, and—perhaps most importantly—convinced the U.S. federal government to guarantee a series of bank loans that would make the company solvent again. The loan guarantees, the union response, and the reaction of the marketplace were due in large measure to Iacocca's leadership style and personal charisma. More recent examples include the return of Starbucks founder Howard Schultz to re-energize and steer his company, and Amazon CEO Jeff Bezos and his ability to innovate during a downturn in the economy.[17]

Exhibit 1.2   Howard Schultz Howard Schultz, executive chairman of Starbucks Corporation, speaks after receiving the Distinguished Business Leadership Award during the Atlantic Council's Distinguished Leadership Awards dinner in Washington, D.C. The awards recognize pillars of the transatlantic relationship for their achievement in the fields of politics, military, business, humanitarian, and artistic leadership. (Credit: Chairman of the Joint Chief of Staff/ flickr/ Attribution 2.0 Generic (CC BY 2.0))

Popular management literature has had little to say about the liaison role until recently. This role, in which managers establish and maintain contacts outside the vertical chain of command, becomes especially important in view of the finding of virtually every study of managerial work that managers spend as much time with peers and other people outside of their units as they do with their own subordinates. Surprisingly, they spend little time with their own superiors. In Rosemary Stewart's study, 160 British middle and top managers spent 47% of their time with peers, 41% of their time with people inside their unit, and only 12% of their time with superiors. Guest's (1956) study of U.S. manufacturing supervisors revealed similar findings.[18]

Informational roles. Managers are required to gather, collate, analyze, store, and disseminate many kinds of information. In doing so, they become information resource centers, often storing huge amounts of information in their own heads, moving quickly from the role of gatherer to the role of disseminator in minutes. Although many business organizations install large, expensive management information systems to perform many of those functions, nothing can match the speed and intuitive power of a well-trained manager's brain for information processing. Not surprisingly, most managers prefer it that way.

As monitors, managers are constantly scanning the environment for information, talking with liaison contacts and subordinates, and receiving unsolicited information, much of it as a result of their network of personal contacts. A good portion of this information arrives in verbal form, often as gossip, hearsay, and speculation.

In the disseminator role, managers pass privileged information directly to subordinates, who might otherwise have no access to it. Managers must not only decide who should receive such information, but how much of it, how often, and in what form. Increasingly, managers are being asked to decide whether subordinates, peers, customers, business partners, and others should have direct access to information 24 hours a day without having to contact the manager directly.

In the spokesperson role, managers send information to people outside of their organizations: an executive makes a speech to lobby for an organizational cause, or a supervisor suggests a product modification to a supplier. Increasingly, managers are also being asked to deal with representatives of the news media, providing both factual and opinion-based responses that will be printed or broadcast to vast unseen audiences, often directly or with little editing. The risks in such circumstances are enormous, but so too are the potential rewards in terms of brand recognition, public image, and organizational visibility.

Decisional roles. Ultimately, managers are charged with the responsibility of making decisions on behalf of both the organization and the stakeholders with an interest in it. Such decisions are often made under circumstances of high ambiguity and with inadequate information. Often, the other two managerial roles—interpersonal and informational—will assist a manager in making difficult decisions in which outcomes are not clear and interests are often conflicting.

In the role of *entrepreneur*, managers seek to improve their businesses, adapt to changing market conditions, and react to opportunities as they present themselves. Managers who take a longer-term view of their responsibilities are among the first to realize that they will need to reinvent themselves, their product and service lines, their marketing strategies, and their ways of doing business as older methods become obsolete and competitors gain advantage.

While the entrepreneur role describes managers who initiate change, the *disturbance or crisis handler* role depicts managers who must involuntarily react to conditions. Crises can arise because bad managers let circumstances deteriorate or spin out of control, but just as often good managers find themselves in the midst of a crisis that they could not have anticipated but must react to just the same.

The third decisional role of *resource allocator* involves managers making decisions about who gets what, how much, when, and why. Resources, including funding, equipment, human labor, office or production space, and even the boss's time are all limited, and demand inevitably outstrips supply. Managers must make sensible decisions about such matters while still retaining, motivating, and developing the best of their employees.

Exhibit 1.3   Thomas Pendergast   Thomas F. Prendergast, the president of the Metropolitan Transit Authority of New York State, updates media on today's labor negotiations with the LIRR unions. In his role negotiating a new contract with the union, he must take on several managerial roles. (Credit: Metropolitan Transit Authority of New York State/ flickr/ Attribution 2.0 Generic (CC BY 2.0))

The final decisional role is that of *negotiator*. Managers spend considerable amounts of time in negotiations: over budget allocations, labor and collective bargaining agreements, and other formal dispute resolutions. In the course of a week, managers will often make dozens of decisions that are the result of brief but important negotiations between and among employees, customers and clients, suppliers, and others with whom managers must deal.[19] A visual interpretation of the roles managers play is illustrated in **Exhibit 1.4**.

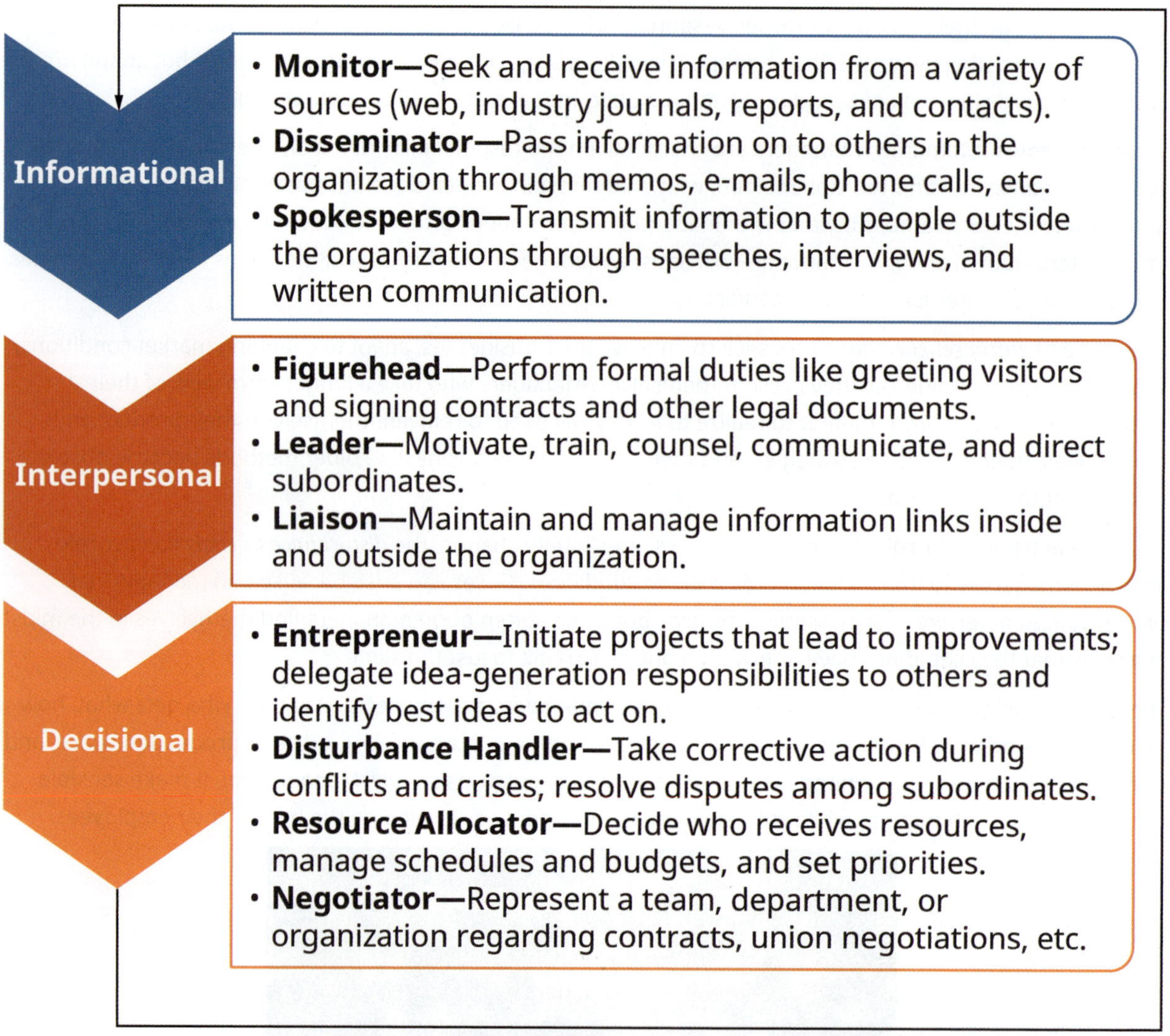

Informational
- **Monitor**—Seek and receive information from a variety of sources (web, industry journals, reports, and contacts).
- **Disseminator**—Pass information on to others in the organization through memos, e-mails, phone calls, etc.
- **Spokesperson**—Transmit information to people outside the organizations through speeches, interviews, and written communication.

Interpersonal
- **Figurehead**—Perform formal duties like greeting visitors and signing contracts and other legal documents.
- **Leader**—Motivate, train, counsel, communicate, and direct subordinates.
- **Liaison**—Maintain and manage information links inside and outside the organization.

Decisional
- **Entrepreneur**—Initiate projects that lead to improvements; delegate idea-generation responsibilities to others and identify best ideas to act on.
- **Disturbance Handler**—Take corrective action during conflicts and crises; resolve disputes among subordinates.
- **Resource Allocator**—Decide who receives resources, manage schedules and budgets, and set priorities.
- **Negotiator**—Represent a team, department, or organization regarding contracts, union negotiations, etc.

Exhibit 1.4   The Roles Managers Play (Attribution: Copyright Rice University, OpenStax, under CC-BY 4.0 license)

CONCEPT CHECK

1. Describe and explain how Mintzberg defines the manager's job.

1.3 | Major Characteristics of the Manager's Job

3. What are the characteristics that effective managers display?

Time is fragmented. Managers have acknowledged from antiquity that they never seem to have enough time to get all those things done that need to be done. In the latter years of the twentieth century, however, a new phenomenon arose: demand for time from those in leadership roles increased, while the number of hours in a day remained constant. Increased work hours was one reaction to such demand, but managers quickly discovered that the day had just 24 hours and that working more of them produced diminishing marginal returns. According to one researcher, "Managers are overburdened with obligations yet cannot easily delegate their tasks. As a result, they are driven to overwork and forced to do many tasks superficially. Brevity, fragmentation, and verbal communication characterize their work."[20]

Values compete and the various roles are in tension. Managers clearly cannot satisfy everyone. Employees want more time to do their jobs; customers want products and services delivered quickly and at high quality levels. Supervisors want more money to spend on equipment, training, and product development; shareholders want returns on investment maximized. A manager caught in the middle cannot deliver to each of these people what each most wants; decisions are often based on the urgency of the need and the proximity of the problem.

The job is overloaded. In recent years, many North American and global businesses were reorganized to make them more efficient, nimble, and competitive. For the most part, this reorganization meant decentralizing many processes along with the wholesale elimination of middle management layers. Many managers who survived such downsizing found that their number of direct reports had doubled. Classical management theory suggests that seven is the maximum number of direct reports a manager can reasonably handle. Today, high-speed information technology and remarkably efficient telecommunication systems mean that many managers have as many as 20 or 30 people reporting to them directly.

Efficiency is a core skill. With less time than they need, with time fragmented into increasingly smaller units during the workday, with the workplace following many managers out the door and even on vacation, and with many more responsibilities loaded onto managers in downsized, flatter organizations, efficiency has become the core management skill of the twenty-first century.

What Varies in a Manager's Job? The Emphasis

The entrepreneur role is gaining importance. Managers must increasingly be aware of threats and opportunities in their environment. Threats include technological breakthroughs on the part of competitors, obsolescence in a manager's organization, and dramatically shortened product cycles. Opportunities might include product or service niches that are underserved, out-of-cycle hiring opportunities, mergers, purchases, or upgrades in equipment, space, or other assets. Managers who are carefully attuned to the marketplace and competitive environment will look for opportunities to gain an advantage.

So is the leader role gaining importance. Managers must be more sophisticated as strategists and mentors. A manager's job involves much more than simple caretaking in a division of a large organization. Unless organizations are able to attract, train, motivate, retain, and promote good people, they cannot possibly hope to gain advantage over the competition. Thus, as leaders, managers must constantly act as mentors to those in the organization with promise and potential. When organizations lose a highly capable worker, all else in their world will come to a halt until they can replace that worker. Even if they find someone ideally suited and superbly qualified for a vacant position, they must still train, motivate, and inspire that new recruit, and live with the knowledge that productivity levels will be lower for a while than they were with their previous employee.

Managerial Responsibilities

An important question often raised about managers is: What responsibilities do managers have in organizations? According to our definition, managers are involved in planning, organizing, directing, and controlling. Managers have described their responsibilities that can be aggregated into nine major types of activity. These include:

1. *Long-range planning*. Managers occupying executive positions are frequently involved in strategic

planning and development.

2. *Controlling.* Managers evaluate and take corrective action concerning the allocation and use of human, financial, and material resources.

3. *Environmental scanning.* Managers must continually watch for changes in the business environment and monitor business indicators such as returns on equity or investment, economic indicators, business cycles, and so forth.

4. *Supervision.* Managers continually oversee the work of their subordinates.

5. *Coordinating.* Managers often must coordinate the work of others both inside the work unit and out.

6. *Customer relations and marketing.* Certain managers are involved in direct contact with customers and potential customers.

7. *Community relations.* Contact must be maintained and nurtured with representatives from various constituencies outside the company, including state and federal agencies, local civic groups, and suppliers.

8. *Internal consulting.* Some managers make use of their technical expertise to solve internal problems, acting as inside consultants for organizational change and development.

9. *Monitoring products and services.* Managers get involved in planning, scheduling, and monitoring the design, development, production, and delivery of the organization's products and services.

As we shall see, not every manager engages in all of these activities. Rather, different managers serve different roles and carry different responsibilities, depending upon where they are in the organizational hierarchy. We will begin by looking at several of the variations in managerial work.

Variations in Managerial Work

Although each manager may have a diverse set of responsibilities, including those mentioned above, the amount of time spent on each activity and the importance of that activity will vary considerably. The two most salient perceptions of a manager are (1) the manager's level in the organizational hierarchy and (2) the type of department or function for which he is responsible. Let us briefly consider each of these.

Management by Level. We can distinguish three general levels of management: executives, **middle management**, and **first-line management** (see **Exhibit 1.3**). **Executive managers** are at the top of the hierarchy and are responsible for the entire organization, especially its strategic direction. Middle managers, who are at the middle of the hierarchy, are responsible for major departments and may supervise other lower-level managers. Finally, first-line managers supervise rank-and-file employees and carry out day-to-day activities within departments.[21]

Executive
Management

Employees at the middle
and first-line level of
management might
also have managerial
responsibilities that
span departments as
the leader of a team.

Middle Management

First-Line Management

Rank-and-File Employees

Exhibit 1.5   Levels in the Management Hierarchy (Attribution: Copyright Rice University, OpenStax, under CC-BY 4.0 license)

Exhibit 1.5 shows differences in managerial activities by hierarchical level. Senior executives will devote more of their time to conceptual issues, while front-line managers will concentrate their efforts on technical issues. For example, top managers rate high on such activities as **long-range planning**, monitoring business indicators, coordinating, and internal consulting. Lower-level managers, by contrast, rate high on supervising because their responsibility is to accomplish tasks through rank-and-file employees. Middle managers rate near the middle for all activities. We can distinguish three types of managerial skills:

1. *Technical skills.* Managers must have the ability to use the tools, procedures, and techniques of their special areas. An accountant must have expertise in accounting principles, whereas a production manager must know operations management. These skills are the mechanics of the job.
2. *Human relations skills.* Human relations skills involve the ability to work with people and understand employee motivation and group processes. These skills allow the manager to become involved with and lead his group.
3. *Conceptual skills.* These skills represent a manager's ability to organize and analyze information in order to improve organizational performance. They include the ability to see the organization as a whole and to understand how various parts fit together to work as an integrated unit. These skills are required to coordinate the departments and divisions successfully so that the entire organization can pull together.

As shown in **Exhibit 1.6**, different levels of these skills are required at different stages of the managerial hierarchy. That is, success in executive positions requires far more conceptual skill and less use of technical skills in most (but not all) situations, whereas first-line managers generally require more technical skills and fewer conceptual skills. Note, however, that human relations skills, or people skills, remain important for success at all three levels in the hierarchy.

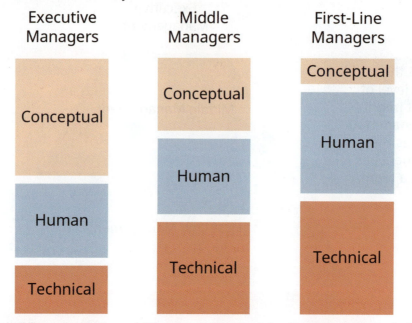

Exhibit 1.6   Difference in Skills Required for Successful Management According to Level in the Hierarchy (Attribution: Copyright Rice University, OpenStax, under CC-BY 4.0 license)

Management by Department or Function. In addition to level in the hierarchy, managerial responsibilities also differ with respect to the type of department or function. There are differences found for quality assurance, manufacturing, marketing, accounting and finance, and human resource management departments. For instance, manufacturing department managers will concentrate their efforts on products and services, controlling, and supervising. Marketing managers, in comparison, focus less on planning, coordinating, and consulting and more on customer relations and external contact. Managers in both accounting and human resource management departments rate high on long-range planning, but will spend less time on the organization's products and service offerings. Managers in accounting and finance are also concerned with controlling and with monitoring performance indicators, while human resource managers provide consulting expertise, coordination, and external contacts. The emphasis on and intensity of managerial activities varies considerably by the department the manager is assigned to.

At a personal level, knowing that the mix of conceptual, human, and technical skills changes over time and that different functional areas require different levels of specific management activities can serve at least two important functions. First, if you choose to become a manager, knowing that the mix of skills changes over time can help you avoid a common complaint that often young employees want to think and act like a CEO before they have mastered being a first-line supervisor. Second, knowing the different mix of management activities by functional area can facilitate your selection of an area or areas that best match your skills and interests.

In many firms managers are rotated through departments as they move up in the hierarchy. In this way they obtain a well-rounded perspective on the responsibilities of the various departments. In their day-to-day tasks they must emphasize the right activities for their departments and their managerial levels. Knowing what types of activity to emphasize is the core of the manager's job. In any event, we shall return to this issue when we address the nature of individual differences in the next chapter.

CONCEPT CHECK

1. Describe and explain the different levels of management.
2. Describe and explain the three types of managerial skills and how they relate to each level of management.

🔑 Key Terms

Decisional role One of the three major roles that a manager assumes in the organization.
executive managers Generally, a *team* of individuals at the highest level of *management* of an organization.
first-line management The level of management directly managing nonmanagerial employees.
Informational role One of the three major roles that a manager assumes in the organization.
Interpersonal role One of the three major roles that a manager assumes in the organization.
middle management The managers in an organization at a level just below that of senior executives.

📋 Summary of Learning Outcomes

1.1 What Do Managers Do?
1. What do managers do to help organizations achieve top performance?

Managers perform a variety of functions in organizations, but amongst one of the most important functions they perform is communicating with direct reports to help their organizations achieve and exceed goals.

1.2 The Roles Managers Play
2. What do managers do to help organizations achieve top performance?

Managers perform a variety of roles in organizations, but amongst one of the most important functions they perform is communicating with direct reports to help their organizations achieve and exceed goals. Managers perform three major types of roles within organizations, interpersonal roles, informational roles, and decisional roles. the extent of each of these roles depends on the manager's position within the organizational hierarchy.

1.3 Major Characteristics of the Manager's Job
3. What are the characteristics that effective managers display?

Management is the process of planning, organizing, directing, and controlling the activities of employees in combination with other resources to accomplish organizational goals. Managerial responsibilities include long-range planning, controlling, environmental scanning, supervision, coordination, customer relations, community relations, internal consulting, and monitoring of products and services. These responsibilities differ by level in the organizational hierarchy and by department or function. The twenty-first-century manager will differ from most current managers in four ways. In essence, he will be a global strategist, a master of technology, a good politician, and a premier leader-motivator.

📖 Chapter Review Questions

1. What are the characteristics and traits that you possess that are common to all successful managers?
2. Why should management be considered an occupation rather than a profession?
3. How do managers learn how to perform the job?
4. Explain the manager's job according to Henry Mintzberg.
5. What responsibilities do managers have towards people within the organization? How do they express these responsibilities?
6. How do managers perform their job according to John Kotter?
7. How do managers make rational decisions?

8. How does the nature of management change according to one's level and function in the organization?
9. Discuss the role of management in the larger societal context. What do you think the managers of the future will be like?
10. Identify what you think are the critical issues facing contemporary management. Explain.

Management Skills Application Exercises

1. During this and your other courses, there will likely be products of your and team-based assignments that can illustrate specific competencies such as the ability to prepare a spreadsheet application, write programming code, or show your communication abilities that demonstrate your skills in a video. It is a good practice to catalog and save these artifacts in a portfolio that will be a useful in demonstrating your skills in future job interviews.

2. Time management is an important skill that will impact your future as a manager. You can categorize the time that you spend as either required or discretionary. You can assess your time management skills by keeping track of your time using a schedule calendar and breaking down the time devoted to each activity over a week. After a week of logging the activity, note whether each activity was required or discretionary and whether the time was used productively or unproductively using a 10-point scale in which 10 is very productive and 1 is completely unproductive. Now write up a plan on how to manage your time by coming up with a list of what to start doing and stop doing and what you can do to manage your discretionary time more productively.

Managerial Decision Exercises

1. You are a manager at a local convenience store that has been the victim of graffiti. Identify the roles you will undertake with both internal employees and others.

2. Here are three job titles. Rank which job would devote the most of its time to conceptual, human, and technical skills.
   a. Vice president of finance at a Fortune 100 company
   b. Coding for a video game producer
   c. General manager at a local McDonald's franchise

Critical Thinking Case

New Management Challenges for the New Age

Today's news is littered with scandals, new allegations of sexual assault, and tragedy. Since 2017 and the #metoo Movement, stemming from the Harvey Weinstein scandal, more and more public figures have been put into the spotlight to defend themselves against allegations from women around the globe.

Not only publically, but privately in companies around the world, there have been firings, and investigations into misconduct from co-workers, managers, and CEOs. It is a relevant topic that is getting long overdue publicity and encouraging more men and women to come forward to discuss openly rather than hide the events and injustices of the past. Other events showcase the tumultuous and on-edge society we are living in, such as the Charlottesville, VA attack, that left 1 dead and 19 injured when a person drove a car through a crowd of protestors during a white nationalist gathering.

With events on a daily business, it is important for companies to take a stand against racial hatred, harassment of any kind, and have firm policies when such events occur. Take Netflix for example, who in July of 2018 fired chief communications officer for saying the "N-word" in full form. This event occurred during an internal meeting, not directing the slur at anyone specific, but claimed it was being made as an emphatic point about offensive words in comedy programming. The "Netflix way", the culture that is built around radical candor and transparency was put to the test during this occurrence.

The offender, Jonathan Friedland attempted to apologize for his misdeed, hoping it would fade away and his apology would be accepted. However, it didn't work that way, instead the anger was palpable between co-workers, and eventually led to the firing of Friedland after a few months of inaction.

Netflixers are given a high level of freedom and responsibility within their "Netflix way" culture. Blunt feedback is encouraged, trust and discretion is the ultimate gate keeper, as employees have access to sensitive information, and are ultimately trusted for how they expense items and take vacation time.

Between the insanely fast-paced streaming services industry, it is hard to keep this culture at a premium, but it is imperative for the success of the company overall. "As you scale a company to become bigger and bigger how do you scale that kind of culture?" said Colin Estep, a former senior engineer who left voluntarily in 2016. "I don't know that we ever had a good answer."

In order to keep up, sometimes the company is seen as harsh in their tactics to keep the best of the best. "I think we're transparent to a fault in our culture and that can come across as cutthroat," said Walta Nemariam, an employee in talent acquisition at Netflix, in the video.

Netflix has stayed true to their cultural values despite the pressures and sometimes negative connotations associated with this "cutthroat" environment. Their ability to remain agile, while displaying no tolerances for societal injustices makes them at the forefront of new age companies. It is a difficult pace to stay in line with, but it seems that they are keeping in stride and remaining true to who they are, for now.

Questions:
1. How have the current cultural environment of our country shaped the way that companies are looking at their own corporate cultural standards?
2. What are the potential downfalls and positive influences of the "Netflix way"?
3. How does Netflix's internal culture negatively or positively affect their ability to stay competitive and deliver cutting edge content?

Sources: B. Stelter, "The Weinstein Effect: Harvey Weinstein scandal sparks movements in Hollywood and beyond," CNN Business, October 20, 2017, https://money.cnn.com/2017/10/20/media/weinstein-effect-harvey-weinstein/; https://www.washingtonpost.com/; L. Hertzler, " Talking #MeToo, one year after bombshell Weinstein allegations," Penn Today, October 30, 2018, https://penntoday.upenn.edu/news/talking-me-too-one-year-later; S. Ramachandaran and J. Flint, " At Netflix, Radical Transparency and Blunt Firings Unsettle the Ranks," Wall Street Journal, October 25, 2018, https://www.wsj.com/articles/at-netflix-radical-transparency-and-blunt-firings-unsettle-the-ranks-1540497174

✎ Introduction

Learning Outcomes

After reading this chapter, you should be able to answer these questions:

1. What are the basic characteristics of managerial decision-making?
2. What are the two systems of decision-making in the brain?
3. What is the difference between programmed and nonprogrammed decisions?
4. What barriers exist that make effective decision-making difficult?
5. How can a manager improve the quality of her individual decision-making?
6. What are the advantages and disadvantages of group decision-making, and how can a manager improve the quality of group decision-making?

EXPLORING MANAGERIAL CAREERS

Up, Up, and Away: How Stephanie Korey and Jen Rubio founded their luggage company

Jen Rubio and Stephanie Korey faced a number of important decisions in starting their luggage company, Away—beginning with the decision to start a business! That decision came about after Rubio's luggage broke on a trip. She found it frustrating that all the luggage options were either inexpensive ($100 or less) but low quality, or high quality but incredibly expensive ($400 and above). There was no midrange option. So in 2015 Rubio and her friend Stephanie Korey began researching the luggage industry. They found that much of the reason for the high prices on quality luggage was because of how it was distributed and sold, through specialty retail shops and department stores. If they opted instead for a model in which they sold directly to consumers, they could provide high-quality luggage at more of a midrange ($200-$300) price. After considerable research, the two were convinced that they had an idea worth pursuing. Rubio and Korey settled on the company name "Away," which is intended to invoke the pleasure that comes from travelling.

Both of the founders had prior experience working for a start-up in the e-commerce space (Warby Parker), which helped them with making sound choices. Rubio's background was more in branding and marketing, while Korey's was in operations and supply chain management—so each was able to bring great expertise to various aspects of the business. They raised money initially from friends and family, but within a few months they sought venture capital funding to ensure that they had enough money to get off to a successful start.

A big decision that Rubio and Korey had to make fairly early in the process of establishing their business was to settle on an initial design for the product. This decision required extensive marketing and consumer research to understand customer needs and wants. They asked hundreds of people what they liked about their existing luggage, and what they found most irritating about their existing luggage. They also contracted with a two-person design team to help create the first prototype. This research and development ultimately led to the design of an attractive hard case that is surprisingly lightweight. It also boasts extremely high-quality wheels (four of them, not two) and high-quality zippers. As a bonus, the carry-on includes a built-in battery for charging phones and other devices.

The two founders also had to choose a partner to manufacture their product. Because their product had a hard, polycarbonate shell, Rubio and Korey discovered that manufacturing in the United States was not a viable option—the vast majority of luggage manufacturers using a polycarbonate shell were based in Asia. They researched a number of possible business partners and asked lots of questions. In addition, they eventually visited all of the factories on their list of options to see what they were actually like. This was an important piece of research, because the companies that looked best on paper didn't always turn out to be the best when they visited in person. Rubio and Korey ended up working with a manufacturing partner in China that also produces luggage for many high-end brands, and they have been extremely pleased with the partnership. They continue to devote time to building and maintaining that relationship, which helps to avoid issues and problems that might otherwise come up.

By the end of 2015, Rubio and Korey had developed their first product. Because the luggage was not going to be available in time for the holiday shopping season, they decided to allow customers to preorder the luggage. To drum up interest, the duo engaged in a unique storytelling effort. They interviewed 40 well-respected members of the creative community about their travel experiences and created a hardcover book of travel memoirs called *The Places We Return To*. Not only was the book interesting and engaging, it also made lots of people in the creative community aware of Away luggage. Starting in November 2015, the travel memoir book was available for free with the purchase of a gift card that could be redeemed in February 2016 for luggage. The book project generated tremendous advance interest in the product, and the 1,200 printed copies sold out. Away generated $12 million in first-year sales.

Stephanie Corey and Jen Rubio faced many important and novel decisions in initially developing and building their business. They have been successful in part because they made those decisions wisely—by relying on shared knowledge, expertise, and lots of research before reaching a decision. They will continue to face many decisions, big and small. They have expanded their product line from one piece of luggage to four, with more luggage—and other travel accessories—in the works for the future. Their company, which is based in New York, has grown to over 60 employees in the first two years. These employees include the two design-team members who were contracted to help create their first prototype; Rubio and Korey appreciated working with them so much, they offered them full-time positions with Away. Each new hire represents new decisions—decisions about what additional work needs to be done and who they should hire to do it. Each new product also brings additional decisions—but it seems Rubio and Korey have positioned themselves (and their business) well for future successes.

Sources: Kendall Baker, "An Interview With the Co-Founder of Away," *The Hustle*, December 5, 2016, https://thehustle.co/episodes; Bond Street Blog, "Up and Away," *Bond Street*, https://bondstreet.com/blog/jen-rubio-interview/; Josh Constine, "Away nears 100k stylish suitcases sold as it raises $20M," *TechCrunch*, May 19, 2017, https://techcrunch.com/; Adeline Duff, " The T&L Carry-On: Away Travel Co-Founders Jen Rubio and Stephanie Korey," Travel & Leisure, March 9, 2017, http://www.travelandleisure.com/; Burt Helm, "How This Company Launched With Zero Products –and Hit $12 Million in First-Year Sales," *Inc.com*, July/August 2017, https://www.inc.com/; Veronique Hyland, "The Duo Trying to Make Travel More Glamorous," *The Cut*, December 22, 2015, https://www.thecut.com/.

Managers and business owners—like Jen Rubio and Stephanie Korey—make decisions on a daily basis. Some are big, like the decision to start a new business, but most are smaller decisions that go into the regular running of the company and are crucial to its long-term success. Some decisions are predictable, and some are unexpected. In this chapter we look at important information about decision-making that can help you make better decisions and, ultimately, be a better manager.

2.1   Overview of Managerial Decision-Making

1. What are the basic characteristics of managerial decision-making?

Decision-making is the action or process of thinking through possible options and selecting one.

It is important to recognize that managers are continually making decisions, and that the quality of their decision-making has an impact—sometimes quite significant—on the effectiveness of the organization and its **stakeholders**. Stakeholders are all the individuals or groups that are affected by an organization (such as customers, employees, shareholders, etc.).

Members of the top management team regularly make decisions that affect the future of the organization and all its stakeholders, such as deciding whether to pursue a new technology or product line. A good decision can enable the organization to thrive and survive long-term, while a poor decision can lead a business into bankruptcy. Managers at lower levels of the organization generally have a smaller impact on the organization's survival, but can still have a tremendous impact on their department and its workers. Consider, for example, a first-line supervisor who is charged with scheduling workers and ordering raw materials for her department. Poor decision-making by lower-level managers is unlikely to drive the entire firm out of existence, but it can lead to many adverse outcomes such as:

*   reduced productivity if there are too few workers or insufficient supplies,
*   increased expenses if there are too many workers or too many supplies, particularly if the supplies have a limited shelf life or are costly to store, and
*   frustration among employees, reduced morale, and increased turnover (which can be costly for the organization) if the decisions involve managing and training workers.

Deciding When to Decide

While some decisions are simple, a manager's decisions are often complex ones that involve a range of options and uncertain outcomes. When deciding among various options and uncertain outcomes, managers need to gather information, which leads them to another necessary decision: how much information is needed to make a good decision? Managers frequently make decisions without complete information; indeed, one of the hallmarks of an effective leader is the ability to determine when to hold off on a decision and gather more information, and when to make a decision with the information at hand. Waiting too long to make a decision can be as harmful for the organization as reaching a decision too quickly. Failing to react quickly enough can lead to missed opportunities, yet acting too quickly can lead to organizational resources being poorly allocated to projects with no chance of success. Effective managers must decide when they have gathered enough information and must be prepared to change course if additional information becomes available that makes it clear that the original decision was a poor one. For individuals with fragile egos, changing course can be challenging because admitting to a mistake can be harder than forging ahead with a bad plan. Effective managers recognize that given the complexity of many tasks, some failures are inevitable. They also realize that it's better to minimize a bad decision's impact on the organization and its stakeholders by recognizing it quickly and correcting it.

What's the Right (Correct) Answer?

It's also worth noting that making decisions as a manager is not at all like taking a multiple-choice test: with a multiple-choice test there is always one right answer. This is rarely the case with management decisions. Sometimes a manager is choosing between multiple good options, and it's not clear which will be the best. Other times there are multiple bad options, and the task is to minimize harm. Often there are individuals in the organization with competing interests, and the manager must make decisions knowing that someone will be upset no matter what decision is reached.

What's the Right (Ethical) Answer?

Sometimes managers are asked to make decisions that go beyond just upsetting someone—they may be asked to make decisions in which harm could be caused to others. These decisions have ethical or moral implications. Ethics and morals refer to our beliefs about what is right vs. wrong, good vs. evil, virtuous vs. corrupt. Implicitly, ethics and morals relate to our interactions with and impact on others—if we never had to interact with another creature, we would not have to think about how our behaviors affected other individuals or groups. All managers, however, make decisions that impact others. It is therefore important to be mindful about whether our decisions have a positive or a negative impact. "Maximizing shareholder wealth" is often used as a rationalization for placing the importance of short-term profits over the needs of others who will be affected by a decision—such as employees, customers, or local citizens (who might be affected, for example, by environmental decisions). Maximizing shareholder wealth is often a short-sighted decision, however, because it can harm the organization's financial viability in the future.[1] Bad publicity, customers boycotting the organization, and government fines are all possible long-term outcomes when managers make choices that cause harm in order to maximize shareholder wealth. More importantly, increasing the wealth of shareholders is not an acceptable reason for causing harm to others.

As you can see from these brief examples, management is not for the faint of heart! It can, however, be incredibly rewarding to be in a position to make decisions that have a positive impact on an organization and its stakeholders. We see a great example of this in the *Sustainability and Responsible Management* box.

SUSTAINABILITY AND RESPONSIBLE MANAGEMENT

Brewing Sustainable Success

The focus of a manager or a business owner is often primarily on doing well (making a profit). Sometimes, though, organizational leaders choose to pursue two big goals at once: doing well, and simultaneously doing good (benefiting society in some way). Why? Generally because they think it's an important thing to do. The business provides an opportunity to pursue another goal that the founders, owners, or managers are also passionate about. In the case of New Belgium Brewing, the company's cofounders, Jeff Lebesch and Kim Jordan, were passionate about two things: making great beer and environmental stewardship. So it should come as no surprise that their brewery is dedicated to reducing its environmental footprint. The brewery has created a culture that fosters sustainability in a wide range of ways, such as by giving employees a bicycle on their one-year anniversary as a way to encourage them to ride bicycles to work. The organization is also active in advocacy efforts, such as the "Save the Colorado" (river) campaign, and it works hard to promote responsible decision-making when it comes to environmental issues. In fact, in 1999, following an employee vote, the brewery began to purchase all of its electricity from wind power, even though it was more expensive than electricity from coal-burning power plants (which meant reduced profitability and less money for employee bonuses).

While the brewery still relies primarily on wind power, it also now generates a portion of its electricity onsite—some from rooftop solar panels, and even more from biogas, the methane gas byproduct that is created by microbes in the brewery's water treatment plant. The company cleans the wastewater generated from beer production, and in doing so it generates the biogas, which is captured and used for energy to help run the brewery.

Brewing is water intensive, so New Belgium works hard to reduce water consumption and to recycle the water that it does use. The company also reduces other types of waste by selling used grain, hops, and yeast to local ranchers for cattle feed. The company, which has been employee owned since 2013, also works with the local utility through a Smart Meter program to reduce their energy consumption at peak times.

All of these efforts at doing good must come at a cost, right? Actually, research shows that companies that are committed to sustainability have superior financial performance, on average, relative to those that are not. In coming up with creative ways to reduce, reuse, and recycle, employees often also find ways to save money (like using biogas). In addition, organizations that strive to do good are often considered attractive and desirable places to work (especially by people who have similar values) and are also valued by the surrounding communities. As a result, employees in those organizations tend to be extremely committed to them, with high levels of engagement, motivation, and productivity. Indeed, it seems clear that the employees at the New Belgium Brewery are passionate about where they work and what they do. This passion generates value for the organization and proves that it is, in fact, possible to do well while having also made the decision to do good. And in the case of New Belgium Brewery, that means working to protect the environment while also making delicious beer.

Discussion Questions

1. What challenges does New Belgium Brewery face in pursuing environmental goals?
2. Can you think of any other examples of companies that try to "do good" while also doing well?
3. Would you like to work for an organization that is committed to something more than just

profitability, even if it meant your salary or bonus would be smaller?

Sources: Karen Crofton, "How New Belgium Brewery leads Colorado's craft brewers in energy," *GreenBiz*, August 1, 2014, https://www.greenbiz.com/. Darren Dahl, "How New Belgium Brewing Has Found Sustainable Success," *Forbes*, February 8, 2016, https://www.forbes.com/. Jenny Foust, "New Belgium Brewing Once Again Named Platinum-Level Bicycle Friendly Business by the League of American Bicyclists," Craft Beer.com, February 18, 2016. Robert G. Eccles, Ioannis Ioannou, & George Serafeim, "The Impact of Corporate Sustainability on Organizational Processes and Performance," *Management Science*, 60, 2014, https://doi.org/10.1287/mnsc.2014.1984. New Belgium Brewery Sustainability web page, http://www.newbelgium.com/sustainability, accessed September 18, 2017.

CONCEPT CHECK

1. What are some positive outcomes of decision-making for an organization? What are some possible negative outcomes?
2. How is managerial decision-making different from a multiple-choice test?
3. In addition to the owners of a business, who are some of the other stakeholders that managers should consider when making decisions?

2.2 How the Brain Processes Information to Make Decisions: Reflective and Reactive Systems

2. What are the two systems of decision-making in the brain?

The human brain processes information for decision-making using one of two routes: a reflective system and a reactive (or reflexive) system.[2,3] The **reflective system** is logical, analytical, deliberate, and methodical, while the **reactive system** is quick, impulsive, and intuitive, relying on emotions or habits to provide cues for what to do next. Research in neuropsychology suggests that the brain can only use one system at a time for processing information [Darlow & Sloman] and that the two systems are directed by different parts of the brain. The prefrontal cortex is more involved in the reflective system, and the basal ganglia and amygdala (more primitive parts of the brain, from an evolutionary perspective) are more involved in the reactive system.[4]

Reactive Decision-Making

We tend to assume that the logical, analytical route leads to superior decisions, but whether this is accurate depends on the situation. The quick, intuitive route can be lifesaving; when we suddenly feel intense fear, a fight-or-flight response kicks in that leads to immediate action without methodically weighing all possible options and their consequences. Additionally, experienced managers can often make decisions very quickly because experience or expertise has taught them what to do in a given situation. These managers might not be able to explain the logic behind their decision, and will instead say they just went with their "gut," or did what "felt" right. Because the manager has faced a similar situation in the past and has figured out how to deal with it, the brain shifts immediately to the quick, intuitive decision-making system.[5]

Reflective Decision-Making

The quick route is not always the best decision-making path to take, however. When faced with novel and complex situations, it is better to process available information logically, analytically, and methodically. As a manager, you need to think about whether a situation requires not a fast, "gut" reaction, but some serious thought prior to making a decision. It is especially important to pay attention to your emotions, because strong emotions can make it difficult to process information rationally. Successful managers recognize the effects of emotions and know to wait and address a volatile situation after their emotions have calmed down. Intense emotions—whether positive or negative—tend to pull us toward the quick, reactive route of decision-making. Have you ever made a large "impulse" purchase that you were excited about, only to regret it later? This speaks to the power our emotions exert on our decision-making. Big decisions should generally not be made impulsively, but reflectively.

The Role of Emotions

Being aware of the role emotions play in decision-making does not mean that we should ignore them. Emotions can serve as powerful signals about what we should do, especially in situations with ethical implications. You can read more about this particular type of decision-making in the *Ethics in Practice* box later in this chapter. Thinking through how we feel about the possible options, and why we feel that way, can greatly enhance our decision-making.[6] Effective decision-making, then, relies on both logic *and* emotions. For this reason, the concept of emotional intelligence has become popular as a characteristic of effective managers. **Emotional intelligence** is the ability to recognize, understand, pay attention to, and manage one's own emotions and the emotions of others. It involves self-awareness and self-regulation—essentially, this is a toggling back and forth between emotions and logic so that we analyze and understand our own emotions and then exert the necessary control to manage them as appropriate for the situation. Emotional intelligence also involves empathy—the ability to understand other peoples' emotions (and an interest in doing so). Finally, emotional intelligence involves social skills to manage the emotional aspects of relationships with others. Managers who are aware of their own emotions can think through what their emotions mean in a given situation and use that information to guide their decision-making. Managers who are aware of the emotions of others can also utilize that information to help groups function more effectively and engage in better group decision-making. While emotional intelligence seems to come easily to some people, it is something that we can develop and improve on with practice. A model of emotional intelligence is presented in **Exhibit 2.2**.

Exhibit 2.2   Emotional Intelligence (Attribution: Copyright Rice University, OpenStax, under CC-BY 4.0 license)

CONCEPT CHECK

1. Explain the two systems used by the brain in decision-making.
2. What is emotional intelligence, and why is it important for decision-making?

2.3 | Programmed and Nonprogrammed Decisions

3. What is the difference between programmed and nonprogrammed decisions?

Because managers have limited time and must use that time wisely to be effective, it is important for them to distinguish between decisions that can have structure and routine applied to them (called programmed decisions) and decisions that are novel and require thought and attention (nonprogrammed decisions).

Programmed Decisions

Programmed decisions are those that are repeated over time and for which an existing set of rules can be developed to guide the process. These decisions might simple, or they could be fairly complex, but the criteria that go into making the decision are all known or can at least be estimated with a reasonable degree of accuracy. For example, deciding how many raw materials to order should be a programmed decision based on anticipated production, existing stock, and anticipated length of time for the delivery of the final product. As another example, consider a retail store manager developing the weekly work schedule for part-time employees. The manager must consider how busy the store is likely to be, taking into account seasonal fluctuations in business. Then, she must consider the availability of the workers by taking into account requests for vacation and for other obligations that employees might have (such as school). Establishing the schedule might be complex, but it is still a programmed decision: it is made on a regular basis based on well-understood criteria, so structure can be applied to the process. For programmed decisions, managers often develop **heuristics**, or mental shortcuts, to help reach a decision. For example, the retail store manager may not know how busy the store will be the week of a big sale, but might routinely increase staff by 30% every time there is a big sale (because this has been fairly effective in the past). Heuristics are efficient—they save time for the decision maker by generating an adequate solution quickly. Heuristics don't necessarily yield the optimal solution—deeper cognitive processing may be required for that. However, they generally yield a good solution. Heuristics are often used for programmed decisions, because experience in making the decision over and over helps the decision maker know what to expect and how to react. Programmed decision-making can also be taught fairly easily to another person. The rules and criteria, and how they relate to outcomes, can be clearly laid out so that a good decision can be reached by the new decision maker. Programmed decisions are also sometimes referred to as *routine* or *low-involvement* decisions because they don't require in-depth mental processing to reach a decision. High- and low-involvement decisions are illustrated in **Exhibit 2.3**.

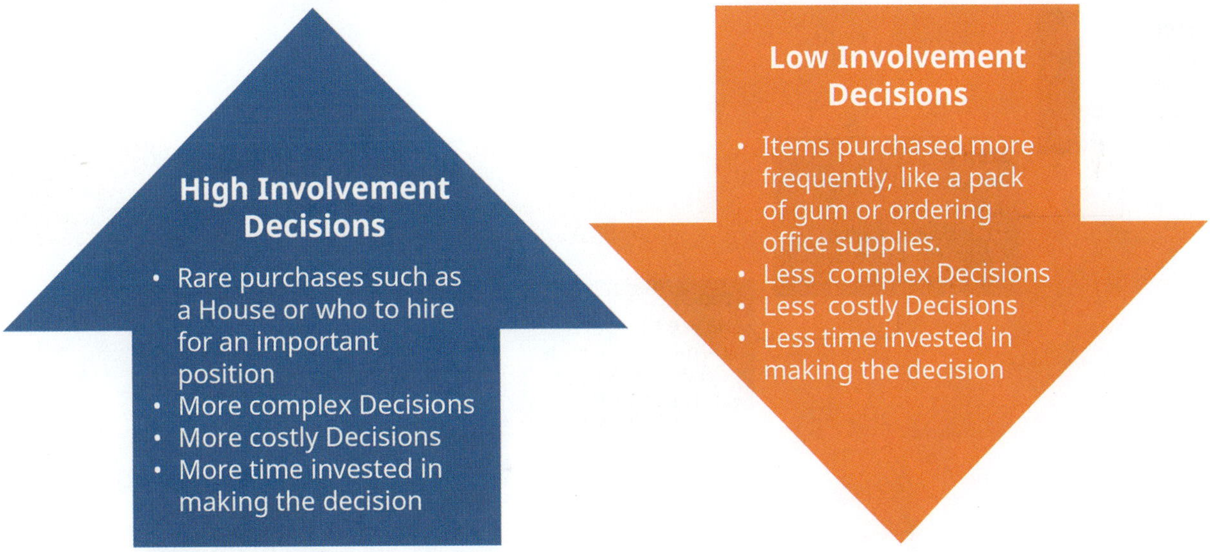

High Involvement Decisions

- Rare purchases such as a House or who to hire for an important position
- More complex Decisions
- More costly Decisions
- More time invested in making the decision

Low Involvement Decisions

- Items purchased more frequently, like a pack of gum or ordering office supplies.
- Less complex Decisions
- Less costly Decisions
- Less time invested in making the decision

Exhibit 2.3 High-Involvement and Low-Involvement Decisions. (Attribution: Copyright Rice University, OpenStax, under CC-BY 4.0 license)

Nonprogrammed Decisions

In contrast, **nonprogrammed decisions** are novel, unstructured decisions that are generally based on criteria that are not well-defined. With nonprogrammed decisions, information is more likely to be ambiguous or incomplete, and the decision maker may need to exercise some thoughtful judgment and creative thinking to reach a good solution. These are also sometimes referred to as *nonroutine* decisions or as *high-involvement* decisions because they require greater involvement and thought on the part of the decision maker. For example, consider a manager trying to decide whether or not to adopt a new technology. There will always be unknowns in situations of this nature. Will the new technology really be better than the existing technology? Will it become widely accepted over time, or will some other technology become the standard? The best the manager can do in this situation is to gather as much relevant information as possible and make an educated guess as to whether the new technology will be worthwhile. Clearly, nonprogrammed decisions present the greater challenge.

The Decision-Making Process

While decisions makers can use mental shortcuts with programmed decisions, they should use a systematic process with nonprogrammed decisions. The decision-making process is illustrated in **Exhibit 2.4** and can be broken down into a series of six steps, as follows:

1. Recognize that a decision needs to be made.
2. Generate multiple alternatives.
3. Analyze the alternatives.
4. Select an alternative.
5. Implement the selected alternative.
6. Evaluate its effectiveness.

While these steps may seem straightforward, individuals often skip steps or spend too little time on some steps. In fact, sometimes people will refuse to acknowledge a problem (Step 1) because they aren't sure how to address it. We'll discuss the steps more later in the chapter, when we review ways to improve the quality of decision-making.

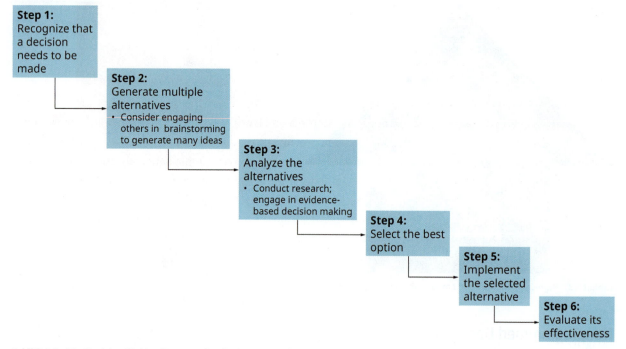

Exhibit 2.4   The Decision-Making Process. (Attribution: Copyright Rice University, OpenStax, under CC-BY 4.0 license)

You may notice similarities between the two systems of decision-making in our brains and the two types of decisions (programmed and nonprogrammed). Nonprogrammed decisions will generally need to be processed via the reflective system in our brains in order for us to reach a good decision. But with programmed decisions, heuristics can allow decision makers to switch to the quick, reactive system and then move along quickly to other issues.

CONCEPT CHECK   ✓

1. Give an example of a programmed decision that a manager might face.
2. Give an example of a nonprogrammed decision.
3. What are heuristics, and when are they helpful?
4. How are programmed and nonprogrammed decisions connected to the reflective and reactive systems in the brain?

2.4 | Barriers to Effective Decision-Making

4. What barriers exist that make effective decision-making difficult?

There are a number of barriers to effective decision-making. Effective managers are aware of these potential barriers and try to overcome them as much as possible.

Bounded Rationality

While we might like to think that we can make completely rational decisions, this is often unrealistic given the complex issues faced by managers. Nonrational decision-making is common, especially with nonprogrammed decisions. Since we haven't faced a particular situation previously, we don't always know what questions to ask or what information to gather. Even when we have gathered all the possible information, we may not be able to make rational sense of all of it, or to accurately forecast or predict the outcomes of our choice. **Bounded rationality** is the idea that for complex issues we cannot be completely rational because we cannot fully grasp all the possible alternatives, nor can we understand all the implications of every possible alternative. Our brains have limitations in terms of the amount of information they can process. Similarly, as was alluded to earlier in the chapter, even when managers have the cognitive ability to process all the relevant information, they often must make decisions without first having time to collect all the relevant data—their information is incomplete.

Escalation of Commitment

Given the lack of complete information, managers don't always make the right decision initially, and it may not be clear that a decision was a bad one until after some time has passed. For example, consider a manager who had to choose between two competing software packages that her organization will use on a daily basis to enhance efficiency. She initially chooses the product that was developed by the larger, more well-established company, reasoning that they will have greater financial resources to invest in ensuring that the technology is good. However, after some time it becomes clear that the competing software package is going to be far superior. While the smaller company's product could be integrated into the organization's existing systems at little additional expense, the larger company's product will require a much greater initial investment, as well as substantial ongoing costs for maintaining it. At this point, however, let's assume that the manager has already paid for the larger company's (inferior) software. Will she abandon the path that she's on, accept the loss on the money that's been invested so far, and switch to the better software? Or will she continue to invest time and money into trying to make the first product work? **Escalation of commitment** is the tendency of decision makers to remain committed to poor decision, even when doing so leads to increasingly negative outcomes. Once we commit to a decision, we may find it difficult to reevaluate that decision rationally. It can seem easier to "stay the course" than to admit (or to recognize) that a decision was poor. It's important to acknowledge that not all decisions are going to be good ones, in spite of our best efforts. Effective managers recognize that progress down the wrong path isn't really progress, and they are willing to reevaluate decisions and change direction when appropriate.

Time Constraints

Managers often face time constraints that can make effective decision-making a challenge. When there is little time available to collect information and to rationally process it, we are much less likely to make a good nonprogrammed decision. Time pressures can cause us to rely on heuristics rather than engage in deep processing. While heuristics save time, however, they don't necessarily lead to the best possible solution. The best managers are constantly assessing the risks associated with acting too quickly against those associated with not acting quickly enough.

Uncertainty

In addition, managers frequently make decisions under conditions of uncertainty—they cannot know the outcome of each alternative until they've actually chosen that alternative. Consider, for example, a manager who is trying to decide between one of two possible marketing campaigns. The first is more conservative but is consistent with what the organization has done in the past. The second is more modern and edgier, and might bring much better results . . . or it might be a spectacular failure. The manager making the decision will ultimately have to choose one campaign and see what happens, without ever knowing what the results would have been with the alternate campaign. That uncertainty can make it difficult for some managers to make decisions, because committing to one option means forgoing other options.

Personal Biases

Our decision-making is also limited by our own biases. We tend to be more comfortable with ideas, concepts, things, and people that are familiar to us or similar to us. We tend to be less comfortable with that which is unfamiliar, new, and different. One of the most common biases that we have, as humans, is the tendency to like other people who we think are similar to us (because we like ourselves).[7] While these similarities can be observable (based on demographic characteristics such as race, gender, and age), they can also be a result of shared experiences (such as attending the same university) or shared interests (such as being in a book club together). This "similar to me" bias and preference for the familiar can lead to a variety of problems for managers: hiring less-qualified applicants because they are similar to the manager in some way, paying more attention to some employees' opinions and ignoring or discounting others, choosing a familiar technology over a new one that is superior, sticking with a supplier that is known over one that has better quality, and so on.

It can be incredibly difficult to overcome our biases because of the way our brains work. The brain excels at organizing information into categories, and it doesn't like to expend the effort to re-arrange once the categories are established. As a result, we tend to pay more attention to information that confirms our existing beliefs and less attention to information that is contrary to our beliefs, a shortcoming that is referred to as **confirmation bias**.[8]

In fact, we don't like our existing beliefs to be challenged. Such challenges feel like a threat, which tends to push our brains towards the reactive system and prevent us from being able to logically process the new information via the reflective system. It is hard to change people's minds about something if they are already confident in their convictions. So, for example, when a manager hires a new employee who she really likes and is convinced is going to be excellent, she will tend to pay attention to examples of excellent performance and ignore examples of poor performance (or attribute those events to things outside the employee's control). The manager will also tend to trust that employee and therefore accept their explanations for poor performance without verifying the truth or accuracy of those statements. The opposite is also true; if we dislike someone, we will pay attention to their negatives and ignore or discount their positives. We are less likely to trust them or believe what they say at face value. This is why politics tend to become very polarized and antagonistic within a two-party system. It can be very difficult to have accurate perceptions of those we like and those we dislike. The effective manager will try to evaluate situations from multiple perspectives and gather multiple opinions to offset this bias when making decisions.

Conflict

Finally, effective decision-making can be difficult because of conflict. Most individuals dislike conflict and will avoid it when possible. However, the best decision might be one that is going to involve some conflict. Consider a manager who has a subordinate who is often late to work, causing others to have to step away from their responsibilities in order to cover for the late employee. The manager needs to have a conversation with that employee to correct the behavior, but the employee is not going to like the conversation and may react in a negative way. Both of them are going to be uncomfortable. The situation is likely to involve conflict, which most people find stressful. Yet, the correct decision is still to have the conversation even if (or especially if) the employee otherwise is an asset to the department.

Exhibit 2.5 Dante Disparte Dante Disparte is the founder and CEO of Risk Cooperative and also coauthor of *Global Risk Agility and Decision Making*. He suggests that unforeseen and unanticipated risks are becoming more frequent and less predictable and are having a greater impact on more people at one time. Credit (New America/ flickr/ Attribution 2.0 Generic (CC BY 2.0))

If the bad behavior is not corrected, it will continue, which is going to cause more problems in the workplace in the long run. Other employees may recognize that this behavior is allowed, and they may also start coming to work late or engaging in other negative behaviors. Eventually, some employees may become sufficiently frustrated that they look for another place to work. It's worth noting that in this situation, the best employees will find new jobs the most quickly. It's important for managers to recognize that while conflict can be uncomfortable (especially in the short-term), there are times when it is necessary for the group, department, or organization to function effectively in the long run.

It is also helpful to think about conflict in terms of process conflict or relationship conflict.[9] **Process conflict,** conflict about the best way to do something, can actually lead to improved performance, as individuals explore various options together in order to identify superior solutions. **Relationship conflict** is conflict between individuals that is more personal and involves attacks on a person rather than an idea. This kind of conflict is generally harmful and should be quelled when possible. The harm from relationship conflict arises at least in part because feeling personally attacked will cause an individual to revert to the reactive system of the brain.

Effective managers should be particularly aware of the possibility of relationship conflict when giving feedback and should keep feedback focused on behaviors and activities (how things are done) rather than on the individual. Being aware of and dealing with relationship conflict points to why emotional intelligence and empathy are beneficial in organizational leaders. Such leaders are more likely to be attentive to the harmful consequences of relationship conflict. The "Managerial Leadership" segment shows how one CEO encourages empathetic collaboration and how that effort is proving beneficial.

MANAGERIAL LEADERSHIP

Satya Nadella's Transformation of Microsoft

When Satya Nadella became the CEO of Microsoft in 2014, he set in motion a major transformation of the organization's culture. He wanted it to shift from a culture that valued "know-it-alls" to one that values "learn-it-all." Instead of employees feeling the need to prove that they were the smartest person in the room, he wanted them to become curious and effective listeners, learners, and communicators. Only through continual learning and collaboration with one another, and with customers, would Microsoft remain able to develop and provide great technology solutions.

One of Nadella's first mandates as CEO was to ask all the members of the top management team to read the book *Nonviolent Communication* by Marshall Rosenberg. The primary focus of the book is on empathetic communication—a kinder, gentler approach than Microsoft employees were accustomed to. Nadella believes that developing empathy leads to a heightened understanding of consumer needs and wants and an enhanced ability to develop better products and services through collaboration.

Nadella has also embraced diversity and inclusion initiatives, though he readily acknowledges that there is more to be done. This is, in part, an extension of his focus on empathy. However, it's also good business, because increasing the diversity of perspectives can help to drive innovation.

This cultural shift is reflected in Microsoft's new mission statement: "To empower every person and every organization on the planet to achieve more." Empowering every person includes Microsoft's own employees. Achieving diversity is particularly a challenge in an industry that is male dominated, and Nadella admits that he has made mistakes based on his own biases. At a Women in Computing conference early in his tenure as CEO, Nadella suggested that women did not need to ask for raises when they deserved them; the system, he said, would work it out. He later admitted that he was wrong and used the mistake as a platform for making greater strides in this arena.

Senior management team meetings at Microsoft have apparently changed dramatically as a result of the culture change driven by Nadella. Previously, members felt the need to constantly prove that they knew all the right answers at team meetings. Nadella has established different norms; he seeks out honest opinions from team members and gives positive feedback on a regular basis. By moving the focus away from always being right and toward a focus of continual learning, the culture at Microsoft has become more collaborative, and employees are more willing to take risks to create something amazing. The culture shift seems to be paying off: Microsoft's products are being described as "cool" and "exciting," its cloud-computing platform is outperforming the competition, and its financial performance has improved dramatically. Transforming the culture of an organization is a massive undertaking, but Nadella's leadership of Microsoft clearly shows that it's a decision that can pay off.

Discussion Questions

1. Do you think a culture focused on learning makes sense for Microsoft? Why or why not?
2. What are the advantages of a culture that emphasizes empathetic communication? Can you think of any disadvantages?
3. The job of CEO means making big decisions that impact the entire organization—like deciding to change the culture. How do you think you prepare for that job?

Sources: Kendall Baker, "Confirmed: Microsoft is a legit threat to Apple," *The Hustle*, March 16, 2017. Bob Evans, "10 Powerful examples of Microsoft CEO Satya Nadella's Transformative Vision," Forbes, July 26, 2017. Harry McCraken, "Satya Nadella Rewrites Microsoft's Code," *Fast Company*, September 18, 2017, https://www.fastcompany.com/40457458/satya-nadella-rewrites-microsofts-code. Annie Palmer, "Microsoft has been reborn under CEO Satya Nadella," *The Street*, September 20, 2017.

CONCEPT CHECK

1. Explain the concept of confirmation bias.
2. List and describe at least three barriers to effective decision-making.
3. When is conflict beneficial, and when is it harmful? Why?

2.5 | Improving the Quality of Decision-Making

5. How can a manager improve the quality of her individual decision-making?

Managers can use a variety of techniques to improve their decision-making by making better-quality decisions or making decisions more quickly. **Table 2.1** summarizes some of these tactics.

Summary of Techniques That May Improve Individual Decision-Making		
Type of Decision	Technique	Benefit
Programmed decisions	Heuristics (mental shortcuts)	Saves time
	Satisficing (choosing first acceptable solution)	Saves time
Nonprogrammed decisions	Systematically go through the six steps of the decision-making process.	Improves quality
	Talk to other people.	Improves quality: generates more options, reduces bias
	Be creative.	Improves quality: generates more options
	Conduct research; engage in evidence-based decision-making.	Improves quality
	Engage in critical thinking.	Improves quality
	Think about the long-term implications.	Improves quality
	Consider the ethical implications.	Improves quality

Table 2.1 (Attribution: Copyright Rice University, OpenStax, under CC-BY 4.0 license)

The Importance of Experience

An often overlooked factor in effective decision-making is experience. Managers with more experience have generally learned more and developed greater expertise that they can draw on when making decisions. Experience helps managers develop methods and heuristics to quickly deal with programmed decisions and helps them know what additional information to seek out before making a nonprogrammed decision.

Techniques for Making Better Programmed Decisions

In addition, experience enables managers to recognize when to minimize the time spent making decisions on issues that are not particularly important but must still be addressed. As discussed previously, heuristics are mental shortcuts that managers take when making programmed (routine, low-involvement) decisions. Another technique that managers use with these types of decisions is satisficing. When **satisficing**, a decision maker selects the first *acceptable* solution without engaging in additional effort to identify the *best* solution. We all engage in satisficing every day. For example, suppose you are shopping for groceries and you don't want to overspend. If you have plenty of time, you might compare prices and figure out the price by weight (or volume) to ensure that every item you select is the cheapest option. But if you are in a hurry, you might just select generic products, knowing that they are cheap enough. This allows you to finish the task quickly at a reasonably low cost.

Techniques for Making Better Nonprogrammed Decisions

For situations in which the quality of the decision is more critical than the time spent on the decision, decision makers can use several tactics. As stated previously, nonprogrammed decisions should be addressed using a systematic process. We therefore discuss these tactics within the context of the decision-making steps. To review, the steps include the following:

1. Recognize that a decision needs to be made.
2. Generate multiple alternatives.
3. Analyze the alternatives.
4. Select an alternative.
5. Implement the selected alternative.
6. Evaluate its effectiveness.

Step 1: Recognizing That a Decision Needs to Be Made

Ineffective managers will sometimes ignore problems because they aren't sure how to address them. However, this tends to lead to more and bigger problems over time. Effective managers will be attentive to problems and to opportunities and will not shy away from making decisions that could make their team, department, or organization more effective and more successful.

Step 2: Generating Multiple Alternatives

Often a manager only spends enough time on Step 2 to generate two alternatives and then quickly moves to Step 3 in order to make a quick decision. A better solution may have been available, but it wasn't even considered. It's important to remember that for nonprogrammed decisions, you don't want to rush the process. Generating many possible options will increase the likelihood of reaching a good decision. Some tactics to help with generating more options include talking to other people (to get their ideas) and thinking creatively about the problem.

Talk to other people

Managers can often improve the quality of their decision-making by involving others in the process, especially when generating alternatives. Other people tend to view problems from different perspectives because they have had different life experiences. This can help generate alternatives that you might not otherwise have considered. Talking through big decisions with a mentor can also be beneficial, especially for new managers who are still learning and developing their expertise; someone with more experience will often be able to suggest more options.

Be creative

We don't always associate management with creativity, but creativity can be quite beneficial in some situations. In decision-making, creativity can be particularly helpful when generating alternatives. **Creativity** is the generation of new or original ideas; it requires the use of imagination and the ability to step back from traditional ways of doing things and seeing the world. While some people seem to be naturally creative, it is a skill that you can develop. Being creative requires letting your mind wander and combining existing knowledge from past experiences in novel ways. Creative inspiration may come when we least expect it (in the shower, for example) because we aren't intensely focused on the problem—we've allowed our minds to wander. Managers who strive to be creative will take the time to view a problem from multiple perspectives, try to combine information in news ways, search for overarching patterns, and use their imaginations to generate new solutions to existing problems. We'll review creativity in more detail in **Chapter 18**.

Step 3: Analyzing Alternatives

When implementing Step 3, it is important to take many factors into consideration. Some alternatives might be more expensive than others, for example, and that information is often essential when analyzing options. Effective managers will ensure that they have collected sufficient information to assess the quality of the various options. They will also utilize the tactics described below: engaging in evidence-based decision-making, thinking critically, talking to other people, and considering long-term and ethical implications.

Do you have the best-quality data and evidence?

Evidence-based decision-making is an approach to decision-making that states that managers should systematically collect the best evidence available to help them make effective decisions. The evidence that is collected might include the decision maker's own expertise, but it is also likely to include external evidence, such as a consideration of other stakeholders, contextual factors relevant to the organization, potential costs and benefits, and other relevant information. With evidence-based decision-making, managers are encouraged to rely on data and information rather than their intuition. This can be particularly beneficial for new managers or for experienced managers who are starting something new. (Consider all the research that Rubio and Korey conducted while starting Away).

Talk to other people

As mentioned previously, it can be worthwhile to get help from others when generating options. Another good time to talk to other people is while analyzing those options; other individuals in the organization may help you assess the quality of your choices. Seeking out the opinions and preferences of others is also a great way to maintain perspective, so getting others involved can help you to be less biased in your decision-making (provided you talk to people whose biases are different from your own).

Are you thinking critically about the options?

Our skill at assessing alternatives can also be improved by a focus on **critical thinking**. Critical thinking is a disciplined process of evaluating the quality of information, especially data collected from other sources and arguments made by other people, to determine whether the source should be trusted or whether the argument is valid.

An important factor in critical thinking is the recognition that a person's analysis of the available information may be flawed by a number of *logical fallacies* that they may use when they are arguing their point or defending their perspective. Learning what those fallacies are and being able to recognize them when they occur can help improve decision-making quality. See **Table 2.2** for several examples of common logical fallacies.

Common Logical Fallacies			
Name	Description	Examples	Ways to Combat This Logical Fallacy
Non sequitur (does not follow)	The conclusion that is presented isn't a logical conclusion or isn't the only logical conclusion based on the argument(s).	Our biggest competitor is spending more on marketing than we are. They have a larger share of the market. Therefore, we should spend more on marketing. _The unspoken assumption:_ They have a larger share of the market BECAUSE they spend more on marketing.	• Examine all the arguments. Are they reasonable? • Look for any assumptions that are being made in the argument sequence. Are they reasonable? • Try to gather evidence that supports or refutes the arguments and/or assumptions. _In this example, you should ask:_ Are there any other reasons, besides their spending on marketing, why our competitor has a larger share of the market?
False cause	Assuming that because two things are related, one caused the other	"Our employees get sick more when we close for holidays. So we should stop closing for holidays."	This is similar to non sequitur; it makes an assumption in the argument sequence. • Ask yourself whether the first thing really causes the second, or if something else may be the cause. In this case, most holidays for which businesses close are in the late fall and winter (Thanksgiving, Christmas), and there are more illnesses at this time of year because of the weather, not because of the business being closed.

Table 2.2 (Attribution: Copyright Rice University, OpenStax, under CC-BY 4.0 license)

Common Logical Fallacies			
Name	Description	Examples	Ways to Combat This Logical Fallacy
Ad hominem (attack the man)	Redirects from the argument itself to attack the person making the argument	"You aren't really going to take John seriously, are you? I heard his biggest client just dropped him for another vendor because he's all talk and no substance." *The goal:* if you stop trusting the person, you'll discount their argument.	• Does the second person have something to gain, a hidden agenda, in trying to make you distrust the first person? • If the first person's argument came from someone else, would it be persuasive?
Genetic fallacy	You can't trust something because of its origins.	"This was made in China, so it must be low quality." "He is a lawyer, so you can't trust anything he says."	This fallacy is based on stereotypes. Stereotypes are generalizations; some are grossly inaccurate, and even those that are accurate in SOME cases are never accurate in ALL cases. Recognize this for what it is—an attempt to prey on existing biases.
Appeal to tradition	If we have always done it one particular way, that must be the right or best way.	"We've always done it this way." "We shouldn't change this; it works fine the way it is."	• Consider whether the situation has changed, calling for a change in the way things are being done. • Consider whether new information suggests that the traditional viewpoint is incorrect. Remember, we used to think that the earth was flat.

Table 2.2 (Attribution: Copyright Rice University, OpenStax, under CC-BY 4.0 license)

Common Logical Fallacies			
Name	Description	Examples	Ways to Combat This Logical Fallacy
Bandwagon approach	If the majority of people are doing it, it must be good.	"Everybody does it." "Our customers don't want to be served by people like that."	• Remember that the majority is sometimes wrong, and what is popular isn't always what is right. • Ask yourself whether "following the pack" is going to get you where you want to be. • Remember that organizations are usually successful by being better than their competitors at something . . . so following the crowd might not be the best approach to success.
Appeal to emotion	Redirects the argument from logic to emotion	"We should do it for [recently deceased] Steve; it's what he would have wanted."	• Develop your awareness of your own emotions, and recognize when someone is trying to use them. • Ask yourself whether the argument stands on its own without the appeal to your emotions.

Table 2.2 (Attribution: Copyright Rice University, OpenStax, under CC-BY 4.0 license)

Have you considered the long-term implications?

A focus on immediate, short-term outcomes—with little consideration for the future—can cause problems. For example, imagine that a manager must decide whether to issue dividends to investors or put that money into research and development to maintain a pipeline of innovative products. It's tempting to just focus on the short-term: providing dividends to investors tends to be good for stock prices. But failing to invest in research and development might mean that in five years the company is unable to compete effectively in the marketplace, and as a result the business closes. Paying attention to the possible long-term outcomes is a crucial part of analyzing alternatives.

Are there ethical implications?

It's important to think about whether the various alternatives available to you are better or worse from an ethical perspective, as well. Sometimes managers make unethical choices because they haven't considered the ethical implications of their actions. In the 1970s, Ford manufactured the Pinto, which had an unfortunate flaw: the car would easily burst into flames when rear-ended. The company did not initially recall the vehicle because they viewed the problem from a financial perspective, without considering the ethical implications.[10] People died as a result of the company's inaction. Unfortunately, these unethical decisions continue to occur—and cause harm—on a regular basis in our society. Effective managers strive to avoid these situations by thinking through the possible ethical implications of their decisions. The decision tree in **Exhibit 2.6** is a great example of a way to make managerial decisions while also taking ethical issues into account.

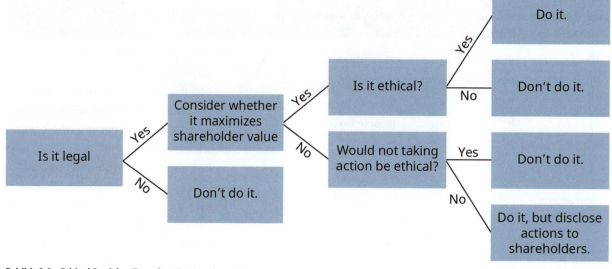

Exhibit 2.6 Ethical Decision Tree (Attribution: Copyright Rice University, OpenStax, under CC-BY 4.0 license)

Thinking through the steps of ethical decision-making may also be helpful as you strive to make good decisions. James Rest's ethical decision-making model[11] identifies four components to ethical decision-making:

1. Moral sensitivity—recognizing that the issue has a moral component;
2. Moral judgment—determining which actions are right vs. wrong;
3. Moral motivation/intention—deciding to do the right thing; and
4. Moral character/action—actually doing what is right.

Note that a failure at any point in the chain can lead to unethical actions! Taking the time to identify possible ethical implications will help you develop moral sensitivity, which is a critical first step to ensuring that you are making ethical decisions.

Once you have determined that a decision has ethical implications, you must consider whether your various alternatives are right or wrong—whether or not they will cause harm, and if so, how much and to whom. This is the moral judgment component. If you aren't sure about whether something is right or wrong, think about how you would feel if that decision ended up on the front page of a major newspaper. If you would feel guilty or ashamed, don't do it! Pay attention to those emotional cues—they are providing important information about the option that you are contemplating.

The third step in the ethical decision-making model involves making a decision to do what is right, and the fourth step involves following through on that decision. These may sound, but consider a situation in which your boss tells you to do something that you know to be wrong. When you push back, your boss makes it clear that you will lose your job if you don't do what you've been told to do. Now, consider that you have family at home who rely on your income. Making the decision to do what you know is right could come at a substantial cost to you personally. In these situations, your best course of action is to find a way to persuade your boss that the unethical action will cause greater harm to the organization in the long-term.

Step 4: Selecting an Alternative

Once alternative options have been generated and analyzed, the decision maker must select one of the options. Sometimes this is easy—one option is clearly superior to the others. Often, however, this is a challenge because there is not a clear "winner" in terms of the best alternative. As mentioned earlier in the chapter, there may be multiple good options, and which one will be best is unclear even after gathering all available evidence. There may not be a single option that doesn't upset some stakeholder group, so you will make someone unhappy no matter what you choose. A weak decision maker may become paralyzed in this situation, unable to select among the various alternatives for lack of a clearly "best" option. They may decide to keep gathering additional information in hopes of making their decision easier. As a manager, it's important to think about whether the benefit of gathering additional information will outweigh the cost of waiting. If there are time pressures, waiting may not be possible.

Recognize that perfection is unattainable

Effective managers recognize that they will not always make optimal (best possible) decisions because they don't have complete information and/or don't have the time or resources to gather and process all the possible information. They accept that their decision-making will not be perfect and strive to make good decisions overall. Recognizing that perfection is impossible will also help managers to adjust and change if they realize later on that the selected alternative was not the best option.

Talk to other people

This is another point in the process at which talking to others can be helpful. Selecting one of the alternatives will ultimately be your responsibility, but when faced with a difficult decision, talking through your choice with someone else may help you clarify that you are indeed making the best possible decision from among the available options. Sharing information verbally also causes our brains to process that information differently, which can provide new insights and bring greater clarity to our decision-making.

Step 5: Implementing the Selected Alternative

After selecting an alternative, you must implement it. This may seem too obvious to even mention, but implementation can sometimes be a challenge, particularly if the decision is going to create conflict or dissatisfaction among some stakeholders. Sometimes we know what we need to do but still try to avoid actually doing it because we know others in the organization will be upset—even if it's the best solution. Follow-through is a necessity, however, to be effective as a manager. If you are not willing to implement a decision, it's a good idea to engage in some self-reflection to understand why. If you know that the decision is going to create conflict, try to think about how you'll address that conflict in a productive way. It's also possible that we feel that there is no good alternative, or we are feeling pressured to make a decision that we know deep down is not right from an ethical perspective. These can be among the most difficult of decisions. You should always strive to make decisions that you feel good about—which means doing the right thing, even in the face of pressures to do wrong.

Step 6: Evaluating the Effectiveness of Your Decision

Managers sometimes skip the last step in the decision-making process because evaluating the effectiveness of a decision takes time, and managers, who are generally busy, may have already moved on to other projects. Yet evaluating effectiveness is important. When we fail to evaluate our own performance and the outcomes of our decisions, we cannot learn from the experience in a way that enables us to improve the quality of our future decisions.

Attending fully to each step in the decision-making process improves the quality of decision-making and, as we've seen, managers can engage in a number of tactics to help them make good decisions. Take a look at the *Ethics in Practice* box to see an example of how one particular manager puts these techniques into practice to make good decisions.

ETHICS IN PRACTICE

Rob Ault, Project Manager, Bayside Community Church
Bradenton, Florida

When it comes to decision-making, ethical dilemmas require particular care. Because managers make many decisions, it should not be surprising that some of those decisions will have ethical implications. With multiple stakeholders to consider, sometimes what is best for one group of stakeholders is not what is best for others. I talked to Rob Ault about his experiences with ethical dilemmas over the course of his career. Rob has been in managerial roles for over 25 years, since he was 19 years old. He told me that he had experienced a number of ethical dilemmas in that time.

Rob has spent most of his career working for for-profit organizations, and for about half of that time he has worked in a union environment. What he has found most frustrating, regardless of environment, was when it was clear to him what was right, but what was right conflicted with what his boss was telling him to do. This included a situation in which he felt an employee should be fired for misbehavior (but wasn't), as well as situation in which he was asked to fire someone undeservedly. What we mostly talked about, though, was his process. How did he go about making decisions in these challenging situations?

Rob clearly stated that his approach to these situations has changed with experience. What he did early in his career is not necessarily what he would do now. He said that it takes experience and some maturity to recognize that, as a leader, the decisions you make affect other people's lives. He also explained that a starting point for the decision-making process is always a recognition of the fact that you have been hired to generate a benefit for your company. So a manager's decisions need to come from the perspective of what is going to be in the best long-term interest of the organization (in addition to what is morally right). This isn't always easy, because short-term consequences are much easier to observe and predict.

I asked Rob who he talked to prior to making decisions in situations with an ethical component. Rob told me that he felt one of the most important things you should do as a leader is to intentionally create and build relationships with people you trust in the organization. That way you have people you know you can talk to when difficult situations come up. He was very clear that you should always talk to your boss, who will tend to have a broader understanding of what is going on in the context of the larger organization. He also told me that he liked to talk to his father, who happened to work in human resource management for a large Fortune 500 organization. His father was always helpful in providing the perspective of how things were likely to play out long-term if one person was allowed to bend the rules. Rob realized eventually that the long-term consequences of this were almost always negative: once one person is allowed to misbehave, others find out about it and realize that they can do the same thing without repercussions. Rob also seeks out the opinions of other individuals in the organization before reaching decisions with an ethical component; he told me that when he worked in a union environment, he tried to make sure he had a good relationship with the union steward, because it was helpful to get the perspective of someone who was committed to the side of the employee.

The biggest ethical dilemma Rob faced was one that he actually couldn't talk to me about. He disagreed with what he was being asked to do, and when it was clear that he had no other choice in the matter, he quit his job rather than do something he felt wasn't right. He accepted a severance package in exchange for signing a nondisclosure agreement, which is why he can't share any details . . . but it was clear from our conversation that he feels he made the right choice. That particular ethical dilemma makes it clear how challenging managerial decision-making can sometimes be.

Discussion Questions

1. If you were faced with an ethical dilemma, from whom would you seek advice?
2. Describe some decisions that might be good for an organization's profitability in the short-term, but bad for the organization in the long-term.
3. What factors would you take into consideration if you were thinking about leaving your job rather than do something unethical?

CONCEPT CHECK

1. Explain what satisficing is and when it may be a good strategy.
2. What are the six steps in the decision-making process?
3. What are the four steps involved in ethical decision-making?

2.6 | Group Decision-Making

6. What are the advantages and disadvantages of group decision-making, and how can a manager improve the quality of group decision-making?

Involving more people in the decision-making process can greatly improve the quality of a manager's decisions and outcomes. However, involving more people can also increase conflict and generate other challenges. We turn now to the advantages and disadvantages of group decision-making.

Advantages of Group Decisions

An advantage to involving groups in decision-making is that you can incorporate different perspectives and ideas. For this advantage to be realized, however, you need a diverse group. In a diverse group, the different group members will each tend to have different preferences, opinions, biases, and stereotypes. Because a variety of viewpoints must be negotiated and worked through, group decision-making creates additional work for a manager, but (provided the group members reflect different perspectives) it also tends to reduce the effects of bias on the outcome. For example, a hiring committee made up of all men might end up hiring a larger proportion of male applicants (simply because they tend to prefer people who are more similar to themselves). But with a hiring committee made up of an equal number of men and women, the bias should be cancelled out, resulting in more applicants being hired based on their qualifications rather than their physical attributes.

Having more people involved in decision-making is also beneficial because each individual brings unique information or knowledge to the group, as well as different perspectives on the problem. Additionally, having the participation of multiple people will often lead to more options being generated and to greater intellectual stimulation as group members discuss the available options. **Brainstorming** is a process of generating as many solutions or options as possible and is a popular technique associated with group decision-making.

All of these factors can lead to superior outcomes when groups are involved in decision-making. Furthermore, involving people who will be affected by a decision in the decision-making process will allow those individuals to have a greater understanding of the issues or problems and a greater commitment to the solutions.

Disadvantages of Group Decisions

Group decision-making is not without challenges. Some groups get bogged down by conflict, while others go to the opposite extreme and push for agreement at the expense of quality discussions. **Groupthink** occurs when group members choose not to voice their concerns or objections because they would rather keep the peace and not annoy or antagonize others. Sometimes groupthink occurs because the group has a positive team spirit and camaraderie, and individual group members don't want that to change by introducing conflict. It can also occur because past successes have made the team complacent.

Often, one individual in the group has more power or exerts more influence than others and discourages those with differing opinions from speaking up (**suppression of dissent**) to ensure that only their own ideas are implemented. If members of the group are not really contributing their ideas and perspectives, however, then the group is not getting the benefits of group decision-making.

How to Form a Quality Group

Effective managers will try to ensure quality group decision-making by forming groups with diverse members so that a variety of perspectives will contribute to the process. They will also encourage everyone to speak up and voice their opinions and thoughts prior to the group reaching a decision. Sometimes groups will also assign a member to play the **devil's advocate** in order to reduce groupthink. The devil's advocate intentionally takes on the role of critic. Their job is to point out flawed logic, to challenge the group's evaluations of various alternatives, and to identify weaknesses in proposed solutions. This pushes the other group members to think more deeply about the advantages and disadvantages of proposed solutions before reaching a decision and implementing it.

Exhibit 2.7   The Devils Advocate   At a meeting of McDonald's franchise owners, attorney Brian Schnell was placed in the audience as a devil's advocate and often would strongly disagree with franchisee attorney Bob Zarco that the National Labor Relations Board (NLRB)'s joint-employer ruling on McDonald's is a boon for franchisees. He would raise his hand often and vehemently, which Zarco had asked him to do before the meeting. In that way, the franchisors' articulate arguments could be heard by all franchisee leaders in attendance, and rebutted. Credit (Mr. Blue MauMau/ flickr/ Attribution 2.0 Generic (CC BY 2.0))

The methods we've just described can all help ensure that groups reach good decisions, but what can a manager do when there is too much conflict within a group? In this situation, managers need to help group members reduce conflict by finding some common ground—areas in which they can agree, such as common interests, values, beliefs, experiences, or goals. Keeping a group focused on a common goal can be a very worthwhile tactic to keep group members working with rather than against one another. **Table 2.3** summarizes the techniques to improve group decision-making.

Summary of Techniques That May Improve Group Decision-Making		
Type of Decision	Technique	Benefit
Group decisions	Have diverse members in the group.	Improves quality: generates more options, reduces bias
	Assign a devil's advocate.	Improves quality: reduces groupthink

Table 2.3 (Attribution: Copyright Rice University, OpenStax, under CC-BY 4.0 license)

Summary of Techniques That May Improve Group Decision-Making		
Type of Decision	Technique	Benefit
	Encourage everyone to speak up and contribute.	Improves quality: generates more options, prevents suppression of dissent
	Help group members find common ground.	Improves quality: reduces personality conflict

Table 2.3 (Attribution: Copyright Rice University, OpenStax, under CC-BY 4.0 license)

Conclusion

Decision-making is a crucial daily activity for managers. Decisions range from small and simple, with straightforward answers, to big and complex, with little clarity about what the best choice will be. Being an effective manager requires learning how to successfully navigate all kinds of decisions. Expertise, which develops gradually through learning and experience, generally improves managerial decision-making, but managers rarely rely solely on their own expertise. They also conduct research and collect information from others; they pay attention to their own biases and to ethical implications; and they think critically about the information that they have received to make decisions that will benefit the organization and its stakeholders.

CONCEPT CHECK

1. Explain why group decision-making can be more effective than individual decision-making.
2. What are some things that can prevent groups from making good decisions?
3. As a manager, what can you do to enhance the quality of group decision-making?

🔑 Key Terms

Bounded rationality The concept that when we make decisions, we cannot be fully rational because we don't have all the possible information or the cognitive processing ability to make fully informed, completely rational decisions.

Brainstorming A process of generating as many ideas or alternatives as possible, often in groups.

Confirmation bias The tendency to pay attention to information that confirms our existing beliefs and to ignore or discount information that conflicts with our existing beliefs.

Creativity The generation of new or original ideas.

Critical thinking A disciplined process of evaluating the quality of information, especially by identifying logical fallacies in arguments.

Decision-making The action or process of thinking through possible options and selecting one.

Devil's advocate A group member who intentionally takes on the role of being critical of the group's ideas in order to discourage groupthink and encourage deep thought and discussion about issues prior to making decisions.

Emotional intelligence The ability to understand and manage emotions in oneself and in others.

Escalation of commitment The tendency of decision makers to remain committed to poor decision, even when doing so leads to increasingly negative outcomes.

Evidence-based decision-making A process of collecting the best available evidence prior to making a decision.

Groupthink The tendency of a group to reach agreement very quickly and without substantive discussion.

Heuristics Mental shortcuts that allow a decision maker to reach a good decision quickly. They are strategies that develop based on prior experience.

Nonprogrammed decisions Decisions that are novel and not based on well-defined or known criteria.

Process conflict Conflict about the best way to do something; conflict that is task-oriented and constructive, and not focused on the individuals involved.

Programmed decisions Decisions that are repeated over time and for which an existing set of rules can be developed.

Reactive system System of decision-making in the brain that is quick and intuitive.

Reflective system System of decision-making in the brain that is logical, analytical, and methodical.

Relationship conflict Conflict between individuals that is based on personal (or personality) differences; this type of conflict tends to be destructive rather than constructive.

Satisficing Choosing the first acceptable solution to minimize time spent on a decision.

Stakeholders Individuals or groups who are impacted by the organization. These include owners, employees, customers, suppliers, and members of the community in which the organization is located.

Suppression of dissent When a group member exerts his or her power to prevent others from voicing their thoughts or opinions.

📖 Summary of Learning Outcomes

2.1 Overview of Managerial Decision-Making
1. What are the basic characteristics of managerial decision-making?

Managers are constantly making decisions, and those decisions often have significant impacts and implications for both the organization and its stakeholders. Managerial decision-making is often characterized by complexity, incomplete information, and time constraints, and there is rarely one right answer. Sometimes there are multiple good options (or multiple bad options), and the manager must try to decide which will generate the most positive outcomes (or the fewest negative outcomes). Managers must weigh the possible consequences of each decision and recognize that there are often multiple stakeholders with conflicting needs and preferences so that it often will be impossible to satisfy everyone. Finally, managerial decision-making can sometimes have ethical implications, and these should be contemplated before reaching a final decision.

2.2 How the Brain Processes Information to Make Decisions: Reflective and Reactive Systems

2. What are the two systems of decision-making in the brain?

The brain processes information to make decisions using one of two systems: either the logical, rational (reflective) system or the quick, reactive system. The reflective system is better for significant and important decisions; these generally should not be rushed. However, the reactive system can be lifesaving when time is of the essence, and it can be much more efficient when based on developed experience and expertise.

2.3 Programmed and Nonprogrammed Decisions

3. What is the difference between programmed and nonprogrammed decisions?

Programmed decisions are those that are based on criteria that are well understood, while nonprogrammed decisions are novel and lack clear guidelines for reaching a solution. Managers can establish rules and guidelines for programmed decisions based on known fact, which enables them to reach decisions quickly. Nonprogrammed decisions require more time to resolve; the decision maker may need to conduct research, collect additional information, gather opinions and ideas from other people, and so on.

2.4 Barriers to Effective Decision-Making

4. What barriers exist that make effective decision-making difficult?

There are numerous barriers to effective decision-making. Managers are limited in their ability to collect comprehensive information, and they are limited in their ability to cognitively process all the information that is available. Managers cannot always know all the possible outcomes of all the possible options, and they often face time constraints that limit their ability to collect all the information that they would like to have. In addition, managers, like all humans, have biases that influence their decision-making, and that can make it difficult for them to make good decisions. One of the most common biases that can confound decision-making is confirmation bias, the tendency for a person to pay attention to information that confirms her existing beliefs and ignore information that conflicts with these existing beliefs. Finally, conflict between individuals in organizations can make it challenging to reach a good decision.

2.5 Improving the Quality of Decision-Making

5. How can a manager improve the quality of her individual decision-making?

Managers tend to get better at decision-making with time and experience, which helps them build expertise. Heuristics and satisficing can also be useful techniques for making programmed decisions quickly. For nonprogrammed decisions, a manager can improve the quality of her decision-making by utilizing a variety of other techniques. Managers should also be careful to not skip steps in the decision-making process, to involve others in the process at various points, and to be creative in generating alternatives. They should also engage in evidence-based decision-making: doing research and collecting data and information on which to base the decision. Effective managers also think critically about the quality of the evidence that they collect, and they carefully consider long-term outcomes and ethical implications prior to making a decision.

2.6 Group Decision-Making

6. What are the advantages and disadvantages of group decision-making, and how can a manager improve the quality of group decision-making?

Groups can make better decisions than individuals because group members can contribute more knowledge and a diversity of perspectives. Groups will tend to generate more options as well, which can lead to better solutions. Also, having people involved in making decisions that will affect them can improve their attitudes about the decision that is made. However, groups sometimes fail to generate added value in the decision-making process as a result of groupthink, conflict, or suppression of dissent.

Managers can improve the quality of group decision-making in a number of ways. First, when forming the group, the manager should ensure that the individual group members are diverse in terms of knowledge and perspectives. The manager may also want to assign a devil's advocate to discourage groupthink. Managers should also encourage all group members to contribute their ideas and opinions, and they should not allow a single voice to dominate. Finally, they should not allow personality conflicts to derail group processes.

Chapter Review Questions

1. What are some of the factors that enabled to Jen Rubio and Stephanie Korey to make good decisions when they established their luggage company, Away?
2. What are the two systems that the brain uses in decision-making? How are they related to programmed and nonprogrammed decisions?
3. What is a heuristic, and when would it be appropriate to use a heuristic for decision-making?
4. What is confirmation bias? Explain how it can be a barrier to effective decision-making.
5. What is a logical fallacy?
6. What are the two types of conflict? Which one is constructive, and which is destructive?
7. What are the steps in the decision-making process? Which ones do people tend to skip or spend insufficient time on?
8. What can individuals do to improve the quality of their decision-making?
9. What can groups or group leaders do to improve the quality of group decision-making?
10. What are the benefits of decision-making in a group, instead of individually?

Management Skills Application Exercises

1. If you wanted to buy a new car, what research would you do first to increase the likelihood of making a good decision? As a manager, do you think you would engage in more research or less research than that prior to making big decisions for the organization?
2. Think about a big decision that you have made. What impact did your emotions have on that decision? Did they help or hinder your decision-making? Would you make the same decision again?
3. If you were faced with an ethical dilemma at work, who would you want to talk to for advice prior to reaching a decision?
4. Which would be better to involve a group with, a programmed or a nonprogrammed decision? Why?
5. If you were manager of a group with a lot of personality conflict, what would you do?

Managerial Decision Exercises

1. Imagine that you are a manager and that two of your employees are blaming one another for a recent project not going well. What factors would you consider in deciding whom to believe? Who else would you

    talk to before making a decision? What would you do to try to reduce the likelihood of this happening again?

2.   You have been asked whether your organization should expand from selling its products only in North America to selling its products in Europe as well. What information would you want to collect? Who would you want to discuss the idea with before making a decision?

3.   You have a colleague who decided the organization should pursue a new technology. Nine months into the project of transitioning to the new technology, based on new information you are convinced that the new technology is not going to work out as anticipated. In fact, you expect it to be a colossal failure. However, when you try to talk to your colleague about the issue, she won't listen to your arguments. She is adamant that this new technology is the correct direction for your organization. Why do you think she is so resistant to seeing reason? Given what you learned in this chapter, what could you do to persuade her?

4.   Your manager has asked you to take the lead on a new and creative project. She has encouraged you to create your own team (from existing employees) to work with you on the project. What factors would you want to consider in deciding who should join your project team? What would you want to do as the team leader to increase the likelihood that the group will be successful?

5.   Identify the logical flaw(s) in this argument:
   - We want to have effective leaders in this organization.
   - Taller individuals tend to be perceived as more leader-like.
   - Men are usually taller than women.
   - So, we should only hire men to be managers in our organization.

Critical Thinking Case

Vinyl Records Make a Comeback

The music industry has seen a series of innovations that have improved audio quality—vinyl records sales were eventually surpassed by compact discs in the 1980s, which were then eclipsed by digital music in the early 2000s. Both of the newer technologies boast superior sound quality to vinyl records. Vinyl should be dead . . . yet it's not. Some say this is simply a result of nostalgia—people love to harken back to older times. However, some audiophiles say that vinyl records produce a "warm" sound that can't be reproduced in any other format. In addition, a vinyl record is a tangible product (you can feel it, touch it, and see it when you own the physical record) and is more attractive, from an aesthetic perspective, than a CD. It is also a format that encourages listening to an entire album at once, rather than just listening to individual tracks, which can change the listening experience.

Whatever the reasons, vinyl is making an impressive comeback. Sales growth has been in the double digits for the last several years (over 50% in 2015 and again in 2016) and is expected to exceed $5 billion in 2017. Sony, which hasn't produced a vinyl record since 1989, recently announced that it is back in the vinyl business.

One of the biggest challenges to making vinyl records is that most of the presses are 40+ years old. In the record-making process, vinyl bits are heated to 170 degrees, and then a specialized machine exerts 150 tons of pressure to press the vinyl into the shape of the record. About a dozen new vinyl record manufacturers have sprung up in the last decade in the United States. Independent Record Pressing, a company based in New Jersey, began producing vinyl records in 2015 using old, existing presses. Their goal upon starting up was to produce over a million records a year. Even at that level of production, though, demand far outstrips the company's capacity to produce because of the limited number of presses available. They could run their machines nonstop, 24 hours a day, and not catch up with demand.

The big question is what the future holds for this industry. Will this just be a passing fad? Will the vinyl record industry remain a small niche market? Or is this the renaissance, the rebirth of a product that can withstand the test of time and alternative technologies? If it's a rebirth, then we should see demand continue to grow at its recent rapid pace . . . and if demand remains strong, then investing in new presses may well be worthwhile. If this is just a short-lived nostalgic return to an outdated media, however, then the large capital investment required to purchase new presses will never be recouped. Even with the recent growth, vinyl records still accounted for only 7% of overall music industry sales in 2015. That may be enough to get old presses running again, but so far it hasn't been enough to promote a lot of investment in new machines. The cost of a new press? Almost half a million dollars.

At least one manufacturer is optimistic about the future of vinyl. GZ Media, based in Czechoslovakia, is currently the world's largest producer of vinyl records. President and owner Zdenek Pelc kept his record factory going during the lean years when vinyl sales bottomed out. He admits that the decision was not wholly logical; he continued in part because of an emotional attachment to the media. After demand for vinyl records practically disappeared, Pelc kept just a few of the presses running to meet the demand that remained. His intention was to be the last remaining manufacturer of vinyl records. Pelc's emotional attachment to vinyl records seems to have served him well, and it's a great example of why basing decisions on pure logic doesn't always lead to the best results. Consumers make purchasing decisions in part based on the emotional appeal of the product, so it shouldn't be surprising that consumers also feel an emotional attachment to vinyl records, as Pelc did.

When demand for vinyl records was low, Pelc stored the company's presses that were no longer in use so that they could be cannibalized for parts as needed. When sales began to grow again in 2005, he started pulling old machines out of storage and even invested in a few new ones. This has made GZ Media not only the largest vinyl record producer in the world, but also one of the only ones with new factory equipment. GZ Media produces over 20 million vinyl records a year, and Pelc is excited to continue that trend and to remain a major manufacturer in what is currently still considered a niche market.

Critical Thinking Questions
1. Why do you think vinyl records are appealing to customers?
2. Do you think the sales growth will continue to be strong for vinyl sales? Why or why not?
3. What research would you want to conduct prior to making a decision to invest in new presses?

Sources: Lee Barron, "Back on record – the reasons behind vinyl's unlikely comeback," *The Conversation*, April 17, 2015, https://theconversation.com/back-on-record-the-reasons-behind-vinyls-unlikely-comeback-39964. Hannah Ellis-Peterson, "Record sales: vinyl hits 25-year high," The Guardian, January 3, 2017, https://www.theguardian.com/music/2017/jan/03/record-sales-vinyl-hits-25-year-high-and-outstrips-streaming. Allan Kozinn, "Weaned on CDs, They're Reaching for Vinyl," *The New York Times*, June 9, 2013. Rick Lyman, "Czech company, pressing hits for years on vinyl, finds it has become one," The New York Times, August 6, 2015. Alec Macfarlane and Chie Kobayashi, "Vinyl comeback: Sony to produce records again after 28-year break," *CNN Money*, June 30, 2017, http://money.cnn.com/2017/06/30/news/sony-music-brings-back-vinyl-records/index.html. Kate Rogers, "Why millennials are buying more vinyl records," CNBC.com, November 6, 2015. https://www.cnbc.com/2015/11/06/why-millennials-are-buying-more-vinyl-records.html. Robert Tait, "In the groove: Czech firm tops list of world's vinyl record producers," *The Guardian*, August 18, 2016.

3

The History of Management

Exhibit 3.1 (Gawler History/ Attribution 2.0 Generic (CC BY 2.0))

 Introduction

Learning Outcomes

After reading this chapter, you should be able to answer these questions:

1. Describe management in the ancient world.
2. How did the Italian Renaissance affect the progression of management theory?
3. How did the Industrial Revolution affect the progression of management theory?
4. How did Frederick Winslow Taylor influence management theory, and how did efficiency in management affect current management theory?
5. How do bureaucratic and administrative management complement scientific management?
6. How did Elton Mayo influence management theory, and how did the human relations movement affect current management theory?
7. How did contingency and systems management transform management thought?

EXPLORING MANAGERIAL CAREERS

Michael Porter: Harvard Professor and Management Consultant, The Monitor Group

Michael Porter is the Bishop William Lawrence University Professor at Harvard Business School and one of the foremost scholars and consultants in business strategy. Dubbed the first "Lord of Strategy," he is one of the most influential management thinkers of all time. Porter's primary contribution is in the field of competition, specifically the question of why some companies profit while others do not. Porter first became interested in competition due to his enthusiasm competing in youth sports (baseball, football, and basketball).

Porter was born in 1947 and graduated from Princeton in 1969 with a degree in aerospace and mechanical engineering. He went on to receive his MBA from Harvard Business School in 1971 and his PhD in business economics from Harvard University in 1973. His book *Competitive Strategy: Techniques for Analyzing Industries and Competitors* (published in 1980) was deemed the ninth most influential work of the 20th century by the Fellows of the Academy of Management. Porter, writing during a period of great economic competition between the United States and Japan, was able to gain a wide and vast audience for his work.

Exhibit 3.2   Michael Porter   Michael E. Porter leads a conversation with three leading public and private investors, Jin-Yong Cai, Tony O. Elumelu, and Arif Naqvi, on the panel "Investing in Prosperity: A Conversation with Global Leaders" at the Shared Value Leadership Summit. (Shared Value Initiative/ flickr/ Attribution 2.0 Generic (CC BY 2.0))

In his 1979 *Harvard Business Review* article "How Competitive Forces Shape Strategy," Porter presented his game management idea that five forces help determine the level of profitability. The five forces are competition in the industry, potential of new entrants into the industry, power of suppliers, power of customers, and threat of substitute products. An unattractive industry is one in which the five forces align themselves to produce a purely competitive industry. In this type of industry, normal profit levels are the highest a firm can expect, which means that the firm can cover its costs and make the owner a profit but cannot make excess profits. Once a firm identifies the five forces in its industry, it can choose between one of three generic strategies for success focus, differentiation, or cost leadership. Depending on where a firm is positioned within the market, the marketplace will determine what strategy it can take. This "five forces, three strategies" framework explains how McDonald's, Morton's Steakhouse, Subway, Wendy's, and TGIF can all be in the same industry and still be profitable. They offer different types of products to different types of customers. These products compete on price, differentiation, focus, or a combination of these. In addition to the five forces model, Porter developed the value-chain model, which describes the unique activities that a corporation performs to make its products valuable to its customers. Porter has also contributed to health-care management, environmental regulation, international competition, and industry-level profits.

Porter's five forces framework is intuitive and has provided managers with an approach to develop actual strategies. His ideas became popular because business leaders wanted to know how their companies could compete. Prior to Porter, management scholars stressed the idiosyncratic nature of business, stressing how each situation faced by each business was different. Other scholars offered business strategy models, but they were not as useful or practical as Porter's. Through his use of industrial-organizational economics and his training in the case method, Porter bridged the gap between theoretical frameworks and the reality of the competitive business world and became one of the most important thinkers on business in the world.

Sources: Bedeian, Arthur G and Wren, Daniel A. (Winter 2001). "Most Influential Management Books of the 20th Century" (PDF). *Organizational Dynamics*. 29 (3): 221–225; Kiechel, Walter (2010). The Lords of Strategy: The Secret Intellectual History of the New Corporate World. *Harvard Business Review Press*; Magretta, Joan (2011). Understanding Michael Porter: The Essential Guide to Competition and Strategy. *Harvard Business Review Press*; and Mathews, J.(2013-02-01). The Competitive Advantage of Michael Porter. In The Oxford Handbook of Management Theorists: *Oxford University Press*.

While you may think that management is a relatively new field, it actually has its roots in the ancient world. In fact, whenever and wherever there has been commerce, there has been management and those thinking about how to do it better. For example, the Seven Wonders of the Ancient World, including the Colossus of Rhodes, the Hanging Gardens of Babylon, and the Great Pyramid, could only have been constructed through the work of a great many people. The size and complexity of these structures suggest that there must have been people (managers) who coordinated the labor and resources needed to execute the construction plans. Similarly, the Romans and the ancient Chinese could not have managed their vast empires without management, nor could the Phoenicians and the Greeks have dominated oceangoing trade without management.

Because management has been around for a while, it makes sense that the study of management is old. This idea is supported by the many managerial insights we can find in political, diplomatic, and military history and in philosophy, poetry, economics, and literature. Anyone familiar with Shakespeare's *King Lear* would recognize the present-day management problem of succession planning! Modern managers have been influenced by the works of Chinese military strategist and philosopher Sun Tzu, Roman general and politician Julius Caesar, and even Genghis Kahn, Mongolian conqueror and ruler of what became the largest land empire in all of history.[1] Mark Zuckerberg[2] of Facebook is a modern admirer of the Caesars and has said that he bases some of his management style on his classical education.

Despite its ancient roots, modern management is less than 150 years old. In fact, a comparison of management before and after the Industrial Revolution shows that the former is only a shadowy comparison to the latter. Prior to the Industrial Revolution, work was performed, with exceptions, mostly in home and on farms by forced labor (slaves or indentured servants) or family members, and the output they produced was often for employers', local, or family consumption. Over the centuries, economics and morality shifted, and laborers could choose where and for whom to work. These changes, in turn, would bring about many changes in how labor and other resources were employed in production.

The two developments that transformed management were the revolutions in how and where goods were sold and the Industrial Revolution. The events combined led to the selling of a wider variety of goods to a wider variety of customers in more distant locations. These events also led to the establishment of vast companies. Competition required the development of economies of scale (i.e., increased production lowering costs) and required coordination and specialization in the use of resources. The combination of coordination and specialization problems encouraged the development of management study as a distinct field.

In this chapter, we trace the evaluation of management from its origins in the ancient world to its form as a modern profession. Understanding how management came to be helps us to understand its principles in a richer, more thorough context and to understand how each concept we discuss is based on evidence produced by a wide range of scholars over many years in the fields of engineering, economics, psychology, sociology, and anthropology.

3.1 | The Early Origins of Management

1. Describe management in the ancient world.

Table 3.1 traces the development of management thought from the ancient world until the 19th century's Industrial Revolution.

Sumer, located in what is today southern Iraq and the first urban-based civilization, contained the genesis of management. Sumer had a flourishing merchant culture in which goods such as grains, livestock, perfumes, and pottery were sold to customers. Rather than bartering (using one good or service, not money, to pay for another good or service), the ancient Sumerians used ancient clay coins to pay. The sizes and shapes of coins represented different amounts of currency and signaled the types of goods for which they could be exchanged.[3]

What made this level of trade and economic activity possible? The introduction of writing made it possible for merchants to keep track of various trades. And the development of a basic form of coins allowed for increased trade because a person wanting to obtain a good or service no longer had to find another person who wanted exactly the good or service he produced. Coordinating the activities of those who provided goods and those who wanted to purchase them often required coordination, one of the main functions of a manager.

Early Contributor	Outcome
Sumerians	Writing and trade
Hammurabi	Written commands and controls
Nebuchadnezzar	Incentives
Ancient Egyptians	Division of labor, coordination and span of control
Sun Tzu	Division of labor, communication and coordination
Han dynasty (206 BC–220 AD)	Development of bureaucracy
Ancient Greeks	Division of labor

Table 3.1 (Attribution: Copyright Rice University, OpenStax, under CC-BY 4.0 license)

Early Contributor	Outcome
Romans	Standardization
Italians	Accounting, corporations, multinational corporations
John Florio	Management to English language
Source: Adapted from George (1972) and Wren & Bedeian (2009)	

Table 3.1 (Attribution: Copyright Rice University, OpenStax, under CC-BY 4.0 license)

Two additional contributions to the early development of management came from the Middle East. The idea of written laws and commands comes from the Babylonian king **Hammurabi** (1810 BC–1750 BC).[4] The Code of Hammurabi was a listing of 282 laws that regulated a wide variety of behaviors, including business dealings, personal behavior, interpersonal relations, and punishments. Law 104 was one of the first instances of accounting and of the need for formal rules for managers and owners. The code also set wages for doctors, bricklayers, stonemasons, boatmen, herdsmen, and other labors. The code did not, however, include the concept of incentive wages because it set wages at a fixed amount. The idea of incentives would come from another, much later, Babylonian king, **Nebuchadnezzar** (605 BC–c. 562 BC),[5] who gave incentives to cloth weavers for production. Weavers were paid in food, and the more cloth they produced, the more food they were given.

Exhibit 3.3   Hammurabi   The Code of Hammurabi is a well-preserved ancient law code, created between 1810 BC and 1750 BC in ancient Babylon. It's a listing of 282 laws that regulated conduct on a wide variety of behaviors, including business dealings, personal behavior, interpersonal relations, and punishments. Law 104 was one of the first instances of accounting and the need for formal rules for owners and managers. (Gabrielle Barni / flickr/ Attribution 2.0 Generic (CC BY 2.0))

The ancient Egyptians made great strides in the building of the great pyramids. The ancient Egyptians were exceptional builders of canals, irrigation projects, and the pyramids, royal tombs whose size and complexity exceeded what the Greeks and Romans[6] were able to build in later centuries. Although we are still uncertain about exactly how the pyramids were constructed, we have some idea that the process required a great number and wide range of slave laborers to construct them. Each laborer would have a different task. Some of the laborers were stonecutters; others were required to push and pull gigantic blocks of stone; still others were required to grease the stones to reduce friction. In this process, we see the management principals of division of labor, coordination, and specialization. These groups of workers were supervised by one individual. In figuring out how best to handle the huge numbers of workers engaged in pyramid building, the ancient Egyptians also pioneered the concept of span of control, that is, the number of workers that a manager controls directly. Anticipating research on this issue in the far, far distant future, Egyptians found the ideal number of workers per supervisor to be ten. In addition, there were various overseers, who had the responsibility to compel workers to produce.

In Asia, the Chinese began to develop the idea of bureaucracy. Bureaucracy has roots in the early dynasties but only became fully developed during the Han dynasty (206 BC–220 AD).[7] The idea was to train scholars in Confucian teachings and use those teachings to make decisions. Unlike modern bureaucracies, this system was not formal but relied upon the discretion of the scholars themselves. Another important development was the idea of meritocracy because selection for and then promotion within a bureaucracy was based on a test of Confucian teaching.

The Greeks (800 BC–400 BC) and Romans (500 BC–476 AD) added a number of important steps in the development of management. Although neither empire was commercially oriented, both Greeks and the Romans undertook a wide range of industrial projects, such as roads and aqueducts, and established various guilds and societies that encouraged trade. The Greeks continued to develop the idea of division of labor based on Plato's recognition of human diversity. The great Greek philosopher Socrates stressed the development of managerial skills such as creating an atmosphere of information sharing and analysis. The Romans' contribution to management was standardization. Because the Romans needed to administer a vast empire, they needed standardization of measures, weights, and coins. Romans also saw the birth of the corporation, in that many Roman companies sold stocks to the public.

Both Greece and Rome saw the continued pestilence of slavery, but due to economic changes that made slavery financially unfeasible, workers were gaining some degree of freedom. They still had masters who determined at what jobs they could work and how those jobs should be done. After the collapse of the Roman Empire, there was a decline in European trade. Scholars refer to this time as the Dark or Middle Ages (500 AD–1000 AD), due its location between the classical world of the Greeks and Romans and the world of the Renaissance. While there was little trade or economic development in Europe during this period, trade flourished in the Muslim and Chinese worlds. Various travelers, such as 13th-century Italian merchant and explorer Marco Polo, provided readers with tales and goods from those booming societies.

CONCEPT CHECK

1. What were the contributions of the following groups to modern management: Sumerians, Babylonians, Egyptians, Chinese, Greeks, and Romans?

3.2 | The Italian Renaissance

2. How did the Italian Renaissance affect the progression of management theory?

In the 11th, 12th, and 13th centuries, Europeans went on a series of military expeditions to recover the Holy Land from the Muslims. These expeditions, called the Crusades, brought wealth and technological advances into Europe from the Muslim world.[8]

In the 14th century, a movement of cultural change and astounding achievements in all spheres of life began in northern Italy. The **Italian Renaissance** saw the reintroduction of classical knowledge and the emergence of new knowledge and learning, much of which had economic and business implications. The emergence of the basic printing press allowed for these ideas and knowledge to spread throughout Europe. The combination of these factors led to the creation of new wealth as a new emphasis on trade and wealth creation developed. In Italy, we see the emergence of modern enterprise and the emergence of the need for people to run these new enterprises. As Muldoon and Marin[9] write:

> Their industrious countrymen were improving mining operations and developing the shipping and banking industries, which created the underlying conditions for the migration of the Italian Renaissance's commercial and intellectual culture from its native Italian soil (Haynes, 1991). The increasing scope and complexity of these commercial activities may well have prompted such inventions as double-entry bookkeeping and motivated companies to hire business managers to coordinate and direct their operations (Witzel, 2002).

Organizations called corporations developed to carry out these commercial activities, not only within a country, but among many countries. The first multinational corporations were located in Italy but had branches across Europe. The Florence Company of Bardi was a multinational bank that provided loans to various kings, including Edward III of England.[10] As their commercial enterprises flourished, the Italians provided manuals for merchants, which spread the ideas of commerce throughout Europe.

CONCEPT CHECK

1. What was the Italian Renaissance?
2. What managerial legacy did it leave?

3.3 | The Industrial Revolution

3. How did the Industrial Revolution affect the progression of management theory?

The Renaissance and its ideals came to England, a backwater power at the time, during the reign of the Tudors (1485–1603).[11] It was during this time that the word *management* came into the English language from Italy through translations by John Florio,[12] an Anglo-Italian member of Queen Elizabeth's court.

The emergence of British power would spawn the third major advance in management, the **Industrial Revolution**. As the British Empire's power grew, so did opportunities for trade. The 18th century saw the emergence of various international corporations, such as the Hudson's Bay Company[13] and the East India Company,[14] which conducted business globally. The Hudson's Bay Company orchestrated fur trade in Canada where pelts were produced and then shipped to England for trade in any part of the globe.

This further development of trade led to the establishment of the marketplace as a dominant means of organizing the exchange of goods. The market would coordinate the actions and activities of various participants, thus allowing resources to flow to their most efficient uses. One of the major intellectual leaders of this period was the economist and moral philosopher **Adam Smith**.[15] In his masterpiece, *The Wealth of Nations*,[16] Smith proposed the idea of specialization and coordination within corporations as a source of economic growth. Specialization and division of labor were Smith's major contributions to management thought. The division of labor meant that a worker specialized in performing one task that was part of a larger series of tasks, at the end of which a product would be produced. The idea of specialization of labor had several important outcomes. Firstly, specialization drastically reduced the cost of goods. Secondly, it drastically reduced the need for training. Instead of learning every aspect of a task, workers needed to learn one portion of it. Thirdly, the need to coordinate all these different tasks required a greater emphasis on management.

Another significant part of the Industrial Revolution involved the development of the steam engine, which played a major role in improving the transportation of goods and raw materials. The steam engine lowered production and transportation costs, thus lowering prices and allowing products to reach more distant markets.[17] All of these factors played a role in the Industrial Revolution, which occurred between 1760 and 1900.[18] The Industrial Revolution saw the emergence of the modern corporation, in which work, usually in a factory setting, was specialized and coordinated by managers.

Prior to the Industrial Revolution, goods and services lacked standardization and were produced at home in small batches.[19] The Industrial Revolution saw work shift from family-led home production to factory production. These factories could employ hundreds and even thousands of workers who produced mass batches of standardized goods more cheaply than they could be produced in homes.

Factory sizes ranged from sections of cities and towns to whole cities, such as Lowell, Massachusetts, which consisted primarily of textile mills. As the Industrial Revolution progressed, small factories transformed into larger ones. In 1849, Harvester in Chicago employed 123 workers and was the largest factory in the United States. McCormick plant by the mid-1850s had 250 workers who made 2,500 reapers per year. After the Great Chicago Fire, McCormick built a new plant with 800 workers and sales well above $1 million. In 1913, Henry Ford's plant in Dearborn employed up to 12,000 workers.[20] As factories grew in size, they provided chances for personnel fulfillment. Not only was the Hawthorne plant in Cicero, Illinois, a place of business, but it also featured sports teams and other social outlets.[21]

The Industrial Revolution shifted from England across the globe and eventually found its way into the United States. The United States starting seeing several notable industrial revolutions from the 1820s until the 1860s. The transportation revolution included the construction of canals and, later, railroads that connected the different parts of the continent. The emergence of a telegraph system allowed for faster communication between various parts of the United States. Previously, it would take weeks to get information from New York to Boston; with the telegraph, it took minutes.[22] The United States also saw the emergence of the Market Revolution. Previously to the Market Revolution, the U.S. economy had been based on small, self-subsistent yeoman farmers who would produce mostly homemade batches. Around 1830, the existence of easy credit and improved transportation established a broad Market Revolution. This spawned a wide variety of corporations that needed managers to coordinate various company offices.[23]

After the period of the American Civil War, which ended in 1865, society witnessed the emergence of gigantic corporations that spanned the continent and factories that were like small cities.[24] Various problems emerged due to the change of production (similar to some of the issues we face today with the change from a manufacturing economy to an information economy). For example, how do you motivate workers? When families controlled labor, it was very easy to motivate workers due to the fact that if family members did not produce, the family may not survive.[25] Yet in the factory, it was possible for workers to avoid work or even destroy machines if they disliked management's ideas. Each worker did the job in a different fashion, workers seemed to be selected without regard to whether they were suited for a particular job, management seemed to be whimsical, and there was little standardization of equipment.

Because production quantity remained an unknown to both management and the worker, management did not explain how they determined what should be produced. Workers believed that management determined what should be produced in haphazard ways.[26] Workers believed that if too much were produced, management would eliminate workers because they believed that there was a finite amount of work in the world. Workers would control production by punishing those workers who produced too much. For example, if a worker produced too much, his equipment would be damaged, or he would be brutalized by his coworkers. Methods of production were similarly haphazard. For example, if you learned how to shovel coal or cut iron, you learned multiple ways to perform the job, which did little for efficiency. Due to managerial inefficiency, various reformers in engineering urged for the establishment of management as a distinct field of study so that some order and logic could be brought to bear on how work was performed. Although this period witnessed enormous changes in technology, management was still lagging behind.[27]

CONCEPT CHECK

1. Why was Adam Smith's specialization of labor so important?
2. What was the economic and managerial legacy of the Industrial Revolution? What were the challenges?

3.4 | Taylor-Made Management

4. How did Frederick Winslow Taylor influence management theory, and how did efficiency in management affect current management theory?

The economic upheaval of the Industrial Revolution also witnessed tremendous social upheavals. The U.S. professional classes (lawyers, administrators, doctors) had numerous concerns.[28] Because more and more people were now working in factories, there was the potential for creating a permanent underclass of poorly educated workers struggling to make a living. Many reformers felt that workers could be radicalized and actively try to better their working conditions, pay, and so on, thus disrupting the status quo of the labor markets, leading to strikes, riots, violence. There were also concerns that money, influence, and pressure from big business were corrupting politics and overriding the will of the people.

The working class had many concerns about their work life. As mentioned earlier, there was a deep fear that work would disappear because of overproduction. There were also concerns over wages, job tenure, and workplace justice. And there was little in the way of standardization when it came to how tasks were to be accomplished.[29] When Frank Gilbreth, a pioneer in scientific management, was apprenticed as a bricklayer in 1885, he noted that he was taught three ways to lay bricks even though there was no need for more than one method.

In the factories, there was little concern for the workers' physical or mental health, and there were no breaks.[30] Management and the workforce were in vicious contention with each other. Management would set the rate of work expected for the day, and in response, workers would band together to limit production. This action, called "soldiering," was a deliberate reduction of productivity on the part of the worker. Those workers who either over- or underproduced could expect that their equipment would be destroyed or that they themselves would be physically harmed. There were very few, if any, incentives provided by management. When managers sought to motivate workers, they did so through physical beatings and other punishments.[31] Neither side had a reason to trust or cooperate with the other.

Compounding management problems, there was now a demand for managers, but there were very few of them to fill this demand, as there was little training provided. Prior to the Industrial Revolution, companies were largely in the hands of a family or a single owner/manager. As companies were getting larger and more complex and the exchange of goods was taking place across more and more regions, most business owners no longer had the expertise to run such vast geographic and financial enterprises.[32] Yet there was little in the way of management training or education. There were no established scholarly journals, such as the *Academy of Management Journal*, or practitioner journals, such as the *Harvard Business Review*. Nor were there business schools until 1881, when the Wharton School of Business at the University of Pennsylvania was established. Business education at this time consisted mostly of classes that taught secretarial work. Allied fields, such as psychology and sociology, were in their infancy. Any management education that did exist was mostly learned from lessons of history and literature. Although there were numerous examples of both excellent and terrible management, this education was anecdotal and not systematic.

The second phase of the Industrial Revolution commenced with the establishment of management as a distinct discipline of knowledge. Management's birth was not in Great Britain, but in the United States.[33] According to management consultant and educator Peter Drucker, the development of management was one of the United States' primary contributions to the world, along with the Declaration of Independence.[34] At the same time management was getting established, sociology and psychology were developing, and the studies of history and economics were becoming more scientific and formal. Management also became formalized as a field of study using the scientific method. Drucker stated that the development of management was one of the factors that held off the development of radicalism in the United States because it increased productivity, lowered prices, and increased wages for workers. The success of scientific management lifted workers into the middle class. This crucial development has been attributed to one person in particular: **Frederick Winslow Taylor**.

Frederick Winslow Taylor (1856–1915) is known as the father of scientific management. He was born to the Quaker aristocracy of Pennsylvania, and initially he planned to go to Harvard and become a lawyer or an executive until he suffered an eye injury that prevented him from reading.[35] With Harvard no longer an option, Taylor went to work at a family friend's factory, the Midvale Steel Company. Taylor took to the work and was promoted quickly from pattern maker to foreman and then to chief engineer. During this time, he witnessed many acts aimed at limiting or reducing production—including having his tools destroyed—and it was he who coined the term *soldiering* to describe this deliberate act.[36] Rather than stand by and see such senseless acts affect the business he worked for, Taylor decided to take action. First, he went to Stevens Institute of Technology to gain a background in engineering. Then he took this knowledge and applied it to his work.

It is important to note that Taylor was not an original thinker. Many of his ideas came from other thinkers, especially the Englishman Charles Babbage (1791–1871).[37] Taylor's contribution was that he advanced a total system of management by uniting the ideas and philosophies of many others. While he may not have invented the scientific study of management, Taylor contributed to the use and synthesis of management by pioneering the use of time studies, division of labor based on function, cost-control systems, written instruction for workers, planning, and standardized equipment. Taylorism is still the basis of modern management, including the use of incentives. For example, Taylor stressed piecework production, meaning that workers were paid for how much they produced. Taylor also stressed the idea of differential piecework, meaning that if workers produced more than a certain amount, they would be paid more. Some compensation systems, such as sales commissions (i.e., being paid for how much you sell), have their bases in Taylor's work.

Taylor's major contribution was that he prized knowledge and science over tradition and rules of thumb. He broke down each act of production into its smallest parts and watched the best workers perform their jobs. Using a stopwatch to time the workers' actions, Taylor determined the most effective and efficient way to accomplish a given task. After breaking down each job into its component parts, Taylor then reconstructed them as they *should* be done. Taylor also developed time management studies to break down a person's workday into a series of activities. He then timed the execution of each activity to see which way was the quickest. He would rebuild the job using only the most efficient ways possible and then train workers to perform the task. And by allowing workers to have rest periods throughout the day, he was able to get workers to work faster and better without making them tired.[38]

Another one of Taylor's significant contributions to the practice and profession of management was the concept of first-class work. When Taylor developed the notion of first-class work, he did so with the idea that workers should do as much work as they are physically and mentally capable of doing. Those who were not physically or mentally capable of keeping up with production and job demands were sent to different areas in the plant where they could work most effectively. First-class work was based not on physical strain or bursts of activity, but on what a worker could realistically be expected to do.

Taylor also developed a task management system that allowed work to occur more efficiently and allowed for breaking up a supervisor's work so that he could function within a discrete area of activities. This focus allowed supervisors to better plan and control the activities for which their workers were responsible. Taylor believed that managers would become better at and more suited to analyzing their specific area of expertise, with authority that came from knowledge and skill and not simply from position or power. He also developed a cost-accounting method that became an integral part of daily planning and control, not something that was applied only to long-term analysis.

Taylorism was based on **four principles of management** illustrated in **Table 3.2**.

Principle 1: A manager should develop a rule of science for each aspect of a job. Following this principal ensures that work is based on objective data gathered through research rather than rules of thumb. For example, many people believed that allowing workers to take breaks would limit how much work could be done. After all, how could a worker produce if he was not working? Taylor changed this attitude through research that demonstrated the benefits of breaks during the workday. Due to Taylor's research, we now enjoy coffee breaks.

Principle 2. Scientifically select and train each worker. When you get to the chapter on human resource management, you will see that Taylor's ideas still hold. Prior to Taylor's work, the selection of workers was made based on favoritism, nepotism, or random choice. Taylor got his job at Midvale because the owner was his father's friend. Likewise, workers were usually selected for a particular job with little consideration of whether they were physically or mentally fit to perform it. Taylor changed this viewpoint by using research to find the best worker for the job.

Principle 3. Management and the workforce should work together to ensure that work is performed according to the principles of management. Taylor's observation went against the long-established principles of both management and the worker who believed that each was the other's enemy. Rather than enmity, Taylor stressed cooperation and the need for the work relationship to be mutually beneficial.

Principle 4. Work and responsibility should be equally divided between management and workers. Previously, management set the directives, and workers obeyed or blocked them. Taylor believed that management and workers had joint responsibilities to each other. Management's responsibility was to scientifically select the quantity of output for the day and provide a fair wage. In return, workers were to provide a fair day's work.

Principles of Scientific Management
First. They develop a science for each element of a man's work, which replaces the old rule-of-thumb method.
Second. They scientifically select and then train, teach, and develop the workman, whereas in the past he chose his own work and trained himself as best he could.
Third. They heartily cooperate with the men so as to ensure all of the work being done in accordance with the principles of the science which has been developed.
Fourth. There is an almost equal division of the work and the responsibility between the management and the workmen. The management take over all work for which they are better fitted than the workmen, while in the past almost all of the work and the greater part of the responsibility were thrown upon the men.

Table 3.2 (Attribution: Copyright Rice University, OpenStax, under CC-BY 4.0 license)

Taylor's Acolytes

In addition to his groundbreaking work on scientific management, Taylor attracted a wide variety of talented individuals who aided him in his research. The first important individual was the mathematician **Carl G. Barth** (1860–1939). Barth made two notable contributions. The first was his work on employee fatigue. He attempted to find what aspects made a worker tired. The second was his use of the slide rule for calculating how much steel to cut. A slide rule is a ruler with a sliding central strip. It makes it possible to perform calculations rapidly and accurately. Barth developed one for cutting steel. Before Barth's work, workers were required to make difficult calculations to determine how much steel to cut. Usually, they guessed, which led to a lot of errors and waste. With the slide rule, however, the number of errors decreased, as did the costs associated with them.

Another notable contributor to Taylor's methods was **Henry Gantt** (1861–1919), who developed the Gantt chart, which allowed for greater and more precise control over the production process. The Gantt chart, illustrated in **Exhibit 3.4**, tracked what was supposed to be done versus what was actually done. Gantt gives two principles for his charts: First, measure the amount of time needed to complete an activity. Second, use the space on the chart to visually represent how much of an activity should have been completed in that given time. Today, the closest thing to a Gantt chart is a scheduling system. These charts allowed management to see how projects were progressing, take steps to see if they were on schedule, and monitor budget concerns.[39] Gantt also pioneered the employee bonus system, in which employees were given a bonus if they completed the task they were assigned.

Gantt Chart for producing OpenStax Principles of Management Project	1/1-1/2	1/2-1/4	1/3-1/8	1/8-1/10	1/10-1/1:	1/1-2/1	2/1-2/2	2/2-2/2	2/3-2/4	2/3-2/5	2/4-2/7
Project Planning											
Author contracting											
Author writing 1st Draft											
Reviewing											
Analysis of content											
Author reviewing of 2nd Draft											
Final Reviews											
Prep for Production											
Copy Editing											
Review of Copy Editing											
Art Creation											
XML											
Proofing											
End of Project											

Exhibit 3.4 Gantt Chart Attribution: Copyright Rice University, OpenStax, under CC BY-NC-SA 4.0 license

The next key contributors to Taylor's system of scientific management were **Frank** (1868–1924) and **Lillian Gilbreth** (1878–1972),[40] a couple that sometimes competed with and sometimes worked with Taylor. Frank Gilbreth was a bricklayer who, before who he heard of Taylor, began to find ways to limit his fatigue and more efficiently lay down more bricks. Unlike Taylor, Gilbreth was concerned with **motion studies**, in which he would film various motions while someone worked on the job. To determine the most efficient way to perform a task, for example, Gilbreth reduced all motions of the hand into some combination of 17 basic motions. Gilbreth would then calculate the most efficient way of carrying out a job. Gilbreth filmed workers performing a wide variety of jobs, including bricklaying, secretarial duties, and even a baseball game.

When working in construction, Gilbreth developed a management system that included rules about no smoking on the job, a ten-dollar prize for the best suggestion in how to improve labor, and a new system of training so that workers were taught only the best way to perform a task. He developed a rule that all accident sites be photographed for use in future lawsuits. Gilbreth also prepared employees for their present and future positions by introducing a plan for promotion, training, and development. This system required charting promotion paths and record keeping for performance appraisals. He wanted to impress upon both workers and managers an understanding of fatigue and of how to improve pay. In his research, Gilbreth realized that monotony came not from the job itself, but from a worker's lack of interest in the job.

Lillian Gilbreth may not have been the originator of the industrial psychology movement, but she brought a human element into the study and practice of management with her training and insight. She stated that to understand how to work better, we must understand the worker. Under scientific management, for example, understanding the worker became a fundamental principle in selecting workers for particular tasks and providing workers with incentives. The object was to develop each person to his fullest potential by strengthening his personal traits, special abilities, and skills. After Frank Gilbreth died, Lillian Gilbreth shifted her focus to increasing domestic efficiency and, in the process, designed the modern kitchen.

Taylor's Shortcomings

Taylor was a monomaniac on a mission to convert as many people to scientific management as possible. Yet despite his conviction and zealousness, Taylor's ideas were poorly understood, and he attracted more enemies than followers.[41] Taylor attracted enmity from unions because he was against them; he believed that unions separated workers from management. Taylor attracted enmity from the workers because he compared them to apes and other beasts of burden. And Taylor gained the distrust and enmity of management because he criticized them for their previous management failures. Taylor had a difficult personality and angered just about everyone.

Additionally, Taylor made several mistakes. Taylorism, despite its claims, was not an overall theory of management, but a management system designed for frontline managers, those immediately supervising. He generally ignored strategy and implementation and thought of workers as machine tools to be manipulated rather than as human beings. Although he was aware of group pressures, he believed that monetary incentives could overcome group pressures. This oversight made him ignore the human aspects of handling workers, those that involved emotions, personality, and attitudes.

While Taylor was certainly a flawed individual, these criticisms do not diminish his great contributions. Taylor dramatically changed management practices and created the modern management world. Future researchers did not replace Taylor, but complemented him. What is remarkable about Taylor was not that he was right in his time and place, but that his vision continues to have meaning and consequence even today.[42] Management was truly Taylor-made.

CONCEPT CHECK

1. List the contributions from Taylor and his associates.
2. How did Taylor change management?

3.5 Administrative and Bureaucratic Management

5. How do bureaucratic and administrative management complement scientific management?

Writing at the same time as Taylor, **Henri Fayol** (1841–1925) and **Max Weber** (1864–1920) wrote complementary contributions to Taylor's four principles of scientific management framework. Whereas Taylor focused on frontline managers, those who handle workers, Fayol focused on top managers, who set strategy, and Weber focused on middle managers, who implement strategy. Although Taylor, Fayol, and Weber viewed management from different perspectives, each stressed the need for logical, rational systems to coordinate and control various types of enterprises.

Henri Fayol was a French mining executive who did the majority of his scholarly work after the Franco-Prussian War of 1870–1871.[43] Fayol sought to develop a theory of administrative theory in order to increase efficiency in order to make the French economy stronger. Like Taylor, Fayol prized knowledge and experience over tradition. Unlike Taylor, however, Fayol focused on overall management of the corporation rather than on individual tasks involved in carrying out a firm's business. Fayol focused on the overall social interactions [between or within what? a company and between companies? or just within a company?] the company. An explanation for this difference is that Taylor was concerned with worker behavior and performance, the domain of the frontline manager. Fayol's focus was on the direction and coordination of the whole organization, which is the domain of the top manager.[44] Another notable difference between the two men was that Taylor emphasized monetary compensation while Fayol recognized that people work for things other than money. Fayol's greatest contribution was that he sought to develop an approach that would aid top managers in setting the direction of their company.

Fayol presented three principal ideas about management.[45] First, Fayol stressed the need for **unity of**

command, that is, that a company's management should speak with only voice. Too often under the Taylor system, a worker could have up to eight managers telling him how to perform a single task. Fayol stressed flexibility and recognized that authority must have responsibility attached to it. Accordingly, he stressed that management should maintain a unity of command, which ensured that each supervisor would explain to each of the employees in his group or division what aspect of his job to focus on. Each supervisor receives direction and information from the managers above him and passes that information down the chain of command.

Fayol's second notable contribution was his recognition that workers focused on the social aspects of their jobs as well as on the monetary compensation they received for doing the job. Taylor was well aware of the social aspects and pressures of work, but he sought to limit them. Fayol sought to use them for the business's benefit by stressing the development of an esprit de corps among workers. *Esprit de corps* refers to the cohesion of workers in a given unit or department, to their commitment to their individual goals and to their coworkers even in the face of adversity, and to the pride that one feels by being a member of the organization. Fayol stressed communication as a means of creating esprit de corps and building commitment between personal goals and organizational goals.

A third important aspect of Fayol's work was his emphasis on the notion of justice within an organization and on the idea that an organization must decide issues fairly and equitably. In this way, managers could limit the ways in which their biases and personal feelings could influence their decisions.

Taken as a whole, Fayol's ideas became what we call today Fayolism, or administrative theory. Fayolism consists of the **14 principles of management**. The 14 principles articulate the types of tasks that managers are supposed to do. These 14 principles are still used today, but how they are used varies with a firm's use of technology and its culture. For example, a society that stresses individual outcomes will have different compensation systems than those that are focused on collective or group outcomes.

Fayol's 14 Principles of Management are:

1. Division of Work
2. Authority
3. Discipline
4. Unity of Command
5. Unity of Direction
6. Subordination of Individual Interest
7. Remuneration
8. Centralization
9. Scalar Chain
10. Order
11. Equity
12. Stability of Tenure of Personnel
13. Initiative—Employees should be given the necessary level of freedom to create and carry out plans.
14. Esprit de Corps

In addition to the 14 principles, Fayol identified the **five functions of management**:

1. Planning
2. Organizing
3. Staffing
4. Controlling
5. Directing

Each of these functions describes what managers should do on a day-to-day basis. The functions of management have changed over the years but have built upon Fayol's structure. Fayol fully described what a manager does and how each activity builds off of the others.

Max Weber was a German sociologist who made significant complementary contributions to Taylor's management system as well as to the disciplines of economics and sociology. Weber did the majority of his work in the early 1890s and then after 1904 when he started writing again. Sociologists hold Weber in such esteem that they regard him as a father of the field.

Weber[46] stressed that social scientists could only understand collectives by understanding the actions of individuals. One of the individual behaviors that Weber did research was the types of leadership, identifying three types of leadership: charismatic domination (familial and religious) traditional domination (patriarchs, patrimonialism, and feudalism) and legal domination (modern law, state, and bureaucracy). Weber's contribution to management is the development and understanding of the legal rationalism model of leadership, which stressed the idea that leaders should make decisions based on law, precedent, and rule, rather than whim. Weber went further than previous scholars and described why we saw the emergence of bureaucracies and other responses to industrialization.

According to Weber, both the industrialization and transportation revolutions allowed for the expanse of territories to be managed. The demands placed on managing larger and larger amounts of territory as well as people facilitated the need for bureaucracy, which is a system of fixed rules that are impartially administered. The expanding market economy required administration that is more efficient. At the same time, the emergence of communication and transportation improvements made improved administration possible.

The most notable contribution Weber provided to modern management was the creation of the **modern bureaucracy**. Weber's principles of the ideal bureaucracy are shown. Although the ancient Chinese had the first bureaucracy, the notable difference of Weber's bureaucracy is that decisions were made on a formal basis, rather than what a manager felt was correct. Weber stressed that knowledge, not birth circumstances, should be the basis of hiring and promotion within a bureaucracy. This attitude stood in sharp contrast to the policies and practices of the time in both Europe and the United States, which stressed birth circumstances. Weber also stressed that bureaucrats need to make decisions based on rules rather than whims. The word *bureaucracy* has negative connotations in the mind of the modern reader, but it was a vast improvement over what had occurred previously. Prior to Weber, management did not have to provide justification for why they made particular decisions, nor did they have to make decisions based on rules. Hiring and promotion were based on nepotism, very different from the modern meritocracy of today.

Principles of the Ideal Bureaucracy:

- Specialized roles
- Recruitment based on merit
- Uniform principles of placement, promotion, and transfer
- Careerism with systematic salary structure
- Hierarchy, responsibility, and accountability
- Subjection of official conduct to strict rules of discipline and control
- Supremacy of abstract rules
- Impersonal authority (i.e., office bearer does not bring the office with him)

There was, however, a downside to this new managerial approach. A bureaucracy could shield bureaucrats from personal responsibility and initiative. Even worse, it could make them willing participants in criminal activities. American sociologist Robert K. Merton noted that in a bureaucracy, rules could become more important than actual goals. Merton wrote:

> An effective bureaucracy demands reliability of response and strict devotion to regulations. (2) Such

devotion to the rules leads to their transformation into absolutes; they are no longer conceived as relative to a set of purposes. (3) This interferes with ready adaptation under special conditions not clearly envisaged by those who drew up the general rules. (4) Thus, the very elements which conduce toward efficiency in general produce inefficiency in specific instances. Full realization of the inadequacy is seldom attained by members of the group who have not divorced themselves from the meanings which the rules have for them. These rules in time become symbolic in cast, rather than strictly utilitarian.[47]

Another particular issue was that bureaucracy placed so much emphasis on legal authority that it ignored several important factors. The first factor is that bureaucratic laws are often incomplete due to problems in communication and understanding. Contracts tend to be abandoned rather than completed. No contract or law can consider every outcome or event. The second issue is that bureaucratic organizations ignored interpersonal authority and often relied only on reason and logic for decision-making. Often people followed their managers because they personally liked them rather than the legal aspect of authority. Managers that only use legal authority to gain performance are going to be really limited in the performance they will be able to garner (please see the chapter on leadership).

Both Fayol and Weber made significant contributions to management. Fayol's ideas are the basis of modern strategy, as he attempted to understand what activities managers should do. His ideas inform management thoughts in terms of the various roles that managers need to undertake to ensure the cooperation of workers. Likewise, Weber's ideas can be seen very clearly in human resource management in that managers should make decisions based on policy rather than whim. We can see that both men's ideas about structure and the line of authority continue to have great influence in management today.

CONCEPT CHECK

1. What were the contributions of Fayol and Weber?
2. How did their work compare to Taylor's?
3. What is the idea of line of authority and structure?

3.6 Human Relations Movement

6. How did Elton Mayo influence management theory, and how did the human relations movement affect current management theory?

The human relations movement was a natural response to some of the issues related to scientific management and the under-socialized view of the worker that ignored social aspects of work. The key uniting characteristics of Taylor, Weber, and Fayol were the ideas of efficiency produced through either operational, legal, or administrative improvements. One of the principal assumptions was an emphasis on rationality.[48] According to scientific management, there was a logic to actions, and formal and knowledge authority were the principal catalysts of workplace motivation. Scientific management tended to downplay the effects of social pressures on human interactions.[49] The human relations movement enhanced scientific management because it acknowledged that peoples' attitudes, perceptions, and desires play a role in their workplace performance. With this acknowledgement, for example, managers began to realize that settling disputes was more difficult than the scientific management approach described.

The major difference between scientific management and human relations theory was that human relations theory recognized that social factors were a source of power in the workplace. While Taylor recognized the existence of social pressures in an organization, he sought to diminish them through pay, that is, compensating workers for production even though social pressure forced workers to reduce production. Fayol recognized the existence of social issues as well, but he emphasized commitment to the organization as a management technique rather than commitment of workers to each other or to their supervisor. Weber placed emphasis on the rule of law and believed that laws and regulations would guide society and corporations. Yet he did not spend enough energy recognizing the outcomes that happen when rules break down. Fayol and Weber did not recognize the role of corporate culture in an organization and did not examine more closely why workers do not follow orders. The human relations movement added more of the social element to the study and theory of work.[50]

Perhaps no research studies have been as misunderstood as the Hawthorne studies. The Hawthorne studies are the most influential, misunderstood, and criticized research experiment in all of the social sciences. The legend goes that **Elton Mayo** (1880–1949) researched, theorized, and developed human relations theory based on a 1924–1932 experiment he conducted at the Hawthorne plant of the Western Electric Company in Cicero Illinois. However, there is very little of the legend that is true. The truth is more complicated and difficult to understand. Most textbooks claim that Mayo researched and conducted the studies. Yet this is fiction. The studies were commenced by scholars from the Massachusetts Institute of Technology. Mayo did not become involved until 1927. Nevertheless, it is Mayo's vision of Hawthorne that has come to dominate the literature.

The first phase of the Hawthorne studies was called the illumination study, and it sought to measure the impact of light upon productivity. The study was inconclusive because there were too many variables other than light that could have affected worker productivity. The researchers had difficulty understanding why productivity increased. The second phase of the study was called the relay-assembly-test-oom, and these experiments were carried out in a room where researchers tested the effect that working conditions such as breaks, length of the workday, company-provided lunches, and payment method had on productivity. They selected six young female workers to be part of a team that produced a phone relay switch. Each woman was young and unlikely to be married any time soon. One woman was assigned to gather the parts to make the switch, and each of the other five women was assigned to assemble one component of the phone relay. The researchers found that production increased regardless of what variable was manipulated. Nevertheless, soldiering still occurred during the experiment. After two workers were fired for a health issue and getting married, production increased even more. The results were surprising to the researchers: they had expected to see a reduction but instead saw a consistent increase.

The Hawthorne executives turned to Elton Mayo, an Australian psychologist from Harvard University, to explain the puzzling results. Most of the controversy regarding the Hawthorne studies stems from Mayo's involvement. Mayo observed that production could be increased if management understood the role of individual workers' attitudes toward work and also took into account how group attitudes affected behavior. Mayo theorized that social issues and attention paid by the supervisor to these issues played a role in increasing production. The Hawthorne women were granted freedoms at work, including the ability to make suggestions regarding their work conditions. Many of the Hawthorne women felt that they were special and that if they performed well on the relay assembly task, they would be treated better by the company's management. Additionally, the Hawthorne women became very friendly with each other. Their connection as a team and increased satisfaction in their work appeared to drive the women to greater performance. Yet the study found that financial incentives were a clear driver of performance as well.

A third study, called the bank wiring room study, was conducted between 1931 and 1932. Rather than being selected to form a new group, participants in the bank wiring room study consisted of an already existing group, one that had a number of bad behaviors. Regardless of financial incentives, group members decided that they would only produce 6,000 to 6,600 connections a day. Workers who produced more were ostracized or hit on the arm to lower production. George Homans summarized the difference in the results of the relay assembly and the bank wiring room experiments:

"Both groups developed an informal social organization, but while the Bank Wiremen were organized in opposition to management, the Relay Assemblers were organized in cooperation with management in the pursuit of a common purpose. Finally, the responses of the two groups to their industrial situation were, on the one hand, restriction of output and, on the other, steady and welcome increase of output. These contrasts carry their own lesson."

Researchers found that cliques were formed that placed informal rules on the workers within a group. According to Homans, the workers also made a connection with one of the managers to control production. The discovery that management could ally themselves with the workforce to limit production was a notable contribution to management thought at the time. It suggests that managerial authority can break down if the manager disagrees with management's policy toward the workers.

Exhibit 3.5 The Hawthorne Electric Plant The Hawthorne studies examined the effects that differences in working conditions (such as the timing and frequency of breaks) had on productivity. The term got its name from the experiments conducted at the Western Electric Hawthorne plant, illustrated here, located in Cicero, Illinois. These studies made popular the idea that attitudes affect performance. Credit: (public domain / flickr / This work is in the public domain in the United States because it was published in the United States between 1923 and 1977 without a copyright notice.)

What did the studies mean? On some level, they were meaningless because they proved little. Indeed, they have been called scientifically worthless. There were too many variables being manipulated; the sample size was too small; observations were collected at random; the Hawthorne researchers viewed the experiments through their own ideological lenses. They made mistakes in assuming that that the wage was insignificant to the workers, when in reality the wage was a significant driving force. Yet these criticisms ignore two major facts about the Hawthorne studies. The first is that the Hawthorne studies were the first to focus on the actual work life of the workers. This was a notable change in sociological research. The second fact is that the studies were intended to generate future research, and future research did discover that attitudes play a major role in determining workplace outcomes. Another important finding concerned the role of the supervisor. Many worker behaviors, attitudes, and emotions have their genesis in their supervisor's actions. Stress and fatigue can be the result of interactions with supervisors and coworkers; they are not just a response to less-than-ideal physical conditions. Finally, the Hawthorne studies showed that work motivation is a function of a wide variety of factors, including pay, social relationships, meaning, interests, and attitudes.

Barnard and the "Zone of Indifference"

Chester Barnard (1886–1961) was president of the New Jersey Bell Telephone Company.[51] As president, he was given an unusual amount of time to conduct research. Barnard had been a student at Harvard, and through his connections there, he found out about some of the industrial research going on. His notable contribution was a book called *The Functions of the Executive*.[52] Barnard argued that an executive's purpose is to gain resources from members within the organization by ensuring that they perform their jobs and that cooperation exists between various groups within the organization. The other notable function of an executive is to hire and retain talented employees. Barnard defined a formal organization as consciously coordinated activities between two or more people but noted that such coordination is not likely to last for very long, a factor that may explain why many companies do not survive for long periods of time.

Barnard believed that executives best exerted authority through communication and the use of incentives. Communication within an organization should include definite channels of communication, and workers should have access to knowledge and information. Communication should be clear, direct, and honest so that members of an organization understand what is expected of them.

Barnard stressed several important outcomes regarding incentives. Some of his incentives reflected the human relations movement's occupation with social outcomes but tempered that movement's emphasis with an understanding that workers labored for pay. The first incentive was that there should be monetary and other material inducements to encourage better performance and production. The second incentive was that there should be nonmaterial incentives, such as recognition. The third incentive was that working conditions should be desirable. The fourth and final incentive was that workers should find pride and meaning in the work they do. Barnard believed that a combination of these elements would ensure cooperation and contributions from organizational members.

While his findings on executive functions, communication, and incentives were significant, Barnard's largest contribution to the study of management involved what he called the "**zone of indifference**." The idea behind the zone of indifference is that workers will comply with orders if they are indifferent to them. This does not mean they have to agree with or support the orders. Rather the zone of indifference suggests that workers need merely to be indifferent to an order to follow it and that workers will follow orders due to an individual's natural tendency to follow authority. The zone of indifference must be reached through the following factors. First, the workers must have the ability to comply with the order. Second, workers must understand the order. Third, the order must be consistent with organizational goals. For both management and the worker to cooperate, their interests must be aligned. Fourth, the order must not violate an individual's personal beliefs. Barnard provided an explanation for why workers do not always obey orders.

Follett and Conflict Resolution

Mary Parker Follett (1868–1933) found a way to use the tenets of the human relations movement to solve some of the problems with the scientific management framework. Follett was a political scientist from Harvard. (Her work on the Speaker of the House remains the classic in the field.) After graduating from Harvard, given the limited opportunities for women, she wound up in the field of social work. She continued to publish works on philosophy and political science, but, based on her social work connections, she soon found herself drifting over to the Taylor Society, a group dedicated to the principles of scientific management. Later in her career, she turned toward business. As Wren and Bedeian note, chronologically she belonged to the scientific management era, but intellectually she belonged to the human relations movement era.[53]

Follett's work was largely ignored for years either because it was too original or because she was a woman; it is likely both factors played a role.[54] Her ideas found little acceptance during the period because in her time, management saw workers only as tools. Her focus was on how to reduce conflict. Follett's contribution was that she pointed out that management should take social concerns into account when dealing with workers.

She asked questions of management: How do we create unity of action? How do we help workers live fuller, richer lives? How do we contribute to group success? Her argument was that individual behavior is affected by and affects others in the group.[55] Accordingly, she argued for the need of the principle of coordination to have a continuous interaction of all factors. What she meant was that both management and the worker should be able to understand the other's viewpoint. She sought to have both management and the worker share power with each other, rather than have power over one another. In addition, unlike Weber and more in line with Taylor, she believed that power should be based on knowledge and expertise.

Follett also argued that there are several ways to resolve conflicts. The first is to have one party dominate the other. In **dominance**, one party dictates the terms of the arrangement. Follett recognized that very few situations in life allow this to be possible and that, for many companies, this approach is impossible without incurring social costs in terms of a disaffected workforce. The second solution is **compromise**. In a compromise, neither side gets exactly everything it wants, and the best each side can do is obtain a result that each can agree too. The problem with this approach is that both sides give up what they really want and settle on what they can agree on. In a compromise, neither side is happy. The third way to solve conflict is **integration**, which occurs when each party states its preferences and attempts to reach an agreement. Follett provided an example of integration:

> In the Harvard Library one day, in one of the smaller rooms, someone wanted the window open. I wanted it shut. We opened the window in the next room where no one was sitting.[56]

It would appear that this situation is a compromise. But closely look at it; Follett wanted the window closed, and her study partner wanted a window open. It just did not have to be in that room. Because they rearranged the problem, they came up with a solution that was satisfactory to both of them.

CONCEPT CHECK

1. What did the Hawthorne studies, Barnard, and Fayol contribute to management thought?
2. What did the works of Follett and Mayo contribute to management thought?

3.7 | Contingency and System Management

7. How did contingency and systems management transform management thought?

The 1950s and 1960s saw the establishment of two schools that competed with and complemented the scientific management and human relations approaches. The first school of thought was the systems school. Some of the leaders of the systems school were Kenneth Boulding, Daniel Katz, Robert Kahn, and Ludwig von Bertalanffy. These men came from diverse disciplines (psychology, economics, sociology, and even biology) and attempted to explain how external factors determine managerial outcomes.[57] The major purpose behind systems school research was to understand the external conditions that organizations face and how to handle these conditions. The major overview of the systems theorists was that firms were an **open system**, that is, a system that interacts with its environment. In this case, the environment interacts with the firm in that it provides and accepts valued resources from the firm. For instance, the raw components of an iPhone are gathered by Apple. Through knowledge, procedures, tools, and resources, Apple takes these components and creates something of value for its customers, after which the consumer purchases the final product. In addition to providing financial resources to the firm, customers provide the firm with information—namely whether they like the product enough to purchase it.

The issue that systems management raises is that the managers' actions are the products of outside factors. For example, if you are a human resource manager, the actions you take are determined by employment law. The law requires corporations to have tests that are both consistent and reliable. When a manager violates this law, the firm can expect a lawsuit. Likewise, the laws of supply and demand determine the salary range that a firm will offer to job applicants. If the firm pays above market, they can expect their pick of the best candidates; below market, they may have a difficult time finding quality workers. From a strategic perspective, how firms compete against each other will be determined, in part, by the general external environment. For example, Apple's ability to sell iPhones is constricted by outside factors, including technology, suppliers, customers, and competitors. Every Android phone sold limits how many iPhones Apple can sell.

The other school that made a contribution to management thought during this time was the **contingency school**. Prior to the development of the contingency school, management scholars sought the one best way of managing. The contingency school changed this by proposing that there are no universal rules in management. External and internal factors create unique situations, and each situation requires a different response. What is the most appropriate response in one situation may not work in another. The key statement of the contingency school is "it depends." One of the major theorists in this school is **Joan Woodward**, a British scholar who did her work in the 1950s and 1960s.[58] She argued that contingencies, such as technology, play a role in how much training workers should receive. For instance, one of the major themes in management today is that workers should be well-trained. Woodward would argue that for low-tech jobs, this might not be the case but that for jobs requiring quite bit of technology, training would be a necessity.

Modern Management

From the 1970s to the present, we have seen the various management schools of thought interwoven. One of the major approaches in modern management is the development of managerial theories. When people hear the word *theory*, they usually assume that it refers to something impractical and disconnected from real life. The reality is that theory is a prediction and an explanation. Since the 1970s, the concept of theory has entered into the management literature and has led to more rigorous research.[59] The body of knowledge explored in this book about concepts such as strategy, organizational behavior, human resource management, and organizational theory has many roots from the 1970s. For example, when you get to job design, you will learn about the Hackman and Oldham model of job design, which was first proposed in 1975. Management has been enriched over the last 40 years by the contributions from researchers in allied fields such as economics, psychology, and sociology.

Based on the theoretical research of the last 40 or so years, scholars such as Stanford University's Jeffrey Pfeffer have now proposed the idea for evidence-based management.[60] The idea is to recommend managerial practices that have been tested. In many ways, this brings us back to Taylor and the need for science-based management. Once again, management thinkers are seeking to use formalized research to eliminate bad management techniques that have been recommended over the last several years.

Exhibit 3.6 indicates how each of the thinkers we discussed in this chapter relates to the others. From Taylor and others, we learned about the basic outcomes of human resource management, control, and some aspects of motivation. From Fayol and Barnard, we began to develop concepts related to strategic management and authority. Mary Parker Follett provided insights into leadership. Elton Mayo and his colleagues launched the field of organizational behavior, and their work continues to have an impact on the fields of motivation, stress, and job design. Weber gave us the start of organizational design and the importance of authority.

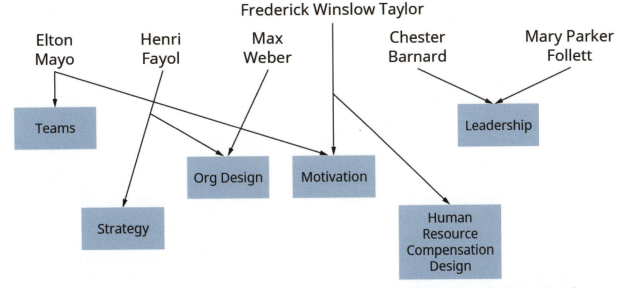

Exhibit 3.6   The Development of Management Thought (Attribution: Copyright Rice University, OpenStax, under CC-BY 4.0 license)

CONCEPT CHECK

1. What is the going contribution of systems and contingency management thought?
2. What is the idea of evidence-based management?

🔑 Key Terms

14 principles of management Created by Henri Fayol.

Adam Smith Adam Smith proposed the ideas of division of labor, specialization, and coordination within a corporation.

Carl G. Barth Carl G. Barth (1860–1939), mathematician, developed a slide rule for calculating how much steel to cut.

Chester Barnard Chester Barnard (1886–1961) argued that the executive purpose was to gain resources from members within the organization by ensuring that they perform their jobs and that cooperation exists between various groups within the organization.

Compromise In a compromise, neither side gets what it wants. The best each side could get is what each can agree too.

Contingency school The contingency school explained that there were no universal laws in management, due to a wide variety of variables that influence relationships and create unique situations, and that each situation required a different response.

Dominance In dominance, one dictates the terms of the arrangement.

Elton Mayo Elton Mayo (1880–1949) researched, theorized, and developed human relations theory based on an experiment at the Hawthorne plant on how to manage workers and to improve production.

Five functions of management Created by Henri Fayol: planning, organizing, staffing, controlling, and directing.

Frank and Lillian Gilbreth Their major contribution was **motion studies**.

Frederick Winslow Taylor Taylor is known as the father of scientific management.

Hammurabi The Code of Hammurabi was a listing of 282 laws that regulated conduct on a wide variety of behaviors, including business dealings, personnel behavior, interpersonal relations, punishments and a wide variety of other outcomes.

Henri Fayol Fayol's administrative theory was the first general statement on management theory.

Henry Gantt Henry Gantt (1861–1919) developed the Gantt chart, which allowed for the process of control to occur.

Industrial Revolution The Industrial Revolution occurred between roughly 1760 and 1900 and saw the emergence of the modern factory.

Integration In integration, both parties state their preferences and attempt to reach an agreement.

Italian Renaissance The Italian Renaissance was a major leap of knowledge and learning that had economic and business implications.

Joan Woodward A British scholar who did her work in the 1950s and 1960s. She argued that contingencies, such as technology, play a role in how much training workers should receive.

Mary Parker Follett Mary Parker Follett (1868–1933) found a way to utilize the tenets of the human relations movement to solve some of the issues with scientific management.

Max Weber Weber developed the idea that organizations should be formalized and legalistic in their operations.

Modern bureaucracy Decisions should be made on a formal basis, rather than what a bureaucrat felt was correct. Weber stressed that knowledge, not birth circumstances, should be the basis of hiring and promotion within a bureaucracy.

Motion studies Film studies of work.

Nebuchadnezzar Nebuchadnezzar (605 BC–c. 562 BC) was a pioneer in the development of incentives in that he gave greater rewards to workers who were productive.

Open system An open system interacts with the environment to gain resources.

Sun Tzu Sun Tzu developed subdivisions, various rankings of authority, and the use of colors as coordination between units.

Unity of command Unity of command stresses that each worker should have only one supervisor.

Zone of indifference Workers would comply with orders if they were indifferent to them. This does not mean they have to agree with the orders. Rather the zone of indifference suggests that workers need merely to be indifferent to an order to follow it.

Summary of Learning Outcomes

3.1 The Early Origins of Management

1. Describe management in the ancient world.

We can track the concept of management from its development under the Sumerians. The Sumerians provided the concepts of writing and record keeping that allowed for an urban economy to develop, which in turn led to the establishment of small businesses. The Egyptians helped to pioneer the ideas of specialization of labor, span of control, and hierarchy of command. Sun Tzu developed subdivisions, various rankings of authority, and coordination. The Greeks and Romans built forerunners of the modern corporation and guilds.

3.2 The Italian Renaissance

2. How did the Italian Renaissance affect the progression of management theory?

The Crusades and various travelers brought new knowledge from both the Muslim and Chinese societies. In addition, there was a rediscovery of trade throughout Europe. These factors led to the establishment of the Renaissance that took place initially in Italy. The development of the printing press saw a distribution of these ideas across Europe. The Renaissance saw a reemergence of trade. The Renaissance also saw the development of the idea of the corporation and double-entry accounting. In fact, some of the first multinational corporations have their genesis in the Italian Renaissance.

3.3 The Industrial Revolution

3. How did the Industrial Revolution affect the progression of management theory?

The Industrial Revolution was a product of a combination of factors, including the spread of learning from the Italian Renaissance, the improvement of transportation, the Market Revolution, and technology. In addition, scholars such as Adam Smith provided support for the ideas of division of labor, specialization, and coordination within a corporation, allowing for the development of factories. This economic shifted created the need for managers.

3.4 Taylor-Made Management

4. How did Frederick Winslow Taylor influence management theory, and how did efficiency in management affect current management theory?

Taylor was the man that added the scientific method to management. He developed the four principles of scientific management and the notion of time study. Henry Gantt developed his famous chart, which allowed managers to track what was done versus supposed to be done. Frank and Lillian Gilbreth added motion study to Taylor's time management.

3.5 Administrative and Bureaucratic Management

5. How do bureaucratic and administrative management complement scientific management?

Henri Fayol and Max Weber made notable contributions to the development of management thought. Fayol focused on top managers, and Weber focused on middle managers. Fayol's administrative theory was the first general statement on management theory. He stressed the need for collective action and vision from top management. Weber developed the idea that organizations should be formalized and legalistic in their operations.

3.6 Human Relations Movement

6. How did Elton Mayo influence management theory, and how did the human relations movement affect current management theory?

Elton Mayo noted the role of nonmonetary motivators and attitudes in terms of the workplace. Barnard developed the idea of the zone of indifference. Follett developed ways to resolve conflict without the use of compromise or domination.

3.7 Contingency and System Management

7. How did contingency and systems management transform management thought?

Systems management developed the concept that management is an open system in that organizations interact with the environment to gain resources. Since organizations require resources from the environment, this constrains what managers can do. The contingency school explained that there were no universal laws in management, due to a wide variety of variables that influence relationships. Modern management is based on theory.

Chapter Review Questions

1. What contributions did ancient civilizations make to management thought?
2. Describe the role of the Renaissance in shaping management thought.
3. How did the Industrial Revolution change business and the economy?
4. Describe scientific management. How was scientific management different from management techniques that came before it?
5. Who were the key contributors to scientific management?
6. Describe the Hawthorne studies. Was Elton Mayo a humanist?
7. What is the zone of indifference?
8. Describe Follett's concept of conflict resolution.
9. What does open systems say about management?
10. What is contingency management?

Managerial Decision Exercises

1. Which management scholar do you find to be the most influential and important, and how would you incorporate their approach into your managerial approach?
2. Based on the reading in this chapter, defend or attack this statement that would be stated by a direct report:
   Management is unethical because it is about manipulating workers.
3. Which management scholar matches your viewpoints on the role of management?

Exhibit 4.1 (Credit: Free-Photos/ Pixabay/ (CC BY 0)), modified from an original image by Ivan Mlinaric

Introduction

Learning Outcomes

After reading this chapter, you should be able to understand these statements:

1. Define the external environment of organizations.
2. Identify contemporary external forces pressuring organizations.
3. Identify different types of organizational structures and their strengths and weaknesses.
4. Explain how organizations organize to meet external market threats and opportunities.
5. Identify the fit between organizational cultures and the external environment.
6. Identify environmental trends, demands, and opportunities facing organizations.

EXPLORING MANAGERIAL CAREERS

Jeff Bezos of Amazon

Amazon's market value was estimated at $1 trillion USD dollars in 2018. The company was recognized as the most innovative company in Fast Company's 2017 list, accounting for 44 percent of all U.S. e-commerce that year—approximately 4 percent of the U.S.'s total retail sales. Amazon market value is greater than the sum of the market capitalizations of Walmart, Target, Best Buy, Nordstrom, Kohl's, JCPenney, Sears, and Macy's. Jeff Bezos, founder and leader, has creatively accomplished what most large companies fail at: meshing size, scale, and external opportunities with agility. Sales figures reached $100 billion in 2015 while the stock price climbed over 300% in the past five years. The company plans on creating over 50,000 new jobs starting in 2018. Bezos has blended his strategy of virtually reaching unlimited numbers of online customers while maintaining land-based distribution centers using Prime's $99-per-year—$119 in 2018—membership. Stephenie Landry, an Amazon's vice president, stated that Prime has reached 49 cities in seven countries. Over 100 million people in 2018 subscribe to the Prime service. She noted that the business has only to answer two questions from customers: "Do you have what I want, and can you get it to me when I need it?" The answer seems to be yes, especially with Bezos's strategy of having high-tech robots already working side by side with human employees—resembling a "factory of the future."

Bezos's digital commerce strategy has led the firm to become the leader of retail commerce. Amazon's digital strategy uses Prime memberships that are supplied and supported by land-based distribution centers; Prime takes in reaching about 60% of the total dollar value of all merchandise sold on the site. That accounts for 60 million customers in the United States who use Prime and who spend $2,500 on Amazon annually. A study of 3,000 independent businesses, half of whom were retailers, listed competition from Amazon as their primary concern. Industry after industry is being disrupted, some replaced, by Bezos's strategy. He has said, "Everybody wants fast delivery. Low prices. I'm serious about this. Our job is to provide a great customer experience, and that is something that is universally desired all over the world".

Still, Amazon faces such challenges as high shipping cost (over $11 billion annually), pressures on employees (especially those working in warehouses that have been criticized for poor working conditions), shipping contractors who go on strike demanding higher wages and reduced workloads, and the possibilities of more governmental regulation (especially with regard to adding drones as a delivery method), as well as pressures to pay more taxes. Bezos has countered these arguments by adding more full-time jobs in different cities, promising to improve working conditions, supporting public spaces for the public, and most importantly, contributing to the U.S. economy.

Sources: https://www.bloomberg.com/news/articles/2018-04-26/amazon-eyes-second-biggest-market-cap-surging-past-microsoft. Noah Robischon, (2017). Why Amazon Is The World's Most Innovative Company Of 2017, https://www.fastcompany.com/3067455/why-amazon-is-the-worlds-most-innovative-company-of-2017; L. Thomas, (2018). Amazon grabbed 4 percent of all US retail sales in 2017, new study says, https://www.cnbc.com/2018/01/03/amazon-grabbed-4-percent-of-all-us-retail-sales-in-2017-new-study.html

Organizations and industries are again at a crossroads when confronting new and challenging external environmental demands. Exceptional companies such as Amazon, in the opening case, Apple, Netflix, and Google/Alphabet Inc. exemplify evolving business models that combine strategic innovation, technological prowess, and organizational cultural agility that not only meet external environmental demands, but also shape them.

Many businesses with traditional business models, however, have failed or are not succeeding strategically, operationally, and organizationally by not realizing and/or adapting to changing external environments. Such firms that were once successful but did not anticipate and then adapt to such changes include Blockbuster, Toys R Us, Borders, Sun Microsystems, Motorola, Digital Equipment Corporation, Polaroid, and Kodak, to name only a few. A sample of contemporary external environmental trends and forces that currently challenge organizations' survival and effectiveness includes:

- *Digital technologies and artificial intelligence (AI)*: Extensions of AI help automate a firm's value chain, thus speeding up and increasing efficient operations and service to customers—as Amazon exemplifies. A current survey showed that 59% of organizations are collecting information to develop AI strategies, while others are moving forward in piloting and/or adopting AI solutions to compete faster and at less cost.[1] However, there are also risks that accompany firms that incorporate new digital and online technologies without adequate security measures. For example, some newer online technologies can expose operational systems to cyberattacks and large-scale manipulation. Hacking is now both an illegal and ongoing "profession" for those who are able to paralyze organizations from accessing their data unless they pay a ransom. While hacking is not new, it is more widespread and lethal, to the point of even threatening national security. Emerging evidence from the U.S. presidential election between Donald Trump and Hillary Clinton suggests that international hackers affected online U.S. election processes. Still, the future of most businesses is using some type of digital and AI technologies.

- The advent of *blockchain* technologies that are interrupting new industry practices. Blockchain is not a single technology; it is "an architecture that allows disparate users to make transactions and then creates an unchangeable record of those transactions." It is "a public electronic ledger—similar to a relational database—that can be openly shared among disparate users and that creates an unchangeable record of their transactions, each one time-stamped and linked to the previous one."[2] These technological inventions will continue to affect almost every business process from procurement to legal management. The banking industry is already using it. It increases speed, security, and accuracy of transactions.

- *Sharing-economy cultural and economic value-added business models* that use information technologies to gain competitive advantage. Companies such as Airbnb and Uber have ushered in new business models that have already disrupted real estate, hotel, taxi, and other industries. Taking out the middle layer of management in transactions to increase efficiencies and customer satisfaction while cutting costs through the use of information and social media technologies will continue. This trend has already had both positive and disruptive effects on companies. Many customers are likely benefitted; businesses with outdated and ineffective business models have either failed or struggle to adapt.

- *Shifts in learning and learning credentials*. Identifying, recruiting, and retaining talent is crucial to organizations. An evolving crisis for the current generation—future talent—is the continued rise in higher educational institutions' tuitions, student debt, and the changing nature of jobs. With the advent of online resources, prospective students' inability to pay creates both a crisis and opportunity for traditional higher educational institutions. While bachelor's degrees remain a requirement for many companies hiring needed higher-level talent, online resources such as Khan Academy, Udacity, and Coursera are gaining recognition and legitimacy toward providing financially challenged students opportunities for entry-level jobs. While many higher-skilled students and professionals may not presently be included in this trend, companies seeking to pay lower wages while offering flexible working conditions are attracting students.[3] Again, how higher educational private, not-for-profit, and even for-profit educational institutions adapt, innovate, and manage their external environments is yet to be seen.

- *Ethics, corporate social responsibility (CSR), and sustainability.* Corruption, lying, and fraud have been and continue to be part of the landscape of governments and public- and private-sector corporations. However, public awareness through social and online media has awakened consumers and corporations to the impending dangers and drawbacks of illegal and unethical activities of certain large corporations. And external environmental problems, created in part by humans, such as pollution and climate change pressure companies to be responsible for their share of the costs associated with these problems.

This small sample of powerful external forces illustrates the continuing pressure companies encounter to innovate in their industries. Basic theories, concepts, and principles are presented in this chapter to help explain elements of external environments and how organizations and corporations can organize and are organizing to survive and thrive in the 21st century.

4.1 The Organization's External Environment

1. Define the external environment of organizations.

To succeed and thrive, organizations must adapt, exploit, and fit with the forces in their external environments. Organizations are groups of people deliberately formed together to serve a purpose through structured and coordinated goals and plans. As such, organizations operate in different external environments and are organized and structured internally to meet both external and internal demands and opportunities. Different types of organizations include not-for-profit, for-profit, public, private, government, voluntary, family owned and operated, and publicly traded on stock exchanges. Organizations are commonly referred to as companies, firms, corporations, institutions, agencies, associations, groups, consortiums, and conglomerates.

While the type, size, scope, location, purpose, and mission of an organization all help determine the external environment in which it operates, it still must meet the requirements and contingencies of that environment to survive and prosper. This chapter is primarily concerned with how organizations fit with their external environments and how organizations are structured to meet challenges and opportunities of these environments. Major takeaways for readers of this chapter include the following: 1) Be able to identify elements in any organization's external—and internal—environment that may interest or affect you as an employee, shareholder, family member, or observer. 2) Gain insights into how to develop strategies and tactics that would help you (and your organization) navigate ways to cope with or try to dominate or appeal to elements (e.g., market segments, stakeholders, political/social/economic/technological issues) in the environment.

The big picture of an organization's **external environment**, also referred to as the *general environment*, is an inclusive concept that involves all outside factors and influences that impact the operation of a business that an organization must respond or react to in order to maintain its flow of operations.[4] **Exhibit 4.2** illustrates types of general macro environments and forces that are interrelated and affect organizations: sociocultural, technological, economic, government and political, natural disasters, and human-induced problems that affect industries and organizations. For example, economic environmental forces generally include such elements in the economy as exchange rates and wages, employment statistics, and related factors such as inflation, recessions, and other shocks—negative and positive. Hiring and unemployment, employee benefits, factors affecting organizational operating costs, revenues, and profits are affected by global, national, regional, and local economies. Other factors discussed here that interact with economic forces include politics and governmental policies, international wars, natural disasters, technological inventions, and sociocultural forces. It is important to keep these dimensions in mind when studying organizations since many if not most or all changes that affect organizations originate from one or more of these sources—many of which are interrelated.

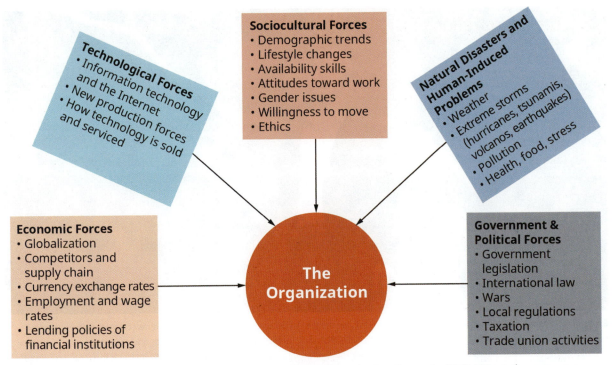

Exhibit 4.2   Macro Forces and Environments (Attribution: Copyright Rice University, OpenStax, under CC-BY 4.0 license)

Globalization is a combination of external forces shaping environments of organizations. Defined as the development of an integrated global economy and characterized by free trade, capital flows, communications, and cheaper foreign labor markets, the processes of globalization underlie the forces in the general international economic environment. This dimension continues to present opportunities and pressures to companies operating locally as well as globally. Globalization continues to affect industries and companies in ways that benefit some and not others. Amazon, for example, is thriving. The firm sells low-end products through its brand AmazonBasics. The company has individual retail websites for the United States, the United Kingdom and Ireland, France, Canada, Germany, Italy, Spain, the Netherlands, Australia, Brazil, Japan, China, India, and Mexico. Uber and Airbnb represent some of the larger sharing-economy companies that operate internationally and have to date prospered in the so-called new but fragmenting global economy.

Exhibit 4.3   Bezos Jeff Bezos' digital commerce strategy has led the firm to become the leader of retail commerce, and forced traditional retailers like Toys R Us to close their operations, and retailers like Walmart, Target, and Sears to reassess their business environment. Amazon's digital strategy uses Prime memberships that are supplied and supported by land-based distribution centers; Prime takes in reaching about 60% of the total dollar value of all merchandise sold on the site. (Credit: Sam Churchill/flickr/ Attribution 2.0 Generic (CC BY 2.0))

In general, countries that have gained from globalization include Japan, South Korea, Taiwan, Malaysia, Singapore, Hong Kong, Thailand, and China. China's markets and growing economic prowess have particularly been noticed. China's GDP (gross domestic product) is estimated at $13.2 trillion in 2018, outpacing the $12.8 trillion combined total of the 19 countries that use the euro.[5] Corporations worldwide, large and small, online and land-based, strive to gain access to sell in China's vast markets. Moreover, China at the beginning of 2018 owns $1.168 trillion of the United States' debt.[6] Japan, in second place, owes $1.07 trillion of this debt. Any instability politically and economically with China could result in increasing inflation and interest rates in the U.S. economy that could, in turn, negatively affect U.S. businesses.

Economic forces

Economically, "The strategic challenge of the next decade is navigating a world that is simultaneously integrating and fragmenting. Stock markets have set new records and economic volatility has fallen to historic lows, while political shocks on a scale unseen for generations have taken place. Seemingly contradictory realities do co-exist."[7] Overall, while economic data indicates that globalization has had a positive effect on the world economy, a dark side also shows that two-thirds of all households in 25 advanced-economy countries had incomes stagnate and/or decline between 2005 and 2014. Moreover, the U.K. and U.S. witnessed falling wages. Wealth distribution in these countries continues to decline. Income inequality globally is also rising. Other trends that also affect the global, regional, and local economies are discussed in this chapter as well as below.

Technological forces are another ubiquitous environmental influence on organizations. Speed, price, service, and quality of products and services are dimensions of organizations' competitive advantage in this era. Information technologies and social media powered by the Internet and used by sharing-economy companies such as Airbnb and Uber have democratized and increased, if not leveled, competition across several industries, such as taxis, real estate rentals, and hospitality services. Companies across industry sectors cannot survive without using the Internet, social media, and sophisticated software in R&D (research and development), operations, marketing, finance, and sales. To manage and use big data in all these functional areas, organizations rely on technology.

Government and political forces also affect industries and organizations. Recent events that have jarred the global economy—and are too early to predict the long-term outcomes of—are the United Kingdom's exit from the European Union, President Trump's nationalistic policies echoed by other presidents in Chile and Argentina,[8] wars in the Middle East, policies that question and disrupt free trade, health-care reform, and immigration—all of which increase uncertainty for businesses while creating opportunities for some industries and instability in others.

Sociocultural forces

Sociocultural environmental forces include different generations' values, beliefs, attitudes, customs and traditions, habits, and lifestyles. More specifically, other aspects of societal cultures are education, language, religion, law, politics, and social organizations. The millennial (ages 20 to 35) workforce, for example, generally seeks work that engages and interests them. Members of this generation are also health conscious and eager to learn. Since this and the newer generation (Generation Z) are adept and accustomed to using technology—social media in particular—organizations must be ready and equipped to provide wellness, interesting, and a variety of learning and work experiences to attract and retain new talent. Millennials are also estimated to be the United States' largest living adult generation in 2019. This generation numbered about 71 million compared with 74 million baby boomers (ages 52 to 70) in 2016. By 2019, an estimated 73 million millennials and 72 million boomers are projected. Because of immigration, millennials are estimated to increase until 2036.[9]

Other general sociocultural trends occurring in the United States and internationally that affect organizations include the following: (1) Sexual harassment at work in the era of #MeToo has pressured organizations to be more transparent about relationships between owners, bosses, and employees. Related to this trend, some surveys show new difficulties for men in workplace interactions and little effect on women's career opportunities taking place in the short term.[10] (2) While fewer immigrants have been entering the United States in recent years, diversity in the U.S. workplace continues. For example, 20 million Asian Americans trace their roots to over 20 countries in East and Southeast Asia and the Indian subcontinent—"each with unique histories, cultures, languages and other characteristics. The 19 largest origin groups together account for 94% of the total Asian population in the U.S."[11] (3) Young adults in the United States are living at home longer. "In 2016, 15% of 25- to 35-year-old Millennials were living in their parents' home. This is 5 percentage points higher than the share of Generation Xers who lived in their parents' home in 2000 when they were the same age (10%), and nearly double the share of the Silent Generation who lived at home in 1964 (8%)."[12] (4) While women have made gains in the workplace, they still comprise a small share of top leadership jobs—across politics and government, academia, the nonprofit sector, and business. Women comprised only about 10% of CEOs (chief executive officers), CFOs (chief financial officers), and the next three highest-paid executives in U.S. companies in 2016–17.[13] A 2018 study by McKinsey & Company "reaffirms the global relevance of the link between diversity—defined as a greater proportion of women and a more mixed ethnic and cultural composition in the leadership of large companies—and company financial outperformance."[14] These and other related sociocultural trends impact organizational cultures and other dimensions involving human talent and diverse workforces.

Natural disasters and human-related problems

Natural disaster and human induced environmental problems are events such as high-impact hurricanes, extreme temperatures and the rise in CO2 emissions as well as 'man-made' environmental disasters such as water and food crises; biodiversity loss and ecosystem collapse; large-scale involuntary migration are a force that affects organizations. The 2018 Global Risks Report identified risks in the environmental category that also affect industries and companies—as well as continents and countries. These risks were ranked higher than average for both likelihood and impact over a 10-year horizon. The report showed that 2017 was characterized by high-impact hurricanes, extreme temperatures, and the first rise in carbon dioxide emissions in four years; "man-made" environmental disasters; water and food crises; biodiversity loss and ecosystem collapse; and large-scale involuntary migration to name a few. Authors of this study noted that "Biodiversity is being lost at mass-extinction rates, agricultural systems are under strain and pollution of the air and sea has become an increasingly pressing threat to human health."[15] Most vulnerable to rising seas are low-lying islands in the Indian and Pacific Oceans. The Republic of the Marshall Islands has more over 1,100 low-lying islands on 29 atolls that include island nations with hundreds of thousands of people. Predictions indicate that rising sea levels could reach 3 feet worldwide by 2300 or sooner. One report stated that in your child's lifetime, Miami, Florida, could be underwater.[16] Large sections of Louisiana's marshes separating the ocean from the coastline are submerging. Oil producers and other related corporations are being sued by that state, claiming that fossil fuel emissions have contributed to natural disasters such as climate change. Many new companies in the United States are already constructing buildings to withstand increasing flooding and predicted rising water levels.

CONCEPT CHECK

1. Define the components of the internal and the external business environments.
2. What factors within the economic environment affect businesses?
3. Why do demographic shifts and technological developments create both challenges and new opportunities for business?

4.2 External Environments and Industries

2. Identify contemporary external forces pressuring organizations.

Industry and organizational leaders monitor environments to identify, predict, and manage trends, issues, and opportunities that their organizations and industries face. Some corporations, such as Amazon, anticipate and even create trends in their environments. Most, however, must adapt. External environments, as identified in the previous section, can be understood by identifying the uncertainty of the environmental forces. **Exhibit 4.4** illustrates a classic and relevant depiction of how scholars portray environment-industry-organization "fit," that is, how well industries and organizations align with and perform in different types of environments.

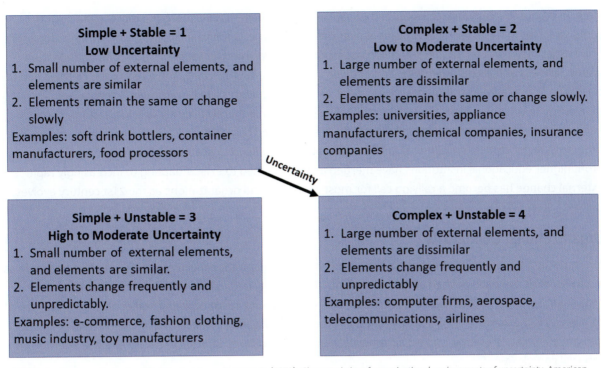

Exhibit 4.4   Company Industry Fit Adapted from: Duncan, R. (1972). *Characteristics of organizational environments of uncertainty*. American Science Quarterly, 17 *(September), 313-327; Daft, R*. Organizational Theory and Design, 12th edition, p. 151, *Mason, OH, Cengage Learning*.

The two dimensions of this figure represent "environmental complexity" (i.e., the number of elements in the environment, such a competitors, suppliers, and customers), which is characterized as either simple or complex, and "environmental change," described as stable or unstable. How available monetary and financial resources are to support an organization's growth is also an important element in this framework.[17] Certain industries—soft drink bottlers, beer distributors, food processors, and container manufacturers—would, hypothetically, fit and align more effectively in a stable (i.e., relative unchanging), simple, and low-uncertainty (i.e., has mostly similar elements) external environment—cell 1 in **Exhibit 4.4**. This is referred to when organizations are in a **simple-stable environment**. Of course unpredicted conditions, such as global and international turmoil, economic downturns, and so on, could affect these industries, but generally, these alignments have served as an ideal type and starting point for understanding the "fit" between environment and industries. In a stable but complex, low- to moderate-uncertainty environment, cell 2 in **Exhibit 4.4**, universities, appliance manufacturers, chemical companies, and insurances companies would generally prosper. This is referred to when organizations are in a **complex-stable environment**. When the external environment has simple but high to moderate uncertainty, cell 3 of **Exhibit 4.4**, e-commerce, music, and fashion clothing industries would operate effectively. This is referred to when organizations are in a **simple-unstable environment**. Whereas in cell 4 of **Exhibit 4.4**, an environment characterized by a high degree of uncertainty with complex and unstable elements, industries and firms such as computer, aerospace, airlines, and telecommunications firms would operate more effectively. This is referred to when organizations are in a **complex-unstable environment**.

Exhibit 4.4 is a starting point for diagnosing the "fit" between types of external environments and industries. As conditions change, industries and organizations must adapt or face consequences. For example, educational institutions that traditionally have been seen to operate best in low- to moderate-uncertainty environments, cell 4 of **Exhibit 4.4**, have during this past decade experienced more high to moderate uncertainty (cell 2)—and even high uncertainty (cell 1). For example, for-profit educational institutions such the University of Phoenix and others—as compared to not-for-profit universities and colleges, such as public state institutions, community colleges, and private nonprofit ones—have undergone more unstable and complex forces in the external environment over the past decade. Under the Obama administration, for-profit universities faced greater scrutiny regarding questionable advertising, graduation rates, and accreditation issues; lawsuits and claims against several of these institutions went forward, and a few of the colleges had to close. The Trump administration has shown signs of alleviating aggressive governmental control and monitoring in this sector. Still, higher educational institutions in general currently face increasingly complex and unstable environments given higher tuition rates, increased competition from less-expensive and online programs, fewer student enrollments, and an overabundance of such institutions. Several private, not-for-profit higher educational institutions have merged and also ceased to exist. Adapting to increasingly rapid external change has become a rallying call for most industries and organizations as the 21st century evolves.

Organizational Complexity

It is important to point out here that external (and internal) organizational complexity is not often as simple as it may seem. It has been defined as "...the amount of complexity derived from the environment where the organisation operates, such as the country, the markets, suppliers, customers and stakeholders; while internal complexity is the amount of complexity that is internal to the organisation itself, i.e. products, technologies, human resources, processes and organisational structure. Therefore, different aspects compose internal and external complexities."[18]

The dilemma that organizational leaders and managers sometimes face is how to deal with external, and internal, complexity? Do you grow and nurture it or reduce it? Some strategies call for reducing and managing it at the local level while nurturing it at the global level—depending on the organization's size, business model, and the nature of the environments. Without going into complicated detail, it is fair to say at the beginning of the chapter that you may want to read through the chapter first, then return here afterward.

In the meantime, here are some simple rules from organizational practitioners De Toni and De Zan to keep in mind for managing high levels of complexity from the external environment, internally, after you have diagnosed the nature of the external complexity—as we discuss throughout in this chapter: first, assemble "...a set of self-managing teams or autonomous business units,[known as modularized units] with an entrepreneurial responsibility to the larger organization." These focused self-organizing teams use creative methods to deal with the diversity to the advantage of the organization. A second method when facing high external environmental complexity when you want to gain value from it is to find and develop "...simple rules to drive out creativity and innovation ... to keep the infrastructure and processes simple, while permitting complex outputs and behaviours." An example offered is found in the rules of the Legos company: "(1) does the proposed product have the Lego look? (2) Will children learn while having fun? (3) Will parents approve? (4) Does the product maintain high quality standards? (5) Does it stimulate creativity?"[19]

A third strategy for dealing with external complexity involves companies' building on their own capabilities manage too much complexity, which otherwise lead to chaos. Some of those strategies include creating open networks internal and outside the organization to promote cooperation and integration and to develop brand and reputation. Also, sharing "...values, vision, strategy, organizational processes and knowledge, through the development of trust and incorporation and promotion of leaders at all levels" can help internal teams exploit external complexity to the organization's advantage. Keep these ideas in mind as you read through the chapter and think about how leaders, managers, employees, and you can learn to read external environmental clues that organizations can use to creatively and proactively use organizational resources to be more competitive, effective, and successful.

CONCEPT CHECK

1. What factors within the economic environment affect businesses?
2. Why do change and shifts and technological developments create both challenges and new opportunities for business?

4.3 | Organizational Designs and Structures

3. Identify different types of organizational structures and their strengths and weaknesses.

A 2017 Deloitte source asked, before answering, "Why has organizational design zoomed to the top of the list as the most important trend in the Global Human Capital Trends survey for two years in a row?"[20] The source continued, "The answer is simple: The way high-performing organizations operate today is radically different from how they operated 10 years ago. Yet many other organizations continue to operate according to industrial-age models that are 100 years old or more."[21]

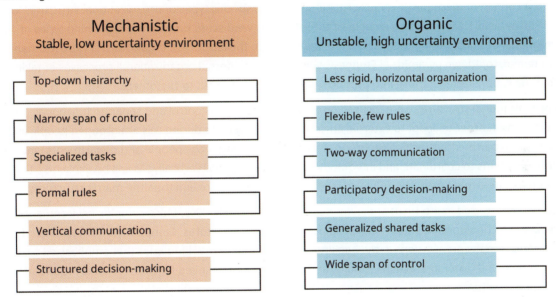

Exhibit 4.5   Mechanistic and Organic Organizations (Attribution: Copyright Rice University, OpenStax, under CC-BY 4.0 license)

Early organizational theorists broadly categorized **organizational structures** and systems as either mechanistic or organic.[22] This broad, generalized characterization of organizations remains relevant. **Mechanistic organizational structures** (**Exhibit 4.5**) are best suited for environments that range from stable and simple to low-moderate uncertainty (**Exhibit 4.4**) and are characterized by top-down hierarchies of control that are rule-based. The chain of command is highly centralized and uses formal authority; tasks are clearly defined and differentiated to be executed by specific specialized experts. Bosses and supervisors have fewer people working directly under them (i.e., a narrow span of control), and the organization is governed by rigid departmentalization (i.e., an organization is divided into different departments that perform specialized tasks according to the departments' expertise). This form of organization represents a traditional type of structure that evolved in environments that were, as noted above, stable with low complexity. Historically, the U.S. Postal

Service and other manufacturing types of industries (**Exhibit 4.4**) were mechanistic. Again, this type of organizational design may still be relevant, as **Exhibit 4.4** suggests, in simple, stable, low-uncertainty environments.

Organic organizational structures and systems, however, have opposite characteristics from mechanistic ones. As **Exhibit 4.4** shows, these organizational forms work best in unstable, complex, changing environments. Their structures are flatter, with participatory communication and decision-making flowing in different directions. There is more fluidity and less-rigid ways of performing tasks; there may also be fewer rules. Tasks are more generalized and shared; there is a wider span of control (i.e., more people reporting to managers). **Exhibit 4.5** offers examples of organically structured industries, such as high tech, computer, aerospace, and telecommunications industries, that must deal with change and uncertainty. Contemporary corporations and firms engaged in fast-paced, highly competitive, rapidly changing, and turbulent environments are becoming more organic in different ways, as we will discuss in this chapter. However, not every organization or every part of most organizations may require an organic type of structure. Understanding different organizational designs and structures is important to discern when, where, and under what circumstances a type of mechanistic system or part of an organization would be needed. The following section discusses five types of structures with variations.

Types of Organizational Structures

Within the context of mechanistic versus organic structures, specific types of organizational structures in the United States historically evolved over at least three eras, as we discuss here before explaining types of organizational designs. During the first era, the mid-1800s to the late 1970s, organizations were mechanistic self-contained, top-down pyramids.[23] Emphasis was placed on internal organizational processes of taking in raw materials, transforming those into products, and turning them out to customers.

Early organizational structures were focused on internal hierarchical control and separate functional specializations in order to adapt to external environments. Structures during this era grouped people into functions or departments, specified reporting relationships among those people and departments, and developed systems to coordinate and integrate work horizontally and vertically. As will be explained, the **functional structure** evolved first, followed by the divisional structure and then the matrix structured.

The second era started in the 1980s and extended through the mid-1990s. More-complex environments, markets, and technologies strained mechanistic organizational structures. Competition from Japan in the auto industry and complex transactions in the banking, insurance, and other industries that emphasized customer value, demand and faster interactions, quality, and results issued the need for more organic organizational designs and structures.

Communication and coordination between and among internal organizational units and external customers, suppliers, and other stakeholders required higher levels of integration and speed of informational processing. Personal computers and networks had also entered the scene. In effect, the so-called "horizontal organization" was born, which emphasized "reengineering along workflow processes that link organizational capabilities to customers and suppliers."[24] Ford, Xerox Corp., Lexmark, and Eastman Kodak Company are examples of early adopters of the **horizontal organizational design**, which, unlike the top-down pyramid structures in the first era, brought flattened hierarchical, hybrid structures and cross-functional teams.

The third era started in the mid-1990s and extends to the present. Several factors contributed to the rise of this era: the Internet; global competition—particularly from China and India with low-cost labor; automation of supply chains; and outsourcing of expertise to speed up production and delivery of products and services. The so-called silos and walls of organizations opened up; everything could not be or did not have to be produced within the confines of an organization, especially if corporations were cutting costs and outsourcing different functions of products to save costs. During this period, further extensions of the horizontal and organic types of structures evolved: the divisional, matrix, global geographic, modular, team-based, and virtual structures were created.

In the following discussion, we identify major types of structures mentioned above and discuss the advantages and disadvantages of each, referenced in **Exhibit 4.6**. Note that in many larger national and international corporations, there is a mix and match among different structures used. There are also advantages and disadvantages of each structure. Again, organizational structures are designed to fit with external environments. Depending on the type of environments from our earlier discussion in which a company operates, the structure should facilitate that organization's capability to achieve its vision, mission, and goals.

Exhibit 4.6 offers a profile of different structures that evolved in our discussion above.

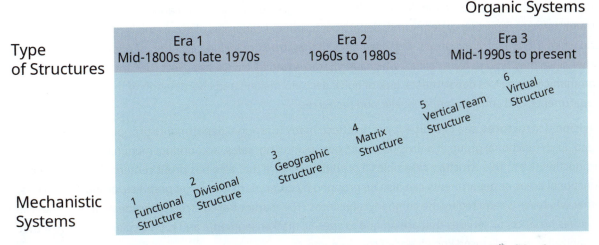

Exhibit 4.6   Evolution of Organizational Structure Adapted from: Daft, R., 2016, Organization Theory and Design, 12th edition, Cengage learning, Chapter 3; Warren, N., "Hitting the Sweet Spot Between Specialization and Integration in Organizational Design", People and Strategy, 34, No. 1, 2012, pp. 24-30.

Note the continuum in **Exhibit 4.6**, showing the earliest form of organizational structure, functional, evolving with more complex environments to divisional, matrix, team-based, and then virtual. This evolution, as discussed above, is presented as a continuum from mechanistic to organic structures—moving from more simple, stable environments to complex, changing ones, as illustrated in **Exhibit 4.6**. The six types of organizational structures discussed here include functional, divisional, geographic, matrix, networked/team, and virtual.[25]

The functional structure, shown in **Exhibit 4.7**, is among the earliest and most used organizational designs. This structure is organized by departments and expertise areas, such as R&D (research & development), production, accounting, and human resources. Functional organizations are referred to as pyramid structures since they are governed as a hierarchical, top-down control system.

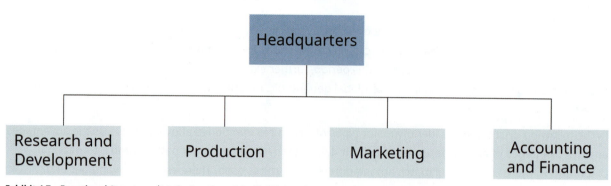

Exhibit 4.7   Functional Structure (Attribution: Copyright Rice University, OpenStax, under CC-BY 4.0 license)

Small companies, start-ups, and organizations working in simple, stable environments use this structure, as do many large government organizations and divisions of large companies for certain tasks.

The functional structure excels in providing for a high degree of specialization and a simple and straightforward reporting system within departments, offers economies of scale, and is not difficult to scale if and when the organization grows. Disadvantages of this structure include isolation of departments from each other since they tend to form "silos," which are characterized by closed mindsets that are not open to communicating across departments, lack of quick decision-making and coordination of tasks across departments, and competition for power and resources.

Divisional structures, see Exhibit 4.8, are, in effect, many functional departments grouped under a division head. Each functional group in a division has its own marketing, sales, accounting, manufacturing, and production team. This structure resembles a product structure that also has profit centers. These smaller functional areas or departments can also be grouped by different markets, geographies, products, services, or other whatever is required by the company's business. The market-based structure is ideal for an organization that has products or services that are unique to specific market segments and is particularly effective if that organization has advanced knowledge of those segments.

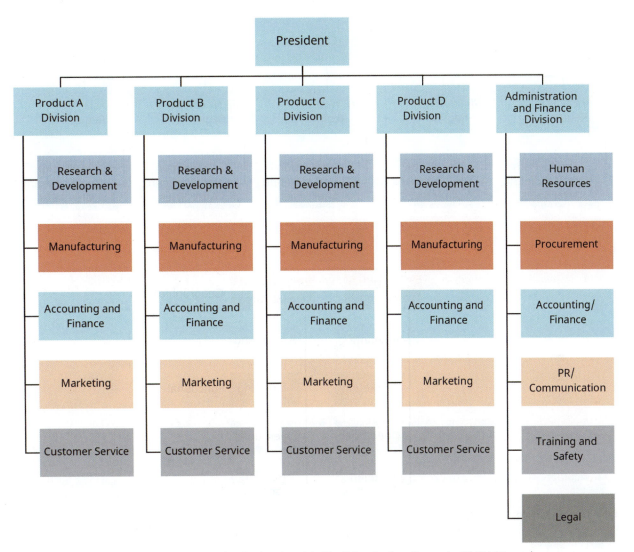

Exhibit 4.8 Divisional Organization Structure (Attribution: Copyright Rice University, OpenStax, under CC-BY 4.0 license)

The advantages of a divisional structure include the following: each specialty area can be more focused on the business segment and budget that it manages; everyone can more easily know their responsibilities and accountability expectations; customer contact and service can be quicker; and coordination within a divisional grouping is easier, since all the functions are accessible. The divisional structure is also helpful for large companies since decentralized decision-making means that headquarters does not have to micromanage all the divisions. The disadvantages of this structure from a headquarters perspective are that divisions can easily become isolated and insular from one another and that different systems, such as accounting, finance, sales, and so on, may suffer from poor and infrequent communication and coordination of enterprise mission, direction, and values. Moreover, incompatibility of systems (technology, accounting, advertising, budgets) can occur, which creates a strain on company strategic goals and objectives.

A **geographic structure**, **Exhibit 4.9**, is another option aimed at moving from a mechanistic to more organic design to serve customers faster and with relevant products and services; as such, this structure is organized by locations of customers that a company serves. This structure evolved as companies became more national, international, and global. Geographic structures resemble and are extensions of the divisional structure.

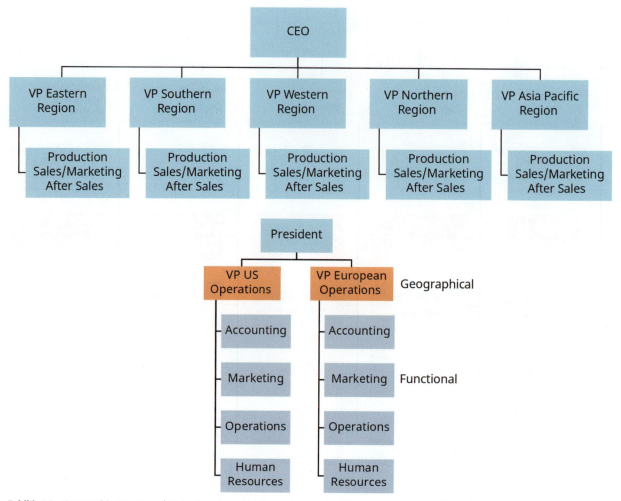

Exhibit 4.9   Geographic Structure (Attribution: Copyright Rice University, OpenStax, under CC-BY 4.0 license)

Organizing geographically enables each geographic organizational unit (like a division) the ability to understand, research, and design products and/or services with the knowledge of customer needs, tastes, and cultural differences. The advantages and disadvantages of the geographic structure are similar to those of the divisional structure. Headquarters must ensure effective coordination and control over each somewhat autonomous geographically self-contained structure.

The main downside of a geographical organizational structure is that it can be easy for decision-making to become decentralized, as geographic divisions (which can be hundreds if not thousands of miles away from corporate headquarters) often have a great deal of autonomy.

Exhibit 4.10   IBM China IBM has chosen a geographic structure which is aimed at moving from a mechanistic to more organic design to serve customers faster and with relevant products and services; as such, this structure is organized by locations of customers that a company serves. This structure evolved as companies became more national, international, and global. Geographic structures resemble and are extensions of the divisional structure. (Credit: Cory Denton/ Flickr/ Attribution 2.0 Generic (CC BY 2.0))

Matrix structures, illustrated in **Exhibit 4.6** and depicted in **Exhibit 4.11**, move closer to organic systems in an attempt to respond to environmental uncertainty, complexity, and instability. The matrix structure actually originated at a time in the 1960s when U.S. aerospace firms contracted with the government. Aerospace firms were required to "develop charts showing the structure of the project management team that would be executing the contract and how this team was related to the overall management structure of the organization." As such, employees would be required to have dual reporting relationships—with the government and the aerospace company.[26] Since that time, this structure has been imitated and used by other industries and companies since it provides flexibility and helps integrate decision-making in functionally organized companies.

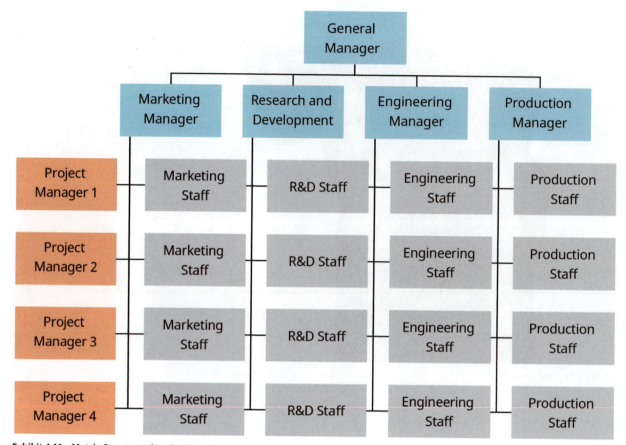

Exhibit 4.11   Matrix Structure (Attribution: Copyright Rice University, OpenStax, under CC-BY 4.0 license)

Matrix designs use teams to combine vertical with horizontal structures. The traditional functional or vertical structure and chain of command maintains control over employees who work on teams that cut across functional areas, creating horizontal coordination that focuses projects that have deadlines and goals to meet within and often times in addition to those of departments. In effect, matrix structures initiated horizontal team-based structures that provided faster information sharing, coordination, and integration between the formal organization and profit-oriented projects and programs.

As **Exhibit 4.11** illustrates, this structure has lines of formal authority along two dimensions: employees report to a functional, departmental boss and simultaneously to a product or project team boss. One of the weaknesses of matrix structures is the confusion and conflicts employees experience in reporting to two bosses. To work effectively, employees (including their bosses and project leaders) who work in dual-authority matrix structures require good interpersonal communication, conflict management, and political skills to manage up and down the organization.

Different types of matrix structures, some resembling virtual team designs, are used in more complex environments.[27] For example, there are cross-functional matrix teams in which team members from other organizational departments report to an "activity leader" who is not their formal supervisor or boss. There are also functional matrix teams where employees from the same department coordinate across another internal matrix team consisting of, for example, HR or other functional area specialists, who come together to develop a limited but focused common short-term goal. There are also global matrix teams consisting of employees from different regions, countries, time zones, and cultures who are assembled to achieve a short-term project goal of a particular customer. Matrix team members have been and are a growing part of horizontal organizations that cut across geographies, time zones, skills, and traditional authority structures to solve customer and even enterprise organizational needs and demands.

As part of the next discussed organizational type of structure, networked teams, organizational members in matrix structures must "learn how to collaborate with colleagues across distance, cultures and other barriers. Matrix team members often suffer from the problem of divided loyalties where they have both team and functional goals that compete for their time and attention, they have multiple bosses and often work on multiple teams at the same time. For some matrix team members this may be the first time they have been given accountability for results that are broader than delivery of their functional goals. Some individuals relish the breath and development that the matrix team offers and others feel exposed and out of control." To succeed in these types of horizontal organizational structures, organizational members "should focus less on the structure and more on behaviors."[28]

Networked team structures are another form of the horizontal organization. Moving beyond the matrix structure, networked teams are more informal and flexible. "[N]etworks have two salient characteristics: clustering and path length. Clustering refers to the degree to which a network is made up of tightly knit groups while path lengths is a measure of distance—the average number of links separating any two nodes in the network."[29] A more technical explanation can be found in this footnote source.[30] For our purposes here, a networked organizational structure is one that naturally forms after being initially assigned. Based on the vision, mission, and needs of a problem or opportunity, team members will find others who can help—if the larger organization and leaders do not prevent or obstruct that process.

There is not one classical depiction of this structure, since different companies initially design teams to solve problems, find opportunities, and discover resources to do so. Stated another way, "The networked organization is one that is connected together by informal networks and the demands of the task, rather than a formal organizational structure. The network organization prioritizes its 'soft structure' of relationships, networks, teams, groups and communities rather than reporting lines."[31] **Exhibit 4.12** is a suggested illustration of this structure.

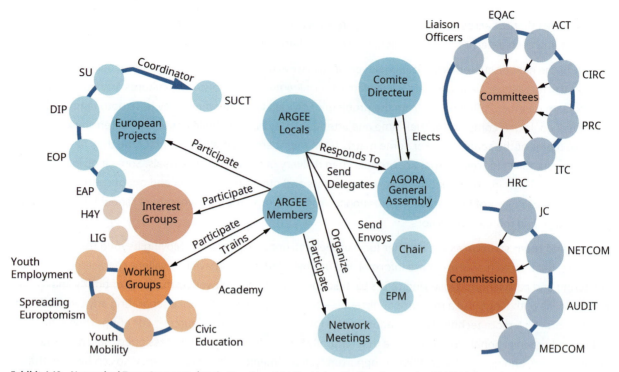

Exhibit 4.12   Networked Team Structure (Attribution: Copyright Rice University, OpenStax, under CC-BY 4.0 license)

A Deloitte source based on the 2017 Global Human Capital Trend study stated that as organizations continue to transition from vertical structures to more organic ones, networked global designs are being adapted to larger companies that require more reach and scope and quicker response time with customers: "Research shows that we spend two orders of magnitude more time with people near our desk than with those more than 50 meters away. Whatever a hierarchical organization chart says, real, day-to-day work gets done in networks. This is why the organization of the future is a 'network of teams.'"[32]

Advantages of networked organizations are similar to those stated earlier with regard to organic, horizontal, and matrix structures. Weaknesses of the networked structure include the following: (1) Establishing clear lines of communication to produce project assignments and due dates to employees is needed. (2) Dependence on technology—Internet connections and phone lines in particular—is necessary. Delays in communication result from computer crashes, network traffic errors and problems; electronic information sharing across country borders can also be difficult. (3) Not having a central physical location where all employees work, or can assemble occasionally to have face-to-face meetings and check results, can result in errors, strained relationships, and lack of on-time project deliverables.[33]

Virtual structures and organizations emerged in the 1990s as a response to requiring more flexibility, solution-based tasks on demand, fewer geographical constraints, and accessibility to dispersed expertise.[34] Virtual structures are depicted in **Exhibit 4.13**. Related to so-called modular and digital organizations, virtual structures are dependent on information communication technologies (ICTs).

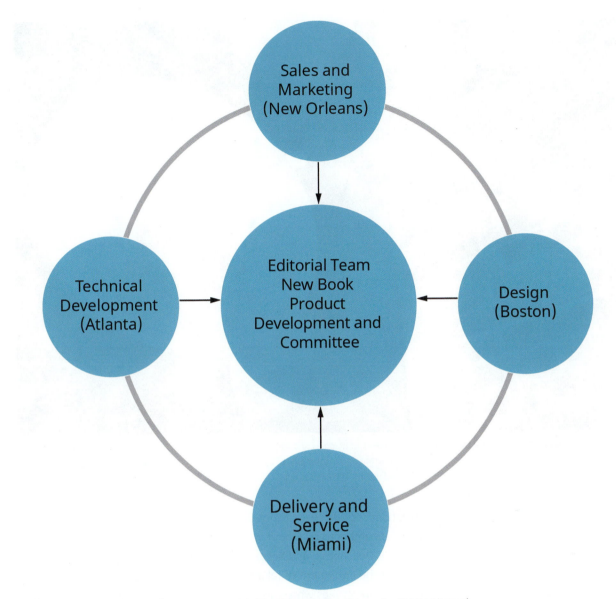

Exhibit 4.13 **Virtual Structure** (Attribution: Copyright Rice University, OpenStax, under CC-BY 4.0 license)

These organizations move beyond network team structures in that the headquarters or home base may be the only or part of part of a stable organizational base. Otherwise, this is a "boundaryless organization." Examples of organizations that use virtual teams are Uber, Airbnb, Amazon, Reebok, Nike, Puma, and Dell. Increasingly, organizations are using different variations of virtual structures with call centers and other outsourced tasks, positions, and even projects.

Exhibit 4.14   Using Technological Disruption Information technologies and social media powered by the internet and used by sharing economy companies such as Airbnb and Uber have democratized and increased, if not leveled, competition across several industries such taxis, real estate rentals, and hospitality services. (Credit: Grid Engine/ flickr/ Attribution 2.0 Generic (CC BY 2.0))

Advantages of virtual teams and organizations include cost savings, decreased response time to customers, greater access to a diverse labor force not encumbered by 8-hour workdays, and less harmful effects on the environment. "The telecommuting policies of Dell, Aetna, and Xerox cumulatively saved 95,294 metric tons of greenhouse gas emissions last year, which is the equivalent of taking 20,000 passenger vehicles off of the road."[35] Disadvantages are social isolation of employees who work virtually, potential for lack of trust among employees and between the company and employees when communication is limited, and reduced collaboration among separated employees and the organization's officers due to lack of social interaction.

In the following section, we turn to internal organizational dimensions that complement structure and are affected by and affect external environments.

CONCEPT CHECK

1. Why does the matrix structure have a dual chain of command?
2. How does a matrix structure increase power struggles or reduce accountability?
3. What are advantages of a formal committee structure? Disadvantages?

4.4 | The Internal Organization and External Environments

4. Explain how organizations organize to meet external market threats and opportunities.

At a basic level of understanding how internal organizations respond to environments, consider the theory of Open Systems, which the organizational theorists Katz and Kahn[36] and Bertalanffy introduced.[37]

Exhibit 4.15 illustrates this theory's view of organizations as open systems that take in resources and raw materials at the "input" phase from the environment in a number of forms, depending on the nature of the organization, industry, and its business. Whatever the input resources are—information, raw materials, students entering a university—to be transformed by the internal processes of the organization. The internal organizational systems then process and transform the input material, which is called "through-put" phase, and move the changed material (resources) to the "outputs" and back into the environment as products, services, graduates, etc.

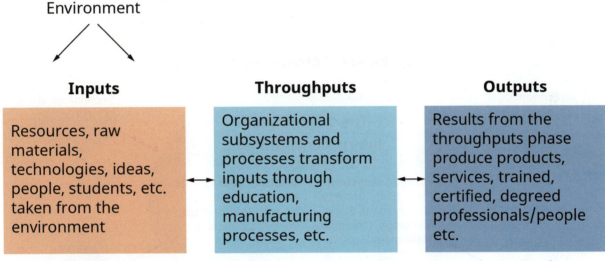

Exhibit 4.15   Open System Model of an Organization (Attribution: Copyright Rice University, OpenStax, under CC-BY 4.0 license)

The open systems model serves as a feedback loop continually taking in resources from the environment, processing and transforming them into outputs that are returned to the environment. This model explains organizational survival that emphasizes long-term goals.

Organizations according to this theory are considered as either Open or Closed systems, (or relatively opened or closed) depending on the organization's sensitivity to the environment. Closed systems are less sensitive to environmental resources and possibilities, and open systems are more responsive and adaptive to environmental changes. For example, during the 1980's the then Big 3 U.S. auto manufacturers (Ford, General Motors and Chrysler) were pressured by Japanese auto manufacturers' successful 4-cylinder car sales that hit the U.S. like a shock wave. The Detroit producers experienced slumping sales, plant closures, and employee lay-offs in response to the Japanese wave of competition. It seemed that the U.S. auto makers had become closed or at least insensitive to changing trends in cars during that time and were unwilling to change manufacturing processes. Similarly, Amazon's business model, discussed earlier, has and continues to pressure retailers to innovate and change processes and practices to compete in this digital era.

Organizations respond to external environments not only through their structures, but also by the domains they choose and the internal dimensions and capabilities they select. An organization defines itself and its niche in an environment by the choice of its **domain**, i.e., what sector or field of the environment it will use its technology, products, and services to compete in and serve. Some of the major sectors of a task environment include marketing, technology, government, financial resources, and human resources.

Presently, several environmental domains that once were considered stable have become more complex and unstable—e.g., toys, public utilities, the U.S. Postal Service, and higher education. And even domains are changing. For example, as referred to earlier, the traditionally stable and somewhat unchanging domain of higher education has become more complex with the entry of for-profit educational institutions, MOOCs (massive open online courses), internal company "universities," and other certification and degree programs outside traditional private institutions. Sharing-economy companies such as Uber and Airbnb have redefined the transportation domain in which taxis operate and the hospitality domain in which hotels and bed and breakfasts serve. New business models that use mobile phones, ICTs (information communication technologies), and apps remove middle management layers in traditional organizations and structures.

With a chosen domain in which to operate, owners and leaders must organize internal dimensions to compete in and serve their markets. For example, hierarchies of authority and chain of command are used by owners and top-level leaders to develop and implement strategic and enterprise decisions; managers are required to provide technologies, training, accounting, legal, and other infrastructure resources; and cultures still count to establish and maintain norms, relationships, legal and ethical practices, and the reputation of organizations.

Exhibit 4.16   Internal Organization (Attribution: Copyright Rice University, OpenStax, under CC-BY 4.0 license)

Exhibit 4.16 shows internal organizational dimensions. These dimensions and systems include leadership, strategy, culture, management, goals, marketing, operations, and structure. Relationships, norms, and politics are also included in the informal organization. There are other internal functions not listed here, such as research and development, accounting and finance, production, and human resources. Another popular depiction of internal organizational dimensions is the **McKinsey 7-S model**, shown in **Exhibit 4.17**. Similarly, *strategy, structure, systems, skills, staff*, and style all revolve around and are interconnected with *shared values* (or culture) in an organization.

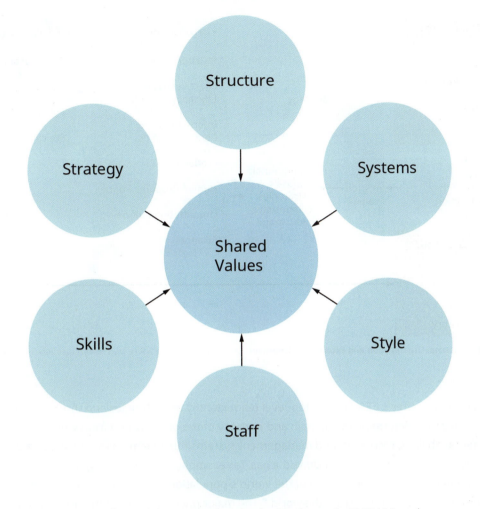

Exhibit 4.17 The McKinsey 7-S Model (Attribution: Copyright Rice University, OpenStax, under CC-BY 4.0 license)

A unifying framework shown in **Exhibit 4.18**, developed by Arie Lewin and Carroll Stephens,[38] illustrates the integration of internal organizational dimensions and how these work in practice to align with the external environment. Note that it is the CEO and other top-level leaders who scan the external environment to identify uncertainties and resources before using a SWOT analysis (identifying strengths, weaknesses, opportunities, and threats) to confirm and update the domain of an organization and then to define the vision, mission, goals, and strategies. Once the enterprise goals and strategies are developed, the organizational culture, structure, and other systems and policies can be established (human resources, technologies, accounting and finance, and so on).

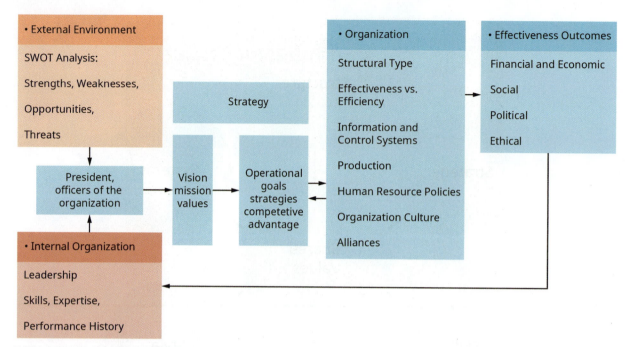

Exhibit 4.18   The Internal Organization and External Environment (Attribution: Copyright Rice University, OpenStax, under CC-BY 4.0 license)

As **Exhibit 4.18** shows, after a CEO and the top-level team identify opportunities and threats in the environment, they then determine the domain and purpose of the organization from which strategies, organizational capabilities, resources, and management systems must be mobilized to support the enterprise's purpose.[39] The company McDonald's has, for example, successfully aligned its enterprise with the global environments it serves, which is "1% of the world's population—more than 70 million customers—every day and in virtually every country across the world." The major operating goal of the firm driving its internal alignment is a "fanatical attention to the design and management of scalable processes, routines, and a working culture by which simple, stand-alone, and standardized products are sold globally at a predictable, and therefore manageable, volume, quality, and cost."[40] A more detailed SWOT analysis of McDonald's operations can be found in endnote.

Exhibit 4.19   McDonald's Processes McDonalds, major operating goal of the firm driving its internal alignment is a "Fanatical attention to the design and management of scalable processes, routines, and a working culture by which simple, stand-alone, and standardized products are sold globally at a predictable, and therefore manageable, volume, quality, and cost." Here employees are reminded of the time that the ingredients should stay on a secondary shelf. (Credit: Walter Lim/ flickr/ Attribution 2.0 Generic (CC BY 2.0))

In practice, no internal organizational alignment with its external environment is perfect or permanent. Quite the opposite. Companies and organizations change leadership and strategies and make structural and systems changes to meet changing competition, market forces, and customers and end users' needs and demands. Even Amazon continues to develop, expand, and change. With a mission statement as bold and broad as Amazon's, change is a constant: "Our vision is to be earth's most customer-centric company; to build a place where people can come to find and discover anything they might want to buy online" (Amazon.com, Apr 15, 2018).

Amazon has a functional organizational structure that focuses on business functions for determining the interactions among the different parts of the company. Amazon's corporate structure is best characterized as global function-based groups (most significant feature), a global hierarchy, and geographic divisions, as **Exhibit 4.20** shows. This structure seems to fit with the size of Amazon's business—43% of 2016 retail sales were in the United States.[41] Seven segments, including information technology, human resources and legal operations, and heads of segments, report to Amazon's CEO. "Senior management team include two CEOs, three Senior Vice Presidents and one Worldwide Controller, who are responsible for various vital aspects of the business reporting directly to Amazon CEO Jeff Bezos." [42] The strategic goal underlying this structure is to facilitate Amazon.com to successfully implement e-commerce operations management throughout the entire organization.[43]

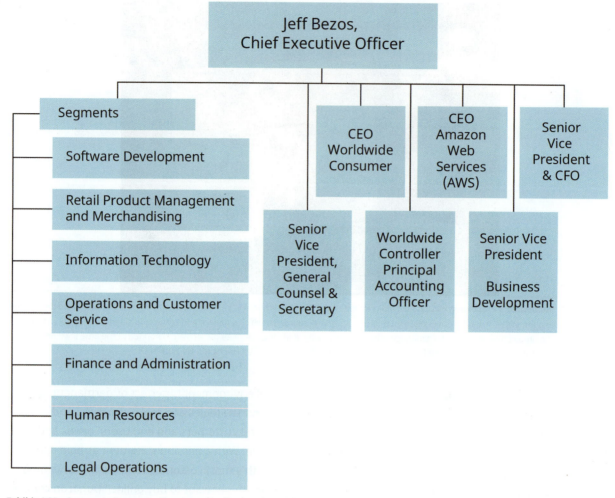

Exhibit 4.20 **Amazon's Corporate Structure** (Attribution: Copyright Rice University, OpenStax, under CC-BY 4.0 license)

Despite the company's exponential growth and success to date, as noted earlier in the section on organizational structures, a disadvantage of structures such as Amazon's, and in this case Amazon's, is that it has limited flexibility and responsiveness even with its current growth. "The dominance of the global function-based groups and global hierarchy characteristics reduces the capacity of Amazon to rapidly respond to new issues and problems encountered in the e-commerce business."[44] Still, Amazon's most outstanding success factor remains its CEO, Jeff Bezos—his ingenuity, vision and foresight, and ability to sustain and even extend the company's competitive advantages. Amazon customers value these factors—customer purchase criteria (CPC) that include price, fast delivery, and reliable service. "Consumers choose Amazon because it does better than its competition on these CPC."[45]

CONCEPT CHECK

1. Identify the six major organizational structures.
2. Explain the McKinsey 7-S model.

4.5 | Corporate Cultures

5. Identify the fit between organizational cultures and the external environment

Organizational culture is considered one of the most important **internal dimensions of an organization**'s effectiveness criteria. Peter Drucker, an influential management guru, once stated, "Culture eats strategy for breakfast."[46] He meant that **corporate culture** is more influential than strategy in terms of motivating employees' beliefs, behaviors, relationships, and ways they work since culture is based on values. Strategy and other **internal dimensions of organization** are also very important, but organizational culture serves two crucial purposes: first, culture helps an organization adapt to and integrate with its external environment by adopting the right values to respond to external threats and opportunities; and secondly, culture creates internal unity by bringing members together so they work more cohesively to achieve common goals. [47]ulture is both the personality and glue that binds an organization. It is also important to note that organizational cultures are generally framed and influenced by the top-level leader or founder. This individual's vision, values, and mission set the "tone at the top," which influences both the ethics and legal foundations, modeling how other officers and employees work and behave. A framework used to study how an organization and its culture fit with the environment is offered in the Competing Values Framework.

The **Competing Values Framework** (CVF) is one of the most cited and tested models for diagnosing an organization's cultural effectiveness and examining its fit with its environment. The CVF, shown in **Exhibit 4.21**, has been tested for over 30 years; the effectiveness criteria offered in the framework were discovered to have made a difference in identifying organizational cultures that fit with particular characteristics of external environments.[48]

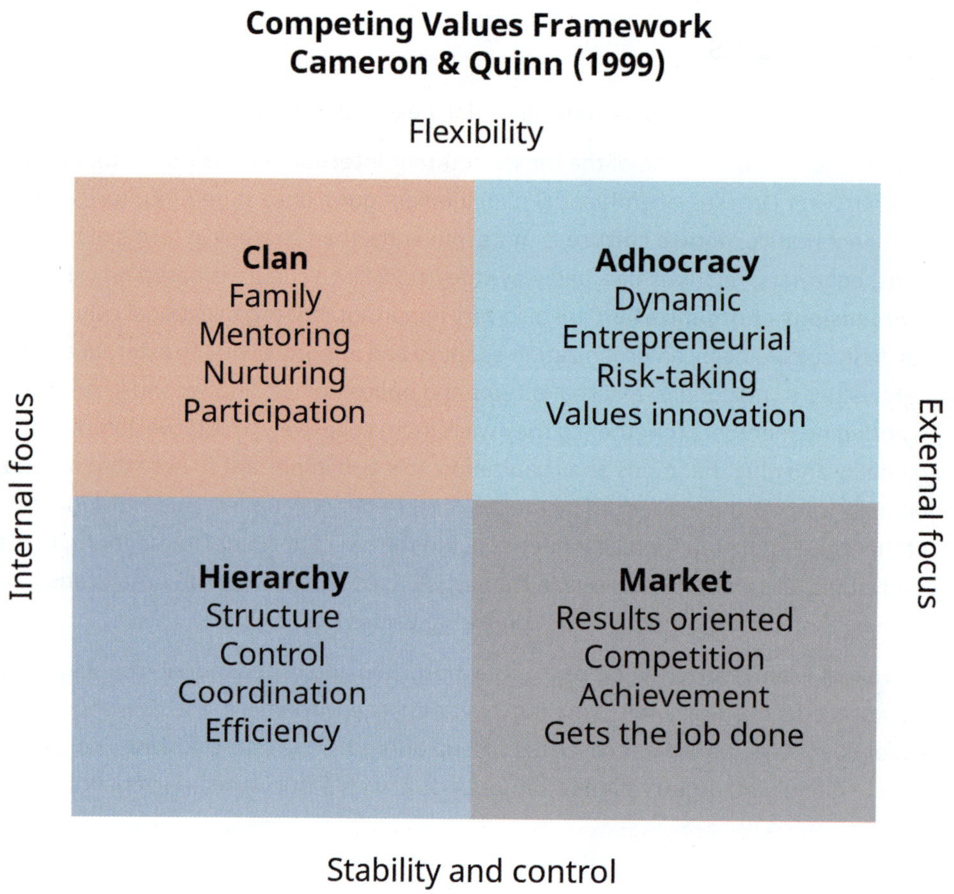

Competing Values Framework
Cameron & Quinn (1999)

Flexibility

Clan Family Mentoring Nurturing Participation	**Adhocracy** Dynamic Entrepreneurial Risk-taking Values innovation
Hierarchy Structure Control Coordination Efficiency	**Market** Results oriented Competition Achievement Gets the job done

Internal focus   External focus

Stability and control

Exhibit 4.21   The Competing Values Framework   Source: Adapted from K. Cameron and R. Quinn, 1999. Diagnosing and Changing Organizational Culture, Addison-Wesley, p. 32.

The two axes in the framework, external focus versus internal focus, indicate whether or not the organization's culture is externally or internally oriented. The other two axes, flexibility versus stability and control, determine whether a culture functions better in a stable, controlled environment or a flexible, fast-paced environment. Combining the axes offers four cultural types: (1) the dynamic, entrepreneurial **Adhocracy Culture**—an external focus with a flexibility orientation; (2) the people-oriented, friendly **Clan Culture**—an internal focus with a flexibility orientation; (3) the process-oriented, structured **Hierarchy Culture**—an internal focus with a stability/control orientation; and (4) the results-oriented, competitive **Market Culture**—an external focus with a stability/control orientation.

The orientation of each of these cultural types is summarized as follows. The **Adhocracy Culture** profile of an organization emphasizes creating, innovating, visioning the future, managing change, risk-taking, rule-breaking, experimentation, entrepreneurship, and uncertainty. This profile culture is often found in such fast-paced industries as filming, consulting, space flight, and software development. Facebook and Google's cultures also match these characteristics.[49] It should be noted, however, that larger organizations may have different cultures for different groupings of professionals, even though the larger culture is still dominant. For example, a different subculture may evolve for hourly workers as compared to PhD research scientists in an organization.

The **Clan Culture** type focuses on relationships, team building, commitment, empowering human development, engagement, mentoring, and coaching. Organizations that focus on human development, human resources, team building, and mentoring would fit this profile. This type of culture fits Tom's of Maine, which has strived to form respectful relationships with employees, customers, suppliers, and the physical environment.

The **Hierarchy Culture** emphasizes efficiency, process and cost control, organizational improvement, technical expertise, precision, problem solving, elimination of errors, logical, cautious and conservative, management and operational analysis, and careful decision-making. This profile would suit a company that is bureaucratic and structured, such as the U.S. Postal Service, the military, and other similar types of government agencies.

The **Market Culture** focuses on delivering value, competing, delivering shareholder value, goal achievement, driving and delivering results, speedy decisions, hard driving through barriers, directive, commanding, and getting things done. This profile suits a marketing-and-sales-oriented company that works on planning and forecasting but also getting products and services to market and sold. Oracle under the dominating, hard-charging executive chairman Larry Ellison characterized this cultural fit.

Amazon illustrates a company that can have a mix of cultures and be effective. For example, Amazon blends a high-performance Adhocracy Culture with regard to its external expansion and Bezos's leadership style; at the same time, Amazon resembles a Hierarchy Culture internally with regard to its tight control over employees at lower levels. The company propelled its domain from an "online bookstore" "to selling everything online to being the pioneering in adopting cloud computing with AWS . . . to adopting the latest robotics in its warehouses to improve productivity . . . to thinking and testing disruptive technologies like drones and so on."[50] It has been criticized, at the same time, for its "toxic cut-throat work environment," asserting that Jeff Bezos is overly demanding and sets very high standards for Amazon employees, as well as for himself. This type of culture extends down to the warehouse employees. Amazon employees have complained that "Work came first, life came second, and trying to find the balance came last." This criticism peaked with an alleged suicide attempt in 2017 of a disgruntled employee who requested a transfer to a different department within in the company but was placed on an employee improvement plan—"a step that could result in his termination from Amazon if his performance didn't improve."[51] Amazon has since changed many of its working rules and regulations for warehouse employees.

CONCEPT CHECK

1. How can employee diversity give a company a competitive advantage?
2. Explain the concept of hiring for fit as it relates to corporate culture.
3. What are some organizational issues that must be addressed when two large firms merge or grow rapidly like Amazon?

4.6 | Organizing for Change in the 21st Century

6. Identify environmental trends, demands, and opportunities facing organizations.

The 2018 annual Global Risks Perception Survey (GRPS) predicts the following trends in the external environment: (1) persistent inequality and unfairness, (2) domestic and international political tensions, (3) environmental dangers, and (4) cyber vulnerabilities. With this context, authors in this report suggest that complex organizations approach their futures with the "nine resilience lens"—i.e., the capacity of a company or other organization to adapt and prosper in the face of high-impact, low-probability risks.[52] The nine lenses are grouped into three categories. First, structural resilience considers the systemic dynamics within the organization itself. The author calls for "system modularity," i.e., structures and designs that are "loosely coupled," which is another way of saying that rigid, mechanistic hierarchies will not function as well in these high-impact environments. Secondly, integrative resilience underlines complex interconnections with the external context. Here the author suggests that organizations must be part of and aware of their contexts: geographically and the health of "individuals, families, neighborhoods, cities, provinces, and countries" that are affected. Relatedly, the author notes that organizations must rely on their social cohesion—such as the social capital an organization has to fall back on in times of crisis—which is a strong source of resilience. Third, transformative resilience requires that mitigating some risks requires transformation. Important to organizations here is the need "to proactively change or it will end up being changed by external circumstances." This process requires organizational foresight, not forecasting. Organizations need to apply different search, environmental scanning, and new discovery techniques "to engage with the uncertainty of multiple futures." They do this through innovation and experimentation. In practice, Google, Amazon, Facebook, SpaceX, Tesla, Airbnb, Uber, and the resilience of other industry and organizational pioneering will be required.

Another trend on the horizon is that "[o]rganizations are no longer judged only for their financial performance, or even the quality of their products or services. Rather, they are being evaluated on the basis of their impact on society at large—transforming them from business enterprises into social enterprises."[53] A recent survey showed that 65 percent of CEOs rated "inclusive growth" as a "top-three strategic concern, more than three times greater than the proportion citing 'shareholder value.'"[54] Deloitte researchers noted that "[a] social enterprise is an organization whose mission combines revenue growth and profit-making with the need to respect and support its environment and stakeholder network. This includes listening to, investing in, and actively managing the trends that are shaping today's world. It is an organization that shoulders its responsibility to be a good citizen (both inside and outside the organization), serving as a role model for its peers and promoting a high degree of collaboration at every level of the organization."[55]

🔑 Key Terms

Adhocracy culture Creates an environment of innovating, visioning the future, accepting of managing change, and risk taking, rule-breaking, experimentation, entrepreneurship, and uncertainty.

Clan culture Focuses on relationships, team building, commitment, empowering human development, engagement, mentoring, and coaching.

Competing Values Framework Developed by Kim Cameron and Robert Quinn this model is used for diagnosing an organization's cultural effectiveness and examining its fit with its environment.

Complex-Stable environments Environments that have a large number of external elements, and elements are dissimilar and where elements remain the same or change slowly.

Complex-Unstable environments Environments that have a large number of external elements, and elements are dissimilar and where elements change frequently and unpredictably

Corporate culture Defines how motivating employees' beliefs, behaviors, relationships, and ways they work creates a culture that is based on the values the organization believes in.

Divisional structure An organizational structure characterized by functional departments grouped under a division head.

Domain The purpose of the organization from which its strategies, organizational capabilities, resources, and management systems are mobilized to support the enterprise's purpose.

Functional structure The earliest and most used organizational designs.

Geographic structure An Organizational option aimed at moving from a mechanistic to more organic design to serve customers faster and with relevant products and services; as such, this structure is organized by locations of customers that a company serves.

Government and political environment forces The global economy and changing political actions increase uncertainty for businesses, while creating opportunities for some industries and instability in others.

Hierarchy culture Emphasizes efficiency, process and cost control, organizational improvement, technical expertise, precision, problem solving, elimination of errors, logical, cautious and conservative, management and operational analysis, careful decision making.

Horizontal organizational structures A "flatter" organizational structure often found in matrix organizations where individuals relish the breath and development that their team offers.

Internal dimensions of organizations How an organization's culture affects and influences its strategy.

Market culture Focuses on delivering value, competing, delivering shareholder value, goal achievement, driving and delivering results, speedy decisions, hard driving through barriers, directive, commanding, competing and getting things done.

Matrix structure An organizational structure close in approach to organic systems that attempt to respond to environmental uncertainty, complexity, and instability.

McKinsey 7-S model A popular depiction of internal organizational dimensions.

Mechanistic organizational structures Best suited for environments that range from stable and simple to low-moderate uncertainty and have a formal "pyramid' structure.

Natural disaster and human induced environmental problems Events such as high-impact hurricanes, extreme temperatures and the rise in CO_2 emissions as well as 'man-made' environmental disasters such as water and food crises; biodiversity loss and ecosystem collapse; large-scale involuntary migration are a force that affects organizations.

Networked-team structure A form of the horizontal organization.

Organic organizational structures The opposite of a functional organizational form that works best in unstable, complex changing environments.

Organizational structures A broad term that covers both mechanistic and organic organizational structures.

Simple-Stable environments Environments that have a small number of external elements, and elements are similar, and the elements remain the same or change slowly.

Simple-Unstable environments Environments that have a small number of external elements, and elements are similar and where elements change frequently and unpredictably.

Socio-cultural environment forces Include different generations' values, beliefs, attitudes and habits, customs and traditions, habits and lifestyles.

Technological forces Environmental influence on organizations where speed, price, service, and quality of products and services are dimensions of organizations' competitive advantage in this era.

Virtual structure A recent organizational structure that has emerged in the 1990's and early 2000's as a response to requiring more flexibility, solution based tasks on demand, less geographical constraints, and accessibility to dispersed expertise.

📖 Summary of Learning Outcomes

4.1 The Organization's External Environment
1. Define the external environment of organizations

Organizations must react and adapt to many forces in their internal and external environments. The context of the firms such as size and geographic location impact how environmental forces affect each organization differently. An understanding of the forces and they currently affecting organizations and pressuring structural change is crucial.

4.2 External Environments and Industries
2. Identify contemporary external forces pressuring organizations

An understanding of the various industries and organizations 'fit' with different types of environment in crucial. There are small and large organizations that face environments that are either stable of unstable and managing the organization by recognizing their environment is a crucial skill.

4.3 Organizational Designs and Structures
3. Identify different types of organizational structures, and their strengths and weaknesses

An understanding of Mechanistic vs Organic Structures and Systems and how they differ and how these major concepts help classify different organizational structures is crucial to recognizing organizational structures. Finally, the issue of organizational complexity and its impact on organizational structure needs to be understood.

You should be able to discuss the evolution of different types of Organizational Structures. You should understand and identify the six types of organizational structures, and the advantages and disadvantages of each: Functional, Divisional, Matrix, Geographic, Networked Team, and Virtual.

4.4 The Internal Organization and External Environments
4. Explain how organizations organize to meet external market threats and opportunities

You should understand and identify the six types of organizational structures, and the advantages and disadvantages of each structure:

- Functional
- Divisional

- Matrix
- Geographic
- Networked Team
- Virtual

You should also understand why the internal dimensions of an organization matter with regard to how it fits with its external environment.

4.5 Corporate Cultures

5. Identify the fit between organizational cultures and the external environment

You should be able to identify and differentiate between the four types of organizational cultures and the fit of each with the external environment and describe the CVF framework. Finally, you can identify the internal dimensions of organizations, the interconnection among the dimensions, and how these affect the 'fit' with external environments.

4.6 Organizing for Change in the 21st Century

6. Identify environmental trends, demands, and opportunities facing organizations.

Among the trends in the external environment: (1) persistent inequality and unfairness, (2) domestic and international political tensions, (3) environmental dangers, and (4) cyber vulnerabilities. Another trend is that organizations will no longer solely be judged only for their financial performance, or even the quality of their products or services. Rather, they will be evaluated on the basis of their impact on society at large—transforming them from business enterprises into social enterprises.

Chapter Review Questions

1. Explain how several current environmental forces are affecting and will affect organizations and organizational structures' effectiveness and efficiency in the near future?
2. What are ways to classify and describe how industries and organizations fit and do not fit with their external environments?
3. What are a few industries and/or organizations that are fitting well with their current environments? What are a few that are not? Why?
4. What are some major differences between organic and mechanistic organizational structures and systems?
5. Which organization would you work best in, an organically or mechanistically structured one, and why?
6. What are some advantages and disadvantages of functional structures?
7. Do you think it's true that every organization has a hidden functional structure in it? Explain your answer.
8. Why have functional structures been criticized for not accommodating new changes in the environment?
9. What are some advantages and disadvantages of divisional structures?
10. How is a product structure one type of a divisional structure? Explain.
11. What are some disadvantages in working in a matrix structure and why?
12. What advantages do matrix structures have compared to functional structures?
13. What advantages do geographic structures have compared to a functional structure?
14. What are issues that working in a networked team structure present?
15. In what ways is a virtual organization and structure different from the other ones discussed in the chapter?
16. What major trends discussed at the end of this chapter are different from previous external environments

and the ways organizations were organized?

17. What purposes does an organization's culture serve when considering the external environment?

18. How does **Exhibit 4.16** facilitate an understanding of how the internal organization functions with external environments?

Management Skills Application Exercises

1. You have just been assigned to lead a functionally structured organization. Explain what types of skills you would need to best perform this function.

2. What types of problems would you expect to have managing a divisionally structured organization? What skills would you need to excel in this undertaking?

3. If you were assigned to work in a matrix team structure, explain the issues and benefits you might expect to experience and why. What skills would help you in this function?

4. .You have just been assigned to work with a strategy team in an organization to predict issues and opportunities that might be expected for the next 2 years. Using this chapter, explain what information you would provide to this team?

5. Use **Exhibit 4.21**, "The Competing Values Framework," to identify the type of organizational culture at IKEA, Home Depot, and Best Buy.

Managerial Decision Exercises

1. You are a manager working in a functionally structured organization. A disgruntled employee is complaining about problems she is having in that structure. Outline a way you would find out more about her complaints with regard to her being in this type of structure and some ways to assist her.

2. You are a manager working in a networked team structured organization. A disgruntled employee is complaining about problems he is having in that structure. Outline a way you would find out more about his complaints with regard to his being in this type of structure and some ways to assist him.

3. You have been selected to lead a team to decide on a different type of structure in your organization to better serve customers who are complaining about poor service that is slow, impersonal, and not meeting their needs to be heard. Presently, the functional structure isn't working well. Outline some information from your knowledge using this chapter that would help the team in its assignment.

4. You witness a senior executive at your firm engaging in overly aggressive methods of pressuring employees to increase their sales quotas beyond reasonable means. You are in a networked team structure that is partly a matrix. You are uncertain about whom to discuss this issue with. What would you do?

5. As a new graduate, you have been hired to help a medium-sized company come into the 21st century. Products need revamping, people aren't sharing information, and customers are gradually leaving. The firm has a traditional top-down managed, vertical hierarchy. It is believed that the firm has very good potential to sell its products, but new markets may be needed. Outline an agenda you would work on to research and make suggestions with regard to this chapter's focus and content.

Critical Thinking Case

Wells Fargo, Crisis and Scandal

The recent widespread scandal at Wells Fargo jolted and shocked the corporate world. How could such internal corrupt and outrageously illegal and unethical activities by professionals have occurred? Wells Fargo is "an American multinational financial services company headquartered in San Francisco, California" with offices nationwide and "the world's second-largest bank by market capitalization and the third largest bank in the U.S. by total assets." In September 2016 it was discovered that the company was continuing to create fake customer accounts to show positive financial activity and gains. 5,000 salespeople had created 2 million fake customer accounts to meet high-pressure internal sales goals, including a monthly report called the "Motivator."

The out-of-control sales leadership pressured sales employees to meet unrealistic, outrageous sales targets. Dramatically unrealistic sales goals propelled by continuous pressure from management coerced employees to open accounts for customers who didn't want or need them. "Some Wells Fargo bankers impersonated their customers and used false email addresses like noname@wellsfargo.com, according to a 2015 lawsuit filed by the city of Los Angeles."

The "abusive sales practices claimed in a lawsuit that Wells Fargo employees probably created 3.5 million bogus accounts" starting in May 2002. Wells Fargo is awaiting final approval to settle that case for $142 million. However, regulators and investigations found that the misconduct was far more "pervasive and persistent" than had been realized. "The bank's culture of misconduct extended well beyond the original revelations." For example, regulators found that the company was (1) "overcharging small businesses for credit card transactions by using a 'deceptive' 63-page contract to confuse them." (2) The company also charged at least 570,000 customers for auto insurance they did not need. (3)The firm admitted that it found 20,000 customers who could have defaulted on their car loans from these bogus actions; (4) The company also had created over 3.5 million fake accounts attributed to customers who had no knowledge of such accounts.

Wells Fargo has had to testify before Congress over these charges, which have amounted to $185 million dollars, and more recently the company has been ordered by regulators to return $3.4 million to brokerage customers who were defrauded. The CEO and management team have been fired and had millions of dollars withheld from their pay.

In the aftermath of the scandal, even though Wells Fargo executives were not imprisoned for the extensive consumer abuses committed by the company, the CFPB (Consumer Financial Protection Bureau) and Office of the Comptroller of the Currency (OCC) imposed a $1 billion fine on Wells Fargo for consumer-related abuses regarding auto loan and mortgage products. The OCC also forced the company to allow regulators the authority to enforce several actions to prevent future abuses, such as and including "imposing business restrictions and making changes to executive officers or members of the bank's board of directors." The new president of the company, Tim Sloan, stated, "What we're trying to do, as we make change in the company and make improvements, is not just fix a problem, but build a better bank, transform the bank for the future."

Sources: https://en.wikipedia.org/wiki/Wells_Fargo; Pasick, Adam, "Warren Buffett Explains the Wells Fargo Scandal," *Quartz*, May 6, 2017. https://qz.com/977778/warren-buffett-explains-the-wells-fargo-scandal/ https://qz.com/977778/warren-buffett-explains-the-wells-fargo-scandal/; Bloomberg, "The Wells Fargo Fake Accounts Scandal Just Got a Lot Worse," *Fortune*, August 21, 2017. http://fortune.com/2017/08/31/wells-fargo-increases-fake-account-estimate/; Horowitz, Julia, "'huge, huge, huge error' in Wells Fargo Handling of Ethics Line Calls, *CNN*, May, 6, 2017. https://money.cnn.com/2017/05/06/investing/buffett-wells-fargo-berkshire-annual-meeting/index.html; http://money.cnn.com/2018/02/05/news/companies/wells-fargo-timeline/index.html; Wattles, Jackie, Grier, Ben, and Egan, Matt, "Wells Fargo's 17 Month Nightmare," *CNN Business*, February 5, 2018. https://money.cnn.com/2018/02/05/news/companies/wells-fargo-timeline/index.html.

Hudson, Caroline, "Wells Fargo Stocks Still Struggling in Wake of Scandal," *Charlotte Business Journal*, April 2, 2018. https://www.bizjournals.com/charlotte/news/2018/04/02/wells-fargo-stocks-still-struggling-in-wake-of.html

Critical Thinking Questions

1. What happened at Wells Fargo with regard to past activities that led to this major scandal?
2. What internal dimensions of the company were part of the problems that occurred?
3. How might the organizational structure of the company have been part of the problems that occurred?
4. . Identify and use relevant concepts from this chapter as well as your own thoughts and analysis to diagnose the scandal at Wells Fargo. How could such a scandal have occurred in the first place? Who and what was at fault?
5. Suggest some solution paths the company might consider, using knowledge from this chapter and your own thoughts/research, to avoid such a scandal from reoccurring.

Ethics, Corporate Responsibility, and Sustainability

Exhibit 5.1 (Credit: Marco Verch /flickr / Attribution 2.0 Generic (CC BY 2.0))

Introduction

Learning Outcomes

After reading this chapter, you should be able to answer these questions:

1. What are ethics and business ethics?
2. What are the types of values that motivate ethics at the individual level?
3. What are major ethical principles that can guide individuals and organizations?
4. Why is ethical leadership important in organizations?
5. What are differences between values-based ethics and compliance in organizations?
6. What purpose can CSR (corporate social responsibility) offer to organizations and society?
7. What ethical issues do organizations and individuals encounter in the global environment?
8. What future near-term forecasts will affect ethical and corporate conduct of organizations?

EXPLORING MANAGERIAL CAREERS

Playing with a Purpose at Hasbro

Hasbro is a global play and entertainment company that takes corporate social responsibility (CSR) very seriously. Founded nearly a century ago in Rhode Island, Hasbro integrates its CSR efforts throughout the organization with the goal of helping to make the world a better place for children of all ages.

In 2017, the company achieved the number one spot in the "100 Best Corporate Citizens" rankings, published annually by *Corporate Responsibility* magazine. Hasbro is no stranger to this achievement; over the past five years Hasbro has consistently been in the top five spots on this prestigious list—and that is no accident.

With more than 5,000 employees, Hasbro relies heavily on its strategic brand blueprint to guide its efforts in CSR, innovation, philanthropy, and product development. With a business portfolio that includes such well-known brands as Nerf, Play-Doh, Transformers, Monopoly, and The Game of Life, the company focuses its CSR efforts on four key areas: product safety, environmental sustainability, human rights and ethical sourcing, and community.

According to the company, product safety is its highest priority. Hasbro uses a five-step quality assurance process that starts with design and then moves to engineering, manufacturing, and packaging. Another key part of product safety at Hasbro is incorporating continuous feedback from both consumers and retailers and insisting that these high standards and quality processes apply to all third-party factories worldwide that manufacture its products.

Hasbro is also committed to finding new ways to reduce its environmental footprint. Over the past several years, the company has reduced energy consumption, cut greenhouse gas emissions, and reduced water consumption and waste production in its production facilities. In addition, Hasbro has totally eliminated the use of wire ties in all of its product packaging, saving more than 34,000 miles of wire tires—more than enough to wrap around the earth's circumference.

Human rights and ethical sourcing remain a key ingredient of Hasbro's CSR success. Treating people fairly is a core company value, as well as working diligently to make great strides in diversity and inclusion at all levels of the organization. Company personnel work closely with third-party factories to ensure that the human rights of all workers in the Hasbro global supply chain are recognized and upheld.

Philanthropy, corporate giving, and employee volunteering are key components of the Hasbro community. Through its various charitable programs, Hasbro made close to $15 million in financial contributions and product donations in 2016, which reached close to an estimated 4 million children around the globe. Several years ago, the company started an annual Global Day of Joy as a way of engaging its employees worldwide in community service. In a recent year, more than 93 percent of Hasbro's employees participated in service projects in more than 40 countries.

Hasbro is in the business of storytelling, and its CSR efforts tell the story of an ethical, responsible organization whose mission is to "create the world's best play experiences." Its ability to be accountable for its actions and to help make the world a better place one experience at time continues to make it a highly successful company.

Sources: Brian Goldner, "Who Are You Really?—Brian Goldner, President & CEO for Hasbro, Inc.," http://insights.ethisphere.com, accessed June 29, 2017; "CSR Fact Sheet," https://csr.hasbro.com, accessed June 23, 2017; "The World's Biggest Public Companies: Hasbro," *Forbes*, https://www.forbes.com, accessed June 23, 2017; "2016 Global Philanthropy & Social Impact," https://csr.hasbro.com, accessed June 23, 2017; Elizabeth Gurdus, "Hasbro CEO Reveals the Magic Behind the Toymaker's Earnings Beat," *CNBC*, http://www.cnbc.com, April 24, 2017; Jade Burke, "Hasbro Reaches Top spot in CSR Listing," *Toy News*, http://www.toynews-online.biz, April 21, 2017; Kathrin Belliveau, "CSR at Hasbro: What It Means to Play with Purpose," *LinkedIn*, https://www.linkedin.com, April 20, 2017.

This chapter will examine the role of ethics and how it affects organizations. Ethics is examined at the individual level, the organizational level, and also examines the role of ethics and leadership. Corporate social responsibility and how it is different than compliance will also be examined. Finally, ethics around the globe and in different cultures and the emerging issues regarding corporate social responsibility and ethics will be discussed.

5.1 Ethics and Business Ethics Defined

1. What are ethics and business ethics?

Ethics essentially involves how we act, live, lead our lives, and treat others. Our choices and decision-making processes and our moral principles and values that govern our behaviors regarding what is right and wrong are also part of ethics.[1]

Normative ethics refers to the field of ethics concerned with our asking how *should* and *ought* we live and act? **Business ethics** is applied ethics that focuses on real-world situations and the context and environment in which transactions occur—How should we apply our values to the way we conduct business?

Ethics and business ethics continue to gain influence in corporations, universities, and colleges nationally and internationally. No longer considered a luxury but a necessity, business ethics has awakened a need in the public consciousness due to crises in many areas. For example, the 2008 subprime lending crisis—economic effects of which still persist—revealed widespread corruption of large investment banks and lending institutions internationally. Unsupported mortgages were fraudulently offered with no legitimate financial backing. Some large financial institutions, such as Lehman Brothers Holdings, Inc., went bankrupt; millions of mortgage holders lost their homes. An estimated cost of that crisis to the global economy is over $22 trillion U.S. dollars.[2]

In the early 2000s, CEOs and top-level leaders from notable corporations such as Enron, Tyco, WorldCom, and others were caught committing outrageously greedy and fraudulent crimes of white-collar theft from their organizations and shareholders. The now classic film *The Smartest Guys in the Room* depict how Enron's leaders during that time, Kenneth Lay (now deceased), Jeff Skilling (still serving prison time), and Andrew Fastow (released from prison in 2011), deceived employees, Wall Street, and shareholders. Enron's crisis took an estimated $67 billion of shareholder wealth out of the U.S. economy.[3] These criminal activities ushered in national laws such as the Sarbanes-Oxley Act, which we discuss below.

While these recent historical crises illustrate the continuing relevance and importance of business ethics, ethical issues are not only concerned with financial and economically motivated crimes and misbehaviors. Fast forward to the rise of artificial intelligence (AI), which also is calling attention to the relevance and need for ethics in scientific institutions, businesses, and governments. The public needs to be informed of potential and actual harmful consequences—as well as all the recognizable benefits—of these technologies that are in large part driven by algorithms ("a sequence of instructions telling a computer what to do").[4] Intentional and unintentional misuses of such designs embedded in artificially intelligent technologies can negatively and harmfully affect individual lives as well as entire societies. For example, studies show that a number of minority members of society are often discriminated against by institutions using faulty algorithms to qualify customers for mortgages and to predict who is at risk of being incarcerated. Often times, racial and low-income minorities are discriminated against by such technology designs.[5]

At a societal level, another now classic film, *The Minority Report*, illustrates how misuses of technology can threaten individual rights, privacy, free will, and choice. While this may sound like science fiction, scientific and business luminaries such as Elon Musk, Stephen Hawking, Bill Gates, and others have openly declared that we as a society must be cautious and ethically aware and active to fend off the ill effects of the control and dominant influences of certain AI algorithms in our lives. Scientific and ethical practices in corporate social responsibility (CSR) are one way that ethicists, business leaders, and consumers can support moral self-regulation of technologies. Some scientific and technological firms have adopted ethics boards to help safeguard against harmful social uses of AI technologies.[6] The European Union (EU) has produced policy studies that are forerunners of laws to safeguard against potentially harmful uses of robotics.[7]

Another timely ethical issue is climate change and the environment. Lack of sustainable environmental practices that curb air pollution and destructive uses of land, water, and natural resources have, according to a large community of reputable scientists, threatened Earth's—and our neighborhoods'—atmosphere.[8] Scientific studies and United Nations reports affirm that changes to the earth's atmosphere, melting glaciers, and rising seas are occurring at accelerated rates. For example, "California's coastline could rise up to 10 feet by 2100, about 30 to 40 times faster than sea-level rise experienced over the last century."[9] While university, business, and local community groups are rallying for legal actions to curtail and reverse environmental polluters, current political executive orders push against such regulations designed to protect against further erosion of the physical environment.[10] The point here is that as these issues described above are not only technological, economic, and political in nature, but also moral and ethical, as the public's health, welfare, and safety are at risk.

Relevant ethical questions can be asked to prevent a crisis: Who is responsible for preventing and addressing what happens to individuals, the public, our institutions, and government and who is responsible for preventing such crises and harmful effects from occurring and reoccurring? At whose and what costs? Whose responsibility is it to protect and preserve the common good of societies? What ethical and moral principles should and can motivate individuals, groups, and society members to act to change course?

Universities and colleges are taking notice. Business ethics and corporate social responsibility courses and offerings are becoming increasingly important. The accrediting national body of business schools, AACSB (Association to Advance Collegiate Schools of Business), reported that "[i]n their curricula, research, and outreach, business schools must be advocates for the human dimension of business, with attention to ethics, diversity, and personal well-being."[11] In addition, NGOs (nongovernmental organizations), emergent groups internationally representing the public's interests and common good, and political action movements are beginning again to give voice to injustices and potentially dangerous ethical as well as fiscal (income inequality), health (the environment), and discriminatory (racism and stereotyping large segments of the society) problems that require **stakeholder** as well as stockholder actions.

In this chapter, we begin by presenting an overview of the dimensions of business ethics at the individual, professional, and leadership levels, followed by the organizational, societal, and global levels.

CONCEPT CHECK

1. What individual and organizational ethical issues can we expect to occur?
2. What are some signs of unethical activities you might notice individually and organizationally?

5.2 | Dimensions of Ethics: The Individual Level

2. What types of values affect business ethics at the individual level?

Ethics is personal and unique to each individual. Ethical decision-making also involves other individuals, groups, organizations, and even nations—stakeholders and stockholders—as we later explain. Kenneth Goodpaster and Laura Nash characterized at least three dimensions or levels of ethics that help explain how individual and group values, norms, and behaviors of different stakeholders interact and respond with the aim of bringing orderly, fair, and just relationships with one another in transactions. This approach is illustrated in **Exhibit 5.2**.

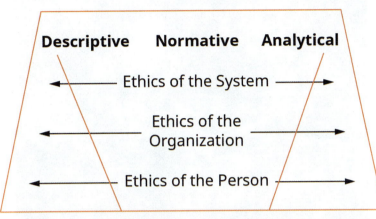

Exhibit 5.2   A Framework for Classifying Levels of Ethical Analysis Source: Adapted from Matthews, John B., Goodpaster, Kenneth E., and Laura L. Nash. (1985). *Policies and persons: A casebook in business ethics*, 509. New York: McGraw-Hill.

Ethical principles generally are codified into laws and regulations when there is societal consensus about such wrongdoing, such as laws against drunk driving, robbery, and murder. These laws, and sometimes unwritten societal norms and values, shape the local environment within which individuals act and conduct business. At the individual level, a person's values and beliefs are influenced by family, community, peers and friends, local and national culture, society, religious—or other types of—communities, and geographic environment. It is important to look at individual values and ethical principles since these influence an individual's decisions and actions, whether it be decisions to act or the failure to act against wrongdoing by others. In organizations, an individual's ethical stance may be affected by peers, subordinates, and supervisors, as well as by the organizational culture. Organizational culture often has a profound influence on individual choices and can support and encourage ethical actions or promote unethical and socially irresponsible behavior.

Ethics and Values: Terminal and Instrumental Values

Of the values that make up an organization's culture, and an individual's motivations, ethical values are now considered among the most important. For instance, when Google took its company public in 2004, its prospectus included an unusual corporate goal: "Don't be evil." That can be a challenge when you're a multibillion-dollar corporation operating around the world, with investors expecting you to produce a profit. Google's operations in the United States and overseas have generated controversy and debate as to how well it's living up to its stated goal. There is a continuing need to integrate ethical values in corporations. The Ethics & Compliance Initiative found 22 percent of global workers reported pressure to compromise their standards.[12] Top corporate managers are under scrutiny from the public as never before, and even small companies are finding a need to put more emphasis on ethics to restore trust among their customers and the community.

Exhibit 5.3   Elon Musk Elon Musk, the CEO of Tesla and SpaceX, pictured here at a TedX conference, is widely admired for his CSR approaches at his companies. Generally, the adoption of electric vehicles, which help reduce pollutants, is viewed as a positive outcome. Musk has, however, come under scrutiny regarding comments about having secured financing to take Tesla private that raise compliance issues. (Credit: Steve Jurvetson/ flickr/ Attribution- 2.0 Generic (CC BY-ND 2.0))

Values can be powerful and motivating guides for individual, group, and organizational behavior. At the individual level, however, a reoccurring issue individuals seem to have with acting ethically is that many people do not consciously know or choose their values. We often act first and think or rationalize later. Secondly and relatedly, the methods and ways we act to reach our goals and objectives are also not always deliberately chosen. Consequently, many times we let the "ends justify the means" and/or "the means justify the ends" in our decisions and actions. **Ethical dilemmas** (i.e., situations and predicaments in which there is not an optimal or desired choice to be made between two options, neither of which solves an issue or delivers an opportunity that is ethical) often originate and occur from an unawareness of how to sort out and think through potential consequences of our actions or inaction. Becoming aware and conscious of our values is a first step toward being able to act ethically and responsibly in order to prevent or lessen harm to ourselves or others.

Toward this end, it is helpful to understand values that have been categorized as terminal and instrumental. **Terminal values** are desired goals, objectives, or end states that individuals wish to pursue. **Instrumental values** are preferred means of behavior used to obtain those goals. Examples of terminal values—at a higher level—are freedom, security, pleasure, social recognition, friendship, accomplishment, comfort, adventure, equality, wisdom, and happiness.[13] Examples of instrumental values are being helpful, honest, courageous, independent, polite, responsible, capable, ambitious, loving, self-contained, and forgiving.[14]

Identifying and separating terminal from instrumental values in any given situation can assist individuals, groups, and work units in distinguishing between the "ends (goals) from the means (methods to reach the goals)" and vice versa in making decisions, thereby helping us choose more ethical options—or at least less unethical ones—in situations. For example, a sales manager has a goal of motivating his sales force to achieve individual sales performance levels at a 17% increase over current levels by the end of the calendar quarter. The means of doing so, according to the manager, are, "Go for it. Use your imagination and fortitude. Just make sure each of you reaches or exceeds that goal." In this case, the terminal value is high achievement to the point of being overly ambitious in order to reach an aggressive financial goal. The instrumental value can also be described as aggressive achievement. Both the terminal and instrumental values in this scenario could very likely create undue pressure and even anxiety for some members of the sales force. The ethical logic underlying this example is to let the "end justify the means." The scenario also raises the question of whether or not individuals in the sales force would choose the values underlying the instruction of the manager if each member identified and reflected on those values.

If the end (terminal) value creates undue pressures and is unrealistic and unobtainable, then the means (instrumental) value would likely create tension and unethical behavior as well. This example in some ways mirrors what actually recently happened at Wells Fargo & Company—an American international banking and financial services holding company headquartered in San Francisco. High pressure and unrealistic sales goals were adopted and implemented from the top down in that organization. A result was that members of that sales force lied, pressured, and misled loyal customers to buy bogus financial products to meet unrealistic sales goals. Such actions when discovered led to and revealed illegal and unethical actions from not only the sales professionals but officers at the top of that organization. Ultimately, the CEO was pressured to resign, 5,300 employees were fired, and several lawsuits ensued.[15]

There are many lessons to take from the Wells Fargo fiasco. From an individual ethical perspective, one insight is to be aware of the underlying values of organizational and other job- and task-related directives issued. Another is to discover your own values and ethical principles that can guide you in work, study, and personal situations so that someone else's problems may not have to become yours. A helpful assessment for discovering your values is the PVA (Personal Values Assessment) found at **https://www.valuescentre.com/ our-products/products-individuals/personal-values-assessment-pva**.

Caroucci found that "five ways organizations needlessly provoke good people to make unethical choices" are the following. (1) People feel psychologically unsafe to speak up. (2) Excessive pressure to reach unrealistic performance targets compromises people's choices. (3) When individuals face conflicting goals, they feel a sense of unfairness and compromise their reasoning. (4) Only talking about ethics when there is a scandal. (5)When there is no positive example available, individuals react instead of choose ethical decisions. Familiarizing yourself with ethical principles in the following section is another way of helping you think through complicated situations to make conscious, values-based decisions to do "the right thing."[16]

CONCEPT CHECK

1. What are terminal and instrumental values?
2. What are ways organizations can employ values to induce people to make ethical choices?

5.3 | Ethical Principles and Responsible Decision-Making

3. What are major ethical principles that can be used by individuals and organizations?

Before turning to organizational and systems levels of ethics, we discuss classical ethical principles that are very relevant now and on which decisions can be and are made by individuals, organizations, and other stakeholders who choose principled, responsible ways of acting toward others.[17]

Ethical principles are different from values in that the former are considered as rules that are more permanent, universal, and unchanging, whereas values are subjective, even personal, and can change with time. Principles help inform and influence values. Some of the principles presented here date back to Plato, Socrates, and even earlier to ancient religious groups. These principles can be, and are, used in combination; different principles are also used in different situations.[18] The principles that we will cover are utilitarianism, universalism, rights/legal, justice, virtue, common good, and ethical relativism approaches. As you read these, ask yourself which principles characterize and underlie your own values, beliefs, behaviors, and actions. It is helpful to ask and if not clear, perhaps identify the principles, you most often use now and those you aspire to use more, and why. Using one or more of these principles and ethical approaches intentionally can also help you examine choices and options before making a decision or solving an ethical dilemma. Becoming familiar with these principles, then, can help inform your moral decision process and help you observe the principles that a team, workgroup, or organization that you now participate in or will be joining may be using. Using creativity is also important when examining difficult moral decisions when sometimes it may seem that there are two "right" ways to act in a situation or perhaps no way seems morally right, which may also signal that not taking an action at that time may be needed, unless taking no action produces worse results.

Utilitarianism: A Consequentialist, "Ends Justifies Means" Approach

The utilitarianism principle basically holds that an action is morally right if it produces the greatest good for the greatest number of people. An action is morally right if the net benefits over costs are greatest for all affected compared with the net benefits of all other possible choices. This, as with all these principles and approaches, is broad in nature and seemingly rather abstract. At the same time, each one has a logic. When we present the specifics and facts of a situation, this and the other principles begin to make sense, although judgement is still required.

Some limitations of this principle suggest that it does not consider individuals, and there is no agreement on the definition of "good for all concerned." In addition, it is difficult to measure "costs and benefits." This is one of the most widely used principles by corporations, institutions, nations, and individuals, given the limitations that accompany it. Use of this principle generally applies when resources are scarce, there is a conflict in priorities, and no clear choice meets everyone's needs—that is, a zero-sum decision is imminent

Universalism: A Duty-Based Approach

Universalism is a principle that considers the welfare and risks of all parties when considering policy decisions and outcomes. Also needs of individuals involved in a decision are identified as well as the choices they have and the information they need to protect their welfare. This principle involves taking human beings, their needs, and their values seriously. It is not only a method to make a decision; it is a way of incorporating a humane consideration of and for individuals and groups when deciding a course of action. As some have asked, "What is a human life worth?"

Cooper, Santora, and Sarros wrote, "Universalism is the outward expression of leadership character and is made manifest by respectfulness for others, fairness, cooperativeness, compassion, spiritual respect, and humility." Corporate leaders in the "World's Most Ethical Companies" strive to set a "tone at the top" to exemplify and embody universal principles in their business practices.[19] Howard Schultz, founder of Starbucks; cofounder Jim Sinegal at Costco; Sheryl Sandberg, chief operating officer of Facebook; and Ursula M. Burns, previous chairperson and CEO of Xerox have demonstrated setting effective ethical tones at the top of organizations.

Limitations here also show that using this principle may not always prove realistic or practical in all situations. In addition, using this principle can require sacrifice of human life—that is, giving one's life to help or save others—which may seem contrary to the principle. The film *The Post*, based on fact, portrays how the daughter of the founder of the famed newspaper, the *Washington Post*, inherited the role of CEO and was forced to make a decision between publishing a whistle-blowers' classified government documents of then top-level generals and officials or keep silent and protect the newspaper. The classified documents contained information proving that generals and other top-level government administrators were lying to the public about the actual status of the United States in the Vietnam War. Those documents revealed that there were doubts the war could be won while thousands of young Americans continued to die fighting. The dilemma for the *Washington Post*'s then CEO centered on her having to choose between exposing the truth based on freedom of speech—which was the mission and foundation of the newspaper—or staying silent and suppressing the classified information. She chose, with the support of and pressure from her editorial staff, to release the classified documents to the public. The Supreme Court upheld her and her staff's decision. A result was enflamed widespread public protests from American youth and others. President Johnson was pressured to resign, Secretary of State McNamara later apologized, and the war eventually ended with U.S. troops withdrawing. So, universalist ethical principles may present difficulties when used in complex situations, but such principles can also save lives, protect the integrity of a nation, and stop meaningless destruction.

Rights: A Moral and Legal Entitlement–Based Approach

This principle is grounded in both legal and moral **rights**. Legal rights are entitlements that are limited to a particular legal system and jurisdiction. In the United States, the Constitution and Declaration of Independence are the basis for citizens' legal rights, for example, the right to life, liberty, and the pursuit of happiness and the right to freedom of speech. Moral (and human) rights, on the other hand, are universal and based on norms in every society, for example, the right not to be enslaved and the right to work.

To get a sense of individual rights in the workplace, log on to one of the "Best Companies to Work For" annual lists (http://fortune.com/best-companies/). Profiles of leaders and organizations' policies, practices, perks, diversity, compensation, and other statistics regarding employee welfare and benefits can be reviewed. The "World's Most Ethical Companies" also provides examples of workforce and workplace legal and moral rights. This principle, as with universalism, can always be used when individuals, groups, and nations are involved in decisions that may violate or harm such rights as life, liberty, the pursuit of happiness, and free speech.

Some limitations when using this principle are (1) it can be used to disguise and manipulate selfish and unjust political interests, (2) it is difficult to determine who deserves what when both parties are "right," and (3) individuals can exaggerate certain entitlements at the expense of others. Still, the U.S. Constitution's Bill of Rights, ratified in 1791, was designed as and remains the foundation of, which is based on freedom and justice to protect the basic rights of all.

Justice: Procedures, Compensation, and Retribution

This principle has at least four major components that are based on the tenets that (1) all individuals should be treated equally; (2) **justice** is served when all persons have equal opportunities and advantages (through their positions and offices) to society's opportunities and burdens; (3) fair decision practices, procedures, and agreements among parties should be practiced; and (4) punishment is served to someone who has inflicted harm on another, and compensation is given to those for a past harm or injustice committed against them.

A simple way of summarizing this principle when examining a moral dilemma is to ask of a proposed action or decision: (1) Is it fair? (2) Is it right? (3) Who gets hurt? (4) Who has to pay for the consequences? (5) Do I/we want to assume responsibility for the consequences? It is interesting to reflect on how many corporate disasters and crises might have been prevented had the leaders and those involved taken such questions seriously before proceeding with decisions. For example, the following precautionary actions might have prevented the disaster: updating the equipment and machinery that failed in the BP and the *Exxon Valdez* oil crises and investment banks and lending institutions following rules not to sell subprime mortgages that could not and would not be paid, actions that led to the near collapse of the global economy.

Limitations when using this principle involve the question of who decides who is right and wrong and who has been harmed in complex situations. This is especially the case when facts are not available and there is no objective external jurisdiction of the state or federal government. In addition, we are sometimes faced with the question, "Who has the moral authority to punish to pay compensation to whom?" Still, as with the other principles discussed here, justice stands as a necessary and invaluable building block of democracies and freedom.

Virtue Ethics: Character-Based Virtues

Virtue ethics is based on character traits such as being truthful, practical wisdom, happiness, flourishing, and well-being. It focuses on the type of person we ought to be, not on specific actions that should be taken. Grounded in good character, motives, and core values, the principle is best exemplified by those whose examples show the virtues to be emulated.

Basically, the possessor of good character is moral, acts morally, feels good, is happy, and flourishes. Altruism is also part of character-based virtue ethics. Practical wisdom, however, is often required to be virtuous.

This principle is related to universalism. Many leaders' character and actions serve as examples of how character-based virtues work. For example, the famous Warren Buffett stands as an icon of good character who demonstrates trustworthy values and practical wisdom. Applying this principle is related to a "quick test" before acting or making a decision by asking, "What would my 'best self' do in this situation?" Others ask the question inserting someone they know or honor highly.

There are some limitations to this ethic. First, some individuals may disagree about who is virtuous in different situations and therefore would refuse to use that person's character as a principle. Also, the issue arises, "Who defines *virtuous*, especially when a complex act or incident is involved that requires factual information and objective criteria to resolve?"

The Common Good

The common good is defined as "the sum of those conditions of social life which allow social groups and their individual members relatively thorough and ready access to their own fulfillment." Decision makers must take into consideration the intent as well as the effects of their actions and decisions on the broader society and the common good of the many.[20]

Identifying and basing decisions on the common good requires us to make goals and take actions that take others, beyond ourselves and our self-interest, into account. Applying the common good principle can also be asked by a simple question: "How will this decision or action affect the broader physical, cultural, and social environment in which I, my family, my friends, and others have to live, breathe, and thrive in now, next week, and beyond?"

A major limitation when using this principle is, "Who determines what the common good is in situations where two or more parties differ over whose interests are violated?" In individualistic and capitalist societies, it is difficult in many cases for individuals to give up their interests and tangible goods for what may not benefit them or may even deprive them.

Ethical Relativism: A Self-Interest Approach

Ethical relativism is really not a "principle" to be followed or modeled. It is an orientation that many use quite frequently. Ethical relativism holds that people set their own moral standards for judging their actions. Only the individual's self-interest and values are relevant for judging his or her behavior. Moreover, moral standards, according to this principle, vary from one culture to another. "When in Rome, do as the Romans do."

Obvious limitations of relativism include following one's blind spots or self-interests that can interfere with facts and reality. Followers of this principle can become absolutists and "true believers"—many times believing and following their own ideology and beliefs. Countries and cultures that follow this orientation can result in dictatorships and absolutist regimes that practice different forms of slavery and abuse to large numbers of people. For example, South Africa's all-white National Party and government after 1948 implemented and enforced a policy of apartheid that consisted of racial segregation. That policy lasted until the 1990s, when several parties negotiated its demise—with the help of Nelson Mandela (**www.history.com/topics/ apartheid**). Until that time, international firms doing business in South Africa were expected to abide by the apartheid policy and its underlying values. Many companies in the United States, Europe, and elsewhere were pressured in the 1980s and before by public interest groups whether or not to continue doing business or leave South Africa.

At the individual level, then, principles and values offer a source of stability and self-control while also affecting job satisfaction and performance. At the organizational level, principled and values-based leadership influences cultures that inspire and motivate ethical behavior and performance. The following section discusses how ethical leadership at the top and throughout organizations affects ethical actions and behaviors.[21]

CONCEPT CHECK

1. What are some ethical guidelines individuals and organizations can use to make ethical choices?
2. Can being aware of the actual values you use to guide your actions make a difference in your choices?

5.4 | Leadership: Ethics at the Organizational Level

4. Why is ethical leadership important in organizations?

Organizational leadership is an important first step toward identifying and enacting purpose and ethical values that are central to internal alignment, external market effectiveness, and responsibility toward stakeholders.[22] The scholar Chester Barnard defined a values-based leadership approach in 1939 as one that inspires "cooperative personal decisions by creating faith in common understanding, faith in the probability of success, faith in the ultimate satisfaction of personal motives, and faith in the integrity of common purpose."[23] **Exhibit 5.4** illustrates how vision, mission, and values are foundational in guiding the identification and implementation of the strategic and operational questions and alignment of an organization—which is a major part of leadership.

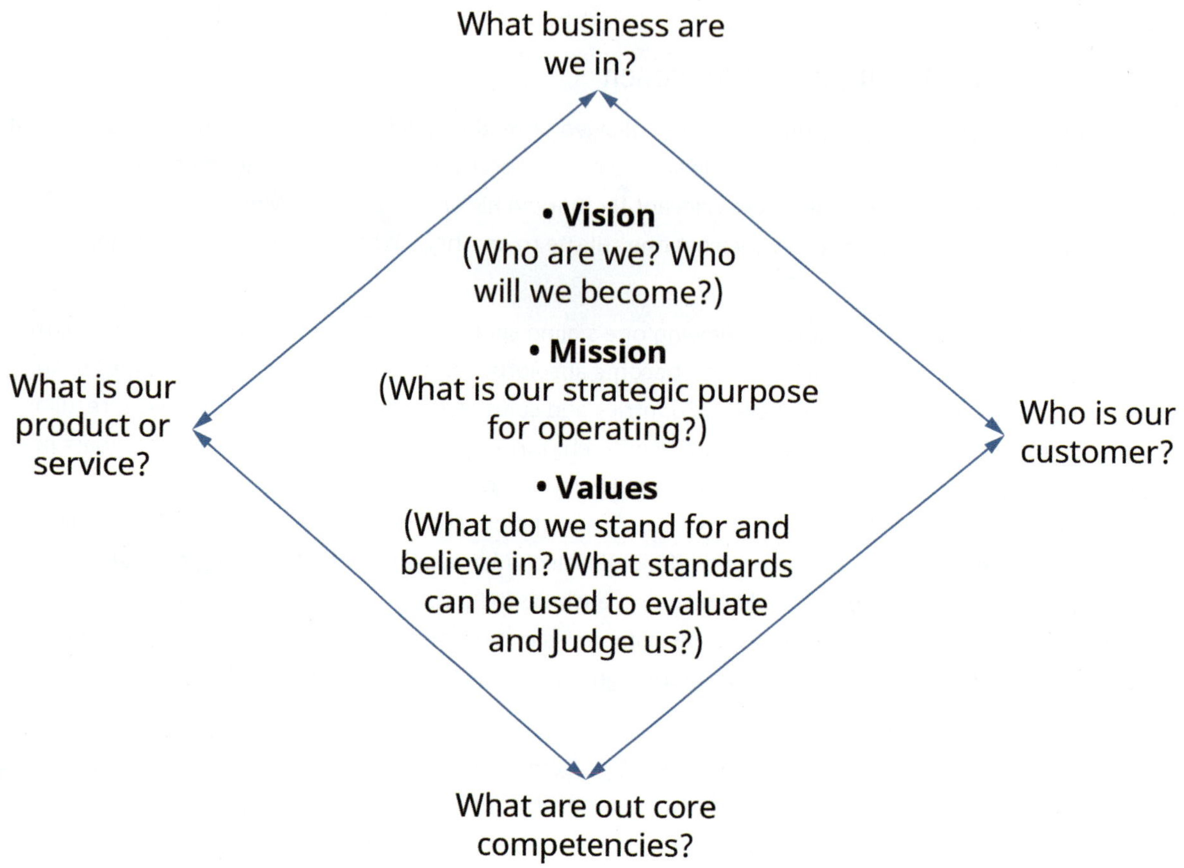

What business are we in?

- **Vision**
(Who are we? Who will we become?)

- **Mission**
(What is our strategic purpose for operating?)

- **Values**
(What do we stand for and believe in? What standards can be used to evaluate and Judge us?)

What is our product or service?

Who is our customer?

What are out core competencies?

Exhibit 5.4   Strategic Organizational Alignment Source: Joseph W. Weiss. © 2014.

Leadership is defined as the ability to influence followers to achieve common goals through shared purposes.[24] Organizational leaders are responsible to a wide range of stakeholders and stockholders as well as employees toward meeting the goals for the organization. How responsibly and ethically they choose to do so depends on a number of factors. From an ethical and related effectiveness perspective, the leader's values count since these generally become the values of an organization. A leader's influence is referred to as "the tone at the top." While a leader's values should align to those of the organization, its vision and mission, this is not always the case, as we know from the crises discussed earlier when referring to the classical failures at Enron, Tyco, WorldCom, Wells Fargo, and other notable companies.

Since leadership is a most important element in forming and directing an organization's strategy, culture, and governance system, it is often a shared responsibility among other officers and followers that cascades throughout the organization. As an example, the widely acknowledged Ethisphere, a private firm that evaluates firms' ethical behavior and responsibilities, uses five criteria that produce a single Ethics Quotient (EQ) score. The first is a company's ethics and compliance program, which accounts for 35% of the EQ. The second criterion is whether or not and the extent to which ethics is embedded into a company's culture. The third element is corporate citizenship and responsibility, elements that measure companies' environmental impact. The fourth component is corporate governance—whether a firm's CEO and board chair are held by one or separate people. An increased focus recently emphasized diversity in board and leadership positions. The fifth criterion is leadership, innovation, and reputation.[25]

There were, according to Ephisphere, 124 honorees in 2017, spanning 5 continents, 19 countries, and 52 industry sectors. Among the 2017 list are 13 eleven-time honorees and 8 first-time honorees. Honorees include "companies who recognize their role in society to influence and drive positive change in the business community and societies around the world. These companies also consider the impact of their actions on their employees, investors, customers and other key stakeholders and leverage values and a culture of integrity as the underpinnings to the decisions they make each day."[26] The top 10 most ethical companies in 2017 as measured by Ethisphere's criteria are shown below in **Table 5.1**.

World's Most Ethical Companies Honorees		
Company	Industry	Country
3M Company	Industrial Manufacturing	USA
Accenture	Consulting Services	IRELAND
Aflac Incorporated	Accident & Life Insurance	USA
Allstate Insurance Company	Property & Casualty Insurance	USA
Alyeska Pipeline Service Co.	Oil & Gas, Renewables	USA
Applied Materials, Inc.	Electronics & Semiconductors	USA
Arthur J. Gallagher & Co.	Insurance Brokers	USA
Avnet, Inc.	Electronics & Semiconductors	USA
Baptist Health South Florida	Healthcare Providers	USA
Source: Adapted from Ephisphere, 2017, https://www.worldsmostethicalcompanies.com/honorees/		

Table 5.1

For ethical leaders, authenticity and integrity, in addition to their values, are also important components of character and behavior that must also be translated into attitude and action toward followers, external stakeholders, and broader communities. Leaders have a responsibility to show respect toward others, treat all stakeholders fairly, work toward a common good, build community, and be honest. These virtue-related values, also referred to as character-related, as discussed earlier, help create an ethical corporation and environment:

Show Respect for Others

Respecting others requires leaders to recognize the intrinsic worth of others and forces them to treat people as ends in themselves—never as means to an end. In other words, people should be seen as valuable because of who they are (a universal principle), not only because of what they can do for others or how they can help others advance. Showing respect for others includes tolerating individual differences and affording followers the freedom to think independently, act as individuals, and pursue their own goals. When a leader shows respect for followers by providing them autonomy, subordinates can feel more useful, valued, and confident. Such a situation often leads to greater loyalty and productivity among subordinates.

Treat All Stakeholders Fairly

Ethical leaders strive to treat everyone their decisions may affect in a fair and just manner. Equality is also a top priority for ethical leaders and needs to factor prominently into their decision-making. Ethical leaders must refrain from offering special treatment to others; failure to do so creates winners and losers—in-groups and out-groups—and can breed resentment between those who receive special treatment and those who do not. The only exception occurs when an individual's specific situation warrants special treatment in order for a just outcome to be realized.

Preventing winners and losers from emerging is not always easy. Some situations require the distribution of benefits and burdens, and such situations can test a leader's ability to ensure that justice is achieved. Beauchamp and Bowie defined the common principles that guide leaders facing such dilemmas; their findings can help leaders allocate responsibilities fairly and justly.[27] These principles stipulate that every person must receive an equal share of opportunity according to his needs, rights, effort, societal contributions, and performance.

Work Toward a Common Good

Mahatma Gandhi offers an example of what striving toward a common good entails. Known for his commitment to nonviolent protests and mass civil disobedience, the Indian activist and ideological leader spent 20 years in South Africa opposing legislation that discriminated against Indians. He spent the remainder of his life in India fighting for independence from foreign rule and working to reduce poverty and taxation, liberate women, and end multiple forms of discrimination.[28] He championed such causes not because he would personally benefit, but because a larger, more substantial population would. Gandhi devoted his life to furthering social causes he believed in and developed a personal sense of purpose and meaning that later translated into a societal and then global ethic.

Ethical leaders strive to further social or institutional goals that are greater than the goals of the individual. This responsibility requires the ethical leader to serve a greater good by attending to the needs of others. This type of behavior is an example of altruism: a steadfast devotion to improving the welfare of others. Altruistic behavior may manifest in a corporate setting through actions such as mentoring, empowerment behaviors (encouraging and enabling others), team building, and citizenship behaviors (such as showing concern for others' welfare), to name a few.

Build Community

Whole Foods Market, recently purchased by Amazon, is well known for its community outreach programs on both local and global scales. Every Whole Foods store donates to community food banks and shelters and throughout the year holds "5% days," when 5% of the day's net sales are donated to local nonprofit or educational organizations. Globally, the company established the Whole Planet Foundation to combat world hunger and supports programs addressing issues such as animal welfare, nutrition, and environmentally friendly production methods.

The effort of Whole Foods to strengthen its stores' local and global neighborhoods is a perfect example of leaders building community. When an ethical leader focuses on the needs of others rather than the self, other people will often follow suit. This can lead to a strong contingent of followers working with the leader to achieve a common goal that is compatible with the desires of all stakeholders. Furthering a common goal means that no one can place his needs ahead of the group's goals and an ethical leader cannot impose his will on others. A successful CEO who works with many charities or other individuals to feed the homeless exemplifies a leader building community.

Be Honest

Honesty is considered desirable by practically everyone, but it is sometimes unclear what honesty actually demands of us. Being honest is not simply telling the truth and avoiding deceitful behaviors; it requires leaders to be as open as possible and to describe reality fully, accurately, and in sufficient detail. Telling the complete truth is not always the most desirable action, however. Leaders must be sensitive to the feelings and beliefs of others and must recognize that the appropriate level of openness and candor varies depending on the situation.

According to a recent survey, 58% of people internationally trust companies, but 42% are less sure. Being more transparent with customers, stakeholders, and stockholders should become a priority for leaders and boards of companies.[29] Dishonesty can be a disastrous practice for a leader. Dishonest leaders distort reality, which can lead to unfavorable outcomes for all stakeholders. Researchers Cialdini, Petia, Petrova, and Goldstein found that dishonest organizations suffer from tarnished reputations, decreased worker productivity, and various damages related to increased surveillance. They concluded that the costs of organizational dishonesty greatly outweigh any short-term gains from such behavior.[30]

Exhibit 5.5 Cialdini Robert Cialdini and other researchers claim that dishonest organizations suffer from tarnished reputations, decreased worker productivity, and various damages related to increased surveillance. They concluded that the costs of organizational dishonesty greatly outweigh any short-term gains from such behavior. (Credit: Dave Dugdale/ flickr/ Attribution-ShareAlike 2.0 Generic (CC BY-SA 2.0))

Stewardship and Servant Leadership Styles

Effective leaders, and followers, who lead by example and demonstrate virtuous practices while demonstrating successful practices are more numerous than the media or press reveal. Such examples are also entrepreneurs who practice both stewardship and servant leadership. Their names are not always recognizable nationally, but their companies, communities, and stakeholders know them well. For example, Inc.com's recent 2017 list of top 10 leaders features four women CEOs who go beyond the "call of duty" to serve others while succeeding in business. For example, Brittany Merrill Underwood started and is CEO of

Akola Jewelry and was named in Yahoo's "Best Person in the World" series in 2014. Her company "reinvests 100 percent of their profits to support work opportunities, training, social programs, and the construction of training centers and water wells in impoverished communities throughout the globe."[31]

A classic example of these leadership styles is also represented by Aaron Feuerstein, a previous CEO of a manufacturing plant in Massachusetts, whose example continues to represent both a steward and servant leadership style.[32]

MANAGERIAL LEADERSHIP

Servant Leadership Personified: Aaron Feuerstein at Malden Mills

Aaron Feuerstein, a third-generation owner of Malden Mills in Lawrence, Massachusetts, suffered his factory burning to the ground on December 11, 1995. Feuerstein had the option of using the insurance money to rebuild the plant, but he instead paid the salaries and complete benefits of all the 3,000 workers for 6 months while the factory was rebuilt. He later said that he had no other option than to help the employees. His action was based on his study of the Talmud, and he presented at Xavier University:

"I have the responsibility to the worker, both blue-collar and white-collar. I have an equal responsibility to the community. It would have been unconscionable to put 3,000 people on the streets and deliver a deathblow to the cities of Lawrence and Methuen. Maybe on paper our company is worthless to Wall Street, but I can tell you it's worth more."

Feuerstein exemplified the two ethical leadership styles of stewardship and servant leadership, which focus specifically on how leaders work with followers. (Ethical leadership as a whole concerns the leader's characteristics and encompasses actions in both the internal and external organizational environment.)

Source: Xavier University News and Events, "Former Malden Mills CEO Aaron Feuerstein speaking at Heroes of Professional Ethics event March 30", March 24, 2009, https://www2.xavier.edu/campusuite25/modules/news.cfm?seo_file=Former-Malden-Mills-CEO-Aaron-Feuerstein-speaking-at-Heroes-of-Professional-Ethics-event-March-30&grp_id=1#.W6FLZPZFyUk

Questions
1. How does Aaron Feuerstein exemplify servant leadership principles?
2. If Feuerstein had decided to use the insurance money for other purposes, would he have not been acting ethically?

Stewardship is concerned with empowering followers to make decisions and gain control over their work. **Servant leadership** involves selflessly working with followers to achieve shared goals that improve collective, rather than individual, welfare. There is a wealth of information on both of these styles. We will briefly address both here, as both involve treating followers with respect—a key component of ethical leadership—and endowing followers with the ability to grow both personally and professionally.

The stewardship approach instructs leaders to lead without dominating followers. Leaders who practice stewardship sincerely care about their followers and help them develop and accomplish individual as well as organizational goals. Effective stewardship breeds a team-oriented environment in which everyone works together. Organizations led by steward leaders are marked by decentralized decision-making—that is, leadership is not centered in one person, group, department, or administrative unity; power is distributed among all stakeholders.[33]

The servant-leadership approach was formulated by Robert K. Greenleaf, who believed that leadership is a natural corollary of service. Servant leadership goes beyond stewardship by requiring leaders to eschew personal accolades and devote themselves entirely to a greater cause. Greenleaf stated, "The essential quality that separates servant leaders from others is that they live by their conscience—the inward moral sense of what is right and wrong. That one quality is the difference between leadership that *works* and leadership—like servant leadership—that endures." The following aspects are central to servant leadership:

1. Placing service before self-interest. The servant leader's primary concern is helping others, not receiving recognition or financial reward.
2. Listening to others. Servant leaders recognize the importance of listening to the ideas and concerns of stakeholders; they never attempt to impose their will on others. This aspect allows servant leaders to strengthen relationships, understand group needs and dynamics, and effectively allocate resources to improve the group's welfare.
3. Inspiring through trust. As we discussed earlier, ethical leaders must be trustworthy. It does not take much effort for servant leaders to be truthful because they usually have strong moral convictions.
4. Working toward feasible goals. Servant leaders realize that many problems cannot be solved by one person. They also tackle the most pressing issues facing their groups.
5. Helping others whenever possible. Servant leaders lend a helping hand when the opportunity arises. An example is the district manager of a fast-food chain who helps part-time employees flip burgers during a lunchtime rush hour. Another is the director of a business unit who observes that a team is short a member and needs help in meeting a deadline; the director joins the team for the afternoon to help meet the deadline.[34]

Another way of understanding the distinguishing characteristics of servant leadership is offered by DeGraaf, Tilley, and Neal:

> The main assumption is that true leadership should call us to serve a higher purpose, something beyond ourselves. One of the most important aspects of leadership is helping organizations and staff identify their higher purpose. The best test of the servant-leadership philosophy is whether or not customers and staff grow as persons! Do customers become healthier, wiser, freer, more autonomous, more likely themselves to become "servants"? And, what is the effect on the least privileged in society? Will they benefit? Or, at least, not be further deprived? To achieve this higher purpose of public organizations, you, as a leader, must be passionate about your desire to improve your community and yourself![35]

Dark Side of Organizational Leadership

However, and as noted earlier, not all leaders lead or model high standards or values. Seven symptoms of the failure of ethical leadership provide a practical lens to examine a leader's shortsightedness:[36]

1. Ethical blindness: They do not perceive ethical issues due to inattention or inability.
2. Ethical muteness: They do not have or use ethical language or principles. They "talk the talk" but do not "walk the talk" on values.
3. Ethical incoherence: They are not able to see inconsistencies among values they say they follow; e.g., they say they value responsibility but reward performance based only on numbers.
4. Ethical paralysis: They are unable to act on their values from lack of knowledge or fear of the consequences of their actions.

5. Ethical hypocrisy: They are not committed to their espoused values. They delegate things they are unwilling or unable to do themselves.

6. Ethical schizophrenia: They do not have a set of coherent values; they act one way at work and another way at home.

7. Ethical complacency: They believe they can do no wrong because of who they are. They believe they are immune.

Examples of highly unethical recent leaders and their dark side leadership practices are described in *Fortune*'s "World's 19 Most Disappointing Leaders." Two illustrations are summarized here. Martin Winterkorn, the former chairman of Volkswagen, who led VW during "a disastrous scandal (which is far from over), as company engineers installed software that manipulated emissions on about 11 million diesel vehicles. Winterkorn has asserted ignorance of any wrongdoing." He is also known as being a micromanager who formed a ruthless culture that emphasized winning over all else. Then there was Rick Snyder, governor of Michigan, who "left the impoverished city of Flint, Mich. with a lead-tainted water supply that is being blamed for illness and brain damage, especially among its youngest residents.". Snyder also blamed "failure of government" and the Environmental Protection Agency for its "dumb and dangerous" rules permitting dangerous amounts of lead in the water systems.

A major takeaway from both the outstanding and undesirable ethical leadership examples presented here is that organizational culture counts and that without an ethical culture both poor and exemplary moral leadership decisions flourish.[37]

CONCEPT CHECK

1. What role does leadership play in how ethically organizations and its members act and perform?
2. Explain what stewardship is and the role of servant leadership.

5.5 Ethics, Corporate Culture, and Compliance

5. What are the differences between values-based ethics and compliance in organizations?

An organization's culture is defined by the shared values and meanings its members hold in common and that are articulated and practiced by an organization's leaders. Purpose, embodied in corporate culture, is embedded in and helps define organizations. Ed Schein, one of the most influential experts on culture, also defined organizational **corporate culture** as "a pattern of shared tacit assumptions learned or developed by a group as it solves its problems of external adaptation and internal integration that have worked well enough to be considered valid and, therefore, to be taught to new members as the correct way to perceive, think, and feel in relation to those problems."[38]

As **Exhibit 5.6** illustrates, culture plays an important integrating role in organizations both externally and internally. Strategy, structure, people, and systems all are affected by an organization's culture, which has been referred to as the "glue" that holds an organization together.[39]

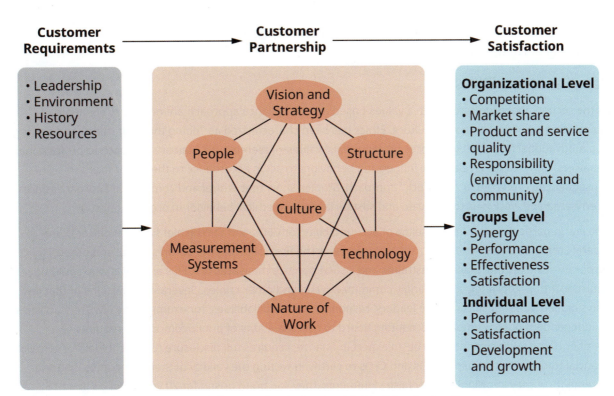

Exhibit 5.6 Role of Culture in Organizational Alignment (Attribution: Copyright Rice University, OpenStax, under CC-BY 4.0 license)

Leadership, in particular, as stated earlier, exerts a powerful influence, along with other factors, on culture. Schein noted that "culture and leadership are two sides of the same coin and one cannot understand one without the other."[40] Culture is transmitted through and by (1) the values and styles that leaders espouse and practice, (2) the heroes and heroines that the company rewards and holds up as models, (3) the rites and symbols that organizations value, and (4) the way that organizational executives and members communicate among themselves and with their stakeholders. Heskett argues that culture "can account for 20–30% of the differential in corporate performance when compared with 'culturally unremarkable' competitors."[41]

While subcultures develop in organizations, the larger organization's culture influences these, especially with strong leaders and leadership teams who set the tone at the top and communicate expectations and performance standards throughout. Other factors that indicate and help create a strong ethical culture include the following, which are based on the reputable assessment firm Ethisphere's experience[42]

An organization models and communicates compliance standards through its values; employees are informed of and familiar with the assets and efforts of the compliance and ethics function.

- The culture sets "enduring and underlying assumptions and norms that determine how things are actually done in the organization."[43]
- "Organizations can effectively identify specific locations, business units, job levels and job functions that may lack a full understanding of available resources, feel unwanted pressure, or perhaps hold negative perceptions."
- Companies and investors believe a company behaves and acts ethically.
- Employees are aware of the conduct, values, and communications of senior leaders.
- Employees are engaged and committed, and organizations regularly survey employees to get a sense of their engagement.
- Employees feel "less pressure to compromise company standards to achieve company goals. And if they do observe misconduct, they are more likely to feel comfortable reporting it."

- "Employees perceive the ethical priorities of their coworkers, the values of their organization and willingness to share opinions."[44]

Compliance and Ethics

As the section above indicates, both a values-based and compliance approach are necessary elements of maintaining an ethical corporate culture. Ethics has been characterized as "doing the right thing" and serving as a motivational force that influences professionals' values—resembling a "carrot" approach to professionals' behaviors. Compliance is related to influencing behaviors to act in accordance to the law or face consequences—referred to as a "stick" approach. Studies show that ethical and compliance approaches are interrelated and work best to motivate and sustain lawful and ethical behavior in organizations.[45]

One law in particular set a new baseline of accountability for CEOs and CFOs (chief financial officers): the federal Sarbanes-Oxley Act of 2002, 2010. This law was the first following the Enron scandal and other corporate scandals that placed constraints and issued punitive measures on CEOs and CFOs who could be punished if they knowingly and willingly committed fraud and other crimes. Several new sections of that law also signaled a change in corporate leaders' responsibilities and liabilities; for example, the law "[e]stablishes an independent public company accounting board to oversee audits of public companies; requires one member of the audit committee to be an expert in finance; requires full disclosure to stockholders of complex financial transactions: requires CEOs and CFOs to certify in writing the validity of their companies' financial statements. If they knowingly certify false statements, they can go to prison for 20 years and be fined $5 million; -Prohibits accounting firms from offering other services, like consulting, while also performing audits" (Federal Sentencing Guidelines, 2004). There are other parts of this law that that further establish compliance regulations.[46]

Because of the widespread corporate scandals discussed at the beginning of the chapter, the U.S. Congress implemented legal and compliance standards to curb and discourage illegal activities in corporations. While self-regulation will always play a major role in corporations' "doing the right thing," compliance has proven to be a necessary but not always sufficient element of corporate governance. Ethics continues to complement compliance, especially since the law cannot, does not, and will not cover every aspect of potentially harmful behaviors. Ethical dimensions and practices such as transparency, privacy, honesty, objectivity, integrity, carefulness, openness, respect for intellectual property, civility, confidentiality, accountability, responsible mentoring, and respect for colleagues are all necessary to motivate organizational behavior.

Ethical values become "actionable" in corporations by corporations first becoming aware of and then assuming responsibility for the corporation's duties toward its stakeholders and stockholders. Social responsibility as a concept originated in 1953 when Howard R. Bowen, known as the "father of corporate social responsibility" (CSR), referred in a book to the "Social Responsibilities of the Businessman."[47]

CONCEPT CHECK

1. In what ways do law and compliance complement ethics in organizations?
2. How does stakeholder management differ from stockholder management?

5.6 | Corporate Social Responsibility (CSR)

6. What value do CSR (corporate social responsibility) programs offer to organizations and society?

CSR contributes to another form of self-regulation that goes further and involves firms taking action to help people and the environment. CSR is described as "a belief that corporations have a social responsibility beyond pure profit." In other words, "Firms are social entities, and so they should play a role in the social issues of the day. They should take seriously their 'obligations to society' and actively try to fulfill them."[48] As such, corporations should employ a decision-making process to achieve more than financial success on the assumption that CSR is integral to an optimum long-term strategy.

In the 21st century, sustainability and corporate social responsibility (CSR) have become strategic imperatives for organizations as fundamental market forces for financial viability and success, where consumers are important stakeholders. Businesses worldwide develop CSR initiatives to become better corporate citizens but also to communicate their activity to both internal and external stakeholders, which may involve a number of groups.

A study by Horizon Media's Finger on the Pulse found that "81 percent of Millennials expect companies to make a public commitment to good corporate citizenship."[49] The 2015 Cone Communications Millennial CSR Study found that "[m]ore than nine-in-10 Millennials would switch brands to one associated with a cause (91% vs. 85% U.S. average), and two-thirds use social media to engage around CSR (66% vs. 53% U.S. average)."[50]

The 3 P's (profit, the people, and the planet), or "the triple bottom line" (TBL), is another concept (closely related to and reflective of the mission of CSR and firm activities.[51] TBL—also known as 3BL—incorporates and assists businesses measure accountability in their funding of and support for social, environmental (ecological), and financial benefits to allow for a greater good. Many corporations have started to add triple bottom line metrics to their business plans in order to evaluate their overall performance and reflect on how companies are contributing to society. A small sample of contemporary CSR initiatives make a difference. For example:

- The GE Foundation gave $88 million to community and educational programs in 2016.
- The 3MGives corporation funded $67 million in 2016 to focus on community and the environment, along with educational initiatives boosting student interest in science and technology.
- Apple was named by the environmental organization Greenpeace as the "greenest tech company in the world" for over three years because that firm's packaging is manufactured with 99 percent recycled paper products.
- Walt Disney Company's social mission to strengthen communities states that "by providing hope, happiness, and comfort to kids and families who need it most". The Walt Disney Company donated more than $400 million to nonprofit organizations in 2016.
- Virgin Atlantic's "Change is in the Air" sustainability initiative states its mission as: "Environment, sustainable design and buying, and community investment." This firm has since 2007 "reduced total aircraft carbon emissions by 22% and [has] partnered with LanzaTech to develop low carbon fuels for the future. Virgin Holidays donates £200,000 annually to the Brandon Center for Entrepreneurship Caribbean to support young entrepreneurs in Jamaica."[52]

Exhibit 5.7   Hasbro Hasbro relies heavily on its strategic brand blueprint to guide its efforts in CSR, innovation, philanthropy, and product development. With a business portfolio that includes such well-known brands as Nerf, Play-Doh, Transformers, and Mr. Potato Head, the company focuses its CSR efforts on four key areas: product safety, environmental sustainability, human rights and ethical sourcing, and community. Here one of its products is featured at the Thanksgiving Day parade in New York City. (Credit: rowenphotography/ flickr/ NoDerivs 2.0 Generic (CC BY-ND 2.0))

Even with the current 2017 U.S. government's executive branch and Congress backing out of international climate change agreements to expand and promote fossil fuel production, taking actions to disable the EPA (Environmental Protection Agency), and not funding the Consumer Financial Protection Bureau, many corporations continue practicing CSR and 3BL principles to support sustainable environmental goals and objectives.[53]

While CSR is not a cure-all that can or will significantly make a difference in ushering in more sustainable environmental practices, help alleviate poverty, and use profits to help lower-income communities, it contributes to both internal and external stakeholder awareness to "do the right thing." For example, Teng and Yazdanifard argue and present evidence that some consumers do take CSR into account while making purchase decision. Also, CSR initiatives and actions have been shown to positively influence both internal and external stakeholders.[54] A study conducted in New Zealand explored the perceptions of internal stakeholders of New Zealand companies to discover the way in which the CSR, sustainability cultures, and identity are communicated internally. It was found that employee behaviors matter, as organizations that are well regarded in the community attract greater external loyalty, have more stable revenues, and face fewer crisis risks. A positive relationship with staff in organizations through CSR policies will not only attract better employees, it will also influence the morale, motivation, and loyalty of existing staff. The effective delivery of CSR initiatives also depends on how responsive employees are. If companies wish to achieve legitimacy by operating within a society's ethical expectations, they must also communicate internally to ensure that CSR activities are integrated into the organizational culture—they cannot "talk the talk" without "walking the walk."[55]

So, does CSR benefit the companies that practice such measures? A meta-analysis of 52 studies with a sample size of 33,878 observations suggested that "corporate virtue in the form of social responsibility and, to a lesser extent, environmental responsibility, is likely to pay off. . . . CSP [corporate social performance] appears to be more highly correlated with accounting-based measures of CFP [corporate financial performance] than with market-based indicators, and CSP reputation indices are more highly correlated with CFP than are other indicators of CSP" . Many business scholars do believe that some of these relationships are positive.[56] Robbins concludes that "[o]n balance, surveys and the research literature suggest that what most executives believe intuitively, that CSR can improve profits, is possible. And almost no large public company today would want to be seen unengaged in CSR. That is clear admission of how important CSR might be to their bottom line, no matter how difficult it may be to define CSR and link it to profits."[57]

Without exception, the managers articulated the importance of communicating CSR initiatives and policy to their employees, as well as recognizing the need to improve their CSR internal communication strategies. According to the managers, CSR initiatives are promoted to create better corporations and a more ethical business environment. These included recycling, carpooling, staff development, and social activities. External initiatives included volunteering, fund-raising, and charitable donations.

Stakeholder Management

CSR and **stakeholder management** are complementary approaches. Stakeholder theory argues that corporations should treat all their constituencies fairly and that doing so can strengthen companies' reputations, customer relations, and performance in the marketplace.[58] "If organizations want to be effective, they will pay attention to all and only those relationships that can affect or be affected by the achievement of the organization's purposes."[59]

The ethical dimension of stakeholder theory is based on the view that profit maximization is constrained by justice, that regard for individual rights should be extended to all constituencies who have a stake in a business, and that organizations are not only "economic" in nature but can also act in socially responsible ways. To this end, companies should act in socially responsible ways, not only because it's the "right thing to do," but also to ensure their legitimacy.[60]

A stakeholder management approach first involves identifying the stakeholders of a company. A **stakeholder** is any group or individual who can affect or is affected by an organization's strategies, major transactions, and activities. Stakeholders include employees, suppliers, customers, shareholders, the government, media, and others. An illustration of the stakeholder relationships is provided in **Exhibit 5.8**. The term *stakeholder* has become commonplace in organizations. Companies and organizations that base their strategic decisions on the principle of duty to earn stakeholder trust "are likely to yield a number of strategic benefits, too, and can help manage political, social, and reputational risk."[61]

Exhibit 5.8   Stakeholder Map Source: Freeman, R. Edward. (1984). *Strategic management: A Stakeholder approach*, 25. Boston: Pitman. Reproduced with permission of the author.

Identifying and Influencing Major Stakeholders

There are several methods for analyzing stakeholder transactions and relationships with an organization that go beyond the purpose of this chapter.[62] Using an ethical perspective, a goal of this approach is for organizations to employ values of transparency, fairness, and consideration of stakeholder interests in strategic decisions and transactions. Toward that end, the following questions can be used from **Exhibit 5.8**.

1. Who are the stakeholders (that is, people who have an interest in supporting or resisting a proposed course of action, resolving an issue, and addressing a change)?
2. What are their stakes in either supporting or resisting the change?
3. What do the supporters stand to gain and lose from the change?
4. What do the resisters stand to gain and lose from the change?
5. What type(s) of power do the supporters have with regard to the change?
6. What type(s) of power do the resisters have with regard to the change?
7. What strategies can we use to keep the support of the supporters?
8. What strategies can we use to neutralize or win over the resisters?

Based on this approach, an organization's leaders and officers inform, involve, obtain feedback from, and influence each of their stakeholders with regard to strategy, issues, or opportunities the organization pursues. The Coca-Cola Company uses an ongoing stakeholder approach that is described on this site: **http://www.coca-colacompany.com/stories/stakeholder-engagement**.

Had BP followed this approach in 2010, the now largest oil spill and rig explosion crisis in the history of such operations that occurred in the Gulf of Mexico, killing 11 workers and damaging over 600 square miles of land and sea, might have been prevented. It appeared that the leadership and culture at BP had been lax and out of touch with its stakeholders—and stockholders. As a consequence, the machinery and equipment were dated and not optimally functioning. One consequence is that employees, workers, communities, and the public may not have suffered that crisis and the continuing after effects.

CSR and stakeholder management have demonstrated benefits to firms' reputations and profitability.[63] The relationship of an organization's ethics and social responsibility to its performance concerns both managers and organization scholars. Studies have shown a positive relationship between ethical and socially responsible behavior and financial results. For example, one study of the financial performance of large U.S. corporations that are considered "best corporate citizens" found that they have both superior reputations and superior financial performance.[64] Similarly, Governance Metrics International, an independent corporate governance ratings agency, found that the stocks of companies run on more selfless principles perform better than those run in a self-serving manner. Top-ranked companies such as Pfizer, Johnson Controls, and Sunoco also outperformed lower-ranking firms on measures such as return on assets, return on investment, and return on capital.[65]

CONCEPT CHECK

1. How do sustainable business practices benefit consumers?
2. Differentiate the roles compliance and CSR programs serve in organizations. Are these the same, or are there differences? Explain.

5.7 | Ethics around the Globe

7. What are ethical issues we encounter in the global environment?

Organizations operating on a global basis often face particularly tough ethical challenges because of various cultural, political, economic, technological, and market factors. The greater the complexity of the environment, the greater the potential for ethical problems and misunderstandings for global organizations.[66] "Think ... of the ethical value systems that shape behavior within and between countries, and the unpredictability that can result when there is a re-evaluation of what is acceptable and unacceptable." Recent and reoccurring global ethical problems and risks that organizations face include cybersecurity and political threats, international conflict and warfare, income inequality, planetary climate and environmental pollution and instability, corruption, and human and diversity rights violations. **Exhibit 5.9** illustrates the wide range of stakeholders and issues related to several of the risks in this figure that MNEs (multinational enterprises) must either prevent from occurring or manage when doing business across and within different country borders.

MNE Global Stakeholder Management Issues and Ethical Concerns

Stakeholder Economic Environmental Issues

Exchange rates, wages, income distribution, balance of payments, import/export levels, taxes, interest rates, GNPs, tranfer pricing

Stakeholder Political Environmental Issues

Governments, media, instability, local laws, antitrust laws, military, foreign policy and treaties, corruption, local competition

MNEs Managing Ethical Concerns

Observing home and host countries' legal and moral codes: e.g., Foreign Corrupt Practices Act, workplace safety, product safety, responsible marketing and advertising standards, moral ecological practices

Stakeholder Ecological Environmental Issues

Air, water, land pollution; toxic wastes and dumping; industrial accidents; use/misuse of natural resources; restoring national environment

Stakeholder Technological Environmental Issues

Intellectual property protection, licensing, agreement fees, technical resources, alliances and sharing of technology

Stakeholder Social and Labor Environmental Issues

Values, attitudes, customs; religious, political, social-class practices and norms; labor unions; availability of skills; expatriate requirements, needs; workplace safety

Exhibit 5.9   MNE Global Stakeholder Management Issues and Ethical Concerns Source: Copyright © Joseph W. Weiss, Bentley University, Waltham, MA. 2014.

Following laws related to doing business abroad is an added challenge for global firms. For example, the FCPA (Foreign Corrupt Practices Act) prohibits American firms from accepting or offering bribes to foreign government officials. U.S. individuals who cannot defend their actions with regard to the FCPA's antibribery provisions can face harsh penalties. "U.S. companies can be fined up to $2 million while U.S. individuals (including officers and directors of companies that have willfully violated the FCPA) can be fined up to $100,000 and imprisoned for up to five years, or both. In addition, civil penalties may be imposed."[67] Recently, the U.S. Department of Justice (DOJ) and the Securities and Exchange Commission (SEC) have been more aggressive in enforcing and prosecuting the bribery section of the FCPA. Halliburton Company in 2017 paid the SEC $29.2 million for bribing a friend of an official in Angola to negotiate a seven oil-field services contracts. The result was a disgorgement fine (i.e., a repayment of illegal gains with penalties imposed on wrongdoers by the courts) for violating the FCPA's records and internal accounting controls provisions.[68]

U.S.-based firms are also expected to not engage in unethical or illegal activities such as discriminating against local populations, violating local laws and norms, and disrespecting property and the environment. MNEs can also assist and add value to local countries. For example, the following practices are encouraged:

- Hiring local labor
- Creating new jobs
- Co-venturing with local entrepreneurs and companies
- Attracting local capital to projects
- Providing for and enhancing technology transfer
- Developing particular industry sectors
- Providing business learning and skills
- Increasing industrial output and productivity
- Helping decrease the country's debt and improve its balance of payments and standard of living.[69]

Globalization

The increasing phenomenon of globalization (an integrated global economy consisting of free trade, capital flows, and cheaper foreign labor markets)[70] also pressures global firms facing international risks to rely on governments, NGOs (nongovernmental organizations), the UN (United Nations), and other business and stakeholder alliances and relationships to help meet nonmarket threats. For example, the ten principles of the UN Global Compact serve as guidelines for international firms doing business in LDCs (least developed countries), and abroad, businesses should (1) support and respect the protection of internationally proclaimed human rights, (2) ensure that they are not complicit in human rights abuses, (3) uphold the freedom of association and the effective recognition of the right to collective bargaining, (4) eliminate of all forms of forced and compulsory labor, (5) abolish child labor, (6) eliminate the discrimination of employment and occupation, (7) support a precautionary approach to environmental challenges, (8) promote greater environmental responsibility through initiatives, (9) encourage the development and diffusion of environmentally friendly technologies, and (10) work against corruption, including extortion and bribery.[71]

While these principles may seem so universal as to be unattainable, they do stand as ethical milestones that protect human life, dignity, and personal welfare and values. However, when companies operate in LDCs and other cultures, it often is necessary to negotiate a balance between fairness, equality, and different local values and standards. U.S. and Western values may differ with local cultural norms, such as child labor and employee rights, in many countries. Donaldson and Dunfee offer methods for such negotiations.[72] A classic example was Levi Strauss doing business in Bangladesh several years ago. Children in that country under the age of 14 were working in two of Levi's local suppliers. This employment practice violated Levi's norms but not the local cultural norms. Firing the children would have prevented the children from being able to get an education and would have placed hardships on their families, who depended on the children's wages. A negotiated agreement (between Levi's universal values and local country norms) involved the suppliers agreeing to pay the children regular wages while they went to school and then hiring them when they turned 15 years old. Levi's agrees to provide for the children's tuition, books, and uniforms.

MNEs Corporate Cultures

MNEs must also create inclusive, ethical corporate cultures while managing both external and internal complexities such as hiring and training a diverse workforce, adapting to local culture norms while balancing home country ethics and values, and ensuring a multicultural approach to doing business across countries.

Hanna identified five strategic questions that relate to organizational cultural sensitivities when doing business abroad as well as in a home country:[73]

1. "What do customers and stakeholders in our market expect from our organization? (Will their standard of living be raised? Will their cultural expectations be violated?)
2. What is our strategy to be successful in this competitive marketplace? (What can we realistically hope to achieve? What results are we willing to commit to?)
3. What are our governing values that define how we will work with stakeholders and with each other?
4. What organizational capabilities do we need in order to achieve these results?
5. What do our work processes, roles, and systems need to do so that we are consistent with all of the above?"

The author maintains that these questions will help bring an awareness to cultural differences and help organizational leaders and staff reach agreement on customizing decisions to fit a particular market while balancing company principles with local values.

Global firms are also sensitized to the recent #MeToo movement in the United States that raises women's awareness and courage to speak out about sexual harassment and assault in companies and workplaces. This movement further highlights the need to diversify and integrate workforces on the basis of gender and other traits that match customers' and population characteristics. This need is not only based on ethical factors such as fairness, equality, rights, and justice, but also on competitive advantage and marketing awareness. To that end, organizational leaders are implementing more gender-balanced talent pools, especially at the early-to-mid-career levels and the mid-to-upper levels globally. Gender balance is beginning to be seen as "a broader, more strategic cultural shift that includes developing leadership teams representing geographically diffuse markets. These leaders are recognizing that this balance drives the innovation and market understanding they need for other key business transformations. Without balance, they simply won't understand the world that's emerging."[74]

For example, Dutch-based Royal DSM—the $8 billion global company in health, nutrition, and materials science—has shifted from a male-run organization to a gender-balanced leadership team in three steps: (1) setting a vision connecting the goal to business success, (2) engaging men of the firm's dominant nationality, and (3) building competencies while working across nationality and gender differences. In 2000, DSM's top 350 executives were 75% Dutch and over 99% male. In 2017, the firm was 40% Dutch and 83% male. The CEO, Feike Sijbesma, plans to decrease the male ratio down by 2% per year and down below 75% by 2025. He is prioritizing sustainability and credibility more than speed.[75]

Govindarajan's research indicated that, even though organizational cultures may vary widely, there are specific components that characterize a global culture. These include an emphasis on multicultural rather than national values, basing status on merit rather than nationality, being open to new ideas from other cultures, showing excitement rather than trepidation when entering new cultural environments and being sensitive to cultural differences without being limited by them.[76] Managers must also think more broadly in terms of ethical issues. Companies are using a wide variety of mechanisms to support and reinforce their ethics initiatives on a global scale. A useful mechanism for building global ethics in an organization is the social audit, which measures and reports the ethical, social, and environmental impact of a company's operations.[77]

Also, as noted earlier in the chapter, Ethisphere—a renowned organization that evaluates the effectiveness of an organization's communication, training, ethics, culture, and compliance efforts to gain insights into employee concerns—continues to survey and publish annual results of "The World's Most Ethical Companies."[78] These surveys offer benchmarks of global and national companies' best ethical practices. A major finding from one of that organization's conferences stated that "[o]ut of the 644 respondents to the

NAVEX Global 2016 Ethics & Compliance Training Benchmark Report, 70 percent said that 'creating a culture of ethics and respect' was one of their top training objectives. When it comes to CEOs, 92 percent agree that a strong corporate culture is important."

CONCEPT CHECK

1. What ways can and do some MNEs demonstrate social responsibility in foreign countries?
2. What are some specific ethical business practices other countries (besides the United States) and regional governing bodies (such as the European Union) practice and demonstrate with regard to the environment and competition?

5.8 Emerging Trends in Ethics, CSR, and Compliance

8. Identify forecasts about contemporary ethical and corporate social responsibility issues.

Predicted trends in ethics, compliance, and corporate social responsibility for Fortune 500 companies, governments, groups, and professionals by Navex Global include:

1. "A shift in the 'power of voice in the story of harassment.'" The #MeToo movement has changed everything. "Bill Cosby, Harvey Weinstein, Charlie Rose, Kevin Spacey, Al Franken, Matt Lauer, and Garrison Keillor" and other high-profile public figures have pressured organizations through public forum social media forums to take action. "Victims of harassment have the power of choice. They can make an internal report and hope that their organization responds properly, or they can choose to take their story public." A clear message for corporations and ethics and compliance officers is, "Create a corporate culture in which employees feel comfortable raising their voices about anything from sexual harassment to feelings of being insulted. This will allow your compliance program to resolve issues before they turn into scandals, and preserve the integrity of your organization's culture internally and its reputation externally. And don't ever tolerate retaliation."
2. The "Glassdoor" effect (when people trust online reviews of their companies more than what companies communicate) and the effect of trust when employee messages go viral on social media. Companies need to create "listen-up" cultures by creating internal reporting systems in which leadership and managers listen to and support employees when they raise their voices for the betterment of the company. "This ensures employees know that their report will be heard, taken seriously, and things will change if necessary."
3. Assisting national disasters that suddenly occur causes havoc not only for vulnerable populations but also for unprepared organizations. Ethics and compliance professionals learned from 2017's natural disasters (hurricanes in particular) to update preparation plans and test emergency hotlines, communications systems, and employee readiness.
4. The acceleration of the need for compliance and ethics programs as economies begin again to grow; "growth without ethics and governance does nobody any favors. Growth with ethics and governance won't simply be a feel-good mantra in 2018, it will be a business imperative."
5. Creating a "culture of compliance" in corporations (a culture of integrity and ethics) over one of "vicious compliance" (an overreliance on laws and regulations). "Finally, and most importantly, leadership accountability is what every employee is watching. In the end, what happens to the top performers who

violate the rules will send the loudest message of all to the organization."

6. An increasing need for compliance's role in prevention and mitigation as cybersecurity evolves. "Compliance must play an integral part in any organization's cross-functional cyber security program to make sure such efforts are enterprise-wide."

7. Giving new voice to whistle-blowers is predicted as "regulatory scrutiny is increasing, and the voice of the whistleblower in the [Silicon] Valley is growing louder as well." Corporations need to listen and resolve whistle-blowers' issues internally before they decide to go outside.

8. Managing culture and free speech in the workplace during "polarizing times" continues about "race, gender, sex, sexual orientation, gender identity, national origin, and religion—and people's right to fair treatment, protection, and the rights and benefits enjoyed by others."

9. Data privacy is becoming a larger concern for chief compliance officers in companies as "privacy laws and the environments they regulate, have evolved." Creating a safe and respectful workplace is needed.

10. The role of the compliance professional evolves and innovates as "old networking models are giving way to online networks that provide new and unprecedented opportunities to share ideas and collaborate."

Ethics and compliance go hand in hand as stated earlier. With a strong ethical culture, compliance is more effective in preventing risks, and without a compliance program, those who deliberately choose to break laws and codes of conduct would create disorder. "Strong cultures have two elements: A high level of agreement about what is valued and a high level of intensity with regard to those values. "In the long run, a positive culture of integrity is the foundation for an effective ethics and compliance program, which, when properly embedded into an organization, can create a competitive advantage and serve as a valuable organizational asset," quoted from Keith Darcy, an independent senior advisor to Deloitte & Touche LLP's Regulatory and Operational Risk practice.[79]

Moral Entrepreneur: A New Component of Ethical Leadership?

An innovative development in ethics and business is the concept of "moral entrepreneur."[80] Brown and Trevino found that people who have been exposed to a **moral entrepreneur** are more likely to become a moral entrepreneur themselves because they have experienced its potential and experienced how it is done. Inspiration certainly takes place, and the person's well-being is improved.[81]

Related to moral entrepreneurship is ethical leadership. Brown and Trevino's ethical leadership is defined as "the demonstration of normatively appropriate conduct through personal actions and interpersonal relationships, and the promotion of such conduct to followers through two-way communication, reinforcement, and decision-making." Examples of such conduct include openness, honesty, and treating employees fairly and thoughtfully. Social learning theory was used to gain an understanding as to why ethical leadership is important to employees and how it is perceived to work.

Ethical leaders are models of ethical conduct who become the targets of identification and emulation for followers. For leaders to be perceived as ethical leaders and to influence ethics-related outcomes, they must be perceived as attractive, credible, and legitimate. They do this by engaging in behavior that is seen as normatively appropriate (e.g., openness and honesty) and motivated by altruism (e.g., treating employees fairly and considerately). Ethical leaders must also gain followers' attention to the ethics message by engaging in explicit ethics-related communication and by using reinforcement to support the ethics message.[82]

In addition to social learning theory, which focuses on why and how supporters follow a leader, a social development approach to the concept of ethical leadership is also needed because it focuses on the direction that leadership should take. Studies on corporate social responsibility are concerned with how companies can contribute to societal development, not only in the sense of solving social problems but also in the sense of improving social welfare, promoting social progress, and creating new social value.

Muel Kaptein argues that there is a third component to ethical leadership—moral entrepreneurship, in addition to the already defined components of the moral person and the moral manager.[83] His belief is that moral entrepreneurship opens avenues for studying various antecedents and outcomes of ethical leadership that hasn't been acknowledged adequately to date.

Studies of the antecedents of ethical leadership, at both the situational and personal levels, have found that leaders who have had ethical role models are more likely to become ethical leaders.[84] These studies have also found that the personality traits of agreeableness and conscientiousness are positively related to ethical leadership. And studies on corporate social responsibility are concerned with how companies can contribute to societal development, not only in the sense of solving social problems, but also in the sense of improving social welfare, promoting social progress, and creating new social value.

According to Kaptein, someone who creates a new ethical norm is called a moral entrepreneur. Becker believes that those people who make moral reform happen are the moral entrepreneurs. He differentiates between two kinds of moral entrepreneurs: those who create new norms and those who enforce new norms. The moral entrepreneur experiences something horrific that prompts him to want to do something to solve the issue, as Kaptein describes, a want to correct by translating a preferred norm into legal prohibitions: however, he risks becoming an outsider themselves if they are not unable to congregate support for the new norm.

Kaptein states that the component of moral entrepreneurship complements the two other components of ethical leadership (moral person and moral manager), because it highlights the creation of new norms instead of only following and implementing current ethical norms. Becker suggests that helping others is important and having the altruistic trait is important for a moral entrepreneur. Yurtsever, in developing a scale for moral entrepreneurship personality, suggests that moral entrepreneurs demonstrate high moral virtues, such as justice and honesty.[85] Moreover, being a moral manager is important to be able to get the support of others to follow the new ethical norm. In order to be successful as a norm creator, one needs the support of others. Even though the three components of ethical leadership complement each other, it is still possible for someone to only exhibit one or two of the components, making ethical leadership a multidimensional construct. For instance, one can be a moral entrepreneur without being a moral manager (what Becker calls the norm creator), or one can be a moral manager without being a moral entrepreneur, what Becker calls the norm enforcer.

Concluding Comments

So, does it pay to be ethical and moral, whether it be entrepreneurs and individuals or corporations and organizations? We have discussed this question in this chapter and presented different arguments with different views. Scholars and ethicists who have debated whether or not corporations can be ethical differ on their responses. One such conference in the INSEAD Business School in France closed with the following statement: "Theoretically, a strong case can be made for the moral responsibility of firms. However, this does not preclude individual moral responsibility for acts as a corporate member. Moreover, it was also evident that considerable concern exists about corporate misconduct going unsanctioned and the possibility that both good and bad corporate behavior is profoundly influenced by the extent to which individuals and corporate entities are held morally responsible."[86]

This statement implies that both corporations and individuals bear the possibility and responsibility for unethical—as well as illegal—acts. While corporations are not individuals, people work and relate in corporate and work settings. That is why organizational leaders and cultures play such important roles in setting the tone and boundaries for what is acceptable (ethically and legally) and what is not. Ethical values and legal, compliance codes of conduct together work to prevent and if necessary seek correction and justice for unlawful actions. As noted earlier, promoting and rewarding ethical actions are more desirable and in the long-term more profitable.

Prooijen and Ellemers's study using social identity analysis found that individuals are attracted to teams and organizations with positive features such as organizational "competence and achievements" and "moral values and ethical conduct." Since these two features do not always cohere working environments, the authors' study had students choose in three different studies which they would prefer in seeking employment, "perceived competence vs morality of a team or organization." They found that "[r]esults of all three studies converge to demonstrate that the perceived morality of the team or organization has a greater impact on its attractiveness to individuals than its perceived competence."[87]

CONCEPT CHECK

1. What are some emerging national and global issues and trends in ethics and business ethics?

🔑 Key Terms

business ethics The area of applied ethics that focuses on real-world situations and the context and environment in which transactions occur.

corporate culture The beliefs and behaviors that determine how a company's employees and management interact inside an organization and also handle outside business transactions. Corporate culture develops organically over time from the cumulative traits of the leaders and the people that the company hires.

ethical dilemma A situation in which a difficult choice has to be made between two courses of action with ethical consequences.

ethical relativism Holds that people set their own moral standards for judging their actions, based on self-interest.

ethics The code of moral principles and values that governs the behaviors of a person or group with respect to what is right or wrong.

instrumental values The preferred means of behavior used to obtain desired goals.

justice Four major tenets: (1) All individuals should be treated equally; (2) Justice is served when all persons have equal opportunities and advantages; (3) Fair decision practices, procedures, and agreements among parties should be practiced; (4) Punishment is served to someone who inflicts harm.

moral entrepreneur Someone who creates a new ethical norm.

normative ethics The field of ethics concerned with our asking how *should* and *ought* we live and act.

rights Legal rights are entitlements that are limited to a particular legal system and jurisdiction, while moral rights are universal and based on norms in every society.

servant leadership Involves selflessly working with followers to achieve shared goals that improve collective, rather than individual, welfare.

stakeholder Any group or individual who can affect or is affected by the achievement of an organization's objectives. The use of the term *stakeholder* has become commonplace in organizations.

stakeholder management The systematic identification, analysis, planning, and implementation of actions designed to engage with stakeholders

stewardship Concerned with empowering followers to make decisions and gain control over their work.

terminal values Desired goals, objectives, or end states that individuals wish to pursue.

virtue ethics Grounded in one's character, focusing on what type of person one ought to be.

📄 Summary of Learning Outcomes

5.1 Ethics and Business Ethics Defined
1. What are ethics and business ethics?

A goal of the chapter is to present ethical principles, guidelines, and questions that inform our individual decision-making and influence actions we can take with regard to questionable ethical situations and dilemmas. We also present and illustrate how business leaders, corporations, and organizations internationally have responded and are responding to questionable ethical problems with the environment in their communities through responsible corporate governance and alliance with concerned stakeholders. Ethics is both local and global; it begins with the individual, moves to the organizational, and reaches to international and global levels of societies.

5.2 Dimensions of Ethics: The Individual Level
2. What are the types of values that motivate ethics at the individual level?

Ethics at an individual level may seem to involve only the individual, but it is a holistic process. There may be high pressure from coworkers, managers, or any other constituent of business culture to be unethical. Individuals may hate such pressures, and they tend to work to avoid the dilemmas.

5.3 Ethical Principles and Responsible Decision-Making

3.   What are the major ethical principles that can guide individuals and organizations?

There are many approaches for both individuals and organizations to take with regard to ethical principles. They are utilitarianism; universalism, which is a duty-based approach; a rights approach, which takes a moral and legal approach; justice; virtue; common good; and finally the ethical relativism approach.

5.4 Leadership: Ethics at the Organizational Level

4.   Why is ethical leadership important in organizations?

After the failures of Enron and other organizations, people have started emphasizing the concept of ethical leadership. An organization can incorporate ethical practices only if its leaders enforce ethical values into the organization. While such basic concepts of ethics such as being honest are crucial to ethical leadership, a modern approach is to take the servant leadership approach, where the leader serves the interests of all stakeholders in an ethical manner.

5.5 Ethics, Corporate Culture, and Compliance

1.   What are the differences between values-based ethics and compliance in organizations?

A compliance-based ethical approach is simple and direct. It provides a basic integrity to the participant since it is spelled out in clear terms. If the individual or organization exhibits destructive behaviors, their rights can be restricted. An integrity-based ethics code fills the receiver with demands based on the highest expectations.

5.6 Corporate Social Responsibility (CSR)

6.   What value do CSR (corporate social responsibility) programs offer to organizations and society?

Corporate social responsibility is about an organization taking responsibility for the impacts of its decisions and activities on all aspects of society, the community, and the environment. Corporate social responsibility is about contributing to the health and welfare of society and operating transparently and ethically. More importantly, this way of operating should be embedded in the business, rather than an afterthought.

5.7 Ethics around the Globe

7.   What are ethical issues we encounter in the global environment?

Some of the most common ethical issues organizations encounter globally include outsourcing, working standards and conditions, workplace diversity and equal opportunity, child labor, trust and integrity, supervisory oversight, human rights, religion, the political arena, the environment, bribery, and corruption.

5.8 Emerging Trends in Ethics, CSR, and Compliance

8.   Identify forecasts about contemporary ethical and corporate social responsibility issues.

Among the emerging issues in the area of ethics are in the area of harassment in the era of #MeToo. Organizations and individuals are also more accepting of their roles in assisting with such things as natural disasters and national emergencies. Finally, there is increasing attention to issues of compliance and governance to ensure that organizations meet their stated ethical standards.

⌷ Chapter Review Questions

1. What is the difference between ethics and business ethics?
2. What is normative ethics?
3. Why are values an important element of ethics for individuals and organizations?
4. What are the differences between instrumental and terminal values?
5. Can an individual be ethical without using ethical principles described in the chapter? Explain.
6. Identify major classical ethical principles.
7. Differentiate between the principle of rights and utilitarianism and between justice and universalism.
8. Why is leadership important for ethical conduct in corporations?
9. Identify two types of ethical leaders and the important role each plays.
10. What is the difference between ethics and compliance in organizations?
11. What is CSR, and why is it important?
12. What is stakeholder management?
13. What is the difference between stakeholders and stockholders?
14. What is different about ethics in a global or international context and ethics in a national context or setting?
15. What are some global issues that corporations must face today, and why are these important?
16. Identify some contemporary ethical and compliance trends affecting corporations, employees, and individuals now.
17. What is a moral entrepreneur?
18. Does ethics pay? Explain.
19. After reading this chapter, what are major insights you have about ethics and CSR?

⚑ Management Skills Application Exercises

1. What are some advantages and disadvantages of leaders, managers, and employees having and working with a principle-centered approach (using some ethical principles in the chapter) rather than taking a "come what may," trust in luck, circumstance and chance approach?
2. Would you rather work for a company that takes a stakeholder or stockholder approach in its dealings with customers, employees, suppliers, and other constituencies in its network? Explain.
3. What are some principles (from the chapter) that leaders and managers can use to guide their actions in ethical ways?
4. What can organizational managers and leaders learn with regard to organizational cultures that would inspire and motivate employees to do the right thing in their work?
5. What type of leaders and leadership styles and practices often lead to problems with employees, customers, and other stakeholders and stockholders?
6. Describe how a leader, manager, and employee might think and act differently if their organization seriously adopted and practiced doing business with a corporate social responsibility mindset.
7. What are some concerns that have ethical implications that a leader, manager, or employee might have when doing business internationally or globally?
8. After reading the section in the chapter on ethical and compliance trends going forward, what top two or three things do you think organizational leaders and managers would want to take action on preparing for now? Why?

Managerial Decision Exercises

1. You are a manager, and your boss—who is also a friend—has reprimanded a fellow employee (also a friend) in ways that are demonstrably unfair and unethical but not illegal. That employee has confided in you with the facts, and you agree. The employee asks you not to mention anything to the boss but to go with her to human resources for support while she reports him for those actions. What would you do, if anything, and why? Explain.

2. One of your direct reports thinks that you are not acting responsibly or in the best interests of the company with him or the department in which you work. The direct report has informed you that your communication and work style are lacking and that this is also causing problems with others in the department. You are upset over this news and realize it could cause you problems with your boss and those above. What would you do, when, why, and how?

3. You learn that a woman in your department has complained about sexually improper advances toward her by your boss and another more senior person above that boss. You know the woman but not well. She may be right in this instance. You have heard rumors that she often exaggerates and sometimes can't be trusted. You don't particularly like her and are concerned about your own reputation if she's wrong. What would you do and why?

4. Your department boss wants you to select a few others in your organization to explore adopting corporate social responsibility practices. Some of your friends think that CSR isn't effective and in fact wastes resources and time of those who get involved. To take on this assignment would require time out of doing your own work. However, you have noticed that your organization's leadership isn't all that responsible and responsive to employees and many customers. Maybe adopting more ethical standards and practices could improve business and some of the questionable leaders' behaviors. What would you do and why?

Critical Thinking Case

Wells Fargo

The Wells Fargo recent crisis over mismanaging customer relationships, fraudulently implementing illegal and unethical sales practices with trusted clients, has cost the company in fines, lost business, and the resignation of the CEO. The following online sources offer a narrative and factual source of what happened, when, to whom, and why. Use these sources to answer and provide evidence to the following questions to present to the class:

1. What were the sources and causes the problems in the first place? Explain.
2. Who were some of the primary decision makers that led to the illegal sales activities?
3. What were these individuals' motives and motivations?
4. How were the illegal and fraudulent activities discovered?
5. Who was to blame?
6. What unethical activities occurred before the illegal actions took place?
7. What would you have done, if anything, had you been one of the sales professionals pressured to engage in unethical, illegal practices there?
8. How would a stakeholder approach, if taken by the company's top leaders and board of directors, have possibly prevented the crisis?

Sources: Comrie, Harley, "Wells Fargo Fake Accounts Scandal", Seven Pillars Institute, March 15, 2017, http://sevenpillarsinstitute.org/case-studies/wells-fargo-fake-accounts-scandal ; "Wells Fargo Banking Scandal a Financial crisis We Can Finally Understand", *The Guardian*, accessed January 2, 2019, https://www.theguardian.com/business/us-money-blog/2016/oct/07/wells-fargo-banking-scandal-financial-crisis; Glazer, Emily, "Wells Fargo's Textbook Case of Botched Crisis Management", The Wall Street Journal, October 13, 2017, https://www.wsj.com/articles/wells-fargos-textbook-case-of-how-not-to-handle-a-crisis-1476380576.

Introduction

Learning Outcomes

After reading this chapter, you should be able to answer these questions:

1. Why is it important to understand and appreciate the importance of international management in today's world?
2. What is culture, and how can culture be understood through Hofstede's cultural framework?
3. How are regions of the world categorized using the GLOBE framework, and how does this categorization enhance understanding of cross-cultural leadership?
4. Why is an understanding of cultural stereotyping important, and what can students do to prepare for cultural stereotyping by looking at social institutions?
5. What steps can you undertake to be better prepared for cross-cultural assignments?
6. What are the main strategies that companies can use to go international?
7. Why might it be necessary for a company to go international, and how might it accomplish this goal?

EXPLORING MANAGERIAL CAREERS

Mike Schlater, Domino's Pizza

Domino's Pizza has more than 14,000 stores worldwide. As executive vice president of Domino's Pizza's international division, Mike Schlater is president of Domino's Canada with more than 440 stores. Originally from Ohio, Schlater started his career with Domino's as a pizza delivery driver and worked his way up into management. Schlater saved his earnings, and with some help from his brother, he was able to accept the opportunity to have the first international Domino's franchise in Winnipeg, Manitoba, in 1983. Within weeks, Schlater's store in Canada reached higher sales than his previous store in Ohio had ever attained.

However, it was not an easy start. Schlater faced a number of challenges going international. First, he had to identify the international suppliers and get them approved to sell their products to Domino's. This shows one of the challenges that organizations face when entering new global markets. To meet quality standards designed to protect a brand, companies must undertake an extensive review of potential new suppliers to ensure consistent product quality.

Second, as discussed in this chapter, a major challenge when opening a business on foreign soil is negotiating the political, cultural, and economic differences of that country. Domino's relies on local master franchisees to take advantage of their local expertise in dealing with marketing strategies, political and regulatory issues, and the local labor market. The master franchisees of Domino's Pizza's international business are individuals or entities who, under a specific licensing agreement with Domino's, control all operations within a specific country. Such master franchisees have deep local knowledge that helped Domino's succeed. For example, it takes local experience to know that only 30 percent of the people in Poland have phones, so carryout needs to be the focus of the business; that Turkey has changed its street names three times in the past 30 years, so delivery is much more challenging; or that, in Japanese, there is no word for pepperoni, the most popular topping worldwide. These are just a few of the challenges that Domino's has had to overcome on the road to becoming the worldwide leader in the pizza delivery business. Under the leadership of people like Schlater, and with the help of dedicated, local master franchisees, Domino's has been able to not only compete in, but lead the global pizza delivery market.

Such an impressive career path might seem like luck to some, but Schlater achieved his success due to determination and attention to detail. Additionally, despite such success, Schlater has been socially responsible. Consider that Schlater recently won $250,000 in a lottery. Since Schlater believes in philanthropy, he donated the entire amount to Cardinal Carter High School in his hometown. Over the years, Schlater has donated millions of dollars to foundations and charities, such as the London Health Sciences Foundation, because he now has the ability to indulge after spending decades climbing the corporate ladder at Domino's Pizza. Such charitable focus has also shone light on his socially responsible tendencies, another critical aspect of success.

Schlater is now president of Domino's of Canada, Ltd., which operates more than 440 stores located in every province, as well as the Yukon and Northwest Territories.

Sources: "Domino's Pizza Corporate Facts," http://phx.corporate-ir.net, accessed June 20, 2017; Domino's Canada website, https://www.dominos.ca, accessed June 20, 2017; Trevor Wilhelm, "Domino's CEO, who lives in Leamington, will donate $250K lotto winnings to high school," *Windsor Star*, February 27, 2015.

The above example shows that Domino's has successfully managed global challenges to become successful internationally. For many business leaders over the past few decades, the business world was becoming "flat" because barriers to trade were slowly disappearing. The expectation was that soon global companies would operate unconstrained by national borders. However, recent trends suggest that the business world is now seeing a barrage of protectionism and nationalism as many countries and their leaders emphasize the negatives of globalization. Consider that the U.K. is currently experiencing the Brexit negotiations and a potential exit from the European Union. The European Union has provided the means to the U.K. to freely trade with a number of other European countries without hindrance. At the same time, rhetoric about policies and practices to protect local industries against global competition and to protect local jobs is increasing. But does this mean globalization is dead? Far from it—experts have analyzed recent trade data and shown that globalization is actually strengthening. The **DHL Global Connected Index**, which tracks the flow of capital, information, trade, and human resources, indicates that the degree of globalization continues to rise.[1] This finding suggests that any serious management scholar will need to be aware of the importance of international management and the need to be able to adapt practices to ensure that management of global operations goes smoothly.

No company is immune to the forces of globalization. Whether you run a small company based in Wisconsin or manage a Fortune 500 company, you are affected by global forces. You may compete with firms from China or India, have coworkers from Egypt, Brazil, or Germany, or have to negotiate with someone from Russia. This chapter will prepare you for the complexities of international management by discussing some of the crucial issues faced by managers of international companies today. The chapter begins by discussing some of the key factors in making the business world global today and why an understanding of international management is so critical. The chapter then explores the importance of national cultures because cross-cultural conflicts can make an international business difficult to navigate and manage. By understanding the countries and the cultures they find themselves in, international managers can better prepare to deal with such differences, including appropriate preparation for cross-cultural assignments, preferred leadership styles around the world, and the potential for stereotyping.

The chapter concludes with coverage about the various approaches to taking a company international, the advantages and disadvantages of each approach, and the types of business strategies available to companies in the international arena.

6.1 | Importance of International Management

1. Why is it important to understand and appreciate the importance of international management in today's world?

International management is a critical area for any serious student of management because of **globalization**, the worldwide phenomenon whereby the countries of the world are becoming more interconnected and where trade barriers among nations are disappearing. Companies of all kinds are no longer limited to producing and selling their goods and services in domestic markets. In fact, companies are encouraged to explore global markets to stay competitive and are thus likely to have business activity anywhere in the world. Globalization is being facilitated by several key factors, and companies that want to succeed in this environment must understand the key factors that are making the business world more globally connected.

Globalization Factor 1: Lowering Trade Barriers

The first critical factor is the lowering of trade barriers through **trade agreements**, government policies through which countries agree to eliminate cross-border barriers to trade and to promote global integration. To understand the importance of trade agreements, it is necessary to note that countries have long used tariffs to protect local industries and companies. **Tariffs** are taxes that are added to the price of imported international products. Because these tariffs are usually passed along to the consumer in the form of higher prices, imposing tariffs on imported goods gives domestic companies a price advantage and protects them from foreign competition.[2] The goal of most trade agreements has been to reduce or eliminate tariffs and other barriers to make cross-border trade easier.

One of the more significant worldwide trade agreements are the rules members in the World Trade Organization (WTO) agree to.[3] The WTO is the only truly global organization that deals with the rules of trade around the world. It was established January 1, 1995, and had 164 country members as of July 2016. The WTO serves many functions, but the four most important are 1) providing the mechanism for countries to negotiate trade agreements, 2) monitoring such agreements, 3) providing the means to handle trade disputes, and 4) providing training to less-developed countries to implement agreements.

Globalization Factor 2: Foreign Direct Investment

Foreign direct investment (FDI) refers to deliberate efforts of a country or company to invest in another country through the form of ownership positions in companies in another country. In 2017, global FDI flows amounted to USD $1.52 trillion.

Exhibit 6.2 shows the top 15 recipients of FDI in 2016. As you can see, many of the world's developed economies, such as the U.S., Germany, Canada, and France, are among the top recipients of FDI. However, it is also important to note that many emerging markets, such as China, Brazil, Mexico, and India, figure prominently on this list. **Emerging markets**, defined as those markets in nondeveloped countries that present tremendous potential for multinationals, have played a critical role in the global business environment for the last decade. Countries such as Brazil, India, China, and South Africa have all experienced tremendous growth and are driving business trends.

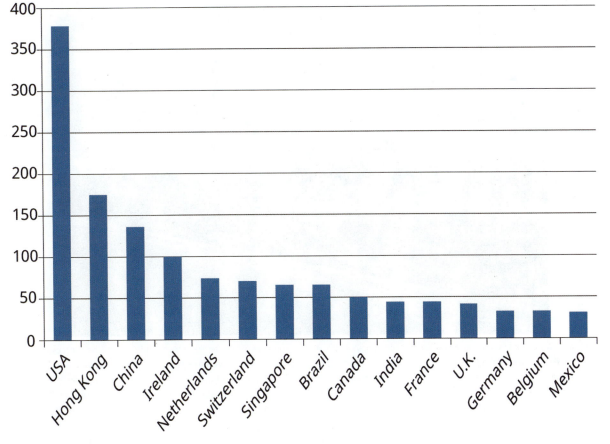

Exhibit 6.2   Foreign Direct Investment Inflows from Other Countries Based on: UNCTAD, 2016, *World Investment Report, 2016*.

An important consequence of the rise of emerging markets has been the growing importance of emerging market multinationals. **Emerging market multinationals** are influential companies from emerging markets that compete head-on with established multinationals and rewrite the rules of competition by using new business models. Consider the case of CEMEX, the Mexican cement manufacturer; Shoprite, the South African retailer; and WIPRO and Infosys, India's leading software companies. These emerging market multinationals are industry leaders in their fields and are pushing more established multinationals to the competitive edge.

Exhibit 6.3   A CEMEX train in Germany   Mexican company CEMEX, whose primary businesses are cement and concrete, has pursued a strategy of differentiation. It defines itself as a provider of solutions for builders and local governments, particularly in emerging economies and for those seeking environmental sustainability. As part of this evolution, CEMEX rebounded from a near bankruptcy during the 2008 economic crisis to regain its position as a leading company in the global construction materials industry. (Credit: Paul Smith/ flickr/ Attribution 2.0 Generic (CC BY 2.0))

The lowering of trade barriers and the increase in foreign direct investment indicate that global trade will continue to stay strong and contribute to globalization. Such trends suggest that companies will need to continue to contend with and take advantage of global opportunities. The rising competition from emerging markets and emerging market multinationals means that companies will need to continue to understand and manage the global environment to compete.

Globalization Factor 3: The Internet

Thanks to the pervasiveness of the Internet today, any company in the world can sell its products to anyone in the world. In fact, the developments in information technology and the reduction in costs of technological equipment mean that any multinational can reach anyone in the world. Social media, such as Twitter and Facebook, also provide a means for multinationals to build relationships with customers worldwide. Data also suggests that even countries that previously had little access to the Internet are now experiencing tremendous growth. To give you more insights on Internet growth, consider **Exhibit 6.4**.

Internet Data

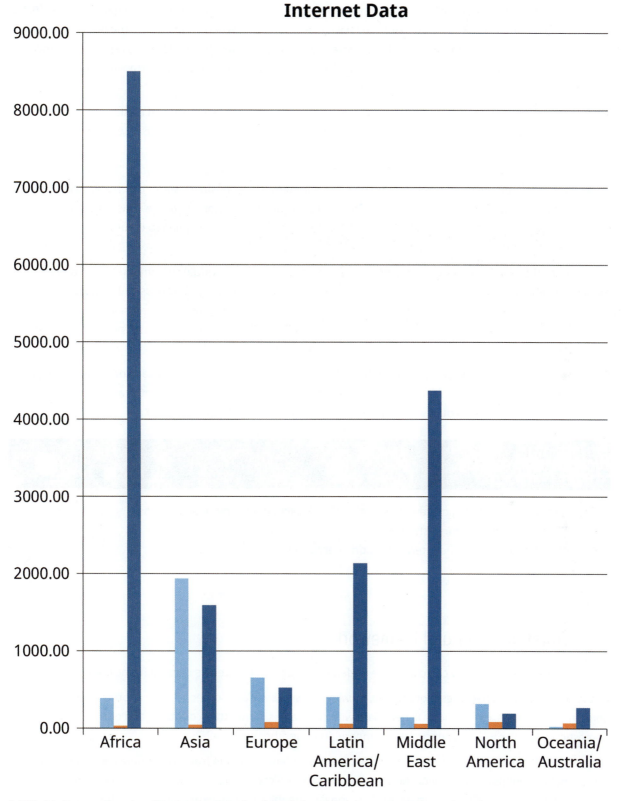

Exhibit 6.4 **Internet Growth and Penetration Rates (% of population with access to Internet)** Based on www.Internetworldstats.com

As **Exhibit 6.4** shows, the pervasiveness of the Internet cannot be ignored. Collectively, Internet users amount to 3.8 billion individuals, representing half of the world's population. Additionally, while the penetration rates in some regions such as Europe and North America are high, the rates of penetration in regions in Asia (46.7%) and Africa (31.2%) suggest that these countries have great potential. When coupled with the dizzying growth rates of the Internet in regions such as Africa (more than 8000% increase from 2000 to 2017), Latin America (2137%), and the Middle East (4374%), any multinationals have to appreciate the importance of the growth of the Internet.

What are the implications of this factor for international management? As mentioned earlier, companies located anywhere in the world will be able to find new markets and new ways to reach new customers. Consider the case of Russian entrepreneur Dmitrii Dvornikov, who was selling jewelry and table clocks made from Russian semiprecious stones.[4] Until 2013, Dvornikov was not able to expand beyond local markets. However, he decided to list his products on eBay. This has allowed his business sales to grow by 30%. Such success was spurred by the implementation of software by eBay's operators in Russia. This software enabled smaller companies to sell anywhere in the world. Such factors have greatly expanded **e-commerce**, the buying and selling of products using the Internet.

E-commerce doesn't necessarily have to be between companies and individual customers. In fact, there are many other forms of e-commerce, such as business-to-consumer (e.g., eBay), business-to-business (B2B, where companies sell to each other), consumer-to-business (C2B, where consumers can sell to businesses), and consumer-to-consumer (C2C, where consumers can sell to other consumers). These forms of e-commerce are all contributing to making the global business world more interconnected.

It is critical for multinationals to appreciate the importance of the Internet. Not only can companies reach new consumers, but they can also improve their business models. Additionally, the Internet provides the opportunity to companies to build relationships with consumers worldwide.

CONCEPT CHECK

1. Describe the lowering of trade barriers and its impact on international business.
2. What is foreign direct investment?
3. What has the role of the Internet had on international business?

6.2 | Hofstede's Cultural Framework

2. What is culture, and how can culture be understood through Hofstede's cultural framework?

As the business world becomes more global, employees will likely face someone from another country at some point in their careers, companies will negotiate with companies from other countries, and even employees of domestic companies will likely encounter someone from another country.

Furthermore, trends suggest that **immigration**, the movement of people from their home country to other countries, will continue to grow worldwide, a process that will contribute to making companies' workforces increasingly diverse. Additionally, many multinational companies rely on expatriates to run their local operations. An **expatriate** is foreign employee who moves to and works in another country for an extended period of time. All of these trends mean that during your career you are likely to encounter someone from a different culture and that the potential for cross-cultural tensions is high. It is therefore important for any international management student to understand culture to better prepare for dealing with such tensions.

According to Geert Hofstede,[5] a Dutch social psychologist, **culture** is "the collective programming of the mind which distinguishes the member of one group or category of people from another." It tells people who they are, which behaviors are appropriate, and which are not acceptable in any society. It affects almost everything we do, see, feel, and believe. In fact, if you have heard of the "American dream," where if one works hard, one can achieve one's dream, you are aware of one characteristic aspect of American culture.

Consider any aspect of your life, and it is likely influenced by your culture. The food you eat, the clothes you wear, and even how you address your boss or teacher are influenced by your culture. Societies develop cultural norms, values, and beliefs to assist their members in adapting to their environments.

Why is an understanding of culture critical to a manager in a global environment? As you have already seen, anyone from any country is likely to encounter someone from another country at the workplace. Such interactions can result in misunderstanding or tensions if not properly managed. Business magazines are full of examples of cross-cultural misunderstandings that have doomed relationships and business. For another example, U.S. managers sent to Beijing, China, get frustrated because they find that their hosts are more interested in socializing than concluding a deal. Understanding Chinese culture would have prevented the latter misunderstanding because the U.S. managers would understand that it is very important for Chinese companies to get to know who they are working with before signing any deal. In this section, you will learn about one of the most powerful tools for understanding cultural differences: **Hofstede's model of national culture**. (See **Table 6.1**)

Hofstede's Model of National Culture				
Countries	Power Distance	Individualism	Uncertainty Avoidance	Masculinity
Australia	Low	High	Low	High
Canada	Low	High	Low	High
China	High	Low	Medium	Medium
Germany	Low	High	Medium	High
Mexico	High	Medium	High	High
France	High	High	High	Low
Spain	Medium	Medium	High	Low
Greece	Medium	Medium	High	Medium
Denmark	Low	High	Low	Low
Finland	Low	High	Medium	Low
Brazil	High	Medium	Medium	Medium
India	High	Medium	Low	Medium
Japan	Low	Medium	High	High

Table 6.1

Hofstede's Model of National Culture				
Countries	Power Distance	Individualism	Uncertainty Avoidance	Masculinity
U.K.	Low	High	Low	High
U.S.A.	Low	High	Low	High
Adapted from Geert Hofstede, "*Culture's consequences: Comparing values, behaviors and institutions across nations*," 2nd edition, 2001, Thousand Oaks, CA: Sage Publications.				

Table 6.1

Although there are several frameworks to understand cultural differences, one of the most powerful is Hofstede's model.[6] Hofstede is a Dutch social scientist who developed his model by surveying over 88,000 employees in IBM subsidiaries from 72 countries. Hofstede developed this cultural model primarily on the basis of differences in values and beliefs regarding work goals. Hofstede's framework is especially useful because it provides important information about differences between countries and how to manage such differences. Recent reviews of research have shown the utility of Hofstede's framework for a wide variety of managerial activities, such as change management, conflict management, leadership, negotiation, and work-related attitudes.[7]

Cultural Dimension 1: Power Distance

Hofstede's original survey of the more than 88,000 employees of the 72 countries revealed four major cultural dimensions. The first cultural dimension is **power distance**, the degree to which members of a society accept differences in power and authority. In societies with **high power distance**, people are more likely to accept that power inequality is good and acceptable. People in high power distance societies are more likely to accept that there are some powerful people who are in charge and that these people are entitled to special benefits. In contrast, societies with **low power distance** tend to consider that all members are equal. Table 6.2 shows the levels of power distance (and the other cultural dimensions discussed later) in 15 selected societies. Hofstede's scores range from 100 (the highest power distance) to 0 (the lowest). In the table, we break Hofstede's scores into high (70–100), medium (40–69), and low (0–39).

Implications of Power Distance		
Type of Work Activity	High Power Distance	Low Power Distance
Organizational structures	• Very centralized • Tall hierarchies with clear levels of managers and subordinates	• Flat organizational hierarchies • Decentralized structures

Table 6.2

Implications of Power Distance		
Type of Work Activity	High Power Distance	Low Power Distance
Managerial authority	• Concentration of authority at the top • Managers rely on formal rules to manage • Authoritative managerial style and decision making	• Dispersed authority • Managers rely on personal experience • More consultative or collaborative forms of decision making
Relationship with supervisors	• Subordinates expect to be told what to do • Perfect boss is seen as one who is an autocrat • Information sharing constrained by hierarchy	• Subordinates often expected to be consulted • Ideal manager is seen as a democratic leader • Openness to sharing information
Other issues	• Wide salary gap between top and bottom of organization • Managers often feel underpaid and dissatisfied with careers	• Low salary gap between top and bottom of company • Managers feel paid adequately and are satisfied

Adapted from Geert Hofstede, "*Culture's consequences: Comparing values, behaviors and institutions across nations*," 2nd edition, 2001, page 107-108, Thousand Oaks, CA: Sage Publications.

Table 6.2

As **Table 6.1** shows, many of the emerging markets in regions such as Asia and Latin America, such as India, Brazil, and Mexico, all have high power distance scores. In such countries, the concern for hierarchy and inequality in organizations is rooted in early socialization in the family and school. In these countries, children are expected to obey their parents and elders. When these children enter school, teachers assume the dominant role. Children must show respect, and they seldom challenge a teacher's authority. As these individuals take on work roles, the allegiance to teachers is transferred to bosses. Thus, people in high power distance societies will seldom question their supervisors. In contrast, Anglo countries such as the United States, Canada, and the United Kingdom have low power distance. In these countries, people do not expect power differences, and everyone is seen as an equal.

Management Implications of Power Distance

What are the implications of power distance for international management? **Table 6.2** shows some of the key differences between high and low power distance societies for work-related issues. As you can see, it is important for managers to express their authority and know-how in high power distance societies. Subordinates expect clear directions from their managers and assume they will be told what to do. In high power distance societies, employees will often equate age with wisdom and seniority. For instance, if a multinational is sending people to negotiate in a high power distance country, they should send higher-level and older managers if they want to be taken seriously.

Cultural Dimension 2: Individualism and Collectivism

The second cultural dimension we consider here is individualism/collectivism. **Individualism** refers to the degree to which a society focuses on the relationship of the individual to the group. **Collectivism** refers to the degree to which a society focuses on the relationship of the group as a whole.

In societies with high individualism (or low collectivism) scores, individuals are valued for their achievements and are rewarded and recognized for such achievements. In contrast, people who live in societies with low individualism (high collectivism) are seen as being part of a wider group, known as the in-group. The in-group includes the family, team, or social class, and how individuals relate to such wider groups is seen as important to their success. In other words, people's success is gauged by how others in their groups view and support them.

Table 6.3 shows the levels of individualism in the same selected 15 nations. We again see similar patterns whereby more Anglo cultures such as the U.S., Canada, and the U.K. have relatively high levels of individualism. In contrast, Asian, Latin American, and many emerging countries tend to have cultures that are either on the medium or low range of the individualism dimension. **Table 6.3** shows some of the implications of individualism for management. The effects of most management practices are determined by whether they are done at a group or individual level. For example, in countries with low individualism, one will find that employees are hired and promoted mostly on the basis of association with a larger group, such as a university or high school. In such societies, emphasis is placed on loyalty, seniority, and age. To operate smoothly in such societies, companies need to appreciate the importance of the larger social group. Additionally, as **Table 6.3** also shows, care should be taken in terms of how rewards are distributed. Rewarding individual team members in low individualism societies can result in tensions because the individual team member may become stigmatized. In such cases, rewards done on a group level may work best.

Implications of Individualism		
Type of Work Activity	Low Individualism/High Collectivism	High Individualism/Low Collectivism
Relationship with companies	• Employees act in the interest of in-group (members of the family or same university) • Employee commitment to company relatively low • Employee-employer relationships is almost like a family link	• Employees act in their own interests • Employee commitment to organizations high • Employee-employer relationship based on the market

Table 6.3

Implications of Individualism		
Type of Work Activity	Low Individualism/High Collectivism	High Individualism/Low Collectivism
Human resource, management	• Hiring and promotion takes in-group into consideration • Better to reward based on equality (give everyone the same reward) rather than equity (base reward on work effort) Relatives of employees preferred in hiring • Training best when focused at group level	• Hiring and promotions based on rules • Family relationships unimportant in hiring • Better to reward based on equity • Training done best individually
Other issues	• Belief in collective decisions • Treating friends better than others is normal • Support of teamwork • Less mobility across occupations • Personal relationships very critical in business	• Belief in individual decision making • Treating friends better than others at the workplace is considered unethical • More mobility across occupations within company • Tasks and company prevail over personal relationships in business
Adapted from Geert Hofstede, "*Culture's consequences: Comparing values, behaviors and institutions across nations*," 2nd edition, 2001, page 169-170, Thousand Oaks, CA: Sage Publications.		

Table 6.3

Cultural Dimension 3: Uncertainty Avoidance

Hofstede's third cultural dimension is **uncertainty avoidance**, the degree to which people in a society are comfortable with risk, uncertainty, and unpredictable situations. People in high uncertainty avoidance societies tend to want to avoid uncertainty and unpredictability. As a result, work environments in such countries try to provide stability and certainty through clear rules and instructions. In contrast, societies with low uncertainty avoidance are comfortable with risk, change, and unpredictability. In these countries, risky and ambiguous situations are less likely to upset people.

Table 6.4 shows details of the levels of uncertainty avoidance for the selected 15 countries. We see that Anglo and Scandinavian countries have relatively lower uncertainty avoidance scores. In contrast, many emerging markets (such as Brazil, Mexico, and China) have medium to high uncertainty avoidance scores. Such findings suggest that companies should adapt their practices to conform to the levels of uncertainty avoidance. In high uncertainty avoidance countries, for example, managers are advised to provide structure and order to reduce uncertainty and ambiguity for subordinates. Companies in these cultures have many written rules and procedures that tell employees exactly what the organization expects of them. Additionally, managers should give clear and explicit directions to their subordinates about exactly what is expected of them in performing their jobs. By reducing any ambiguity, subordinates are less anxious.

In contrast, in low uncertainty avoidance countries, subordinates are much more comfortable and ambiguity. Managers can therefore give more flexibility and freedom to employees. Design of organizations also allows for fewer rules and regulations.

Table 6.4 provides more detail on the implications of uncertainty avoidance on several managerial aspects.

Implications of Uncertainty Avoidance		
Type of Work Activity	Low Uncertainty Avoidance	High Uncertainty Avoidance
Relationship with companies	• Weak loyalty to companies • Average duration of employment shorter • Preference for smaller organizations	• Strong loyalty to employing organizations • Employment are long term in duration • Preference for larger companies
Characteristics of supervisors/managers	• Superiors optimistic about subordinate ambition and leadership abilities • Top managers usually involved in strategy • Power of superiors based on relationships and position • Transformational leaders preferred	• Superiors pessimistic about subordinate ambition • Top managers often involved in operations • Power of superiors based on control of uncertainties • Hierarchical control roles preferred
Entrepreneurship and innovation	• Innovators feel less constrained by rules • Renegade championing • Tolerance for ambiguity in procedures and structures • Innovation welcomed	• Innovators feel constrained by rules • Rational championing • Formalized management structures • Innovation resisted
Based on Geert Hofstede, *"Culture's consequences: Comparing values, behaviors and institutions across nations,"* 2nd edition, 2001, page 169-170, Thousand Oaks, CA: Sage Publications.		

Table 6.4

Cultural Dimension 4: Masculinity

The fourth and final dimension we consider is **masculinity**, the degree to which a society emphasizes traditional masculine qualities such as advancement and earnings. In high masculinity societies, work tends to be very important to people, gender roles are clear, and work takes priority over other aspects of a person's life, such as family and leisure. In addition, masculine societies emphasize earnings and achievements, and employees tend to work very long hours and take very little vacation time.

Table 6.5 shows the masculine scores for selected societies. As the table shows, Anglo cultures such as the U.S. and Canada tend to have high masculinity. This is not surprising given that both the U.S. and Canada tend to have some of the highest number of hours worked. In contrast, Latin European countries such as France and Spain have much lower masculinity as reflected in the importance of leisure in these societies. Scandinavian cultures also reflect low masculinity, a characteristic that is consistent with the preference for quality of life in such countries. We also see that many of the emerging nations have medium to high masculinity.

Table 6.5 provides some more insights into the implications of masculinity differences for work-related issues. As you can see, companies in high masculinity societies can count on very work-oriented employees. Multinationals are therefore advised to motivate their employees through pay and security. In contrast, individuals in more feminine societies tend to prefer interesting work and more leisure. Strong motivational policies in these societies emphasize a balance between work and leisure, and multinationals in such societies tend to have stronger policies catering to both genders.

Implications of Masculinity		
Type of Work Activity	High Masculinity	Low Masculinity
Relationship with work	• Live in order to work • Preference for high pay • Workers look for security, pay and interesting work	• Work in order to live • Preference for lower number of work hours • Workers look for better working conditions and relationships in work
Managers' characteristics	• Managers seen as cultural heroes • Successful managers primarily exhibit male characteristics • Managers need to be competitive, firm, aggressive, and decisive Managers are very ambitious • Fewer women in management • Managers prepared to move family for career reasons	• Managers are employees like others • Successful managers are seen as possessing both male and female characteristics • Managers hold fairly modest career ambition • More women in management • Managers less prepared to uproot family because of career move

Table 6.5

Implications of Masculinity		
Type of Work Activity	High Masculinity	Low Masculinity
Other issues	• Large pay gap between genders Job applicants oversell their abilities • Absences due to sickness lower • General preference for larger companies • Conflicts are resolved through fighting until the best "man" wins	• Low salary gap between top and bottom of company [what about gender gap?] • Managers feel paid adequately and are satisfied • Absences because of sickness higher • Preference for smaller organizations • Conflicts are resolved through compromise and negotiations
Based on Geert Hofstede, "*Culture's consequences: Comparing values, behaviors and institutions across nations*," 2nd edition, 2001, page 318, Thousand Oaks, CA: Sage Publications.		

Table 6.5

One of the underlying themes of cross-cultural research is that countries tend to cluster around cultural dimensions. For instance, we saw how Anglo cultures, Latin American cultures, and Scandinavian cultures countries tend to share similar cultural characteristics. Such categorizations are useful because they help managers simplify their organizational world.

CONCEPT CHECK

1. Describe Hofstede's approach to defining national culture.
2. Describe power distance and its implications for managers in in cultural contexts.
3. Describe individualism versus collectivism and its implications for managers in cultural contexts.
4. Sescribe uncertainty avoidance and its implications for managers in in cultural contexts.

6.3 | The GLOBE Framework

3. How are regions of the world categorized using the GLOBE framework, and how does this categorization enhance understanding of cross-cultural leadership?

A second important cultural framework, the Global Leadership and Organizational Behavior Effectiveness (GLOBE) project provides managers with an additional lens through which they can better understand how to perform well in an international environment. While the Hofstede framework was developed in the 1960s, the **GLOBE project developed in the 1990s** is a more recent attempt to understand cultural dimensions.[8] The GLOBE project involves 170 researchers from over 60 countries who collected data on 17,000 managers from

62 countries around the world.

Similar to Hofstede, the GLOBE researchers uncovered nine cultural dimensions. However, basing their work on Hofstede's cultural dimensions, it is not surprising to note that five of these dimensions are similar to those uncovered by Hofstede, namely 1) uncertainty avoidance, 2) power distance, 3) future orientation (degree to which society values the long term) 4) assertiveness orientation (masculinity), 5) gender egalitarianism (femininity), 6) institutional, and 7) societal collectivism (similar to individualism/collectivism). The only two cultural dimensions unique to the GLOBE project are **performance orientation** (degree to which societies emphasize performance and achievement) and **humane orientation** (extent to which societies places importance on fairness, altruism, and caring).

Similar to Hofstede, the GLOBE researchers categorized countries into **clusters** of countries with similar cultural characteristics. This categorization provides a convenient way to summarize cultural information for a larger number of countries and simplifies the task of the international manager attempting to manage effectively in countries within clusters. Because the clusters include societies with similar cultural profiles, similar cultural adaptations can be made. Although the GLOBE study identified ten clusters, we will discuss only the seven clusters most relevant for international managers: the Anglo cluster, the Confucian Asia cluster, the Germanic Europe cluster, the Nordic Europe cluster, the Latin America cluster, the Middle East cluster, and the sub-Saharan cluster. **Table 6.6** shows these various clusters and the countries in each cluster.

Country Clusters						
Anglo	Confucian Asia	Germanic Europe	Latin America	Nordic Europe	Middle East	Sub-Saharan Africa
Australia	China	Austria	Argentina	Denmark	Qatar	Namibia
Canada	Hong Kong	Switzerland	Bolivia	Finland	Morocco	Nigeria
Ireland	Japan	Netherlands	Brazil	Sweden	Turkey	South Africa (Black)
New Zealand	Singapore	Germany (former East)	Colombia		Egypt	Zambia
South Africa (White)	South Korea	Germany (former West)	Costa Rica		Kuwait	Zimbabwe
United Kingdom	Taiwan		El Salvador			
United States			Guatemala			
			Mexico			
			Venezuela			

Based on Dorfman, P., Paul J. Hanges, and F. C. Brodbeck. 2004. "Leadership and cultural variation: The identification of culturally endorsed leadership profiles." In R. J. House, P. J. Hanges, M. Javidan, P. W. Dorfman, and V. Gupta, eds. *Culture, Leadership, and Organizations.* Thousand Oaks, CA: Sage Publications, 669–720.

Table 6.6

To compare how the different clusters rate different forms of leadership, the GLOBE researchers considered six leadership profiles:

- charismatic type (degree to which the leader can inspire and motivate others)

- team oriented (degree to which the leader can foster a high functioning team),
- participative type (degree to which leaders involve others in decision-making)
- humane-oriented type (degree to which the leader shows compassion and generosity)
- autonomous (degree to which the leader reflects independent and individualistic leadership)
- self-protective (degree to which the leader is self-centered and uses a face-saving approach)

Table 6.7 shows how the various clusters rank these leadership types.

Country Clusters and Preferred Leadership Styles							
Leadership Style	Anglo	Confucian Asia	Germanic Europe	Latin America	Middle East	Nordic Europe	Sub-Saharan Africa
Charismatic	High	Medium	High	High	Low	High	Medium
Team-oriented	Medium	Medium/High	Medium/Low	High	Low	Medium	Medium
Participative	High	Low	High	Medium	Low	High	High
Humane-oriented	High	Medium/High	Medium	Medium	Medium	Low	Medium
Autonomous	Medium	Medium	High	Low	Medium	Medium	Low
Self-protective	Low	High	Low	Medium/High	High	Low	Medium

Based on Dorfman, P., Paul J. Hanges, and F. C. Brodbeck. 2004. "Leadership and cultural variation: The identification of culturally endorsed leadership profiles." In R. J. House, P. J. Hanges, M. Javidan, P. W. Dorfman, and V. Gupta, eds. *Culture, Leadership, and Organizations.* Thousand Oaks, CA: Sage Publications, 669–720.

Table 6.7

Table 6.7 provides further insights to understand how cultural differences affect preferences for leadership styles.[9] Consider, for example, the Nordic Europe cluster, including Scandinavian countries such as Denmark, Finland, and Sweden. These countries have low levels of masculinity, low levels of power, and high individualism. It is therefore not surprising to see that individuals in such societies prefer leaders who are more charismatic and who demonstrate participative leadership tendencies. The least preferred style for this cluster is the self-protective leader, which is more representative of individualist cultures.

Countries in the Latin American cluster (which includes some of the emerging markets of Argentina, Mexico, and Brazil) tend to be more collective, have high power distance, and have high uncertainty avoidance. It is therefore not surprising that leaders who are successful in this cluster are those who make decisions collectively, who treat their subordinates with formality, and who display charisma.

The countries in the Middle East cluster (which includes countries such as Egypt, Morocco, and Turkey) tend to score high on uncertainty avoidance, high on collectivism, and medium on power distance. As a result, because of the high levels of uncertainty avoidance, subordinates are often reluctant to make decisions that involve risk, thereby explaining the high ranking for autonomous leadership style. Thus, it is not surprising that the Middle East cluster prefers leaders who are less participative. Furthermore, the preferred leadership style in this cluster behaves in a collective manner and tries to maintain harmony because of the high level of collectivism.

Although there are cultural differences between clusters, it is important to see that the clusters do share some similarities. For example, the charismatic leadership style is preferred in all clusters except the Middle East cluster. In addition, **Table 6.8** shows that the humane-oriented leadership style is preferred in all but the Nordic Europe cluster.

In contrast, leadership styles based on individualist tendencies, such as the autonomous and the self-protective types, tend to be least preferred.

Traits and Behaviors That Are Universally Admired and Disliked	
Positively-Regarded Traits and Behaviors across the World	
Trustworthy	Dependable
Intelligent	Just
Honest	Decisive
Plans ahead	Effective bargainer
Encouraging	Win-win problem solver
Positive	Skilled administrator
Dynamic	Communicator
Motivator	Informed
Confidence builder	Team builder
Negatively-Regarded Traits and Behaviors across the World	
Loner	Egocentric
Antisocial[what does this mean? is it different from antisocial?]	Ruthless
Not cooperative	Dictatorial
Nonexplicit	
Based on Den Hartog, Deanne N., Robert J. House, Paul J. Hanges, Peter W. Dorfman, S. Antonio Ruiz-Quintanna, and 170 associates. 1999. "Culture specific and cross-culturally generalizable implicit leadership theories: Are attributes of charismatic/transformational leadership universally endorsed?" *Leadership Quarterly*, 10, 219–256.	

Table 6.8

The GLOBE team also found that a number of traits, such as being honest, trustworthy, positive, and dynamic, were viewed positively worldwide and were endorsed irrespective of national culture. Similarly, leadership behaviors such as being a loner, egocentric, and dictatorial were viewed in a negative light by all clusters.

Table 6.8 shows which traits are viewed as positive and which are viewed as negative by the various clusters.

Summary

In this section, we have learned about the various tools that managers can use to understand and prepare for cross-national differences and how they impact behaviors of employees across multinational corporations. We've also seen that there are many similarities among cultures. Relying solely on such frameworks to understand a culture can be misleading, however. In the next section, we discuss some of the dangers of cultural stereotyping and examine the need to be cautious and to take into account the interaction between a nation's culture and its social institutions.

CONCEPT CHECK

1. Describe how the GLOBE tools can be used by managers to prepare for cross-national situations.
2. What are the similarities and differences among clusters?

MANAGING CHANGE

Negotiations in Malaysia and China

You are a rising star in your company, and your CEO asks you to accept an exciting and promising assignment in Malaysia and China, during which you will meet with representatives of your company's local affiliates. In Malaysia, you are introduced to the company executives in a flashy ceremony. You understand that the affiliate's CEO is named Roger, and you have a great time socializing with him. You even decide to show your fondness for him by calling him "Rog." However, later you find that your host's name is actually Rajah.

After your trip to Malaysia, you go to China. You are welcomed lavishly by the local affiliate's executives and are invited to several important meals. Over the next few days, you seem to be spending time mostly at lunches or dinners. Whenever you try to discuss specifics of your products, you find that your hosts are more interested in eating and drinking. You attempt to provide your hosts with contracts that your company has drafted, but you are not successful.

Despite your reservations, you return home feeling strongly about your efforts. However, your CEO soon asks to meet with you. During the meeting, she mentions that neither the Malaysian company nor the Chinese company is interested in doing further business with your company. In fact, both companies decide to go with competitors. The CEO wants to know what happened, and you need to figure out what went wrong.

Discussion Questions

1. Discuss where the United States, Malaysia, and China stand on Hofstede's cultural dimensions.
2. What are the implications of the above differences for how business is conducted in Malaysia and China?
3. How can these cultural differences explain why you were not successful? What should you have

done differently?

6.4 | Cultural Stereotyping and Social Institutions

4. Why is an understanding of cultural stereotyping important, and what can students do to prepare for cultural stereotyping by looking at social institutions?

The above sections provided you with some strong insights into cultural differences. However, despite these observations, cultural scholars often find examples where cultural realities don't necessarily fit neatly or completely into the categories proposed by models. Consider, for instance, that American managers tend to think of themselves as very egalitarian and will typically ask their subordinates to address them by their first name. American managers will also encourage subordinates to share their views on work-related matters. In contrast, Japanese managers are often seen as autocratic, and decisions are driven by those at the top. The implications of such preferences suggest that American managers are more likely to make decisions that reflect the egalitarian position of incorporating subordinates' views. In contrast, the Japanese managers are expected to make decisions on their own, with little input from subordinates. As a result, when American teams and Japanese teams work together, there is often intense confusion. Such confusion stems from the observation that although American managers tend to be viewed as egalitarian, in reality they are not, and decisions are often made unilaterally by those at the top. At the same time, Japanese managers tend to prefer consensus-based decisions even though they are seen as autocratic.

As detailed by Erin Meyer, a professor at INSEAD,[10] the above preferences are often sources of friction when American and Japanese teams work together. Such confusion often occurs because American managers believe that Japanese managers have authority because of the Japanese culture's autocratic preferences. The incident of what happened when Suntory, a Japanese whisky manufacturer, became the majority holder of Jim Beam, an American bourbon maker, clearly illustrates the resulting conflict. When a critical decision had to be made, a Jim Beam manager went to Japan to present the proposal to a Japanese manager, thinking that the manager would have the authority to make the decision. However, the Jim Bean manager found that he was not able to have any effect during the meeting because a decision had already been made by consensus.

The above example shows an instance of a **cultural paradox**, where the insights from an understanding of culture may not necessarily coincide with reality.[11] Why would Japanese managers, who are often perceived as autocratic, take the time to make decisions by consensus? As another example of cultural paradox, the Japanese tend to have a low tolerance for uncertainty because of their high uncertainty avoidance, yet they will often have contracts that incorporate significant ambiguity. In contrast, Americans, who are much more comfortable with uncertainty, write very explicit contracts.

If an international management student or manager doesn't appreciate the importance of cultural paradoxes, she can engage in cultural stereotyping. **Cultural stereotyping** occurs when one assumes that all people within a culture act, think, and behave the same way. While national cultures can provide a lens to gain insights into a country, broad generalizations may not necessarily be helpful. In such cases, it is much more prudent to be cautious and to understand that there are significant differences among people within a culture.

The Role of Social Institutions in International Management

Recent research examining Hofstede's work provides some evidence of the need to be cautious about using culture as the only source of understanding of societies.[12] The researchers examined the ongoing assumption that that all residents of a given country will behave according to broad cultural norms and found that 80% of variation in cultural values is actually *within* countries. In other words, the assumption that people between countries are more different than people within a country may not be accurate. The researchers actually found that other cultural factors pertaining to people's occupations or the country's wealth also play a critical role. These findings suggest that other factors besides national culture need to be examined. One of these factors is a country's social institutions.

A **social institution** is "a complex of positions, roles, norms, and values lodged in particular types of social structures and organizing relatively stable patterns of human resources with respect to fundamental problems in . . . sustaining viable societal structures within a given environment."[13] In other words, as you see below, social institutions such as education and the degree of social inequality have an impact on how individuals within a society behave.

Similar to national cultures, social institutions have strong effects on how people think, act, and behave. While there are many social institutions in any given country or culture, we limit ourselves to the three institutions that are most relevant in the workplace: social stratification, level of education, and religion.

Social Stratification

Social stratification refers to the degree to which "social benefits are unequally distributed and those patterns . . . are perpetuated for life."[14] These social benefits include wealth and distribution of income. Through school and parenting, children are taught to accept such inequality, and over time, it becomes a solidly established, taken-for-granted fact of life. Because the level of social stratification in a country impacts how work elements are perceived, it is important for managers to understand a country's level of social stratification.

Current research suggests that the level of social stratification typically results in societies where only the privileged few have access to jobs with work-related advantages such as the ability to work at enriched jobs that can contribute to personal growth or that may not be under close supervision. In countries with a high level of social stratification, employees may not have a very positive outlook of work. The same research shows that employees in countries with high levels of social inequality tend to have lower levels of attachment to their work. Thus, it is important for multinational managers to understand employee attitudes toward work in the society in which the company operates. **Exhibit 6.5** shows the level of social inequality worldwide as represented by the GINI index, which measures the degree to which income is unequally distributed within a nation. Countries such as South Africa, Lesotho, Namibia, Hong Kong, and Colombia have some of the highest GINI indices, indicating great social inequality. In contrast, countries such as Finland, Moldova, and Germany have among the lowest degrees of social inequality. International management students can use these indices to gain another level of understanding in any society.

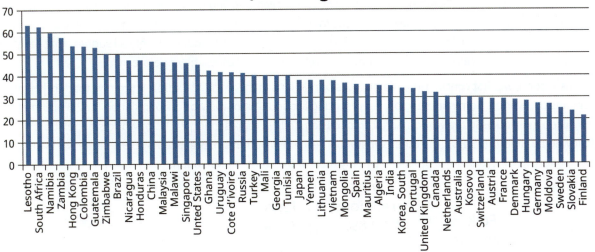

Exhibit 6.5   Level of Social Inequality Based on CIA World Factbook - https://www.cia.gov/library/publications/the-world-factbook/rankorder/2172rank.html

Education

A second social institution is **education**, the socializing experiences which prepare individuals to act in society. Education plays a critical role in socializing individuals into expected norms in their society. One of the critical ways countries differ is on the level of education. In some countries, such as the United States and Western European countries, education is accessible to most members of societies. In other societies, such as many found in Western Africa, South Asia, and Latin America, however, education may be much more elitist and not as accessible to the members of the population.

How does education affect the workplace? Research shows that education has an impact on many aspects of work, including employee attachment to work and gender roles. For example, in a study of 30,270 individuals from 26 countries, the findings show that the more accessible education is, the less likely people are to attach to work.[15] The researchers argue that the more individuals have access to education, the more likely they have the means to feel satisfaction in life and the less likely work plays a critical role. In contrast, where education is less accessible, individuals have to rely on their work to achieve desired rewards.

Another study shows that education also affects how managers view gender roles.[16] Examining a sample of over 1,500 managers located in 19 countries, the study finds that greater accessibility to education affects managers' perception of gender roles. Specifically, in societies with more access to education, managers had less traditional views about the role of women in society and were therefore more open-minded about women in the workplace.

The above findings also point to the importance of education as an influence in society. Societies and individuals that have similar levels of education accessibility may behave more similarly irrespective of cultural differences. Astute international managers are therefore well advised to take such issues into consideration when managing international operations.

Religion

The final social institution we consider is **religion**, the shared set of beliefs, activities, and institutions based on faith in supernatural forces.[17] Religion has always been and continues to be an extremely critical aspect of the international business environment. Most countries have seen a strong growth in popularity of religions. For instance, Islam continues to gain new adherents in many parts of the world. Similarly, the tremendous growth of Protestantism in Latin America and the sustained role of Hinduism in Indian society all suggest that religion has significant influences on societal members as well as the businesses they operate in.

In this section, we first consider the major types of religions in the world.[18] **Exhibit 6.6** shows that Christianity remains the world's dominant religion, representing around 31% of the world's population (or 2.3 billion of the 7.3 billion individuals in the world). Adherents of Islam follow, representing 24.1% of world's population, followed by Hindus (15.1%). The other substantial religion is Buddhism, practiced by 6.9% of the world's population. Finally, Judaism is practiced by only 0.2% of the world's population.

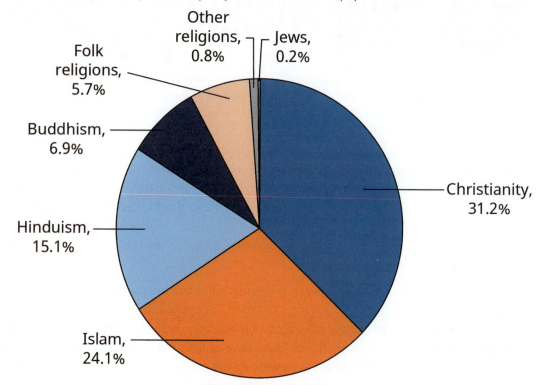

Exhibit 6.6   Religions of the World Based on Pew Research: http://www.pewresearch.org/fact-tank/2017/04/05/christians-remain-worlds-largest-religious-group-but-they-are-declining-in-europe/

Given that Christianity, Islam, and Hinduism represent around 70% of the world's population, we will look at a brief description of each of these religions and their implications for the workplace.[19]

Christianity

Christianity is a faith based on the life, teachings, death, and resurrection of Jesus. Adherents of Christianity all share the same belief that Jesus is the incarnation of God who was sent to clean the sinfulness of humanity. Jesus is often associated with the possibility of humans to connect with God through penance, confessions of one's sins, self-discipline, and purification.

Christianity has strong influences on the workplace. For example, the impact of Protestantism, a branch of Christianity, on the development of capitalism is seen as evidence of the link between religion and the economic structuring of societies. Through Protestantism, wealth and hard work were for the glory of God. This emphasis therefore allowed a focus on goals attached to economic development and wealth accumulation. This belief explains much of the sustained development of capitalism in the Western Protestant societies.

International management scholars recognize that Christianity is generally supportive of business and wealth, and so multinationals located in countries where a majority of people are Christian should expect to face an environment in which work and accumulation of wealth are celebrated. Additionally, recent research also shows that Christianity even affects levels of entrepreneurship in a society.[20] In that study, researchers examined data from a sample of 9,266 individuals from 27 predominantly Christian countries. The study looked at the impact of different manifestations of Christianity on entrepreneurship and found that Christianity encouraged entrepreneurship, especially in societies characterized by strong knowledge investments in research and development. This study provides further evidence that Christianity supports economic development.

Islam

The essence of **Islam**, the second largest of the world's religions, is described in the Qur'an as the submission to the will of Allah (God). It has adherents primarily in Africa, the Middle East, China, Malaysia, and the Far East but is growing rapidly in many countries, especially in Europe. Current evidence suggests that Islamic societies are generally supportive of work and accumulation of wealth as well as entrepreneurship. However, there are some Islamic principles to which multinationals must adhere if they are to succeed in primarily Islamic nations.

Muslim society is very heavily influenced by Islamic standards and norms. Islam provides encompassing guidance in all spheres of life, both social and economic. In fact, the practicing Muslim lives by adhering to the five major pillars of sharia law:

- *Shahada*, or confession (believing and professing the message of Allah)
- prayer (must pray five times a day while facing Mecca, the spiritual home of Islam)
- *Zakat*, or almsgiving (the need to donate a portion of one's income to others to help reduce greed and inequality)
- fasting (the avoidance of eating, including the obligatory fast during the month of Ramadan)
- the *hajj*, or pilgrimage to Mecca (all Muslims who can make the pilgrimage are expected to do so at least once in their lifetime).

These are all important aspects of Islam that have significant implications for the business environment.

For the multinational operating in Islamic nations, these pillars provide important guidance. For instance, managers are advised to provide employees with space and the opportunity to pray. Additionally, adherents of Islam also fast for a month during the month of Ramadan. During that month, Muslim employees are not allowed to eat, drink, smoke, or even take medicines from dawn until dusk. Ramadan is considered holy, and multinational companies should expect their workers to be more concerned with sacred matters and a heightened spiritual atmosphere during this time. Therefore, multinational managers are advised to take steps to ensure that business activities are not disrupted during Ramadan.

Another implication of Islam for global business is that interest is viewed as profits generated without wealth and is therefore prohibited. In most Islamic countries, governments have instituted financial laws that therefore see interest as illegal. For any company with operations in a Muslim country, the prohibition of interest presents a serious challenge both in terms of access to loans as well as repayment of obligations. Multinational companies are therefore strongly advised to work with local banks and financial institutions to find creative ways to pay interest in the form of profit sharing or other financial transactions.

Hinduism

Finally, **Hinduism** is represented by all those who honor the ancient scriptures called the Vedas. There are currently around 760 million Hindus residing in India, Malaysia, Nepal, Suriname, and Sri Lanka. Unlike Christianity or Islam, Hinduism has significant variations in practices and rituals, leading some experts to suggest that there are no central traditions. Other experts suggest that the quest for Brahman, the ultimate reality and truth and the sacred power that pervades and maintains all things, is the ultimate quest for many Hindus.

Similar to the other religions, Hinduism has implications for the way business is conducted. One of the facets of Hinduism is the caste system, which refers to the ordering of Indian society based on four occupational groups: 1) priests, 2) kings and warriors, 3) merchants and farmers, and 4) manual laborers and artisans. Although the caste system is illegal in India today, its original purpose was to create a system that would subordinate individual interests to the collective good.

Unfortunately, the caste system became a legitimate way to discriminate against the lower castes. The system remains a dominant feature of life in India today, and multinational companies operating in India must be aware of it. For instance, having a member of a lower caste supervise higher-caste individuals can be problematic. Additionally, members of lower castes may face promotion ceilings in organizations because of their caste membership. Nevertheless, it is critical for multinationals to play a critical role in reducing discrimination that is fostered by the caste system. Many companies located in India, such as Infosys, have implemented programs to train lower-caste members to get jobs.

Finally, it is important for multinational managers to appreciate Hindu beliefs. One of the most relevant beliefs is that Hindus consider cows sacred. Companies such as McDonald's have been very careful to honor this belief and only offer foods that do not include beef products. Multinational managers also need to be aware of the various Hindu festivals and celebrations because employees generally expect time off and gifts for holidays such as Diwali, the festival of lights.

Summary

This section presented some of the social institutions that may bring a deeper understanding of cross-national differences. Relying solely on national culture dimensions may not be useful in the presence of cultural paradoxes. Carefully understanding a nation's social institutions can therefore bring additional insights into better international management.

CONCEPT CHECK

1. Describe the social institutions that can provide a deeper understanding of cross-national differences.

---

2. How can managers use insights from Hofstede and GLOBE in conjunction with an understanding of social institutions?

6.5 | Cross-Cultural Assignments

5. What steps can you take to be better prepared for cross-cultural assignments?

At some point in your career, you are very likely to be asked to be involved in cross-cultural operations. You may encounter employees from other countries in the local company you work for, or your company may send you to another country to run international operations. When these situations arise, you will need to be prepared to manage cultural differences. In this section, we discuss some of the things companies and individuals can do to better prepare for cross-national differences.

One of the goals of any cross-cultural training is to increase an employee's cultural intelligence. **Cultural intelligence** refers to "individuals' capabilities to function and manage effectively in culturally diverse settings."[21] The culturally intelligent manager is someone who can operate without difficulty in cross-national settings. Recent research suggests that cultural intelligence is made up of four dimensions:

*   a **cognitive dimension**, focusing on the individual's knowledge of values and practices inherent in the new culture acquired through education and personal experiences
*   a **meta-cognitive dimension**, which reflects an individual's ability to use cross-cultural knowledge to understand and adapt to the cultural environment they are exposed to
*   a **motivational dimension**, which reflects the ability and desire to continuously learn new aspects of cultures and adapt to them
*   a **behavioral dimension**, based on the ability of the individual to exhibit the appropriate forms of verbal and nonverbal behaviors when interacting with people from another culture

To give you more insights into the cultural intelligence measure, **Table 6.9** provides some representative statements used to gauge a person's understanding of these four dimensions of cultural intelligence various aspects of cross-cultural interactions.

Cultural Intelligence Statements	
Metacognitive	• I am conscious of the cultural knowledge I use when interacting with people with different cultural backgrounds. • I am conscious of the cultural knowledge I apply to cross-cultural interactions.
Cognitive	• I know the legal and economic systems of other cultures. • I know the cultural values and religious beliefs of other cultures.
Motivational	• I enjoy interacting with people from different cultures. • I enjoy living in cultures that are unfamiliar to me.

Table 6.9

Cultural Intelligence Statements	
Behavioral	• I change my non-verbal behavior when a cross-cultural interaction requires it. • I alter my facial expressions when a cross-cultural interaction requires it.

Based on Jacob Eisenberg, Hyun-Jung Lee, Frank Bruck, Barbara Brenner, Marie-Therese Claes, Jacek Mironski and Roger Bell, "Can business schools make students culturally competent? Effects of cross-cultural management courses on cultural intelligence," *Academy of Management Learning and Education*, 2013, Vol. 12, pp. 603-621.

Table 6.9

Cross-Cultural Training through Education and Personal Experience: Low and High Rigor

Current research suggests that cross-cultural training can influence cultural intelligence. At a basic level, you can acquire cultural intelligence by taking classes in your program. Research has shown that taking cross-cultural management courses can enhance cultural intelligence.[22] For example, in a study of 152 MBA students, researchers found that cultural intelligence of the students increased after they took a cross-cultural management course. In another longitudinal study, researchers found that study abroad has significant impact on the cognitive and metacognitive aspects of cultural intelligence. How do multinationals approach cross-cultural training? The above provides examples of **low-rigor training**, in which individuals are exposed to critical information to help them understand the realities of a different culture but are not actively and directly engaged with the culture.[23] In such cases, instructors transfer basic information and knowledge to students through lectures, books, and case studies.

Low-rigor training has several important disadvantages. Participants often just receive information; they learn that differences exist but do not necessarily learn how to deal with cultural differences in a real-life situation. Furthermore, cross-cultural differences can be very subtle and nuanced, and this method cannot expose participants to such nuances. Balancing these significant disadvantages is one key advantage: low-rigor training tends to be the most cost effective.

Companies can also rely on **high-rigor** methods of training, in which participants are actively engaged in the process and can learn some tacit aspects of cross-cultural differences.[24] Examples of high-rigor training include classroom language training, case studies, and sensitivity training. High-rigor training also includes more experiential approaches such as role-playing, simulations, and field experiences. Some MNCs (multi-national corporations) also offer on-the-job training, during which employees are coached and trained while working at their jobs. This method allows the trainee not only to see the new culture, but also to learn how that culture interacts with the work environment. The advantage of this method is that it enables the participant to be much more actively engaged in learning, thereby facilitating transfer of knowledge. But as you might have guessed, high-rigor training is much more expensive to provide.

Which method works best? Experts agree that it depends on the nature of the assignment. Longer and more complex international assignments benefit from higher-rigor training.[25] Furthermore, because international work assignments tend to be more short-term in nature, ways to enhance the metacognitive aspects of cultural intelligence are necessary.[26] Today, because more managers tend to have more frequent but shorter assignments to international companies, having metacognitive skills is critical. As a result, brief lectures or other low-rigor methods that simply provide information may be useful in helping develop the cognitive aspect but not metacognition. In such cases, high-rigor methods that allow participants to be much more actively engaged with a culture will work well.

When Should Cross-Cultural Training Occur?

Another important aspect of cross-cultural training is the timing of the training. Some multinationals offer **predeparture cross-cultural training**, which provides individuals with learning opportunities prior to their departure.[27] Such training can take the form of 1- to 12-week programs, although two- to three-day programs are also very popular. After such training, the expatriate has a good understanding of expectations, what the local culture looks and feels like, and how to manage any local shocks when they arrive. This approach also makes individuals about to go to another country less anxious about the unknown.

Multinationals will also often opt for **postarrival cross-cultural training**, which occurs after an expatriate has arrived in the foreign country and can address issues in "real time." Armed with local cultural knowledge and training, the expatriate can delve into work issues without worrying about daily living issues.

Recent research provides evidence of the utility of cross-cultural training. For example, a recent study of 114 expatriates showed that both predeparture and postarrival training had positive effects on several aspects of their success.[28] Specifically, in a study in Vietnam, the findings show that both predeparture and postarrival training positively impacted the ability of expatriates to adjust to their work and general environment. Additionally, such training was also effective in enhancing the ability of expatriates to better interact with locals. The researchers also examined the impact of language training. Not surprisingly, expatriates who received training in the local language were better able to adjust to local interaction than others.

The above study shows that both predeparture and postarrival training are important for success in cross-cultural management. While the study shows that it is most effective for MNCs to provide more than one type of training, the findings also show that postarrival training has the most impact on the types of cross-cultural adjustment. While companies tend to shy away from the more expensive postarrival training, the study suggests that the investment may be worthwhile if it enables expatriates to succeed.

Best practices advise that the optimal time for predeparture training programs is around three to five weeks prior to the international assignment. Training provided too far ahead of time may not be very effective because the expatriate may not activate all learning readiness and may forget the training if it occurs too far ahead of the assignment. Best practices also suggest that postarrival training is best delivered 8 to 12 weeks after arrival. This allows the expatriate to experience cross-cultural interaction and phenomena and to be better ready to gain the most from the training.

Adapting Behavior to the Culture

A final issue that managers need to address is that the training should not focus only on identifying and teaching about differences.[29] Experts agree that this focus on differences is a problem in current cross-cultural training approaches. While identifying and understanding cultural differences is useful and necessary, trainers often don't provide guidance as to how the participants should adapt and react to such cultural differences. It is therefore necessary for the multinational to take the necessary steps to teach cross-cultural sojourners to adapt their behaviors so that they act and react in culturally appropriate ways. Experts also suggest that such training should not be static and limited to web pages or documentation. Training should be integrated with the actual work that the employee is engaging in.

CONCEPT CHECK ✓

1. How should training to manage cultural and regional differences occur?
2. How should training for cross-cultural assignments be implemented?

6.6 | Strategies for Expanding Globally

6. What are the main strategies that companies can use to go international?

In the previous sections, you have learned about the need for a serious international management student to appreciate how countries differ and some possible ways to address these differences. Any company involved in business today also needs to understand the global business environment and how it can play a role in this environment. In the final two sections of the chapter, we look at the three main strategies available to companies as they internationalize and learn how companies can use these strategies to enter global markets.

Global Strategy

Companies can choose to pursue one of three main strategies:

- a **global strategy**, whereby all operations and activities are managed fairly similarly worldwide
- a **regional strategy**, whereby activities and operations are adapted to regional requirements
- a **local strategy**, whereby the company's operations are adapted to fit specific countries.

Global strategy

A global strategy is based on the assumption that the world is extremely interconnected and that patterns of consumption and production are fairly homogeneous worldwide.[30] In such cases, the company simply extends its domestic strategy to the global arena.

Global strategies represent a potential solution to reduce costs. Using standardized products and processes in each of the markets it enters allows a company to possibly achieve economies of scale and scope. The global company will scan the world for opportunities and respond by expanding into those areas where there is potential. Furthermore, it will deploy those activities worldwide depending on where most value is achieved.

A good example of a global strategy is the one pursued by Ford Motor Company.[31] Ford has decided that electric cars will be the vehicles of the future, and it is therefore pursuing a "global electrification strategy," whereby it will use a global platform across many different models and styles. For instance, Ford is now using the "C-platform" to make a variety of vehicles ranging from compact cars (e.g., the Ford Focus) to larger five-passenger cars (e.g., the C-Max). This platform can also be used to build hybrid electric and battery electric cars.

Exhibit 6.7   Electric and Hybrid Vehicles In addition to Ford, many automobile manufacturers have taken a strategic decision to provide electric and hybrid vehicles for the global market. Pictured here is the Toyota Prius hybrid electric vehicle. Toyota takes a regional approach to its global operations. (Credit: Mariordo59/ flickr/ Attribution 2.0 Generic (CC BY 2.0))

Why do some companies pursue global strategies? One major reason is the nature of the industry in which they operate. For instance, the automotive industry lends itself to global approaches because the use of the product and the product being sold are similar worldwide. Thus, if there is the possibility of global markets where global customer needs can be met, a global strategy works well. Additionally, as mentioned earlier, a global strategy also enables cost savings. Because activities are not being adapted to local needs, a company can enjoy the benefits of having the same operations worldwide and enjoying synergistic benefits.

Current discussion of research suggests that few companies are truly global. A recent examination of the Fortune Global 500 companies found that only nine companies were truly global as measured by how sales were globally distributed across a number of countries. These companies include Canon, Coca-Cola, Flextronics, IBM, Intel, LVMH, Nokia, Philips, and Sony.

Regional Strategy

A regional strategy is one in which the company decides that it makes sense to organize its functional activities, such as marketing, finance, etc., around geographical regions that play a critical role in terms of sales. Toyota is an example of a company that has successfully implemented a regional strategy. Because regions such as Europe and North America are sufficiently large but different markets, Toyota has decided that it is worth customizing its operations by regions. In this case, the company has several regional offices that operate independently of Japanese headquarters.

A regional strategy is appropriate if companies find that the benefits from dispersing their activities far outweigh the benefits of coordination. For Toyota, having independent units based on regions makes a lot of sense because each region has specific needs that can better be addressed with a regional rather than a global approach. For instance, consider that the price of gasoline is significantly higher in Europe than in the United States. Using a regional approach to the design and manufacture of more- or less-fuel-efficient cars makes much more sense than having a "one size fits all" car designed for a global market.

Local Strategy

The local strategy is the one in which a company adapts its products to meet the needs of the local market. For instance, experts argue that despite the perception that customers want global products, significant cultural and national value differences still suggest that some level of customization is necessary. This is especially critical for some functional areas, such as marketing. People across cultures have different purchasing and usage habits. Furthermore, they respond differently to promotional campaigns and other advertising messages. In such cases, a local strategy may be necessary.

An example of a local strategy is McDonald's product offerings in India.[32] Given the taste and vegetarian preference of India as well as the consideration that cows are sacred, the company famous for its hamburgers does not offer any beef or pork products. Rather than offend its customers, McDonald's restaurants in India offer burgers made of potatoes and peas (McAloo Tikki); burgers made of beans, green peas, onions, and carrots (McVeggie); and burgers made of paneer, India's cheese (McSpicy Paneer). The only meats that McDonald's sells at its restaurants in India are chicken (McChicken) and fish. Furthermore, the products are adapted to fit the local preference for spicy foods, and offerings such as the Masala Grill chicken and the McSpicy Chicken.

Despite the attractiveness of a local strategy, it is not without disadvantages. The local strategy is much more costly because it requires companies to duplicate resources and departments around the world. Additionally, because of the differences in local activities and operations, it may be difficult for the company to achieve learning or cost savings across subsidiaries. The nature of some markets, however, may require that a local strategy be adopted.

MANAGERIAL LEADERSHIP

From Regional to Global

Bayer Crop Science is a division of Bayer, a leading global company based in Leverkusen Germany. The Crop Science division's main goal "is to be able to produce enough food, feed, fiber and renewable raw materials for a growing world population on the limited land available."[33] It has been involved in many of the latest innovations in agriculture, such as developing apps for farmers to help them understand their crops, climates, and so on and developing the ability to use drones to assess crop quality.

One of Bayer Crop Science's units is the Global Public and Government Affairs (GPGA) division, which is in charge of monitoring and proactively complying with local government policies. In 2012, Bayer Crop Science had a large number of independent country GPGA divisions that acted independently, thereby limiting collaboration and cooperation. As a result of this regional strategy as described earlier, critical information about policy priorities from different regions was slow to reach headquarters, and Bayer

Crop Science was not able to quickly address policy challenges worldwide.

In 2013, Bayer Crop Science hired Lisa Coen to implement a more global strategy in the GPGA division.[34] Her main task was to make the GPGA division a truly global organization. To accomplish her task, she first travelled extensively around the world to meet with the business unit leaders and the public affairs team members. Through this process, she wanted to engage with the key stakeholders to prevent any resistance to change from building up. During these meetings, she discovered that the various local and regional GPGA units had deep knowledge that would greatly help Bayer Crop Science face and manage public policy issues all over the world. The meetings also allowed her to come up with the best strategy to turn the various regional units into a global unit.

To build a more collaborative organization, Coen had to move from a traditional and hierarchical organization based on regions to a globalized network of units. To demonstrate the need for such a system, Coen invited key individuals to a global meeting to work collectively on public policy issues. Through this exercise, she was able to show the group the critical importance of a network organization. Through team-building exercises, Coen showed how the entire group had to move around to meet with the key people in each region. This interaction allowed the group to commit to a network model that would support and build a global organization.

Discussion Questions

1. Why did Bayer Crop Science decide to move from its original regional organization of units to a more global network of units? What were the advantages and disadvantages of this approach?
2. How did Coen build support for the change? Do you believe this was an appropriate way?
3. What challenges do you anticipate as Coen continues to build a network organization?**

Summary

Companies choose international strategies based on their capabilities and skills as well as on the structure and nature of the industry in which they operate. Companies choose regional strategies if they feel that the regions have differences significant enough to justify such an approach. In contrast, companies elect a global strategy if they believe they have global products that can satisfy global consumer needs.

It is important to note, however, that companies rarely adopt the pure forms of strategy as we've described them. Many companies adopt hybrid structures, where some functional areas may be approached globally while other activities may be approached more regionally or locally.

CONCEPT CHECK

1. How and why do companies take various approaches to global operations?

6.7 | The Necessity of Global Markets

7. Why might it be necessary for a company to go international, and how might it accomplish this goal?

In this section, we explore some of the methods companies can use to go international and how they might implement them. As we have seen so many times before, each method for entering international markets has its advantages and disadvantages, and it is up to the international management team to figure out which is most suitable for its company and for the countries in which it operates.

Reasons for Internationalization

Before we get into how companies can go international, let's look at why a company might want to expand internationally in the first place. Because navigating cross-cultural environments is fraught with dangers but holds the possibility of great success, we must understand the compelling reasons to go international.

Trade Facilitation

At a basic level, relying on a domestic market can be problematic. Because of the many factors enhancing globalization, companies of all sizes and types want to take advantage of global markets to expand and achieve sustainable competitive advantage. Despite some slowdown in trade, business-to-consumer e-commerce is expected to double to $2.2 trillion over the span 2018 to 2021 due to improvements in IT and the use of the web.

Growth Opportunities

Another critical factor that supports internationalization is that emerging markets such as China, India, Brazil, and Malaysia will continue to grow and present companies with tremendous opportunities. Research from the Boston Consulting Group suggests that such emerging markets experienced growth (as measured by GDP growth rate), surpassing more developed economies by 2.2%.[35] Furthermore, this research predicted that economic growth in emerging markets accounted for 68% of worldwide growth in 2013 despite an economic slowdown. Finally, experts also predict that incomes in emerging markets will continue to rise.

How to Go International 1: Exporting

Given that it is critical for companies to go global, there are various means that companies can use to do so. The most basic and cost-effective approach is **exporting**, whereby a company sends its product to an international market and fills the order just as it fills a domestic order. Our earlier example of Dmitrii Dvornikov (who was selling jewelry and table clocks made from Russian semiprecious stones to international customers on Russia's eBay) is a simple example of exporting. However, companies can also become more involved in the process and have dedicated offices in another country to tackle exports. In fact, some companies may find that exporting is so critical that they create a dedicated export department.

Because exporting is one of the easiest ways to go international, it can bring many benefits.[36] Current research suggests that companies that export tend to be 17% more profitable than companies that don't. Additionally, exporting provides the ability for companies to defend their markets by becoming more competitive in other markets. Furthermore, by exploring international markets, a company can acquire critical cross-cultural management skills, thereby increasing the value of the company. Consider the case of DeFeet International, a U.S. maker of socks for cyclists.[37] Despite several major disasters during the company's existence (it burned down in 2006), DeFeet has been able to survive and expand thanks to the global market. The company hired an international marketing manager to get advice on how to develop a market strategy for Europe. Because of its strong research and development, DeFeet International has been able to develop the best socks for cycling. While production still takes place in the U.S., exporting has resulted in distributors in over 35 countries.

Despite the many benefits of exporting, companies are often reluctant to do so. Much of such fear is based on some assumptions about how business is done. For instance, managers often assume that exporting can be too risky, but some argue that selling only to domestic markets is just as risky. Some companies believe that exporting is too cumbersome or that getting paid for exports is too complicated and not worth the time. However, experts believe that exporting is not as complicated and can be easily done through the right channels. Finally, some companies believe that they are too small to export. However, research shows that nearly 30% of all U.S. exporters in 2005 had 19 employees or less.[38] This finding suggests that exporting is a viable strategy, even for small firms. To give you more insights into these assumptions, **Table 6.10** summarizes some of these myths and counterarguments.

Myths About Exporting and Counterarguments	
Myths	Reality
Exporting is risky.	Selling domestically is as difficult as exporting to some markets. Additionally, not all markets are necessarily risky.
It is difficult to get paid for exports.	Buying and selling internationally is now fairly routine. There are numerous ways to ensure reliable payment.
Exporting is so complicated.	Exporting requires minimal paperwork. It is now very easy to search for buyers using the internet. There are many intermediaries available to help with exports.
I can't succeed because I don't speak another language.	As mentioned in the chapter, there are many organizations offering help with translation etc. Setting up global websites can be seamless now.
My product won't do well in other markets.	If you do well in the U.S., your product will probably do well in other countries. There are many services available to test the market.
Based on U.S Department of Commerce, "A basic guide to exporting," 11th edition, 2015, https://www.export.gov/article?id=Why-Companies-should-export	

Table 6.10

Solving a Disadvantage of Exporting through Licensing and Franchising

Although exporting is an easy way to go international, it has some disadvantages. Exporting does not give much control to the company in terms of how the product is presented in the international market. For instance, if the company decides to use an international intermediary to sell its product abroad, it is at the mercy of that intermediary. Additionally, exporting sometimes requires travelling and other tasks that may take managers away from domestic activities. In the light of such disadvantages, companies will often resort to licensing.

Licensing is a contractual agreement whereby, in exchange for a royalty or fee, a company gives the right to another company to use a trademark, know-how, or other proprietary technology. Similar to exporting, licensing is an easy way for a company to enter an international market quickly and without the need for laying out much capital. A licensor often has some asset that it can offer to the licensee in exchange for a fee. This asset might include a valuable patent, a trademark, technological know-how, or a company name that the licensor provides to the licensee in return for a payment.

A recent study of European firms' entry to the Vietnamese market shows that these companies relied on licensing.[39] For instance, consider Haymarket Media, one of the largest publishers in the United Kingdom. Haymarket enters into simple licensing agreements with the local affiliates to provide generic content to all worldwide licensees. This content is similar in all overseas editions of its magazines. However, through this licensing arrangement, the country affiliate adds local content. In this way, Haymarket has been able to increase sales of existing content by selling it in new global markets.

International franchising takes licensing up a notch. Rather than simply license some specific aspect of the value chain, a company will license the complete business model. The business model usually includes trademarks, business organization structures, technologies and know-how, and training. Similar to licensing, the franchisor owns a trademark that the franchisee pays a royalty for. Additionally, the franchisee will usually pay for the right to use the business model of the franchisor.

Many fast food companies have relied on franchising agreements to enter the Indian market.[40] As India has experienced economic growth, more people have greater amounts of disposable income. In addition, because more couples are now busy working, they rely more on fast food as a meal option. Companies such as McDonald's, KFC, Domino's Pizza, and Pizza Hut have all entered franchising agreements with local companies to sell their products. This move has proven to be very successful because the franchisors have been able to expand their markets while the franchisees have seen significant profits in the local Indian markets.

Similar to other forms of entry, licensing and franchising have benefits and disadvantages. In terms of benefits, both forms of entry provide the receiving company with an established brand or some other technological know-how that has already proved itself. The recipient of the franchise agreement doesn't need to build a new reputation but can rely on a well-known international competitor. For the franchisor, this often provides a quick way to expand revenue from an existing business model. Additionally, while licensing and franchising are cost effective ways to go international, the companies granting the license or franchise still retain control over their product. If things don't work out as planned, the licensor can end the agreement. For the franchisee, an added benefit is that corporate support is provided to help the company succeed.

Disadvantages of Licensing and Franchising

Both licensing and franchising have disadvantages that can affect both the recipient of the agreement and the grantor of the agreement. For instance, a study of Indian entrepreneurs entering into franchise agreements with fast food companies in the United States reported that the master franchisor had too much control.[41] Furthermore, a franchise agreement can be risky and capital intensive for the local companies. For the licensor or franchisor, the biggest disadvantage is that the company can create a new competitor. While the host country laws may dictate the terms of agreement, local enforcement of these laws may not always be strong. Thus, a local company can therefore use the business model for its own purpose. Furthermore, compared to exporting, the licensor gives up additional control. Once the agreement is signed, it is possible for the licensee to sell the product at a lower price or with lower quality. This has the potential to affect reputation of the licensor.

How to Go International 2: Strategic Alliances

Because of some of the dangers of licensing and franchising, companies can often get even more involved in global operations by engaging in strategic alliances. **International strategic alliances** occur when two or more companies from different countries enter into an agreement to conduct joint business activities. Strategic alliances are often the preferred means of entry in emerging markets because they make it easier to do business in the country. A strategic alliance is a way for a foreign company to bypass barriers imposed by local governments.

A prominent example of one of the most successful strategic alliances is the one entered into by Nissan and Renault in 1999.[42] In this case, both companies were facing situations in which finding an international partner made sense. Nissan had historically low profitability and needed to find a partner. In contrast, Renault had just ended a failed relationship with Volvo and also needed to expand globally. Furthermore, both companies had what the other partner needed. For instance, Nissan had a strong presence in North America, providing a much-needed boost to Renault's global ambition. Nissan also had strong engineering abilities that would benefit Renault. In contrast, Renault had ample cash and superior design capabilities, both of which Nissan needed.

The Nissan-Renault example shows some of the benefits of strategic alliances. Strategic alliances often provide both partners with sorely needed skills or capabilities. Strategic alliances also often provide access to new markets and customers. In terms of going global, a company may not always have the necessary know-how or financial assets to enter an international market. Strategic alliances therefore provide the means for a company to spring into the international domain. In that context, China remains an attractive destination for many multinationals. China's market presents tremendous potential given the increase in disposable income. A recent study sheds some light on the many aspects of entering alliances in China.[43] **Exhibit 6.8** therefore provides you with some of the main benefits foreign companies expect to gain from strategic alliances.

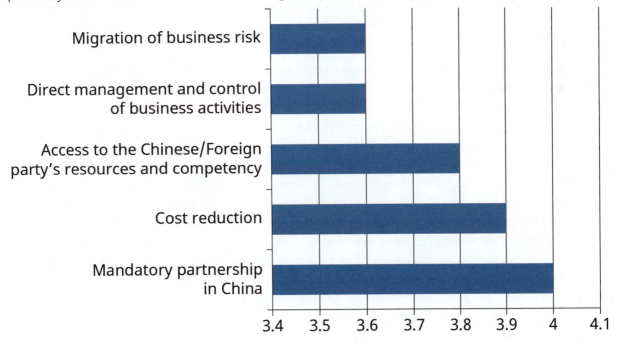

Exhibit 6.8   Reasons to Enter Strategic Alliances Based on PWC, 2015, "Courting China Inc: Expectations, pitfalls, and success factors of Sino-foreign business partnerships in China," http://www.pwccn.com/webmedia/doc/635705701963346674_china_joint_venture.pdf

Strategic alliances also enable companies to share resources to develop new technologies and make technological advances. This issue is acknowledged by the South Korean government, which encourages South Korean small and medium enterprises to enter into strategic alliances with foreign partners as a way to gain access to advanced technology as well as getting management skills to expand internationally. A recent study examined data from South Korea and found that entering strategic alliances also allowed companies to enjoy higher productivity.[44]

Disadvantages of Strategic Alliances

Despite these advantages, strategic alliances are notorious for high failure rates. A major reason is that strategic alliances are very difficult to manage. Additionally, strategic alliances often present partners with the possibility of acting opportunistically. This can occur when a partner tries to access technological know-how that they were not originally privy too. Alliance partners may also decide to refuse to agree to the original terms of the strategic alliance contracts. Finally, strategic alliances inevitably involve ambiguity and uncertainty. Properly managing such ambiguity is also necessary to avoid disadvantages associated with such alliances.

MANAGERIAL LEADERSHIP

McDonald's in India

McDonald's has had significant success in India. In 1996, it opened its first restaurant. Today, it has over 380 restaurants in India. McDonald's has been successful because it adequately examined cultural differences and found ways to address cultural challenges. As mentioned earlier, the practice of Hinduism, the dominant religion in India, results in preferences for vegetarian meals. McDonald's therefore developed many vegetarian menu items while also integrating local foods. It also recognized the very diverse nature of Indian society and offers appropriate regional and local foods in different regions.

To enter the Indian market, McDonald's entered into strategic alliances with two companies that were responsible for different parts of India.[45] However, despite the success, McDonald's is currently embroiled in a business war with one of two individuals who helped McDonald's come to India. In 1996, McDonald's entered into a 50-50 joint venture with Vikram Bakshi of Connaught Place Restaurants Limited. Over the subsequent decades, Bakshi was able to expand McDonald's significantly in the east and north of India. However, in 2008, McDonald's tried to buy back Bakshi's share for $7 million. Bakshi used evidence from an accounting firm to argue that his share was worth $331 million. In the face of this challenge, McDonald's had Bakshi fired as an alliance partner in 2013. Baskhi has been fighting McDonald's in Indian courts. He sued to be reinstated and to be able to run his stores without interference from McDonald's corporate headquarters. When McDonald's tried to take Bakshi to the London Court of International Arbitration, he was able to get a local Indian court to agree that he was being subjected to "oppression and mismanagement." Although another court has agreed to allow McDonald's to sue Bakshi in London, he is now appealing in another Indian court. This experience has revealed some of the worst fear of multinationals about the dangers of strategic alliances and the need to respect the local courts.

Discussion Questions

1. Why did McDonald's choose to use strategic alliances to enter India? Why not use exporting or other means?
2. Why is McDonald's facing challenges in India? What disadvantages of strategic alliances do these challenges reflect?
3. What can McDonald's do to address Bakshi's concerns?
4. What can McDonald's do about Bakshi's use of local Indian courts? How can multinationals adequately prepare for such situations?**

How to Go International 3: Foreign Direct Investment

Given the difficulties associated with strategic alliances, some companies elect to be wholly vested in the host country. This final form of international entry, which we discussed at the beginning of the chapter, is **foreign direct investment (FDI)**, which occurs when a company invests in another country by constructing facilities and buildings in that country. FDI can also occur through mergers and acquisitions, whereby a multinational company fully acquires a company in another country. Many car companies, such as Toyota, Honda, BMW, and Nissan, have fully operational plants in the United States. For example, many of the BMW SUVs, such as the BMW X3 and X5, are fully built in the BMW plant in Spartanburg, South Carolina.

Why do some companies choose FDI as a means of international entry? For BMW, FDI allows the company to be closer to its customers and to also sell the car as an American car. Additionally, because some countries may impose tariffs on imported products or otherwise discourage imports, building a plant locally allows a company to bypass such restrictions. Furthermore, FDI can also provide access to local expertise or to cheaper costs of labor, both of which can help a company become more competitive through reduced costs.

Disadvantages of FDI

As you might expect, FDI as an entry mode is not without difficulties. While this method gives the company the most control, it is also the most capital intensive. A multinational engaged in FDI is also exposed to the **political risk** of a country, the degree to which political decisions can impact a business's ability to survive in that country. For instance, throughout history, countries such as Venezuela have used governmental decrees to appropriate investment from U.S. oil companies. Finally, it is important to note that FDI also involves additional coordination risks and can drain resources from local operations. A company that engages in FDI must be able to coordinate and integrate foreign and domestic operations.

The Incremental Path to Internationalization: The Uppsala Model

The above sections also provided some insights into how some companies can start small (say, with exporting) and eventually have FDI activities in some countries. One of the most popular ways to understand this development path of internationalization is the **Uppsala model**, which argues that "as firms learn more about a specific market, they become more committed by investing more resources into that market."[46] In this model, companies adopt an incremental approach to internationalizing. First, they develop a solid domestic market base. After they have a strong domestic foundation, they start exploring international markets and eventually export products to markets that they feel have close psychic distance. **Psychic distance** refers to the many differences that exist between countries because of language, cultural characteristics, social institutions, and business practices. Countries with close psychic distance are similar to each other in all these variables; those with greater psychic distance are less similar. As a firm continues to gain international experience, it will start exporting to countries with greater psychic distance. As the firm gains even more international experience and knowledge of international markets, it will eventually want to have production facilities in the overseas market.[47]

The Uppsala model has been criticized on many fronts. Experts argue that this approach may oversimplify a very complex process. It is also criticized as being too deterministic because some companies may skip stages. The latter criticism is valid when we consider the case of **born globals**, companies that operate internationally from the day they are created.

The All-In Approach to Internalization: Born Globals

Born globals are considered key to most countries' economic development. A recent report suggests that born globals were significant contributors to exports in countries such as Poland and Australia. Additionally, the Organisation for Economic Co-operation and Development (OECD), a leading international organization comprising many of the world's leading economies, has argued that born globals were key engines that tackled the economic downturn that occurred after the financial crisis of 2007. It is therefore critical for the international management student to understand born globals.

Born globals have been made possible because of the many factors we discussed earlier that are making the world more global: the rapid development and decreasing costs of many types of information technologies have allowed companies to go international from the day they are created. Consider the case of M-PESA, the world's leading mobile-money company, created in 2007 in Kenya.[48] Because of M-PESA, it is now easier to pay for a taxi ride using your mobile phone in Nairobi, Kenya, than in New York. M-PESA was created by Safaricom, Kenya's largest mobile-network operator. A customer can sign up for the service at one of the 40,000 agents throughout Kenya and place money in the account. Money can then be transferred to others by using a mobile phone. This has proved to be very useful because so many people work in Kenya's major cities and need to transfer money to their family, who often life far away in rural areas. The mobile-money service provides a safe and convenient way to move money around in unsafe environments. The development in IT has also allowed M-PESA to quickly expand globally. Today it has 30 million users in 10 countries.[49]

Current research suggests that born globals are unique in many ways.[50] When compared to other start-ups, born globals tend to have higher employment and job growth rates. Born globals also serve a wider global market than domestic start-ups. Additionally, while born globals tend to experience similar internationalization patterns of smaller entrepreneurial firms, they have much more aggressive learning strategies as a result of becoming global much faster than others.[51]

Given the critical importance of born globals, what are the factors that contribute to their success? Current research suggests that a number of factors, such as marketing competence, effective pricing, advertising and distribution capabilities, product quality, and so on, all contribute to the success of such companies.[52] Studies also show that prior experience of managers in combining resources from different countries and having a global vision are also important. To give you more insights, **Table 6.11** discusses the success factors for born globals based on several studies.

Success Factors of Born Globals	
Study Sample	Key Success Factors
21 British firms	• Product uniqueness • New product development ability • Ability to meet customer specification • Company reputation
Companies based in U.S. and Denmark	• Marketing competence • Control of marketing processes • Effective pricing • Advertising and distribution • Product quality and differentiation
New ventures in Irish shellfish sector	• Maintaining closer relationship with international customers • Product differentiation • Proactive personality and global mindset of company founder
Irish low-technology International New Ventures	• Dynamic capability - ability for firms to constantly develop new capabilities to identify opportunities and respond
Polish born globals	• Product quality • Product pricing

Based on studies reviewed in Lidia Danik and Izabela Kowalik, "Success factors and development barriers perceived by the Polish born global companies. Empirical study results," *Journal for East European Management Studies,* 2015, Vol. 20, pp. 360-390.

Table 6.11

Summary

In the above sections, you have learned about the different ways in which a company can go international. Some companies have minimal engagement and only export. Others are fully vested and build production plants overseas. Yet others choose to go global from inception. Each entry mode has its benefits and costs, advantages and disadvantages. How do companies choose among these entry types?

The primary factors in the internalization decision are how much control the company wants to have over operations and how much of the company's resources (physical, financial, natural, human) it wants to expend to go international. For example, if a company doesn't want to invest or spend too much to access global markets but still wants to explore them, it can simply export. But with this method, the company has less control over operations, such as how the product is marketed and sold. However, if companies want to control all activities and if they have the resources, they can get involved in FDI. In such cases, the companies have significant control but at much higher costs.

A recent study of banks provides further insight into this issue.[53] For instance, the more a bank required local resources in the form of local reputation or the availability of a local branch network to offer services, the more likely the company was to use joint ventures or acquisitions as forms of international entry. If a bank wanted to have greater control in terms of being able to manage its activities to achieve its goals, it would be more likely to acquire local firms. In some cases, banks needed this degree of control so that they could coordinate the activities to achieve economies of scale.

To become born globals, companies need to understand whether they have many of the success factors discussed in **Table 6.11**. Furthermore, all companies going international face risks, such as the barriers to export initiation (such as insufficient finances and knowledge of international market) and other complexities associated with transferring money across borders (fluctuation in exchange rates, payment delays, etc.).[54] Companies also face political risk in terms of foreign government intervention in the form of tariffs or foreign exchange controls. Companies need to determine whether they can work around these barriers.

CONCEPT CHECK

1. What are the factors and approaches that organizations can take when deciding to go global?
2. Explain the term *born global* and why it is important for companies to take this approach.

🔑 Key Terms

Born globals Companies that operate internationally from the day that they are created.

Christianity Faith based on the life, teachings, death, and resurrection of Jesus.

Clusters Representing countries that share similar cultural characteristics.

Cultural intelligence Refers to the individuals' capabilities to function and manage effectively in culturally diverse settings.

Cultural paradox Insights from an understanding of culture may not necessarily coincide with reality in that culture.

Cultural stereotyping Occurs when one assumes that all people within a culture act, think, and behave the same way.

DHL Global Connected Index Index tracking the flow of capital, information, trade, and human resources and representing the degree of globalization.

E-commerce Buying and selling of products using the Internet.

Education Socializing experiences that prepare individuals to act in society.

Emerging market multinationals Influential companies from emerging markets that are competing head-on with established multinationals and rewriting the rules of competition by using new business models.

Emerging markets Those markets in countries that present tremendous potential for multinationals.

Expatriate Foreign employee who moves and works in another country for an extended period of time.

Exporting International entry mode where a company sends a product to an international market and fills the order like a domestic order.

Foreign direct investment (FDI) Refers to deliberate efforts of a country or company to invest in another country through the form of ownership positions in companies in another country.

Foreign direct investment (FDI) Involves a company investing in another country through the construction of facilities and buildings in another country.

Global strategy Where all operations and activities are managed fairly similarly worldwide.

Globalization Worldwide phenomenon whereby the countries of the world are becoming more interconnected and where trade barriers are disappearing.

GLOBE project More recent cultural project involving 170 researchers who collected data on 17,000 managers from 62 countries around the world.

High-rigor cross-cultural training Methods of training where participants are much more actively engaged in the training process and can learn some tacit aspects of cross-cultural differences.

Hinduism Represented by all those who honor the ancient scriptures called the Vedas.

Hofstede model of national culture Project involving survey of over 88,000 employees in IBM subsidiaries from 72 countries.

Immigration Movement of people from their home country to other countries; will continue to grow worldwide.

Individualism Degree to which a society focuses on the relationship of the individual to the group.

International franchising Where a company will license the complete business model.

International strategic alliances Two or more companies from different countries enter into an agreement to conduct joint business activities.

Islam Religion whose essence is described in the Qur'an as the submission to the will of Allah (God).

Licensing Contractual agreement whereby a company is given the right to another company's trademarks, know-how, and other intangible assets in return for a royalty or a fee.

Local strategy Company's operations are adapted to fit some specific countries.

Low-rigor cross-cultural training Training where individuals are exposed to critical information to help them understand the realities of a different culture but are not actively engaged in their learning.

Masculinity Degree to which a society emphasizes traditional masculine qualities, such as advancement and earnings.

Political risk Degree to which political decisions can impact a business's ability to survive in a country.

Postarrival cross-cultural training Training provided after the expatriate has arrived to the intended destination.

Power distance Refers to the degree to which societies accept power differences and authority in society.

Predeparture cross-cultural training Learning opportunities provided prior to departure.

Regional strategy Where the multinational adapts activities and operations to regional requirements.

Religion Shared set of beliefs, activities, and institutions based on faith in supernatural forces.

Social institution Complex of positions, roles, norms, and values lodged in particular types of social structures and organizing relatively stable patterns of human resources with respect to fundamental problems in . . . sustaining viable societal structures within a given environment.

Social stratification Degree to which social benefits are unequally distributed; those patterns are perpetuated for life.

Tariffs Extra charges that are added to the price of international products in the form of additional taxes or higher prices as a way to give domestic companies a price advantage while also protecting these companies from foreign competition.

Trade agreements Popular policy instruments that countries agree on to eliminate cross-border barriers to trade and to promote global integration.

Uncertainty avoidance Refers to the degree to which people in a society are comfortable with uncertainty and unpredictable situations.

Uppsala model of internationalization Model that argues that as firms learn more about a specific market, they become more committed by investing more resources into that market.

▣ Summary of Learning Outcomes

6.1 Importance of International Management

1. Why is it important to understand and appreciate the importance of international management in today's world?

Any serious management student needs to understand and appreciate the importance of international management in today's global business environment. Whether you work for a domestic company or a foreign company, you will likely need to interact with someone from another country or do business in another country. Understanding international management is therefore critical to address future challenges.

In this section, you learned about the many factors contributing to making globalization a reality: the growth of trade between countries, the growing importance of foreign direct investment, the growing competition from emerging market multinationals, and the globalization-fueling pervasiveness of the Internet. These factors all contribute to making the business world more global.

6.2 Hofstede's Cultural Framework

2. What is culture, and how can culture be understood through Hofsetde's cultural framework?

Given the importance of globalization, any serious international management students will need to be able to understand the cultural aspects of a society in which they may find themselves and will need to learn how to adapt to various cultural conditions. The most popular cultural framework, the Hofstede scheme, was developed by Geert Hofstede, a Dutch social scientist who surveyed over 88,000 employees in 72 countries in which IBM had subsidiaries. He developed this cultural model primarily on the basis of differences in values and beliefs regarding work goals. This effort resulted in four main dimensions: power distance (the degree to which societies accept power differences and authority in society), individualism (the degree to which a society focuses on the relationship of the individual to the group), uncertainty avoidance (the degree to which people in a society are comfortable with uncertainty and unpredictable situations), and masculinity (degree to which a society emphasizes traditional masculine qualities such as advancement and earnings).

6.3 The GLOBE Framework

3. How are regions of the world categorized using the GLOBE framework, and how does this categorization enhance understanding of cross-cultural leadership?

The GLOBE project cultural framework is a much more recent effort that involved 170 researchers who collected data on 17,000 managers from 62 countries around the world. The focus of the GLOBE project was to understand how national cultures have preferences for different leadership styles. One of the strengths of the GLOBE project is that it clusters societies that share similar characteristics. The seven important clusters of the GLOBE project are the Anglo cluster, the Confucian Asia cluster, the Germanic Europe cluster, the Latin America cluster, the Middle East cluster, the Nordic Europe cluster, and the Sub-Saharan cluster. Each cluster rates differently the styles of leadership that the GLOBE researchers considered. The six leadership profiles are charismatic types (degree to which the leader can inspire and motivate others), participative type (degree to which leaders involve others in decision making), humane-oriented type (degree to which the leader shows compassion and generosity), autonomous (degree to which the leader reflects independent and individualistic leadership), and self-protective (degree to which the leader is self-centered and uses a face-saving approach). The various clusters show preferences for specific leadership styles that are consistent with the cultural aspects emphasized in each cluster.

6.4 Cultural Stereotyping and Social Institutions

4. Why is an understanding of cultural stereotyping important, and what can students do to prepare for cultural stereotyping by looking at social institutions?

While the Hofstede and GLOBE culture frameworks are certainly useful and can provide a solid basis for understanding cultural differences, relying solely on cultural dimensions can lead to problems when managers are confronted with cultural paradoxes (when reality doesn't coincide with expectations based on cultural dimensions) and cultural stereotyping (when it is assumed that everyone within the same culture acts and behaves similarly).

To broaden your understanding of cultural differences, you must also take into account a country's social institutions.

While there are a large number of social institutions that can impact international business, we examined three main types of social institutions that affect how people act and behave: social stratification (degree to which social benefits are unequally distributed and those patterns are perpetuated for life), education (the socializing experiences which prepare individuals to act in society), and religion (the shared set of beliefs, activities, and institutions based on faith in supernatural forces).

6.5 Cross-Cultural Assignments

5. What steps can you undertake to be better prepared for cross-cultural assignments?

While the above sections provided you with many diagnostic tools to understand how to evaluate cross-cultural differences, this section presented you with the ways to prepare for cross-cultural assignments. The goal of any training is to increase cultural intelligence, the ability to function and manage effectively in culturally diverse settings. To understand what companies can do to increase cultural intelligence, you learned about various types of training: low-rigor training (where individuals are exposed to critical information but are not necessarily actively engaged in their learning) and high-rigor training (methods of training where participants are much more actively engaged in the training process). You also learned that multinationals can also provide training before someone goes on an international assignment or while someone is already on the assignment.

6.6 Strategies for Expanding Globally

6.   What are the main strategies that companies can use to go international?

As companies explore expanding into international markets, they adopt one of three main strategies, each of which has its advantages and disadvantages depending on the company's and country's characteristics. The three strategies are 1) the global strategy, in which all operations and activities are managed fairly similarly worldwide; 2) the regional strategy, in which the multinational adapts activities and operations to regional requirements; and 3) the local strategy, in which the company's operations are adapted to fit some specific countries.

6.7 The Necessity of Global Markets

7.   Why might it be necessary for a company to go international, and how might it accomplish this goal?

In the final section of the chapter, you first read about the need for companies to go international and learned that some markets present strong potential while others have floundered.

Companies can go international in many ways: exporting (an entry mode where a company sends a product to an international market and fills the order like a domestic order), licensing and franchising (a contractual agreement whereby a company is given the right to another company's trademarks, know-how, and other intangible assets in return for a royalty or a fee), strategic alliances (where two or more companies from different countries enter into an agreement to conduct joint business activities), and foreign direct investment (which involves a company investing in another country through the construction of facilities and buildings in another country).

With each of these methods of entry, there is a trade-off between the cost of a means of entry and the amount of control a company has over its operations. For example, exporting is usually the cheapest way to go international but offers the company the least amount of control. Born globals do not have to think about how or when to go global because they are international from the day they are created.

⌨ Chapter Review Questions

1.   Why is international management a critical area that all management students should be aware of?
2.   Briefly describe the main cultural dimensions of Hofstede's framework. Where does the U.S. stand on each of the dimensions?
3.   What is power distance? What are the implications of power distance for how management is conducted in different societies?
4.   How is the GLOBE project different from the Hofstede project of cultural dimensions? What are the main findings of the study?
5.   What are country clusters? Pick any three clusters and discuss some of the leadership preferences for each cluster.
6.   Compare and contrast low-rigor versus high-rigor cross-cultural training. Provide some examples of each type of training.
7.   What is predeparture cross-cultural training? What is postarrival cross-cultural training? Which method

works best and why?

8. What is a global strategy? When do companies prefer a global strategy?

9. Compare and contrast a global, regional, and local strategy. Discuss some advantages and disadvantages of each method.

10. What are the various means available to companies to go international? When is an exporting strategy most appropriate?

Management Skills Application Exercises

1. Your manager is currently considering negotiations in China, and given your international management knowledge, you are asked for advice. How would you approach preparing to advise her? What type of information will you provide to her?

2. You have a new product, and you are considering exporting the product. Visit the government's export website at **https://www.export.gov/article?id=Why-Companies-should-export**. What are some of the key issues to take into consideration when exporting?

3. You are in charge of HR in your company, and the company will soon need to send an expatriate to Japan. You will need to design a training program to better prepare your employee. What type of training program will you provide? What essential elements will the program include?

4. You are considering investing in Saudi Arabia and know that the business culture there is influenced by religion. Using your knowledge of Islam, what should you expect? How can you better prepare for the investment?

5. You have designed a new surfboard that presents significant advantages over current models. How can you determine whether you are ready to launch your company as a born global?

Managerial Decision Exercises

1. You are the CEO of a company that produces high-end laptops for gaming. You have heard that there is interest in your product from international customers. You need to decide how to enter the international market. What issues do you take into consideration when deciding among the different means of entry? Which approach do you think would work best?

2. Visit Hofstede's cultural dimensions website at **https://www.hofstede-insights.com/models/national-culture/**. Pick two countries and compare them with the United States on the cultural dimensions. How would you manage cultural differences in these countries?

3. Your company is interesting in exploring international expansion into Africa. Visit the African Union's website at **https://au.int/en/**. What are some of the countries included in the African Union? How easy will it be to approach entering these markets?

4. Your company is interested in exploring investments in several sectors in Zimbabwe. Because of political instability, you are obviously very reluctant given the risks of doing business in that country. Using data from **https://www.marsh.com/us/campaigns/political-risk-map-2017.html**, discuss the concept of political risk. When can you decide that investing in Zimbabwe is a good idea?

5. You will be sending one of your employees to several new countries for short-term assignments. You need to decide between low-rigor cross-cultural training and high-rigor cross-cultural training. Which method would work best? How would you decide between the two, and what elements would your training involve?

Critical Thinking Case

SAP and the American CEO of a German Multinational

SAP is a German multinational specializing in enterprise application software. The company was founded by five engineers, and the company is now the world's leading business software maker. Through its software, SAP helps its customers streamline production processes. SAP also provides forecasting services to its customers to help them predict customer trends. It currently has over 87,000 employees in 130 countries assisting over 335,000 customers worldwide.

For the first time in its history, the company is currently headed by an American, Bill McDermott. McDermott's training was in sales, and that provided him with significant expertise to become SAP's current CEO. In 2010, SAP was facing declining revenue worldwide and needed a turnaround. Initially, McDermott was co-CEO with Jim Hagemann Snabe, a Danish executive who was one of the company's cofounders. The arrangement worked well, and when Snabe retired in 2014, McDermott became CEO.

McDermott's success came from the many changes he instituted to better adapt to cultural differences. For instance, he quickly discovered that sales were not very effective in the United States because the salespeople were more interested in focusing on the engineering aspects of SAP's products at the expense of listening to American customers. Such experiences led to the development of more customer-focused innovation and a more empathetic approach to customer needs, things McDermott strongly believes in.

In visiting his German counterparts, McDermott also saw other potential sources of cross-cultural conflict. For instance, he saw that presentations in the United States were much more effective if the presentation quickly engaged the audience and got them excited. In contrast, a German audience preferred a more disciplined, fact-based presentation. McDermott also discovered key differences between the way U.S. companies are managed in comparison to German companies. For example, he found that while U.S. public companies are pressured by quarterly results, SAP was much more interested in 30-year cycles as opposed to 90-day stock price movements.

McDermott's success at managing cross-cultural differences is no surprise. When he was a teenager, he purchased a distressed deli shop in Long Island. Long Island was already a melting pot of immigrants, and he learned how to deal with a diverse group of customers. When he was first hired at 27 to sell Xerox copy machines, he found that American customers do not have a long time for a sales pitch. He learned to be quick and to the point. In contrast, in Asia, he found that you had to focus on developing relationships rather than focus on the product. At the age of 29, he was asked to turn around business in Puerto Rico. There he found employee morale to be very low because of cost-cutting measures. Rather than blindly implementing American management, he listened to the local employees and implemented many measures to improve operations. For instance, he worked to improve customer service. Most importantly, he reinstated a Christmas party that had been canceled as a cost-cutting measure. This lifted morale and led to the turnaround.

McDermott has many important lessons for aspiring cross-cultural leaders. He advises that leaders be respectful of cross-cultural differences. Additionally, because SAP has one global vision, he can have all employees focus on that vision. He therefore also suggests that leaders and managers adopt a compelling vision that can be readily shared with all employees. He also believes that the customer experience is what is critical. Finally, he recommends that the savvy manager be human and empathetic and show humility.

Critical Thinking Questions

1. What are some of the sources of McDermott's excellence at managing cross-cultural differences? How did his experience managing a deli store at a young age help him develop cross-cultural management skills?

2. What are some of the cross-cultural differences he discovered? Using your knowledge of culture, explain some of these differences.

3. What is your assessment of his lessons for cross-cultural managers? Relate these lessons to the GLOBE findings of the effective global leader.

Sources: Geoff Colvin, " A CEO's plan to defy disruption," *Fortune,* November 2014, pp. 36; Michal Lev-Ram, "Inside SAP's radical make-over," Fortune, April 9th, 2012, Issue 5, pp. 35-38; Bill McDermott, "SAP's CEO on being the American head of a German multinational," *Harvard Business Review,* 2016, November, https://hbr.org/2016/11/saps-ceo-on-being-the-american-head-of-a-german-multinational; SAP Corporate Website https://www.sap.com/index.html.

Exhibit 7.1 (Credit: Christian Heilmann / flickr / Attribution 2.0 Generic (CC BY 2.0))

✏️ Introduction

Learning Outcomes

After reading this chapter, you should be able to answer these questions:

1. Why do people become entrepreneurs, and what are the different types of entrepreneurs?
2. What characteristics do successful entrepreneurs share?
3. How do small businesses contribute to the U.S. economy?
4. What are the first steps to take if you are starting your own business?
5. Why does managing a small business present special challenges for the owner?
6. What are the advantages and disadvantages facing owners of small businesses?
7. How does the Small Business Administration help small businesses?
8. What trends are shaping entrepreneurship and small-business ownership?

EXPLORING MANAGERIAL CAREERS

Natalie Tessler, Spa Space

Natalie Tessler has always had an entrepreneurial spirit. After she graduated from New York University's law school, she began working as a tax attorney for a large firm in Chicago. But Tessler soon realized that this left her feeling unfulfilled. She didn't want to practice law, and she didn't want to work for someone else. "I wanted to wake up and be excited for my day," Tessler said. Not until one night, though, when she was having dinner with a friend who recently had begun a writing career, did she realize it was time. "I was listening to her talk about how much she loved her job. Her passion and excitement—I wanted that. I wanted something that grabbed me and propelled me through the day—and being a lawyer wasn't it."

She began searching for what "it" was. She had a tremendous passion and talent for hospitality, entertaining others, and presentation. Seeking an outlet for that flair, she found the spa industry, and the idea for Spa Space was born.

"People think that, owning a spa, I'm able to live this glamorous lifestyle," she laughs. "Owning a spa is nothing like going to one—my nails always are broken from fixing equipment; my back is usually in pain from sitting hunched over a computer trying to figure out the budget or our next marketing promotion." Tessler is a true entrepreneur, embodying the spirit and drive necessary to see her vision become a reality.

Tessler wanted to design a spa that focused on something new: creating a comfortable, personalized environment of indulgence while not neglecting the medical technology of proper skin care. "My father's a dermatologist, so we discussed the importance of making this more than a spa where you can get a frou-frou, smell-good treatment that might actually harm your skin. We both thought it was important to create an experience that is as beneficial for people's skin as it is for their emotional well-being." To address this need, Spa Space has a medical advisory board that helps with product selection, treatment design, and staff training.

Armed with a vision and a plan, Tessler turned her sights toward making it a reality. Spa Space opened in 2001 and has received a great deal of national recognition for its service excellence, unique treatments and products, and its fresh approach to appealing to both men and women. But it hasn't always been smooth sailing for Spa Space. Tessler had to steer the business through several obstacles, including the 9/11 tragedy just three months after the spa's grand opening, and then the Great Recession. Tessler learned to adapt her strategy by refining her target market and the services Spa Space offered. Her resiliency enabled the company to not only survive difficult economic periods, but to thrive and grow 17 years later into what the press recognizes as Chicago's best spa.

Tessler recently turned the reins over to Ilana Alberico, another entrepreneur and founder of Innovative Spa Management, a company that has been named twice to *Inc.* magazine's list of fastest growing companies. When Alberico met Natalie Tessler and learned about her vision, she was inspired to invest in Spa Space. "Natalie's vision still resonates . . . I'm inspired to champion her vision into the future."

Sources: "Our Team," https://spaspace.com, accessed February 1, 2018; Jennifer Keishin Armstrong, "Spa Reviews: Spa Space in Chicago," *Day Spa* magazine, http://www.dayspamagazine.com, accessed February 1, 2018; "About Us," https://ismspa.com, accessed February 1, 2018.

Typical of many who catch the entrepreneurial bug, Natalie Tessler had a vision and pursued it single-mindedly. She is just one of thousands of entrepreneurs from all age groups and backgrounds. Even kids are starting businesses and high-tech firms. College graduates are shunning the corporate world to head out on their own. Downsized employees, midcareer executives, and retirees who have worked for others all their lives are forming the companies they have always wanted to own.

Companies started by entrepreneurs and small-business owners make significant contributions to the U.S. and global economies. Hotbeds of innovation, these small businesses take leadership roles in technological change and the development of new goods and services. Just how important are small businesses to our economy? Table 7.1 provides insight into the role of small business in today's economy.

You may be one of the millions of Americans who's considering joining the ranks of business owners. As you read this chapter, you'll learn why entrepreneurship continues to be one of the hottest areas of business activity. Then you'll get the information and tools you need to help you decide whether owning your own company is the right career path for you. Next you'll discover what characteristics you'll need to become a successful entrepreneur. Then we'll look at the importance of small businesses in the economy, guidelines for starting and managing a small business, the many reasons small businesses continue to thrive in the United States, and the role of the Small Business Administration. Finally, the chapter explores the trends that shape entrepreneurship and small-business ownership today.

7.1 | Entrepreneurship

1. Why do people become entrepreneurs, and what are the different types of entrepreneurs?

Brothers Fernando and Santiago Aguerre exhibited entrepreneurial tendencies at an early age. At 8 and 9 years old respectively, they sold strawberries and radishes from a vacant lot near their parents' home in Plata del Mar on the Atlantic coast of Argentina. At 11 and 12, they provided a surfboard repair service from their garage. As teenagers, Fer and Santi, as they call each other, opened Argentina's first surf shop, which led to their most ambitious entrepreneurial venture of all.

The flat-footed brothers found that traipsing across hot sand in flip-flops was uncomfortable, so in 1984 they sank their $4,000 savings into manufacturing their own line of beach sandals. Now offering sandals and footwear for women, men, and children, as well as clothing for men, Reef sandals have become the world's hottest beach footwear, with a presence in nearly every surf shop in the United States.[1]

The Economic Impact of Small Business
Most U.S. Businesses Are Small:

- 80% (approximately 23.8 million) of the nearly 29.7 million businesses have no employees (businesses run by individuals or small groups of partners, such as married couples).
- 89% (approximately 5.2 million) of the nearly 5.8 million businesses with employees have fewer than 20 employees.
- 99.6% (approximately 5.7 million) of all businesses have 0–99 employees—98% have 0–20 workers.
- Approximately 5.8 million businesses have fewer than 500 employees.
- Only about 19,000 businesses in the United States have more than 500 employees.
- Companies with fewer than 50 employees pay more than 20% of America's payroll.
- Companies with fewer than 500 employees pay more than 41% of America's payroll.
- 32.5 million people (1 employee in 4) work for businesses with fewer than 50 employees.
- These businesses also pay tens of millions of owners, not included in employment statistics.

Table 7.1 Source: "Firm Size Data: 2014," https://www.sba.gov, accessed February 1, 2018.

CATCHING THE ENTREPRENEURIAL SPIRIT

Young Entrepreneur Living the Dream

Jack Bonneau is the quintessential entrepreneur. In the three years he has been in business, he has expanded his product line, opened multiple locations, established strategic partnerships, and secured sponsorship from several national brands. His business has garnered publicity from *The New York Times*, *The Denver Post*, *The Today Show*, *Good Morning America*, and numerous other media. He has shared his business success on several stages, speaking at TechStars and the Aspen Ideas Festival, and recently delivered the closing keynote speech at a national STEM conference. He even landed a gig on *Shark Tank*.

Jack Bonneau is smart, charismatic, an excellent spokesperson, and persistent in his mission. And he is only 11 years old—which also makes him very adorable.

Jack's business was born from a need that most kids have: a desire for toys. He asked his dad, Steve Bonneau, for a LEGO Star Wars Death Star. The problem was that it cost $400. Jack's dad said he could have it but only if he paid for it himself. This led Jack to do what a lot of kids do to earn some extra cash. He opened a lemonade stand. But he quickly learned that this would never help him realize his dream, so, with the advice and help of his father, he decided to open a lemonade stand at a local farmers market. "There were lots of people who wanted to buy great lemonade from an eight-year-old," says Jack. In no time, Jack had earned enough to buy his LEGO Death Star. "I had sales of around $2,000, and my total profit was $900," Jack said.

Jack realized that he was on to something. Adults love to buy things from cute kids. What if he could make even more money by opening more locations? Jack developed an expansion plan to open three new "Jack Stands" the following spring. Realizing that he would need more working capital, he secured a $5,000 loan from Young Americas Bank, a bank in Denver that specializes in loans to children. Jack made $25,000 in 2015.

The following year, Jack wanted to expand operations, so he secured a second loan for $12,000. He opened stands in several more locations, including shopping malls during the holiday season, selling apple cider and hot chocolate instead of lemonade. He also added additional shop space and recruited other young entrepreneurial kids to sell their products in his space, changing the name to Jack's Stands and Marketplace. One of his first partnerships was Sweet Bee Sisters, a lip balm and lotion company founded by Lily, Chloe, and Sophie Warren. He also worked with 18 other young entrepreneurs who sell a range of products from organic dog treats to scarves and headbands.

Jack's strategy worked, and the business brought in more than $100,000 last year. This year, he became the spokesperson for Santa Cruz Organic Lemonade, and he's now looking at expanding into other cities such as Detroit and New Orleans.

Even though Jack is only 11 years old, he has already mastered financial literacy, customer service, marketing and sales, social skills, and other sound business practices—all the qualities of a successful entrepreneur.

Critical Thinking Questions

1. What do you think enabled Jack Bonneau to start and grow a successful business at such a young age?
2. What personal characteristics and values will Jack need to continue running his business while also attending school full-time?

Sources: "About Jack's Stands & Marketplaces," https://www.jackstands.com, accessed February 1, 2018; Peter Gasca, "This 11-Year-Old Founder's Advice Is As Profound as Any You Could Receive," *Inc.,* https://www.inc.com, July 27, 2017; Claire Martin, "Some Kids Sell Lemonade. He Starts a Chain," *The New York Times,* https://www.nytimes.com, February 26, 2016.

Christy Glass Lowe, who monitors surf apparel for USBX Advisory Services LLC, notes, "They [Reef] built a brand from nothing and now they're the dominant market share leader."

The Aguerres, who currently live two blocks from each other in La Jolla, California, sold Reef to VF Corporation for more than $100 million in 2005. In selling Reef, "We've finally found our freedom," Fernando says. "We traded money for time," adds Santiago. Fernando remains active with surfing organizations, serving as president of the International Surfing Association, where he became known as "Ambassador of the Wave" for his efforts in getting all 90 worldwide members of the International Olympic Committee to unanimously vote in favor of including surfing in the 2020 Olympic Games.[2] He has also been named "Waterman of the Year" by the Surf Industry Manufacturers Association two times in 24 years.[3] Santi raises funds for his favorite not-for-profit, SurfAid. Both brothers are enjoying serving an industry that has served them so well.

The United States is blessed with a wealth of entrepreneurs such as the Aguerres who want to start a **small business**. According to research by the Small Business Administration, two-thirds of college students intend to be entrepreneurs at some point in their careers, aspiring to become the next Bill Gates or Jeff Bezos, founder of Amazon.com. But before you put out any money or expend energy and time, you'd be wise to check out **Table 7.2** for some preliminary advice.

The desire to be one's own boss cuts across all age, gender, and ethnic lines. Results of a recent U.S. Census Bureau survey of business owners show that minority groups and women are becoming business owners at a much higher rate than the national average. **Exhibit 7.4** illustrates these minority-owned business demographics.

Why has entrepreneurship remained such a strong part of the foundation of the U.S. business system for so many years? Because today's global economy rewards innovative, flexible companies that can respond quickly to changes in the business environment. Such companies are started by **entrepreneurs**, people with vision, drive, and creativity, who are willing to take the risk of starting and managing a business to make a profit.

Are You Ready to Be an Entrepreneur?

Here are some questions would-be entrepreneurs should ask themselves:

1. What is new and novel about your idea? Are you solving a problem or unmet need?
2. Are there similar products/services out there? If so, what makes yours better?
3. Who is your target market? How many people would use your product or service?
4. Have you talked with potential customers to get their feedback? Would they buy your product/service?
5. What about production costs? How much do you think the market will pay?
6. How defensible is the concept? Is there good intellectual property?
7. Is this innovation strategic to my business?
8. Is the innovation easy to communicate?
9. How might this product evolve over time? Would it be possible to expand it into a product line? Can it be updated/enhanced in future versions?
10. Where would someone buy this product/service?
11. How will the product/service be marketed? What are the costs to sell and market it?
12. What are the challenges involved in developing this product/service?

Table 7.2 Sources: Jess Ekstrom, "5 Questions to Ask Yourself Before You Start a Business," *Entrepreneur,* https://www.entrepreneur.com, accessed February 1, 2018; "Resources," http://www.marketsmarter.com, accessed February 1, 2018; Monique Reece, *Real-Time Marketing for Business Growth: How to Use Social Media, Measure Marketing, and Create a Culture of Execution* (Upper Saddle River, NJ: FT Press/Pearson, 2010); Mike Collins, "Before You Start–Innovator's Inventory," *The Wall Street Journal,* May 9, 2005, p. R4.

Statistics for Minority-Owned Businesses

- The number of Hispanic-owned businesses almost tripled between 1997 (1.2 million) and 2012 (3.3 million).
- The percentage of U.S. businesses with 1 to 50 employees owned by African Americans increased by 50% between 1996 and 2015.
- Almost a million firms with employees are minority owned: 53% are Asian American owned, 11% are African American owned, and almost a third are Hispanic owned.
- 19% of all companies with employees are owned by women.

Table 7.3 Sources: Robert Bernstein, "Hispanic-Owned Businesses on the Upswing," International Trade Management Division, U.S. Census, https://www.census.gov, December 1, 2016; The Kauffman Index of Main Street Entrepreneurship, https://www.kauffman.org, November 2016.

Entrepreneur or Small-Business Owner?

The term *entrepreneur* is often used in a broad sense to include most small-business owners. The two groups share some of the same characteristics, and we'll see that some of the reasons for becoming an entrepreneur or a small-business owner are very similar. But there is a difference between entrepreneurship and small-business management. Entrepreneurship involves taking a risk, either to create a new business or to greatly change the scope and direction of an existing one. Entrepreneurs typically are innovators who start companies to pursue their ideas for a new product or service. They are visionaries who spot trends.

Although entrepreneurs may be small-business owners, not all small-business owners are entrepreneurs. Small-business owners are managers or people with technical expertise who started a business or bought an existing business and made a conscious decision to stay small. For example, the proprietor of your local independent bookstore is a small-business owner. Jeff Bezos, founder of Amazon.com, also sells books. But Bezos is an entrepreneur: He developed a new model—web-based book retailing—that revolutionized the bookselling world and then moved on to change retailing in general. Entrepreneurs are less likely to accept the status quo, and they generally take a longer-term view than the small-business owner.

Types of Entrepreneurs

Entrepreneurs fall into several categories: classic entrepreneurs, multipreneurs, and intrapreneurs.

Classic Entrepreneurs

Classic entrepreneurs are risk-takers who start their own companies based on innovative ideas. Some classic entrepreneurs are *micropreneurs* who start small and plan to stay small. They often start businesses just for personal satisfaction and the lifestyle. Miho Inagi is a good example of a micropreneur. On a visit to New York with college friends in 1998, Inagi fell in love with the city's bagels. "I just didn't think anything like a bagel could taste so good," she said. Her passion for bagels led the young office assistant to quit her job and pursue her dream of one day opening her own bagel shop in Tokyo. Although her parents tried to talk her out of it, and bagels were virtually unknown in Japan, nothing deterred her. Other trips to New York followed, including an unpaid six-month apprenticeship at Ess-a-Bagel, where Inagi took orders, cleared trays, and swept floors. On weekends, owner Florence Wilpon let her make dough.

In August 2004, using $20,000 of her own savings and a $30,000 loan from her parents, Inagi finally opened tiny Maruichi Bagel. The timing was fortuitous, as Japan was about to experience a bagel boom. After a slow start, a favorable review on a local bagel website brought customers flocking for what are considered the best bagels in Tokyo. Inagi earns only about $2,300 a month after expenses, the same amount she was making as a company employee. "Before I opened this store I had no goals," she says, "but now I feel so satisfied."[4]

In contrast, *growth-oriented entrepreneurs* want their business to grow into a major corporation. Most high-tech companies are formed by growth-oriented entrepreneurs. Jeff Bezos recognized that with Internet technology he could compete with large chains of traditional book retailers. Bezos's goal was to build his company into a high-growth enterprise—and he chose a name that reflected his strategy: Amazon.com. Once his company succeeded in the book sector, Bezos applied his online retailing model to other product lines, from toys and house and garden items to tools, apparel, music, and services. In partnership with other retailers, Bezos is well on his way to making Amazon's vision "to be Earth's most customer-centric company; to build a place where people can come to find and discover anything they might want to buy online."—a reality.[5]

Multipreneurs

Then there are *multipreneurs,* entrepreneurs who start a series of companies. They thrive on the challenge of building a business and watching it grow. In fact, over half of the chief executives at *Inc.* 500 companies say they would start another company if they sold their current one. Brothers Jeff and Rich Sloan are a good example of multipreneurs, having turned numerous improbable ideas into successful companies. Over the past 20-plus years, they have renovated houses, owned a horse breeding and marketing business, invented a device to prevent car batteries from dying, and so on. Their latest venture, a multimedia company called StartupNation, helps individuals realize their entrepreneurial dreams. And the brothers know what company they want to start next: yours.[6]

Exhibit 7.2 If there is one person responsible for the mainstream success of solar energy and electric vehicles in the past 10 years, it's Elon Musk, founder and CEO of Tesla. Since the 2000s when he founded Tesla, launching innovation in solar technology, and commercial space exploration with SpaceX, Musk has pioneered countless innovations and has challenged traditional automobile, trucking, and energy companies to challenge and rethink their businesses. *What entrepreneurial type best describes Elon Musk?* (Credit: Steve Jurvetson/ Flickr/ Attribution 2.0 Generic (CC BY 2.0))

Intrapreneurs

Some entrepreneurs don't own their own companies but apply their creativity, vision, and risk-taking within a large corporation. Called **intrapreneurs**, these employees enjoy the freedom to nurture their ideas and develop new products, while their employers provide regular salaries and financial backing. Intrapreneurs have a high degree of autonomy to run their own minicompanies within the larger enterprise. They share many of the same personality traits as classic entrepreneurs, but they take less personal risk. According to Gifford Pinchot, who coined the term *intrapreneur* in his book of the same name, large companies provide seed funds that finance in-house entrepreneurial efforts. These include Intel, IBM, Texas Instruments (a pioneering intrapreneurial company), Salesforce.com, and Xerox.

Why Become an Entrepreneur?

As the examples in this chapter show, entrepreneurs are found in all industries and have different motives for starting companies. The most common reason cited by CEOs of the *Inc.* 500, the magazine's annual list of fastest-growing private companies, is the challenge of building a business, followed by the desire to control their own destiny. Other reasons include financial independence and the frustration of working for someone else. Two important motives mentioned in other surveys are a feeling of personal satisfaction with their work, and creating the lifestyle that they want. Do entrepreneurs feel that going into business for themselves was worth it? The answer is a resounding yes. Most say they would do it again.

CONCEPT CHECK

1. Describe several types of entrepreneurs.
2. What differentiates an entrepreneur from a small-business owner?
3. What are some major factors that motivate entrepreneurs to start businesses?

7.2 Characteristics of Successful Entrepreneurs

2. What characteristics do successful entrepreneurs share?

Do you have what it takes to become an entrepreneur? Having a great concept is not enough. An entrepreneur must be able to develop and manage the company that implements his or her idea. Being an entrepreneur requires special drive, perseverance, passion, and a spirit of adventure, in addition to managerial and technical ability. Entrepreneurs *are* the company; they tend to work longer hours, take fewer vacations, and cannot leave problems at the office at the end of the day. They also share other common characteristics as described in the next section.

The Entrepreneurial Personality

Studies of the entrepreneurial personality find that entrepreneurs share certain key traits. Most entrepreneurs are

- *Ambitious:* They are competitive and have a high need for achievement.
- *Independent:* They are individualists and self-starters who prefer to lead rather than follow.
- *Self-confident:* They understand the challenges of starting and operating a business and are decisive and confident in their ability to solve problems.
- *Risk-takers:* Although they are not averse to risk, most successful entrepreneurs favor business opportunities that carry a moderate degree of risk where they can better control the outcome over highly risky ventures where luck plays a large role.
- *Visionary:* Their ability to spot trends and act on them sets entrepreneurs apart from small-business owners and managers.
- *Creative:* To compete with larger firms, entrepreneurs need to have creative product designs, bold marketing strategies, and innovative solutions to managerial problems.
- *Energetic:* Starting and operating a business takes long hours. Even so, some entrepreneurs start their companies while still employed full-time elsewhere.
- *Passionate.* Entrepreneurs love their work, as Miho Inagi demonstrated by opening a bagel shop in Tokyo despite the odds against it being a success.
- *Committed.* Because they are so committed to their companies, entrepreneurs are willing to make

personal sacrifices to achieve their goals.

ETHICS IN PRACTICE

Ethical Choices Transform Family Business into International Brand

Ever since Apollonia Poilâne was a young girl growing up in Paris, she always knew what she wanted to do when she grew up: take over the family business. But she didn't anticipate how quickly this would happen. When her father—Lionel Poilâne—and her mother died in a helicopter crash in 2002, France lost its most celebrated baker, and Apollonia stepped into the role. She was just 18 years old at the time with plans to matriculate to Harvard in the fall, but the moment her parents had prepared her for had come. As her Harvard admissions essay said, "The work of several generations is at stake."

With organization and determination, Apollonia managed one of the best French bakeries in the world—based in Paris—from her apartment in Cambridge, Massachusetts. She would usually wake up an extra two hours before classes to make sure she would get all the phone calls done for work. "After classes I check on any business regarding the company and then do my homework," she says. "Before I go to bed I call my production manager in Paris to check the quality of the bread." Because the name Poilâne has earned a place with a very small group of prestige bakers, the 18-year-old was determined to continue the tradition of customer satisfaction and quality her grandfather established in 1932. When her grandfather suffered a stroke in 1973, his 28-year-old son, Lionel, poured his heart into the business and made the family bread into the global brand it is today. Lionel opened two more bakeries in Paris and another in London. He developed and nurtured a worldwide network of retailers and celebrities where bread is shipped daily via FedEx to upscale restaurants and wealthy clients around the world.

Experimenting with sourdough is what distinguished Poilâne's products from bread produced by Paris's other bakers, and it has remained the company's signature product. It is baked with a "P" carved into the crust, a throwback to the days when the use of communal ovens forced bakers to identify their loaves, and it also ensures that the loaf doesn't burst while it's baking. Today, Poilâne also sells croissants, pastries, and a few specialty breads, but the company's signature item is still the four-pound *miche*, a wheel of sourdough, a country bread, *pain Poilâne*.

"Apollonia is definitely passionate about her job," says Juliette Sarrazin, manager of the successful Poilâne Bakery in London. "She really believes in the work of her father and the company, and she is looking at the future, which is very good."

Apollonia's work ethic and passion fueled her drive even when she was a student. Each day presented a juggling act of new problems to solve in Paris while other Harvard students slept. As Apollonia told a student reporter from *The Harvard Crimson* writing a story about her, "The one or two hours you spend procrastinating I spend working. It's nothing demanding at all. It was always my dream to run the company."

Her dedication paid off, and Apollonia retained control of important decisions, strategy, and business goals, describing herself as the "commander of the ship," determining the company's overall direction. Today, Poilâne is an $18 million business that employs 160 people. Poilâne runs three restaurants called Cuisine de Bar in Paris and in London, serving casual meals such as soups, salads, and open-faced *tartines*. The company ships more than 200,000 loaves a year to clients in 20 countries, including the United States, Japan, and Saudi Arabia. "More people understand what makes the quality of the bread, what my father spent years studying, so I am thrilled about that," says Apollonia.

Critical Thinking Questions

1. What type of entrepreneur is Apollonia Poilâne?
2. What personal ethics drove Apollonia's decision to take over the family business?

Sources: "About Us," https://www.poilane.com, accessed February 1, 2018; Meg Bortin, "Apollonia Poilâne Builds on Her Family's Legacy," *The New York Times,* https://www.nytimes.com, accessed February 1, 2018; Lauren Collins, "Bread Winner: A Daughter Upholds the Traditions of France's Premier Baking Dynasty," *The New Yorker,* https://www.newyorker.com, December 3, 2012; Gregory Katz, "Her Daily Bread," *American Way* magazine, July 15, 2005, p. 34; Clarel Antoine, "No Time to Loaf Around," *Harvard Crimson,* http://www.thecrimson.com, October 16, 2003.

Most entrepreneurs combine many of the above characteristics. Sarah Levy, 23, loved her job as a restaurant pastry chef but not the low pay, high stress, and long hours of a commercial kitchen. So she found a new one—in her parents' home—and launched Sarah's Pastries and Candies. Part-time staffers help her fill pastry and candy orders to the soothing sounds of music videos playing in the background. Cornell University graduate Conor McDonough started his own web design firm, OffThePathMedia.com, after becoming disillusioned with the rigid structure of his job. "There wasn't enough room for my own expression," he says. "Freelancing keeps me on my toes," says busy graphic artist Ana Sanchez. "It forces me to do my best work because I know my next job depends on my performance."[7]

Exhibit 7.3   Celebrity Ashton Kutcher is more than just a pretty face. The actor-mogul is an active investor in technology-based start-ups such as Airbnb, Skype, and Foursquare with an empire estimated at $200 million dollars. *What personality traits are common to successful young entrepreneurs such as Kutcher?* (Credit: TechCrunch/ Flickr/ Attribution 2.0 Generic (CC BY 2.0))

Managerial Ability and Technical Knowledge

A person with all the characteristics of an entrepreneur might still lack the necessary business skills to run a successful company. Entrepreneurs need the technical knowledge to carry out their ideas and the managerial ability to organize a company, develop operating strategies, obtain financing, and supervise day-to-day activities. Jim Crane, who built Eagle Global Logistics from a start-up into a $250 million company, addressed a group at a meeting saying, "I have never run a $250 million company before so you guys are going to have to start running this business."[8]

Good interpersonal and communication skills are important in dealing with employees, customers, and other business associates such as bankers, accountants, and attorneys. As we will discuss later in the chapter, entrepreneurs believe they can learn these much-needed skills. When Jim Steiner started his toner cartridge remanufacturing business, Quality Imaging Products, his initial investment was $400. He spent $200 on a consultant to teach him the business and $200 on materials to rebuild his first printer cartridges. He made sales calls from 8.00 a.m. to noon and made deliveries to customers from noon until 5:00 p.m. After a quick dinner, he moved to the garage, where he filled copier cartridges until midnight, when he collapsed into bed, sometimes covered with carbon soot. And this was not something he did for a couple of months until he got the business off the ground—this was his life for 18 months.[9] But entrepreneurs usually soon learn that they can't do it all themselves. Often they choose to focus on what they do best and hire others to do the rest.

7.3 | Small Business

3. How do small businesses contribute to the U.S. economy?

Although large corporations dominated the business scene for many decades, in recent years small businesses have once again come to the forefront. Downsizings that accompany economic downturns have caused many people to look toward smaller companies for employment, and they have plenty to choose from. Small businesses play an important role in the U.S. economy, representing about half of U.S. economic output, employing about half the private sector workforce, and giving individuals from all walks of life a chance to succeed.

What Is a Small Business?

How many small businesses are there in the United States? Estimates range from 5 million to over 22 million, depending on the size limits government agencies and other groups use to define a small business or the number of businesses with or without employees. The Small Business Administration (SBA) established size standards to define whether a business entity is small and therefore eligible for government programs and preferences that are reserved for "small businesses." Size standards are based on the types of economic activity or industry, generally matched to the North American Industry Classification System (NAICS).[10]

Small businesses are defined in many ways. Statistics for small businesses vary based on criteria such as new/start-up businesses, the number of employees, total revenue, length of time in business, nonemployees, businesses with employees, geographic location, and so on. Due to the complexity and need for consistent statistics and reporting for small businesses, several organizations are now working together to combine comprehensive data sources to get a clear and accurate picture of small businesses in the United States. **Table 7.4** provides a more detailed look at small-business owners.

Snapshot of Small-Business Owners
• Start-up activity has risen sharply over the last three years, from an all-time low of minus 0.87% in 2013 to positive 0.48% in 2016.
• Between 1996 and 2011, the rate of business ownership dropped for both men and women; however, business ownership has increased every year since 2014.
• The Kauffman Index of Startup Activity, an early indicator of new entrepreneurship in the United States, rose again slightly in 2016 following sharp increases two years in a row.
• New entrepreneurs who started businesses to pursue opportunity rather than from necessity reached 86.3%, more than 12 percentage points higher than in 2009 at the height of the Great Recession.
• For the first time, Main Street entrepreneurship activity was higher in 2016 than before the onset of the Great Recession. This increase was driven by a jump in business survival rates, which reached a three-decade high of 48.7%. Nearly half of new businesses are making it to their fifth year of operation.
• 47% of U.S. businesses have been in business for 11 or more years.
• In 2016, about 25% of all employing firms had revenues over $1 million, but 2% had revenues under $10,000.

Table 7.4 Sources: "The Kauffman Index: Main Street Entrepreneurship: National Trends," http://www.kauffman.org, November 2016; "Kauffman Index of Startup Activity, 2016 (calculations based from CPS, BDS, and BED)," http://www.kauffman.org; "America's Entrepreneurs: September 2016," https://www.census.gov; "Nearly 1 in 10 Businesses with Employees Are New, According to Inaugural Annual Survey of Entrepreneurs," https://www.census.gov, September 1, 2016.

One of the best sources to track U.S. entrepreneurial growth activity is the Ewing Marion Kauffman Foundation. The Kauffman Foundation is among the largest private foundations in the country, with an asset base of approximately $2 billion, and focuses on projects that encourage entrepreneurship and support education through grants and research activities. They distributed over $17 million in grants in 2013.[11]

The Kauffman Foundation supports new business creation in the United States through two research programs. The annual Kauffman Index of Entrepreneurship series measures and interprets indicators of U.S. entrepreneurial activity at the national, state, and metropolitan level. The foundation also contributes to the cost of the Annual Survey of Entrepreneurs (ASE), which is a public–private partnership between the foundation, the U.S. Census Bureau, and the Minority Business Development Agency. The ASE provides annual data on select economic and demographic characteristics of employer businesses and their owners by gender, ethnicity, race, and veteran status.[12] The Kauffman Index of Entrepreneurship series is an umbrella of annual reports that measures how people and businesses contribute to America's overall economy. What is unique about the Kauffman reports is that the indexes don't focus on only inputs (as most small-business reporting has been done in the past); it reports primarily on entrepreneurial outputs—the actual results of entrepreneurial activity, such as new companies, business density, and growth rates. The reports also include comprehensive, interactive data visualizations that enable users to slice and dice a myriad of data nationally, at the state level, and for the 40 largest metropolitan areas.[13]

The Kauffman Index series consists of three in-depth studies—Start-up Activity, Main Street Entrepreneurship, and Growth Entrepreneurship.

• The Kauffman Index of Startup Activity is an early indicator of new entrepreneurship in the United States.

It focuses on new business creation activity and people engaging in business start-up activity, using three components: the rate of new entrepreneurs, the opportunity share of new entrepreneurs, and start-up density.

- The Kauffman Index of Main Street Entrepreneurship measures established small-business activity—focusing on U.S. businesses more than five years old with less than 50 employees from 1997 to 2016. Established in 2015, it takes into account three components of local, small-business activity: the rate of businesses owners in the economy, the five-year survival rate of businesses, and the established small-business density.

- The Kauffman Growth Entrepreneurship Index is a composite measure of entrepreneurial business growth in the United States that captures growth entrepreneurship in all industries and measures business growth from both revenue and job perspectives. Established in 2016, it includes three component measures of business growth: rate of start-up growth, share of scale-ups, and high-growth company density.

Data sources for the Kauffman Index calculations are based on Current Population Survey (CPS), with sample sizes of more than 900,000 observations, and the Business Dynamics Statistics (BDS), which covers approximately 5 million businesses. The Growth Entrepreneurship Index also includes *Inc.* 500/5000 data).

Small businesses in the United States can be found in almost every industry, including services, retail, construction, wholesale, manufacturing, finance and insurance, agriculture and mining, transportation, and warehousing. Established small businesses are defined as companies that have been in business at least five years and employ at least one, but less than 50, employees. **Table 7.5** provides the number of employees by the size of established business. More than half of small businesses have between one and four employees.

Number of Employees, by Percentage of Established Small Businesses	
Established small businesses are defined as businesses over the age of five employing at least one, but less than 50, employees.	
Number of Employees	**Percentage of Businesses**
1–4 employees	53.07%
5–9 employees	23.23%
10–19 employees	14.36%
20–49 employees	9.33%

Table 7.5 Source: Kauffman Foundation calculations from Business Dynamics Statistics, yearly measures. November 2016.

CONCEPT CHECK

1. What are three ways small businesses can be defined?
2. What social and economic factors have prompted the rise in small business?

7.4 Start Your Own Business

4. What are the first steps to take if you are starting your own business?

You have decided that you'd like to go into business for yourself. What is the best way to go about it? Start from scratch? Buy an existing business? Or buy a franchise? About 75 percent of business start-ups involve brand-new organizations, with the remaining 25 percent representing purchased companies or franchises. Franchising may have been discussed elsewhere in your course, so we'll cover the other two options in this section.

Getting Started

The first step in starting your own business is a self-assessment to determine whether you have the personal traits you need to succeed and, if so, what type of business would be best for you. **Table 7.6** provides a checklist to consider before starting your business.

Finding the Idea

Entrepreneurs get ideas for their businesses from many sources. It is not surprising that about 80 percent of *Inc.* 500 executives got the idea for their company while working in the same or a related industry. Starting a firm in a field where you have experience improves your chances of success. Other sources of inspiration are personal experiences as a consumer; hobbies and personal interests; suggestions from customers, family, and friends; industry conferences; and college courses or other education.

Checklist for Starting a Business
Before you start your own small business, consider the following checklist: • Identify your reasons • Self-analysis • Personal skills and experience • Finding a niche • Conduct market research • Plan your start-up: write a business plan • Finances: how to fund your business

Table 7.6 Source: "10 Steps to Start Your Business," https://www.sba.gov, accessed February 2, 2018.

An excellent way to keep up with small-business trends is by reading entrepreneurship and small-business magazines and visiting their websites. With articles on everything from idea generation to selling a business, they provide an invaluable resource and profile some of the young entrepreneurs and their successful business ventures (**Table 7.7**).[14]

Successful Entrepreneurs	
Name and Age	Company and Description
Philip Kimmey, 27	Kimmey's dog-sitting and dog-walking network, Rover.com, raised almost $100 million in venture capital and was valued at $300 million in 2017.
Max Mankin, 27	Mankin cofounded Modern Electron and raised $10 million in venture capital to create "advanced thermionic energy converters" that will generate "cheap, scalable, and reliable electricity." Modern Electron will turn every home into a power station.
Alexandra Cristin White, 28	In her early 20s, White founded Glam Seamless, which sells tape-in hair extensions. In 2016, her self-funded company grossed $2.5 million.
Steph Korey, 29; Jen Rubio, 29	Korey and Rubio founded Away, selling "first-class luggage at a coach price" in 2015. They raised $31 million in funding and grossed $12 million in sales in 2016.
Allen Gannet, 26	Gannet founded TrackMaven, a web-marketing analytics company, in 2012; by 2016, his company was grossing $6.7 million a year.
Jake Kassan, 25; Kramer LaPlante, 25	Kassan and Kramer launched their company, MVMT, through Indiegogo, raising $300,000, and in 2016 grossed $60 million, selling primarily watches and sunglasses.
Brian Streem, 29	Streem's company, Aerobo, provides drone services to the film industry, selling "professional aerial filming and drone cinematography." Aerobo grossed $1 million in 2016, its first full year of business.
Natalya Bailey, 30; Louis Perna, 29	Accion Systems began in 2014, raised $10 million in venture funding, and grossed $4.5 million in 2016, making tiny propulsion systems for satellites.
Jessy Dover, 29	Dover is the cofounder of Dagne Dover, a company making storage-efficient handbags for professional women. She and her cofounders grossed $4.5 million in 2016 and debuted on Nordstrom.com in 2017.

Table 7.7 (Attribution: Copyright Rice University, OpenStax, under CC-BY 4. license)

These dynamic individuals, who are already so successful in their 20s and 30s, came up with unique ideas and concepts and found the right niche for their businesses.

Interesting ideas are all around you. Many successful businesses get started because someone identifies a need and then finds a way to fill it. Do you have a problem that you need to solve? Or a product that doesn't work as well as you'd like? Raising questions about the way things are done and seeing opportunity in adversity are great ways to generate ideas.

Choosing a Form of Business Organization

A key decision for a person starting a new business is whether it will be a sole proprietorship, partnership, corporation, or limited liability company. As discussed earlier, each type of business organization has advantages and disadvantages. The choice depends on the type of business, number of employees, capital requirements, tax considerations, and level of risk involved.

Developing the Business Plan

Once you have the basic concept for a product or service, you must develop a plan to create the business. This planning process, culminating in a sound **business plan**, is one of the most important steps in starting a business. It can help to attract appropriate loan financing, minimize the risks involved, and be a critical determinant in whether a firm succeeds or fails. Many people do not venture out on their own because they are overwhelmed with doubts and concerns. A comprehensive business plan lets you run various "what if" analyses and evaluate your business without any financial outlay or risk. You can also develop strategies to overcome problems well before starting the business.

Taking the time to develop a good business plan pays off. A venture that seems sound at the idea stage may not look so good on paper. A well-prepared, comprehensive, written business plan forces entrepreneurs to take an objective and critical look at their business venture and analyze their concept carefully; make decisions about marketing, sales, operations, production, staffing, budgeting and financing; and set goals that will help them manage and monitor its growth and performance.

Exhibit 7.4 Each year, a variety of organizations hold business plan competitions to engage the growing number of college students starting their own businesses. The University of Essex and the iLearn entrepreneurship curriculum developed by the University of Texas in Austin, which partnered with Trisakti University in Jakarta, Indonesia, and the U.S. embassy to help run an entrepreneurship course and competition are examples of such competitions. Seven students from "iLearn: Entrepreneurship" were selected as finalists to pitch their business plans to a panel of Indonesian business leaders and embassy representatives. The winning business plan, which was an ecotourism concept, earned $1,000 in seed money. *What research goes into a winning business plan?* (Credit: University of Essex /flickr/ Attribution 2.0 Generic (CC BY 2.0))

The business plan also serves as the initial operating plan for the business. Writing a good business plan takes time. But many businesspeople neglect this critical planning tool in their eagerness to begin doing business, getting caught up in the day-to-day operations instead.

The key features of a business plan are a general description of the company, the qualifications of the owner(s), a description of the products or services, an analysis of the market (demand, customers, competition), sales and distribution channels, and a financial plan. The sections should work together to demonstrate why the business will be successful, while focusing on the uniqueness of the business and why it will attract customers. **Table 7.8** describes the essential elements of a business plan.

A common use of a business plan is to persuade lenders and investors to finance the venture. The detailed information in the plan helps them assess whether to invest. Even though a business plan may take months to write, it must capture potential investors' interest within minutes. For that reason, the basic business plan should be written with a particular reader in mind. Then you can fine-tune and tailor it to fit the investment goals of the investor(s) you plan to approach.

Key Elements of a Business Plan
Executive summary provides an overview of the total business plan. Written after the other sections are completed, it highlights significant points and, ideally, creates enough excitement to motivate the reader to continue reading.
Vision and mission statement concisely describe the intended strategy and business philosophy for making the vision happen. Company values can also be included in this section.
Company overview explains the type of company, such as manufacturing, retail, or service; provides background information on the company if it already exists; and describes the proposed form of organization—sole proprietorship, partnership, or corporation. This section should include company name and location, company objectives, nature and primary product or service of the business, current status (start-up, buyout, or expansion) and history (if applicable), and legal form of organization.
Product and/or service plan describes the product and/or service and points out any unique features, as well as explains why people will buy the product or service. This section should offer the following descriptions: product and/or service; features and benefits of the product or service that provide a competitive advantage; available legal protection—patents, copyrights, and trademarks.
Marketing plan shows who the firm's customers will be and what type of competition it will face; outlines the marketing strategy and specifies the firm's competitive edge; and describes the strengths, weaknesses, opportunities, and threats of the business. This section should offer the following descriptions: analysis of target market and profile of target customer; methods of identifying, attracting, and retaining customers; a concise description of the value proposition; selling approach, type of sales force, and distribution channels; types of marketing and sales promotions, advertising, and projected marketing budget; product and/or service pricing strategy; and credit and pricing policies.
Management plan identifies the key players—active investors, management team, board members, and advisors— citing the experience and competence they possess. This section should offer the following descriptions: management team, outside investors and/or directors and their qualifications, outside resource people and their qualifications, and plans for recruiting and training employees.
Operating plan explains the type of manufacturing or operating system to be used and describes the facilities, labor, raw materials, and product-processing requirements. This section should offer the following descriptions: operating or manufacturing methods, operating facilities (location, space, and equipment), quality-control methods, procedures to control inventory and operations, sources of supply, and purchasing procedures.

Table 7.8 Sources: "7 Elements of a Business Plan," https://quickbooks.intuit.com, accessed February 2, 2018; David Ciccarelli, "Write a Winning Business Plan with These 8 Key Elements," *Entrepreneur*, https://www.entrepreneur.com, accessed February 2, 2018; Patrick Hull, "10 Essential Business Plan Components," *Forbes*, https://www.forbes.com, accessed February 2, 2018; Justin G. Longenecker, J. William Petty, Leslie E. Palich, and Frank Hoy, *Small Business Management: Launching & Growing Entrepreneurial Ventures,* 18th edition (Mason, OH: Cengage, 2017); Monique Reece, *Real-Time Marketing for Business Growth: How to Use Social Media, Measure Marketing, and Create a Culture of Execution* (Upper Saddle River, NJ: FT Press/Pearson, 2010).

Key Elements of a Business Plan
Financial plan specifies financial needs and contemplated sources of financing, as well as presents projections of revenues, costs, and profits. This section should offer the following descriptions: historical financial statements for the last 3–5 years or as available; pro forma financial statements for 3–5 years, including income statements, balance sheets, cash flow statements, and cash budgets (monthly for first year and quarterly for second year); financial assumptions; breakeven analysis of profits and cash flows; and planned sources of financing.
Appendix of supporting documents provides materials supplementary to the plan. This section should offer the following descriptions: management team biographies; the company's values; information about the company culture (if it's unique and contributes to employee retention); and any other important data that support the information in the business plan, such as detailed competitive analysis, customer testimonials, and research summaries.

Table 7.8 Sources: "7 Elements of a Business Plan," https://quickbooks.intuit.com, accessed February 2, 2018; David Ciccarelli, "Write a Winning Business Plan with These 8 Key Elements," *Entrepreneur,* https://www.entrepreneur.com, accessed February 2, 2018; Patrick Hull, "10 Essential Business Plan Components," *Forbes,* https://www.forbes.com, accessed February 2, 2018; Justin G. Longenecker, J. William Petty, Leslie E. Palich, and Frank Hoy, *Small Business Management: Launching & Growing Entrepreneurial Ventures,* 18th edition (Mason, OH: Cengage, 2017); Monique Reece, *Real-Time Marketing for Business Growth: How to Use Social Media, Measure Marketing, and Create a Culture of Execution* (Upper Saddle River, NJ: FT Press/Pearson, 2010).

But don't think you can set aside your business plan once you obtain financing and begin operating your company. Entrepreneurs who think their business plan is only for raising money make a big mistake. Business plans should be dynamic documents, reviewed and updated on a regular basis—monthly, quarterly, or annually, depending on how the business progresses and the particular industry changes.

Owners should adjust their sales and profit projections up or down as they analyze their markets and operating results. Reviewing your plan on a constant basis will help you identify strengths and weaknesses in your marketing and management strategies and help you evaluate possible opportunities for expansion in light of both your original mission and goals, current market trends, and business results. The Small Business Administration (SBA) offers sample business plans and online guidance for business plan preparation under the "Business Guide" tab at **https://www.sba.gov**.

Financing the Business

Once the business plan is complete, the next step is to obtain financing to set up your company. The funding required depends on the type of business and the entrepreneur's own investment. Businesses started by lifestyle entrepreneurs require less financing than growth-oriented businesses, and manufacturing and high-tech companies generally require a large initial investment.

Who provides start-up funding for small companies? Like Miho Inagi and her Tokyo bagel shop, 94 percent of business owners raise start-up funds from personal accounts, family, and friends. Personal assets and money from family and friends are important for new firms, whereas funding from financial institutions may become more important as companies grow. Three-quarters of *Inc.* 500 companies have been funded on $100,000 or less.[15]

The two forms of business financing are **debt**, borrowed funds that must be repaid with interest over a stated time period, and **equity**, funds raised through the sale of stock (i.e., ownership) in the business. Those who provide equity funds get a share of the business's profits. Because lenders usually limit debt financing to no more than a quarter to a third of the firm's total needs, equity financing often amounts to about 65 to 75 percent of total start-up financing.

Exhibit 7.5   FUBU started when a young entrepreneur from Hollis, Queens, began making tie-top skullcaps at home with some friends. With funding from a $100,000 mortgage and a later investment from the Samsung Corporation, CEO Daymond John, turned his home into a successful sportswear company. The FUBU brand tops the list for today's fashionistas who don everything from FUBU's classic Fat Albert line to swanky FUBU suits and tuxedos. *How do start-ups obtain funding?* (Credit: U.S. Embasy Nairobi/ flickr/ Attribution 2.0 Generic (CC BY 2.0))

One way to finance a start-up company is bootstrapping, which is basically funding the operation with your own resources. If the resources needed are not available to an individual, there are other options. Two sources of equity financing for young companies are angel investors and venture-capital firms. **Angel investors** are individual investors or groups of experienced investors who provide financing for start-up businesses by investing their own money, often referred to as "seed capital." This gives the investors more flexibility on what they can and will invest in, but because it is their own money, angels are careful. Angel investors often invest early in a company's development, and they want to see an idea they understand and can have confidence in. **Table 7.9** offers some guidelines on how to attract angel financing.

Making a Heavenly Deal
You need financing for your start-up business. How do you get angels interested in investing in your business venture? <ul><li>Show them something they understand, ideally a business from an industry they've been associated with.</li><li>Know your business details: Information important to potential investors includes annual sales, gross profit, profit margin, and expenses.</li><li>Be able to describe your business—what it does and who it sells to—in less than a minute. Limit PowerPoint presentations to 10 slides.</li><li>Angels can always leave their money in the bank, so an investment must interest them. It should be something they're passionate about. And timing is important—knowing when to reach out to an angel can make a huge difference.</li><li>They need to see management they trust, respect, and like. Present a competent management team with a strong, experienced leader who can explain the business and answer questions from potential investors with specifics.</li><li>Angels prefer something they can bring added value to. Those who invest could be involved with your company for a long time or perhaps take a seat on your board of directors.</li><li>They are more partial to deals that don't require huge sums of money or additional infusions of angel cash.</li><li>Emphasize the likely exits for investors and know who the competition is, why your solution is better, and how you are going to gain market share with an infusion of cash.</li></ul>

Table 7.9 Sources: Guy Kawasaki, "The Art of Raising Angel Capital," https://guykawasaki.com, accessed February 2, 2018; Murray Newlands, "How to Raise an Angel Funding Round," *Forbes,* https://www.forbes.com, March 16, 2017; Melinda Emerson, "5 Tips for Attracting Angel Investors," *Small Business Trends,* https://smallbiztrends.com, July 26, 2016; Nicole Fallon, "5 Tips for Attracting Angel Investors," *Business News Daily,* https://www.businessnewsdaily.com, January 2, 2014; Stacy Zhao, "9 Tips for Winning over Angels," *Inc.,* https://www.inc.com, June 15, 2005; Rhonda Abrams, "What Does It Take to Impress an Angel Investor?" *Inc.,* https://www.inc.com, March 29, 2001.

Venture capital is financing obtained from *venture capitalists,* investment firms that specialize in financing small, high-growth companies. Venture capitalists receive an ownership interest and a voice in management in return for their money. They typically invest at a later stage than angel investors. We'll discuss venture capital in greater detail when discussing financing the enterprise.

Buying a Small Business

Another route to small-business ownership is buying an existing business. Although this approach is less risky, many of the same steps for starting a business from scratch apply to buying an existing company. It still requires careful and thorough analysis. The potential buyer must answer several important questions: Why is the owner selling? Does he or she want to retire or move on to a new challenge, or are there problems with the business? Is the business operating at a profit? If not, can this be corrected? On what basis has the owner valued the company, and is it a fair price? What are the owner's plans after selling the company? Will he or she be available to provide assistance through the change of ownership of the business? And depending on the type of business it is, will customers be more loyal to the owner than to the product or service being offered? Customers could leave the firm if the current owner decides to open a similar business. To protect against this, many purchasers include a *noncompete clause* in the contract of sale, which generally means that the owner of the company being sold may not be allowed to compete in the same industry of the acquired business for a specific amount of time.

You should prepare a business plan that thoroughly analyzes all aspects of the business. Get answers to all your questions, and determine, via the business plan, whether the business is a sound one. Then you must negotiate the price and other terms of purchase and obtain appropriate financing. This can be a complicated process and may require the use of a consultant or business broker.

Risky Business

Running your own business may not be as easy as it sounds. Despite the many advantages of being your own boss, the risks are great as well. Over a period of five years, nearly 50% percent of small businesses fail according to the Kauffman Foundation.[16]

Businesses close down for many reasons—and not all are failures. Some businesses that close are financially successful and close for nonfinancial reasons. But the causes of business failure can be interrelated. For example, low sales and high expenses are often directly related to poor management. Some common causes of business closure are:

- Economic factors—business downturns and high interest rates
- Financial causes—inadequate capital, low cash balances, and high expenses
- Lack of experience—inadequate business knowledge, management experience, and technical expertise
- Personal reasons—the owners may decide to sell the business or move on to other opportunities

Inadequate early planning is often at the core of later business problems. As described earlier, a thorough feasibility analysis, from market assessment to financing, is critical to business success. Yet even with the best plans, business conditions change and unexpected challenges arise. An entrepreneur may start a company based on a terrific new product only to find that a larger firm with more marketing, financing, and distribution clout introduces a similar item.

The stress of managing a business can also take its toll. The business can consume your whole life. Owners may find themselves in over their heads and unable to cope with the pressures of business operations, from the long hours to being the main decision maker. Even successful businesses have to deal with ongoing challenges. Growing too quickly can cause as many problems as sluggish sales. Growth can strain a company's finances when additional capital is required to fund expanding operations, from hiring additional staff to purchasing more raw material or equipment. Successful business owners must respond quickly and develop plans to manage its growth.

So, how do you know when it is time to quit? "Never give up" may be a good motivational catchphrase, but it is not always good advice for a small-business owner. Yet, some small-business owners keep going no matter what the cost. For example, Ian White's company was trying to market a new kind of city map. White maxed out 11 credit cards and ran up more than $100,000 in debt after starting his company. He ultimately declared personal bankruptcy and was forced to find a job so that he could pay his bills. Maria Martz didn't realize her small business would become a casualty until she saw her tax return showing her company's losses in black and white—for the second year in a row. It convinced her that enough was enough and she gave up her gift-basket business to become a full-time homemaker. But once the decision is made, it may be tough to stick to. "I got calls from people asking how come I wasn't in business anymore. It was tempting to say I'd make their basket but I had to tell myself it is finished now."[17]

1. How can potential business owners find new business ideas?
2. Why is it important to develop a business plan? What should such a plan include?
3. What financing options do small-business owners have? What risks do they face?

7.5 Managing a Small Business

5. Why does managing a small business present special challenges for the owner?

Managing a small business is quite a challenge. Whether you start a business from scratch or buy an existing one, you must be able to keep it going. The small-business owner must be ready to solve problems as they arise and move quickly if market conditions change.

MANAGING CHANGE

Learning How to Pivot

Most small business owners either use, or at least know of, the iconic email service MailChimp, a company that is growing by more than $120 million every year and is on track to bring in $525 million over the coming year. But Ben Chestnut, the CEO and cofounder, says it took MailChimp several years to figure out what it did well.

When Chestnut was laid off from his job at the Cox Media Group in Atlanta, he founded Rocket Science Group, a web design firm. Cofounder Dan Kurzius (who taught himself to code) joined Chestnut, and they began to focus their sales efforts on tech companies. But when the tech bubble burst, they pivoted to focus on selling to airline and travel companies. Then 9/11 hit, and they needed to change focus again, this time on the real estate market. However, both Chestnut and Kurzius discovered they didn't enjoy sales (and they weren't very good at it), nor did they like the bureaucracy of working with large companies. "The only companies we could relate to were small businesses, and they always asked for email marketing."

This insight helped Chestnut to recall a product feature the Rocket Science Group had previously developed for an email greeting card project. So Chestnut and Kurzius evaluated the marketing software and began to test it with small businesses. "Our day jobs felt like going to these big organizations and pitching to them, and it was miserable," Chestnut says. "But we really loved our nighttime jobs, which were helping the small businesses use this email marketing app." Their passion, along with market feedback, led to their decision to completely focus on email marketing for small businesses. But it wasn't until almost 2009 that MailChimp found its sweet spot. The founders initially wanted to give away one product that collected subscribers and then charge for another, which was sending emails, but it would have been very difficult to divide the product into two pieces. That's when they landed on the Freemium idea. "Let's just make the whole thing free," said Chestnut.

The idea was that if they made it cheap and easy for small businesses to try MailChimp, their business would grow and they would be happy to pay for MailChimp services. MailChimp allows customers to send an email for free to 1,999 people at once but charges for emails sent to over 2,000 people and for premium features. MailChimp charges a monthly recurring fee starting at $10 for sending more than 12,000 emails a month.

The idea quickly proved to be a huge success. MailChimp went from a few hundred thousand users to 1 million users in a year. The next year they added another million users.

The MailChimp founders learned a lot of lessons during their 17 years in business. One of their most important lessons is knowing when to change. When you see an opportunity, don't be afraid to pivot and change course, especially if it means focusing on a market you're passionate about. Listening to market feedback and following their passion earned MailChimp's founders \recognition as "2017 Business of the Year" by *Inc.* magazine.

Critical Thinking Questions
1. What led MailChimp's founders to change its focus on the customers they were selling to?
2. What was MailChimp's "big idea" that changed the business, and why was it so successful?

Sources: Maria Aspan, "Want Proof That Patience Pays Off? Ask the Founders of This 17-Year-Old $525 Million Email Empire," *Inc.*, https://www.inc.com, Winter 2017/January 2018 issue; "MailChimp: From Startup to Inc. Magazine's Top Company," *CNBC,* https://www.cnbc.com, December 12, 2017; Farhad Manjoo, "MailChimp and the Un-Silicon Valley Way to Make It as a Start-Up," *The New York Times,* https://www.nytimes.com, October 5, 2016.

A sound business plan is key to keeping the small-business owner in touch with all areas of his or her business. Hiring, training, and managing employees is another important responsibility because the owner's role may change over time. As the company grows, others will make many of the day-to-day decisions while the owner focuses on managing employees and planning for the firm's long-term success. The owner must constantly evaluate company performance and policies in light of changing market and economic conditions and develop new policies as required. He or she must also nurture a continual flow of ideas to keep the business growing. The types of employees needed may change too as the firm grows. For instance, a larger firm may need more managerial talent and technical expertise.

Using Outside Consultants

One way to ease the burden of managing a business is to hire outside consultants. Nearly all small businesses need a good certified public accountant (CPA) who can help with financial record keeping, decision-making, and tax planning. An accountant who works closely with the owner to help the business grow is a valuable asset. An attorney who knows about small-business law can provide legal advice and draw up essential contracts and documents. Consultants in areas such as marketing, employee benefits, and insurance can be used on an as-needed basis. Outside directors with business experience are another way for small companies to get advice. Resources such as these free the small-business owner to concentrate on medium- and long-range planning and day-to-day operations.

Some aspects of business can be outsourced or contracted out to specialists. Among the more common departments that use outsourcing are information technology, marketing, customer service, order fulfillment, payroll, and human resources. Hiring an outside company—in many cases another small business—can save money because the purchasing firm buys just the services it needs and makes no investment in expensive technology. Management should review outsourced functions as the business grows because at some point it may be more cost-effective to bring them in-house.

Hiring and Retaining Employees

It is important to identify all the costs involved in hiring an employee to make sure your business can afford it. Recruiting, help-wanted ads, extra space, and taxes will easily add about 10–15 percent to their salary, and employee benefits will add even more. Hiring an employee may also mean more work for you in terms of training and management. It's a catch-22: To grow you need to hire more people, but making the shift from solo worker to boss can be stressful.

Attracting good employees is more difficult for a small firm, which may not be able to match the higher salaries, better benefits, and advancement potential offered by larger firms. Small companies need to be creative to attract the right employees and convince applicants to join their firm. Once they hire an employee, small-business owners must make employee satisfaction a top priority in order to retain good people. A company culture that nurtures a comfortable environment for workers, flexible hours, employee benefit programs, opportunities to help make decisions, and a share in profits and ownership are some ways to do this.

Duane Ruh figured out how to build a $1.2 million business in a town with just 650 residents. It's all about treating employees right. The log birdhouse and bird feeder manufacturer, Little Log Co., located in Sargent, Nebraska, boasts employee-friendly policies you read about but rarely see put into practice. Ruh offers his employees a flexible schedule that gives them plenty of time for their personal lives. During a slow period last summer, Ruh cut back on hours rather than lay anyone off. There just aren't that many jobs in that part of Nebraska that his employees could go to, so when he received a buyout offer that would have closed his facility but kept him in place with an enviable salary, he turned it down. Ruh also encourages his employees to pursue side or summer jobs if they need to make extra money, assuring them that their Little Log jobs are safe.[18]

Going Global with Exporting

More and more small businesses are discovering the benefits of looking beyond the United States for market opportunities. The global marketplace represents a huge opportunity for U.S. businesses, both large and small. Small businesses' decision to export is driven by many factors, one of which is the desire for increased sales and higher profits. U.S. goods are less expensive for overseas buyers when the value of the U.S. dollar declines against foreign currencies, and this creates opportunities for U.S. companies to sell globally. In addition, economic conditions such as a domestic recession, foreign competition within the United States, or new markets opening up in foreign countries may also encourage U.S. companies to export.

Like any major business decision, exporting requires careful planning. Small businesses may hire international-trade consultants or distributors to get started selling overseas. These specialists have the time, knowledge, and resources that most small businesses lack. Export trading companies (ETCs) buy goods at a discount from small businesses and resell them abroad. Export management companies (EMCs) act on a company's behalf. For fees of 5–15 percent of gross sales and multiyear contracts, they handle all aspects of exporting, including finding customers, billing, shipping, and helping the company comply with foreign regulations.

Many online resources are also available to identify potential markets for your goods and services, as well as to decipher the complexities involved in preparing to sell in a foreign country. The Small Business Association's Office of International Trade has links to many valuable sites. The Department of Commerce offers services for small businesses that want to sell abroad. Contact its Trade Information Center, 1-800-USA-TRADE, or its Export Center (**http://www.export.gov**).

CONCEPT CHECK

1. How does the small-business owner's role change over time?
2. How does managing a small business contribute to its growth?
3. What are the benefits to small firms of doing business internationally, and what steps can small businesses take to explore their options?

7.6 | The Large Impact of Small Business

6. What are the advantages and disadvantages facing owners of small businesses?

An uncertain economy has not stopped people from starting new companies. The National Federation of Independent Businesses reports that 85 percent of Americans view small businesses as a positive influence on American life. This is not surprising when you consider the many reasons why small businesses continue to thrive in the United States:

- *Independence and a better lifestyle:* Large corporations no longer represent job security or offer the fast-track career opportunities they once did. Mid-career employees leave the corporate world—either voluntarily or as a result of downsizing—in search of the new opportunities that self-employment provides. Many new college and business school graduates shun the corporate world altogether to start their own companies or look for work in smaller firms.
- *Personal satisfaction from work:* Many small-business owners cite this as one of the primary reasons for starting their companies. They love what they do.
- *Best route to success:* Business ownership provides greater advancement opportunities for women and minorities, as we will discuss later in this chapter. It also offers small-business owners the potential for profit.
- *Rapidly changing technology:* Technology advances and decreased costs provide individuals and small companies with the power to compete in industries that were formerly closed to them.
- *Major corporate restructuring and downsizing:* These force many employees to look for other jobs or careers. They may also provide the opportunity to buy a business unit that a company no longer wants.
- *Outsourcing:* As a result of downsizing, corporations may contract with outside firms for services they used to provide in-house. Outsourcing creates opportunities for smaller companies that offer these specialized goods and services.
- *Small businesses are resilient:* They are able to respond fairly quickly to changing economic conditions by refocusing their operations.

There are several cities and regions that are regarded as the best locations for start-up businesses and entrepreneurs. Among them are Tulsa, Oklahoma; Tampa, Florida; Atlanta, Georgia; Raleigh, North Carolina; Oklahoma City, Oklahoma; Seattle, Washington; Minneapolis, Minnesota; and Austin, Texas.[19]

Why Stay Small?

Owners of small businesses recognize that being small offers special advantages. Greater flexibility and an uncomplicated company structure allow small businesses to react more quickly to changing market forces. Innovative product ideas can be developed and brought to market more quickly, using fewer financial resources and personnel than would be needed in a larger company. And operating more efficiently keeps costs down as well. Small companies can also serve specialized markets that may not be cost-effective for large companies. Another feature is the opportunity to provide a higher level of personal service. Such attention brings many customers back to small businesses such as gourmet restaurants, health clubs, spas, fashion boutiques, and travel agencies.

Steve Niewulis played in baseball's minor leagues before an injury to his rotator cuff cut short his career. Niewulis decided to combine his love of the game with a clever idea that has elevated him to the big leagues. The fact that players had trouble keeping their hands dry while batting inspired his big idea: a sweat-busting rosin bag attached to a wristband so that a player can dry the bat handle between pitches. In less than two years, Niewulis's Fort Lauderdale, Florida, company, Tap It! Inc., sold thousands of Just Tap It! wristbands. The product, which retails for $12.95, is used by baseball players, basketball players, tennis players, golfers, and even rock climbers. His secret to success? Find a small distribution network that allows small companies, with just one product line, to succeed.[20]

On the other hand, being small is not always an asset. The founders may have limited managerial skills or encounter difficulties obtaining adequate financing, potential obstacles to growing a company. Complying with federal regulations is also more expensive for small firms. Those with fewer than 20 employees spend about twice as much per employee on compliance than do larger firms. In addition, starting and managing a small business requires a major commitment by the owner. Long hours, the need for owners to do much of the work themselves, and the stress of being personally responsible for the success of the business can take a toll.

But managing your company's growing pains doesn't need to be a one-person job. Four years after he started DrinkWorks (now Whirley DrinkWorks), a company that makes custom drinking cups, Richard Humphrey was logging 100-hour weeks. "I was concerned that if I wasn't there every minute, the company would fall apart." Humphrey got sick, lost weight, and had his engagement fall apart. When forced by a family emergency to leave the company in the hands of his five employees, Humphrey was amazed at how well they managed in his absence. "They stepped up to the plate and it worked out," he says. "After that the whole company balanced out."[21]

CONCEPT CHECK

1. Why are small businesses becoming so popular?
2. Discuss the major advantages and disadvantages of small businesses.

7.7 | The Small Business Administration

7. How does the Small Business Administration help small businesses?

Many small-business owners turn to the **Small Business Administration (SBA)** for assistance. The SBA's mission is to speak on behalf of small business, and through its national network of local offices it helps people start and manage small businesses, advises them in the areas of finance and management, and helps them win federal contracts. Its toll-free number—1-800-U-ASK-SBA (1-800-827-5722)—provides general information, and its website at **http://www.sba.gov** offers details on all its programs.[22]

Financial Assistance Programs

The SBA offers financial assistance to qualified small businesses that cannot obtain financing on reasonable terms through normal lending channels. This assistance takes the form of guarantees on loans made by private lenders. (The SBA no longer provides direct loans.) These loans can be used for most business purposes, including purchasing real estate, equipment, and materials. The SBA has been responsible for a significant amount of small-business financing in the United States. In the fiscal year ending on September 30, 2017, the SBA backed more than $25 billion in loans to almost 68,000 small businesses, including about $9 billion to minority-owned firms and $7.5 billion in loans to businesses owned by women. It also provided more than $1.7 billion in home and business disaster loans.[23]

Other SBA programs include the New Markets Venture Capital Program, which promotes economic development and job opportunities in low-income geographic areas, while other programs offer export financing and assistance to firms that suffer economic harm after natural or other disasters.

More than 300 SBA-licensed **Small Business Investment Companies (SBICs)** provide about $6 billion each year in long-term financing for small businesses. The SBA's website suggests seeking angel investors and using SBA-guaranteed loans as a way to fund the start-up. These privately owned and managed investment companies hope to earn a substantial return on their investments as the small businesses grow.

SCORE-ing with Management Assistance Programs

The SBA also provides a wide range of management advice. Its Business Development Library has publications on most business topics. Its "Starting Out" series offers brochures on how to start a wide variety of businesses—from ice-cream stores to fish farms.

Business development officers at the Office of Business Development and local Small Business Development Centers counsel many thousands of small-business owners each year, offering advice, training, and educational programs. The SBA also offers free management consulting through two volunteer groups: the Service Corps of Retired Executives (SCORE), and the Active Corps of Executives (ACE). Executives in these programs use their own business backgrounds to help small-business owners. SCORE has expanded its outreach into new markets by offering email counseling through its website (**http://www.score.org**). The SBA also offers free online resources and courses for small-business owners and aspiring entrepreneurs in its Learning Center, located on the SBA website under the "Learning Center" tab.

Assistance for Women and Minorities

The SBA is committed to helping women and minorities increase their business participation. It offers a minority small-business program, microloans, and the publication of Spanish-language informational materials. It has increased its responsiveness to small businesses by giving regional offices more decision authority and creating high-tech tools for grants, loan transactions, and eligibility reviews.

The SBA offers special programs and support services for socially and economically disadvantaged persons, including women, Native Americans, and Hispanics through its Minority Business Development Agency. It also makes a special effort to help veterans go into business for themselves.

CONCEPT CHECK ✓

1. What is the Small Business Administration (SBA)?
2. Describe the financial and management assistance programs offered by the SBA.

7.8 Trends in Entrepreneurship and Small-Business Ownership

8. What trends are shaping entrepreneurship and small-business ownership?

Entrepreneurship has changed since the heady days of the late 1990s, when starting a dot-com while still in college seemed a quick route to riches and stock options. Much entrepreneurial opportunity comes from major changes in demographics, society, and technology, and at present there is a confluence of all three. A major demographic group is moving into a significantly different stage in life, and minorities are increasing their business ownership in remarkable numbers. We have created a society in which we expect to have our problems taken care of, and the technological revolution stands ready with already-developed solutions. Evolving social and demographic trends, combined with the challenge of operating in a fast-paced technology-dominated business climate, are changing the face of entrepreneurship and small-business ownership.

Into the Future: Start-ups Drive the Economy

Did new business ventures drive the economic recovery from the 2001–2002 and 2007–2009 to recessions, and are they continuing to make significant contributions to the U.S. economy? The economists who review Department of Labor employment surveys and SBA statistics think so. "Small business drives the American economy," says Dr. Chad Moutray, former chief economist for the SBA's Office of Advocacy. "Main Street provides the jobs and spurs our economic growth. American entrepreneurs are creative and productive." Numbers alone do not tell the whole story, however. Are these newly self-employed workers profiting from their ventures, or are they just biding their time during a period of unemployment?

U.S. small businesses employed 57.9 million people in 2016, representing nearly 48 percent of the workforce. The number of net new jobs added to the economy was 1.4 million.[24]

The highest rate of growth is coming from women-owned firms, which continues to rise at rates higher than the national average—and with even stronger growth rates since the recession. There were an estimated 11.6 million women-owned businesses employing nearly 9 million people in 2016, generating more than $1.7 trillion in revenue.[25]

Between 2007 and 2017, women-owned firms increased by 114 percent, compared to a 44 percent increase among all businesses. This means that growth rates for women-owned businesses are 2.5 times faster than the national average. Employment growth was also stronger than national rates. Women-owned businesses increased 27 percent over the past 20 years, while overall business employment has increased by 13 percent since 2007.[26]

These trends show that more workers are striking out on their own and earning money doing it. It has become very clear that encouraging small-business activity leads to continued strong overall economic growth.

Changing Demographics Create Entrepreneurial Diversity

The mantra, "60 is the new 40," describes today's Baby Boomers who indulge in much less knitting and golf in their retirement years. The AARP predicts that silver-haired entrepreneurs will continue to rise in the coming years. According to a recent study by the Kauffman Foundation, Baby Boomers are twice as likely as Millennials to start a new business. In fact, close to 25 percent of all new entrepreneurs fall between the ages of 55 and 64.[27] This has created a ripple effect in the way we work. Boomers have accelerated the growing acceptance of working from home, adding to the millions of U.S. workers already showing up to work in their slippers. In addition, the ongoing corporate brain drain could mean that small businesses will be able to tap into the expertise of seasoned free agents at less-than-corporate prices—and that seniors themselves will become independent consultants to businesses of all sizes.[28]

The growing numbers of Baby Boomer entrepreneurs has prompted some forward-thinking companies to recognize business opportunities in technology. At one time there was a concern that the aging of the population would create a drag on the economy. Conventional wisdom says that the early parenthood years are the big spending years. As we age, we spend less and, because Boomers are such a big demographic group, this was going to create a long-term economic decline. Not true, it now appears. The Boomer generation has built sizable wealth, and they are not afraid to spend it to make their lives more comfortable.

Minorities are also adding to the entrepreneurial mix. As we saw in **Exhibit 7.4**, minority groups and women are increasing business ownership at a much faster rate than the national average, reflecting their confidence in the U.S. economy. These overwhelming increases in minority business ownership paralleled the demand for U.S. Small Business Administration loan products. Loans to minority business owners in fiscal year 2017 set a record—more than $9.5 billion, or 31 percent, of SBA's total loan portfolio.[29]

The latest Kauffman Foundation Index of Startup Activity found that immigrants and Latinos have swelled the growing numbers of self-employed Americans in recent years, increasing the diversity of the country's entrepreneurial class. Overall, minority-owned businesses increased 38 percent. The SBA notes that the number of Hispanic-owned businesses has increased more than 46 percent between 2007 and 2012.[30]

Exhibit 7.6 The popularity of home businesses such as Rodan+Fields, eBay, and other e-commerce sites has given rise to a new kind of entrepreneur: the "mompreneur." Typically ex-corporate professionals, these web-driven women launch home businesses specializing in the sale of antiques, jewelry, thrift-store fashions, and other items. Aided by digital photography, wireless technology, and friendly postal workers, these savvy moms are one of the fastest-growing segments of entrepreneurs building successful businesses on the web. *Why are many professional women leaving the workplace to start entrepreneurial ventures online?* (Credit: Amanda nobles/ Flickr/ Attribution 2.0 Generic (CC BY 2.0))

How Far Will You Go to Get Rich?

With enough intelligence and determination, people can get rich almost anywhere in the United States. Whether you own chains of dry cleaners in Queens, car dealerships in Chicago, or oil wells in West Texas, fortunes have been made in every state in the Union. There are some places, however, where the chances of creating wealth are much greater than others. That is the reason why people who hope to strike it rich move to places such as Manhattan or Palo Alto. It's not because the cost of living is low or the quality of life as a struggling entrepreneur is fun. Whether starting a software or soft-drink company, entrepreneurs tend to follow the money

But not all companies follow the herd. Guild Education, founded in 2015 by Rachel Carlson and Brittany Stich at Stanford University, left San Francisco due to the high cost of living that could slow down the company's growth. "We have a lot of women who are executives and department heads here, starting with myself and my cofounder," CEO Rachel Carlson said. "So when we left, we deliberately chose a place where you can have a family."[31] Guild Education's mission is to help large employers offer college education and tuition reimbursement as a benefit to the 64 million working-age adults who lack a college degree.

Since moving to Denver, Guild Education has raised another $21 million in venture capital, bringing the total funding to $31.5 million with a company valuation of $125 million.[32] The company headquarters in Denver is next door to a Montessori school and employs 58 employees. "We were joking that we're the polar opposite of Apple," said Carlson. "Remember when the new 'mothership' came out? Every single parent noticed that it had a huge gym but not a day care."

According to PwC's quarterly venture capital study, "MoneyTree Report," the top regions in the United States for venture-backed deals in the third quarter of 2017 were San Francisco ($4.1 billion), New York Metro ($4.2 billion), Silicon Valley (Bay Area $2.2 billion), and New England ($1.8 billion). [33]

In 2017, equity financing in U.S. start-ups rose for the third straight quarter, reaching $19 billion, according to the PwC/CB Insights "MoneyTree Report Q3 2017." "Financing was boosted by a large number of mega-rounds," says Tom Ciccolella, Partner, U.S. Ventures Leader at PwC.[34] Twenty-six mega-rounds of $100 million in companies such as WeWork, 23andMe, Fanatics, and NAUTO contributed to the strong activity levels in the first three quarters of 2017. The top five U.S. industry sectors with the most deals and funding were Internet, Healthcare, Mobile and Telecommunications, Software (Non-Internet/Mobile), and Consumer Products.

CONCEPT CHECK

1. What significant trends are occurring in the small-business arena?
2. How is entrepreneurial diversity impacting small business and the economy?
3. How do ethics impact decision-making with small-business owners?

🔑 Key Terms

angel investors Individual investors or groups of experienced investors who provide financing for start-up businesses by investing their own funds.

business plan A formal written statement that describes in detail the idea for a new business and how it will be carried out; includes a general description of the company, the qualifications of the owner(s), a description of the product or service, an analysis of the market, and a financial plan.

debt A form of business financing consisting of borrowed funds that must be repaid with interest over a stated time period.

entrepreneurs People with vision, drive, and creativity who are willing to take the risk of starting and managing a business to make a profit, or greatly changing the scope and direction of an existing firm.

equity A form of business financing consisting of funds raised through the sale of stock (i.e., ownership) in a business.

intrapreneurs Entrepreneurs who apply their creativity, vision, and risk-taking within a large corporation, rather than starting a company of their own.

small business A business with under 500 employees that is independently managed, is owned by an individual or a small group of investors, is based locally, and is not a dominant company in its industry.

Small Business Administration (SBA) A government agency that speaks on behalf of small business; specifically it helps people start and manage small businesses, advises them in the areas of finance and management, and helps them win federal contracts.

Small Business Investment Company (SBIC) Privately owned and managed investment companies that are licensed by the Small Business Administration and provide long-term financing for small businesses.

venture capital Financing obtained from venture capitalists, investment firms that specialize in financing small, high-growth companies and receive an ownership interest and a voice in management in return for their money.

📑 Summary of Learning Outcomes

7.1 Entrepreneurship

1. Why do people become entrepreneurs, and what are the different types of entrepreneurs?

Entrepreneurs are innovators who take the risk of starting and managing a business to make a profit. Most want to develop a company that will grow into a major corporation. People become entrepreneurs for four main reasons: the opportunity for profit, independence, personal satisfaction, and lifestyle. Classic entrepreneurs may be micropreneurs, who plan to keep their businesses small, or growth-oriented entrepreneurs. Multipreneurs start multiple companies, while intrapreneurs work within large corporations.

7.2 Characteristics of Successful Entrepreneurs

2. What characteristics do successful entrepreneurs share?

Successful entrepreneurs are ambitious, independent, self-confident, creative, energetic, passionate, and committed. They have a high need for achievement and a willingness to take moderate risks. Good managerial, interpersonal, and communication skills, as well as technical knowledge are important for entrepreneurial success.

7.3 Small Business

3. How do small businesses contribute to the U.S. economy?

Small businesses play an important role in the economy. They account for over 99 percent of all employer firms and produce about half of U.S. economic output. Most new private-sector jobs created in the United States over the past decade were in small firms. The Small Business Administration defines a small business as independently owned and operated, with a local base of operations, and not dominant in its field. It also defines small business by size, according to its industry. Small businesses are found in every field, but they dominate the service, construction, wholesale, and retail categories.

7.4 Start Your Own Business

4. What are the first steps to take if you are starting your own business?

After finding an idea that satisfies a market need, the small-business owner should choose a form of business organization. Preparing a formal business plan helps the business owner analyze the feasibility of his or her idea. The written plan describes in detail the idea for the business and how it will be implemented and operated. The plan also helps the owner obtain both debt and equity financing for the new business.

7.5 Managing a Small Business

5. Why does managing a small business present special challenges for the owner?

At first, small-business owners are involved in all aspects of the firm's operations. Hiring and retaining key employees and the wise use of outside consultants can free up an owner's time to focus on planning, strategizing, and monitoring market conditions, in addition to overseeing day-to-day operations. Expanding into global markets can be a profitable growth strategy for a small business.

7.6 The Large Impact of Small Business

6. What are the advantages and disadvantages facing owners of small businesses?

Because of their streamlined staffing and structure, small businesses can be efficiently operated. They have the flexibility to respond to changing market conditions. Small firms can serve specialized markets more profitably than large firms, and they provide a higher level of personal service. Disadvantages include limited managerial skill, difficulty in raising capital needed for start-up or expansion, the burden of complying with increasing levels of government regulation, and the major personal commitment that is required by the owner.

7.7 The Small Business Administration

7. How does the Small Business Administration help small businesses?

The Small Business Administration is the main federal agency serving small businesses. It provides guarantees of private-lender loans for small businesses. The SBA also offers a wide range of management assistance services, including courses, publications, and consulting. It has special programs for women, minorities, and veterans.

7.8 Trends in Entrepreneurship and Small-Business Ownership

8. What trends are shaping entrepreneurship and small-business ownership?

Changes in demographics, society, and technology are shaping the future of entrepreneurship and small business in America. More than ever, opportunities exist for entrepreneurs of all ages and backgrounds. The numbers of women and minority business owners continues to rise, and older entrepreneurs are changing the small-business landscape. Catering to the needs of an older population and a surge in web-based companies fuel continues technology growth. Entrepreneurs typically follow the money and set up shop in places where there is venture capital money easily available.

Chapter Review Questions

1. What are the differences between classic, multipreneurs, and intrapreneurs?
2. What differentiates an entrepreneur from a small-business owner?
3. What are some major factors that motivate entrepreneurs to start businesses?
4. How can potential business owners find new business ideas?
5. Why is it important to develop a business plan? What should such a plan include?
6. What financing options do small-business owners have? What risks do they face?
7. How do the small-business owner's and entrepreneur's roles change over time?
8. What are the benefits to small firms of doing business internationally, and what steps can small businesses take to explore their options?
9. Describe the financial and management assistance programs offered by the SBA.
10. What significant trends are occurring in the small-business arena?
11. How is entrepreneurial diversity impacting small business and the economy?
12. How do ethics impact decision-making with small-business owners?

Management Skills Application Exercises

1. After working in software development with a major food company for 12 years, you are becoming impatient with corporate "red tape" (regulations and routines). You have an idea for a new snack product for nutrition-conscious consumers and are thinking of starting your own company. What entrepreneurial characteristics do you need to succeed? What other factors should you consider before quitting your job? Working with a partner, choose one to be the entrepreneurial employee and one to play the role of his current boss. Develop notes for a script. The employee will focus on why this is a good idea—reasons he will succeed—and the employer will play devil's advocate to convince him that staying on at the large company is a better idea. Then switch roles and repeat the discussion.

2. What does it really take to become an entrepreneur? Find out by interviewing a local entrepreneur or researching an entrepreneur you've read about in this chapter or in the business press. Get answers to the following questions, as well as any others you'd like to ask:
   - How did you research the feasibility of your idea?
   - How did you develop your vision for the company?
   - How long did it take you to prepare your business plan?
   - Where did you obtain financing for the company?
   - Where did you learn the business skills you needed to run and grow the company?
   - What are the most important entrepreneurial characteristics that helped you succeed?
   - What were the biggest challenges you had to overcome?
   - What are the most important lessons you learned by starting this company?
   - What advice do you have for would-be entrepreneurs?

3. Your class decides to participate in a local business plan competition. Divide the class into small groups, and choose one of the following ideas:
   - A new computer game based on the stock market
   - A company with an innovative design for a skateboard
   - Travel services for college and high school students

   Prepare a detailed outline for the business plan, including the objectives for the business and the types of information you would need to develop product, marketing, and financing strategies. Each group will then present its outline for the class to critique.

Managerial Decision Exercises

1. A small catering business in your city is for sale for $250,000. The company specializes in business luncheons and small social events. The owner has been running the business for four years from her home but is expecting her first child and wants to sell. You will need outside investors to help you purchase the business. Develop questions to ask the owner about the business and its prospects, as well as a list of documents you want to see. What other types of information would you need before making a decision to buy this company? Summarize your findings in a memo to a potential investor that explains the appeal of the business for you and how you plan to investigate the feasibility of the purchase.

2. As the owner of a small factory that makes plastic sheeting, you are constantly seeking ways to increase profits. As the new year begins, one of your goals is to find additional funds to offer annual productivity and/or merit bonuses to your loyal, hardworking employees. Then a letter from a large national manufacturer of shower curtains seems to provide an answer. As part of a new "supplier diversity" program it is putting in place, the manufacturer is offering substantial purchase contracts to minority-owned suppliers. Even though the letter clearly states that the business must be minority owned to qualify for the program, you convince yourself to apply for it based on the fact that all your employees are Latino. You justify your decision by deciding they will benefit from the increased revenue a larger contract will bring, some of which you plan to pass on to them in the form of bonuses later in the year. Using a web search tool, locate articles about this topic, and then write responses to the following question. Be sure to support your arguments and cite your sources.

    a. Is it wrong for this business owner to apply for this program even though it will end up benefiting his employees as well as his business?

Critical Thinking Case

Fostering Entrepreneurship in Unlikely Places

Vic Ahmed is no stranger to business start-ups; he's been involved in at least 15 or 20. But his latest venture is a start-up … for start-ups. Ahmed founded Innovation Pavilion, a business incubator in Centennial, Colorado (Denver's Tech Center), in 2011. A typical business incubator provides start-up companies with workspace, mentoring, training, and sometimes a path to funding, but Innovation Pavilion goes further.

Innovation Pavilion (IP) is an 80,000 square foot "entrepreneurial ecosystem," housing dozens of start-ups and renting out desks, office space, and event space. But it also hosts meetups, educational workshops, and a Toastmasters group designed specifically for entrepreneurs. It contains a makerspace (a workspace providing shared tools and manufacturing equipment for prototyping products) and encourages the growth of niche entrepreneurial communities based on specific industries. For example, IP has a space for IoT (the Internet of Things), one for health care, and another for aerospace. These communities bring together people in an industry to learn from and collaborate with each other.

While IP has a traditional incubator program, with companies housed within the IP campus, it has a semi-virtual hypergrowth accelerator program for more mature firms, too, which is open to companies around the country. It also seeks out educational partnerships, working with the Highland's Ranch STEM program, for instance, and has its own educational spin-off, Xuno Innovative Learning, designed to help companies train their staff and find new employees with the skills they need. IP operates its own streaming TV service, filming educational events and interviews with entrepreneurs.

Innovation Pavilion has national expansion plans—and several signed agreements with specific cities—targeting not the giant metropolitan areas but also second tier and "ring" cities across the country, such as Joliet, Illinois, and Olathe, Kansas, smaller cities that don't get the attention of the larger cities yet have plenty of educated and creative people.

IP is in discussions with 20 cities around the nation, with the goal of building 200,000-square-foot campuses providing incubator services, office space, makerspace, education and training, outreach to young entrepreneurs, conference centers, retail space, and even housing. Entrepreneurs will be able to live and work in a space with everything they need, providing a complete entrepreneurial ecosystem in smaller cities across the nation.

Steve Case, the cofounder of America Online (AOL), shares Vic Ahmed's vision for entrepreneurship in mid-America. His "Rise of the Rest" bus tour has traveled 8,000 miles over the last three years, investing in local start-ups in 33 cities across the country. Case hosts a pitch competition with the best start-ups in each city, and one lucky winner receives a $100,000 investment from Case.

Media attention has focused on the entrepreneurial engines of America's coastal cities, but Ahmed and Case have a more expansive entrepreneurial vision, in which smaller cities throughout the nation rise up alongside larger, start-up hot spots.

Critical Thinking Questions
1. What characteristics made Vic Ahmed a successful entrepreneurs?
2. How did their Ahmed and Steven Case's partnership and shared vision of "Rise of the Rest" serve their business goals?
3. Is focusing on smaller cities rather than areas like silicon valley a good strategy, why?

Sources: Innovation Pavilion website http://www.innovationpavilion.com/ accessed February, 13, 2018; Tamara Chuang, Centennial incubator plans coworking office expansion to Illinois, complete with STEM school, housing," Denver Post, August 1, 2017, https://www.denverpost.com/2017/08/01/innovation-pavilion-illinois-expansion/; Jan Wondra, Innovation Pavilion Expands Base," The Villager, November 29, 2017, https://villagerpublishing.com/innovation-pavilion-expands-geographic-base/.

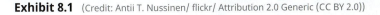

Strategic Analysis: Understanding a Firm's Competitive Environment

Exhibit 8.1 (Credit: Antii T. Nussinen/ flickr/ Attribution 2.0 Generic (CC BY 2.0))

Introduction

Learning Outcomes

After reading this chapter, you should be able to answer these questions:

1. What is strategic analysis and why do firms need to analyze their competitive environment?
2. What is a SWOT analysis and what can it reveal about a firm?
3. What makes up a firm's external macro environment, and what tools do strategists use to understand it?
4. What makes up a firm's external micro environment, and what tools do strategists use to understand it?
5. How and why do managers conduct an internal analysis of their firms?
6. What does it mean to compete with other firms in a business environment, what does it mean when a firm has a competitive advantage over its rivals, and what generic strategies can a firm implement to gain advantage over its rivals?
7. What elements go into determining a firm's strategic position?

EXPLORING MANAGERIAL CAREERS

Lauri Goodman Lampson, Planning Design Research Corporation

Lauri Goodman Lampson is president and CEO of Planning Design Research Corporation,[1] a firm that analyzes work environments to understand how employees work and what kind of spaces and facilities they need to do their best, most productive work. Lampson was hired by Accenture, a consulting firm, to evaluate and improve its location in Houston. Accenture's Houston office was a three-story, 66,000-square-foot building that served 800 employees.[2] Accenture employees are consultants themselves, and they typically spend up to two-thirds of their working time away from the office serving clients.

Lampson worked with Accenture director of workplaces Dan Johnson and Steelcase, an office furniture manufacturer, to study how Accenture was using its Houston space. Lampson's "focus is on gaining a deep understanding of the business and its strategy for success and then developing strategic workplace solutions that enable those goals."[3] To achieve this outcome, Lampson and Steelcase analyzed employee demographics and expectations and studied how employees actually interacted with each other and performed tasks in the workplace. Accenture wanted to have a workspace that fostered its corporate goals of: worker innovation, collaboration, and flexibility.[4]

Exhibit 8.2   American General Center The American General Center is a complex of several office buildings in Houston, Texas, and home offices for Accenture. (Credit: Ken Luncd/ flickr/ Attribution-ShareAlike 2.0 Generic (CC BY-SA 2.0))

Understanding a firm's strengths is an important step in strategic analysis, and Lampson's focus on supporting those strengths in the workplace environment led to Workplace 2.0, Accenture's reimagined facility. Not only does the new workspace provide better physical and technological support for collaboration among Accenture employees, but Lampson and Steelcase were able to identify opportunities for Accenture to significantly reduce the size of its offices. Accenture saves money by using less space (it was able to downsize to a single floor of 25,000 square feet to serve the same number of workers) and supports worker interaction and engagement by providing a more effective workspace. You can watch a video of this transformation here: **https://www.youtube.com/watch?v=y4oIlY3HJfo**

8.1 | Gaining Advantages by Understanding the Competitive Environment

1. What is strategic analysis, and why do firms need to analyze their competitive environment?

Strategic analysis is the process that firms use to study and understand the many different layers and aspects of their competitive environment. Why do firms spend time and money trying to understand what is going on around them? Firms do not operate in a vacuum. They are impacted by forces and factors from inside their organizations and outside in the world at large. Understanding these forces and factors is crucial to achieving success as a business. For example, the growth in the Spanish-speaking population in the United States has led many firms to change the signage in their stores and labels on their products to include Spanish, in order to make their stores easier to shop in and their products easier to identify for this growing market. The external environment is continually changing, and the most successful firms are able to prepare for and adapt to environmental changes because they have done their homework and understand how external forces impact their operations.

To react to change more easily and develop products consumers want, managers and consultants engage in **environmental scanning**—the systematic and intentional analysis of both a firm's internal state and its external, competitive environment. From a local coffee shop to an international corporation, firms of all sizes benefit from strategic analysis. Let's examine some important strategic factors in more detail.

The Competitive Environment

A firm's **competitive environment** includes components inside the firm and outside the firm. **External factors** are things in the global environment that may impact a firm's operations or success, examples are a rise in interest rates, or a natural disaster. External factors cannot be controlled, but they must be managed effectively and to understand them so that the firm can be as successful. For example, the unemployment rate will affect a firm's ability to hire qualified employees at a reasonable rate of pay. If unemployment is high, meaning that a lot of people are looking for jobs, then a firm will probably have a lot of applicants for any positions it needs to fill. It will be able to choose more highly qualified applicants to hire and may be able to hire them at a lower pay rate because the employee would rather work for a lower pay rate than not have a job at all. On the other hand, when unemployment is low, meaning that not many people are looking for jobs, firms may have to offer higher pay or settle for lower qualifications to find someone to fill a position.

Internal factors are characteristics of the firm itself. To plan to compete against other firms, a firm needs to understand what physical, financial, and human resources it has, what it is good at, and how it is organized. For example, Walmart has a sophisticated IT system that tracks inventory and automatically orders products before they run out, by calculating how long it will take for the new product to arrive and comparing that to the rate at which the product is selling off the shelves. The system orders new product so that it will arrive just as the product on the shelves is running out, so that Walmart stores do not need to have storage space for inventory. All Walmart inventory is on the store shelves, ready to be sold to customers. How does this system benefit Walmart? It does not have to spend money on storing or keeping track of inventory, all products in the store can generate revenue because they are available for customers to buy, and when the system is working optimally, the store never runs out of items customers want.

8.2 Using SWOT for Strategic Analysis

2. What is a SWOT analysis, and what can it reveal about a firm?

You may already have heard of one very common tool firms use to analyze their strategic and competitive situations: **SWOT**, which is an acronym for **s**trengths, **w**eaknesses, **o**pportunities, and **t**hreats. Firms use SWOT analysis to get a general understanding of what they are good or bad at and what factors outside their doors might present chances for success or difficulty. Let's take a look at SWOT analysis piece by piece (**Exhibit 8.3**).

Strengths	Weaknesses	Opportunities	Threats
• Employees • Patents • Cash • Brand • Unique capabilites	• Outdated technology • Employee skill gaps • High operating costs	• Underserved markets • New social trends • Technological advances	• Competitor actions • Economic downturns • Government regulations

Inside the firm .... *Outside the firm*

Exhibit 8.3   The Components of SWOT (Attribution: Copyright Rice University, OpenStax, under CC-BY 4.0 license)

Strengths

A firm's **strengths** are, to put it simply, what it is good at. Nike is good at marketing sports products, McDonald's is good at making food quickly and inexpensively, and Ferrari is good at making beautiful fast cars. When a firm analyzes its strengths, it compiles a list of its capabilities and assets. Does the firm have a lot of cash available? That is a strength. Does the firm have highly skilled employees? Another strength. Knowing exactly what it is good at allows a firm to make plans that exploit those strengths. Nike can plan to expand its business by making products for a sport it doesn't currently serve. Its sports marketing expertise will help it successfully launch that new product line.

Weaknesses

A firm's **weaknesses** are what it is not good at—things that it does not have the capabilities to perform well.

Weaknesses are not necessarily faults—remember that not all firms can be great at all things. When a firm understands its weaknesses, it will avoid trying to do things it does not have the skills or assets to succeed in, or it will find ways to improve its weaknesses before undertaking something new. A firm's weaknesses are simply gaps in capabilities, and those gaps do not always have to be filled within the firm.

SWOT analysis alerts firms to the gaps in their capabilities so they can work around them, find help in those areas, or develop capabilities to fill the gaps. For example, Paychex is a firm that handles payroll for over 600,000 firms.[5] Paychex processes hours, pay rates, tax and benefits deductions, and direct deposit for firms that would rather not have to perform those tasks themselves. A large firm would need to have a team of employees dedicated to fulfilling that task and equip that team with software systems to do the job efficiently and accurately. For Paychex, these capabilities are a company strength—that's what it does. Other companies that do not have the resources to develop this capability or may not be interested in doing so can hire Paychex to do the job for them.

Opportunities

While strengths and weaknesses are internal to an organization, but opportunities and threats are always external. An **opportunity** is a potential situation that a firm is equipped to take advantage of. Think of opportunities in terms of things that happen in the market. Opportunities offer positive potential, however sometimes a firm is not equipped to take advantage of an opportunity which is why considering the entire SWOT is important before deciding what to do. For example, as cities are becoming more populated, parking is becoming scarcer. Younger consumers who live in cities are starting to question whether it makes sense to own a car at all, when public transportation is available and parking is not. Sometimes, however, a person might need a car to travel outside the city or transport a special purchase. Daimler, the manufacturer of Mercedes-Benz and Smart cars, started a car-sharing service in Europe, North America, and China called Car2Go to offer cars to this new market of part-time drivers. By establishing Car2Go, Daimler has found a way to sell the use of its products to people who would not buy them outright.

Threats

When a manager assesses the external competitive environment, she labels anything that would make it harder for her firm to be successful as a **threat**. A wide variety of situations and scenarios can threaten a firm's chances of success, from a downturn in the economy to a competitor launching a better version of a product the firm also offers. A good threat assessment looks thoroughly at the external environment and identifies threats to the firm's business so it can be prepared to meet them. Opportunities and threats can also be a matter of perspective or interpretation: the Car2Go service that Daimler developed to serve young urban customers who don't own cars could also be cast as a defensive response to the trend away from car ownership in this customer group. Daimler could have identified decreasing sales among young urban professionals as a threat and developed Car2Go as an alternative way to gain revenue from these otherwise lost customers.

The Limitations of SWOT Analysis

Although a SWOT analysis can identify important factors and situations that affect a firm, it only works as well as the person doing the analysis. SWOT can generate a good evaluation of the firm's internal and external environments, but it is more likely to overlook key issues because it is difficult to identify or imagine everything that could, for example, be a threat to the firm. That's why the remainder of this chapter will present tools for developing a strategic analysis that is more thorough and systematic in examining both the internal and external environments that firms operate in.

1. Explain the elements of a SWOT analysis.
2. What information does a SWOT analysis provide managers? What information might it miss?

8.3 A Firm's External Macro Environment: PESTEL

3. What makes up a firm's external macro environment, and what tools do strategists use to understand it?

The world at large forms the **external environment** for businesses. A firm must confront, adapt to, take advantage of, and defend itself against what is happening in the world around it to succeed. To make gathering and interpreting information about the external environment easier, strategic analysts have defined several general categories of activities and groups that managers should examine and understand. **Exhibit 8.4** illustrates layers and categories found in a firm's environment.

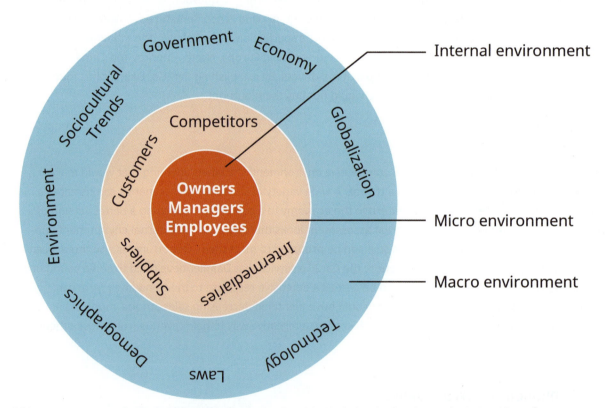

Exhibit 8.4   Components of a Firm's Environment (Attribution: Copyright Rice University, OpenStax, under CC-BY 4.0 license)

A firm's **macro environment** contains elements that can impact the firm but are generally beyond its direct control. These elements are characteristics of the world at large and are factors that all businesses must contend with, regardless of the industry they are in or type of business they are. In the **Exhibit 8.4**, the macro environment is indicated in blue. Note that the terms contained in the blue ring are all "big-picture" items that exist independently of business activities. That is not to say that they do not affect firms or that firm activities cannot affect macro environmental elements; both can and do happen, but firms are largely unable to directly change things in the macro environment.

Strategists study the macro environment to learn about facts and trends that may present opportunities or threats to their firms. However, they do not usually just think in terms of SWOT. Strategists have developed more discerning tools to examine the external environment.

PESTEL

PESTEL is a tool that reminds managers to look at several distinct categories in the macro environment. Like SWOT, PESTEL is an acronym. In this case, the letters represent the categories to examine: **p**olitical factors, **e**conomic factors, **s**ociocultural factors, **t**echnological factors, **e**nvironmental factors, and **l**egal factors. When using PESTEL to analyze a specific firm's situation, overlap between different categories of PESTEL factors can sometimes happen just as it can with SWOT.

Remember our earlier example: When urban millennials decide that car ownership is no longer attractive, car manufacturers' sales are threatened. However, those same manufacturers might be able to adapt their sales methods to offer millennials car-sharing services, taking advantage of the opportunity to earn revenue from millennials who want access to cars for vacations or big shopping trips. PESTEL can also reveal multiple impacts from a single element in the external environment. For example, decreasing interest in car ownership among urban millennials would be a sociocultural trend. However, the technological connectedness of those same urban millennials is exactly what makes it possible for ride-sharing services such as Uber and Lyft to thrive: their services are app based and provide convenience both by connecting drivers and passengers quickly and by making transactions cashless.

Exhibit 8.5 illustrates the components of PESTEL, which will be discussed individually below.

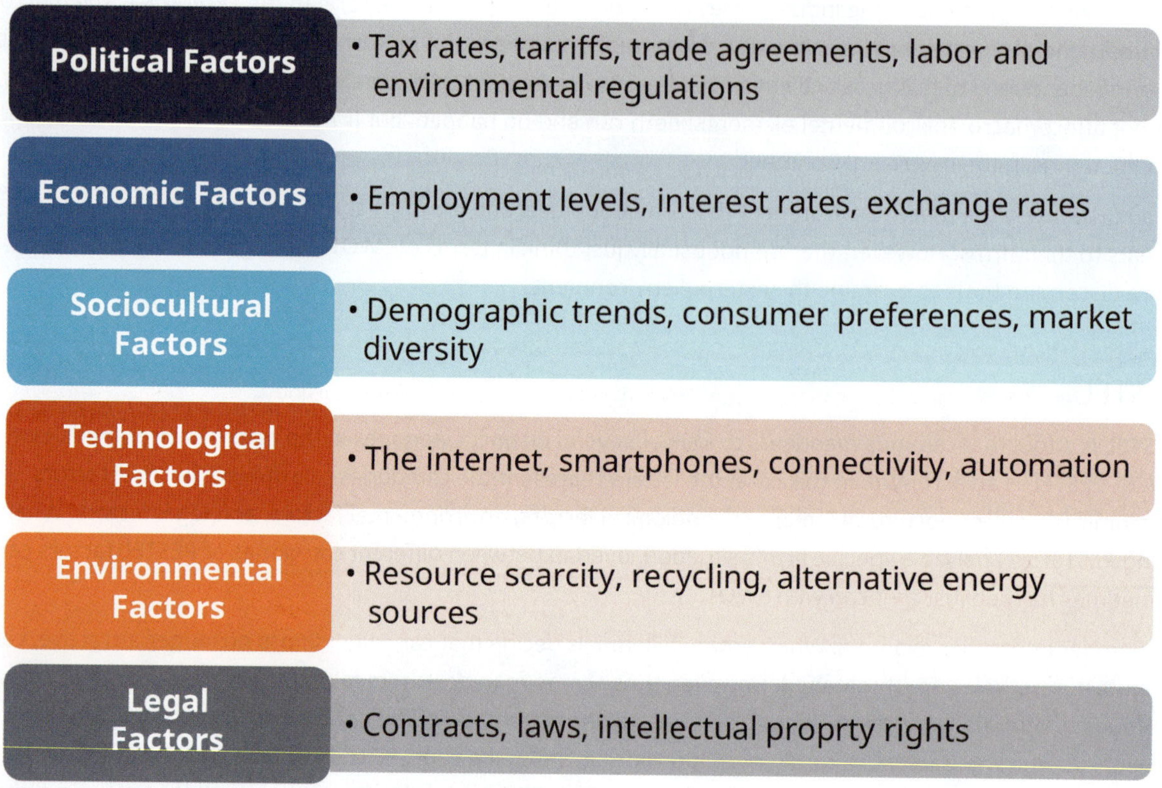

Political Factors	• Tax rates, tarriffs, trade agreements, labor and environmental regulations
Economic Factors	• Employment levels, interest rates, exchange rates
Sociocultural Factors	• Demographic trends, consumer preferences, market diversity
Technological Factors	• The internet, smartphones, connectivity, automation
Environmental Factors	• Resource scarcity, recycling, alternative energy sources
Legal Factors	• Contracts, laws, intellectual proprty rights

Exhibit 8.5   The PESTEL Model for External Environmental Analysis (Attribution: Copyright Rice University, OpenStax, under CC-BY 4.0 license)

Political Factors

Political factors in the macro environment include taxation, tariffs, trade agreements, labor regulations, and environmental regulations. Note that in PESTEL, factors are not characterized as opportunities or threats. They are simply things that a firm can take advantage of or treat as problems, depending on its own interpretation or abilities. American Electric Power, a large company that generates and distributes electricity, may be negatively impacted by environmental regulations that restrict its ability to use coal to generate electricity because of pollution caused by burning coal. However, another energy firm has taken advantage of the government's interest in reducing coal emissions by developing a way to capture the emissions while producing power. The Petra Nova plant, near Houston, was developed by NRG and JX Nippon, who received Energy Department grants to help fund the project.[6] Although firms do not directly make government policy decisions, many industries and firms invest in lobbying efforts to try to influence government policy development to create opportunities or reduce threats.

Economic Factors

All firms are impacted by the state of the national and global economies. The increased interdependence of individual country economies has made evaluating the **economic factors** in a firm's macro environment more complex. Firms analyze economic indicators to make decisions about entering or exiting geographic markets, investing in expansion, and hiring or laying off employees. As discussed earlier in this chapter, employment rates impact the quantity, quality, and cost of employees available to firms. Interest rates impact sales of big-ticket items that consumers normally finance, such as appliances, cars, and homes. Interest rates also impact the cost of capital for firms that want to invest in expansion. Exchange rates present risks and opportunities to all firms that operate across national borders, and the price of oil impacts many industries, from airlines and transportation companies to solar panel producers and plastic recycling companies. Once again, any scenario can be a threat to one firm and an opportunity to another, so economic forces should not be assumed to be intrinsically good or bad.

Sociocultural Factors

Quite possibly the largest category of macro environmental factors an analyst might examine are **sociocultural factors**. This broad category encompasses everything from changing national demographics to fashion trends and many things in between. **Demographics**, a subset of this category, includes facts about income, education levels, age groups, and the ethnic and racial composition of a population. All of these facts present market challenges and possibilities. Firms can target products to specific market segments by studying the needs and preferences of demographic groups, such as working women (they might need day-care services but not watch daytime television), college students (who would be interested in affordable textbooks but couldn't afford to buy new cars), or the elderly (who would be willing to pay for lawn-mowing services but might not be interested in adventure tourism).

Changes in people's values and interests are also included in this category. Environmental awareness has spurred demand for solar panels and electric and hybrid cars. A general interest in health and fitness has created industries in gyms, home gym equipment, and organic food. The popularity of social media has created an enormous demand for instant access to information and services, not to mention smartphones. Values and interests are constantly changing and vary from country to country, creating new market opportunities as well as communication challenges for companies trying to enter unfamiliar new markets.

Technological Factors

The rise of the Internet may be the most disruptive technological change of the last century. The globe has become more interconnected and interdependent because of the fast, low-cost communications the Internet provides. Customer service agents in India can serve customers in Kansas because technology has advanced to the point that the customer's account information can be instantly accessed by the service provider in India. Entrepreneurs around the world can reach customers anywhere through companies such as eBay, Alibaba, and Etsy, and they can get paid, regardless of their customers' currency, through PayPal. The Internet has enabled Jeff Bezos, who started an online bookselling company called Amazon in 1994, to transform how consumers shop for goods.

How else have **technological factors** impacted business? The Internet is not the only technological advance that has transformed how businesses operate. Automation has increased efficiency for manufacturers. MRP (materials requirement planning) systems have changed how companies and their suppliers work together, and global-positioning technology has helped construction engineers manage large projects more accurately. Consumers and firms have nearly unlimited access to information, and this access has empowered consumers to make more-informed buying decisions and challenged firms to develop ways to analyze the large amounts of data their businesses generate.

Environmental Factors

The physical environment, which provides natural resources for manufacturing and energy production, has always been a key part of human business activity. As resources become scarcer and more expensive,

environmental factors impact businesses more every day. Firms are developing technology to operate more cleanly and using fewer resources. Political pressure on businesses to reduce their impact on the natural environment has increased globally and dramatically in the 21st century. In 2017, London, Barcelona, and Paris announced their plans to ban cars with internal combustion engines over the next few decades, in order to combat air-quality issues.[7]

This external environment category often overlaps with others in PESTEL because concern for the environment is also a sociocultural trend, as more consumers look for recycled products and buy electric and hybrid cars. On the political front, firms are facing increased regulation around the world on their carbon emissions and natural resource use. Although SWOT would characterize these factors as either opportunities or threats, PESTEL simply identifies them as aspects of the external environment that firms must consider when planning for their futures.

Legal Factors

Legal factors in the external environment often coincide with political factors because laws are enacted by government entities. This does not mean that the categories identify the same issues, however. Although labor laws and environmental regulations have deep political connections, other legal factors can impact business success. For example, in the streaming video industry, licensing fees are a significant cost for firms. Netflix pays billions of dollars every year to movie and television studios for the right to broadcast their content. In addition to the legal requirement to pay the studios, Netflix must consider that consumers may find illegal ways to view the movies they want to see, making them less willing to pay to subscribe to Netflix. Intellectual property rights and patents are major issues in the legal realm.

Note that some external factors are difficult to categorize in PESTEL. For instance tariffs can be viewed as either a political or economic factor while the influence of the internet could be viewed as either a technological or social factor. While some issues can overlap two or more PESTEL areas, it does not diminish the value of PESTEL as an analytical tool,

CONCEPT CHECK

1. Describe a firm's macro environment.
2. What does PESTEL stand for? How do managers use PESTEL to understand their firm's macro environment?

ETHICS IN PRACTICE

Sustainability and Responsible Management: *Can LEGO Give up Plastic?*

"In 2012, the LEGO Group first shared its ambition to find and implement sustainable alternatives to the current raw materials used to manufacture LEGO products by 2030. The ambition is part of the LEGO Group's work to reduce its environmental footprint and leave a positive impact on the planet our children will inherit."[8]

Danish toy company LEGO announced in 2015 that it would invest almost $160 million dollars into its efforts to meet the goal it announced in 2012. You know LEGO—they are the colored plastic bricks that snap together to make toys ranging from Harry Potter castles to Star Wars fighter craft. The family-owned company was founded in 1932 by Ole Kirk Christiansen and has since grown to be the world's number one toy brand.[9]

Given that LEGO and plastic seem to go hand in hand, why would the company want to give up on the material that makes their toys so successful? LEGO's manufacturing process relies on plastic to make highly precise plastic bricks that always fit together securely and easily. Replacing the plastic with another material that is durable, can be brightly colored, and can be molded as precisely is a difficult task. LEGO's leadership has decided that a strategic position based on fossil fuels is not sustainable and is making plans now to transition to a more environmentally friendly material to manufacture its products.

Switching from oil-based plastic might make economic sense as well. Manufacturers who rely on petroleum-based products must weather volatile oil prices. LEGO's raw materials costs could skyrocket overnight if the price of oil climbs again as it did in 2011. That price spike was due to conflict in Libya and other parts of the Arab world,[10] something entirely beyond the control of any business.

Technological innovations in bio-based plastics may be the answer for LEGO,[11] which is working with university researchers around the globe to find a solution to its carbon-footprint problem.

Sources: Trangbæk, Roar Rude (2016). "LEGO Group to invest 1 Billion DKK Boosting Search for Sustainable Materials." https://www.lego.com/en-us/aboutus/news-room/2015/june/sustainable-materials-centre. Accessed July 29, 2017; Brand Finance (2017). "Toys 25 2016." http://brandfinance.com/images/upload/brand_finance_toys_25_2017_report_locked.pdf Accessed July 29, 2017; Holodny, Elena (2016). TIMELINE: The tumultuous 155-year history of oil prices. *Business Insider*. http://www.businessinsider.com/timeline-155-year-history-of-oil-prices-2016-12 Accessed July 29, 2017; and Peters, Adele (2015). "Why LEGO is Spending Millions to Ditch Oil-Based Plastic." *Fast Company*. https://www.fastcompany.com/3048017/why-lego-is-spending-millions-to-ditch-oil-based-plastic Accessed July 29, 2017.

Critical Thinking Questions
1. How would you approach this issue if you were the manager in charge of sourcing raw materials for LEGO? How would PESTEL analysis inform your actions?
2. What PESTEL challenges is LEGO trying to address by changing the raw materials used in its products?
3. Explain what favorable PESTEL factors support LEGO's efforts.

8.4 | A Firm's Micro Environment: Porter's Five Forces

4. What makes up a firm's external micro environment, and what tools do strategists use to understand it?

A firm's **micro environment** is illustrated in the green circle in **Exhibit 8.4**. These entities are all directly connected to the firm in some way, and firms must understand the micro environment in order to successfully compete in an industry. All firms are part of an **industry**—a group of firms all making similar products or offering similar services, for example automobile manufacturers or airlines. Firms in an industry may or may not compete directly against one another, as we'll discuss shortly, but they all face similar situations in terms of customer interests, supplier relations, and industry growth or decline.

Harvard strategy professor Michael Porter developed an analysis tool to evaluate a firm's micro environment. **Porter's Five Forces** is a tool used to examine different micro-environmental groups in order to understand the impact each group has on a firm in an industry (**Exhibit 8.6**). Each of the forces represents an aspect of competition that affects a firm's potential to be successful in its industry. It is important to note that this tool is different than Porter's generic strategy typology that we will discuss later.

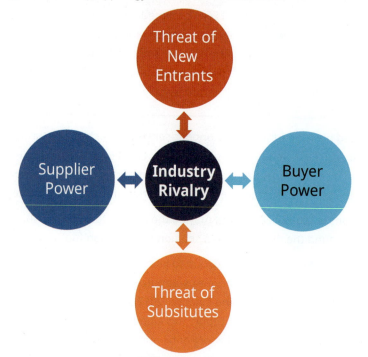

Exhibit 8.6   Porter's Five Forces Model of Industry Competition (Attribution: Copyright Rice University, OpenStax, under CC-BY 4.0 license)

Industry Rivalry

Industry rivalry, the first of Porter's forces, is in the center of the diagram. Note that the arrows in the diagram show two-way relationships between rivalry and all of the other forces. This is because each force can affect how hard firms in an industry must compete against each other to gain customers, establish favorable supplier relationships, and defend themselves against new firms entering the industry.

When using Porter's model, an analyst will determine if each force has a strong or weak impact on industry firms. In the case of rivalry, the question of strength focuses on how hard firms must fight against industry rivals (competitors) to gain customers and market share. Strong rivalry in an industry reduces the profit potential for all firms because consumers have many firms from which to purchase products or services and can make at least part of their purchasing decisions based on prices. An industry with weak rivalry will have few firms, meaning that there are enough customers for everyone, or will have firms that have each staked out a unique position in the industry, meaning that customers will be more loyal to the firm that best meets their particular needs.

The Threat of New Entrants

In an industry, there are incumbent (existing) firms that compete against each other as rivals. If an industry has a growing market or is very profitable, however, it may attract **new entrants**. These either are firms that start up in the industry as new companies or are firms from another industry that expand their capabilities or target markets to compete in an industry that is new to them.

Different industries may be easier or harder to enter depending on **barriers to entry**, factors that prevent new firms from successfully competing in the industry. Common barriers to entry include cost, brand loyalty, and industry growth. For example, the firms in the airline industry rarely face threats from new entrants because it is very expensive to obtain the equipment, airport landing rights, and expertise to start up a new airline.

Brand loyalty can also keep new firms from entering an industry, because customers who are familiar with a strong brand name may be unwilling to try a new, unknown brand. Industry growth can increase or decrease the chances a new entrant will succeed. In an industry with low growth, new customers are scarce, and a firm can only gain market share by attracting customers of other firms. Think of all the ads you see and hear from competing cell phone providers. Cell phone companies are facing lower industry growth and must offer consumers incentives to switch from another provider. On the other hand, high-growth industries have an increasing number of customers, and new firms can successfully appeal to new customers by offering them something existing firms do not offer. It is important to note that barriers to entry are not always external, firms often lobby politicians for regulations that can be a barrier to entry. These types of barriers will be covered in greater depth in more upper level courses.

Threat of Substitutes

In the context of Porter's model, a **substitute** is any other product or service that can satisfy the same need for a customer as an industry's offerings. Be careful not to confuse substitutes with rivals. Rivals offer similar products or services and directly compete with one another. Substitutes are completely different products or services that consumers would be willing to use instead of the product they currently use. For example, the fast food industry offers quickly prepared, convenient, low-cost meals. Customers can go to McDonald's, Wendy's, Burger King, or Taco Bell—all of these firms compete against each other for business. However, their customers are really just hungry people. What else could you do if you were hungry? You could go to the grocery store and buy food to prepare at home. McDonald's does not directly compete against Kroger for customers, because they are in different industries, but McDonald's does face a threat from grocery stores because they both sell food. How does McDonald's defend itself from the threat of Kroger as a substitute? By making sure their food is already prepared and convenient to purchase—your burger or salad is ready to eat and available without even getting out of your car.

Exhibit 8.7   McDonalds A drive-through menu at this McDonald's is designed to help customers choose their meal quickly and have it ready for pickup at the drive-through window. (Credit: Caribb/ flickr/ Public Domain)

Supplier Power

Virtually all firms have suppliers who sell parts, materials, labor, or products. **Supplier power** refers to the balance of power in the relationship between firms and their suppliers in an industry. Suppliers can have the upper hand in a relationship if they offer specialized products or control rare resources. For example, when Sony develops a new PlayStation model, it often works with a single supplier to develop the most advanced processor chip it can for their game console. That means its supplier will be able to command a fairly high price for the processors, an indication that the supplier has power. On the other hand, a firm that needs commodity resources such as oil, wheat, or aluminum in its operations will have many suppliers to choose from and can easily switch suppliers if price or quality is better from a new partner. Commodity suppliers usually have low power.

Buyer Power

The last of Porter's forces is **buyer power**, which refers to the balance of power in the relationship between a firm and its customers. If a firm provides a unique good or service, it will have the power to charge its customers premium prices, because those customers have no choice but to buy from the firm if they need that product. In contrast, when customers have many potential sources for a product, firms will need to attract customers by offering better prices or better value for the money if they want to sell their products. One protection firms have against buyer power is **switching costs**, the penalty consumers face when they choose to use a particular product made by a different company. Switching costs can be financial (the extra price paid to choose a different product) or practical (the time or hassle required to switch to a different product). For example, think about your smartphone. If you have an iPhone now, what would be the penalty for you to switch to a non-Apple smartphone? Would it just be the cost of the new phone? Smartphones are not inexpensive, but even when cell phone service providers offer free phones to new customers, many people still don't switch. The loss of compatibility with other Apple products, the need to transfer apps and phone settings to another system, and the loss of favorite iPhone features, such as iMessage, are enough to keep many people loyal to their iPhones.

CONCEPT CHECK

1. Describe each of Porter's Five Forces. What information does each provide a manager trying to understand her firm's micro environment?

8.5 | The Internal Environment

5. How and why do managers conduct an internal analysis of their firms?

A firm's internal environment is illustrated in **Exhibit 8.4** by the innermost orange circle. The **internal environment** consists of members of the firm itself, investors in the firm, and the assets a firm has. Employees and managers are good examples; they are firm members who have skills and knowledge that are valuable assets to their firms. Evaluating a firm's internal environment is not just a matter of counting heads, however. Successful firms have a wide range of resources and capabilities that they can use to maintain their success and grow into new ventures. A thorough analysis of a firm's internal situation provides a manager with an understanding of the resources available to pursue new initiatives, innovate, and plan for future success.

Resources and Capabilities

A firm's resources and capacities are the unique skills and assets it possesses. **Resources** are things a firm has to work with, such as equipment, facilities, raw materials, employees, and cash. **Capabilities** are things a firm can do, such as deliver good customer service or develop innovative products to create value. Both are the building blocks of a firm's plans and activities, and both are required if a firm is going to compete successfully against its rivals. Firms use their resources and leverage their capabilities to create products and services that have some advantage over competitors' products. For example, a firm might offer its customers a product with higher quality, better features, or lower prices. Not all resources and capabilities are equally helpful in creating success, though. Internal analysis identifies exactly which assets bring the most value to the firm.

The Value Chain

Before examining the role of resources and capabilities in firm success, let's take a look at the importance of how a firm uses those factors in its operations. A firm's **value chain** is the progression of activities it undertakes to create a product or service that consumers will pay for. A firm should be adding value at each of the chain of steps it follows to create its product. The goal is for the firm to add enough value so that its customers will believe that the product is worth buying for a price that is higher than the costs the firm incurs in making it. As an example, **Exhibit 8.8** illustrates a hypothetical value chain for some of Walmart's activities.

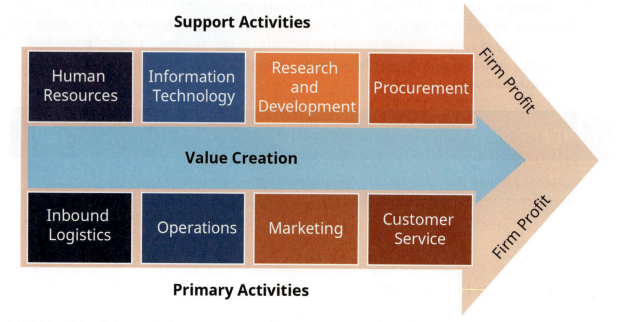

Exhibit 8.8   A Value Chain Example (Attribution: Copyright Rice University, OpenStax, under CC-BY 4.0 license)

In this example, note that value increases from left to right as Walmart performs more activities. If it adds enough value through its efforts, it will profit when it finally sells its services to customers. By working with product suppliers (procurement), getting those products to store locations efficiently (inbound logistics), and automatically keeping track of sales and inventory (information technology), Walmart is able to offer its customers a wide variety of products in one store at low prices, a service customers value. **Primary activities**, the ones across the bottom half of the diagram, are the actions a firm takes to directly provide a product or service to customers. **Support activities**, the ones across the top of the diagram, are actions required to sustain the firm that are not directly part of product or service creation.

Using Resources and Capabilities to Build an Advantage over Rivals

A firm's resources and capabilities are not just a list of equipment and things it can do. Instead, resources and capabilities are the distinctive assets and activities that separate firms from each other. Firms that can amass critical resources and develop superior capabilities will succeed in competition over rivals in their industry. Strategists evaluate firm resources and capabilities to determine if they are sufficiently special to help the firm succeed in a competitive industry.

Using VRIO

The analytical tool used to assess resources and capabilities is called **VRIO**. As usual, this is an acronym developed to remind managers of the questions to ask when evaluating their firms' resources and capabilities. The four questions of VRIO, which focus on **v**alue, **r**arity, **i**mitation, and **o**rganization, are illustrated in **Exhibit**

8.9.

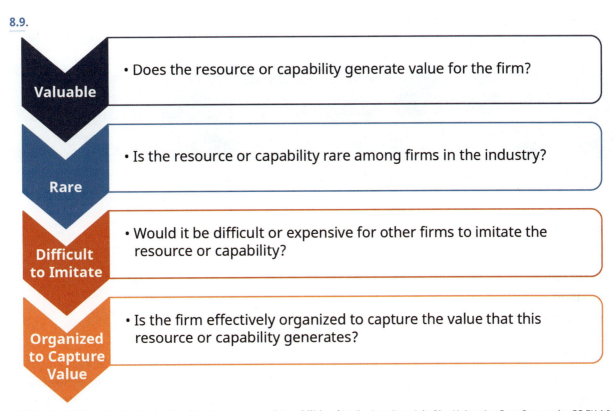

Exhibit 8.9 VRIO, a Tool for Evaluating Firm Resources and Capabilities (Attribution: Copyright Rice University, OpenStax, under CC-BY 4.0 license)

If each question can be answered with a "yes," then the resource or capability being evaluated can be the source of a competitive advantage for the firm. An example will help you better understand the VRIO process.

Imagine that you are a top manager for Starbucks and you want to understand why you are able to be successful against rivals in the coffee industry. You make a list of some of Starbucks' resources and capabilities and use VRIO to determine which ones are key to your success. These are shown in **Table 8.1**.

Starbucks' Resources and Capabilities	
Resources	Capabilities
Brand name	Making quality coffee drinks
Thousands of locations worldwide	Delivering excellent customer service
Cash	Training excellent staff
Loyal customers	Paying above-average wages
Well-trained employees	Retaining quality employees

Table 8.1 (Attribution: Copyright Rice University, OpenStax, under CC-BY 4.0 license)

You look at your list and decide to pick a few of the entries to evaluate with VRIO (**Table 8.2**):

Evaluating Starbucks' VRIO					
Resource/Capability	Is it valuable?	Is it rare?	Is it difficult to imitate?	Is Starbucks organized to capture its value?	Can it be a basis for competitive advantage?
Brand name	Yes	Yes	Yes	Yes	Yes
Delivering excellent customer service	Yes	Yes	Yes	Yes	Yes
Thousands of locations worldwide	Yes	No	No	Yes	No

Table 8.2 (Attribution: Copyright Rice University, OpenStax, under CC-BY 4.0 license)

According to the evaluation above, Starbucks' brand helps it compete and succeed against rivals, as does its excellent customer service. However, simply having a lot of locations globally isn't enough to beat rivals—McDonald's and Subway also have thousands of worldwide locations, and both serve coffee. Starbucks succeeds against them because of their brand and customer service.

CONCEPT CHECK

1. What are firm resources and capabilities?
2. Describe a value chain and what the activities in the chain represent.
3. What is VRIO? What questions do the letters stand for, and how does using VRIO help a manager make decisions?

MANAGING CHANGE

Technology and Innovation: Uber, Lyft, and the Self-Driving Car: The Transportation of the Future Is Coming Soon

Although the ride-sharing industry is still relatively new, it has seen explosive growth, and its two main rivals, Uber and Lyft, are looking for ways to increase their capacity to serve riders. Both firms, and rivals like them, operate in basically the same way. A person needing a ride uses a smartphone app to alert a nearby person with a car of their location. The driver, usually an independent contractor for the service (meaning they are just a person with a car that has signed up to provide rides in exchange for a portion of the fare the customer pays), picks up the customer and drives them to their destination. Paying for the ride is also handled through the app, and the driver receives about 75–80% of the fare, with Uber or Lyft keeping the balance.[12]

Exhibit 8.10 Rideshare pickup area The ride-share pickup area at Pierre Elliott Trudeau Airport in Montreal. Due to the popularity of ride sharing with companies such as Uber and Lyft, municipalities and airports have had to accommodate the changing demands of customers. (Credit: Quinn Dombroski/ flickr/ Attribution-ShareAlike2.0 Generic (CC BY-NC 2.0))

The popularity of ride-sharing services has soared, and both companies are constantly recruiting more drivers. However, both companies have also explored alternatives to independent drivers: self-driving cars. Uber and Lyft have taken different paths to develop this capability. Uber has worked to internally develop its own software technology and self-driving car technology, while Lyft has focused on software interfaces that can accommodate other companies' self-driving cars.[13] Lyft's partnerships with firms such as Google and GM that are already developing self-driving cars has put it ahead of Uber in the race to get driverless vehicles into its ride-sharing network, and it was able to test self-driving cars in Boston by partnering with NuTonomy in 2017.[14] Lyft offered a demonstration to journalists at the Consumer Electronics Show in Las Vegas in 2018, offering rides in self-driving cars developed by Aptiv.[15] Uber had been testing similar technology in Pittsburgh but suspended its self-driving car program after a fatal pedestrian accident in Arizona.[16]

Sources: Ridester (2017). "How Much do Uber Drivers Actually Make? The Inside Scoop." *Ridester.com.* https://www.ridester.com/how-much-do-uber-drivers-make/ Accessed July 29, 2017; Bensinger, Greg

(2017). "Lyft Shifts Gears With New Driverless-Car Division; San Francisco company to hire hundreds of engineers and open new Silicon Valley office." *The Wall Street Journal*. July 21, 2017; Edelstein, Stephen (2017). "Lyft Finally Launches Its Boston Self-Driving Car Pilot Program." *The Drive*. Dec. 17, 2017. http://www.thedrive.com/tech/16779/lyft-finally-launches-its-boston-self-driving-car-pilot-program; O'Kane, Sean (2018). "I took a gamble by riding in a self-driving Lyft in Las Vegas." *The Verge*. January 8, 2018. https://www.theverge.com/2018/1/8/16860590/self-driving-lyft-las-vegas-ces-2018; and Korosec, Kristen (2018). "Uber self-driving cars back on public roads, but in manual mode/" *Tech Crunch*. July 24, 2018. https://techcrunch.com/2018/07/24/uber-self-driving-cars-back-on-public-roads-but-in-manual-mode/.

Critical Thinking Questions
1. What resource or capability challenges have Uber and Lyft faced because their fast company growth?
2. What PESTEL factors do you think are contributing to the popularity of ride-sharing services?
3. What industry challenges (think of Porter's Five Forces) does the use of self-driving cars address?

8.6 | Competition, Strategy, and Competitive Advantage

6. What does it mean to compete with other firms in a business environment, what does it mean when a firm has a competitive advantage over its rivals, and what generic strategies can a firm implement to gain advantage over its rivals?

Now that you understand more about the environment that businesses operate in, let's take a deeper look at exactly how they operate. Businesses exist to make profits by offering goods and services in the marketplace at prices that are higher than the costs they incurred creating those goods and services. Businesses rarely exist alone in an industry; **competition** is a usually a key part of any marketplace. This means that businesses must find ways to attract customers to their products and away from competitors' products. **Strategy** is the process of planning and implementing actions that will lead to success in competition.

The analytical tools we discuss here are part of the strategic planning process. Managers cannot successfully plan to compete in an industry if they don't understand its competitive landscape. It is also unlikely that a firm planning to launch a new product they are not equipped to make will be successful.

Competition

Porter's Five Forces model is centered around rivalry, a synonym for competition. In any industry, multiple firms compete against each other for customers by offering better or cheaper products than their rivals. Firms use PESTEL to understand what consumers are interested in and use VRIO to evaluate their own resources and capabilities so that they can figure out how to offer products and services that match those consumer interests and that are better in quality and price than the products offered by their competitors.

A firm is described as having a **competitive advantage** when it successfully attracts more customers, earns more profit, or returns more value to its shareholders than rival firms do. A firm achieves a competitive advantage by adding value to its products and services or reducing its own costs more effectively than its rivals in the industry.

Generic Business-Level Competitive Strategies

When discussing business strategy, a business is a firm or a unit of a firm that centers its activities around one primary type of product or service line. Business-level strategy is the general way that a business organizes its activities to compete against rivals in its product's industry. Michael Porter (the same Harvard professor who developed the Five Forces Model) defined three **generic business-level strategies** that outline the basic methods of organizing to compete in a product market. He called the strategies "generic" because these ways of organizing can be used by any firm in any industry.

Cost Leadership

When pursuing a **cost-leadership strategy**, a firm offers customers its product or service at a lower price than its rivals can. To achieve a competitive advantage over rivals in the industry, the successful cost leader tightly controls costs throughout its value chain activities. Supplier relationships are managed to guarantee the lowest prices for parts, manufacturing is conducted in the least expensive labor markets, and operations may be automated for maximum efficiency. A cost leader must spend as little as possible producing a product or providing a service so that it will still be profitable when selling that product or service at the lowest price. Walmart is the master of cost leadership, offering a wide variety of products at lower prices than competitors because it does not spend money on fancy stores, it extracts low prices from its suppliers, and its pays its employees relatively low wages.

Differentiation

Not all products or services in the marketplace are offered at low prices, of course. A **differentiation strategy** is exactly the opposite of a cost-leadership strategy. While firms do not look to spend as much as possible to produce their output, firms that differentiate try to add value to their products and services so they can attract customers who are willing to pay a higher price. At each step in the value chain, the differentiator increases the quality, features, and overall attractiveness of its products or services. Research and development efforts focus on innovation, customer service is excellent, and marketing bolsters the value of the firm brand. These efforts guarantee that the successful differentiator can still profit even though its production costs are higher than a cost leader's. Starbucks is a good example of a differentiator: it makes coffee, but its customers are willing to pay premium prices for a cup of Starbucks coffee because they value the restaurant atmosphere, customer service, product quality, and brand.

Porter's typology assumes that firms can succeed through either cost leadership or differentiation. Trying to combine these two, Porter suggests, can lead to a firm being stuck in the middle.

Focus

Porter's third generic competitive strategy, **focus**, is a little different from the other two. A firm that focuses still must choose one of the other strategies to organize its activities. It will still strive to lower costs or add value. The difference here is that a firm choosing to implement a focused strategy will concentrate its marketing and selling efforts on a smaller market than a broad cost leader or differentiator. A firm following a focus-differentiation strategy, for example, will add value to its product or service that a few customers will value highly, either because the product is specifically suited to a particular use or because it is a luxury product that few can afford. For example, Flux is a company that offers custom-made bindings for your snowboard. Flux is a focus differentiator because it makes a specialized product that is valued by a small market of customers who are willing to pay premium prices for high-quality, customized snowboarding equipment.

Exhibit 8.11   Snowboard bindings The Flux premium bindings on this snowboard are an example of a product on a focus-driven company. Snowboard bindings are the only products Flux markets. (Credit: Ted and dani Percival/ flickr/ Attribution 2.0 Generic (CC BY 2.0))

Strategic Groups

When managers analyze their competitive environment and examine rivalry within their industry, they are not confronted by an infinite variety of competitors. Although there are millions of businesses of all sizes around the globe, a single business usually competes mainly against other businesses offering similar products or services and following the same generic competitive strategy. Groups of businesses that follow similar strategies in the same industry are called **strategic groups**, and it is important that a manager know the other firms in their strategic group. Rivalry is fiercest within a strategic group, and the actions of one firm in a group will elicit responses from other group members, who don't want to lose market share in the industry. Take a look at **Exhibit 8.12**: although all of the firms shown are in the retail industry, they don't all compete directly against one another.

Exhibit 8.12 Strategic Groups in the Retail Industry (Attribution: Copyright Rice University, OpenStax, under CC-BY 4.0 license)

Although some cross competition can occur (for example, you could buy a Kate Spade wallet at Nordstrom), firms in different strategic groups tend to compete more with each other than against firms outside their group. Although Walmart and Neiman Marcus both offer a wide variety of products, the two firms do not cater to the same customers, and their managers do not lose sleep at night wondering what each might do next. On the other hand, a Walmart manager would be concerned with the products or prices offered at Target; if laundry detergent is on sale at Target, the Walmart manager might lose sales from customers who buy it at Target instead, and so the Walmart manager might respond to Target's sale price by discounting the same detergent at Walmart.

CONCEPT CHECK

1. What is competition, and what is the role of strategy in competition?
2. When does a firm have a competitive advantage over its rivals?
3. Explain the differences between the three business-level generic competitive strategies.

8.7 Strategic Positioning

7. What elements go into determining a firm's strategic position?

A manager who has done all of the analysis described so far in this chapter has some decisions to make based on all of the information the analysis has revealed. A firm's decisions on how to serve customers and compete against rivals is called **strategic positioning**. In order to develop its position, a firm combines its understanding of the competitive environment, including the firm's own resources and capabilities, its industry situation, and facts about the macro environment. A strategic position includes a choice of generic competitive strategy, which a firm selects based on its own capabilities and in response to the positions already staked out by its industry rivals. The firm also determines which customers to serve and what those customers are willing to pay for. A strategic position also includes decisions about what geographic markets to participate in.

Most importantly, a firm's strategic position should try to be unique in some way that competitors cannot imitate quickly or easily. Competitive advantage is achieved when a firm attracts more customers or makes more profit than rivals. This cannot happen unless the firm organizes its activities to provide customers with better value than rivals.

CONCEPT CHECK

1. How does strategic analysis help a firm develop its own strategic position?

🔑 Key Terms

barriers to entry Industry factors (such as high start-up costs) that can prevent new firms from successfully launching new operations in that industry.

buyer power In the relationship between a firm and its customers, buyers with high power can negotiate product price or features, while buyers with low power cannot.

capabilities A firm's skill at coordinating and leveraging resources to create value.

competition Business actions a firm undertakes to attract customers to its products and away from competitors' products.

competitive advantage When a firm successfully attracts more customers, earns more profit, or returns more value to its shareholders than rival firms do.

competitive environment Factors and situations both inside the firm and outside the firm that have the potential to impact its operations and success.

cost-leadership strategy A generic business-level strategy in which a firm tightly controls costs throughout its value chain activities in order to offer customers low-priced goods and services at a profit.

demographics Part of PESTEL that includes facts about the income, education, age, and ethnic and racial composition of a population.

differentiation strategy A generic business-level strategy in which firms add value to their products and services in order to attract customers who are willing to pay a higher price.

economic factors PESTEL category that includes facts (such as unemployment rates, interest rates, and commodity prices) about the state of the local, national, or global economy.

environmental factors PESTEL category that examines a firm's external situation with respect to the natural environment, including pollution, natural resource availability and preservation, and alternative energy.

environmental scanning The systematic and intentional analysis of a firm's internal state and its external environment.

external environment The aspects of the world at large and of a firm's industry that can impact its operations.

external factors Things in the world or industry environments that may impact a firm's operations or success, such as the economy, government actions, or supplier power. Strategic decisions can be made in response to these things but normally cannot directly influence or change them.

focus strategy A generic business-level competitive strategy that firms use in combination with either a cost-leadership or differentiation strategy in order to target a smaller demographic or geographic market with specialized products or services.

generic business-level strategies Basic methods of organizing firm value chain activities to compete in a product market that can be used by any sized firm in any industry.

industry A group of firms all offering products or services in a single category, for example restaurants or athletic equipment.

industry rivalry One of Porter's Five Forces; refers to the intensity of competition between firms in an industry.

internal environment Innermost layer of a firm's competitive environment, including members of the firm itself (such as employees and managers), investors in the firm, and the resources and capabilities of a firm.

internal factors Characteristics of a firm itself, such as resources and capabilities, that the firm can use to successfully compete against its rivals.

legal factors In PESTEL, the laws impacting business, such as those governing contracts and intellectual property rights and illegal activities, such as online piracy.

macro environment The outermost layer of elements in a firm's external environment that can impact a business but are generally beyond the firm's direct control, such as the economy and political activity.

micro environment The middle layer of elements in a firm's external environment, primarily concerned with a firm's industry situation.

new entrants One of Porter's Five Forces, the threat of new entrants assesses the potential that a new firm will start operations in an industry.

opportunity A situation that a firm has the resources and capabilities to take advantage of.

PESTEL A strategic analysis tool that examines several distinct categories in the macro environment: **p**olitical, **e**conomic, **s**ociocultural, **t**echnological, **e**nvironmental, and **l**egal.

political factors PESTEL factor that identifies political activities in the macro environment that may be relevant to a firm's operations.

Porter's Five Forces Evaluates the interconnected relationships between various actors in an industry, including competing firms, their suppliers, and their customers, by examining five forces: industry rivalry, threat of new entrants, threat of substitutes, supplier power, and buyer power.

primary activities Firm activities on the value chain that are directly responsible for creating, selling, or servicing a product or service, such as manufacturing and marketing.

resources Things a firm has, such as cash and skilled employees, that it can use to create products or services.

sociocultural factors PESTEL category that identifies trends, facts, and changes in society's composition, tastes, and behaviors, including demographics.

strategic analysis Process that firms use to study and understand their competitive environment.

strategic group Businesses offering similar products or services and following the same generic competitive strategy.

strategic positioning Firm's decisions on how to organize its actions and operate to effectively serve customers and compete against rivals.

strategy Process of planning and implementing actions that will lead to success in competition.

strengths Resources and capabilities of a firm; what it is good at.

substitutes One of Porter's Five Forces; products or services outside a firm's industry that can satisfy the same customer needs as industry products or services can.

supplier power One of Porter's Five Forces; describes the balance of power in the relationship between firms in an industry and their suppliers.

support activities Value chain activities that a firm performs to sustain itself; do not directly create a product or service but are necessary to support the firm's existence, such as accounting and human resources.

switching costs Penalty, financial or otherwise, that a consumer bears when giving up the use of a product currently being used to select a competing product or service.

SWOT Strategic analysis tool used to examine a firm's situation by looking at its **s**trengths, **w**eaknesses, **o**pportunities, and **t**hreats.

technological factors PESTEL category that includes factors such as the Internet, social media, automation, and other innovations that impact how businesses compete or how they manufacture, market, or sell their goods or services.

threat Anything in the competitive environment that would make it harder for a firm to be successful.

value chain Sequence of activities that firms perform to turn inputs (parts or supplies) into outputs (goods or services).

VRIO analytical tool that evaluates a firm's resources and capabilities to determine whether or not it can support an advantage for the firm in the competitive environment: **v**alue, **r**arity, **i**mitation, and **o**rganization.

weaknesses Things that a firm does not have good capabilities to perform or gaps in firm resources.

Summary of Learning Outcomes

8.1 Gaining Advantages by Understanding the Competitive Environment

1. What is strategic analysis, and why do firms need to analyze their competitive environment?

Strategic analysis is a systematic evaluation of a firm's situation, both internally and with respect to what is happening in the outside world. This analysis examines what the firm itself is good or bad at, how rivals in its industry are competing against it for customers, and what factors in the world environment, such as economic indicators or demographic changes, might impact the firm's ability to be successful.

Firms need to conduct this analysis in order to be aware of and prepared for changes in their competitive environment and to maximize their chance of successfully competing against rivals and sustaining their profitability and market share in their industry.

8.2 Using SWOT for Strategic Analysis

2. What is a SWOT analysis, and what can it reveal about a firm?

SWOT is a traditional analytical tool that identifies a firm's **s**trengths, **w**eaknesses, **o**pportunities, and **t**hreats (SWOT is an acronym of these four factors). It is useful for conducting a quick look at the internal capabilities (strengths and weaknesses) and external events and situations (opportunities and threats) a firm is facing.

SWOT is not a comprehensive analytical tool, because the four categories for analysis are too broad and will not necessarily identify all of the factors important to a firm's success that a more thorough analysis would.

8.3 A Firm's External Macro Environment: PESTEL

3. What makes up a firm's external macro environment, and what tools do strategists use to understand it?

The external environment of a firm is composed of two primary layers: the macro environment and the micro environment. The macro environment includes facts and situations that a firm must be aware of but cannot always influence. The macro environment is analyzed using the PESTEL analytical tool that considers a firm's political and legal aspects, economic indicators, sociocultural trends, demographic facts, technological changes, and environmental aspects.

8.4 A Firm's Micro Environment: Porter's Five Forces

4. What makes up a firm's external micro environment, and what tools do strategists use to understand it?

The second layer of a firm's external environment is its micro environment, which includes the components of a firm's industry, such as competitors, suppliers, and customers. Porter's Five Forces of industry competition (industry rivalry, threat of new entrants, threat of substitutes, supplier power, and buyer power) capture the dynamic relationships between these components.

8.5 The Internal Environment

5. How and why do managers conduct an internal analysis of their firms?

Managers cannot lead their firms to success without understanding what the firm is able to do. An analysis of the firm's resources and capabilities, as well as its gaps, is essential in determining the best path forward for the firm. A good strategy for competitive advantage capitalizes on a firm's key resources and capabilities, as identified and evaluated using the VRIO (**v**alue, **r**arity, **i**mitation, and **o**rganization) analytical tool.

Resources and capabilities that satisfy VRIO criteria are the key things that a firm is best at, and these should be leveraged so the firm can compete against rivals.

8.6 Competition, Strategy, and Competitive Advantage

6. What does it mean to compete with other firms in a business environment, and what does it mean when a firm has a competitive advantage over its rivals and what generic strategies can a firm implement to gain advantage over its rivals?

Competition is the battle for customers. Firms compete against rivals offering similar products and services and try to attract customers by making sure their product or service is a little better or less expensive than those of their competitors. The firm that is most successful in this battle, measured in terms of profitability or in terms of market share, has a competitive advantage.

Generic competitive strategies are the basic templates for organizing firm activities in order to achieve competitive advantage in an industry. A firm will perform value chain activities, such as marketing and research and development, in order to support the overall competitive strategy it has chosen.

Following a generic cost-leadership strategy requires that a firm try to save money throughout the value chain so that it can offer customers low-priced goods and services. In contrast, differentiators add value to their products and services while performing value chain activities so that they can charge premium prices to consumers.

A third generic competitive strategy, focus, is chosen in combination with one of the other two strategies by firms who decide to target smaller geographic or demographic customer groups.

8.7 Strategic Positioning

7. What elements go into determining a firm's strategic position?

A firm develops a strategic position in response to the factors present in its competitive environment. Strategic analysis is essential in identifying and understanding the factors that a strategic position must address. The choice of strategic position factors in a firm's key resources and capabilities when choosing a generic competitive strategy, product or service to be offered, target market, and geographic reach to compete successfully against rivals in an industry. To be successful in allowing a firm to achieve a competitive advantage in its industry, a firm's strategic position should be different from its competitors' positions in the same industry and should be hard for competitors to copy so that the firm's competitive advantage lasts.

Chapter Review Questions

1. Why do managers use strategic analysis?
2. What information does a SWOT analysis provide managers? What information might it miss?
3. Describe a firm's macro environment and how managers use PESTEL to understand it.
4. What is a firm's micro environment, and why is it important?
5. What is an industry, and how do Porter's Five Forces help a manager trying to understand a firm's industry environment?
6. What are firm resources and capabilities, and what information does VRIO provide about them?
7. When does a firm have a competitive advantage over its rivals?
8. What are generic competitive strategies, and how are they implemented in a firm's value chain activities?
9. What do strategic group members have in common with each other? What impact do firms outside a strategic group have on those in that group?
10. How does strategic analysis help a firm develop its own strategic position? Why should that position be unique?

👥 Management Skills Application Exercises

1. (Analytical Skills) Assume that you have been hired by a local small-business consulting firm. You have been asked by your boss to review a proposal from a client who is considering opening a new Pilates and yoga studio in a trendy part of town. Because you know SWOT analysis, you have been asked to group the following attributes about the proposed business into a SWOT analysis:

    a. The proposed location is on the same street corner as the main subway line station and three blocks from a ferry terminal that commuters use go to work.

    b. The proposed location has a vestibule and a new HVAC system.

    c. The street that the location is situated on has many small shops, restaurants, and bars and is a popular gathering place.

    d. There are many historic structures that are in need of updates, but some owners are reluctant to invest in these aging structures.

    e. The area has become gentrified over the past decade, and there is more disposable income than in the past.

    f. In addition to the young professionals, a large number of 55 and over retirees who are now empty nesters have been moving into the neighborhood.

    g. With the young professionals and empty nesters, this area has one of the lowest birth rates in the nation.

    h. The two-year lease is affordable for the business plan, but there is no guarantee of renewal after the term.

    i. There is a rumor of a spin studio opening two blocks away.

    j. The building has been updated with ramps and restrooms to accommodate disabled patrons.

    k. The local paper has interviewed the client and will be running a "Pilates Craze" feature in the upcoming weekend newspaper.

2. (Interpersonal Skills) Your instructor may assign you to a small group, and you will receive either a "Team A" or "Team B" assignment. Team A groups will need to meet for 15 minutes in a face-to-face setting, while Team B members will meet electronically either by setting up a meeting via Skype or using text messaging on their cell phones. Team A members will need to set up a time and location for their meeting while Team B members will need to share their contact information with a team leader.
Your instructor will assign a company to discuss and report on. Team A will discuss a firm's internal environment while team B will discuss the firm's external environment. In class, each team will report its conclusions about its assignment and report on the benefits and challenges that meeting in person or electronically posed.

3. (Communication) Set up an interview with a manager at a local business who is involved in the strategic planning process at her company. Ask her what type of planning she is involved in (strategic, operational). Discover if she involves the employees who report to her in the planning process and how planning is tied to goal setting. Write a report on your findings. The interview should take no more than 15 minutes.

🔱 Managerial Decision Exercises

1. Select three different businesses from different industries, such as a hospitality business (hotel, restaurant, fitness center), a manufacturing company, and a not-for-profit business. Perform a SWOT analysis for each business.

2. Perform a quick PESTEL analysis of the companies listed below. What is the largest risk for each of the

companies? Assume that you had $100,000 to invest in one of more of these companies. Explain how you would allocate your investment and why you chose this particular allocation.

   a. Uber

   b. Tesla

   c. General Motors

3. Technology has the ability to disrupt industries. You are involved in an industry that is undergoing change and disruption by taking this class. The traditional textbook industry is being disrupted by the availability of digital textbooks, and free textbooks such as this one are further impacting traditional textbook publishers. Place the following statements into Porter's Five Forces model.

   a. Students have access to the material at a greatly reduced cost.

   b. Authorship is funded through philanthropic donations rather than royalties paid from textbook sales revenue.

   c. More students have access to the Internet than ever before.

   d. Companies, governments, and students invest large sums of money in their education.

   e. Traditional public educational institutions are adapting their delivery models for online learning.

   f. Private companies such as Apollo (University of Phoenix) are offering lower-cost education options.

   g. Bookstores now offer traditional textbooks as well as used and rental options.

   h. Government legislation is urging faculty to consider lower-cost options.

Critical Thinking Case

Tesla Aims for the Mass Market

Elon Musk cofounded Tesla in 2003 with the vision of making electric cars that could rival, and even replace, traditional gas-engine cars in the consumer marketplace. At the start of the 21st century, the external environment was beginning to show favorable signs for the development of electric cars: people were becoming more concerned about the environment and their carbon footprints, and gas prices were beginning a steep climb that had already spurred the sales of hybrid gas-electric cars such as the Toyota Prius.

The automobile industry was not responding to these environmental trends, instead relying on the fact that trucks such as the Ford F-150 and Chevrolet Silverado were still the two top-selling vehicles in America in 2003. Musk saw a different future for vehicles, and Tesla introduced the all-electric Roadster in 2008. Four years later, the more practical Model S was introduced, and Tesla sales began to climb.

As a new entrant in the automobile industry, though, Tesla faced several challenges. Manufacturing and distribution in this industry are extremely expensive, and Tesla had to develop the capability of efficiently manufacturing large quantities of cars. Tesla also had to establish dealerships for its cars, although it also decided to sell cars online, taking advantage of tech-savvy consumers' comfort with online shopping. Perhaps Tesla's greatest challenge was convincing consumers to trust the new technology of all-electric cars. *Range anxiety* became an actual term, describing people's fear that their car batteries would run out before they reached their destinations. To combat this, Tesla developed an extensive network of charging stations so consumers could be confident that they could charge their cars conveniently.

Elon Musk has been a master of raising money to fund Tesla's efforts to successfully enter the mainstream automobile manufacturing industry; so far, Tesla's entry has cost billions of dollars. Tesla has also taken advantage of tax incentives to develop its charging stations and to sell its cars, because Tesla customers receive tax credits for the purchase of their cars. Tesla cars are not inexpensive, however, and that has limited their marketability. Most Americans cannot afford the Model S or more recent Model X's high prices (up to and exceeding $100,000).

In 2017, Tesla launched the Model 3, designed to transform the car industry by being its first mass-market, affordable model. The company started taking "reservations" for the model in 2016, promising that it would arrive with a $35,000 price tag. By mid-2017, the reservations list had reached half a million customers, creating a new problem for Tesla. How could it possibly manufacture that many cars when production levels for all of 2016 were less than 84,000 cars?

Exhibit 8.13   Tesla 3 The Tesla Model 3. (Credit: Brian Doyle/ flickr/ Attribution 2.0 Generic (CC BY 2.0))

Critical Thinking Questions

1. What PESTEL factors supported Tesla's success? Which factors posed challenges?
2. How has Tesla's strategic position changed since it was founded in 2003?
3. What kind of responses would you expect from Tesla's rivals in the automobile manufacturing industry to the Model 3's popularity?

Sources: Tesla company website: https://www.tesla.com/ and investor relations site: http://ir.tesla.com/; Edmunds, "Top 10 Best Selling Cars in 2003." https://www.edmunds.com/car-reviews/top-10/top-10-best-selling-vehicles-in-2003.html (updated May 12, 2009); Bill Vlasic, "In Pivotal Moment, Tesla Unveils its First Mass Market Sedan." New York Times, July 29, 2017, https://www.nytimes.com/2017/07/29/business/tesla-model-3-elon-musk.html?ref=business.

9

The Strategic Management Process: Achieving and Sustaining Competitive Advantage

Exhibit 9.1 (Credit: Steve Pisano/ flickr/ Attribution 2.0 Generic (CC BY 2.0))

 Introduction

Learning Outcomes

After reading this chapter, you should be able to answer these questions:

1. What is the strategic management process?
2. What is the difference between a firm's vision and its mission?
3. Why is strategic analysis important to strategy formulation?
4. What are strategic objectives, levels of strategy, and a grand strategy? How are they related?
5. How and why do managers plan? Why are goals important in the planning process?
6. How and why do managers evaluate the effectiveness of strategic plans?

EXPLORING MANAGERIAL CAREERS

Chieh Huang, Boxed

As a successful entrepreneur, Chieh Huang knows how spot a business opportunity. His current business venture, Boxed, ships warehouse-club type products directly to customers' homes. The company has grown from $8 million in revenue to more than $100 million in just three years. How has Huang achieved this success? He started "basically trying to solve a problem that I myself have. I grew up in the burbs, and every other weekend would go to the Price Club, and then I went to the city and didn't have a car anymore. Am I just supposed to get ripped off?"[1] Huang thought that other millennials might be in the same situation and developed a company to offer bulk items like paper towels and energy bars at warehouse-club prices to millennials who want app-based shopping convenience.

Exhibit 9.2   Chieh Huang Chieh Huang, founder and CEO of Boxed. (Credit: Boxed.com / Attribution 2.0 Generic (CC BY 2.0))

Huang explained his entrepreneurial approach this way: "With repeat entrepreneurs, you not only solve a problem, you look for changes taking place in the world that become tailwinds to help the business exponentially grow."[2] Environmental analysis might reveal an opportunity, but strategic planning is what makes it grow. Huang has managed growth by obtaining the resources necessary to serve more customers. As CEO of Boxed, Huang has raised money to build distribution centers, hired employees, developed private-label products to offer customers low prices, and expanded supplier relationships.

What is the strategy at Boxed? Huang discussed the company's position in an interview on CNBC. He acknowledged that today's selling environment is focused on "value, convenience, and brand,"[3] and said that when companies sell at similar low prices and offer similar delivery services, the only real differentiator left is brand. Huang has worked hard to develop the Boxed brand, promoting it on CNN, MSNBC, and the Today Show. The Boxed brand is also enhanced by reports of the benefits Huang offers employees. The CEO pays college tuition for employees' children and even pays for employee weddings. For millennials, a company's values have become part of its value, and if the price and convenience offered by Boxed match other sellers, Boxed's values may be their best asset in attracting customers. This YouTube video is a CNBC story about Boxed with an interview with Huang.

https://www.youtube.com/watch?v=3ANAe1vLAIw

9.1 | Strategic Management

1. What is the strategic management process?

In the previous chapter we focused on analyzing and understanding a firm's competitive environment. In this chapter, we see how the information strategic analysis provides gets put to work. The **strategic management process** is the set of activities that firm managers undertake in order to try to put their firms in the best possible position to compete successfully in the marketplace. Strategic management is made up of several distinct activities, shown in **Exhibit 9.3**. This chapter will detail the role each activity plays in developing and sustaining a successful competitive position.

While **Exhibit 9.3** presents strategic management as an orderly process. However, most top managers deal with all of the steps simultaneously; they engage in environmental scanning to update their analytical view of the firm, they are executing strategies formulated in the past, they are formulating strategies to execute in the future, and so on. While it is useful to discuss the strategic management process in a stepwise fashion, it's important to point out that the cycle occurs such that everything is being done at once.

Exhibit 9.3 The Strategy Cycle (Attribution: Copyright Rice University, OpenStax, under CC-BY 4.0 license)

CONCEPT CHECK

1. What activities make up the strategic management process?

9.2 | Firm Vision and Mission

2. What is the difference between a firm's vision and its mission?

The first step in the process of developing a successful strategic position should be part of the founding of the firm itself. When entrepreneurs decide to start a business, they usually have a reason for starting it, a reason that answers the question "What is the point of this business?" Even if an entrepreneur initially thinks of starting a business in order to be their own boss, they must also have an idea about what their business will do. Overall, entrepreneurs start businesses for a variety of reasons. A **vision statement** is an expression of what a business's founders want that business to accomplish. The vision statement is usually very broad, and it does not even have to mention a product or service. The vision statement does not describe the strategy a firm will use to follow its vision—it is simply a sentence or two that states why the business exists.

While a firm's vision statement is a general statement about its values, a firm's **mission statement** is more specific. The mission statement takes the *why* of a vision statement and gives a broad description of *how* the firm will try to make its vision a reality. A mission statement is still not exactly a strategy, but it focuses on describing the products a firm plans to offer or the target markets it plans to serve.

Exhibit 9.4 gives examples of vision and mission statements for the Walt Disney Company and for Ikea. Notice that in both cases, the vision statement is very broad and is not something a business could use as a strategy because there's simply not enough information to exhibit out what kind of business they might be. The mission statements, on the other hand, describe the products and services each company plans to offer and the customers each company plans to serve in order to fulfill their vision.

Vision ➡ Mission		
	Broad: *Why do we exist?*	**Focused: *How will we accomplish our vision?***
Disney	**"To make people happy."**	"The mission of The Walt Disney Company is to be one of the world's leading producers and providers of entertainment and information. Using our portfolio of brands to differentiate our content, services and consumer products, we seek to develop the most creative, innovative and profitable entertainment experiences and related products in the world."
Ikea	**"To create a better everyday life for the many people."**	"We shall offer a wide range of well-designed, functional home furnishing products at prices so low that as many people as possible will be able to afford them."

Exhibit 9.4   Vision and Mission Statements (Attribution: Copyright Rice University, OpenStax, under CC-BY 4.0 license)

An interesting thing to note about vision and mission statements is that many companies confuse them, calling a very broad statement their mission. For example, Microsoft says that its mission is "to help people around the world realize their full potential."[4] By the description above, this would be a good vision statement. However, Microsoft's official vision statement is to "empower people through great software anytime, anyplace, and on any device."[5] Although the second statement is also quite broad, it does say *how* Microsoft wants to achieve the first statement, which makes it a better mission statement than vision statement.

Why are vision and mission statements important to a firm's strategy for developing a competitive advantage? To put it simply, you can't make a plan or strategy unless you know what you want to accomplish. Vision and mission statements together are the first building blocks in defining why a firm exists and in developing a plan to accomplish what the firm wants to accomplish.

CONCEPT CHECK

1. What does a mission statement explain about a firm that a vision statement does not?
2. What are the similarities and differences between vision and mission?

9.3 The Role of Strategic Analysis in Formulating a Strategy

3. Why is strategic analysis important to strategy formulation?

In the previous chapter, you read about the various levels of analysis that a manager carries out in order to understand their firm's competitive environment. A **strategic analysis** of a firm's external environment (the world, competitors) and internal environment (firm capabilities and resources) gives its managers a clear picture of what they have to work with and also what needs to be addressed when developing a plan for the firm's success. Analysis comes early in the strategic process because the information a manager gets from the analysis informs the decision-making that follows. The information is so critical that entrepreneurs writing business plans (before the business even exists) do this analysis to understand if their business idea is feasible, and to understand how to position their business relative to existing competitors or potential customers in order to maximize their odds of success. **Exhibit 9.5** outlines just a few of the questions that strategic analysis tools can help answer.

PESTEL	Porter's 5 Forces	Resources and Capabilities
• What techological opportunities exist for my business? • What sociocultural trends provide opportunities for my business? • Are there laws or regulations that affect what I can sell or how I can make my product?	• Are other firms in the industry competing based on price or on differentiation? • Are new firms coming into this market? • Do buyers have attractive substitute options for my offerings? • Are suppliers available for the supplies I need?	• Do we have any special resources or capabilities that our competitors don't? • Do we need any resources or capabilities in order to compete with other firms in the industry?

Exhibit 9.5   **Some Questions That Strategic Analysis Should Answer**

As an example of how the strategic tools help inform decisions, look back at the Walt Disney mission and vision in **Exhibit 9.4**. Imagine if you were Mr. Walt Disney today, and you wanted to start a company with a vision of making people happy in the 21st century. What products or services would you plan to offer? A PESTEL analysis would tell you that technology is an important part of entertainment and that sociocultural trends include people's preference for on-demand entertainment, to be convenient and compatible with their busy schedules. Disney's mission statement is broad enough about products and services to include a wide variety of offerings (they are thinking about the future too!), but if you were starting this company today, where would you start? Would you make movies for movie theaters, or develop a way to offer video entertainment online? Would you make console video games or phone apps? Who would your competition be, and what do they offer? How could you offer something better or cheaper?

Managers learn about the conditions that their business will have to operate in by doing strategic analysis, and understanding those conditions is required in order to develop the plans and actions that will lead to success.

CONCEPT CHECK

1. What strategic analysis tools from the previous chapter would a manager use when planning a strategy for an existing business? What tools would be most helpful for a start-up business?

9.4 Strategic Objectives and Levels of Strategy

4. What are strategic objectives, levels of strategy, and a grand strategy? How are they related?

Once a strategic analysis has been completed, the next step in the strategy process is to establish strategic objectives. At this point, the manager has decided why the company exists and how it will try to fulfill its mission. Strategic analysis has provided information about customer preferences, competitors, and the firm's resources and capabilities. Now it is time to start planning for success.

Strategic objectives

Strategic objectives are the big-picture goals for the company: they describe what the company will do to try to fulfill its mission. Strategic objectives are usually some sort of performance goal—for example, to launch a new product, increase profitability, or grow market share for the company's product.

Exhibit 9.6 shows what might be some strategic objectives for Disney. To make people happy (Disney's vision), Disney focuses on entertainment (its mission). Top executives then decide each year what entertainment products the company will offer. Because Disney is a large corporation (more on that shortly), it has a variety of resources available to create entertainment products to offer. For example, they may decide to release three movies this year, as well as build a new theme park and create five new shows for their television network. In reality, the strategic objectives at Disney are much more complex than this, because some of these choices involve long-term efforts (they cannot build a theme park in one year).

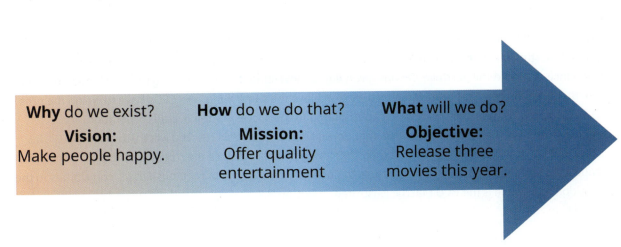

Exhibit 9.6   A Possible Strategic Path from Vision to Objective for Disney (Attribution: Copyright Rice University, OpenStax, under CC-BY 4.0 license)

Levels of Strategies

Once a firm has set its objectives, it then must turn to the question of how it will achieve them. A **business-level strategy** is the framework a firm uses to organize its activities, and it is developed by the firm's top managers. Examples of business-level strategies include cost leadership and differentiation. These strategies are pursued by businesses with a single product or a range of products.

For example, imagine that you own a coffee shop. You aren't Starbucks—you are a local shop in your neighborhood, and you run it yourself. You have employees, but you are the manager, owner, and all-around decision maker. While developing your vision and mission statements, you have already made some basic decisions about how your shop will operate. For example, you have chosen to either offer quick, inexpensive coffee (cost leadership) or a full-service coffee experience (differentiation). That decision impacts whether or not you choose premium or discount suppliers, how your shop is decorated, and how many employees you have to offer attention (service) to your customers. A business-level strategy guides a company in how they approach the activities in the value chain. Operations, for example, would focus on efficiency for a cost leader and focus on adding value for a differentiator.

When you develop strategic objectives for your shop, you will decide whether or not you want to try to attract more customers (grow), maintain your business at its current level, or shrink your business (perhaps you feel you don't have enough time to spend with your family). If you decide that your objective is to grow, for example, you should set a specific target, say, to grow revenue by 10%. Once you set that specific objective, you can exhibit out exactly what business-level actions you will need to take to reach that target.

Even if a business is much larger than a local coffee shop, the strategic objectives pursued by these larger companies are not significantly different in concept. Large companies like Nike or Apple, which have many different business units, develop strategies at several levels. Each individual business unit (say Nike Basketball) will have a manager who decides the objectives for that unit, just as in the coffee shop example. However, the company as a whole will have a chief executive officer (the top manager for the company) who develops strategy for the entire corporation. **Corporate strategy** is the broadest level of strategy, and is concerned with decisions about growing, maintaining, or shrinking very large companies. At this level, business-level strategy activities, such as an advertising campaign to attract new customers for a single product line, are not going to be enough to significantly impact the company as a whole.

The corporate CEO essentially manages a group of businesses (unless the firm operates as one business unit) and develops strategies to create success for the overall group. Think of the group of businesses as an investment portfolio: investors try to have a diverse set of investments to spread risk and maximize the performance of the overall portfolio. On any given day, an investment that isn't doing so well should be offset by one that is doing well. Corporate strategy tries to achieve the same thing, and CEOs have to weigh the pros and cons of each business unit and how it is contributing to the success of the overall corporation. For example, a company that has business units that do well in the winter (ski resorts) will try to also have business units that will perform in the summer (swimming pools) to reduce the risk of having periods of low revenue. One tool that corporate strategists use to understand how each of their businesses contributes to the corporation as a whole is the **BCG Matrix**, illustrated in **Exhibit 9.7**.

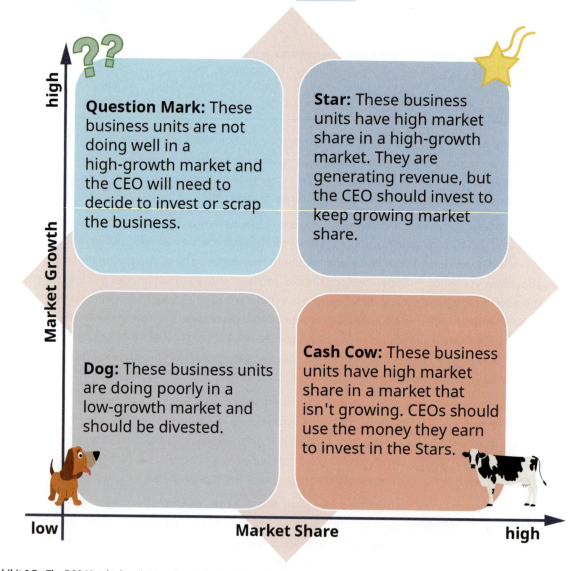

Exhibit 9.7   The BCG Matrix (Attribution: Copyright Rice University, OpenStax, under CC-BY 4.0 license)

The BCG Matrix gives managers a quick picture of which business units are doing well and which are not. The tool has recommendations for businesses in each quadrant—for example, a business in the dog quadrant should be sold or closed. Cash cows provide income to the corporation, and stars provide growth. A CEO is always trying to balance the group of business units throughout the quadrants to maximize overall corporate performance. Note that the BCG Matrix is not applicable for firm's that operate in one business unit.

In order to achieve the scale of growth necessary to meet corporate strategic objectives, a CEO must find ways to develop entirely new business units or reach brand-new markets. For example, for Walmart to grow their 2017 revenue by 5%, they would need to add $25 billion in new revenue. That's more revenue than opening some new stores could generate. CEOs have several ways of growing their corporations, as shown in **Table 9.1**.

How Grand Strategies Are Translated into Objectives and Actions			
	Grand Strategy	Strategic Objective	Potential Action
Business-Level Strategy	Growth	Increase business revenue by 25%	• Introduce a new product. • Expand to a new location.
Corporate-Level Strategy	Growth	Increase corporate revenue by 10%	• Acquire a competitor. • Expand to a new country. • Develop a business in a new industry.
International Strategy	Growth	Attract 10% overall market share in a new country	• Export products to that country. • Acquire a local company in that country to gain their customers.

Table 9.1 (Attribution: Copyright Rice University, OpenStax, under CC-BY 4.0 license)

In Walmart's case, for example, growing has meant expanding their online capabilities to better compete with Amazon. They have acquired new companies to support this goal, including Shoebuy, Jet, ModCloth, and Flipkart to reach customers and increase their online product selection, as well as Parcel, to build delivery services.[6]

International strategy is similar to corporate strategy because it is concerned with the large-scale actions involved in entering a brand-new geographic market. For companies operating internationally, strategic questions focus on how to successfully enter and compete in a foreign market. International strategy can combine with business-level or corporate-level strategies because a growth strategy at either scale can involve entering new markets in order to reach new customers.

The Grand Strategy

At all three levels, companies choose a **grand strategy** in response to the first question they should ask themselves: does the firm want to grow, strive for stability, or take a defensive position in the marketplace? Often, the choice of a grand strategy is based on conditions in the business environment because firms generally want to grow unless something (like a recession) makes that difficult. Note that a grand strategy and a corporate strategy can overlap significantly.

- A **growth strategy** involves developing plans to increase the size of the firm in terms of revenue, market share, or geographic reach (often a combination of these, as they can overlap significantly). Walmart is implementing a growth strategy with the acquisitions discussed in the corporate strategy section.
- A **stability strategy** is a strategy for a company to maintain its current income, market share, or geographic reach. A firm usually works to maintain a stable position when the alternative is to lose

ground in one of those categories, for example because of competition or economic factors. In today's business environment, publicly held firms rarely aim solely to maintain the status quo, because shareholders and the stock market reward firm growth.

- Firms pursue **defensive strategies** in the face of challenges. A company that is struggling may decide to shrink its operations to reduce costs in order to survive, for example. A company facing strong new competition may have to radically rethink its product offerings or pricing in order not to lose too much market share to the newcomer. A technological innovation may make a company's products obsolete (or at least less attractive), forcing it to work to catch up to the new technology. Ford made a defensive decision when it recently decided to stop selling sedans in the United States because of slow sales compared to trucks and SUVs.

Operationalizing a Grand Strategy

A firm operationalizes its choice of a grand strategy differently at each level of strategy (business, corporate, international). At the business level, a growth strategy means that the manager will have to develop ways to grow the business by developing new products or expanding the customer base for existing products, either at home or abroad. Expanding a corporation can take a wider variety of forms. The CEO can develop new businesses, expand to new countries, acquire or merge with competitors, or perform previously outsourced activities. International expansion can be accomplished by exporting goods to another country or by acquiring a similar firm in another country to establish the company's presence in that country. In all three of these cases, the grand strategy would be growth, and the strategic objectives could be expressed in terms of revenue growth, profit growth, market share growth, or even share price growth. **Table 9.1** outlines how a grand strategy can be used to develop specific company actions.

CONCEPT CHECK

1. What is the difference between strategic objectives and a strategy?
2. Describe the three levels of strategy and what a manager developing strategy at each level is concerned with.
3. What is a grand strategy, and how does it relate to strategic objectives and the three levels of strategy?
4. What are the three grand strategies, and why would firms pursue each of them?

9.5 | Planning Firm Actions to Implement Strategies

5. How and why do managers plan? Why are goals important in the planning process?

When managers create strategies, they are making plans for how their firm will compete in the marketplace and what actions the firm will have to undertake to compete. A **plan** is a decision to carry out a particular action in order to achieve a specific goal. A plan includes decisions about when and how actions should be accomplished and what resources will be required to complete the actions. Because planning is one of the basic functions of management, a good manager should have good goal-setting skills, technical knowledge about the tasks necessary to reach goals, time-management skills, and the organizational skills required to arrange company resources to be available to complete the planned tasks. Planning is a combination of deciding what needs to be done, figuring out how to do it, assigning roles to people and providing them the resources to complete their tasks, and overseeing the work to make sure it gets done correctly and in a timely manner.

MANAGING CHANGE

Technology and Innovation: Amazon Puts Brick-and-Mortar Retailers on the Defensive

Amazon.com has become the place everyone buys from. It wasn't always that way, though. In 1995, Jeff Bezos founded Amazon in the garage of his house as an online book-selling company. Even then, however, he had a bigger mission: he wanted Amazon to be "an everything store." In a little over two decades, Bezos has achieved his vision by growing Amazon in almost every possible way. Amazon reaches across international borders, with 14 country-specific websites, and has expanded product offerings to include almost anything a shopper might be looking for. They have developed their own products, like the Kindle reader and Echo/Alexa digital home assistant, and now, with the acquisition of Whole Foods grocery stores, Amazon operates physical "brick-and-mortar" stores. Amazon uses the expertise it has developed along the way to serve other online retailers by hosting their stores and also by offering other tech services.

Amazon's online business model has transformed how people shop, which has impacted the retail industry. Malls and brick-and-mortar stores have struggled to match Amazon's prices, selection, and convenience. **Exhibit 9.8** shows the stock market's reaction to retail's struggles: Amazon's share price has soared even as shares of stores such as Macy's and Best Buy have lost value.

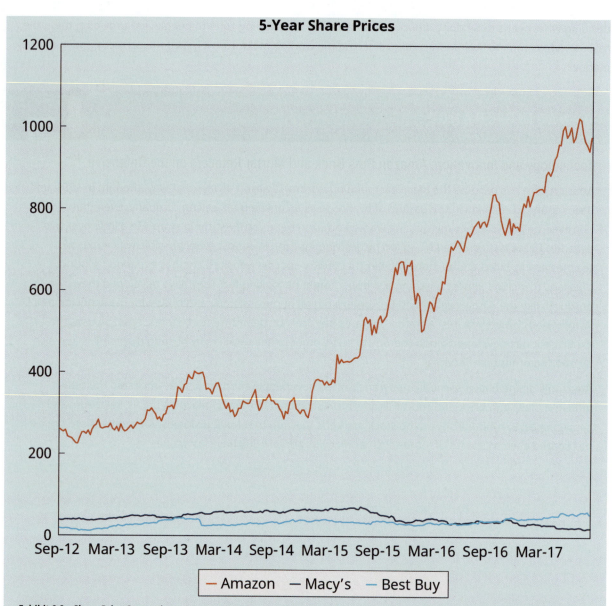

Exhibit 9.8   Share Price Comparison: Amazon, Best Buy, and Macy's (Attribution: Copyright Rice University, OpenStax, under CC-BY 4.0 license)

How have traditional brick-and-mortar retailers adjusted their strategies and objectives in response to changing customer shopping habits? Clothing retailers like Macy's have had to adopt defensive strategies by lowering prices, reducing the number of locations, and expanding their own online sales capabilities. Big-box stores like Best Buy, in an effort to sustain their business, have fought back against "showrooming," the process that occurs when a customer visits a brick-and-mortar store to check out a product in person and then goes home to order it online. To combat this practice, big-box stores offer installation services and price match the online retailers.

The transformation of the retail industry has hurt some stores, like Macy's, whose share price has declined as they shrink their operations in order to try to survive. Best Buy, on the other hand, is trying to adapt by choosing defensive actions that will maintain their operations. Best Buy has had some success in figuring out how to attract buyers in the era of online retail, and market investors have approved their actions, as shown in their share price increases. Will these retailers survive over the long term? It's hard to say. Macy's and JCPenney have announced that they are closing stores, and Sears recently filed for bankruptcy. Analysts have predicted the death of Best Buy for years and still think that over the long term, physical retail stores are going to have to become service providers to differentiate themselves from product retailers like Amazon. For example, in 2002, Best Buy acquired Geek Squad, a computer-repair company, in order to provide in-home computer repair services.

Sources: Hartmans, Avery (2017). "15 fascinating facts you probably didn't know about Amazon." *Business Insider*. http://www.businessinsider.com/jeff-bezos-amazon-history-facts-2017-4/#amazon-wasnt-the-companys-original-name-1. Accessed September 4, 2017; Amazon.com (2017). https://www.amazon.com/p/feature/rzekmvyjojcp6uc ; Radial (2016). "Best Buy Omnichannel Strategy: A Model for Other Brick-and-Mortar Retailers?" Radial.com. https://www.radial.com/insights/best-buy-omnichannel-strategy-model-other-brick-and-mortar-retailers. Accessed September 4, 2017; Garfield, Leanna (2017). "17 photos show the meteoric rise and fall of Macy's, JCPenney, and Sears." *Business Insider*. http://www.businessinsider.com/department-store-sears-macys-jcpenney-closures-history-2017-8. Accessed September 4, 2017; Isidore, Chris (2018). "Sears, the Store that Changed America, Declares Bankruptcy." *CNN Business*. https://www.cnn.com/2018/10/15/business/sears-bankruptcy/index.html . October 15, 2018; Kline, Daniel B. (2016). "Here's Why Even a Well-Run Best Buy Can't Compete." The Motley Fool. https://www.fool.com/investing/general/2016/01/23/heres-why-even-a-well-run-best-buy-cant-compete.aspx. Accessed September 4, 2017; Innosight, Clayton Christensen and (2007). "Mega-Merger Fever." *Forbes*. https://www.forbes.com/2007/08/31/christensen-megamergers-att-pf-guru_in_cc_0904christensen_inl.html#4f3a915a7f69. Accessed October 14, 2018.

Critical Thinking Questions

1. What PESTEL forces (see **Chapter 8**) have contributed to the transformation of the retail industry?
2. Amazon has entered into the brick-and-mortar store business with the acquisition of Whole Foods. Do you think this is a good move or a bad move for Amazon? Why?
3. What strategic actions do you think a store like Macy's can undertake to survive in the current retail industry?

Exhibit 9.9   Amazon's aggressive strategy has forced retailers like Macy's to shutter some of their underperforming stores, like this one in downtown Miami. (Credit: Phillip Pessar/ Flickr/ Attribution 2.0 Generic (CC BY 2.0))

Goal Setting

To examine the planning process, we need to start by understanding what the planning is for. A **goal** is something that you are trying to accomplish, and any firm will have many items on its list of things to accomplish. Consider the situation of a Walmart store in a college town. When it's time for students to arrive back to school in the fall, the store needs to be ready with all the products students need when they move in. The Walmart store manager will plan months in advance and use information learned from the previous year's sales to decide what products to order and how many, and when to have extra staff in the store to efficiently check out increased numbers of shoppers. Note that since Walmart is a global firm, goals will likely be prescribed from a higher level and the store manager's responsibility would be to functional strategy response.

The manager's plans will take into account the lead time for ordering products to make sure that mini-refrigerators and twin XL sheets arrive and can be stocked in the store in time for the back-to-school rush. Preparing for the back-to-school season may involve reducing prices on other items to get them out of the way to make room for all those small refrigerators, and hiring and training additional employees so that there will be enough associates to help students and their parents. The manager's ultimate goal is to have a successful back-to-school sales season, but achieving that goal will involve completing tasks such as making product-selection decisions, meeting ordering deadlines, and setting intermediate goals for hiring and training additional employees.

Setting Good Goals: The SMART Framework

Good goals have a few common characteristics, and **Exhibit 9.10** presents a framework for creating good goals.

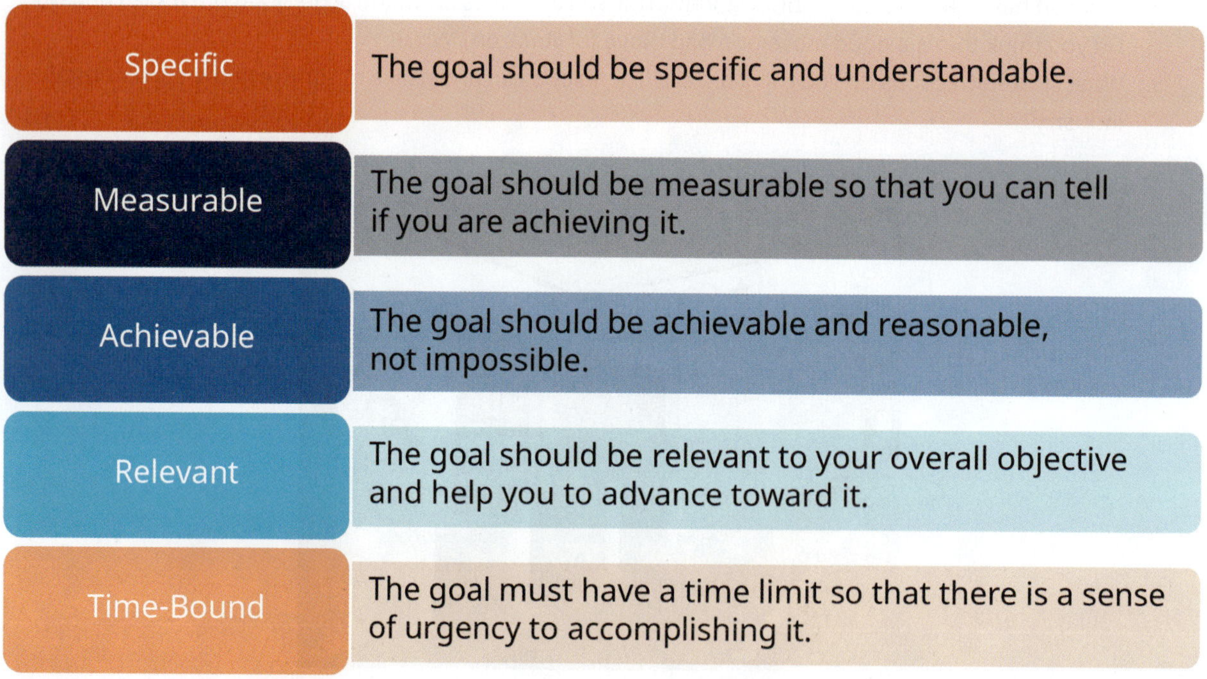

Specific	The goal should be specific and understandable.
Measurable	The goal should be measurable so that you can tell if you are achieving it.
Achievable	The goal should be achievable and reasonable, not impossible.
Relevant	The goal should be relevant to your overall objective and help you to advance toward it.
Time-Bound	The goal must have a time limit so that there is a sense of urgency to accomplishing it.

Exhibit 9.10 SMART Goals (Attribution: Copyright Rice University, OpenStax, under CC-BY 4.0 license)

The **SMART framework** can be applied to business or personal goals. A good goal should be **s**pecific, **m**easurable, **a**chievable, **r**elevant, and **t**ime-bound.

Say you want to do well in this class. You need to turn that into a specific goal, because "doing well" is a little vague. Make the goal more *specific* by stating that your goal is to get an A in this course. Is this goal *measurable*? Well, yes: grades are good examples of performance measures. Is your goal *achievable*? That's something you have to think about yourself: Do you usually get good grades? Are you able to put in the time to study the course material? Is the goal *relevant* to the achievement of a larger objective such as graduating with a good overall grade point average? If so, then getting an A in this class would contribute to that larger goal. Will you have *time* to accomplish your goal? Class-grade goals are inherently time-bound because the class ends on a certain date. So it's possible that getting an A in this class is an overall SMART goal. To achieve it, however, you have to set some shorter term goals—for example, you should set a SMART goal for getting an A on the next exam.

The Planning Process

Exhibit 9.11 illustrates the planning cycle. It looks a lot like the strategy cycle shown in **Exhibit 9.3** because they have a lot in common. In fact, the planning process is an integral part of the strategy cycle, since developing objectives, creating strategies, and implementing firm-wide activities all require extensive planning.

The first step in planning is to set a goal to be accomplished. Making sure that the goal checks off all of the SMART criteria will help make the planning process easier and more likely to be successful, so be sure to spend some time developing a good goal.

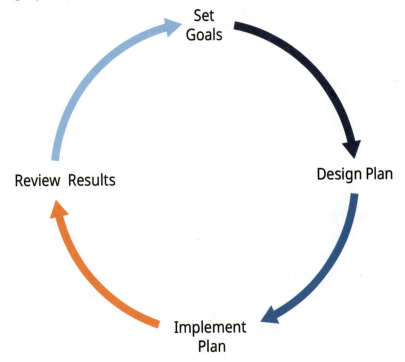

Exhibit 9.11   The Planning Cycle (Attribution: Copyright Rice University, OpenStax, under CC-BY 4.0 license)

Once you've figured out your goal, the next step is to design the plan. "Designing the plan" involves several distinct activities, so let's break it down into what needs to happen. Think of planning as a problem-solving exercise. A plan is a set of actions developed to accomplish a goal, and *planning* is essentially figuring out what those actions should be. The goal is the end point, and the plan answers the question "How do we get there?"

When designing a plan, a manager may think of many ways to achieve a goal. He or she can have a group of employees brainstorm to come up with ideas. Not all of the potential ideas are likely to be feasible, however. Part of the manager's task in designing a plan is to coordinate various ideas with a firm's resources and capabilities and its time constraints (see **Exhibit 9.12**). When does the goal need to be accomplished? What other resources does the firm need to complete the project?

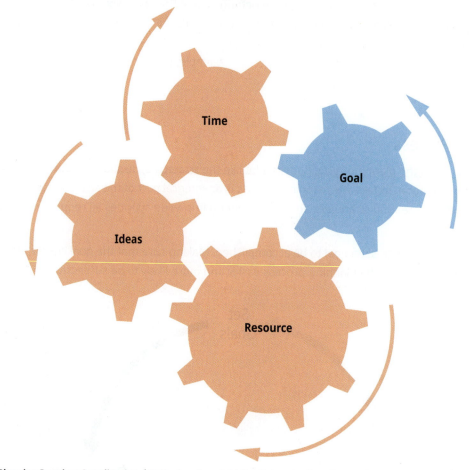

Exhibit 9.12   Planning Requires Coordination (Attribution: Copyright Rice University, OpenStax, under CC-BY 4.0 license)

Designing the plan becomes a puzzle of figuring out what is the best way to reach a goal with the resources the firm has or can reasonably get in the time available. There is no prescription for this, and the best way to learn how to plan is to practice. Fortunately, you probably have a pretty good amount of practice already, because you've been planning in one form or another for a long time. You have planned study time, team practices, club events, and even meals. Strategic planning uses the same skills in a new context. Planning a product launch may sound complicated, but so is planning a wedding. The scale and scope of the things a manager must coordinate in order to reach company goals may be larger than what you are used to, but the specific skills are likely not new at all.

For example, let's take a look at the challenge Tesla is currently facing.

Tesla has developed a mass-market car and has a line of about half a million customers waiting to buy one. Until now, Tesla has been more of a boutique car maker, manufacturing small numbers of cars that they are able to sell at high prices. The Model 3, however, has been specifically conceived as an affordable car that almost anyone can buy. The brand and reputation Tesla has built with its premium cars has generated a lot of enthusiasm and demand for this new model. So Elon Musk, CEO of Tesla, is planning to make cars in larger numbers and more quickly than ever before.

What's Tesla's goal? Manufacture cars at a rate of 500,000 per year in order to meet demand. Is this a SMART goal? Analysts around the world are arguing over this (is it achievable?), but it's the goal that Tesla is focusing on, so Musk has to design a plan to reach that goal. What resources does Tesla need in order to reach this level of production? They developed a car that is easy to manufacture, because they knew that they would want to build it in large numbers. Still, they need manufacturing facilities, parts, and production employees. To get these resources, they need money. Elon Musk is a spectacular fundraiser, but they need billions of dollars to develop manufacturing capabilities on this scale. So while Tesla builds the world's largest factory in Nevada, called the Gigafactory, Musk continues to raise funds.

Components (specifically the batteries) are also an issue for the Model 3, and Musk has built his giant factory in part to manufacture the hundreds of thousands of batteries needed to power the Model 3. Tesla's planning involves many interrelated activities, and figuring out what the activities are, what resources Tesla needs to perform the activities, and how to obtain resources that they need but don't have yet are the challenges Elon Musk is tackling. Tesla is a fascinating company that is multifaceted. There have been serious questions raised about their ability to produce enough cars and an examination of more recent commentary is encouraged.

Implementing Plans for Different Levels of Firm Activity and Time Horizons

Developing plans happens simultaneously at multiple levels in any company. Plans, as in our earlier grade example, often require different steps in order to achieve a large-scale objective. If a firm decides on growth as a grand strategy, actions at every level of firm activity should contribute to firm growth, and managers at all of those levels should develop plans so that their part of the firm is working to implement the growth strategy. A grand strategy cascades throughout the company, becoming more and more specific, until front-line employees are working on specific tasks that support the grand strategy.

Time is an important consideration when top managers develop company goals and the plans to achieve them. In general, firms have two time spans that they plan for: short term and long term. A **short-term strategic plan** is one that can be accomplished in a year or sooner. A **long-term strategic plan** is developed when an objective cannot be accomplished in less than a year. Companies generally have both scales of plans in place at any given time: short-term plans might involve quarterly sales goals, for example, but a firm might have a longer-term goal of establishing operations in another country or building a new facility. Tesla's Gigafactory and Apple's new headquarters at Apple Park in Cupertino, California, are both multiyear, multibillion dollar projects, and so would be good examples of long-term plans. In Tesla's case, the Gigafactory was initially planned many years ago when the company knew that it wanted to mass-produce cars at the scale required for the Model 3.[7]

Scale Levels of Planning

Another dimension that impacts strategic planning is scale. We have already looked at some large-scale planning concepts, such as business-level and grand strategies. However, the day-to-day planning that managers do to take steps toward those bigger objectives is key to achieving success. **Exhibit 9.13** shows the typical levels of planning going on in a company at any given time.

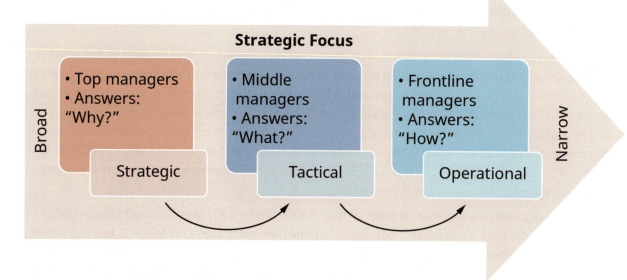

Exhibit 9.13   Levels of Strategic Planning (Attribution: Copyright Rice University, OpenStax, under CC-BY 4.0 license)

Notice that, if you compare **Exhibit 9.13** to **Exhibit 9.6**, the "what" and "how" are switched. The switch is a scale switch. Vision and mission are both conceived at the broadest scale, and so even the "how" of the mission is a large-scale idea. In contrast, when managers are planning, the "how" of operational planning lays out precise actions and steps to follow to achieve a specific objective.

Let's look at the levels one by one. **Strategic planning** is what we've been discussing so far. It's the high-level planning performed by company executives in order to set the overall direction of the company. Grand strategies are part of strategic planning, as are business-level strategies such as cost leadership. Strategic planning connects the company's actions back to its vision and mission statements (the "why does this company exist" question).

Tactical planning is mid-level planning that consists of broad ideas of what the company should do to pursue its mission. This is the sort of planning done by division managers. For example, Walmart division managers carry out the company's growth and cost-leadership strategies by finding ways for the company to grow and continue to be able to offer low prices. They may decide where to locate distribution centers to maximize store-stocking efficiency, which manufacturers of goods they can buy inventory from at low prices, and where to build new stores to attract more customers.

Operational planning lays out the front-line activities that each employee in the company will do to advance the tactical plans. A McDonald's restaurant manager develops operational plans, but you might recognize them more as employee schedules or promotional plans. Operational plans are the daily activities required for the company to function, including ordering inventory or supplies, scheduling workers and defining their work tasks, and developing sales goals and promotions to help achieve those goals. At McDonald's, as at other companies that pursue a cost-leadership strategy, scheduling enough employees to work in the restaurant at specific times to keep the store functioning smoothly without scheduling more than you need (and incurring excess labor costs) is a critical task for the manager, and doing that task successfully is how the manager contributes to the company's larger cost-leadership strategy.

Implementing Planned Strategies

Implementation of planned strategies refers to the execution of a strategy by assigning tasks for people to carry out to accomplish the company's strategic goals. Although a manager may talk about "implementing a differentiation strategy," the real implementation of a strategy happens at the bottom of not just the strategy hierarchy, but the organizational hierarchy, in the actions of operational employees who carry out planned tasks that add value to the company's product. Such tasks include research and development to add unique features, monitoring manufacturing to ensure company products meet high quality standards, and marketing the product to add brand value in the eyes of consumers.

CONCEPT CHECK

1. What are the three levels of planning, and what kinds of plans do managers develop at each level?
2. Why is strategic implementation most commonly carried out at the operational level?

9.6 Measuring and Evaluating Strategic Performance

6. How and why do managers evaluate the effectiveness of strategic plans?

The last step in the strategy cycle in **Exhibit 9.3** is measuring and evaluating performance. The "M" in SMART goals is also about measurement. A company's actions need to be measured so that managers can understand if the firm's strategic plans are working. Any action in a plan should be designed so that the people performing the action and the manager who is supervising employees can understand whether or not the action is accomplishing what it was designed to. You have been living in this sort of framework all of your life. For many life goals, standards exist to measure achievements. For example, students are given standardized tests to see if they are learning what they are expected to, and the results are used to assess the effectiveness of education at all levels.

In businesses, measurement is also a fact of life. Investors decide whether or not to invest in a particular company based on its performance, and publicly held companies are required to disclose their financial performance so investors can make informed decisions. So the overall performance of a business is often defined by its financial measures, but how do they make sure their financial performance will make investors happy? Strategy. Firms make strategic plans in order to be successful. This chapter has explained the steps of making those plans, but a final step closes the circle of the strategy cycle. Checking to see if that success is happening is as important as making the plans in the first place.

Performance measurement comes in many forms, from financial reports to quality measures like defect rates. Any activity a firm can perform can have a performance measure developed to evaluate the success of that activity. **Table 9.2** lists a few common firm objectives and how actions to achieve them might be evaluated. Evaluation involves setting a performance standard, measuring the results of firm activities, and comparing the results to the standard. One specific form of evaluation is called **benchmarking**, a process in which the performance standard is based on another firm's superior performance. In the hospitality industry, for example, Disney theme park operations are used as standards for other companies in the theme park industry. Universal theme parks, for example, likely compare their customer satisfaction to Disney's in order to evaluate whether or not they are also offering a superior park experience to their customers.

Three Different Actions to Support a Differentiation Strategy and Ways to Measure Results			
Strategic Plan	Tactical Plan	Operational Plan	Performance Measure
Product differentiation	Innovation	Hire three engineers to develop new products.	Number of new products launched
Product differentiation	Increase customer satisfaction	Improve customer service with hiring and training program for customer service associates.	Customer complaints per 10,000 products sold
Product differentiation	Quality improvement	Reduce defective products by improving manufacturing process accuracy.	Defect rate per 10,000 units produced

Table 9.2 (Attribution: Copyright Rice University, OpenStax, under CC-BY 4.0 license)

Performance evaluation closes the strategy cycle because of what managers do with the feedback they get in the evaluation process. When a manager compares performance to a standard, he is deciding whether or not the performance is acceptable or needs to be improved. The strategy cycle is a process managers use to achieve an advantage in the marketplace, and the measurement and evaluation stage tells managers whether the advantage is being achieved. If firm performance meets or exceeds objectives, then the manager reports the success to middle and upper-level managers. The company CEO may develop more ambitious objectives based on that success, and the strategy cycle starts over. If performance fails to meet objectives, the operational manager must develop new actions to try to meet the objectives or report to higher-level managers that the objectives cannot be met. In this case, a new round of operational planning begins, or upper managers examine their strategic plan to see if they need to make adjustments.

The strategy process is always circular. Performance feedback becomes part of the strategic analysis of the firm's capabilities and resources, and firm leadership uses the information to help develop better strategies for firm success.

CONCEPT CHECK

1. Why is performance evaluation critical in strategic planning?
2. How does the strategic planning process inform itself?

🔑 Key Terms

BCG matrix a tool used to evaluate the various business units in a corporation.

benchmarking a performance evaluation technique where the standard for a firm's performance is based on another firm's superior performance.

business-level strategy ways that single-product firms organize their activities to succeed against rivals; at this level, include cost leadership and differentiation.

corporate strategy the broadest level of strategy, concerned with decisions about growing, maintaining, or shrinking very large companies.

defensive strategy a grand strategy pursued by companies facing challenges.

goal something that a firm is trying to accomplish; can also be called an objective.

growth strategy a grand strategy to increase the size of the firm in terms of revenue, market share, geographic reach, or a combination of these elements.

implementation the execution of a strategy by planning and assigning actions to employees to carry out in order to accomplish the company's strategic objectives.

international strategy the level of strategy concerned with the large-scale actions involved in entering a brand-new geographic market.

long-term strategic plan company actions to achieve an objective that will take a year or longer to accomplish.

mission statement a general description of how the firm will try to accomplish the firm's vision.

operational planning first-line strategic planning consisting of specific daily and short-term actions that employees will perform to make the company function.

performance measurement the evaluation of firm activities to determine the success of that activity in helping the firm reach its strategic objectives.

plan a decision to carry out a particular action in order to achieve a specific goal, including decisions about when and how the action should be accomplished and what resources will be required to carry out the action.

short-term strategic plan company actions to achieve an objective in a time frame of a year or less.

SMART framework an acronym for the characteristics of good goals: specific, measurable, achievable, relevant, and time-bound.

stability strategy a grand strategy for a company that wants maintain its current income, market share, or geographic reach.

strategic analysis the systematic examination of a firm's internal and external situation that informs managerial decision-making.

strategic management process the set of activities that firm managers undertake in order to try to put their firms in the best possible position to compete successfully in the marketplace.

strategic objectives the big-picture goals for the company: what the company will do to try to fulfill its mission.

strategic planning connects the company's actions back to its vision and mission statements.

tactical planning mid-level strategic planning consisting of broad ideas of what a company should do to pursue its mission.

vision statement a broad expression of what a business's founders want that business to accomplish.

📖 Summary of Learning Outcomes

9.1 Strategic Management

1. What is the strategic management process?

The strategic management process is the set of activities that firm managers undertake to put their firms in the best possible position to compete successfully in the marketplace. Strategic management is made up of several distinct activities: developing the firm's vision and mission; strategic analysis; developing objectives; creating, choosing, and implementing strategies; and measuring and evaluating performance.

9.2 Firm Vision and Mission

2. What is the difference between a firm's vision and its mission?

A firm's vision is a broad statement expressing the reason for the firm's existence and what it hopes to accomplish. The mission statement explains (still broadly) how the firm intends to fulfill its vision—for example, by stating what products or services the firm will offer or what customers it wants to serve.

9.3 The Role of Strategic Analysis in Formulating a Strategy

3. Why is strategic analysis important to strategy formulation?

Strategic analysis produces information that managers need in order to develop appropriate strategies for their firms. A good strategy should use a firm's resources and capabilities to stake out a position in the marketplace that sets it apart from competitors and enables it to successfully compete in the external environment.

9.4 Strategic Objectives and Levels of Strategy

4. What are strategic objectives, levels of strategy, and a grand strategy? How are they related?

Strategic objectives are the big-picture goals for the company: what the company will do to try to fulfill its mission. These goals are broad and are developed based on top management's choice of a generic competitive strategy and grand strategy for the firm. For example, cost-leadership and growth competitive and grand strategies will require managers to develop objectives for growing the firm in a low-cost way.

Business-level strategy is concerned with positioning a single company or business unit that focuses on a single product or product line. The primary business-level strategies are cost leadership and differentiation, as well as focus, which is combined with one of the other two strategies (focus-cost leadership, focus-differentiation).

Corporate-level strategy is concerned with the management and direction of multi-business corporations. These large firms make decisions about what businesses and industries to operate in so they can improve their overall performance and reduce the risk they would face if all of their operations were concentrated in a single business or industry. Corporate CEOs use the BCG Matrix to evaluate their portfolio of businesses and use corporate actions like acquisitions to make significant changes to their companies.

International strategy can be combined with either of the previous two strategies to incorporate international operations into a business or corporation. International strategy answers questions of what country or countries to operate in and how to be successful in foreign operations.

Grand strategies outline an approach to firm growth. The three grand strategies are growth, stability, and defensive, and a firm chooses one of these approaches in addition to their choice of business-level, corporate, and/or international strategies. The choice of grand strategy is often dictated by conditions in the business environment such as recessions or competitor activities.

9.5 Planning Firm Actions to Implement Strategies

5. How and why do managers plan? Why are goals important in the planning process?

Managers plan in order to decide what actions the firm will perform in order to achieve a specific goal. Planning includes decisions about when and how the goal should be accomplished and what resources will be required to perform the planned action. Planning is one of the basic functions of management, along with organizing, leading, and controlling.

Firms typically have several levels of planning happening simultaneously: one based on time and another based on detail. The time scale is expressed in terms of short-term (within the year) or long-term (over a yearlong) planning. Planning details become more specific as the manager moves downward in the hierarchy of planning levels. Strategic planning is the responsibility of firm leadership (CEO), while unit or division managers take the CEO's broad plans and focus them to be more suitable for their own units (tactical planning). Operational planning is the frontline manager's domain—he develops specific action plans for operational employees so that their work advances the entire firm towards the large-scale strategic goal.

Good goals are specific, measurable, achievable, relevant, and time-bound. These terms can be remembered by using the acronym SMART. Goals are critical to planning because they focus firm activities on specific objectives or outcomes.

9.6 Measuring and Evaluating Strategic Performance

7. How and why do managers evaluate the effectiveness of strategic plans?

Performance evaluation is to determine if plans have been successful and identify any changes that might be necessary. This is done both at the end and the beginning of strategic planning because when managers measure firm activities and progress towards objectives, the information they learn by doing that measurement becomes part of the analysis they use to develop improved plans and objectives to keep the firm on track to fulfill their mission and improve their overall performance.

Chapter Review Questions

1. What does a mission statement explain about a firm that a vision statement does not?
2. Describe the three levels of strategy and what a manager developing strategy at each level is concerned with.
3. Give an example for why a firm would pursue each of the three grand strategies.
4. What actions can help a firm grow?
5. What managerial skills and actions are included in the planning process?
6. Why are good goals important to the planning process?
7. What are the strategic planning time frames? How do they work together?
8. Why is performance measurement often the start of new strategy development?

Management Skills Application Exercises

1. (Analytical Skills) You have recently completed a leadership development program, and your company has given you a retail store to manage. The employees at your store are diverse in terms of age, race, gender, and fluency in English. Your company has told you to set individual performance objectives for your employees to increase your store's profitability.
   A. What specific types of actions do you think you should include in a plan to increase profitability in a retail environment?
   B. Would you set the same performance objectives for different store roles, for example sales

associates and cashiers?

   C. Should your employees be involved in creating their own performance objectives? Why or why not?

   D. Should your communication of performance goals be adapted for the diversity of the employees you supervise? How and why (or why not)?

2. (Ethical skills) You have probably experienced a situation in which you were not happy with the service you received as a customer of a business. Put yourself in the shoes of the manager of a business, and think about the following:

   A. How does a company's vision and mission impact your approach to trying to appease an unhappy customer?

   B. Imagine that the company follows a cost-leadership strategy and has a "no cash refunds" policy in order to reduce company costs. What kind of plan or rules would you develop for your employees to follow to deliver consistent customer service if a customer wants a refund?

   C. When might it be ethical to violate the rules you developed in (b) above in order to deliver the right response to a customer service problem?

3. (Personal skills) Use the strategy cycle (**Exhibit 9.3**) to outline a strategy for yourself. What is your personal vision and mission? Analyze your current situation, and develop three personal, professional, or educational goals or objectives that you would like to reach within the next five years. Brainstorm some strategies to achieve those goals. Even though you can't really implement them in the context of this exercise, think about performance measures you might use to track your progress towards your objectives.

Y Managerial Decision Exercises

1. Each of the following statements is a goal or objective, but it is not expressed very clearly. Rewrite each statement as a SMART goal, and be ready to explain what you had to change to make it SMART.

   a. Amazon wants to improve product delivery times.

   b. Starbucks baristas should make customized drinks more quickly.

   c. Sales associates should sell more cars this month.

   d. McDonald's needs more customers at dinnertime.

   e. FedEx wants to compete with UPS.

   f. Boxed wants to reach more customers.

   g. Lyft wants to increase revenue.

2. Entrepreneurs must be strategic thinkers in order to develop the plans and objectives necessary to start a business that will last. Imagine you are starting a new music-streaming service. You have decided to differentiate your service from the others already in the marketplace. Think of three ways to add value to your service and also the performance measures you'll need to use in order to know if your added value is really valued by customers.

💡 Critical Thinking Case

Interface Inc.'s Strategy for Sustainability

Watch Interface CEO Ray Anderson present his vision for Interface, Inc.:

https://www.youtube.com/watch?v=NskixbVn0BE

Interface, Inc. is the world's largest manufacturer of carpet tile. Headquartered in Atlanta, Georgia, the global company manufactures the kind of carpet that millions of commercial buildings of all types have on their floors. Carpet manufacturing is a historically dirty business. Not only is commercial carpet a petroleum-based product, the manufacturing process is water-intensive, and carpet squares are installed using toxic glue. Because this carpet is aimed at the commercial market (think schools, libraries, malls, office buildings), it usually does not have a long life span. Malls and schools regularly remove and replace carpet after just a few years because of fading and wear from daily foot traffic. This puts millions of square feet of old carpet into landfills annually.

In 1994, Ray Anderson, the founder of Interface, was put on the spot when he was asked what his company was doing to be sustainable. He realized that the answer to the question was, unfortunately, "not much." Anderson realized that in order to improve the company's sustainability performance, Interface was going to have to radically reimagine every part of their business.

Unlike what many CEOs in his position might have done, Anderson decided to do just that. He gave Interface a new vision, which he called Mission Zero. The objective was to reduce Interface's environmental impact to zero by the year 2020. To accomplish this vision, the company looked at every aspect of its operations and developed what it called the "Seven Fronts of Sustainability":

Front #1—Eliminate Waste: Eliminate all forms of waste in every area of the business.

Front #2—Benign Emissions: Eliminate toxic substances from products, vehicles, and facilities.

Front #3—Renewable Energy: Operate facilities with 100% renewable energy.

Front #4—Closing the Loop: Redesign processes and products to close the technical loop using recycled and biobased materials.

Front #5—Efficient Transportation: Transport people and products efficiently to eliminate waste and emissions.

Front #6—Sensitizing Stakeholders: Create a culture that uses sustainability principles to improve the lives and livelihoods of all of our stakeholders.

Front #7—Redesign Commerce: Create a new business model that demonstrates and supports the value of sustainability-based commerce.

To achieve the seven sustainability goals, Interface needed to redesign their operations from start to finish and even reconsider what constituted the start and finish for their products. Anderson empowered employees and invested in research to develop new ways to design, manufacture, and install carpet tiles. Interface also reimagined how its clients would use and dispose of carpet tiles.

Changing the strategy of a successful company is always risky, but Anderson felt he had to take the risk. Developing action plans for such a radical change meant that every step of the business had to be rethought, and Interface is on the way to achieving Ray Anderson's vision. "Since January 2014, Interface's plants in Holland and Northern Ireland have been using around 90% less carbon and 95% less water than in 1996, with no waste going to landfill. Its plant in Scherpenzeel, Netherlands, has hit two of its zero targets."

How has Interface made these changes? In addition to changing the way they thought about their product's life cycle, Interface has implemented performance measures to track its progress and it has incentivized employees to be part of the company's successful redesign. Connecting company actions to real cost savings was a key part of Ray Anderson's vision. "Over time, programs that linked bonuses for employees at all company levels to reductions in waste started to put meat on the bones of Ray's 'business case for sustainability.'" Interface's costs have dropped as they have learned to use fewer resources to manufacture their products, and the cost savings have improved profitability even as Interface continues to invest in Mission Zero.

Critical Thinking Questions

1. What reaction do you think employees had when Ray Anderson announced he wanted to change the company's mission?

2. How would you turn the Seven Fronts of Sustainability into SMART goals?

3. How is tying rewards to improved sustainability performance a form of strategic control?

Sources: Interface Inc. company website: http://www.interfaceglobal.com/Company.aspx and sustainability site: http://www.interfaceglobal.com/Sustainability.aspx ; Thorpe, Lorna (2014). "Interface is a carpet-tile revolutionary." The Guardian Sustainable Business. https://www.theguardian.com/sustainable-business/sustainability-case-studies-interface-carpet-tile-revolutionary; Davis, Mikhail (2014). "Radical Industrialists: 20 years later, Interface looks back on Ray Anderson's legacy." Greenbiz.com. https://www.greenbiz.com/blog/2014/09/03/20-years-later-interface-looks-back-ray-andersons-legacy.

Organizational Structure and Change

Exhibit 10.1 (Credit: GLady/ Pixabay/ (CC BY 0))

Introduction

Learning Outcomes

After reading this chapter, you should be able to answer these questions:

1. What are mechanistic versus organic organizational structures?
2. What are the fundamental dimensions of change?
3. How do managers deal with change?

EXPLORING MANAGERIAL CAREERS

Jackie Smith, CareSource University

Jackie Smith is a human resources, training and organizational development professional with more than 20 years of experience. She has worked in a variety of organizations and industries in both the for-profit and not-for-profit sectors.

Jackie is vice president of CareSource University at CareSource, a Medicaid managed care organization. She oversees CareSource University as well as the company's performance management, succession, and goal-setting processes. In 2017 CSU delivered more than 240,000 learning hours, coached 300 leaders, and onboarded 1,100 new hires. CareSource University has been nationally recognized for seven years as one of *Training* magazine's Top 125 training organizations, ranking in the top 19 for six years. In 2017, CSU was named to the global Learning Elite, ranking 18th among worldwide organizations. Prior to CareSource, Jackie was president of Reflections on Learning, a performance-consulting firm, and worked as a senior organizational development consultant, regional human resources manager, training specialist, and manager in the financial services, retail, and transportation industries.

Jackie's instructional focus has been in the area of leadership development, designing programs including:

- Developing Your Leadership Vision
- Leading through Extraordinary Change
- Transforming Team Performance through Dialogue
- Building Sustainable Strategy with Appreciative Inquiry

Her educational background includes a BS in education from Miami University, Ohio and Luxembourg and an MS in organizational development and leadership from St. Joseph's University in Philadelphia. In addition, she has served as an adjunct faculty member at Antioch McGregor University and is a certified facilitator in a variety of training and development programs, organizational assessments, and Myers-Briggs profiling. She also serves as a team leader facilitating business strategy sessions in countries around the world including Ecuador, Jordan, Guinea, and Senegal.

This chapter will cover several concepts that deal with how leaders develop and shape organizations. An understanding of the concepts in this chapter is essential for leaders who need to pull people together to accomplish the essential work of a business in a consistent process over time. We will address the essential ideas.

10.1 | Organizational Structures and Design

1. What are mechanistic versus organic organizational structures?

First, an **organizational structure** is a system for accomplishing and connecting the activities that occur within a work organization. People rely on structures to know what work they should do, how their work supports or relies on other employees, and how these work activities fulfill the purpose of the organization itself.

Second, **organizational design** is the process of setting up organizational structures to address the needs of an organization and account for the complexity involved in accomplishing business objectives.

Next, **organizational change** refers to the constant shifts that occur within an organizational system—for example, as people enter or leave the organization, market conditions shift, supply sources change, or adaptations are introduced in the processes for accomplishing work. Through **managed change**, leaders in an organization can intentionally shape how these shifts occur over time.

Finally, **organizational development (OD)** is the label for a field that specializes in change management. OD specialists draw on social science to guide change processes that simultaneously help a business achieve its objectives while generating well-being for employees and sustainable benefits for society. An understanding of OD practices is essential for leaders who want to maximize the potential of their organizations over a long period of time.

Together, an understanding of these concepts can help managers know how to create and direct organizations that are positioned to successfully accomplish strategic goals and objectives.[1]

To understand the role of organizational structure, consider the experience of Justin, a young manager who worked for a logistics and transportation company. His success at leading change in the United States gave his leaders the confidence that he could handle a challenging assignment: organize a new supply chain and distribution system for a company in Northern Europe. Almost overnight, Justin was responsible for hiring competent people, forming them into a coherent organization, training them, and establishing the needed infrastructure for sustained success in this new market.

If you were given this assignment, what would you do? How would you organize your employees? How would you help them understand the challenge of setting up a new organization and system? These are the kinds of questions that require an understanding of organizational structure, organizational design, organizational change, and organizational development.

One of the first issues Justin will need to address deals with how he will organize the system he will manage. "The decisions about the structure of an organization are all related to the concept of organizational design. There are two fundamental forms of structure to remember when designing an organization.

To address these questions, we need to be familiar with two fundamental ways of building an organization.

The **formal organization** is an officially defined set of relationships, responsibilities, and connections that exist across an organization. The traditional organizational chart, as illustrated in **Exhibit 10.2**, is perhaps the most common way of depicting the formal organization. The typical organization has a hierarchical form with clearly defined roles and responsibilities.

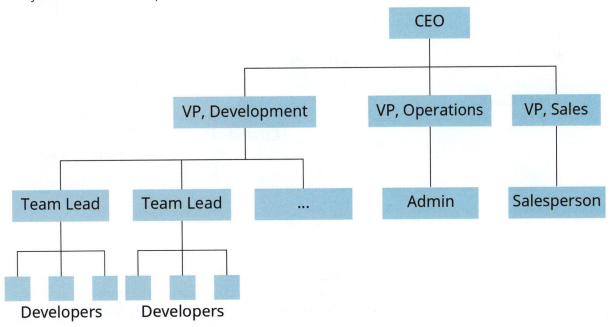

Exhibit 10.2 Formal Organizational Chart (Attribution: Copyright Rice University, OpenStax, under CC-BY 4.0 license)

When Justin sets up his formal organization, he will need to design the administrative responsibilities and communication structures that should function within an organizational system. The formal systems describe how flow of information and resources should occur within an organization. To establish the formal organization, he will identify the essential functions that need to be part of the system, and he will hire people to fill these functions. He will then need to help employees learn their functions and how these functions should relate to one another.

The **informal organization** is sometimes referred to as the invisible network of interpersonal relationships that shape how people actually connect with one another to carry out their activities. The informal organization is emergent, meaning that it is formed through the common conversations and relationships that often naturally occur as people interact with one another in their day-to-day relationships. It is usually complex, impossible to control, and has the potential to significantly influence an organization's success.

As depicted in **Exhibit 10.3**, the informal organization can also be mapped, but it is usually very different than the formal organization. The chart you see in this example is called a network map, because it depicts the relationships that exist between different members of a system. Some members are more central than others, and the strength of relationships may vary between any two pairs or groups of individuals. These relationships are constantly in flux, as people interact with new individuals, current relationships evolve, and the organization itself changes over time.[2]

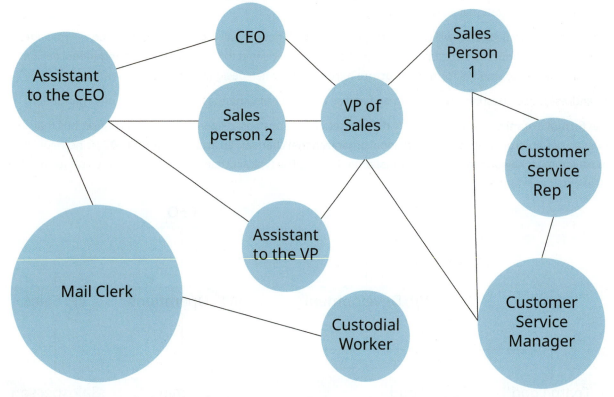

Exhibit 10.3 Informal Organizational Chart (Attribution: Copyright Rice University, OpenStax, under CC-BY 4.0 license)

The informal organization in Justin's design will form as people begin interacting with one another to accomplish their work. As this occurs, people will begin connecting with one another as they make sense of their new roles and relationships. Usually, the informal organization closely mirrors the formal organization, but often it is different. People quickly learn who the key influencers are within the system, and they will begin to rely on these individuals to accomplish the work of the organization. The informal organization can either help or hinder an organization's overall success.

In sum, the formal organization explains how an organization *should* function, while the informal organization is how the organizational *actually* functions. Formal organization will come as Justin hires and assigns people to different roles. He can influence the shape of the informal organization by giving people opportunities to build relationships as they work together. Both types of structures shape the patterns of influence, administration, and leadership that may occur through an organizational system.

As we continue our discussion of structure and design, we will next examine different ways of understanding formal structure.

Types of Formal Organizational Structures

Now, Justin will need to choose and implement an administrative system for delegating duties, establishing oversight, and reporting on performance. He will do this by designing a formal structure that defines the responsibilities and accountability that correspond to specific duties throughout an organizational system. In this section, we'll discuss the factors that any manager should consider when designing an organizational structure.

Exhibit 10.4   Smoke coming out of chapel chimney Almost all organizations have established organizational hierarchies and customs. As an older, large organization, the Catholic Church has a tall global structure with the pope in the Vatican at the apex. A process of succession has the cardinals voting on a new pope, and white smoke billowing out of the Sistine Chapel signals that they have chosen the new pope. (Credit: Jeffrey Bruno/ flickr/ Attribution 2.0 Generic (CC BY 2.0))

Bureaucracy

One of the most common frameworks for thinking about these issues is called the **bureaucratic model**. It was developed by Max Weber, a 19th-century sociologist. Weber's central assumption was that organizations will find efficiencies when they divide the duties of labor, allow people to specialize, and create structure for coordinating their differentiated efforts, usually within a hierarchy of responsibility. He proposed five elements of bureaucracy that serve as a foundation for determining an appropriate structure: specialization, command-and-control, span of control, centralization, and formalization.[3]

Specialization

The degree to which people are organized into subunits according to their expertise is referred to as

specialization—for example, human resources, finance, marketing, or manufacturing. It may also include specialization within those functions. For instance, people who work in a manufacturing facility may be well-versed in every part of a manufacturing process, or they may be organized into specialty units that focus on different parts of the manufacturing process, such as procurement, material preparation, assembly, quality control, and the like.

Command-and-Control

The next element to consider is the reporting and oversight structure of the organization. **Command-and-control** refers to the way in which people report to one another or connect to coordinate their efforts in accomplishing the work of the organization.

Span of Control

Another question addresses the scope of the work that any one person in the organization will be accountable for, referred to as **span of control**. For instance, top-level leaders are usually responsible for all of the work of their subordinates, mid-level leaders are responsible for a narrower set of responsibilities, and ground-level employees usually perform very specific tasks. Each manager in a hierarchy works within the span of control of another manager at a level of the organization.

Centralization

The next element to consider is how to manage the flows of resources and information in an organization, or its **centralization**. A highly centralized organization concentrates resources in only one or very few locations, or only a few individuals are authorized to make decisions about the use of resources. In contrast, a diffuse organization distributes resources more broadly throughout an organizational system along with the authority to make decisions about how to use those resources.

Formalization

The last element of bureaucracy, **formalization**, refers to the degree of definition in the roles that exist throughout an organization. A highly formalized system (e.g., the military) has a very defined organization, a tightly structured system, in which all of the jobs, responsibilities, and accountability structures are very clearly understood. In contrast, a loosely structured system (e.g., a small, volunteer nonprofit) relies heavily on the emergent relationships of informal organization.

Mechanistic and Organic Structures

Using the principles of bureaucracy outlined above, managers like Justin have experimented with many different structures as way to shape the formal organization and potentially to capture some of the advantages of the informal organization. Generally, the application of these principles leads to some combination of the two kinds of structures that can be seen as anchors on a continuum (see **Table 10.1**).

Elements of Organizational Structure and Their Relationship to Mechanistic and Organic Forms		
Mechanistic	←——————→	Organic
Highly formalized	**Standardization**	Low
High/Narrow	**Specialization**	Low/Broad
Centralized	**Centralization**	Decentralized
Functional	**Departmentalization**	Divisional

Table 10.1 (Attribution: Copyright Rice University, OpenStax, under CC-BY 4.0 license)

On one end of the continuum is **mechanistic bureaucratic structure**. This is a strongly hierarchical form of organizing that is designed to generate a high degree of standardization and control. Mechanistic organizations are often characterized by a highly **vertical organizational structure**, or a "tall" structure, due to the presence of many levels of management. A mechanistic structure tends to dictate roles and procedure through strong routines and standard operating practices.

In contrast, an **organic bureaucratic structure** relies on the ability of people to self-organize and make decisions without much direction such that they can adapt quickly to changing circumstances. In an organic organization, it is common to see a **horizontal organizational structure**, in which many individuals across the whole system are empowered to make organizational decision. An organization with a horizontal structure is also known as a **flat organization** because it often features only a few levels of organizational hierarchy.

The principles of bureaucracy outlined earlier can be applied in different ways, depending on the context of the organization and the managers' objectives, to create structures that have features of either mechanistic or organic structures.

For example, the degree of specialization required in an organization depends both on the complexity of the activities the organization needs to account for and on the scale of the organization. A more organic organization may encourage employees to be both specialists and generalists so that they are more aware of opportunities for innovation within a system. A mechanistic organization may emphasize a strong degree of specialization so that essential procedures or practices are carried out with consistency and predictable precision. Thus, an organization's overall objectives drive how specialization should be viewed. For example, an organization that produces innovation needs to be more organic, while an organization that seeks reliability needs to be more mechanistic.

Similarly, the need for a strong environment of command-and-control varies by the circumstances of each organization. An organization that has a strong command-and-control system usually requires a vertical, tall organizational administrative structure. Organizations that exist in loosely defined or ambiguous environments need to distribute decision-making authority to employees, and thus will often feature a flat organizational structure.

The span of control assigned to any specific manager is commonly used to encourage either mechanistic or organic bureaucracy. Any manager's ability to attend to responsibilities has limits; indeed, the amount of work anyone can accomplish is finite. A manager in an organic structure usually has a broad span of control, forcing her to rely more on subordinates to make decisions. A manager in a mechanistic structure usually has a narrow span of control so that she can provide more oversight. Thus, increasing span of control for a manager tends to flatten the hierarchy while narrowing span of control tends to reinforce the hierarchy.

Centralization addresses assumptions about how an organization can best achieve efficiencies in its operations. In a mechanistic structure, it is assumed that efficiencies will occur in the system if the resources and decisions flow through in a centralized way. In an organic system, it is assumed that greater efficiencies will be seen by distributing those resources and having the resources sorted by the users of the resources. Either perspective may work, depending on the circumstances.

Finally, managers also have discretion in how tightly they choose to define the formal roles and responsibilities of individuals within an organization. Managers who want to encourage organic bureaucracy will resist the idea of writing out and tightly defining roles and responsibilities. They will encourage and empower employees to self-organize and define for themselves the roles they wish to fill. In contrast, managers who wish to encourage more mechanistic bureaucracy will use tools such as standard operating procedures (SOPs) or written policies to set expectations and exercise clear controls around those expectations for employees.

When a bureaucratic structure works well, an organization achieves an appropriate balance across all of these considerations. Employees specialize in and become highly advanced in their ability to perform specific functions while also attending to broader organizational needs. They receive sufficient guidance from managers to stay aligned with overall organizational goals. The span of control given to any one manager encourages them to provide appropriate oversight while also relying on employees to do their part. The resources and decision-making necessary to accomplish the goals of the organization are efficiently managed. There is an appropriate balance between compliance with formal policy and innovative action.

Functional Structures

Aside from the considerations outlined above, organizations will often set structures according to the functional needs of the organization. A functional need refers to a feature of the organization or its environment that is necessary for organizational success. A functional structure is designed to address these organizational needs. There are two common examples of functional structures illustrated here.

Product structures exist where the business organizes its employees according to product lines or lines of business. For example, employees in a car company might be organized according to the model of the vehicle that they help to support or produce. Employees in a consulting firm might be organized around a particular kind of practice that they work in or support. Where a functional structure exists, employees become highly attuned to their own line of business or their own product.

Geographic structures exist where organizations are set up to deliver a range of products within a geographic area or region. Here, the business is set up based on a territory or region. Managers of a particular unit oversee all of the operations of the business for that geographical area.

In either functional structure, the manager will oversee all the activities that correspond to that function: marketing, manufacturing, delivery, client support systems, and so forth. In some ways, a functional structure is like a smaller version of the larger organization—a smaller version of the bureaucracy that exists within the larger organization.

One common weakness of a bureaucratic structure is that people can become so focused on their own part of the organization that they fail to understand or connect with broader organizational activities. In the extreme, bureaucracy separates and alienates workers from one another. These problems can occur when different parts of an organization fail to communicate effectively with one another.

Some organizations set up a **matrix structure** to minimize the potential for these problems. A matrix structure describes an organization that has multiple reporting lines of authority. For example, an employee who specializes in a particular product might have both the functional reporting line and a geographic reporting line. This employee has accountability in both directions. The functional responsibility has to do with her specialty as it correlates with the strategy of the company as a whole. However, her geographic accountability is to the manager who is responsible for the region or part of the organization in which she is currently working. The challenge is that an employee may be accountable to two or more managers, and this can create conflict if those managers are not aligned. The potential benefit, however, is that employees may be more inclined to pay attention to the needs of multiple parts of the business simultaneously.

CONCEPT CHECK

1. What is an organizational structure?
2. What are different types of organizational structures?
3. What is organizational design?
4. What concepts should guide decisions about how to design structures?

10.2 Organizational Change

2. What are the fundamental dimensions of change?

Our discussion about organizational structure to this point has focused on the forms that an organization might take and the options that are available to managers as they design structures for their organizations. However, organizations are constantly evolving. One common refrain is that "there is nothing so constant as change." Because of this, there is no one best way to organize in all circumstances. Effective managers need to be aware of the various factors that drive the need for change. There advantages and disadvantages of each the various forms of organizing we have discussed. Managers need to adapt the organization so that it is ideally situated to accomplish current organizational goals. Thus, effective managers need to know how to plan and implement change to achieve organizational success.

We will begin this section by reviewing the types of changes that may occur in an organization. Then we will explore the organizational life cycle model, which explains how the structural needs of an organization evolve over time.[4]

Types of Change

There are many different types of changes in organizations. The first, consistent with what we talked about so far in this chapter, is **structural change**. This has to do with the changes in the overall formal relationships within an organization. Examples of structural change include reorganizing departments or business units, adding employee positions, or revising job roles and assignments. These changes should be made to support broader objectives such as to centralize or decentralize operations, empower employees, or find greater efficiencies.

Another common type of change is **technological change**. Implementation of new technologies is often forced upon an organization as the environment shifts. For example, an industry upgrade in a commonly used software platform may require that employees learn new ways of working. Upgraded machinery or hardware may require employees to learn new procedures or restructure the way that they interact with one another. The advent of web-based cloud technologies is an example from the last decade and an example of ways which new forms of collaboration are becoming more available. Technological change often induces structural change because it requires different ways of connecting across an organizational system.

A third type of organizational change is **culture change**. Organizational culture refers to the common patterns of thinking and behaving within an organization. Culture is rooted in the underlying beliefs and assumptions that people hold of themselves and of the organization. These beliefs and assumptions create mindsets that shape the culture. Culture change is among the most difficult kinds of changes to create within an organizational system. It often involves reshaping and reimagining the core identity of the organization. A typical culture change process, if it is successful, requires many years to achieve.[5]

The Organizational Life Cycle

Most organizations begin as very small systems that feature very loose structures. In a new venture, nearly every employee might contribute to many aspects of an organization's work. As the business grows, the workload increases, and more workers are needed. Naturally, as the organization hires more and more people, employees being to specialize. Over time, these areas of specialization mature through **differentiation**, the process of organizing employees into groups that focus on specific functions in the organization. Usually, differentiated tasks should be organized in a way that makes them complementary, where each employee contributes an essential activity that supports the work and outputs of others in the organization.

The patterns and structures that appear in an organization need to evolve over time as an organization grows or declines, through four predictable phases (see **Exhibit 10.5**). In the **entrepreneurship** phase, the organization is usually very small and agile, focusing on new products and markets. The founders typically focus on a variety of responsibilities, and they often share frequent and informal communication with all employees in the new company. Employees enjoy a very informal relationship, and the work assignments are very flexible. Usually, there is a loose, organic organizational structure in this phase.

	Entrepreneurship	Survival and Early Success	Sustained Success	Renewal (or Decline)
Organization				
Extent of formal systems	Minimal to nonexistent	Minimal	Basic/Developing/ Maturing	Extensive
Key Ideas	• Marshalling of resources • Lots of ideas • Entrepreneurial activities • Little planning and coordination • Formaion of a ''niche'' • "Prime mover" has power	• Informal communication and structure • Sense of collectivity • Long hours spent • Sense of mission • Innovation continues • High commitment	• Formalization of rules • Stable structure • Emphasis on efficiency and maintenance • Conservatism • Institutionalized procedures	• Elaboration (or reduction) of structure • Decentralization (or centralization) • Domain expansion (or reduction) • Adaptation (or stagnation) • Renewal (or decline

Exhibit 10.5   Organizational Life Cycle (Attribution: Copyright Rice University, OpenStax, under CC-BY 4.0 license)

The second phase, *survival and early success*, occurs as an organization begins to scale up and find continuing success. The organization develops more formal structures around more specialized job assignments. Incentives and work standards are adopted. The communication shifts to a more formal tone with the introduction of hierarchy with upper- and lower-level managers. It becomes impossible for every employee to have personal relationships with every other employee in the organization. At this stage, it becomes appropriate for introduce mechanistic structures that support the standardization and formalization required to create effective coordination across the organization.

In a third phase, *sustained success* or *maturity*, the organization expands and the hierarchy deepens, now with multiple levels of employees. Lower-level managers are given greater responsibility, and managers for significant areas of responsibility may be identified. Top executives begin to rely almost exclusively on lower-level leaders to handle administrative issues so that they can focus on strategic decisions that affect the overall organization. At this stage, the mechanistic structures of the organization are strengthened, and functional structures may be introduced. Often, tension emerges over how to find balance in the structure. Most organizations at this stage of development need to have elements of a mechanistic bureaucracy while maintaining an environment that allows for the innovation and flexibility that is a feature of an organic structure.

A transition to the fourth phase, *renewal* or *decline*, occurs when an organization expands to the point that its operations are far-flung and need to operate somewhat autonomously. Functional structures become almost essential, and subunits may begin to operate as independent businesses. Often, the tensions in the company between mechanistic and organic inclinations may be out of balance. To address these issues, the organization has to be reorganized or restructured to achieve higher levels of coordination between and among different groups or subunits. Managers may need to address fundamental questions about the overall direction and administration of the organization.

To summarize, the key insight about the organizational life cycle is that the needs of an organization will evolve over time. Different structures are needed at different stages as an organization develops. The needs of employees will also change. An understanding of the organizational life cycle provides a framework for thinking about changes that may be needed over time.

Dimensions of Change

When considering how to assess the need for change in an organization, it can be helpful to think of three dimensions: the scope of change, the level of change, and the intentionality of change.

The first, the **scope of change** refers to the degree to which the required change will disrupt current patterns and routines. **Incremental change** refers to small refinements in current organizational practices or routines that do not challenge, but rather build on or improve, existing aspects and practices within the organization. Common incremental change practices are LEAN and Six Sigma, which are used to find relatively small changes that can generate greater efficiencies in a process. An organization can improve its product-line efficiencies by identifying small discrepancies in process, then fixing them in a systematic way. Incremental change does not typically challenge people to be at the edge of their comfort zone.[6]

In contrast, **transformational change** refers to significant shifts in an organizational system that may cause significant disruption to some underlying aspect of the organization, its processes, or structures. Transformational change can be invigorating for some employees, but also highly disruptive and stressful for others. Examples of transformational change include large systems changes and organizational restructuring. Culture change often requires transformational change to be successful.[7]

Finally, a **strategic change** is a change, either incremental or transformational, that helps align an organization's operations with its strategic mission and objectives. This kind of change is necessary for an organization to achieve the focus it needs to make needed transfer missions and work it does feel to stay competitive in the current or larger organization, larger market environment, or societal environment.

Exhibit 10.6   Uber Eats on bicycle An example of a small organizational structure is exemplified by jobs in the sharing economy like Uber and Lyft drivers. Here an Uber Eats food delivery driver cycles along a very busy Oxford Road in Manchester, England. (Credit: Shopblocks/ flickr/ Attribution 2.0 Generic (CC BY 2.0))

The **level of change** refers to the breadth of the systems that need to be changed within an organization. **Individual-level change** focuses on how to help employees to improve some active aspect of their performance or the knowledge they need to continue to contribute to the organization in an effective manner. Individual-level change programs include leadership development, training, and performance management. **Group-level change** centers on the relationships between people and usually focuses on helping people to work more effectively together. Team development, or teambuilding, is one of the most common forms of a team change process. **Organization-level change** is a change that affects an entire organizational system or several of its units. Strategic planning and implementation is perhaps the most common type of organization-level change. Higher-level change programs usually require changes at lower levels—an organization-level change may require change at both team and individual levels as well.

Intentionality is the final dimension of change and refers to the degree to which the change is intentionally designed or purposefully implemented. **Planned change** is an intentional activity or set of intentional activities that are designed to create movement toward a specific goal or end. Planned change processes often involve large groups of people and step-by-step or phase-by-phase activities that unfold over a period of time. Usually, effective leaders identify clear objectives for the change, the specific activities that will achieve those objectives, and the indicators of success.

In contrast, **unplanned change** is unintentional and is usually the result of informal organizing. It may or may not serve the aims of the organization as a whole. Unplanned change may be completely spontaneous, occurring simply because employees in some part of an organization want to initiate change. But sometimes it occurs as a byproduct of a planned change process. This is because it is difficult for leaders to anticipate all the consequences of a planned change effort. Employees react in unpredictable ways, technologies don't work as expected, changes in the marketplace don't happen as expected, or other actors may react in unanticipated ways.

As we will discuss below, some change models are designed to take advantage of the potential for spontaneous organizing among employees. Unplanned change can be harnessed as a positive force when employees are invited to be proactive about working toward common organizational goals.

CONCEPT CHECK

1. What is organizational change?
2. What are the fundamental dimensions of change?

10.3 Managing Change

3. How do managers deal with change?

To this point in the chapter, we have focused on factors that influence the need for change. We have also discussed how to think about the dimensions of change that may be needed. In this section, we will describe different approaches to designing and implementing change.

Change management is the process of designing and implementing change. Most leaders are responsible for some degree of change management. In addition, as indicated in the introduction, **organizational development (OD)** is a specialized field that focuses on how to design and manage change.[8]

An **OD consultant** is someone who has expertise in change management processes. An internal consultant is someone who works as an employee of an organization and focuses on how to create change from within that organization. An external consultant is an OD specialist hired to provide outside expertise for a short period of time, usually for a major change effort. Leaders are more effective in managing change if they understand the common practices for managing change as well as the perspectives and practices used by OD specialists.

Basic Assumptions about Change

There are numerous models of change available to managers, and it can be difficult to discern the differences between them when creating a planned change process. Many approaches and methodologies for developing organizations and managing change have been developed and practiced during the last century. Indeed, it can be daunting and confusing to sort through and understand which models are most appropriate and relevant for a particular situation. Every model of change has its strengths and its limitations, and it is important to understand what these may be. The type of change methodology used in a particular situation should be matched to the needs of that situation.

It may be helpful to use several questions when deciding on the appropriate approach to use in a planned change process.

A first question has to do with the starting place for the change: *Is the organization in a state of deficiency that needs significant fixing, or is it in a state of high performance, where there exists a need for refining and tweaking?*

One common motivation for change is the perception that an organization may be in some state of dysfunction with significant and serious problems, somewhat like a patient in a hospital in need of serious medical attention. A dysfunctional organization may require transformational change, in which the fundamental assumptions, beliefs, and organizing ideas of the organization are thoroughly challenged and altered. This set of perceptions often leads to **deficit-based change**, in which leaders assume that employees will change if they know they will otherwise face negative consequences.

In contrast, leaders may perceive that an organization is highly functional, much like an Olympic athlete or highly accomplished team. A high-performing organization may require incremental change as the organization continues to build on solid fundamentals to refine and add to its capacity for high performance. This set of perceptions often leads to **abundance-based change**, in which leaders assume that employees will change if they can be inspired to aim for greater degrees of excellence in their work.

A second important question addresses the mechanisms of change: *What are our assumptions about how to create change?* This question is crucial, because the answers determine the preferred designs for planned change and the perceptions of the effectiveness of the change.

Top-down change approaches rely on mechanistic assumptions about the nature of an organization. In this approach, a relatively small group of individuals in the organization will design a process and instruct others throughout the organization as to how the process of change should unfold. Most employees in the top-down approach play a passive role during the design process and are generally expected to follow the directions given to them by leaders in the organization. In other words, this approach to change relies on the formal organization to drive the legitimacy of the change.

The opposite of the top-down change approach is the **emergent or bottom-up approach**. This approach relies on the belief that employees will be more invested in change if they play some role in the process of designing the change. **Participatory management**, the inclusion of employees in the deliberations about key business decisions, is a common practice that aligns with the emergent approach to change.

The differences between top-down and bottom-up approaches can be dramatic. For example, following the top-down approach, leaders might determine that the organizational structure needs to be reconfigured to better accommodate a significant shift in its business. They might assume that they can implement the new structure and that employee routines and patterns of behavior will then change in a natural progression.

The bottom-up approach may reverse this logic. Employees might first work together to explore the tasks that are essential to a specific business problem, they might experiment with potential changes, and *then* managers might rearrange structures to match the new, emergent way of doing work. In contrast to the top-down approach, in a bottom-up process a shift in structure may be a last step.

A challenge for many managers in the bottom-up approach is a perception that they cannot directly control planned changes. Rather, they must rely on processes that draw employees together and expect that employees will respond. This requires a leap of faith, trusting that the process of involving people will lead to desirable emergent changes.

In practice, top-down and bottom-up practices often work together. For example, leaders might exercise top-down authority to define and declare what change is necessary. Then, they might design processes that engage and empower employees throughout an organization to design how the change will be brought about. Working toward a generally defined goal, employees at all levels are highly engaged in the change process from beginning to end. This approach has the effect of encourage self-organizing through the informal organization as employees make and implement decisions with minimal direction.

As a general rule of thumb, the more complex the potential change, the greater the need to involve employees in the process of planning and implementing change.

A final question addresses the mindset for change: What are our fundamental beliefs about people and change?

Again, a simplistic dichotomy is helpful for defining the approach that may be employed to create change. In the **conventional mindset**, leaders assume that most people are inclined to resist change and therefore they need to be managed in a way that encourages them to accept change. In this view, people in an organization may be seen as objects, sometimes even as obstacles, that need to be managed or controlled. When leaders use conventional methods, they demonstrate a tendency to assume that their perspectives are more informed sound and logical than the perspectives of employees. They will work hard to convince employees about the correctness of their decisions, relying on logic to prove the point. They may be inclined to use methods that may be seen by employees as manipulative or coercive. Some authors claim that the conventional mindset is the default, or dominant mode of change in most organizations.[9]

In contrast, in the **positive or appreciative mindset**, leaders assume that people are inclined to embrace change when they are respected as individuals with intrinsic worth, agency, and capability. In this view, employees in an organization may be seen as partners, sometimes even as champions of change, who can do significant things. When leaders use appreciative methods, they involve employees through meaningful dialogue and seek to lead with a sense of purpose. They may start the change process by highlighting the values that people may hold in common to establish an environment in which employees develop a strong sense of connection with one another. With a strong social infrastructure, they involve employees through participatory processes that allow them to develop common goals and processes for achieving significant changes.

Exhibit 10.7   IBM building in China IBM is a U.S.-based company with several divisions organized geographically. Pictured here is the "Dragon Building," their China-based headquarters. (Credit: bfishshadow/ flickr/ Attribution 2.0 Generic (CC BY 2.0))

The three questions we have raised here can lead to many variations in the way that leaders design and implement change. For example, it is possible for a change process to be deficit-based, top-down, and conventional, while another change process may be abundance-based, bottom-up, and positive. Other change processes may be mixed in their design and delivery—for example, starting with a deficit-based perspective yet choosing to use an abundance-based design to create transformational change through a bottom-up, participatory, appreciative process. In today's business environment, it is rare to find an approach that purely fits any of these categories.

We will next turn to a discussion of common change models that may be analyzed through the three questions just raised.

SUSTAINABILITY AND RESPONSIBLE MANAGEMENT

Why Is the National Hockey League Interested in Climate Change, and Why Did They Hire Kim Davis?

Because of demographics, with most of their employees coming from northern U.S. states, Canada, and northern European countries, there was probably no organization more racially uniform than the National Hockey League. In these days of increased attention on social issues and changing demographics, the NHL needed a drastic shift in its approach to inclusivity and the social issues it addresses. Two of the best people to usher in change, they decided, were an accomplished executive untouched by old-guard hockey culture and a former player.

Kim Davis knew that she was different from many executives, managers, coaches, and players in the National Hockey League. She welcomed the challenge, and it was a major attraction that led her to accept the position. She looks like no one else holding the position of executive vice president at the NHL, which has primarily been run by (a) men and (b) white men in its over-100-year history. The league signaled a long-overdue shift in thinking when it named Davis, a black woman, as executive vice president of social impact, growth initiatives, and legislative affairs.

In a time when the NHL is trying to adapt and become more welcoming to those who feel they don't belong or haven't been allowed to belong in the sport, the perfect person to initiate change was someone from the outside, someone free of a hockey culture that has become stale by current social standards.

Especially compared to the other major North American pro sports, hockey sometimes unfairly gets accused of being tone-deaf or at least resistant to change. The league is working hard to improve its commitment to inclusivity, with initiatives like the Declaration of Principles and Hockey Is For Everyone, but change doesn't come easy for players, coaches, administrators, and fans of the sport. Davis represents the NHL's attempt to shepherd the game through social change—internally and externally. That's been her area of expertise throughout her professional life. At JPMorgan Chase she endured nine different mergers, and her job was to help her employees prepare for change.

"Most people aren't comfortable with change, and often when they say that, what they really mean is that they are comfortable with change, but they aren't comfortable with change happening to *them*," she said. "It's all about what happens to us, so how as a leader do you help people get through that?

"We may not be able to control that fan and that microcosm of society that is over-indexed in our sport," she said. "Over time it will change as we introduce new fans, and guess what? Even that classic model of our fans, that white male, generationally, their kids, they're not buying into that even if their parents are."

"Find another hockey executive who will touch a topic like that without tapdancing." And that's why Kim Davis is here. She's the outsider turned insider, the voice of those formerly neglected. And she's just getting started.

Regarding climate change, why did the NHL attend the historic climate change conference in Paris? As NHL President Gary Bettman states: "Our game, which is probably unique to most other professional sports, is so tied to the environment. We need cold weather; we need fresh water to play. Therefore, our game is directly impacted by climate change and fresh water scarcity. So, we developed NHL Green, a mandate to promote this type of awareness across all our organizations. Over the course of the last five years, we've done everything from a food recovery initiative, which was taking all the unused food that we prepare in our arenas and donating it to local food banks ... to a water restoration program. All of that culminated in the release of a sustainability report in 2014, which was the first of its kind from any U.S. pro sports league. It's important to us."

The NHL players are also interested. One individual is recently retired player Andrew Ference, who introduced green initiatives like the NHL Players Association Carbon Neutral Challenge. While he was a player with the Stanley Cup champion Boston Bruins, he knew that he wanted a career after retirement from the NHL and decided to attend the Harvard Business School, where he earned a certificate in Corporate Sustainability and Innovation. Since he really prioritized sustainability in his life, it was a natural progression to a second career after his retirement. Ference says, "I've had a lifelong passion for the environment and sustainability issues. But, before leaving the NHL, I wanted to back that up with some formal education. When I signed up for that first class, I knew in my gut it was a big moment."

Commissioner Gary Bettman says that the next stage regarding sustainability is to "...engage more players around this issue because when we put out stuff on our social media platforms, 12 million followers on social media, that definitely gets messaging out to fans. But when you get an Andrew Ference, that's when you get a lot more engagement. We need to educate our athletes on this issue because they grew up on frozen ponds, they get the connection between learning to play outside and environmental issues. They get it."

Sources: Matt Larkin, "Kim Davis is the kind of Leader the NHL Needs in 2018: A Hockey Outsider," *The Hockey News*, April 6, 2018, http://www.thehockeynews.com/news/article/kim-davis-is-the-kind-of-leader-the-nhl-needs-in-2018-a-hockey-outsider; Kevin Blackistone, "Why the NHL is getting involved in climate-change efforts, *The Chicago Tribune*, January 3, 2016, http://www.chicagotribune.com/sports/hockey/ct-nhl-climate-change-epa-20160103-story.html; Miranda Green, "NHL Report Finds that Climate Change Hurts the Sport," *The Hill*, March 28, 2018, http://thehill.com/policy/energy-environment/380648-national-hockey-league-report-finds-climate-change-hurts-the-sport; "Andrew Ference; Student Spotlight," *Harvard University Extension- Inside Insight*, Accessed March 15, 2018, https://www.extension.harvard.edu/inside-extension/andrew-ference; Amalie Benjamin, "Andrew Ference Excited About New Sustainability Role," *NHL.com*, March 13, 2017, https://www.nhl.com/news/andrew-ference-flourishing-in-role-with-nhl-green/c-287680614.

1. What types of changes that Kim Davis is addressing for the National Hockey League, such as demographics, "hockey culture," and climate change, relate to the concepts in this chapter?
2. How are the roles of Kim Davis, Gary Bettman, and the players regarding change defined in the concepts of this chapter?

Common Change Models

In this section, we will share four common approaches to OD and organizational change. Lewin's model and Kotter's model are common planned change processes that usually rely on the mechanisms of formal organization.[10] The other two models, Cooperrider's Appreciative Inquiry model[11] and the Olson and Eoyang Complex Adaptive Systems model,[12] are designed to promote informal organizing and emergent change.

Lewin's Change Model

Psychologist Kurt Lewin proposed one of the first models of change. **Lewin's change model** shows organizational change occurring in three phases (see **Exhibit 10.8**).

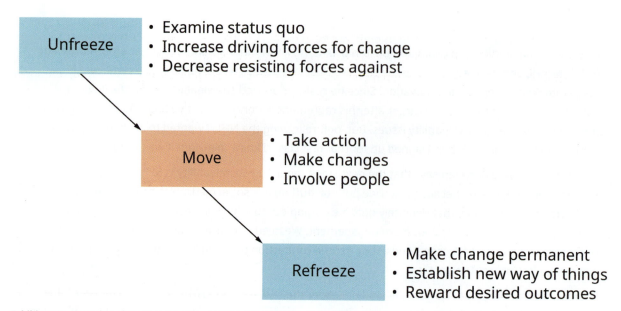

Exhibit 10.8   Summary of Kurt Lewin's Change Model (Attribution: Copyright Rice University, OpenStax, under CC-BY 4.0 license)

First, an organization must be "unfrozen" in that existing norms, routines, and practices need to be disrupted. This can be done in several ways. For example, structural changes that cause a disruption in the system can be introduced to the organization. Similarly, the introduction of a new technology or policy can cause an organization to "unfreeze." Whatever the cause, unfreezing sets the stage for change.

Next, changes are introduced in the organization to shift the system to a new state or reality. Typically, people react to moments of disorder by creating a new form of order. As changes are introduced, managers might provide a number of interventions that help people adjust to the new norms of reality they are facing. For example, they might require employees to go through a training program, or they might hold discussion sessions or town-hall meetings with people talk about the changes and troubleshoot. The intent of this phase is to help people adjust to the expected change.

The final phase is to "refreeze" the organization. That is, leaders of the organization reinforce the new norms or practices that should accompany the change. They might adjust the resources, policies, and routines to fit the new expected norms.

Lewin's model explains a very basic process that accompanies most organizational changes. That is, many people prefer a stable, predictable organization, and they become accustomed to the routines that exist in their organizational environment. For this reason, common routines and behaviors need to be disrupted. When past routines and behaviors are no longer available, people naturally adjust. As they react to a new reality, they establish new routines and patterns of behavior.

However, Lewin's model is most understandable when we assume that an organization is generally stable unless otherwise acted upon. That is, this model seems to fit in organizations in which any change is likely to last for a long period of time. Such a stable organizational context is increasingly rare in contemporary society.

Still, Lewin's model really describes a basic pattern of change that plays out in all organizational systems: stability gives way to instability, something shifts in the system, then stability emerges once again. An understanding of this pattern can be viewed through either deficit-based or abundance-based lenses, and it applies in either top-down or bottom-up approaches.

Kotter's Change Model

Kotter's change model is one of the most widely used in organizations today. Generally, it aligns with mechanistic view of structure and thus it may be especially useful in organizations where there is a strong, hierarchical structure. This is an eight-step model, shown in **Exhibit 10.9**, that relies on a centralized, top-down process for creating planned change.

Kotter's Model

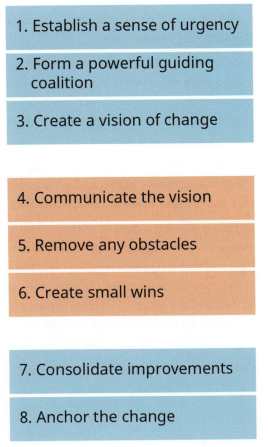

1. Establish a sense of urgency

2. Form a powerful guiding coalition

3. Create a vision of change

4. Communicate the vision

5. Remove any obstacles

6. Create small wins

7. Consolidate improvements

8. Anchor the change

Exhibit 10.9   Summary of John Kotter's Change Model (Attribution: Copyright Rice University, OpenStax, under CC-BY 4.0 license)

In the first step, managers *establish a sense of urgency*. They do this by creating a narrative about why the change is necessary. Top managers often use diagnostic tools to gather data that supports the case for change. They strive to convince key organizational leaders and employees that the change is absolutely necessary. A common metaphor is to "create a burning platform," or to make it clear that the organization cannot survive if it continues doing what it has done.

In the second step, *form a powerful guiding coalition*, managers assemble a group of influential people to help shape the planned change. Ideally, the guiding coalition should represent the areas of an organization that will be affected by the change. The guiding coalition should become ambassadors for the change as it unfolds.

In the third phase, *create a vision of change*, the manager and guiding coalition together create a vision of the expected change. They outline the scope of the change, the reason for the change, and what will be better or different as a result of the change.

The fourth step is to *communicate the vision*—reach out to all members of the organization and communicate the vision for change. Ideally, they connect with all the key areas of the organization that will be affected. They clearly explain why the change is needed and how the change should unfold. If needed, they answer questions and clarify problems.

The fifth step is to *remove any obstacles.* This step is intended to reduce the resistance to change and/or to provide the necessary resources to make the change successful. The success of this step helps to smooth the way for successful implementation.

The sixth step is to *create small wins*. A very powerful way to encourage people to support changes to help them to see the path to success. Short wins signal to the organization that a change is possible and that tangible benefits will come once the change is fully implemented.

The seventh step is to *consolidate improvements*. Small changes build up over time and become big changes. As the organization successfully moves toward implementation, it is important to consolidate and solidify successes. Managers should reinforce and celebrate small wins and milestones. The unfolding success of the change helps to convince all members of the organization that the change is real and will produce its intended benefits.

The last step is to *anchor the changes.* In this step, the new norms and practices that accompany the change are standardized and refined. The mode of change moves from transformational to incremental. Refinements are implemented to fine-tune the change and to capture all the intended benefits.

Kotter's model is especially useful in situations where the desired change is reasonably predictable and where leaders are empowered to drive the change down through an organization. One challenge is that many employees may resist change if they have had no hand in shaping the plans. This is especially true if they do not fully comprehend the urgency of the change or the vision for the change. In this regard, it tends to be used when leaders hold a deficit-based view and are generally inclined to take a top-down approach from a conventional perspective. Still, where leaders need to clearly define and implement a large-scale change, Kotter's model may work very effectively.

A comparison and contrast of Lewin's and Kotter's models is illustrated in **Exhibit 10.10**.

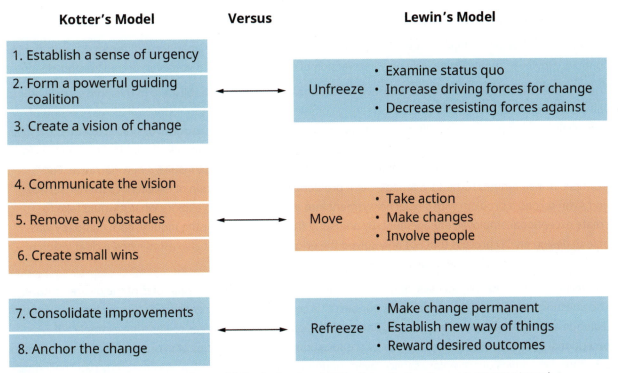

Kotter's Model   **Versus**   **Lewin's Model**

1. Establish a sense of urgency

2. Form a powerful guiding coalition   ← → Unfreeze
   • Examine status quo
   • Increase driving forces for change
   • Decrease resisting forces against

3. Create a vision of change

4. Communicate the vision

5. Remove any obstacles   ← → Move
   • Take action
   • Make changes
   • Involve people

6. Create small wins

7. Consolidate improvements   ← → Refreeze
   • Make change permanent
   • Establish new way of things
   • Reward desired outcomes

8. Anchor the change

Exhibit 10.10   Kotter's Model versus Lewin's Model (Attribution: Copyright Rice University, OpenStax, under CC-BY 4.0 license)

Appreciative Inquiry

The **Appreciative Inquiry (AI) model** is a model specifically designed as an abundance-based, bottom-up, positive approach. An Appreciative Inquiry, broadly defined, can be any question-focused, participatory approach to change that creates an appreciative effective on people and organizations.[13] That is, the process of asking and discussing questions (inquiry) causes people to appreciate the people around them, the strengths of their organization, and the opportunities before them. Simultaneously, the process of having conversations expands the social capital of the organization, or the ability of people to work effectively together.

Developed in the 1980s by David Cooperrider at Case Western Reserve University, AI relies on the assumption that people continuously create their organizations through an emergent process that occurs in the common conversations of organizational life. These conversations are shaped by "narratives" about the reality of the organization in which people find themselves. For example, a dominant narrative might be that an organization's leaders are corrupt and intent on exploiting employees, or in contrast, that an organization's leaders are compassionate, forward-thinking, and innovative. Whatever the narrative, employees tend to justify actions that align with their views. Over time, a narrative can become a self-reinforcing reality. Based in this understanding of organizations as a socially constructed system, the key to creating change is to change the dominant narratives of an organization.

In AI, group dialogue is the primary mechanism for helping people to create new narratives.[14] Specifically, **appreciative conversations** are intense, positively framed discussions that help people to develop common ground as they work together to co-create a positive vision of an ideal future for their organization. When leaders use appreciative inquiry, they intentionally invite dialogue that generates a narrative for a positive organizational reality. This shift in narrative will inspire a shift in the actions that employees initiate in their daily work. While this approach may sound somewhat ambitious and abstract, in reality it is simply an opportunity for employees to envision the future changes they would like to see, then work together to design how they will make these changes a reality.

OD consultants have developed many different variations of AI practices that address different organizational contexts. However, most of them rely on some version of a 5-D cycle: define, discover, dream, design, destiny.

The first phase is *define*, in which the objective for change and inquiry is established. In this phase, the leaders will create a guiding group, often called a steering committee. This group should include a cross-section of perspectives that represent the different parts of the organization where change is desired. Together, they will decide on a compelling way of describing an objective that invites people to think about ideal possibilities for the organization. In this process, they might turn a problem upside down to inspire a new narrative. For example, British Airlines turned a baggage-claim problem into an exploration of excellent customer service, and Avon turned a problem with sexual harassment into an opportunity to explore what it would take to create exceptional employee engagement. By adjusting the perspective for the inquiry, each company was able to design an OD process that not only solved the original problem but also established a clear vision of what they most wanted as the positive alternative.

The second phase, *discover,* focuses on questions that explore ideal, existing examples of the desired future. The question "who are we when we are at our best?" is commonly used to encourage this exploration through dialogue among employees. For example, British Airways asked its employees to describe examples of exceptional customer service anywhere in its organization. By sharing stories of exceptional customer service, they found examples of exemplary service, even though the dominant narrative was that they had challenges in this area. Finding existing examples of the desired future—no matter how small—causes people to see that a positive alternative is possible. Such examples also provide the data for documenting the strengths of an organization and the factors that make success possible.

The third phase, *dream*, is an exploration of ideal future possibilities for the organization. The strengths and factors revealed in the discovery phase provide a foundation this discussion. Employees are invited to think creatively about what the organization might do if it were to build on its strengths. "What could be?" is a commonly used question to encourage this exploration. Many organizations have used creative techniques to encourage employees to innovate about the future. They might have employees work in groups to design prototypes of a process or write a mock newspaper article about a future successful project. The idea of the dream phase is to encourage employees to think as expansively as possible about the possibilities for change, usually in a fun and inviting way.

The fourth phase, *design*, starts with a process of prioritizing the ideas that have been developed in the dream phase. Employees might work together to brainstorm a list of all the possible areas for action that might help them to accomplish the objective. Then they use a collective process to identify the ideas that have the most promise. Usually senior leaders will add their voice to endorse the ideas that they want to encourage as actual action initiatives. Employees might be invited to join project teams that will carry out specific actions to develop and implement key actions.

The final phase, *destiny*, occurs as employees implement the plans they have developed. Project groups will continue to work on the agreed-upon action steps for a period of time. Typically, they will meet with other employee-based groups to check in, report on progress, and adjust their plans. Some organizations will also create celebrative events to commemorate key successes.

The appreciative inquiry cycle can become an intrinsic part of an organization's culture. Some companies will go through the AI process on an annual basis as an integral part of strategic planning. Other organizations use it only as needed when major transformational changes are desired. Though the examples in this section illustrate appreciative inquiry as used to change organizations as a whole, the model can also be applied at any level of organization—for example, in work with individuals and teams.

Complex Adaptive Systems

The final model we will review builds on the assumption that all organizations are **complex adaptive systems (CAS)**.[15] That is, an organization is constantly developing and adapting to its environment, much like a living organism. A CAS approach emphasizes the bottom-up, emergent approach to the design of change, relying on the ability of people to self-manage and adapt to their local circumstances. Before reviewing the CAS model in more depth, perhaps it would be helpful to examine a change process that is grounded in the CAS model.

One common CAS-based approach is Open Space Technology, a technique in which dozens of people may be involved.[16] To set the stage, let's suppose that we want to create a series of innovations to improve the culture of innovation in an organization. The first task would be to invite as many interested stakeholders as possible to participate in a discussion on various topics related to the culture of innovation, perhaps over a two-day period. At the beginning of the first session, a leader in the organization might greet the participants and invite them to be part of an open-ended exploration of ideas and solutions. A facilitator would then distribute a single sheet of paper and a marker to each participant. She would ask each person to propose a topic or question for discussion, explaining that the purpose of this exercise is to attract other people to join a discussion.

Then she will go around the room, giving each person in turn up to 30 seconds to propose a topic or question and describe the significance and urgency of the idea. The go-around continues until a variety of topics are identified. Next, the facilitator works with participants to define a list of topics for discussion. The facilitator then designates times and locations for discussions on those topics. Finally, participants "vote with their feet" to choose groups that they want to join for discussion. Typically, each discussion in an Open Space meeting will include an exploration of key questions, actions related to those questions, and proposals for resolving key questions.

As shown by this example, this approach is similar to AI in that it focuses on creating the conditions for people to self-organize in ways that align with the overall objectives of an organizational system. However, one big difference is that it relies less on step-by-step processes for creating change and more on principles that can be applied in many variations to shape the conditions for change in an organization.

The CAS approach provides a useful perspective on how organic organizational structures emerge and develop through the informal organization. An understanding of CAS, therefore, provides leaders with the key knowledge they need to influence the direction of the informal organization, even if they cannot directly control it.

To use the CAS approach, it is essential to understand a few key features about how self-organizing occurs among employees.[17] To begin, the direction of any organization is emergent and requires involvement from many people. Yet, when people react to change, their exact behaviors may be unknowable, unpredictable, and uncontrollable. Most often, people react to change based on the perceptions of the people in their immediate circle of relationships within the organization. Every person in an organization is both influencing others and being influenced by others. This means that a key locus of change must involve the relationships that people have with one another. From the perspective of CAS, a change in the nature or patterns of interpersonal relationships in an organization will lead to changes in the outcomes of that organization. Leaders, in this regard, should think of themselves as facilitators of relationships and as supporters of employees who are constantly engaged in self-organizing to create needed changes.

So, how can a leader (as a facilitator) influence the way in which self-organizing occurs? For starters, a leader needs to pay attention to the key conditions that allow for informal self-organizing to occur. There are three basic questions to consider.

First, to what degree do people feel empowered to act as **change agents** in the system? Self-organizing originates in the people who comprise the organization. If they view themselves as agents who have discretion to act, they are more likely to take initiative, engaging in nondirected activities that may benefit the organization. Do people feel empowered as agents of the organization? If not, interventions may be designed to help people understand their own capacities and competencies.

Second, *how connected are people to one another* in the organization? Relationships are the building blocks of all informal organizational activities. The more connected people feel to one another, the more likely they are to work with others in self-directed activity. Do people feel like they have high-quality relationships with coworkers? Are people regularly connecting with other individuals that they do not know very well? If the answers to these questions are negative, then interventions can be designed to strengthen the quality and configurations of connections within and across an organization.

Third, to what extent are *flows* of information and energy passing through the connections that exist between people? Both informal and formal feedback loops provide a mechanism whereby people receive information about what is working and or not in their activities. Do people quickly receive information about breakdowns or successes in the system? Is the emotional energy in the system generating a positive dynamic that encourages people to be engaged? Again, if the answers to these questions are negative, then processes or initiatives should be designed that will help people to communicate more effectively across their relationships.

Aside from examining these basic conditions for self-organizing, the CAS approach assumes that every organizational outcome is the product of an indeterminable number of variables. No one cause produces a single outcome. For instance, the accurate delivery of a product to a customer is caused by a whole system of interrelated factors, each influencing the other. Therefore, where broad changes in outcomes are desired, the whole system of interrelated factors needs to be engaged at once. The preferred method of doing this is to engage broad groups of stakeholders simultaneously, using dialogue and conversation to help people develop their sense of agency, their connections with others, and the processes that need to be adjusted to create desired changes in outcomes. Appreciative inquiry is one method that works especially well to accomplish all these impacts.

In addition, leaders may also influence the structures that shape patterns of self-organizing. From a CAS perspective, a structure is anything that causes people to engage in a particular pattern of activity. Structures can be physical, such as the work environment, or they can be assumptions or beliefs that are broadly held, such as the ideas about bureaucracy we discussed earlier in this chapter. To create change, leaders can change the structures that are producing current patterns of organization.

There are three ways in which self-organizing structures can be altered.[18] First, a leader can influence the **boundary conditions** that establish the limits for emergent activity. Boundary conditions define the degree of discretion that is available to employees for self-directed action. Giving employees more responsibility, empowering them to make decisions at the local level, and providing them with more discretion in the work they do are some of the ways that the boundary conditions may be expanded. The more undefined the boundaries, the more self-organizing can be expected.

Second, self-organizing is altered through the introduction of **disturbances** to the system. Sometimes this can be as simple as helping employees learn about the tensions that exist within an organization around existing patterns of self-organizing activity. For example, there are nearly always significant differences in perspective among different subgroups in an organization. Helping employees to have conversations with others who have significantly different perspectives can introduce a positive disturbance that causes people to reorganize their activities to overcome hidden structures. In manufacturing organizations, for instance, it is common for engineering and production departments to be isolated from one another. Dialogue that includes and connects the employees from such groups can help them overcome and change the structural assumptions that may cause them to self-organize in ways that antagonize the other. The conversation itself can be a catalyst for change.

One final suggestion is a reminder to pay particular attention to the flows and connections that exist among employees across an organizational system. It is essential to healthy organizing to regularly create opportunities for transformational connections, in which employees are able to learn about the perspectives of other areas of an organization. As they develop and maintain healthy connections, they will empathize with and consider those perspectives as they engage in their own self-organizing activities.

The CAS approach, as indicated earlier, provides both a perspective and a set of principles that can be used in many ways. Many methodologies build on the assumptions of the CAS approach. These include appreciative inquiry and others such as Open Space Technology, Whole Systems Change, Future Search, and more. In this section, we have barely scratched the surface of the variety of practices that can be used to catalyze change.

Planning a Change Management Process

The perspectives we have reviewed in this section provide a very brief menu of the options that are available to leaders as they consider how to manage change. In reality, many of these can be used together, and they should not be considered as mutually exclusive. For example, Kotter's model can be seen as an overall framework for designing a long-term change process. The Open Space or appreciative inquiry models can be used in certain parts of the Kotter process—for example, in the creation of a guiding coalition or creating a vision for the change.

Moreover, there are many, many practices and methodologies that may align in different ways to the framework of questions provided in this section. These can be used in different combinations to design change processes that meet the needs of a particular context.

CONCEPT CHECK

1. What are organizational development (OD) and change management?
2. What questions may be used to guide OD and change management?
3. What are the common models of OD and change management?

🔑 Key Terms

abundance-based change Leaders assume that employees will change if they can be inspired to aim for greater degrees of excellence in their work.

appreciative conversations Intense, positively framed discussions that help people to develop common ground as they work together to cocreate a positive vision of an ideal future for their organization.

Appreciative Inquiry model A model specifically designed as an abundance-based, bottom-up, positive approach.

boundary conditions Define the degree of discretion that is available to employees for self-directed action.

bureaucratic model Max Weber's model that states that organizations will find efficiencies when they divide the duties of labor, allow people to specialize, and create structure for coordinating their differentiated efforts within a hierarchy of responsibility.

centralization The concentration of control of an activity or organization under a single authority.

change agents People in the organization who view themselves as agents who have discretion to act.

change management The process of designing and implementing change.

command-and-control The way in which people report to one another or connect to coordinate their efforts in accomplishing the work of the organization.

Complex Adaptive Systems (CAS) A model that views organizations as constantly developing and adapting to their environment, much like a living organism.

conventional mindset Leaders assume that most people are inclined to resist change and therefore need to be managed in a way that encourages them to accept change.

culture change Involves reshaping and reimagining the core identity of the organization.

deficit-based change Leaders assume that employees will change if they know they will otherwise face negative consequences.

differentiation The process of organizing employees into groups that focus on specific functions in the organization.

disturbances Can cause tension amongst employees, but can also be positive and a catalyst for change.

emergent or bottom-up approach Organizations exist as socially constructed systems in which people are constantly making sense of and enacting an organizational reality as they interact with others in a system.

entrepreneurship The process of designing, launching, and running a new business.

flat organization A horizontal organizational structure in which many individuals across the whole system are empowered to make organizational decisions.

formal organization A fixed set of rules of organizational procedures and structures.

formalization The process of making a status formal for the practice of formal acceptance.

geographic structures Occur when organizations are set up to deliver a range of products within a geographic area or region.

group-level change Centers on the relationships between people and focuses on helping people to work more effectively together.

horizontal organizational structure Flat organizational structure in which many individuals across the whole system are empowered to make organizational decisions.

incremental change Small refinements in current organizational practices or routines that do not challenge, but rather build on or improve, existing aspects and practices within the organization.

individual-level change Focuses on how to help employees to improve some active aspect of their performance or the knowledge they need to continue to contribute to the organization in an effective manner.

informal organization The connecting social structure in organizations that denotes the evolving network of interactions among its employees, unrelated to the firm's formal authority structure.

intentionality The degree to which the change is intentionally designed or purposefully implemented.

Kotter's change model An overall framework for designing a long-term change process.

level of organization The breadth of the systems that need to be changed within an organization.

Lewin's change model Explains a very basic process that accompanies most organizational changes.

managed change How leaders in an organization intentionally shape shifts that occur in the organization when market conditions shift, supply sources change, or adaptations are introduced in the processes for accomplishing work over time.

matrix structure An organizational structure that groups people by function and by product team simultaneously.

mechanistic bureaucratic structure Describes organizations characterized by (1) centralized authority, (2) formalized procedures and practices, and (3) specialized functions. They are usually resistant to change.

OD consultant Someone who has expertise in change management processes.

organic bureaucratic structure Used in organizations that face unstable and dynamic environments and need to quickly adapt to change.

organization development (OD) Techniques and methods that managers can use to increase the adaptability of their organization.

organization-level change A change that affects an entire organizational system or several of its units.

Organizational change The movement that organizations take as they move from one state to a future state.

organizational design The process by which managers define organizational structure and culture so that the organization can achieve its goals.

organizational development (OD) Specialized field that focuses on how to design and manage change.

organizational structure The system of task and reporting relationships that control and motivate colleagues to achieve organizational goals.

participatory management Includes employees in deliberations about key business decisions.

planned change An intentional activity or set of intentional activities that are designed to create movement toward a specific goal or end.

positive or appreciative mindset Leaders assume that people are inclined to embrace change when they are respected as individuals with intrinsic worth, agency, and capability.

product structures Occurs when businesses organize their employees according to product lines or lines of business.

scope of change The degree to which the required change will disrupt current patterns and routines.

span of control The scope of the work that any one person in the organization will be accountable for.

specialization The degree to which people are organized into subunits according to their expertise—for example, human resources, finance, marketing, or manufacturing.

strategic change A change, either incremental or transformational, that helps align an organization's operations with its strategic mission and objectives.

structural change Changes in the overall formal relationships, or the architecture of relationships, within an organization.

technological change Implementation of new technologies often forces organizations to change.

top-down change Relies on mechanistic assumptions about the nature of an organization.

transformational change Significant shifts in an organizational system that may cause significant disruption to some underlying aspect of the organization, its processes, or its structures.

unplanned change An unintentional activity that is usually the result of informal organizing.

vertical organizational structure Organizational structures found in large mechanistic organizations; also called "tall" structures due to the presence of many levels of management.

Summary of Learning Outcomes

10.1 Organizational Structures and Design
1. What are mechanistic versus organic organizational structures?

The organizational structure is designed from both the mechanistic and the organic points of view, and the structure depends upon the extent to which it is rigid or flexible. Flexible structures are also viewed as more humanistic than mechanistic structures. The mechanistic organizational structure is similar to Max Weber's bureaucratic organization. Organic structures are more flexible in order to cope with rapidly changing environments. These structures are more effective if the environment is dynamic, requiring frequent changes within the organization in order to adjust to change. It is also considered to be a better form of organization when employees seek autonomy, openness, change, support for creativity and innovation, and opportunities to try new approaches.

All organizations need structures to accomplish their work, and they need an ability to change in order to sustain and renew themselves over time

10.2 Organizational Change
2. What are the fundamental dimensions of change?

It is often said that the only constant is change. Managers need to have the ability to understand the dimensions of change, know what drives change, and know how to implement changes to meet and exceed organizational goals. The three types of change are structural, technological, and culture changes. Managers need to understand change as organizations evolve and grow over time.

One of the key responsibilities of management is to design organizational structures that will allow an organization to accomplish its primary objectives. The structure should always match the need for coordination. Often, managers cannot tell what form the organization should take until they experience the informal organization that determines how work is actually accomplished. Only then can they understand how to draw on the concepts of bureaucracy to appropriately design a structure that will maximize the likelihood of organizational success.

10.3 Managing Change
3. How do managers deal with change?

As an organization grows and matures, change becomes necessary to its sustained viability. Thus, another key responsibility for most leaders is the task of designing and managing change. We have reviewed several questions that should be considered when designing a change process, and we have explored several approaches that may be used to guide the development of organizational change.

The field of knowledge about how to change and develop organizations is vast and can be somewhat confusing to the novice learner. The material presented in this chapter provides an overview of key ideas, but there is so much more to learn. Should you wish to become an influential leader of change, it is important to learn more about this very important field of research and practice.

Chapter Review Questions

1. What is an organizational structure?

2. What are different types of organizational structures?
3. What is organizational design?
4. What concepts should guide decisions about how to design structures?
5. What is organizational change?
6. What are the fundamental dimensions of change?
7. What are organizational development (OD) and change management?
8. What questions may be used to guide OD and change management?
9. What are the common models of OD and change management?

Management Skills Application Exercises

1. Refer to **Exhibit 10.2**, **Exhibit 10.3**, and **Exhibit 10.5** for this exercise. Pick a business that you are familiar with, and draw their existing organizational chart. You may be able to infer much of the information from their website or through a short interview with someone in their organization. After completing this task, construct an alternative organizational chart and comment on why it may be more effective than the current organizational structure and what risks that new structure may have.

2. You have been assigned the task of working with a company that had a traditional, functional organizational structure with sales, marketing, product development, finance and accounting, and operations teams each reporting to a VP, who then reported to the CEO. The company wants to move to a matrix organization that will retain the efficiencies of the functional organization but also groups employees by product teams. You have been asked to comment on how to manage this change and how to communicate and respond to employee concerns. Specifically, you need to address: What are the desired impacts or benefits of this project on the organization? What are the emotions that your employees may have about this organizational change? How could the employee emotions impact the organization or its operations? How can the organization manage these emotions, or in what ways do you think they should manage these emotions to get desired outcome?

Managerial Decision Exercises

1. Place yourself in the position of a CEO who is contemplating a reorganization of your company and has received conflicting opinions from two of your trusted reports. Presently you are a wholesaler with 45 regional warehouses who acquires products from manufacturers and distributes them to retailers and service establishments. You have over 100,000 SKUs (stock keeping unit) ranging from ACE bandages to Ziploc bags. You have 825 field-based sales representatives who represent all the products within a geographic area.

   One of the ideas that has been brought up by the vice president of marketing is to specialize the salesforce into three groups, fashion retail, general retail, and services. Basically, individual sales representatives would be able to specialize with greater expertise and product knowledge to better serve customers. The vice president of sales fears that many of her salespeople will leave due to the expanded geography that this change would require.

   What process would you take to address the concerns of your managers? How would you implement the plan? What customer considerations would you need to address?

2. You have recently accepted the position of director for a full-service retirement home that has three components. The first component is for retired individuals and married couples who can still manage on

their own but appreciate the amenities such as medical care and having other residents that they interact with through planned activities. The second is for residents who are still relatively healthy but do need assistance for specific tasks such as mobility and the like. The third section is for individuals with chronic health issues and palliative care patients.

You have learned during the interview process that the facility has performance and morale issues and that the previous director had a rigid structure, did not allow workers from different roles to interact, and wanted all decisions to be directed to her. This has led to dramatic staff turnover and a larger number of empty units compared to other facilities.

As the incoming new director, you will need to address the staff, and your new assistant asks whether you would like to address the staff in one large room or in smaller meeting rooms with employees from the different functional units. She also asks how to handle the workers who are from different shifts. Make your communication decisions, and write up an opening statement to make to the employees before you open the meeting to questions.

Critical Thinking Case

Danny Meyer Leads His Company through the Challenges of Eliminating Tips

What happens when your CEO wants to remove the tip structure from your restaurant? Do you complain about the new prices as a customer? Do you worry about your paychecks as a server?

Danny Meyer, CEO of Union Square Hospitality (home to some of the most successful New York restaurants), discovered these answers when he began eliminating the tip structure in most of his restaurants. He had seen firsthand the largest negative impact of a tipping culture: employees stuck in front-line positions with no chance to advance to management without taking significant pay cuts.

Meyer began by first involving the affected employees in town-hall talks. These town halls happened months before any publicity was released. Meyer then hosted town halls with customers to explain the importance of fair wages for all his employees at the restaurant, not just the few who served the food. The transition period for each restaurant to eliminate tips was usually three to six months.

As a result of eliminating the tip structure in most of his restaurants, Meyer has been able to increase the pay structure for cooks at those locations, which enables him to fill more cook positions and address a common industry shortage. Meyer has also been able to hire employees with a purpose to deliver exceptional hospitality. Meyer encourages his employees to take care of each other first, and to then take care of the customer, which creates a virtuous cycle of hospitality.

Meyer constantly uses feedback from his employees even after the tip structure was eliminated. He wants to ensure that each employee feels their voice is heard and understood. Employees continue to have access to town-hall meetings and internal feedback channels to offer honest feedback.

Critical Thinking Questions

1. What type of change is this: transformational or incremental? Why?
2. What level(s) of change is Meyer aiming for in this case?
3. What models are consistent with Meyer's process for designing and implementing change?

Sources: Mark Matousek, Dannu Meyer Banned Tipping at his Restaurants- But Employees Say it has Led to Lower Pay and High Turnover," *Business Insider*, October 20, 2017, http://www.businessinsider.com/danny-meyers-no-tip-policy-struggles-2017-10; Loren Feldman, "Danny Meyer On Eliminating Tipping: "It Takes a

Year to Get The Math Right," *Forbes*, January 14, 2018, https://www.forbes.com/sites/lorenfeldman/2018/01/14/danny-meyer-on-eliminating-tipping-it-takes-a-year-to-get-the-math-right/#189bd5c8431f; Elizabeth Dunn, "The Limitations of American Restaurants' No-Tipping Experience," *The New Yorker*, February 24, 2018, https://www.newyorker.com/culture/annals-of-gastronomy/the-limitations-of-american-restaurants-no-tipping-experiment.

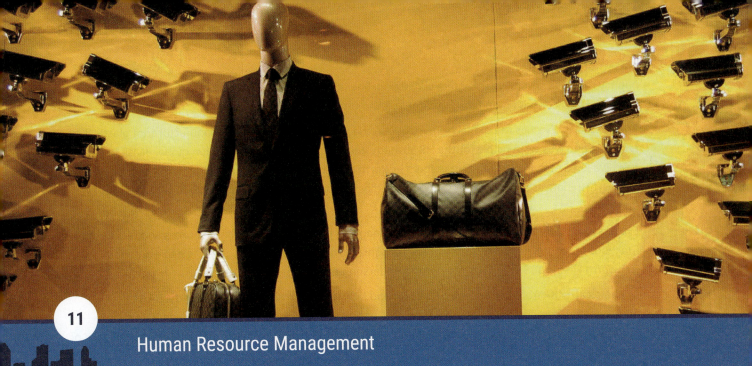

Exhibit 11.1 (Credit: Ludovic Bertron /flickr / Attribution 2.0 Generic (CC BY 2.0))

Introduction

Learning Outcomes

After reading this chapter, you should be able to answer these questions:

1. What has been the evolution of human resource management over the years, and what is the current value it provides to an organization?
2. How does the human resources compliance role of HR provide value to a company?
3. How do performance management practices impact company performance?
4. How do companies use rewards strategies to influence employee performance and motivation?
5. What is talent acquisition, and how can it create a competitive advantage for a company?
6. What are the benefits of talent development and succession planning?

EXPLORING MANAGERIAL CAREERS

Eva Hartmann, Trellis LLC

Eva Hartmann has nearly 20 years of experience as a strategic, results-driven, innovative leader with significant expertise in human resources strategy, talent and leadership development, and organizational effectiveness. She has worked in a variety of industries, from manufacturing to Fortune 500 consulting. Eva is a transformational change agent who has developed and led strategic human capital programs and talent initiatives in multiple challenging environments globally. Eva is passionate about enhancing both individual and organizational performance.

Eva began her career in one of the large "Big 6" management consulting firms at the time, and she happily returned several years ago to consulting. She is the founder and president of Trellis LLC, a human capital consulting and staffing firm in Richmond, Virginia.

Prior to Trellis, Eva was the global human resources leader for a large global manufacturer of plastic film products and was responsible for the HR strategy and operations of a $600 million global division. In this role, Eva led a global team of HR managers in North and South America, Europe, and Asia to support global HR initiatives to drive business results and build human capital and performance across the division.

Eva has also held a variety of leadership and managerial roles in both human resources and quality functions at several nationally and globally recognized companies, including Wachovia Securities, Genworth Financial, Sun Microsystems, and Andersen Consulting (now Accenture).

Eva holds an MBA from the College of William and Mary in Williamsburg, Virginia, and a BA in anthropology from the University of Virginia in Charlottesville, Virginia. She is also an adjunct faculty member with the University of Richmond Robins School of Business. Eva currently serves on the board of the Society of Human Resource Management (SHRM) of Richmond, Virginia.

Human resource management is an area that has evolved a great deal over the last few decades. From the days of the very tactical "personnel" management to the current and more strategic state of human resources, businesses and HR professionals alike have changed the way they see the function. In the current economy, human capital assets (i.e., people) are the greatest value creators. Companies compete for talent, and they distinguish themselves in their business performance by the talent they have in their ranks. Human resource management, therefore, becomes a key lever companies can utilize to find, recruit, develop, and grow talent for competitive advantage. This chapter discusses the value and benefits that human resource management brings to an organization, as well as the challenges that the function still faces as a strategic partner to the business.

11.1 | An Introduction to Human Resource Management

1. What has been the evolution of human resource management (HRM) over the years, and what is the current value it provides to an organization?

Human resource management over the years has served many purposes within an organization. From its earliest inception as a primarily compliance-type function, it has further expanded and evolved into its current state as a key driver of human capital development. In the book *HR From the Outside In* (Ulrich, Younger, Brockbank, Younger, 2012), the authors describe the evolution of HR work in "waves".[1] Wave 1 focused on the administrative work of HR personnel, such as the terms and conditions of work, delivery of HR services, and regulatory compliance. This administrative side still exists in HR today, but it is often accomplished differently via technology and outsourcing solutions. The quality of HR services and HR's credibility came from the ability to run administrative processes and solve administrative issues effectively. Wave 2 focused on the design of innovative HR practice areas such as compensation, learning, communication, and sourcing. The HR professionals in these practice areas began to interact and share with each other to build a consistent approach to human resource management. The HR credibility in Wave 2 came from the delivery of best-practice HR solutions.

Wave 3 HR, over the last 15–20 years or so, has focused on the integration of HR strategy with the overall business strategy. Human resources appropriately began to look at the business strategy to determine what

HR priorities to work on and how to best use resources. HR began to be a true partner to the business, and the credibility of HR was dependent upon HR having a seat at the table when the business was having strategic discussions. In Wave 4, HR continues to be a partner to the business, but has also become a competitive practice for responding to external business conditions. HR looks outside their organizations to customers, investors, and communities to define success—in the form of customer share, investor confidence, and community reputation. HR's credibility is thus defined in terms of its ability to support and drive these external metrics. Although each "wave" of HR's evolution is important and must be managed effectively, it is the "outside in" perspective that allows the human resource management function to shine via the external reputation and successes of the organization.

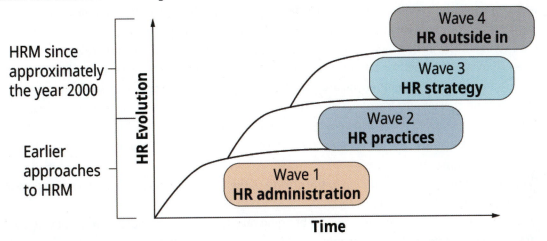

Exhibit 11.2   Evolution of HR Work in Waves (Attribution: Copyright Rice University, OpenStax, under CC-BY 4.0 license)

CATCHING THE ENTREPRENEURIAL SPIRIT

Human Resources Outsourcing—Entrepreneurial Ventures

Human resources is a key function within any company, but not all companies are able to afford or justify full-time HR staff. Over the last decade, HR outsourcing has become a good business decision for many small companies whose current staff doesn't have the bandwidth or expertise to take on the risks of employee relations issues, benefits and payroll, or HR compliance responsibilities. This has led many HR practitioners to try out their entrepreneurial skills in the areas of HR outsourcing and "fractional HR."

Human resources outsourcing is very commonly used by smaller companies (and often large companies too) to cover such tasks as benefits and payroll management. This is an area that has been outsourced to third parties for many years. More recent is the trend to have "fractional HR" resources to help with the daily/weekly/monthly HR compliance, employee relations, and talent management issues that companies need to address. Fractional HR is a growing industry, and it has become the service offering of many entrepreneurial HR ventures. Fractional HR is essentially as it sounds—it is the offering of HR services to a company on a part-time or intermittent basis when the company may not be able to justify the cost of a full-time HR resource. An HR professional can be available onsite for a specified number of hours or days weekly or monthly, depending on the company's needs and budget. The HR professional handles everything from HR compliance issues and training to employee issues support. Also, for companies that are keen on development of employees, the HR resource can drive the talent management processes—such as performance management, succession planning, training, and development—for companies who require more than just basic HR compliance services.

How does a business leader decide whether HR outsourcing is needed? There are generally two factors that drive a leader to consider fractional HR or HR outsourcing—time and risk. If a leader is spending too much time on HR issues and employee relations, he may decide that it is a smart tradeoff to outsource these tasks to a professional. In addition, the risk inherent in some HR issues can be very great, so the threat of having a lawsuit or feeling that the company is exposed can lead the company to seek help from a fractional HR professional.

HR entrepreneurs have taken full advantage of this important trend, which many say will likely continue as small companies grow and large companies decide to off-load HR work to third parties. Some HR companies offer fractional HR as part of their stated HR services, in addition to payroll and benefits support, compensation, and other HR programmatic support. Having a fractional HR resource in place will often illuminate the need for other HR services and program builds, which are generally supported by those same companies. Whether you are an individual HR practitioner or have a small company of HR practitioners and consultants, fractional HR and HR outsourcing can be a very viable and financially rewarding business model. It can also be very personally rewarding, as the HR professional enables smaller companies to grow and thrive, knowing that its HR compliance and processes are covered.

Discussion Questions

1. What do you believe is contributing to the growth of the fractional HR and HR outsourcing trend? Do you expect this trend to continue?
2. At what point should a company consider bringing on a full-time HR resource instead of using a fractional HR resource? What questions should the company ask itself?

Human resource management provides value to an organization, to a large extent, via its management of the overall **employee life cycle** that employees follow—from hiring and onboarding, to performance management and talent development, all the way through to transitions such as job change and promotion, to retirement and exit. **Human capital** is a key competitive advantage to companies, and those who utilize their human resource partners effectively to drive their human capital strategy will reap the benefits.

Human resource management includes the leadership and facilitation of the following key life cycle process areas:

- Human resources compliance
- Employee selection, hiring, and onboarding
- Performance management
- Compensation rewards and benefits
- Talent development and succession planning

Human resources is responsible for driving the strategy and policies in these areas to be in accordance with and in support of the overall business strategy. Each of these areas provides a key benefit to the organization and impacts the organization's value proposition to its employees.

CONCEPT CHECK

1. How has the function of human resource management evolved over the years?
2. In what way do you usually interact with human resources?

11.2 | Human Resource Management and Compliance

2.   How does the human resources compliance role of HR add value to an organization?

Human resources compliance is an area that traces back to the very origin of the human resources function—to administrative and regulatory functions. Compliance continues to be a very important area that HR manages, and there are numerous regulations and laws that govern the employment relationship. HR professionals must be able to understand and navigate these laws to help their organizations remain compliant and avoid having to pay fines or penalties. The additional threat of reputational harm to the organization is another reason that HR needs to be aware and alert to any potential gaps in compliance.

Some of the most common examples of laws and regulations that govern the **employer-employee relationship** include the following (SHRM.org):

- Age Discrimination in Employment Act (ADEA)
- Americans with Disabilities Act (ADA)
- Fair Labor Standards Act (FLSA)
- Family and Medical Leave Act (FMLA)
- National Labor Relations Act (NLRA)
- Worker Adjustment and Retraining Notification Act (WARN)

The Age Discrimination in Employment Act (ADEA) of 1967 protects individuals who are 40 years of age or older from employment discrimination based on age. These protections apply to both employees and job applicants. It also makes it unlawful to discriminate based on age with respect to any terms of employment, such as hiring, firing, promotion, layoff, compensation, benefits, job assignments, and training.

The Americans with Disabilities Act (ADA) of 1990 prohibits private employers, state and local governments, employment agencies, and labor unions from discriminating against qualified individuals with disabilities. The ADA defines an individual with a disability as a person who: 1) has a mental or physical impairment that substantially limits one or more major life activities, 2) has a record of such impairment, or 3) is regarded as having such impairment. An employer is required to make a reasonable accommodation to the known disability of a qualified applicant or employee if it would not impose an "undue hardship" on the operation of the employer's business.

The Fair Labor Standards Act (FLSA) of 1938 establishes the minimum wage, overtime pay, recordkeeping, and youth employment standards affecting full-time and part-time workers in the private sector and in federal, state, and local governments. Special rules apply to state and local government employment involving fire protection and law enforcement activities, volunteer services, and compensatory time off instead of cash overtime pay.

The Family and Medical Leave Act (FMLA) of 1993 entitles eligible employees to take up to 12 weeks of unpaid, job-protected leave in a 12-month period for specified family and medical reasons. FMLA applies to all public agencies, including state, local, and federal employers, local education agencies (schools), and private-sector employers who employed 50 or more employees in 20 or more workweeks in the current or preceding calendar year, including joint employers and successors of covered employers.

The National Labor Relations Act (NLRA) of 1947 extends rights to many private-sector employees, including the right to organize and bargain with their employer collectively. Employees covered by the act are protected from certain types of employer and union misconduct and have the right to attempt to form a union where none exists.

The Worker Adjustment and Retraining Notification Act (WARN) of 1988 generally covers employers with 100 or more employees, not counting those who have worked less than six months in the last 12 months and those who work an average of less than 20 hours a week. Regular federal, state, and local government entities that provide public services are not covered. WARN protects workers, their families, and communities by requiring employers to provide notification 60 calendar days in advance of plant closings and mass layoffs.

These are just a few of the key regulatory federal statutes, regulations, and guidance that human resources professionals need to understand to confirm organizational compliance. For additional information on HR compliance resources, the **Society of Human Resource Management (SHRM)** at SHRM.org maintains a plethora of resources for the HR professional and the businesses that they support.

To ensure the successful management and oversight of the many compliance rules and regulations, the human resources team must utilize best practices to inform and hold employees accountable to HR compliance practices. Some of these best practices include education and training, documentation, and audit. Each of these is described in greater detail, and will help HR achieve its important goal of maintaining HR compliance for the organization.

Education and training in the areas of compliance and labor law is critical to ensure that all applicable laws and regulations are being followed. These laws can change from year to year, so the HR professionals in the organization need to ensure that they are engaged in ongoing education and training. It is not just imperative for the HR professional to receive training. In many organizations, managers receive training on key rules and regulations (such as FMLA or ADA, to name a few) so that they have a foundation of knowledge when dealing with employee situations and potential risk areas. Human resources and management need to partner to ensure alignment on compliance issues—especially when there is a risk that an employee situation treads into compliance regulation territory. See **Table 11.1** for a partial list of federal labor laws by number of employees, as displayed on the Society for Human Resource Management website.

Refer to **Table 11.1**: Federal Labor Laws by Number of Employees.

Federal Labor Laws by Number of Employees
American Taxpayer Relief Act of 2012
Consumer Credit Protection Act of 1968
Employee Polygraph Protection Act of 1988
Employee Retirement Income Security Act of 1974 (ERISA)
Equal Pay Act of 1963
Fair and Accurate Credit Transaction Act of 2003 (FACT)
Fair Credit Reporting Act of 1969
Fair Labor Standards Act of 1938
Federal Insurance Contributions Act of 1935 (Social Security) (FICA)
Health Insurance Portability and Accountability Act of 1996 (if a company offers benefits) (HIPPA)
Immigration Reform and Control Act of 1986

Table 11.1 (Attribution: Copyright Rice University, OpenStax, under CC-BY 4.0 license)

Federal Labor Laws by Number of Employees
These federal laws cover all employees of all organizations. Several other factors may apply in determining employer coverage, such as whether the employer is public or private, whether the employer offers health insurance, and whether the employer uses a third party to conduct background checks. Source: SHRM website, https://www.shrm.org/, accessed October 20, 2018.

Table 11.1 (Attribution: Copyright Rice University, OpenStax, under CC-BY 4.0 license)

Documentation of the rules and regulations—in the form of an employee handbook—can be one of the most important resources that HR can provide to the organization to mitigate compliance risk. The handbook should be updated regularly and should detail the organization's policies and procedures and how business is to be conducted. Legal counsel should review any such documentation before it is distributed to ensure that it is up-to-date and appropriate for the audience.

Scheduling HR compliance audits should be part of the company's overall strategy to avoid legal risk. Noncompliance can cause enormous financial and reputational risk to a company, so it is important to have audits that test the organization's controls and preparedness. When the human resources function takes the lead in implementing audits and other best practices, they create real value for the organization.

CONCEPT CHECK

1. What are some of the key regulations that guide the compliance work of human resource management?
2. What does an employee handbook provide to an organization?

11.3 Performance Management

3. How do performance management practices impact company performance?

Performance management practices and processes are among the most important that human resources manages, yet they are also among the most contentious processes in an organization. Many people view performance management as a human resources role and believe that it is in some parallel path with the business. On the contrary, for the process to be successful, it should not only be human resources that is responsible for driving performance. For the (typically) annual performance management process, human resources and line management should partner on the implementation and ongoing communication of the process. Although HR is responsible for creating and facilitating the performance management processes, it is the organizational managers that need to strongly support the process and communicate the linkage of performance management to overall organizational goals and performance. In my experience, it was helpful when business leadership emphasized that performance management isn't a human resources process—it is a mission-critical business process. If a business manager can't track and drive performance at the individual level, then the overall organization won't know how it's tracking on overall organizational goals. Performance Management Before discussing the state of performance management in the workplace today, it is important to understand the origin of performance management. Performance management began as a simple tool to drive accountability (as it still does) but has evolved more recently into a tool used for employee development.

Performance management can be tracked back to the U.S. military's "merit rating" system, which was created during World War I to identify poor performers for discharge or transfer ("The Performance Management Revolution," Harvard Business Review, October 2016).[2] After World War II, about 60% of all U.S. companies were using a performance appraisal process. (By the 1960s nearly 90% of all U.S. companies were using them.) Although the rules around job seniority determined pay increases and promotions for the unionized worker population, strong performance management scores meant good advancement prospects for managers. In the beginning, the notion of using this type of system to *improve* performance was more of an afterthought, and not the main purpose. By the 1960s or so, when we started to see a shortage of managerial talent, companies began to use performance systems to develop employees into supervisors, and managers into executives.

In 1981, when Jack Welch became CEO of General Electric, he championed the forced-ranking system—another military creation. He did this to deal with the long-standing concern that supervisors failed to label real differences in performance (HBR, The Performance Management Revolution). GE utilized this performance management system to shed the people at the bottom. They equated performance with people's inherent capabilities and ignored their potential to grow. People were categorized as "A" players (to be rewarded), "B" players (to be accommodated), and "C" players (to be dismissed). In the GE system, development was reserved for the "A" players—and those with high potential were chosen to advance to senior positions. Since the days of GE's forced ranking, many companies have implemented a similar forced-ranking system, but many have backed away from the practice. After Jack Welch retired, GE backed away from the practice as well. Companies, GE included, saw that it negatively fostered internal competition and undermined collaboration and teamwork and thus decided to drop forced ranking from their performance management processes.

Most people agree, in theory, that performance management is important. What people may *not* agree on is *how* performance management should be implemented. As the dissatisfaction with performance management processes began to increase, some companies began to change the way they thought about performance. In 2001, an "Agile Manifesto" was developed by software developers and "emphasized principles of collaboration, self-organization, self-direction, and regular reflection on how to work more effectively, with the aim of prototyping more quickly and responding in real-time to customer feedback and changes in requirements." (Performance Management Revolution, HBR). The impact on performance management was clear, and companies started to think about performance management processes that were less cumbersome, incorporated frequent feedback, and delivered performance impacts.

In a recent public survey by Deloitte Services, 58% of executives surveyed believed that their current performance management approach drives neither employee engagement nor high performance. They need something more nimble, real-time, and individualized—and focused on fueling performance in the future rather than assessing it in the past.[3] ("*Reinventing Performance Management*," Harvard Business Review, Buckingham and Goodall, 2015). In light of this study, Deloitte became one of the companies that has recently sought to redesign their performance processes. As part of their "radical redesign," they seek to see performance at the individual level, and thus they ask team leaders about their own future actions and decisions with respect to each individual. They ask leaders what they'd do with their team members, not what they think of them ("Reinventing Performance Management," HBR). The four questions that Deloitte asks of its managers are as follows:

- Given what I know of this person's performance, and if it were my money, I would award this person the highest possible compensation increase and bonus.
- Given what I know of this person's performance, I would always want him or her on my team.
- This person is at risk for low performance.
- This person is ready for promotion today.

Although there has been some discussion over the last several years about some companies wanting to drop performance appraisals completely, most of the research seems to support that the total absence of performance management doesn't help either. A recent global survey by CEB Global reports that more than 9,000 managers and employees think that not having performance evaluations is worse than having them.[4] ("Let's Not Kill Performance Evaluations Yet," HBR, Nov 2016, Goler, Gale, Grant). Their findings indicate that even though every organization has people who are unhappy with their bonuses or disappointed that they weren't promoted, research shows that employees are more willing to accept an undesirable outcome when the process is fair. The key question really becomes: how can HR help the business create a process to fairly evaluate performance and enhance employee development while *not* burdening the business with undue bureaucracy and non-value-added activities?

MANAGING CHANGE

Global versus Local HR

Multinational companies are always challenged to determine the balance between global and local needs when creating a human resource management strategy. Some large companies weigh heavily on the side of centralization, with very few local deviations from the global strategy. Others may allow more localization of processes and decision-making if there are very specific local cultural needs that must be addressed. In either case, companies are well-served by maintaining global standards while also allowing for local market adaptation in the human resources areas where it makes the most sense.

According to the *MIT Sloan Management Review* article "Six Principles of Effective Global Talent Management" (Winter 2012), most multinational companies introduce global performance standards, competency profiles, and performance management tools and processes. These are the human resources areas that are most closely linked to the overall strategies and goals, and thus remain at the global level. Those HR processes that are not perceived as being as closely linked to the strategy and that may need to have local market inputs include processes such as training and compensation. Hiring practices may also need to be locally adapted, due to country-specific labor laws and challenges. One caveat, however, is that a company may limit itself in terms of its global talent management if it has too many country-specific adaptations to hiring, assessment, and development processes for top talent. It is important that the company takes a global approach to talent management so that cross-learning opportunities and cross-cultural development opportunities can take place.

One of the most important aspects of global talent management is that a company can break down silos and pollinate the business with talented employees from around the globe. Some companies even have global leadership programs that bring together high-potential leaders from across the organization to build camaraderie, share knowledge, and engage in learning. Others have created rotational programs for leaders to be able to experience new roles in other cultures in order to build their personal resumes and cultural intelligence. Human resources can have an enormous impact on the company's ability to harness the power of a global talent pool when they create a global network for talent while also balancing this with the requirements of the local market.

Discussion Questions
1. What are the challenges of a company developing a different competency model or performance management process for each of its local offices?
2. Why might compensation programs and hiring practices need to have local adaptation? What would be the risks if these were not adapted to local markets?

As organizations evaluate their options for a performance management system, human resources and business leadership need to consider several challenges that will need to be addressed—no matter what the system.[5] ("*The Performance Management Revolution*," Capelli and Tavis, HBR, pp. 9-11).

The first is the challenge of aligning individual and company goals. Traditionally, the model has been to "cascade" goals down through the organization, and employees are supposed to create goals that reflect and support the direction set at the top. The notion of SMART goals (Specific, Measurable, Achievable, Relevant, Timebound) has made the rounds over the years, but goal setting can still be challenging if business goals are complex or if employee goals seem more relatable to specific project work than to the overall top-line goals. The business and the individual need to be able to respond to goal shifts, which occur very often in response to the rapid rate of change and changing customer needs. This is an ongoing issue that human resources and business leadership will need to reconcile.

The next key challenge to think about when designing a performance management process is rewarding performance. Reward structures are discussed later in this chapter, but reward systems must be rooted in performance management systems. Currently, the companies that are redesigning their performance processes are trying to figure out how their new practices will impact their **pay-for-performance** models. Companies don't appear to be abandoning the concept of rewarding employees based on and driven by their performance, so the linkage between the two will need to be redefined as the systems are changed.

The identification of poor performers is a challenge that has existed since the earliest days of performance management, and even the most formal performance management process doesn't seem to be particularly good at weeding out poor performers. A lot of this is due to the managers who evaluate employees and are reluctant to address the poor performers that they're seeing. Also, the annual performance management process tends to make some managers feel that the poor performance should be overlooked during the year and only addressed (often ineffectively) during a one-per-year review. Whatever new performance management models an organization adopts, they will have to ensure that poor performance is dealt with in real time and is communicated, documented, and managed closely.

Avoiding legal troubles is another ongoing challenge for organizations and is another reason for real-time communication and documentation of performance issues. Human resources supports managers as they deal with employee relations issues, and the thought of not having a formal, numerical ratings system is unfathomable for some people who worry about defending themselves against litigation. However, because even formal performance processes can be subjective and may reveal ratings bias, neither the traditional formal process nor some of the radical new approaches can guarantee that legal troubles will never develop. From my experience, the best strategy for effective and fair performance management is real-time communication and documentation of issues. The employee is told about his or her performance issues (in as close to real time as possible), and the manager has documented the performance issues and conversations objectively and has engaged human resources with any larger or more complex issues.

"Managing the feedback firehose" and keeping conversations, documentation, and feedback in a place where it can be tracked and utilized is an ongoing challenge. The typical annual performance process is not conducive to capturing ongoing feedback and conversations. There have been some new technologies introduced (such as apps) that can be used to capture ongoing conversations between managers and employees. General Electric uses an app called PD@GE (PD = performance development) that allows managers to pull up notes and materials from prior conversations with employees. IBM has a similar app that allows peer-to-peer feedback. Although there are clearly some technology solutions that can be used to help communicate and collect feedback, human resources will need to continue to communicate and reinforce rules around objectivity and appropriate use of the tools.

Performance management processes—traditional and inventive new approaches alike—will face the same challenges over time. Human resource management professionals need to be aware of these challenges and design a performance management system that addresses them in the format and within the context of their culture.

CONCEPT CHECK

1. Where did the concept of performance management originate?
2. What are some of the key challenges of any performance management process?

11.4 | Influencing Employee Performance and Motivation

4. How do companies use rewards strategies to influence employee performance and motivation?

Both performance management and rewards systems are key levers that can be used to motivate and drive individual and group performance ... which leads to overall organizational performance, productivity, and growth. Performance and rewards systems are also "cultural" in that they provide a glimpse into the way a company manages the performance (or nonperformance) of its employees, and to what extent they are willing to differentiate and reward for that performance. There has been a great deal of discussion over the years to identify best practices in the ways we differentiate and reward employees, which will also drive employee performance and motivation.

Before we can talk about best practices and findings in rewards and motivation systems, we must first define the terms. Rewards systems are the framework that an organization (generally via human resources) creates and manages to ensure that employee performance is reciprocated with some sort of reward (e.g., monetary or other extrinsic) that will drive and motivate the employee to continue to perform for the organization. Rewards programs consist primarily of compensation programs and policies, but can also include employee benefits and other extrinsic rewards that fulfill employee needs.

Within human resource management, the primary focus of a rewards program in an organization is to successfully implement a compensation system. Most organizations strive to implement a **pay-for-performance** compensation program that offers competitive pay in the marketplace and allows differentiation of compensation based on employee performance. Pay for performance begins with a philosophy that an organization adopts that states that they seek to reward the best-performing employees to enhance business performance and take care of those who can have the greatest impact.

In the 2011 SHRM article by Stephen Miller, entitled "Study: Pay for Performance Pays Off," Miller says that companies' top four drivers for moving to a pay-for-performance strategy are to:

- Recognize and reward high performers (46.9%)
- Increase the likelihood of achieving corporate goals (32.5%)
- Improve productivity (7.8%)
- Move away from an entitlement culture (7.8%)

The study also showed that the drivers differed depending on whether the company was high performing or lower performing.[6] Almost half of high-performing organizations indicated that recognizing and rewarding top performers was the main driver of their pay-for-performance strategy, making it number one on the list of primary drivers. Lower-performing organizations did not appear to be as sure about the drivers behind their strategy. The number one driver among this group was achieving corporate goals. It appears that those top-performing organizations that implement a pay-for-performance strategy truly believe in the idea of differentiating among different levels of performance.

According to the 2015 World at Work "Compensation Programs and Practices Report," pay for performance continues to thrive with better than 7 in 10 (72%) companies saying that they directly tie pay increases to job performance, and two-thirds (67%) indicating increases for top performers are at least 1.5 times the increase for average performers. In addition, the results of the survey seem to indicate that employees' understanding of the organization's compensation philosophy improves when there is higher differentiation in increases between average and top performers. The greater differentiation of increases is more visible and drives home the point that the company is serious about pay for performance.[7]

A pay-for-performance program may have many components, and the human resources organization has the challenge of designing, analyzing, communicating, and managing the different components to ensure that the philosophy and the practices themselves are being carried out appropriately and legally. Human resource management's role in establishing pay for performance is that HR must engage business leadership to establish the following elements of the framework:

1. Define the organization's pay philosophy. Leadership needs to agree that they will promote a culture that rewards employees for strong performance.
2. Review the financial impacts of creating pay-for-performance changes. How much differentiation of performance will we have? What is the cost of doing this?
3. Identify any gaps that exist in the current processes. If any of the current human resources and compensation policies conflict with pay for performance, they should be reviewed and changed. Examples may lie in the performance management process, the merit increase process, and the short-term and long-term bonus processes. If the performance management process has gaps, these should be corrected before pay for performance is implemented; otherwise this will generate more distrust in the system. The salary structure should also be benchmarked with market data to ensure that the organization is compensating according to where it wishes to be in the marketplace.
4. Update compensation processes with new pay for-performance elements. This includes the design of a **merit matrix** that ties employee annual pay increases to performance. Other areas of focus should be the design of a short-term bonus matrix and a long-term bonus pay-for-performance strategy. In other words, how does performance drive the bonus payouts? What is the differential (or multiplier) for each level?
5. Communicate and train managers and employees on the pay for-performance philosophy and process changes. Explain the changes in the context of the overall culture of the organization. This is a long-term investment in talent and performance.

Human resource management professionals play a key role in the rewards processes, and employee compensation is only one piece (although a key piece!) of the "total rewards" pie. World at Work defines *total rewards* as a "dynamic relationship between employers and employees." World at Work also defines a **total rewards strategy** as the six elements of total rewards that "collectively define an organization's strategy to attract, motivate, retain and engage employees." These six elements include:

- Compensation—Pay provided by an employer to its employees for services rendered (i.e., time, effort, and skill). This includes both fixed and variable pay tied to performance levels.
- Benefits—Programs an employer uses to supplement the cash compensation employees receive. These health, income protection, savings, and retirement programs provide security for employees and their families.
- Work-life effectiveness—A specific set of organizational practices, policies, and programs, plus a philosophy that actively supports efforts to help employees achieve success at both work and home.

- Recognition—Formal or informal programs that acknowledge or give special attention to employee actions, efforts, behavior, or performance and support business strategy by reinforcing behaviors (e.g., extraordinary accomplishments) that contribute to organizational success.
- Performance management—The alignment of organizational, team, and individual efforts toward the achievement of business goals and organizational success. Performance management includes establishing expectations, skill demonstration, assessment, feedback, and continuous improvement.
- Talent development—Provides the opportunity and tools for employees to advance their skills and competencies in both their short- and long-term careers.

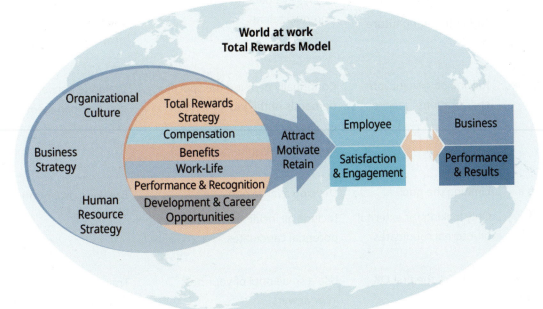

Exhibit 11.3 **Total Rewards Model, World at Work** (Attribution: Copyright Rice University, OpenStax, under CC-BY 4.0 license)

Human resource management is responsible for defining and driving the various elements of an organization's total rewards strategy and ensuring that it is engaging enough to attract and retain good employees. It is easy to see that there are many different types of rewards that can motivate individuals for many different reasons. In the HBR article "Employee Motivation: A Powerful New Model" (Nohria, Groysberg, Lee), August 2008, the authors describe four different drives that underlie motivation. They assert that these are hardwired into our brains and directly affect our emotions and behaviors. These include the drives to acquire, bond, comprehend, and defend. **Table 11.2** illustrates each of these drives, the primary levers found in an organization to address those drives, and the actions that should be taken to support the primary levers.[8]

Hiring Top-Level Executives			
Steps in the Process	Poor Practices	Best Practices	Challenges
Anticipate.	Hiring only when you have an opening Poor succession plan Not anticipating future needs	Conduct ongoing analysis of future needs. Always evaluate the pool of potential talent.	Linking the talent plan to the strategic plan Incorporating HR into the strategic planning process
Specify the job.	Relying on generic job specifications	Continually defining the specific demands of the job Specifying specific skills and experience requirements	Dialogue between HR and top management
Develop a pool.	Limiting the pool Only looking for external or internal candidates	Develop a large pool. Include all inside and outside potential candidates.	Breaking organizational silos
Assess the candidates.	Don't pick the first OK choice. Don't only use your "gut."	Use a small pool of your best interviewers. Conduct robust background checks.	Training senior managers on interviewing techniques
Hire the choice.	Don't assume money is the only issue. Don't only discuss the positives of the job.	Show active support of the candidates' interests. Realistically describe the job. Ensure that offered compensation is fair to other employees.	Getting commitment of top managers Ensuring compensation equity
Integrate the new hire.	Don't assume that the new hire is a "plug and play."	Use a "top performer" as a mentor. Check in often early in the process even if no problems seem imminent.	Rewarding mentors

Table 11.2 (Attribution: Copyright Rice University, OpenStax, under CC-BY 4.0 license)

Hiring Top-Level Executives			
Steps in the Process	Poor Practices	Best Practices	Challenges
Review the process.	Don't hang on to bad hires.	Remove bad hires early on. Review the recruiting practices. Reward your best interviewers.	Institutionalizing audit and review practices Admitting mistakes and moving on
Adapted from "The Definitive Guide to Recruiting in Good Times and Bad," from article "Hiring Top Executives: A Comprehensive End-to-End Process," Harvard Business Review, May 2009.			

Table 11.2 (Attribution: Copyright Rice University, OpenStax, under CC-BY 4.0 license)

The drive to acquire describes the notion that we are all driven to acquire scarce goods that bolster our sense of well-being. This drive also seems to be relative (we compare ourselves to others in what we have) and insatiable (we always want more). Within an organization, the primary lever to address this drive is the reward system, and the actions are to differentiate levels of performance, link performance to rewards, and pay competitively.

The drive to bond describes the idea that humans extend connections beyond just individuals, to organizations, associations, and nations. In organizations, this drive is fulfilled when employees feel proud to be a part of the company and enjoy being a member of their team. Within an organization, the primary lever to address this drive is culture, and the actions are to foster mutual reliance and friendships, to value collaboration and teamwork, and to encourage best practice sharing.

The drive to comprehend is the concept of all of us wanting to make sense of the world around us and producing different theories and accounts to explain things. People are motivated by the idea of figuring out challenges and making a contribution. In organizations, the primary lever to address this drive is job design, and the actions are to design jobs that have distinct and important roles in the organization, as well as jobs that are meaningful and foster a sense of contribution.

The drive to defend is our instinct to defend ourselves, our families, and our friends, and it describes our defensiveness against external threats. This drive also tells us a lot about our level of resistance to change, and why some employees have especially guarded or emotional reactions. In organizations, the primary levers that address this drive are performance management and resource-allocation processes, and the actions are to increase process transparency and fairness, and to build trust by being just in granting rewards, assignments, and other recognition.

Within human resource management, the area of compensation and reward systems is exceedingly complicated. In organizations, we think primarily of compensation rewards, which are very important drivers and motivators for most people. We need to also remember the other aspects of the total rewards strategy, as well as the drives and levers we can utilize to motivate employees.

11.5 Building an Organization for the Future

5. What is talent acquisition, and how can it create a competitive advantage for a company?

We've discussed some of the key focus areas that human resource management professionals need to address to ensure that employees are performing their roles well and are being fairly rewarded for their contributions. We haven't yet addressed how we think about where these employees come from—Whom do we hire? What skills do we need now and in the future? Where will we even look for these employees? What are some best practices? **Talent acquisition** is the area within human resource management that defines the strategy for selection, recruiting, and hiring processes, and helps the organization fight the **"war for talent"** during good times and bad.

Hiring strong talent is a key source of competitive advantage for a company, yet so many companies do it poorly. Often, the recruiting and hiring processes happen reactively—someone leaves the organization and then people scramble to fill the gap. Very few companies take a longer-term, proactive approach and work to create a strategic plan for talent acquisition. In the article "The Definitive Guide to Recruiting in Good Times and Bad" (Fernandez-Araoz, Groysberg, Nohria, HBR, 2009), the authors advocate for a rigorous and strategic recruiting process that includes the following critical actions:

- Anticipate your future leadership needs based on your strategic business plan.
- Identify the specific competencies required in each position you need to fill.
- Develop a sufficiently large candidate pool.

In organizations today, there are often pieces of the talent acquisition process that are outsourced to external recruiters, as opposed to being managed internally by human resources employees.[9] While outsourcing specific searches is not an issue, there must be internal HR/talent acquisition employees responsible for creating the overall strategic plan for the recruiting function. Contract recruiters may then take responsibility for a piece of the overall process by leveraging the strategy and competencies that the HR team puts forth.[10]

Recruiting and hiring of high-level leadership candidates has special risks and rewards associated with it. The risk that a key leadership position is vacant or becoming vacant poses a risk to the organization if it is left open for too long. These high-level positions are often harder to fill, with fewer candidates being available and the selection of the right talent being so critical to the organization's future. The reward, however, is that with due diligence and clear goals and competencies/skills defined for the position, the HR/talent acquisition professional can create a competitive advantage through the recruitment of key high-level talent.

The following best practices illustrate the key steps for effective recruiting of key leadership hires. Both human resources and business leadership should partner to discuss and define each of the elements to ensure alignment and support of the recruiting plan and process (Definitive Guide to Recruiting, HBR, 2009).

Anticipate your needs. Every two to three years there should be a review of high-level leadership requirements based on the strategic plan. Some of the questions to answer here are:

- How many people will we need, and in what positions, in the next few years?
- What will the organizational structure look like?

• What must our leadership pipeline contain today to ensure that we find and develop tomorrow's leaders?

Specify the job. For each leadership position identified, specify competencies needed in each role. For example:

• Job-based: What capabilities will the job require?
• Team-based: Will the applicant need to manage political dynamics?
• Firm-based: What resources (supporting, talent, technology) will the organization need to provide the person who fills this role?

Develop the pool. Cast a wide net for candidates by asking suppliers, customers, board members, professional service provides, and trusted insiders for suggestions. It helps to start this process even before you have a role that you're hiring for. During succession planning and talent discussions internally, it helps to start making of list of internal *and* external contacts and potential candidates before the need arises.

Assess the candidates. Have the hiring manager, the second-level manager, and the top HR manager conduct a "behavioral event interview" with each candidate. Candidates will describe experiences they've had that are like situations they'll face in the organization. Gain an understanding of how the candidate acted and the reasoning behind their actions. Make sure to evaluate a broad range of references to ask about results the candidate achieved.

Exhibit 11.4   The Job Fair A job fair, career fair, or career expo, like this one at the College of DuPage, is an event in which employers, recruiters, and schools give information to potential employees and job seekers attend hoping to make a good impression on potential employers. They also interact with potential coworkers by speaking face-to-face, exchanging résumés, and asking questions in an attempt to get a good feel for the work needed. Likewise, online job fairs give seekers another way to get in contact with probable employers using the Internet. (Credit: Taavi Burns/ flickr/ Attribution 2.0 Generic (CC BY 2.0))

Close the deal. Once you have chosen the final candidate, you can increase the chance that the job offer will be accepted by:

- Sharing passion about the company and role, and showing genuine interest in the candidate
- Acknowledging the opportunities and challenges of the role, differentiating the opportunities at your organization from those of your competitor
- Striking a creative balance between salary, bonuses, and other long-term incentives

Integrate the newcomer. It is important to integrate new hires into the company's culture:

- During the first few months, have the managers and the HR team check in with each new hire.
- Assign a mentor (star employee) to provide ongoing support to each new hire.
- Check in with the new hire to ensure that they are getting enough support, and inquire about what other support might be needed. Ensure that new hires are adequately building new relationships throughout the organization.

Refer to **Table 11.2**: Hiring Top-Level Executives, adapted from "The Definitive Guide to Recruiting in Good Times and Bad," from the article "Hiring Top Executives: A Comprehensive End-to-End Process," *Harvard Business Review*, May 2009.

By following these best practices, human resources and business leadership can ensure that the new hire is integrating well and has the best possible start in the new role. Talent acquisition is a key element of any human resource management program, and the right process can mean the difference between a poor hire and a distinct competitive advantage gained through top talent.

CONCEPT CHECK

1. What are some best practices for recruiting and hiring leadership candidates?
2. How can we ensure a more successful integration of the new hire?

11.6 Talent Development and Succession Planning

6. What are the benefits of talent development and succession planning?

Talent development and **succession planning** are, in my opinion, two of the most critical human resource management processes within an organization. You can work tirelessly to recruit and hire the right people, and you can spend a lot of time defining and redesigning your performance and rewards programs, but if you can't make decisions that effectively assess and develop the key talent that you have, then everything else feels like a wasted effort. Talent development describes all process and programs that an organization utilizes to assess and develop talent. Succession planning is the process for reviewing key roles and determining the readiness levels of potential internal (and external!) candidates to fill these roles. It is an important process that is a key link between talent development and talent acquisition/recruiting.

The human resources function facilitates talent development activities and processes, but they are also heavily reliant on business inputs and support. Each of the talent development processes that will be discussed require heavy involvement and feedback from the business. Like performance management, talent development is a process that HR owns and facilitates, but it is a true business process that has a fundamental impact on an organization's performance. Talent is a competitive advantage, and in the age of the "war for talent," an organization needs to have a plan for developing its key talent.

One of the key tools that is used in talent development is the talent review. This process generally follows an organization's performance management process (which is primarily focused on *current* employee performance) and is more focused on employee development and potential for the *future*. Talent reviews often employ the use of a **9-box** template, which plots employee performance versus employee potential and provides the reviewer with nine distinct options, or boxes, to categorize where the employee is.

Refer to **Table 11.3**: Performance and Potential Grid.

Performance and Potential Grid			
		Potential	
		Lowest potential rating	Middle potential rating	Highest potential rating
Performance over time	**Highest**	John Smith Melanie Roper Keegan Flanagan	Chieh Zhang Edgar Orrelana	Rory Collins Aimee Terranova
	Medium	Joseph Campbell Alina Dramon Alex Joiner Lauren Gress	Christina Martin Thomas Weimeister	Richard Collins
	Lowest	Marty Hilton		

Table 11.3

The performance axis ratings are low/medium/high and based on the employee's recent performance management rating. Low = below target, medium = at target, and high = above target. Like the performance rating, this reflects performance against objectives and the skills and competencies required in the employee's current role and function. Performance can change over time (for example, with a promotion or job change). Performance is overall a more objective rating than potential, which leaves the rater to make some assumptions about the future.

Potential is defined as an employee's ability to demonstrate the behaviors necessary to be successful at the next highest level within the company. **Competencies** and behaviors are a good indicator of an employee's potential. Higher-potential employees, no matter what the level, often display the following competencies: business acumen, strategic thinking, leadership skills, people skills, learning agility, and technology skills. Other indicators of potential may include:

- Top performance in current job
- Success in other positions held (within or outside of the company)
- Education/certifications
- Significant accomplishments/events
- Willingness and desire to advance

MANAGING CHANGE

Tech in Human Resources

There has been a boom in HR technology and innovation over the last several years—and it is making some of the traditional HR systems from last decade seem enormously outdated. Some of the trends that are driving this HR tech innovation include mobile technology, social media, data analytics, and learning management. Human resources professionals need to be aware of some of the key technology innovations that have emerged as a result of these trends because there's no sign that they will be going away any time soon.

Josh Bersin of Bersin by Deloitte, Deloitte Consulting LLP, wrote about some of these HR technology innovations in his SHRM.org article "9 HR Tech Trends for 2017" (Jan. 2017). One of these technology innovations is the "performance management revolution" and the new focus on managing performance by team and not just by hierarchy. Performance management technologies have become more agile and real time, with built-in pulse surveys and easy goal tracking. Now, instead of the formal, once-a-year process that brings everything to a halt, these performance management technologies allow ongoing, real-time, and dynamic input and tracking of performance data.

Another HR tech trend named is the "rise of people analytics." Data analytics has become such a huge field, and HR's adoption of it is no exception. Some disruptive technologies in this area are predictive—they allow analysis of job change data and the prediction of successful versus unsuccessful outcomes. Predictive analytics technologies can also analyze patterns of e-mails and communications for good time-management practices, or to predict where a security leak is likely to occur. One other incredible analytics application consists of a badge that monitors employees' voices and predicts when an employee is experiencing stress. That is either really cool or really eerie, if you ask me.

The "maturation of the learning market" is a fascinating trend to me, as an HR professional who grew up in the days of multiple in-class trainings and week-long leadership programs. Learning processes have changed greatly with the advent of some of these innovative HR technologies. Although many larger companies have legacy learning management systems (like Cornerstone, Saba, and SuccessFactors), there are many new and competitive options that focus on scaling video learning to the entire organization. The shift has gone from learning management to learning—with the ability to not only register and track courses online, but to take courses online. Many companies are realizing that these YouTube-like learning applications are a great complement to their existing learning systems, and it is predicted that the demand will continue to grow.

Other trends of note include technologies that manage the contingent workforce, manage wellness, and automate HR processes via artificial intelligence. It is amazing to think about so many interesting and innovative technologies that are being designed for Human Resources. The investment in human capital is one of the most critical investments that a company makes, and it is refreshing to see that this level of innovation is being created to manage, engage, and develop this investment.

Discussion Questions

1. How does real-time performance management compare to the traditional annual performance process? How can a real-time process help an employee be more effective? What are some potential drawbacks?

2. Why do you think learning systems evolved in this way? Is there still a place for group classroom training? What types of learning might require classroom training, and what is better suited for

online and YouTube-style learning?

In the talent review, the potential axis equates to potential for advancement within the organization: low = not ready to advance, medium = close to ready, and high = ready to advance. Potential does *not* equate to the value of an individual within the organization, nor does it state the quality of individual. There are likely many strong performers (top contributors) in every company who prefer to stay in their current role for years and be specialists of their own processes. A specialist or expert may not want to manage people, and thus would be rated as low on potential due to the lack of interest in advancement. Advancement may also mean relocation or lifestyle change that an employee is not willing to make at that time, so the employee would be rated low on potential for that reason. Potential can certainly change over time, given people's individual situations and life circumstances. Potential tends to be the more subjective ratings axis, as it involves some assumptions into what a team member could be capable of based on limited information that is available now.

Exhibit 11.5   This is a flight simulator for a Boeing 737 aircraft. There is a drastic shortage of aircraft pilots, and training future pilots is a critical function with the challenge of limited actual flight training time. Consider how technology helps companies develop skilled workers both on and off the job. (Credit: Michael Coghlan/Flickr/ Attribution 2.0 Generic (CC BY 2.0))

A human resources team member should absolutely facilitate the talent review process and provide leaders with clear session objectives and specific instructions in order maintain the integrity and confidentiality of this important talent process. The book *One Page Talent Management* (Effron and Ort, HBS Press, 2010) describes the talent review meeting as a **talent review calibration process** that "ensures objective performance and potential evaluations, clear development plans, and an understanding of what high potential means in your company. A calibration meeting brings together a manager and her team members to discuss their talent. Each team member presents the performance and potential (PxP) grid that he prepared on direct reports and briefly describes how each person is rated. Other team members contribute their opinions based on their firsthand interactions with that person. The discussion concludes after they have discussed each person, agreed on their final placement, and identified key development steps for them."[11]

After everyone being discussed has been placed in one of the boxes on the 9-box template, the leadership team should discuss key development actions for each employee. (If there isn't time to discuss development activities for each employee, the group should start with the high-potential employees.) After the talent review calibration process is complete, human resources should keep a master list of the documented outcomes, as well as the development activities that were suggested for everyone. HR should follow up with each of the leaders to help with the planning and execution of the development activities as needed. The key outputs of the talent review process include:

- Identification of the "high-potential" employees in the organization
- Definition of development actions/action plans for each employee
- Insight into talent gaps and issues
- Input into the succession planning process

Succession planning generally follows shortly after (if not right after) a talent review because human resources and organizational leadership now have fresh information on the performance and potential of employees in the organization. Succession planning is a key process used to identify the depth of talent on the "bench" and the readiness of that talent to move into new roles. The process can be used to identify gaps or a lack of bench strength at any levels of the organization, but it is usually reserved for leadership roles and other key roles in the organization. In succession planning, human resources will generally sit down with the group leader to discuss succession planning for his group and create a defined list of leadership and other critical roles that will be reviewed for potential successors.

Once the roles for succession planning analysis have been defined, both HR and the business leader will define the following elements for each role:

- Name of incumbent
- Attrition risk of incumbent
- Names of short-term successor candidates (ready in <1 year)
- Names of mid-term successor candidates (ready in 1–3 years)
- Names of long-term successor candidates (ready in 3+ years)
- Optional—9-box rating next to each successor candidate's name

The names of longer-term successor candidates are not as critical, but it is always helpful to understand the depth of the bench. With the information recently collected during the talent review process, HR and management will have a lot of quality information on the internal successor candidates. It is important to include external successor candidates in the succession planning analysis as well. If there are no candidates that are identified as short-, mid-, or long-term successor candidates for a role, then the word "EXTERNAL" should automatically be placed next to that role. Even if there are internal candidates named, any external successor candidates should still be captured in the analysis as appropriate.

Talent reviews and succession planning processes both generate excellent discussions and very insightful information on the state of talent in the organization. Human resources facilitates both processes, in very close partnership with the business, and ultimately keeps the output information from the sessions—i.e., the final succession plan, the final 9-box, and the follow-up development actions and activities as defined in the talent review session. With this information, human resources possesses a level of knowledge that will allow it to drive talent development and coach managers on the follow-up actions that they need to set in motion. Some examples of follow-up development activities that may be appropriate based on the outputs of the succession and 9-box events include **training, stretch assignments, individual assessments,** and **individual development plans**. Training and training plans identify the learning events that an individual would benefit from, either in a classroom or online format. Stretch assignments may be an appropriate development action for an employee who is being tested for or who wants to take on additional responsibility. Individual assessments, such as a **360 assessment** for managers, is a good developmental tool to provide feedback from manager, peers, direct reports, customers, or others who interact with the employee regularly. Finally, an individual development plan is an important document that employees should use to map out their personal development goals and actions, and to track their own status and progress toward those goals.

Talent development is a collection of organization-wide processes that help to evaluate talent strengths and gaps within the organization. Although many of the processes are carried out in a group setting, the output of talent development needs to be very individualized via a collection of development tools and strategies to enhance performance. Human resources is a key resource and partner for these tools and strategies, and thus plays a critical role in the future of talent for the organization.

Conclusion

Human resource management is a complex and often difficult field because of the nature of the key area of focus—people. In working with people, we begin to understand both the expressed and the hidden drives—intentions and emotions that add complexity and additional context to the processes and tasks that we set forth. We also begin to understand that an organization is a group of individuals, and that human resources plays a critical role in ensuring that there are philosophies, structures, and processes in place to guide, teach, and motivate individual employees to perform at their best possible levels.

CONCEPT CHECK

1. What is the difference between the performance and potential categories used in the talent review?
2. What roles should an organization discuss as part of the succession planning process?

🔑 Key Terms

360 assessment An evaluation tool that collects feedback from manager, peers, direct reports, and customers.

9-box A matrix tool used to evaluate an organization's talent pool based on performance and potential factors.

Competencies A set of defined behaviors that an organization might utilize to define standards for success.

Employee life cycle The various stages of engagement of an employee—attraction, recruitment, onboarding, development, retention, separation.

Employer-employee relationship The employment relationship; the legal link between employers and employees that exists when a person performs work or services under specific conditions in return for payment.

Human capital The skills, knowledge, and experience of an individual or group, and that value to an organization.

Human resource management The management of people within organizations, focusing on the touchpoints of the employee life cycle.

Human resources compliance The HR role to ensure adherence to laws and regulations that govern the employment relationship.

Merit matrix A calculation table that provides a framework for merit increases based on performance levels.

Pay-for-performance model The process and structure for tying individual performance levels to rewards levels

Performance management The process by which an organization ensures that its overall goals are being met by evaluating the performance of individuals within that organization.

Society for Human Resource Management The world's largest HR professional society, with more than 285,000 members in more than 165 countries. It is a leading provider of resources serving the needs of HR professionals.

Succession planning The process of identifying and developing new leaders and high-potential employees to replace current employees at a future time.

Talent acquisition The process of finding and acquiring skilled candidates for employment within a company; it generally refers to a long-term view of building talent pipelines, rather than short-term recruitment.

Talent development Integrated HR processes that are created to attract, develop, motivate, and retain employees.

Talent review calibration process The meeting in which an organization's 9-box matrix is reviewed and discussed, with input and sharing from organizational leadership.

Total rewards strategy As coined by World at Work, includes compensation, benefits, work-life effectiveness, recognition, performance management, and talent development.

Training, stretch assignments, individual assessments, individual development plans These are tools that may be used in talent development:

Training—a forum for learning in person or online

Stretch assignments—challenge roles for high-potential employees

Individual assessments—personality and work style inventories of employees

Individual development plans—documents that highlight an individual employee's opportunities for growth and path of action

War for talent Coined by McKinsey & Company in 1997, it refers to the increasing competition for recruiting and retaining talented employees.

📖 Summary of Learning Outcomes

11.1 An Introduction to Human Resource Management

1. What has been the evolution of human resource management over the years, and what is the current value it provides to an organization?

Human resource management began in its first "wave" as a primarily compliance-type function, with the HR staff charged with enforcing compliance of employees and running the ongoing administrative processes. In the second wave, HR became focused on the design of HR practice areas, which could be built upon best-practice models. Wave 3 of HR brought with it the concept that HR should be a true partner to the business and should support the business strategy through its programs and services. Finally, in the fourth wave, HR is still a partner to the business, but it looks outside of the business to customers, investors, and communities to see how it can be competitive in terms of customer share, investor confidence, and community reputation.

Some key areas that HR supports within the employee life cycle process include: human resources compliance, employee selection and hiring, performance management, compensation rewards, and talent development and succession planning.

11.2 Human Resource Management and Compliance

2. How does the human resources compliance role of HR provide value to a company?

Human resources helps protect the company and its employees to ensure that they are adhering to the numerous regulations and laws that govern the employment relationship. The impact of noncompliance can be very costly and can be in the form of financial, legal, or reputational cost. Some of the key legislation that HR manages compliance around includes the Fair Labor Standards Act (FLSA), the Age Discrimination in Employment Act (ADEA), the Americans with Disabilities Act (ADA), and the Family and Medical Leave Act (FMLA), among others.

Some of the best practices for informing and holding employees accountable are to provide education and training to explain the regulations, to provide reference documentation for guidance with the regulations, and to schedule regular compliance audits to ensure that processes are being followed. Scheduling regular internal HR audits help the organization plan and feel comfortable with its level of preparedness and illustrates the value that a strong HR group can bring to the organization.

11.3 Performance Management

3. How do performance management practices impact company performance?

Performance management is a critical business process that the human resources group manages for the business. Performance management aligns the work of individual groups with the overall business objectives and enables the business to work toward its goals. Performance management should also help the company differentiate between different levels of employee performance through the management of feedback and a rewards structure.

Performance management also allows a company to identify its poor performers and provides a consistent process for tracking and managing poor performance in a manner that is fair and consistent with the law. There has been much discussion of best practices for a performance management process beyond a formal, annual process that often feels cumbersome to the business. However formal or informal, human resource management needs to ensure that the process helps to differentiate different levels of performance, manages the flow of feedback, and is consistent and fair for all employees.

11.4 Influencing Employee Performance and Motivation

4. How do companies use rewards strategies to influence employee performance and motivation?

Companies use rewards strategies to influence employee performance and motivation by differentiating between the various levels of performance. This strategy is called pay for performance, and it ties the employee's performance level to a consistent framework of rewards at each level. Research indicates that the primary reason that companies implement pay for performance is to be able to recognize and reward their high performers.

To implement a pay-for-performance structure, HR and the organization first need to define a compensation philosophy, then perform a review of the financial implications of such a system. Gaps in the current system must be identified, and compensation practices should be updated in accordance with the determined pay-for-performance design. Finally, communication and training are key to help employees understand the context and philosophy, as well as the specific methodology.

11.5 Building an Organization for the Future

5. What is talent acquisition, and how can it create a competitive advantage for a company?

Human resource management plays the important role of managing the talent processes for an organization, and it is critical in the process of acquiring talent from the outside. Talent acquisition is the process of determining what roles are still needed in the organization, where to find people, and whom to hire. Hiring top talent is a key source of competitive advantage for a company, and not all organizations are good at doing it.

The impact of hiring is especially magnified when you talk about top leadership talent. The right leadership candidate can make all the difference in an organization's growth, performance, and trajectory over the years. HR should work with the business to assess need and specifics of the job, develop a pool of candidates, and then assess candidates for the right person to bring into the organization.

11.6 Talent Development and Succession Planning

6. What are the benefits of talent development and succession planning?

Talent development and succession planning processes provide organizations with the systems needed to assess and develop employees and to make the appropriate decisions on their internal movement and development. One important talent development process involves a talent review, in which leadership discusses the employees in its groups in terms of their performance and potential. Performance is based on current performance management evaluations on the current role. Potential is based on behavioral indications that would predict future high performance and promotability in an organization. There is then a discussion on the follow-up actions and development plans for the employees, based on where they fall in the performance/potential matrix. The benefit of this process is that the organization gains a better understanding of where the top talent is within the organization and can make plans to manage the development of that talent.

Another key process for managing talent is succession planning. In this process, leadership and HR meet to identify leadership roles and other critical roles in the organization, and then they discuss a potential pipeline of internal and external successor candidates at different levels of readiness for the role. The output of succession planning is that an organization gets to understand the depth of its talent bench and knows the gap areas where it may need to focus on developing or acquiring additional candidates.

Chapter Review Questions

1. What are the four "waves" of the human resource management evolution?
2. What are some of the key regulations that human resources must manage compliance with?
3. What are some of the unintended consequences of a forced ranking system?
4. What are some of the performance management challenges that must be addressed, no matter what the system?
5. Why are many companies interested in moving to a pay-for-performance strategy?
6. What are the main process steps for implementing pay for performance?
7. What are some best practices for recruiting new leadership candidates?
8. Describe the steps of a talent review session.
9. What is the difference between performance and potential?
10. How can you tell if a candidate has potential?

Management Skills Application Exercises

1. How has human resource management's evolution over the years helped to make it a better partner to the business? In what way would you expect HRM to continue to evolve over the years?
2. Do you believe that a formal, annual performance management process is necessary to help an organization reach its goals? Why or why not? What are the minimum process requirements that must be met to successfully evaluate performance?
3. .Is it possible for an organization to reward people fairly without implementing a pay-for-performance process? Why or why not? Do you see any pitfalls to a pay-for-performance process?
4. How does the "war for talent" impact talent acquisition processes? How can HR be more successful working with the business to navigate the competitive talent landscape?
5. What are the benefits of having talent review calibration processes? What is the downside of the process? Should an organization let employees know what their talent review "rating" is? Why or why not?

Managerial Decision Exercises

1. You have been hired as a new Finance VP, and you oversee a team of almost 30 people. Your HR manager has recently informed you that there have been several employee relations in your group in the recent past, and you are concerned about the level of knowledge that your management team has around dealing with these issues. What could you do to close the gap in knowledge and mitigate the risk of issues in your group?
2. Your company has decided to drop their formal, annual performance management process and move to a system based on ongoing feedback and communication with employees. You are concerned because you have always been careful to differentiate your employees by performance level, and you're worried that this will hurt your stronger employees. How can use ensure that your feedback and communication with employees provides performance management, despite the lack of a formal system?
3. Your company has recently implemented a pay-for-performance model for compensation. This worries you because you know that your employees will be even more upset with their performance ratings if they know that they are tied to compensation. What actions can you take to start to prepare for this change?
4. You are the director of an engineering organization and have been fighting the "war for talent" for a while. It seems that whenever you have a role vacancy, you let HR know but it takes forever to find

someone—and the candidate often turns down the job. What are some ways to better partner with HR to get ahead of the curve for the next time?

5. You are the VP of a line of business at an international manufacturing company. You and several of your long-time colleagues will be retiring over the next few years, and you need to start thinking about talent and succession planning. You are going into a talent review discussion next week, and you're realizing that you have a dearth of potential within your organization. What are some actions you (and HR) can take now to ensure that your business unit isn't floundering when you leave for retirement?

Critical Thinking Case

Zappos, Holacracy, and Human Resource Management

In 2013, Zappos was performing well under the leadership of Tony Hsieh and was getting ready to take on a new challenge that would, among other things, push the boundaries of traditional human resource management. Although business was booming, Tony Hsieh was not a man who wanted to be in status quo mode for too long, so he set out to implement an organizational and cultural change called Holacracy. Zappos was the largest and best known of the 300 companies worldwide that had adopted Holacracy—a new form of hierarchy that is a "flexible, self-governing structure, where there are no fixed jobs but simply temporary functional roles."

In a Holacracy, the main unit is called the "circle," which is a distinct yet fluid team. Leadership became similarly fluid with the changing circles. Circles are designed to meet certain goals and are created and disbanded as project needs change. The intent is that people self-select to work on projects that they want to work on and that they have the skills for. Tony also removed all previous titles. The role of manager went away and was replaced with three roles: "lead links" would focus on guiding the work in the circles; "mentors" would work on employee growth and development; and "compensation appraisers" would work on determining employees' salaries. In 2015, he decided to further break down the divisions between many of the functions, changing them all to business-centric circles. There were changes to almost every human resource management structure that you can think of, and there were quite a few growing pains within the organization. Zappos began to look at employee pay, and Holacracy seemed to have a steep learning curve for many people, even though a "constitution" was created to provide guidance. Zappos was also facing 14% attrition, as some of the rapid and excessive changes were wearing on employees. Tony was a visionary, but for a lot of people it was hard to catch up and see the same vision.

From a human resource management perspective, there could be some positive attributes of a Holacracy if it were to succeed—such as building engagement and helping to build talent and skill sets. There were also a few risks that needed to be dealt with carefully. When you create an organization in which people don't have set teams or projects but instead determine what they want to work on, one of the big challenges is going to be determining the level and nature of their role, as well as the compensation for that role. If Holacracy is compared to a consulting organization, in which consultants are brought into different projects with different requirements, it is critical to first determine the level of their consultant role (based on their education, skills, experience, etc.) so that they can properly move from project to project yet maintain a role of a certain level. That level is then tied to a specific pay scale, so the same consultant will receive the same salary no matter which project he is on. If that consultant is "on the bench," or not placed on a project (or self-placed, in the case of Holacracy), then after a certain defined period that consultant may be at risk of termination.

Holacracy is in some ways a challenging concept to think about, and self-management may not be able to work in all environments. A company that is implementing a Holacracy may find that they are able to master the process of self-selection of work in the "circles." The "task" part of the equation may not be much of an issue once people figure out how to navigate the circles. However, the "people" part of the equation may need some work. The greatest challenge may lie in the structures and processes of human resource management that ultimately define the employer-employee relationship.

Critical Thinking Questions

1. What are some of the human resource management processes that might be enhanced by a Holacracy? What processes will be challenged?

2. Do you think that a Holacracy can be compared to a consulting company? How are they similar,s and how are they different? Can you think of work areas or industries in which Holacracy would be very difficult to implement?

Sources: Askin and Petriglieri, *"Tony Hsieh at Zappos: Structure, Culture, and Change"*, INSEAD Business School Press, 2016.

Introduction

Learning Outcomes

After reading this chapter, you should be able to answer these questions:

1. What is diversity?
2. How diverse is the workforce?
3. How does diversity impact companies and the workforce?
4. What is workplace discrimination, and how does it affect different social identity groups?
5. What key theories help managers understand the benefits and challenges of managing the diverse workforce?
6. How can managers reap benefits from diversity and mitigate its challenges?
7. What can organizations do to ensure applicants, employees, and customers from all backgrounds are valued?

EXPLORING MANAGERIAL CAREERS

Dr. Tamara A. Johnson, Assistant Chancellor for Equity, Diversity, and Inclusion at University of Wisconsin-Eau Claire

Dr. Tamara Johnson's role as assistant chancellor for equity, diversity, and inclusion at the University of Wisconsin-Eau Claire involves supervising and collaborating with various campus entities to ensure their operations continue to support the university's initiatives to foster diversity and equity within the university community. Dr. Johnson oversees the Affirmative Action, Blugold Beginnings (pre-college program), Gender and Sexuality Resource Center, Office of Multicultural Affairs, Ronald E. McNair Program, Services for Students with Disabilities, Student Support Services, University Police, and Upward Bound units and leads campus-wide initiatives to educate and train faculty, students, and staff about cultural awareness, diversity, and institutional equity.

Dr. Johnson's journey to her current role began more than 20 years ago when she worked as a counselor for the Office of Multicultural Student Affairs at the University of Illinois. Her role in this office launched her on a path through university service—Dr. Johnson went on to work as the associate director for University Career Services at Illinois State University, the director for multicultural student affairs at Northwestern University, and the director for faculty diversity initiatives at the University of Chicago. As faculty at the Chicago School of Professional Psychology, Argosy University, and Northwestern University, Dr. Johnson taught counseling courses at the undergraduate, master's, and doctorate levels.

Dr. Johnson's work at the University of Wisconsin-Eau Claire involves developing a program and protocols to ensure all faculty and staff across the institution receive baseline diversity training. In addition, one of her goals is to include criteria related to diversity factors in the evaluations of all faculty/staff. A primary issue that she seeks to address is to increase the awareness of the challenges experienced by underrepresented students. This includes individuals who may come from backgrounds of low income, students of color, first-generation students, and other marginalized groups such as lesbian, gay, bisexual, and transgender students. Dr. Johnson understands the importance of creating initiatives to support individuals in those groups so their specific concerns may be addressed in multiple ways. As you will learn in this chapter, when leaders proactively create an inclusive and supportive climate that values diversity, benefits are produced that result in in positive outcomes for organizations.

12.1 | An Introduction to Workplace Diversity

1. What is diversity?

Diversity refers to identity-based differences among and between two or more people[1] that affect their lives as applicants, employees, and customers. These identity-based differences include such things as race and ethnicity, gender, sexual orientation, and age. Groups in society based on these individual differences are referred to as **identity groups**. These differences are related to discrimination and disparities between groups in areas such as education, housing, healthcare, and employment. The term **managing diversity** is commonly used to refer to ways in which organizations seek to ensure that members of diverse groups are valued and treated fairly within organizations[2] in all areas including hiring, compensation, performance evaluation, and customer service activities. The term *valuing diversity* is often used to reflect ways in which organizations show appreciation for diversity among job applicants, employees, and customers.[3] **Inclusion**, which represents the degree to which employees are accepted and treated fairly by their organization,[4] is one way in which companies demonstrate how they value diversity. In the context of today's rapidly changing organizational environment, it is more important than ever to understand diversity in organizational contexts and make progressive strides toward a more inclusive, equitable, and representative workforce.

Three kinds of diversity exist in the workplace (see **Table 12.1**). **Surface-level diversity** represents an individual's visible characteristics, including, but not limited to, age, body size, visible disabilities, race, or sex.[5] A collective of individuals who share these characteristics is known as an identity group. **Deep-level diversity** includes traits that are nonobservable such as attitudes, values, and beliefs.[6] **Hidden diversity** includes traits that are deep-level but may be concealed or revealed at the discretion of individuals who possess them.[7]

These hidden traits are called **invisible social identities**[8] and may include sexual orientation, a hidden disability (such as a mental illness or chronic disease), mixed racial heritage,[9] or socioeconomic status. Researchers investigate these different types of diversity in order to understand how diversity may benefit or hinder organizational outcomes.

Diversity presents challenges that may include managing dysfunctional conflict that can arise from inappropriate interactions between individuals from different groups. Diversity also presents advantages such as broader perspectives and viewpoints. Knowledge about how to manage diversity helps managers mitigate some of its challenges and reap some of its benefits.

Types of Diversity	
Surface-level diversity	Diversity in the form of characteristics of individuals that are readily visible including, but not limited to, age, body size, visible disabilities, race or sex.
Deep-level diversity	Diversity in characteristics that are nonobservable such as attitudes, values, and beliefs, such as religion.
Hidden diversity	Diversity in characteristics that are deep-level but may be concealed or revealed at discretion by individuals who possess them, such as sexual orientation.

Table 12.1 (Attribution: Copyright Rice University, OpenStax, under CC-BY 4.0 license)

CONCEPT CHECK

1. What is diversity?
2. What are the three types of diversity encountered in the workplace?

12.2 | Diversity and the Workforce

2. How diverse is the workforce?

In 1997, researchers estimated that by the year 2020, 14% of the workforce would be Latino, 11% Black, and 6% Asian.[10] Because of an increase in the number of racial minorities entering the workforce over the past 20 years, most of those projections have been surpassed as of 2016, with a workforce composition of 17% Hispanic or Latino of any race, followed by 12% Black and 6% Asian (see **Exhibit 12.2**). American Indians, Alaska Natives, Native Hawaiians, and Other Pacific Islanders together made up a little over 1% of the labor force, while people of two or more races made up about 2% of the labor force.[11] Women constitute approximately 47% of the workforce compared to approximately 53% for men,[12] and the average age of individuals participating in the labor force has also increased because more employees retire at a later age.[13] Although Whites still predominantly make up the workforce with a 78% share,[14] the U.S. workforce is becoming increasingly more diverse, a trend that presents both opportunities and challenges. These demographic shifts in the labor market affect the workforce in a number of ways due to an increasing variety of workers who differ by sex, race, age, sexual orientation, disability status, and immigrant status.

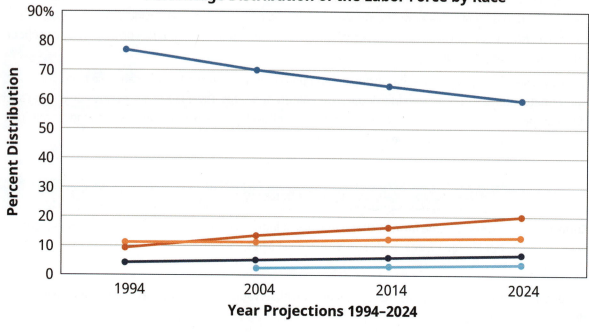

Exhibit 12.2 Percentage distribution of the labor force by race (Attribution: Copyright Rice University, OpenStax, under CC-BY 4.0 license)

Gender

Increasingly more women are entering the workforce.[15] Compared to 59% in 1977, the labor force participation rate for men is now approximately 53% and is expected to decrease through 2024 to 52%.[16] As the labor force participation rate decreases for men, the labor force growth rate for women will be faster. Their percentage of the workforce has steadily risen, as can be seen in **Exhibit 12.3**, which compares the percentage of the workforce by gender in 1977 to 2017.[17]

Although more women are entering the labor force and earning bachelor's degrees at a higher rate than men,[18] women still face a number of challenges at work. The lack of advancement opportunities awarded to qualified women is an example of a major challenge that women face called the **glass ceiling**,[19] which is an invisible barrier based on the prejudicial beliefs that underlie organizational decisions that prevent women from moving beyond certain levels within a company. Additionally, in organizations in which the upper-level managers and decision makers are predominantly men, women are less likely to find mentors, which are instrumental for networking and learning about career opportunities. Organizations can mitigate this challenge by providing mentors for all new employees. Such a policy would help create a more equal playing field for all employees as they learn to orient themselves and navigate within the organization.

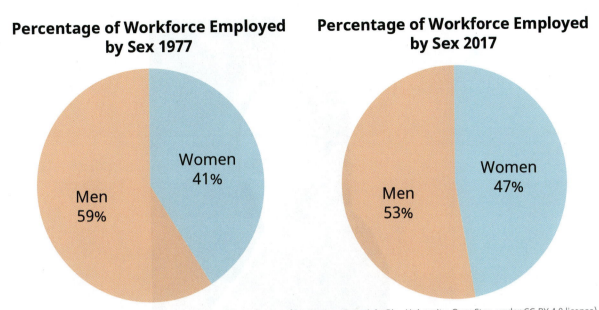

Exhibit 12.3 **Percentage Distribution of the Labor Force by Sex** (Attribution: Copyright Rice University, OpenStax, under CC-BY 4.0 license)

One factor that greatly affects women in organizations is **sexual harassment**. Sexual harassment is illegal, and workers are protected from it by federal legislation.[20] Two forms of sexual harassment that can occur at work are quid pro quo and hostile environment.[21] Quid pro quo harassment refers to the exchange of rewards for sexual favors or punishments for refusal to grant sexual favors. Harassment that creates a hostile environment refers to behaviors that create an abusive work climate. If employees are penalized (for example by being demoted or transferred to another department) for refusing to respond to repeated sexual advances, quid pro quo sexual harassment has taken place. The telling of lewd jokes, the posting of pornographic material at work, or making offensive comments about women in general are actions that are considered to create a hostile work environment. According to the Equal Employment Opportunity Commission, sexual harassment is defined as the "unwelcome sexual advances, requests for sexual favors, and other verbal or physical harassment of a sexual nature. Harassment can also include offensive remarks about a person's sex."[22] Although both men and women can be sexually harassed, women are sexually harassed at work more often.[23] In addition, Black and other minority women are especially likely to be subjected to sexual discrimination and harassment.[24]

Exhibit 12.4 Tamara Johnson The treatment of women in business has become a hot topic in corporate boardrooms, human resources departments, and investment committees. Tamara Johnson, who is profiled in the opening feature to this chapter, moves beyond simply acknowledging widespread discrimination to focusing on solutions. Also on the agenda: the need to improve diversity and inclusion across the board and breaking through the glass ceiling. (Credit: Tamara Johnson/ Attribution 2.0 Generic (CC BY 2.0))

Because employees who experience sexual harassment are more likely to quit their jobs and experience emotional distress that can negatively impact their performance,[25] it is in the organization's best interest to prevent sexual harassment at work from occurring. Ways to do this include companies providing ongoing (e.g., annual) training so that employees are able to recognize sexual harassment. Employees should know what constitutes acceptable and unacceptable behavior and what channels and protocols are in place for reporting unacceptable behaviors. Managers should understand their role and responsibilities regarding harassment prevention, and a clear and understandable policy should be communicated throughout the organization.

Race

Another important demographic shift in workforce diversity is the distribution of race. (Note that we are using categories defined by the U.S. Census Bureau. It uses the term "Black (African-American)" to categorize U.S. residents. In this chapter, we use the term "Black.")

While the White non-Hispanic share of the workforce continues to shrink, the share of racial and ethnic minority groups will continue to grow.[26] Specifically, Hispanics and Asians will grow at a faster rate than other racial minorities, and Hispanics are projected to make up almost one-fifth of the labor force by 2024.[27] The projected changes in labor force composition between 2014 and 2024 are as follows:

White non-Hispanic participation in the labor force will decline by 3%. Other groups' share of the labor force is expected to increase: Black (10.1%), Hispanic (28%), Asian (23.2%), and Other groups (i.e., multiracial, American Indian, Alaska Native, Native Hawaiian, and Other Pacific Islanders) labor force share is expected to increase by 22.2%.[28] With the workforce changing, managers will need to be mindful of issues employees encounter that are uniquely tied to their experiences based on race and ethnicity, including harassment, discrimination, stereotyping, and differential treatment by coworkers and decision makers in organizations.

Discrimination Against Black Employees

Race is one of the most frequent grounds for discrimination.[29] Although Blacks do not make up the largest share of the workforce for racial minorities, research studies show they face discrimination more often than other racial minorities. As a matter of fact, some experts believe that hiring discrimination against Blacks has not declined over the past 25 years while workplace discrimination against other racial minority groups has declined.[30]

ETHICS IN PRACTICE

Discrimination in the Sharing Economy—#AirbnbWhileBlack

Airbnb, a popular home-sharing website founded in San Francisco in 2008, offers millions of homes for short-term rental in more than 190 countries. This company has revolutionized the sharing economy in the same way that ride-sharing services such as Uber and Lyft have, and according to the company, the site's drive to connect hosts and potential renters has been able to contribute to the quality of life of both homeowners and travelers. According to Airbnb's press releases and information campaigns, their services can reduce housing costs for travelers on a budget and can provide unique experiences for adventurous travelers who wish to have the flexibility to experience a city like a local. The organization also claims that most of its users are homeowners looking to supplement their incomes by renting out rooms in their homes or by occasionally renting out their whole homes. According to a statement, most of the listings on the site are rented out fewer than 50 nights per year.

Despite the carefully crafted messages Airbnb has presented to the public, in 2016 the company came under intense scrutiny when independent analyses by researchers and journalists revealed something startling: While some Airbnb hosts did in fact use the services only occasionally, a significant number of hosts were using the services as though they were hotels. These hosts purchased a large number of properties and continuously rented them, a practice that affected the availability of affordable housing in cities and, because these hosts were not officially registered as hoteliers, made it possible for Airbnb hosts to avoid paying the taxes and abiding by the laws that hotels are subject to.

Title II of the Civil Rights Act of 1964 mandates that hotels and other public accommodations must not discriminate based on race, national origin, sex, or religion, and Title VIII of the Civil Rights Act of 1968 (also known as the Fair Housing Act [FHA]) prohibits discrimination specifically in housing. However, Airbnb's unique structure allows it to circumvent those laws. The company also claims that while it encourages hosts to comply with local and federal laws, it is absolved from responsibility if any of its hosts break these laws. In 2017, researcher Ben Edelman conducted a field experiment and found that Airbnb users looking to rent homes were 16% less likely to have their requests to book accepted if they had traditionally African American sounding names like Tamika, Darnell, and Rasheed.

These findings, coupled with a viral social media campaign, #AirbnbWhileBlack, in which users claimed they were denied housing requests based on their race, prompted the state of California's Department of Fair Employment and Housing (DFEH) to file a complaint against the company. In an effort to resolve the complaint, Airbnb reported banning any hosts who were found to have engaged in discriminatory practices, and they hired former U.S. Attorney General Eric Holder and former ACLU official Laura Murphy to investigate any claims of discrimination within the company.[31] In 2016, Airbnb released a statement outlining changes to company practices and policies to combat discrimination, and while they initially resisted demands by the DFEH to conduct an audit of their practices, the company eventually agreed to an audit of roughly 6,000 of the hosts in California who have the highest volume of properties listed on the site.

Sources: AirBnB Press Room, accessed December 24, 2018, https://press.atairbnb.com/about-us/; "Airbnb's data shows that Airbnb helps the middle class. But does it?", *The Guardian*, accessed December 23, 2018, https://www.theguardian.com/technology/2016/jul/27/airbnb-panel-democratic-national-convention-survey ; and Quittner, Jeremy, "Airbnb and Discrimination: Why It's All So Confusing", *Fortune*, June 23, 2016, http://fortune.com/2016/06/23/airbnb-discrimination-laws/.

Discussion Questions

1. What are some efforts companies in the sharing economy can take before problems of discrimination threaten to disrupt operations?
2. Should Airbnb be held responsible for discriminatory actions of its hosts?

Currently, White men have higher participation rates in the workforce than do Black men,[32] and Black women have slightly higher participation rates than White women.[33] Despite growth and gains in both Black education and Black employment, a Black person is considerably more likely to be unemployed than a White person, even when the White person has a lower level of education[34] or a criminal record.[35]

Blacks frequently experience discrimination in the workplace in spite of extensive legislation in place to prohibit such discrimination. Research has shown that stereotypes and prejudices about Blacks can cause them to be denied the opportunity for employment when compared to equally qualified Whites.[36] It is estimated that about 25% of businesses have no minority workers and another 25% have less than 10% minority workers.[37] In terms of employed Blacks, research has shown that, regardless of managers' race, managers tended to give significantly higher performance ratings to employees who were racially similar to them. Because Whites are much more likely to be managers than Blacks, this similarity effect tends to advantage White employees over Black employees.[38] Blacks are also significantly more likely to be hired in positions that require low skills, offer little to no room for growth, and pay less. These negative employment experiences affect both the mental and physical health of Black employees.[39]

Hispanics

Hispanics are the second-fastest-growing minority group in the United States behind Asians,[40] and they make up 17% of the labor force.[41] Despite this and the fact that Hispanics have the highest labor participation rate of all the minority groups, they still face discrimination and harassment in similar ways to other minority groups.

Hispanics can be of any race.[42] As a matter of fact, increasingly more Hispanics are identifying racially as White. In 2004 almost half of Hispanics identified themselves racially as White, while just under half identified themselves as "some other race."[43] More than 10 years later, approximately 66% of Hispanics now identify themselves racially as White while only 26% identify themselves as "some other race."[44] The remaining Hispanic population, totaling approximately 7%, identify as either Black, American Indian, Asian, Alaskan

Native, Pacific Islander, or Native Hawaiian.[45]

Why would a minority identity group identify racially as White? A Pew study found that the longer Hispanic families lived in the United States, the more likely they were to claim White as their race even if they had not done so in the past.[46] This suggests that upward mobility in America may be perceived by some Hispanics to be equated with "Whiteness."[47] Consequently, Hispanics who self-identify racially as White experience higher rates of education and salary, and lower rates of unemployment.[48] Additionally, only 29% of Hispanics polled by the Pew Hispanic Center believe they share a common culture.[49] According to the Pew Research Center, this finding may be due to the fact that the Hispanic ethnic group in the United States is made up of at least 14 Hispanic origin groups (such as Puerto Rican, Cuban, Spanish, Mexican, Dominican, and Guatemalan, among many others).[50] Each of these groups has its own culture with different customs, values, and norms.

These cultural differences among the various Hispanic groups, combined with different self-perceptions of race, may also affect attitudes toward their workplace environment. For example, one study found that the absenteeism rate among Blacks was related to the level of diversity policies and activities visible in the organization, while the absenteeism rate among Hispanics was similar to that of Whites and not related to those diversity cues.[51] Results from this study suggest that managers need to be aware of how diversity impacts their workplace, namely addressing the relationship between Hispanic job seekers or workers and organizational outcomes concerning diversity policies as it may differ from that of other racial minorities.

Asians

Asians are the fastest-growing ethnic group in the United States, growing 72% between 2000 and 2015.[52] Compared to the rest of the U.S. population overall, households headed by Asian Americans earn more money and are more likely to have household members who hold a bachelor's degree.[53] However, there is a wide range of income levels among the Asian population that differs between the more than 19 groups of Asian origin in the United States.[54]

Similar to other racial and ethnic minority groups, Asians are stereotyped and face discrimination at work. Society through media often stereotypes Asian men as having limited English-speaking skills and as being highly educated, affluent, analytical, and good at math and science.[55] Asian women are often portrayed as weak and docile.[56] For Asian women, and other minority women as well, social stereotypes depicting them as exotic contribute to reports of sexual harassment from women minority groups.[57]

The **model minority myth**[58] is a reflection of perceptions targeting Asians and Asian Americans that contrast the stereotypes of "conformity" and "success" of Asian men with stereotypes of "rebelliousness" and "laziness" of other minority men. It also contrasts the stereotyped "exotic" and "obedient" nature of Asian women against the stereotypical beliefs that White women are "independent" and "pure."[59] These perceptions are used not only to invalidate injustice that occurs among other racial minorities, but also to create barriers for Asians seeking leadership opportunities as they are steered toward "behind the scenes" positions that require less engagement with others. These stereotypes also relegate Asian women into submissive roles in organizations, making it challenging for Asian men and women to advance in rank at the same rate as White male employees.[60]

Multiracial

Although the U.S. Census Bureau estimates that approximately 2% of the U.S. population describes themselves as belonging to more than one race, the Pew Research Center estimates that number should be higher, with around 7% of the U.S. population considered multiracial.[61] This is due to the fact that some individuals may claim one race for themselves even though they have parents from different racial backgrounds. To complicate matters even more, when collecting data from multiracial group members, racial identity for individuals in this group may change over time because race is a social construct that is not necessarily based on a shared culture or country of origin in the same way as ethnicity. As a result, multiracial individuals (and Hispanics) have admitted to changing their racial identity over the course of their life and even based on the situation. Approximately 30% of multiracial individuals polled by the Pew Research Center say that they have varied between viewing themselves as belonging to one race or belonging to multiple races. Within the group polled, the order in which they first racially identified as belonging to one racial group versus belonging to more than one group varied.[62]

Despite the fact that multiracial births have risen tenfold between 1970 and 2013,[63] their participation in the labor force is only around 2%.[64] Additionally, multiracial individuals with a White racial background are still considered a racial minority unless they identify themselves solely as White, and approximately 56% of them on average say they have been subjected to racial jokes and slurs.[65] Discrimination also varies when multiracial groups are broken down further, with Black–American Indians having the highest percentage of individuals reporting discrimination and White–Asians having the lowest percentage.[66]

At work, multiracial employees are sometimes mistaken for races other than their own. If their racial minority background is visible to others, they may experience negative differential treatment. Sometimes they are not identified as having a racial or ethnic minority background and are privy to disparaging comments from unsuspecting coworkers about their own race, which can be demoralizing and can lead to lower organizational attachment and emotional strain related to concealing their identity.[67]

Other Groups

Approximately 1% of the labor force identifies as American Indian, Alaska Native, Native Hawaiian or Pacific Islander, or some other race.[68]

Age

The age distribution of an organization's workforce is an important dimension of workplace diversity as the working population gets older. Some primary factors contributing to an older population include the aging of the large Baby Boomer generation (people born between 1946 and 1964), lower birth rates, and longer life expectancies[69] due to advances in medical technology and access to health care. As a result, many individuals work past the traditional age of retirement (65 years old) and work more years than previous generations in order to maintain their cost of living.

Exhibit 12.5 compares the percentage of the population over the age of 65 to those under the age of 18 between 2010 and 2016. The number of older individuals has increased and is projected to reach 20.6% by the year 2030 while the number of younger individuals has steadily decreased within that time period. These numbers imply that organizations will increasingly have employees across a wide range of ages, and cross-generational interaction can be difficult manage. Although older workers are viewed as agreeable and comfortable to work with, they are also stereotyped by some employees as incompetent[70] and less interested in learning new tasks at work compared to younger workers.[71] Studies have found support for the proposition that age negatively relates to cognitive functioning.[72] However, if managers offer less opportunity to older workers solely because of declining cognitive functioning, it can be detrimental to organizational performance because older workers outperform younger workers on a number of other job performance measures. Compared to younger workers, older workers are more likely to perform above their job expectations and follow safety protocols. They are also less likely to be tardy, absent, or abuse drugs or alcohol at work compared to their younger counterparts.

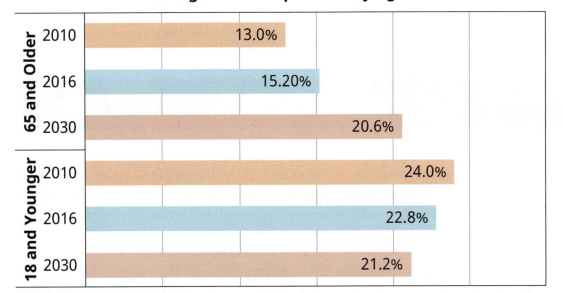

Exhibit 12.5   Change in U.S. population by age (Attribution: Copyright Rice University, OpenStax, under CC-BY 4.0 license)

Sexual Orientation

Sexual orientation diversity is increasing in the workforce.[73] However, only 21 states and Washington D.C. prohibit discrimination based on sexual orientation.[74] Without federal protection, individuals who do not live in these states could be overlooked for employment or fired for their sexual orientation unless their employer has policies to protect them.[75] Many employers are beginning to understand that being perceived as inclusive will make them more attractive to a larger pool of job applicants.[76] So although the Civil Rights Act does not explicitly provide federal protection to lesbian, gay, bisexual, and transgender (LGBT) employees, more than half of the Fortune 500 companies have corporate policies that protect sexual minorities from discrimination at work and offer domestic-partner benefits.[77]

Unfortunately, the percentage of hate crimes relating to sexual orientation discrimination has increased.[78] Indeed, LGBT employees are stigmatized so much that in a recent study, researchers found that straight-identifying participants were more attracted to employers with no job security to offer them compared to gay-friendly employers.[79] In other words, individuals would waive job security to avoid working with sexual minorities. Also, compared to heterosexuals, sexual minorities have higher education levels[80] but still face hiring and treatment discrimination frequently.[81]

LGBT employees are often faced with the decision of whether or not to be truthful about their sexual orientation at work for fear of being stigmatized and treated unfairly. The decision to not disclose is called **passing**, and for some it involves a great risk of emotional strain that can affect performance.[82] Individuals who pass may distance themselves from coworkers or clients to avoid disclosure about their personal life. This behavior can also result in decreased networking and mentoring opportunities, which over time can limit advancement opportunities. The decision to be transparent about sexual orientation is called **revealing**.[83] Just like passing, revealing has its own set of risks including being ostracized, stigmatized, and subjected to other forms of discrimination at work. However, compared to passing, the benefits of building relationships at work and using their identity as a catalyst for tolerance and progressive organizational change may outweigh the risks when LGBT employees decide to reveal.

Research shows that when local or state laws are passed to prevent sexual orientation discrimination, incidents of workplace discrimination decrease.[84] This same effect occurs when firms adopt policies that protect the rights of sexual minority employees.[85] By creating a safe and inclusive work environment for LGBT employees, companies can create a culture of tolerance for all employees regardless of their sexual orientation or gender identity.

MANAGING CHANGE

Blind Recruiting

An increasing number of companies are testing a new and innovative way of recruiting. *Blind recruiting* is a process by which firms remove any identifying information about applicants during the recruitment process. An example of this may include anonymous applications that omit fields requesting information such as an applicant's name or age. Using computer application technology, some companies like Google administer surveys to their anonymous applicants that measure the abilities required for the job before they are considered in the next step of the recruitment process. Alternatively, companies may request that applicants remove identifying information such as names and address from their resumes before applying for positions. As resumes are received, hiring managers can assign a temporary identification number.

Although more companies are using this method of recruiting, the idea is not new for symphony orchestras, many of which have been using blind auditioning since the 1970s. In some instances musicians audition behind screens so they are evaluated only by their music. This process removes bias associated with race and gender because the performer cannot be seen and only heard. A study investigating this practice examined 11 symphony orchestras that varied on the use of blind auditions. Researchers found that blind auditions increased the likelihood that a woman would be hired by between 25 and 46%. A recruitment process like this can help organizations attract more candidates, hire the best talent, increase their workplace diversity, and avoid discrimination liability.

Sources: Grothaus, M. (Mar 14 2016). How "blind" recruitment works and why you should consider it. Fast Company. Retrieved from https://www.fastcompany.com/3057631/how-blind-recruitment-works-and-why-you-should-consider; and MIller, C.C. (Feb 25 2016). Is blind hiring the best hiring? The New York Times Magazine. Retrieved from https://www.nytimes.com/2016/02/28/magazine/is-blind-hiring-the-best-hiring.html.

Discussion Questions

1. Should all companies use blind recruiting in place of traditional recruiting, or are there exceptions that must be considered?
2. If blind recruiting helps eliminate bias during the recruitment process, then what does that say about social media platforms such as Linked In that are commonly used for recruiting applicants? Will using those platforms expose companies to greater liability compared to using more traditional means of recruiting?
3. How does blind recruiting help organizations? How may it hinder organizations?

Immigrant Workers

Every year a new record is set for the time it takes to reach the U.S. cap of H-1B visas granted to employers.[86] H- 1B visas are a type of **work visa**, a temporary documented status that authorizes individuals to permanently or temporarily live and work in the United States.[87] As a result of the demand for work visas by employers, the number of immigrant workers in the U.S. workforce has steadily grown within the last decade from 15% in 2005 to 17% in 2016.[88] Compared to those born in the United States, the immigrant population in America is growing significantly faster.[89] This is partly because of the U.S. demand for workers who are proficient in math and science[90] and wish to work in America.

Although a huge demand for immigrant labor exists in the United States, immigrant labor exploitation occurs, with immigrant employees receiving lower wages and working longer hours compared to American workers.[91] Foreign-born job seekers are attracted to companies that emphasize work visa sponsorship for international employees, yet they are still mindful of their vulnerability to unethical employers who may try to exploit them. For example, Lambert and colleagues found that some of the job-seeking MBA students from the Philippines in their study believed that companies perceived to value international diversity and sponsor H-1B visas signaled a company wishing to exploit workers.[92] Others believed that those types of companies might yield diminishing returns to each Filipino in the company because their token value becomes limited. In news stories, companies have been accused of drastically shortchanging foreign student interns on their weekly wages.[93] In another case, Infosys, a technology consulting company, paid $34 million to settle allegations of visa fraud due to suspicion of underpaying foreign workers to increase profits.[94]

Other Forms of Diversity at Work

Workers with disabilities are projected to experience a 10% increase in job growth through the year 2022.[95] This means that more public and corporate policies will be revised to allow greater access to training for workers with disabilities and employers.[96] Also, more companies will use technology and emphasize educating employees about physical and mental disabilities as workplace accommodations are used more often.

In the past, the United States has traditionally been a country with citizens who predominantly practice the Christian faith. However, over the past almost 30 years the percentage of Americans who identify as Christian has significantly decreased—by approximately 12%. Over that same time period, affiliation with other religions overall increased by approximately 25%.[97] The increase in immigrant workers from Asian and Middle Eastern countries means that employers must be prepared to accommodate religious beliefs other than Christianity. Although federal legislation protects employees from discrimination on the basis of race, religion, and disability status, many employers have put in place policies of their own to deal with the variety of diversity that is increasingly entering the workforce.

CONCEPT CHECK

1. How is diversity defined in relation to the workplace?
2. What are the components that make up a diverse workplace and workforce?

12.3 Diversity and Its Impact on Companies

3. How does diversity impact companies and the workforce?

Due to trends in globalization and increasing ethnic and gender diversity, it is imperative that employers learn how to manage cultural differences and individual work attitudes. As the labor force becomes more diverse there are both opportunities and challenges to managing employees in a diverse work climate. Opportunities include gaining a competitive edge by embracing change in the marketplace and the labor force. Challenges include effectively managing employees with different attitudes, values, and beliefs, in addition to avoiding liability when leadership handles various work situations improperly.

Reaping the Advantages of Diversity

The business case for diversity introduced by Taylor Cox and Stacy Blake outlines how companies may obtain a competitive advantage by embracing workplace diversity.[98] Six opportunities that companies may receive when pursuing a strategy that values diversity include cost advantages, improved resource acquisition, greater marketing ability, system flexibility, and enhanced creativity and better problem solving (see **Exhibit 12.6**).

Exhibit 12.6   Managing Cultural Diversity (Attribution: Copyright Rice University, OpenStax, under CC-BY 4.0 license)

Cost Advantages

Traits such as race, gender, age, and religion are protected by federal legislation against various forms of discrimination (covered later in this chapter). Organizations that have policies and procedures in place that encourage tolerance for a work climate of diversity and protect female and minority employees and applicants from discrimination may reduce their likelihood of being sued due to workplace discrimination. Cox and Blake identify this decreased liability as an opportunity for organizations to reduce potential expenses in lawsuit damages compared to other organizations that do not have such policies in place.

Additionally, organizations with a more visible climate of diversity experience lower turnover among women and minorities compared to companies that are perceived to not value diversity.[99] Turnover costs can be substantial for companies over time, and diverse companies may ameliorate turnover by retaining their female and minority employees. Although there is also research showing that organizations that value diversity experience a higher turnover of White employees and male employees compared to companies that are less diverse,[100] some experts believe this is due to a lack of understanding of how to effectively manage diversity. Also, some research shows that Whites with a strong ethnic identity are attracted to diverse organizations similarly to non-Whites.[101]

Resource Acquisition

Human capital is an important resource of organizations, and it is acquired through the knowledge, skills, and abilities of employees. Organizations perceived to value diversity attract more women and minority job applicants to hire as employees. Studies show that women and minorities have greater job-pursuit intentions and higher attraction toward organizations that promote workplace diversity in their recruitment materials compared to organizations that do not.[102] When employers attract minority applicants, their labor pool increases in size compared to organizations that are not attractive to them. As organizations attract more job candidates, the chances of hiring quality employees increases, especially for jobs that demand highly skilled labor. In summary, organizations gain a competitive advantage by enlarging their labor pool by attracting women and minorities.

Marketing

When organizations employ individuals from different backgrounds, they gain broad perspectives regarding consumer preferences of different cultures. Organizations can gain insightful knowledge and feedback from demographic markets about the products and services they provide. Additionally, organizations that value diversity enhance their reputation with the market they serve, thereby attracting new customers.

System Flexibility

When employees are placed in a culturally diverse work environment, they learn to interact effectively with individuals who possess different attitudes, values, and beliefs. Cox and Blake contend that the ability to effectively interact with individuals who differ from oneself builds *cognitive flexibility*, the ability to think about things differently and adapt one's perspective. When employees possess cognitive flexibility, system flexibility develops at the organizational level. Employees learn from each other how to tolerate differences in opinions and ideas, which allows communication to flow more freely and group interaction to be more effective.

Creativity and Problem Solving

Teams from diverse backgrounds produce multiple points of view, which can lead to innovative ideas. Different perspectives lead to a greater number of choices to select from when addressing a problem or issue.

Life experience varies from person to person, sometimes based on race, age, or sex. Creativity has the opportunity to flourish when those experiences are shared. Diverse teams not only produce more alternatives, but generate a broader range of perspectives to address tasks and problems. One way in which diverse teams enhance problem-solving ability is by preventing **groupthink**,[103] a dysfunction in decision-making that occurs in homogeneous groups as a result of group pressures and group members' desire for conformity and consensus. Diverse group membership prevents groupthink because individuals from varied backgrounds with different values, attitudes, and beliefs can test the assumptions and reasoning of group members' ideas.

Aligning Diversity Programs with an Organization's Mission and Strategic Goals

Diversity helps organizations perform best when it is aligned with a specific business strategy. For example, when companies use heterogeneous management teams that are directed by an entrepreneurial strategy focusing on innovation, the companies' productivity increases.

When an entrepreneurial strategy is not present, however, team diversity has little effect on productivity.[104] An entrepreneurial strategy includes innovation that reflects a company's commitment to being creative, supporting new ideas, and supporting experimentation as a way to gain a competitive advantage. In other words, managers may properly utilize the multiple perspectives that emerge from heterogeneous teams by integrating them as a resource for pursuing the overall strategy of the organization.

Using Human Resources Tools Strategically

To effectively align diversity with an organization's strategy, the human resources function must be able to engage employees at dynamic levels. Using a strategic human resources management approach to an organization can successfully integrate diversity with the organization's goals and objectives.[105] **Strategic human resources management (SHRM)** is a system of activities arranged to engage employees in a manner that assists the organization in achieving a sustainable competitive advantage. SHRM practices vertically integrate with the mission and strategy of the organization while horizontally integrating human resources activities across its functional areas. By doing so, a unique set of resources can be made available to specific to the needs of the organization. Furthermore, when human resources becomes a part of the strategic planning process instead of just providing ancillary services, improved communication, knowledge sharing, and greater synergy between decision makers can occur within the organization to improve organizational functioning.

The **resource-based view** of the firm has been used to support the argument for diversity because it demonstrates how a diverse workforce can create a sustainable competitive advantage for organizations. Based on the resource-based view of the firm, when companies possess resources that are rare, valuable, difficult to imitate, and non-substitutable, a sustained competitive advantage can be attained.[106] The SHRM approach assumes that human capital—the current and potential knowledge, skills, and abilities of employees—is instrumental to every organization's success and sustainability and longevity.

If a diverse composition of employees within organizations is rare, employing minorities in positions of leadership is even rarer. One exception is Northern Trust, an investment management firm that was recently listed on Forbes magazine's 2018 Best Employers for Diversity list.[107] Thirty-eight percent of Northern Trust's top executives are women, which is impressive because it matches the average percentage of women in full-time one-year MBA programs over the past five years.[108] The average for S&P 500 companies is just 27%. In addition, African Americans make up 23% of Northern Trust's board, which also demonstrates the commitment Northern Trust has to diversity. This rare degree of diversity helps Northern Trust become an employer of choice for minorities and women. In turn, attracting minority applicants increases the labor pool available to Northern Trust and increases its ability to find good talent.

Exhibit 12.7   Bank staff watching presentation The Disability Awareness Players present to the staff at Northern Trust. (Credit: JJ's List/ flickr/ Attribution 2.0 Generic (CC BY 2.0))

Diverse companies may capitalize on the multiple perspectives that employees from different backgrounds contribute to problem solving and idea generation. In group settings, members from collectivist cultures from Asia and South America, for example, engage with others on tasks differently than members from North America. Similarly, Asians, Blacks, and Hispanics usually act more collectively and engage more interdependently than Whites, who are generally more individualistic. More harmonious working interactions benefit group cohesion and team performance,[109] and employees can grasp better ways of doing things when there is a diverse population to learn from.

For a company to attain a sustained competitive advantage, its human resource practices must be difficult to copy or imitate. As we will see later in the chapter, companies may hold one of three perspectives on workplace diversity. The integration and learning perspective results in the best outcomes for employees and the organization. However, it is not easy to become an employer that can effectively manage diversity and avoid the challenges we learned about earlier in this chapter. Historical conditions and often-complex interplay between various organizational units over time can contribute to a company's ability to perform effectively as a diverse organization. Best practices for targeting diverse applicants or resolving conflicts based on cultural differences between employees may occur organically and later become codified into the organizational culture. Sometimes, however, the origin of diversity practices is unknown because they arose from cooperation among different functional areas (e.g., marketing and human resources working strategically with leadership to develop recruitment ideas) that occurred so long ago that not even the company itself, let alone other companies, could replicate the process.

Diversity and Organizational Performance

Research indicates that having diversity in an organization produces mixed results for its success. Some studies show a positive relationship, some show a negative relationship, and others show no relationship between diversity and performance. Some researchers believe that although findings regarding a direct relationship between diversity and success in the marketplace may be inconsistent, the relationship may be due to other variables not taken into account.

Taking the resource-based view perspective, Richard and colleagues demonstrated that racially diverse banking institutions focused on innovation experienced greater performance than did racially diverse banks with a low focus on innovation.[110] These findings suggest that for the potential of racial diversity to be fully realized, companies should properly manage the system flexibility, creativity, and problem-solving abilities used in an innovative strategy. Other studies show that when top management includes female leadership, firm performance improves when organizations are innovation driven.[111]

CONCEPT CHECK

1. What are the challenges and opportunities that diversity provides to companies?
2. What are the responsibilities of human resources regarding diversity?
3. Can diversity be a strategic advantage to organizations?

12.4 | Challenges of Diversity

4. What is workplace discrimination, and how does it affect different social identity groups?

Although diversity has it benefits, there are also challenges that managers must face that can only be addressed with proper leadership. Some of the most common challenges observed in organizations and studied in research include lower organizational attachment and misunderstanding work diversity initiatives and programs.

Lower Organizational Attachment

Although diversity programs attract and retain women and minorities, they may have the opposite effect on other, nonminority employees. When diversity is not managed effectively, White and male employees can feel alienated from or targeted by the organization as diversity programs are put in place. A study that examined 151 work groups across three large organizations investigated whether the proportion of group membership based on race or sex affected the group members' absentee rates, psychological attachment to their work group, and turnover intentions,[112] three factors that play significant roles in an employee's attachment to their organization. Results showed a positive relationship between group heterogeneity and lower organizational attachment, higher turnover intentions, and greater frequency of absences for men and for White group members. In other words, as work group diversity increased, White employees and male employees felt less attached to the organization and were more likely to quit. Because heterogeneous groups improve creativity and judgement, managers should not avoid using them because they may be challenging to manage. Instead, employers need to make sure they understand the communication structure and decision-making styles of their work groups and seek feedback from employees to learn how dominant group members may adjust to diversity.

Legal Challenges and Diversity

The legal system is used to combat discrimination. Among the ways that we will cover here are reverse discrimination, workplace discrimination, harassment, age discrimination, disability discrimination, national origin discrimination, pregnancy discrimination, race/color discrimination, religious discrimination, sex-based discrimination and other forms of discrimination.

Reverse Discrimination

As research shows, workplace discrimination against women and racial or ethnic minorities is common. **Reverse discrimination** is a term that has been used to describe a situation in which dominant group members perceive that they are experiencing discrimination based on their race or sex. This type of discrimination is uncommon, but is usually claimed when the dominant group perceives that members of a protected (diverse) class of citizens are given preference in workplace or educational opportunities based not on their merit or talents, but on a prescribed preferential treatment awarded only on the basis of race or sex.

Research conducted in the 1990s shows that only six federal cases of reverse discrimination were upheld over a four-year period (1990–1994), and only 100 of the 3,000 cases for discrimination over that same four-year period were claims of reverse discrimination.[113] Interestingly, a recent poll administered by the Robert Wood Johnson Foundation and the Harvard T.H. Chan School of Public Health found that a little more than half of White Americans believe that White people face discrimination overall, and 19% believe they have experienced hiring discrimination due to the color of their skin.[114] This misperception stems in part from the recalibration of the labor force as it become more balanced due to increased equal employment opportunities for everyone. Members of dominant identity groups, Whites and men, perceive fewer opportunities for themselves when they observe the workforce becoming more diverse. In reality, the workforce of a majority of companies is still predominantly White and male employees. The only difference is that legislation protecting employees from discrimination and improvements in equal access to education have created opportunities for minority group members when before there were none.

Workplace Discrimination

Workplace discrimination occurs when an employee or an applicant is treated unfairly at work or in the job-hiring process due to an identity group, condition, or personal characteristic such as the ones mentioned above. Discrimination can occur through marital status, for example when a person experiences workplace discrimination because of the characteristics of a person to whom they are married. Discrimination can also occur when the offender is of the same protected status of the victim, for example when someone discriminates against someone based on a national origin that they both share.

The **Equal Employment Opportunity Commission** (EEOC) was created by Title VII of the Civil Rights Act of 1964 with the primary goal of making it illegal to discriminate against someone in the workplace due to their race, national origin, sex, disability, religion, or pregnancy status.[115] The EEOC enforces laws and issues guidelines for employment-related treatment. It also has the authority to investigate charges of workplace discrimination, attempt to settle the charges, and, if necessary, file lawsuits when the law has been broken.

All types of workplace discrimination are prohibited under different laws enacted and enforced by the EEOC, which also considers workplace harassment and sexual harassment forms of workplace discrimination and mandates that men and women must be given the same pay for equal work.[116]

The provision for equal pay is covered under the **Equal Pay Act of 1963**, which was an amendment to the Fair Labor Standards Act of 1938. Virtually all employers are subject to the provisions of the act, which was an attempt to address pay inequities between men and women. More than 50 years later, however, women still earn about 80 cents to every dollar that men earn, even while performing the same or similar jobs.[117]

Harassment

Harassment is any unwelcome conduct that is based on characteristics such as age, race, national origin, disability, sex, or pregnancy status. Harassment is a form of workplace discrimination that violates Title VII of the Civil Rights Act of 1964, the Age Discrimination in Employment Act of 1967, and the Americans with Disabilities Act of 1990.[118]

Sexual harassment specifically refers to harassment based on a person's sex, and it can (but does not have to) include unwanted sexual advances, requests for sexual favors, or physical and verbal acts of a sexual nature. Though members of any sex can be the victim of sexual harassment, women are the primary targets of this type of harassment.[119]

Age Discrimination

Age discrimination consists of treating an employee or applicant less favorably due to their age. The **Age Discrimination in Employment Act (ADEA)** forbids discrimination against individuals who are age 40 and above. The act prohibits harassment because of age, which can include offensive or derogatory remarks that create a hostile work environment.[120]

Disability Discrimination

A person with a disability is a person who has a physical or mental impairment that limits one or more of the person's life actions. **Disability discrimination** occurs when an employee or applicant who is covered by the **Americans with Disabilities Act (ADA)** is treated unfavorably due to their physical or mental disability. The ADA is a civil rights law that prohibits discrimination in employment, public services, public accommodations, and telecommunications against people with disabilities.[121] To be covered under the ADA, individuals must be able to perform the essential functions of their job with or without reasonable accommodations. Research has shown that reasonable accommodations are typically of no or low cost (less than $100) to employers.[122]

National Origin Discrimination

National origin discrimination involves treating someone unfavorably because of their country of origin, accent, ethnicity, or appearance. EEOC regulations make it illegal to implement an employment practice or policy that applies to everyone if it has a negative impact on people of a certain national origin. For example, employers cannot institute an "English-only" language policy unless speaking English at all times is essential to ensure the safe and efficient operation of the business. Employers also cannot mandate employees be fluent in English unless fluency in English is essential to satisfactory job performance. The EEOC also prohibits businesses from hiring only U.S. citizens or lawful residents unless the business is required by law to do so.[123]

Pregnancy Discrimination

Pregnancy discrimination involves treating an employee or applicant unfairly because of pregnancy status, childbirth, or medical conditions related to pregnancy or childbirth. The **Pregnancy Discrimination Act (PDA)** prohibits any discrimination as it relates to pregnancy in any of the following areas: hiring, firing, compensation, training, job assignment, insurance, or any other employment conditions. Further, certain conditions that result from pregnancy may be protected under the ADA, which means employers may need to make reasonable accommodations for any employee with disabilities related to pregnancy.

Under the **Family and Medical Leave Act (FMLA)**, new parents, including adoptive and foster parents, may be eligible for 12 weeks of unpaid leave (or paid leave only if earned by the employee) to care for the new child. Also, nursing mothers have the right to express milk on workplace premises.[124]

Race/Color Discrimination

Race/color discrimination involves treating employees or applicants unfairly because of their race or because of physical characteristics typically associated with race such as skin color, hair color, hair texture, or certain facial features.

As with national origin discrimination, certain workplace policies that apply to all employees may be unlawful if they unfairly disadvantage employees of a certain race. Policies that specify that certain hairstyles must or must not be worn, for example, may unfairly impact African American employees, and such policies are prohibited unless their enforcement is necessary to the operations of the business.[125]

Religious Discrimination

Religious discrimination occurs when employees or applicants are treated unfairly because of their religious beliefs. The laws protect those who belong to traditional organized religions and those who do not belong to organized religions but hold strong religious, ethical, or moral beliefs of some kind. Employers must make reasonable accommodations for employees' religious beliefs, which may include flexible scheduling or modifications to workplace practices. Employees are also permitted accommodation when it comes to religious dress and grooming practices, unless such accommodations will place an undue burden on the employer. Employees are also protected from having to participate (or not participate) in certain religious practices as terms of their employment.[126]

Sex-Based Discrimination

Sex-based discrimination occurs when employees or applicants are treated unfairly because of their sex. This form of discrimination includes unfair treatment due to gender, transgender status, and sexual orientation. Harassment and policies that unfairly impact certain groups protected under sex discrimination laws are prohibited under EEOC legislation.[127]

The key diversity-related federal laws are summarized in **Table 12.2**.

Key Diversity Related Legislation	
Title VII of the Civil Rights Act of 1964	Created the Equal Employment Opportunity Commission with the primary role of making it illegal to discriminate against someone in the workplace due to their race, national origin, sex, disability, religion, or pregnancy status.
Equal Pay Act of 1963	Mandates that men and women must be given the same pay for equal work
Age Discrimination in Employment Act (ADEA)	Forbids discrimination against individuals who are age 40 and above.
Americans with Disabilities Act (ADA)	Prohibits discrimination against people with disabilities in employment, public services, public accommodations, and in telecommunications
Pregnancy Discrimination Act (PDA)	Prohibits any discrimination as it relates to pregnancy, including hiring, firing, compensation, training, job assignment, insurance, or any other employment conditions.
Family and Medical Leave Act (FMLA)	Grants new parents up to 12 weeks of paid or unpaid leave to care for the new child, and gives nursing mothers the right to express milk on workplace premises.

Table 12.2 (Attribution: Copyright Rice University, OpenStax, under CC-BY 4.0 license)

Other Types of Discrimination

Beyond the key types of discrimination outlined by the EEOC, diversity and management scholars have identified other types of discrimination that frequently impact certain identity groups more than others. **Access discrimination** is a catchall term that describes when people are denied employment opportunities because of their identity group or personal characteristics such as sex, race, age, or other factors. **Treatment discrimination** describes a situation in which people are employed but are treated differently while employed, mainly by receiving different and unequal job-related opportunities or rewards.[128] Scholars have also identified a form of discrimination called **interpersonal** or **covert discrimination** that involves discrimination that manifests itself in ways that are not visible or readily identifiable, yet is serious because it can impact interpersonal interactions between employees, employees and customers, and other important workplace relationships.

This type of discrimination poses unique challenges because it is difficult to identify. For example, one study examining customer service and discrimination found that obese customers were more likely to experience interpersonal discrimination than average-weight customers. Salespersons spent less time interacting with obese customers than average-weight customers, and average-weight customers reported more positive interactions with salespeople when asked about standard customer service metrics such as being smiled at, receiving eye contact, and perceived friendliness.[129]

1. What is the role of the EEOC?
2. What are the types of discrimination encountered in the workplace?

12.5 | Key Diversity Theories

5. What key theories help managers understand the benefits and challenges of managing the diverse workforce?

Many theories relevant to managing the diverse workforce center on an individual's reactions (such as categorization and assessment of the characteristics of others) to people who are different from the individual. Competing viewpoints attempt to explain how diversity is either harmful or beneficial to organizational outcomes.

- The **cognitive diversity hypothesis** suggests that multiple perspectives stemming from the cultural differences between group or organizational members result in creative problem solving and innovation.
- The **similarity-attraction paradigm** and **social identity theory** hold that individuals' preferences for interacting with others like themselves can result in diversity having a negative effect on group and organizational outcomes.
- The **justification-suppression model** explains under what conditions individuals act on their prejudices.

Cognitive Diversity Hypothesis

Some research shows that diversity has no relationship to group performance, and some shows that there is a relationship. Of the latter research, some shows a negative relationship (greater diversity means poorer group performance, less diversity means better group performance) and some shows a positive relationship.

These various findings may be due to the difference in how diversity can affect group members. **Cognitive diversity** refers to differences between team members in characteristics such as expertise, experiences, and perspectives.[130] Many researchers contend that physical diversity characteristics such as race, age, or sex (also known as bio-demographic diversity) positively influence performance because team members contribute unique cognitive attributes based on their experiences stemming from their demographic background.[131]

There is research that supports the relationship between group performance and task-related diversity as reflected in characteristics not readily detectable such as ability, occupational expertise, or education. However, the relationship between bio-demographic diversity and group performance has produced mixed results.[132] For example, Watson and colleagues studied the comparison of group performance between culturally homogeneous and culturally heterogeneous groups. Groups were assigned business cases to analyze, and their group performance was measured over time based on four factors: the range of perspectives generated, the number of problems identified in the case, the number of alternatives produced, and the quality of the solution. Overall performance was also calculated as the average of all the factors. The factors were measured at four intervals: Interval 1 (at 5 weeks), Interval 2 (at 9 weeks), Interval 3 (at 13 weeks), and Interval 4 (at 17 weeks).

For Intervals 1 and 2, the overall performance of homogeneous groups was higher than heterogeneous groups. However, by Intervals 3 and 4, there were no significant differences in overall performance between the groups, but the heterogeneous group outperformed the homogeneous group in generating a greater range of perspectives and producing a greater number of alternatives.

This research suggests that although homogeneous groups may initially outperform culturally diverse groups, over time diverse groups benefit from a wider range of ideas to choose from when solving a problem. Based on the cognitive diversity hypothesis, these benefits stem from the multiple perspectives generated by the cultural diversity of group members. On the other hand, it takes time for members of diverse groups to work together effectively due to their unfamiliarity with one another, which explains why homogeneous groups outperform heterogeneous groups in the early stages of group functioning. (This is related to the similarity-attraction paradigm, discussed in the next section.) Other studies have shown that ethnically diverse groups cooperate better than homogeneous groups at tasks that require decision-making and are more creative and innovative. While homogeneous groups may be more efficient, heterogeneous groups sacrifice efficiency for effectiveness in other areas.

Similarity-Attraction Paradigm

The cognitive diversity hypothesis explains how diversity benefits organizational outcomes. The similarity-attraction paradigm explains how diversity can have negative outcomes for an organization.

Some research has shown that members who belong to diverse work units may become less attached, are absent from work more often, and are more likely to quit.[133] There is also evidence that diversity may produce conflict and higher employee turnover. Similarity-attraction theory is one of the foundational theories that attempts to explain why this occurs; it posits that individuals are attracted to others with whom they share attitude similarity.[134]

Attitudes and beliefs are common antecedents to interpersonal attraction. However, other traits such as race, age, sex, and socioeconomic status can serve as signals to reveal deep-level traits about ourselves. For example, numerous studies investigating job-seeker behaviors have shown that individuals are more attracted to companies whose recruitment literature includes statements and images that reflect their own identity group. One study showed that companies perceived to value diversity based on their recruitment literature are more attractive to racial minorities and women compared to Whites.[135] Another study showed that when organizations use recruitment materials that target sexual minorities, the attraction of study participants weakened among heterosexuals.[136] Even foreign-born potential job candidates are more attracted to organizations that depict international employees in their job ads.[137]

Social Cognitive Theory

Social cognitive theory is another theory that seeks to explain how diversity can result in negative outcomes in a group or organization. Social cognitive theory suggests that people use categorization to simplify and cope with large amounts of information. These categories allow us to quickly and easily compartmentalize data, and people are often categorized by their visible characteristics, such as race, sex, and age. Thus, when someone sees a person of a particular race, automatic processing occurs and beliefs about this particular race are activated. Even when the person is not visible, he or she can be subject to this automatic categorization. For example, when sorting through resumes a hiring manager might engage in sex categorization because the person's name provides information about the person's sex or racial categorization because the person's name provides information about their race.[138] **Stereotypes** are related to this categorization, and refer to the overgeneralization of characteristics about large groups. Stereotypes are the basis for prejudice and discrimination. In a job-related context, using categorization and stereotyping in employment decision-making is often illegal. Whether illegal or not, this approach is inconsistent with a valuing-diversity approach.

Social Identity Theory

Social identity theory is another explanation of why diversity may have a negative outcome. Social identity theory suggests that when we first come into contact with others, we categorize them as belonging to an in-group (i.e., the same group as us) or an out-group (not belonging to our group).[139] We tend to see members of our in-group as heterogeneous but out-group members as homogeneous. That is, we perceive out-group members as having similar attitudes, behaviors, and characteristics (i.e., fitting stereotypes).

Researchers posit that this perspective may occur because of the breadth of interactions we have with people from our in-group as opposed to out-groups. There is often strong in-group favoritism and, sometimes, derogation of out-group members. In some cases, however, minority group members do not favor members of their own group.[140] This may happen because of being continually exposed to widespread beliefs about the positive attributes of Whites or men and to common negative beliefs about some minorities and women. When in-group favoritism does occur, majority-group members will be hired, promoted, and rewarded at the expense of minority-group members, often in violation of various laws.

Schema Theory

Schema theory explains how individuals encode information about others based on their demographic characteristics.[141] Units of information and knowledge experienced by individuals are stored as having patterns and interrelationships, thus creating schemas that can be used to evaluate one's self or others. As a result of the prior perceived knowledge or beliefs embodied in such schemas, individuals categorize people, events, and objects. They then use these categories to evaluate newly encountered people and make decisions regarding their interaction with them.

Based on schema theory, employees develop schemas about coworkers based on race, gender, and other diversity traits. They also form schemas about organizational policies, leadership, and work climates. Schemas formed can be positive or negative and will affect the attitudes and behaviors employees have toward one another.

Justification-Suppression Model

The **justification-suppression model** explains the circumstances in which prejudiced people might act on their prejudices. The process by which people experience their prejudice is characterized as a "two-step" process in which people are prejudiced against a certain group or individual but experience conflicting emotions in regard to that prejudice and are motivated to suppress their prejudice rather than act upon it.[142] Theory about prejudice suggests that all people have prejudices of some sort, that they learn their prejudices from an early age, and that they have a hard time departing from them as they grow older. Prejudices are often reinforced by intimate others, and individuals use different methods to justify those prejudices.

Most people will attempt to suppress any outward manifestations of their prejudices. This suppression can come from internal factors like empathy, compassion, or personal beliefs regarding proper treatment of others. Suppression can also come from societal pressures; overt displays of prejudice are no longer socially acceptable, and in some cases are illegal.

At times, however, prejudiced individuals will look for reasons to justify acting on their prejudiced beliefs. Research has shown people are more likely to act in prejudiced ways when they are physically or emotionally tired, when they can do so and remain anonymous, or when social norms are weak enough that their prejudiced behavior will not be received negatively.

CONCEPT CHECK ✔

1. What are the theories that can help managers understand diversity?

12.6 | Benefits and Challenges of Workplace Diversity

6. How can managers reap benefits from diversity and mitigate its challenges?

Much theoretical work has espoused the benefits of workplace diversity, but empirical studies have often had conflicting results, which have shown researchers that certain conditions can affect how successful initiatives to increase and enhance workplace diversity are. Managers can work to make sure that the efforts and initiatives they enact to increase diversity in the workplace come from a perspective that ensures and strives for equity and fairness, and not simply from the perspective of only benefitting the company's bottom line. By approaching diversity and diversity issues in a thoughtful, purposeful way, managers can mitigate the challenges posed by a diverse workforce and enhance the benefits a diverse workforce can offer.

Three Perspectives on Workplace Diversity

Ely and Thomas's work on cultural diversity was designed to theoretically and empirically support some of the hypothesized relationships between diversity and workplace outcomes. Their research yielded a paradigm that identifies three perspectives regarding workplace diversity:[143] integration and learning, access and legitimacy, and discrimination and fairness.

The Integration-and-Learning Perspective

The **integration-and-learning perspective** posits that the different life experiences, skills, and perspectives that members of diverse cultural identity groups possess can be a valuable resource in the context of work groups. Under this perspective, the members of a culturally diverse workgroup can use their collective differences to think critically about work issues, strategies, products, and practices in a way that will allow the group to be successful in its business operations. The assumption under this perspective is that members of different cultural identity groups can learn from each other and work together to best achieve shared goals. This perspective values cultural identity and strongly links diversity of the group to the success of the firm.

Downfalls of the integration-and-learning perspective can be that White members of the work group can feel marginalized when they are not asked to join in on diversity-related projects or discussions. Similarly, workforce members of color might experience burnout if they are always expected to work on those projects and discussions that specifically deal with diversity issues.

The Access-and-Legitimacy Perspective

The **access-and-legitimacy perspective** focuses on the benefit that a diverse workforce can bring to a business that wishes to operate within a diverse set of markets or with culturally diverse clients. Work groups that operate under this perspective are doing so in order to gain access to diverse markets and because their diversity affords them some level of legitimacy when attempting to gain access to diverse markets. This type of workplace diversity is more of a functional type of diversity that does not attempt to integrate or value diversity at the business's core. The danger of this diversity perspective is that it can limit the roles of certain minority groups by valuing members of these groups only because they can increase the access to diverse markets and clients and not because they can make other potentially valuable contributions.[144]

The Discrimination-and-Fairness Perspective

The **discrimination-and-fairness perspective** stems from a belief that a culturally diverse workforce is a moral duty that must be maintained in order to create a just and fair society. This perspective is characterized by a commitment to equal opportunities in hiring and promotions, and does not directly link a work group's productivity or success with diversity. Many times firms operating under this perspective will have a spoken or unspoken assumption that assimilation into the dominant (White) culture should take place by the members of other cultural identity groups. One drawback of this perspective is that because it measures progress by the recruitment and retention of diverse people, employees of traditionally underrepresented groups can feel devalued. Often, assimilation is pushed on diverse employees under the guise of reducing conflict or in an effort to demonstrate that differences between cultural identity groups are unimportant.[145]

Exhibit 12.8 shows the degrees of effectiveness and benefits for each perspective.

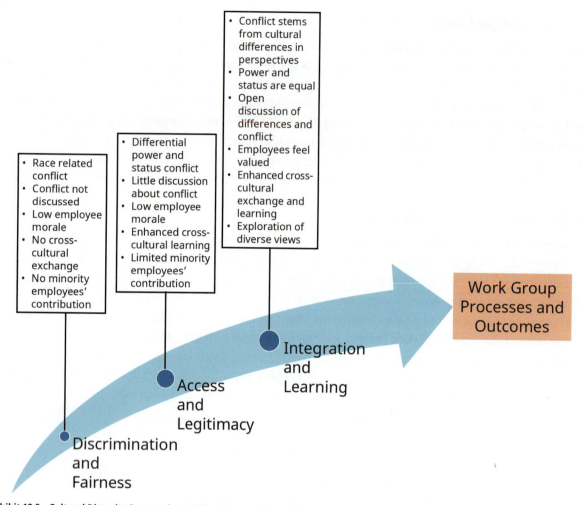

Exhibit 12.8   Cultural Diversity Perspectives at Work   Source: Adapted from Ely, Robin J., and David A. Thomas. "Cultural diversity at work: The effects of diversity perspectives on work group processes and outcomes." Administrative science quarterly. 46.2 (2001): 229-273.

CONCEPT CHECK ✓

1. How can managers reap the benefits of diversity?
2. How can managers mitigate the challenges of diversity?
3. What is the access-and-legitimacy perspective? Differentiate it from the discrimination-and-fairness perspective.

12.7   Recommendations for Managing Diversity

7. What can organizations do to ensure applicants, employees, and customers from all backgrounds are valued?

Organizations that are committed to equality and inclusion must take steps to combat the examples of discrimination and harassment that have been covered in this chapter. And they must take steps to make diversity a goal in the pre-employment stages as well as in the post-employment stages. Anyone with managerial or supervisory responsibilities should pay careful attention to hiring and performance-rewarding practices, and make sure to rely on relevant information for making decisions and ignore race-based stereotypes. The following are examples of what leaders and organizations can do make sure employees feel valued.

Interview Selection Process

To ensure fairness for all applicants, organizations should use **highly structured interviews** during the selection process to avoid bias based on race or gender.[146] Highly structured interviews consists of the following 15 characteristics: "(1) job analysis, (2) same questions, (3) limited prompting, (4) better questions, (5) longer interviews, (6) control of ancillary information, (7) limited questions from candidates, (8) multiple rating scales, (9) anchored rating scales, (10) detailed notes, (11) multiple interviewers, (12) consistent interviewers, (13) no discussion between interviews, (14) training, and (15) statistical prediction."[147] Similarity bias can occur when interviewers prefer interviewees with whom they share similar traits. Organizations can mitigate this challenge if all 15 characteristics of a structured interview are used consistently with each job applicant.

Diversified Mentoring Relationships

Thanks to the rapid growth of international travel and globalization, managers are often called upon to manage a workforce that is increasingly diverse. Research has shown that racially and ethnically diverse firms have better financial performance than more homogeneous firms, because, as mentioned, employees from different backgrounds and with different experiences can give the firm a competitive advantage in various ways. It is necessary, however, that managers and those in positions of power are adequately equipped to manage diverse workforces in ways that are beneficial to all. **Diversified mentoring relationships** are relationships in which the mentor and the mentee differ in terms of their status within the company and within larger society. The differences could be in terms of race, gender, class, disability, sexual orientation, or other status. Research has found that these types of relationships are mutually beneficial and that the mentor and the mentee both have positive outcomes in terms of knowledge, empathy, and skills related to interactions with people from different power groups.[148]

MANAGERIAL LEADERSHIP

Diversity Training Programs

As the workforce becomes increasingly more diverse, managers will face a major challenge in understanding how to manage diversity. One of many decisions to be made is whether an organization should offer diversity training and, if so, what topics and issues should be addressed based on the organizational goals.

There has been a debate over the effectiveness of corporate diversity training since the Civil Rights Act of 1964 helped prompt corporate diversity training with the organizational goal of simply being compliant with the law. Prior research shows that it can be effective, ineffective, or even detrimental for employees, but as diversity training has evolved through the years, it has become an important factor in helping employers manage diversity.

In the 1980s through the late 1990s, diversity training evolved from focusing solely on compliance to addressing the needs of women and minorities as they entered the workforce at a faster rate. Unfortunately, this type of training was perceived by Whites and men as singling them out as the problem; sometimes such training was even formatted as "confession" sessions for White employees to express their complicity in institutional racism. Not unexpectedly, this type of training would often backfire and would further separate employees from each other, the exact opposite of its intention.

Recently, diversity training has evolved to focus on (1) building cultural competencies regarding fellow employees, (2) valuing differences, and (3) learning how diversity helps make better business decisions. This perspective toward diversity training is more effective than simply focusing on causes of a lack of diversity and the historical roots of discrimination. Understanding how to comply with the law is still important, but training has a greater effect when the other factors are also included.

A recent study investigated various diversity-training methods, including having participants engage in activities on perspective taking and goal setting. For perspective-taking activities, participants were asked to write a few sentences about the challenges they believed minority group members might experience. Goal-setting activities involved writing specific and measurable goals related to workplace diversity such as crafting future policies or engaging in future behaviors. Researchers found that when these activities were used as a diversity-training method, pro-diversity attitudes and behavioral intentions persisted months later.

Issues regarding employee sexual orientation have also been introduced into corporate diversity training in recent years. Because employees' religious beliefs are protected by Title VII of the Civil Rights Act, employers should be sensitive to balancing the rights of lesbian, gay, and bisexual employees and employees' religious rights. Attempting to protect the rights of one group and not be perceived to disrespect another is a difficult situation for managers. In order to mitigate any backlash from some employees, employers should seek feedback from all groups to learn the best ways to accommodate them, and should assess the organizational climate. Additionally, managers should explain how diversity based on sexual orientation aligns with the company's strategic objectives and explain the company's legal position with supportive reasoning. Lastly, based on their organizational climate and how it reshapes itself over time, some companies may wish to address diversity training on sexual orientation in a voluntary training separate from other diversity issues.

Sources: Young, Cheri A., Badiah Haffejee, and David L. Corsun. "Developing Cultural Intelligence and Empathy Through Diversified Mentoring Relationships." *Journal of Management Education* (2017): 1052562917710687; Bezrukova, K., Jehn, K.A., & Spell, C.S. (2012). Reviewing diversity training: Where we have been and where we should go. *Academy of Management Learning & Education*, 11 (2): 207-227; Anand, R., & Winters, M. (2008). A retrospective view of corporate diversity training from 1964 to the present. *Academy of Management Learning & Education*, 7 (3): 356-372; Lindsey, A., King, E., Membere, A., & Cheung, H.K. (July 28, 2017). Two types of diversity training that really work. *Harvard Business Review*.

Discussion Questions
1. Why do you believe diversity training is resisted by some employees?
2. Do you believe there will always be a need for workplace diversity training?
3. How would you determine what types of diversity training are needed at your company?

Visible Leadership

Another key to ensure that employees are treated fairly is utilizing appropriate leadership strategies.[149] Leadership must sincerely value variety of opinions, and organizational culture must encourage openness and make workers feel valued. Organizations must also have a well-articulated and widely understood mission and a relatively egalitarian, nonbureaucratic structure. Having such a work environment will ensure that the attitudes and values of employees are aligned with those of the organization. In this way culture serves as a control mechanism for shaping behaviors.

Strategies for Employees

Individuals can increase positive employment outcomes by obtaining high levels of education, because for all groups education is a predictor of employment and increased earnings. Individuals can also seek employment in larger firms, which are more likely to have formal hiring programs and specific diversity provisions in place. Individuals of any race or ethnic background can also take steps to eliminate discrimination by being aware of their own personal stereotypes or biases and taking steps to challenge and address them.

CONCEPT CHECK

1. How can managers ensure fairness in the interviewing and selection process regarding diversity?
2. What is the role of leadership regarding diversity?

🔑 Key Terms

access discrimination A catchall term that describes when people are denied employment opportunities because of their identity group or personal characteristics such as sex, race, or age.

access-and-legitimacy perspective Focuses on the benefits that a diverse workforce can bring to a business that wishes to operate within a diverse set of markets or with culturally diverse clients.

age discrimination Treating an employee or applicant less favorably due to their age.

Age Discrimination in Employment Act (ADEA) Forbids discrimination against individuals who are age 40 and above, including offensive or derogatory remarks that create a hostile work environment.

Americans with Disabilities Act (ADA) Prohibits discrimination in employment, public services, public accommodations, and telecommunications against people with disabilities.

cognitive diversity Differences between team members regarding characteristics such as expertise, experiences, and perspectives.

cognitive diversity hypothesis Multiple perspectives stemming from the cultural differences between group or organizational members result in creative problem-solving and innovation.

covert discrimination (interpersonal) An interpersonal form of discrimination that manifests in ways that are not visible or readily identifiable.

deep-level diversity Diversity in characteristics that are nonobservable such as attitudes, values, and beliefs, such as religion.

disability discrimination Occurs when an employee or applicant is treated unfavorably due to their physical or mental disability.

discrimination-and-fairness perspective A culturally diverse workforce is a moral duty that must be maintained in order to create a just and fair society.

diversified mentoring relationships Relationships in which the mentor and the mentee differ in terms of their status within the company and within larger society.

diversity Identity-based differences among and between people that affect their lives as applicants, employees, and customers.

Equal Employment Opportunity Commission An organization that enforces laws and issues guidelines for employment-related treatment according to Title VII of the Civil Rights Act of 1964.

Equal Pay Act of 1963 An amendment to the Fair Labor Standards Act of 1938.

Family and Medical Leave Act (FMLA) Provides new parents, including adoptive and foster parents, with 12 weeks of unpaid leave (or paid leave only if earned by the employee) to care for the new child and requires that nursing mothers have the right to express milk on workplace premises.

glass ceiling An invisible barrier based on the prejudicial beliefs of organizational decision makers that prevents women from moving beyond certain levels within a company.

groupthink A dysfunction in decision-making that is common in homogeneous groups due to group pressures and group members' desire for conformity and consensus.

harassment Any unwelcome conduct that is based on characteristics such as age, race, national origin, disability, sex, or pregnancy status.

hidden diversity Differences in traits that are deep-level and may be concealed or revealed at discretion by individuals who possess them.

highly structured interviews Interviews that are be structured objectively to remove bias from the selection process.

identity group A collective of individuals who share the same demographic characteristics such as race, sex, or age.

inclusion The degree to which employees are accepted and treated fairly by their organization.

integration-and-learning perspective Posits that the different life experiences, skills, and perspectives that members of diverse cultural identity groups possess can be a valuable resource in the context of work groups.

invisible social identities Membership in an identity group based on hidden diversity traits such as sexual orientation or a nonobservable disability that may be concealed or revealed.

justification-suppression model Explains the circumstances in which prejudiced people might act on their prejudices.

justification-suppression model Explains under what conditions individuals act on their prejudices.

managing diversity Ways in which organizations seek to ensure that members of diverse groups are valued and treated fairly within organizations.

model minority myth A stereotype that portrays Asian men and women as obedient and successful and is often used to justify socioeconomic disparities between other racial minority groups.

national origin discrimination Treating someone unfavorably because of their country of origin, accent, ethnicity, or appearance.

passing The decision to not disclose one's invisible social identity.

pregnancy discrimination Treating an employee or applicant unfairly because of pregnancy status, childbirth, or medical conditions related to pregnancy or childbirth.

Pregnancy Discrimination Act (PDA) Prohibits any discrimination as it relates to pregnancy in hiring, firing, compensation, training, job assignment, insurance, or any other employment conditions.

race/color discrimination Treating employees or applicants unfairly because of their race or because of physical characteristics typically associated with race such as skin color, hair color, hair texture, or certain facial features.

religious discrimination When employees or applicants are treated unfairly because of their religious beliefs.

resource-based view Demonstrates how a diverse workforce can create a sustainable competitive advantage for organizations.

revealing The decision to disclose one's invisible social identity.

reverse discrimination Describes a situation in which dominant group members perceive that they are experiencing discrimination based on their race or sex.

schema theory Explains how individuals encode information about others based on their demographic characteristics.

sex-based discrimination When employees or applicants are treated unfairly because of their sex, including unfair treatment due to gender, transgender status, or sexual orientation.

sexual harassment Harassment based on a person's sex, and can (but does not have to) include unwanted sexual advances, requests for sexual favors, or physical and verbal acts of a sexual nature.

sexual harassment Harassment based on a person's sex; it can (but does not have to) include unwanted sexual advances, requests for sexual favors, or physical and verbal acts of a sexual nature.

similarity-attraction paradigm Individuals' preferences for interacting with others like themselves can result in diversity having a negative effect on group and organizational outcomes.

social identity theory Self-concept based on an individual's physical, social, and mental characteristics.

stereotypes Overgeneralization of characteristics about groups that are the basis for prejudice and discrimination.

strategic human resources management (SHRM) System of activities arranged to engage employees in a manner that assists the organization in achieving a sustainable competitive advantage.

surface-level diversity Diversity in the form of characteristics of individuals that are readily visible, including, but not limited to, age, body size, visible disabilities, race, or sex.

treatment discrimination A situation in which people are employed but are treated differently while employed, mainly by receiving different and unequal job-related opportunities or rewards.

work visa A temporary documented status that authorizes individuals from other countries to permanently or temporarily live and work in the United States.

workplace discrimination Unfair treatment in the job hiring process or at work that is based on the identity group, physical or mental condition, or personal characteristic of an applicant or employee.

📖 Summary of Learning Outcomes

12.1 An Introduction to Workplace Diversity
1. What is diversity?

Diversity refers to identity-based differences among and between people that affect their lives as applicants, employees, and customers. Surface-level diversity represents characteristics of individuals that are readily visible, including, but not limited to, age, body size, visible disabilities, race, or sex. Deep-level diversity includes traits that are nonobservable such as attitudes, values, and beliefs. Finally, hidden diversity includes traits that are deep-level but may be concealed or revealed at the discretion of individuals who possess them.

12.2 Diversity and the Workforce
2. How diverse is the workforce?

In analyzing the diversity of the workforce, several measures can be used. Demographic measures such as gender and race can be used to measure group sizes. Measures of such things as discrimination toward specific groups can be analyzed to gauge the diversity of the workforce. Other measures of diversity in the workforce can include examination of differences in age and sexual orientation.

12.3 Diversity and Its Impact on Companies
3. How does diversity impact companies and the workforce?

The demography of the labor force is changing in many ways as it becomes racially diverse and older and includes more women and individuals with disabilities. Diversity affects how organizations understand that employing people who hold multiple perspectives increases the need to mitigate conflict between workers from different identity groups, enhances creativity and problem solving in teams, and serves as a resource to create a competitive advantage for the organization.

12.4 Challenges of Diversity
4. What is workplace discrimination, and how does it affect different social identity groups?

Workplace discrimination occurs when an employee or an applicant is treated unfairly at work or in the job-hiring process due to an identity group, condition, or personal characteristic such as age, race, national origin, sex, disability, religion, or pregnancy status. The Equal Employment Opportunity Commission enforces laws and legislation related to individuals with those protected statuses.

Harassment is any unwelcome conduct that is based on the protected characteristics listed above. Sexual harassment refers specifically to harassment based on a person's sex, and it can (but does not have to) include unwanted sexual advances, requests for sexual favors, or physical and verbal acts of a sexual nature.

12.5 Key Diversity Theories
5. What key theories help managers understand the benefits and challenges of managing the diverse workforce?

The cognitive-diversity hypothesis suggests that multiple perspectives stemming from the cultural differences between groups or organizational members result in creative problem solving and innovation. The similarity-attraction paradigm and social identity theory explain how, because individuals prefer to interact with others like themselves, diversity may have a negative effect on group and organizational outcomes. The justification-suppression model explains under what conditions individuals act on their prejudice.

12.6 Benefits and Challenges of Workplace Diversity

6. How can managers reap benefits from diversity and mitigate its challenges?

By approaching diversity and diversity issues in a thoughtful, purposeful way, managers can mitigate the challenges posed by a diverse workforce and enhance the benefits a diverse workforce can offer.

Managers can work to make sure that the efforts and initiatives they enact to increase diversity in the workplace come from a perspective that ensures and strives for equity and fairness, not simply one that will benefit the company's bottom line.

Using an integration-and-learning perspective strongly links diversity to the work and success of the firm by viewing cultural identity, different life experiences, skills, and perspectives from members of diverse cultural identity groups as a valuable resource.

12.7 Recommendations for Managing Diversity

7. What can organizations do to ensure applicants, employees, and customers from all backgrounds are valued?

Organizations should use objective and fair recruitment and selection tools and policies.

Leadership should make employees feel valued, be open to varied perspectives, and encourage a culture of open dialogue. Women and racial minorities can increase positive employment outcomes by pursuing higher levels of education and seeking employment in larger organizations. All individuals should be willing to listen, empathize with others, and seek to better understand sensitive issues that affect different identity groups.

Chapter Review Questions

1. Define the three types of diversity and compare them using examples for each type.
2. How are demographics of the workforce changing?
3. What are some major challenges that women face in organizations?
4. What is the model minority myth? How does it compare to how Blacks and Hispanics are stereotyped?
5. What are some benefits of hiring older workers?
6. Why would an employee "pass" or "reveal" at work? What are the positive and negative consequences of doing so?
7. Explain the six benefits of workplace diversity described by Cox and Blake's business case for diversity.
8. Compare how the cognitive diversity hypothesis and the similarity-attraction paradigm relate to diversity outcomes.
9. Based on the justification-suppression model, explain why individuals act on their prejudicial beliefs.
10. Describe challenges that managers must face when managing diversity.
11. How can employees ensure they are compliant with the laws and legislation enforced by the EEOC?
12. What are some recommendations for managing diversity?

Management Skills Application Exercises

1. Do you agree that diversity can be a source of greater benefit than harm to organizations? Why or why not?

2. Have you ever worked in a diverse team setting before? If so, did you encounter any attitudes or behaviors that could potentially cause conflict? If not, how would you manage conflict stemming from diversity?

3. List three organizational goals you would implement to create an organizational culture of diversity and inclusion.

4. Have you or has someone you know experienced discrimination? How did that affect you or that person emotionally, physically, or financially?

5. Pick an identity group (e.g., gay, Black, or woman) other than your own. Imagine and list the negative experiences and interactions you believe you might encounter at work. What policies or strategies could an organization implement to prevent those negative experiences from occurring?

6. Provide a concrete example of how different perspectives stemming from diversity can positively impact an organization or work group. You may use a real-life personal example or make one up.

Managerial Decision Exercises

1. As a manager for a hospital, you oversee a staff of marketing associates. Their job is to find doctors and persuade them to refer their patients to your hospital. Associates have a very flexible work schedule and manage their own time. They report to you weekly concerning their activities in the field. Trusting them is very important, and it is impossible to track and confirm all of their activities. Your assistant, Nancy, manages the support staff for the associates, works very closely with them, and often serves as your eyes and ears to keep you informed as to how well they are performing.

   One day, Nancy comes into your office crying and tells you that your top-performing associate, Susan, has for the past few weeks repeatedly asked her out to dinner and she has repeatedly refused. Susan is a lesbian and Nancy is not. Today, when she refused, Susan patted her on the bottom and said, "I know, you are just playing hard to get."

   After Nancy calms down, you tell her that you will fill out the paperwork to report a sexual harassment case. Nancy says that she does not want to report it because it would be too embarrassing if word of the incident got out. To impress upon you how strongly she feels, she tells you that she will consider resigning if you report the incident. Nancy is essential to the effective operation of your group, and you dread how difficult it would be to get things done without her assisting you.

   What do you do? Do you report the case, lose Nancy's trust, and jeopardize losing a high-performing employee? Or do you not report it, thereby protecting what Nancy believes to be her right to privacy?

2. Recently your company has begun to promote its diversity efforts, including same-sex (and heterosexual) partner benefits and a nonharassment policy that includes sexual orientation, among other things. Your department now has new posters on the walls with photos of employees who represent different aspects of diversity (e.g., Black, Hispanic, gay). One of your employees is upset about the diversity initiative and has begun posting religious scriptures condemning homosexuality on his cubicle in large type for everyone to see. When asked to remove them, your employee tells you that the posters promoting diversity offend Christian and Muslim employees. What should you do?

3. You are a recently hired supervisor at a paper mill factory. During your second week on the job, you learn about a White employee who has been using a racial slur during lunch breaks when discussing some of her Black coworkers with others. You ask the person who reported it to you about the woman and learn that she is an older woman, around 67 years old, and has worked at the factory for more than 40 years.

You talk to your boss about it, and he tells you that she means no harm by it, she is just from another era and that is just her personality. What would you do in this situation?

4. You are a nurse manager who oversees the triage for the emergency room, and today is a slow day with very few patients. During the downtime, one of your subordinates is talking with another coworker about her new boyfriend. You observe her showing her coworkers explicit images of him that he emailed her on her phone. Everyone is joking and laughing about the ordeal. Even though it appears no one is offended, should you address it? What would you say?

5. You work for a company that has primarily Black and Hispanic customers. Although you employ many racial minorities and women, you notice that all of your leaders are White men. This does not necessarily mean that your organization engages in discriminatory practices, but how would you know if your organization was managing diversity well? What information would you need to determine this, and how would you collect it?

6. Your company's founder believes that younger workers are more energetic and serve better in sales positions. Before posting a new job ad for your sales division, he recommends that you list an age requirement of the position for applicants between ages 18 and 25. Is his recommendation a good one? Why or why not?

7. You work for a real estate broker who recently hired two gay realtors, Steven and Shauna, to be a part of the team. During a staff meeting, your boss mentions an article she read about gay clients feeling ostracized in the real estate market. She tells the new employees she hired them to help facilitate the home-buying process for gay buyers and sellers. She specifically instructs them to focus on recruiting gay clients, even telling them that they should pass along any straight customers to one of the straight realtors on the team. A few weeks later, Shauna reports that she has made her first sale to a straight couple that is expecting a baby. During the next staff meeting, your boss congratulates Shauna on her sale, but again reiterates that Shauna and Steven should pass along straight clients to another realtor so they can focus on recruiting gay clients. After the meeting, Shauna tells you that she thinks it is unfair that she should have to focus on gay clients and that she is thinking of filing a discrimination complaint with HR. Do you think that Shauna is correct in her assessment of the situation? Is there merit to your boss's desire to have the gay realtors focus on recruiting gay clients? What might be a better solution to help gay clients feel more comfortable in the home-buying and -selling process?

Critical Thinking Case

Uber Pays the Price

Nine years ago, Uber revolutionized the taxi industry and the way people commute. With the simple mission "to bring transportation—for everyone, everywhere," today Uber has reached a valuation of around $70 billion and claimed a market share high of almost 90% in 2015. However, in June 2017 Uber experienced a series of bad press regarding an alleged culture of sexual harassment, which is what most experts believe caused their market share to fall to 75%.

In February of 2017 a former software engineer, Susan Fowler, wrote a lengthy post on her website regarding her experience of being harassed by a manager who was not disciplined by human resources for his behavior. In her post, Fowler wrote that Uber's HR department and members of upper management told her that because it was the man's first offense, they would only give him a warning. During her meeting with HR about the incident, Fowler was also advised that she should transfer to another department within the organization. According to Fowler, she was ultimately left no choice but to transfer to another department, despite having specific expertise in the department in which she had originally been working.

As her time at the company went on, she began meeting other women who worked for the company who relayed their own stories of harassment. To her surprise, many of the women reported being harassed by the same person who had harassed her. As she noted in her blog, "It became obvious that both HR and management had been lying about this being his 'first offense.'" Fowler also reported a number of other instances that she identified as sexist and inappropriate within the organization and claims that she was disciplined severely for continuing to speak out. Fowler eventually left Uber after about two years of working for the company, noting that during her time at Uber the percentage of women working there had dropped to 6% of the workforce, down from 25% when she first started.

Following the fallout from Fowler's lengthy description of the workplace on her website, Uber's chief executive Travis Kalanick publicly condemned the behavior described by Fowler, calling it "abhorrent and against everything Uber stands for and believes in." But later in March, Uber board member Arianna Huffington claimed that she believed "sexual harassment was not a systemic problem at the company." Amid pressure from bad media attention and the company's falling market share, Uber made some changes after an independent investigation resulted in 215 complaints. As a result, 20 employees were fired for reasons ranging from sexual harassment to bullying to retaliation to discrimination, and Kalanick announced that he would hire a chief operating officer to help manage the company. In an effort to provide the leadership team with more diversity, two senior female executives were hired to fill the positions of chief brand officer and senior vice president for leadership and strategy.

Critical Thinking Questions

1. Based on Cox's business case for diversity, what are some positive outcomes that may result in changes to Uber's leadership team?
2. Under what form of federal legislation was Fowler protected?
3. What strategies should have been put in place to help prevent sexual harassment incidents like this from happening in the first place?

Sources: Uber corporate Website, https://www.uber.com/newsroom/company-info/ (February, 2017); Marco della Cava, "Uber has lost market share to Lyft during crisis," *USA Today*, June 13, 2017, https://www.usatoday.com/story/tech/news/2017/06/13/uber-market-share-customer-image-hit-string-scandals/102795024/; Tracey Lien, "Uber fires 20 workers after harassment investigation," *Los Angeles Times*, Jun 6, 2017, http://www.latimes.com/business/la-fi-tn-uber-sexual-harassment-20170606-story.html; Susan Fowler, "Reflecting On One Very, Very Strange Year At Uber," February 19, 2017, https://www.susanjfowler.com/blog/2017/2/19/reflecting-on-one-very-strange-year-at-uber.

Exhibit 13.1 (Credit: Tambako the Jaguar/ flickr/ Attribution 2.0 Generic (CC BY 2.0))

Introduction

Learning Outcomes

After reading this chapter, you should be able to answer these questions:

1. What is the nature of leadership and the leadership process?
2. What are the processes associated with people coming to leadership positions?
3. How do leaders influence and move their followers to action?
4. What are the trait perspectives on leadership?
5. What are the behavioral perspectives on leadership?
6. What are the situational perspectives on leadership?
7. What does the concept "substitute for leadership" mean?
8. What are the characteristics of transactional, transformational, and charismatic leadership?
9. How do different approaches and styles of leadership impact what is needed now?

EXPLORING MANAGERIAL CAREERS

John Arroyo: Springfield Sea Lions

John Arroyo is thrilled with his new position as general manager of the Springfield Sea Lions, a minor league baseball team in. Arroyo has been a baseball fan all of his life, and now his diligent work and his degree in sports management are paying off.

Arroyo knew he had a hard act to follow. The general manager whom John replaced, "T.J." Grevin, was a much-loved old-timer who had been with the Sea Lions since their inception 14 years ago. John knew it would be difficult for whoever followed T.J., but he didn't realize how ostracized and powerless he would feel. He tried a pep talk: "I'm the general manager—the CEO of this ball club! In time, the staff *will* respect me." [Not a very good pep talk!]

After his first season ends, Arroyo is discouraged. Ticket and concession sales are down, and some long-time employees are rumored to be thinking about leaving. If John doesn't turn things around, he knows his tenure with the Sea Lions will be short.

Questions: Is John correct in assuming that the staff will learn to respect him in time? What can John do to earn the loyalty of his staff and improve the ball club's performance?

Outcomes: During the winter, John thinks long and hard about how he can earn the respect of the Sea Lions staff. Before the next season opener, John announces his plan: "So I can better understand what your day is like, I'm going to spend one day in each of your shoes. I'm trading places with each of you. I will be a ticket taker, a roving hot dog vendor, and a janitor. And I will be a marketer, and an accountant—for a day. You in turn will have the day off so you can enjoy the game from the general manager's box." The staff laughs and whistles appreciatively. Then the Springfield mascot, Sparky the Sea Lion, speaks up: "Hey Mr. Arroyo, are you going to spend a day in my flippers?" "You bet!" says John, laughing. The entire staff cheers.

John continues. "At the close of the season, we will honor a staff member with the T.J. Grevin Award for outstanding contributions to the Sea Lions organization. T.J. was such a great guy, it's only right that we honor him." The meeting ends, but John's staff linger to tell him how excited they are about his ideas. Amidst the handshakes, he hopes that this year may be the best year yet for the Sea Lions.

Sarah Elizabeth Roisland is the manager of a district claims office for a large insurance company. Fourteen people work for her. The results of a recent attitude survey indicate that her employees have extremely high job satisfaction and motivation. Conflict is rare in Sarah's office. Furthermore, productivity measures place her group among the most productive in the entire company. Her success has brought the company's vice president of human resources to her office in an attempt to discover the secret to her success. Sarah's peers, superiors, and workers all give the same answer: she is more than a good manager—she is an outstanding leader. She continually gets high performance from her employees and does so in such a way that they enjoy working for her.

There is no magic formula for becoming a good leader. There are, however, many identifiable reasons why some people are better and more effective leaders. Leaders, especially effective leaders, are not created by simply attending a one-day leadership workshop. Yet effective leadership skills are not something most people are born with. You can become an effective leader if you are willing to invest the time and energy to develop all of the "right stuff."

According to Louise Axon, director of content strategy, and her colleagues at Harvard Business Publishing, in seeking management talent, *leadership* is an urgently needed quality in all managerial roles.[1] Good leaders and good leadership are rare. Harvard management professor John P. Kotter notes that "there is a leadership crisis in the U.S. today,"[2] and the late USC Professor Warren Bennis states that many of our organizations are overmanaged and underled.[3]

13.1 | The Nature of Leadership

1. What is the nature of leadership and the leadership process?

The many definitions of leadership each have a different emphasis. Some definitions consider leadership an act or behavior, such as initiating structure so group members know how to complete a task. Others consider a leader to be the center or nucleus of group activity, an instrument of goal achievement who has a certain personality, a form of persuasion and power, and the art of inducing compliance.[4] Some look at leadership in terms of the management of group processes. In this view, a good leader develops a vision for the group, communicates that vision,[5] orchestrates the group's energy and activity toward goal attainment, "[turns] a group of individuals into a team," and "[transforms] good intentions into positive actions."[6]

Leadership is frequently defined as a social (interpersonal) influence relationship between two or more persons who depend on each other to attain certain mutual goals in a group situation.[7] Effective leadership helps individuals and groups achieve their goals by focusing on the group's *maintenance needs* (the need for individuals to fit and work together by having, for example, shared norms) and *task needs* (the need for the group to make progress toward attaining the goal that brought them together).

Exhibit 13.2   Joe Madden at pitcher mound   Joe Maddon, manager of the Chicago Cubs baseball team, is lauded for both his managerial and leadership skills. Maddon is a role model for managers competing in the business world. Managers can learn and profit from the Cubs skipper's philosophy of instilling an upbeat attitude with the team, staying loose but staying productive, and avoiding being the center of attention.

Leader versus Manager

The two dual concepts, leader and manager, leadership and management, are not interchangeable, nor are they redundant. The differences between the two can, however, be confusing. In many instances, to be a good manager one needs to be an effective leader. Many CEOs have been hired in the hope that their leadership skills, their ability to formulate a vision and get others to "buy into" that vision, will propel the organization forward. In addition, effective leadership often necessitates the ability to manage—to set goals; plan, devise, and implement strategy; make decisions and solve problems; and organize and control. For our purposes, the two sets of concepts can be contrasted in several ways.

First, we define the two concepts differently. In **Chapter 1**, we defined management as a process consisting of planning, organizing, directing, and controlling. Here we define leadership as a social (interpersonal) influence relationship between two or more people who are dependent on each another for goal attainment.

Second, managers and leaders are commonly differentiated in terms of the processes through which they initially come to their position. Managers are generally appointed to their role. Even though many organizations appoint people to positions of leadership, leadership per se is a relationship that revolves around the followers' acceptance or rejection of the leader.[8] Thus, leaders often emerge out of events that unfold among members of a group.

Third, managers and leaders often differ in terms of the types and sources of the power they exercise. Managers commonly derive their power from the larger organization. Virtually all organizations legitimize the use of certain "carrots and sticks" (rewards and punishments) as ways of securing the compliance of their employees. In other words, by virtue of the position that a manager occupies (president, vice president, department head, supervisor), certain "rights to act" (schedule production, contract to sell a product, hire and fire) accompany the position and its place within the hierarchy of authority. Leaders can also secure power and the ability to exercise influence using carrots and sticks; however, it is much more common for leaders to derive power from followers' perception of their knowledge (expertise), their personality and attractiveness, and the working relationship that has developed between leaders and followers.

From the perspective of those who are under the leader's and manager's influence, the motivation to comply often has a different base. The subordinate to a manager frequently complies because of the role authority of the manager, and because of the carrots and sticks that managers have at their disposal. The followers of a leader comply because they want to. Thus, leaders motivate primarily through intrinsic processes, while managers motivate primarily through extrinsic processes.

Finally, it is important to note that while managers may be successful in directing and supervising their subordinates, they often succeed or fail because of their ability or inability to lead.[9] As noted above, effective leadership often calls for the ability to manage, and effective management often requires leadership.

CONCEPT CHECK

1. What is the nature of leadership and the leadership process?

13.2 | The Leadership Process

2. What are the processes associated with people coming to leadership positions?

Leadership is a process, a complex and dynamic exchange relationship built over time between leader and follower and between leader and the group of followers who depend on each other to attain a mutually desired goal.[10] There are several key components to this "working relationship": the leader, the followers, the context (situation), the leadership process per se, and the consequences (outcomes) (see **Exhibit 13.3**).[11] Across time, each component interacts with and influences the other components, and whatever consequences (such as leader-follower trust) are created influence future interactions. As any one of the components changes, so too will leadership.[12]

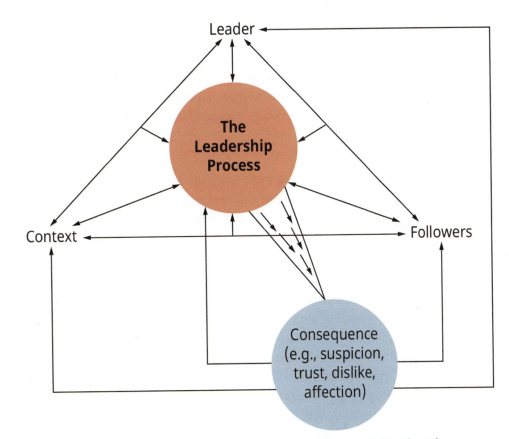

The Leader

Leaders are people who take charge of or guide the activities of others. They are often seen as the focus or orchestrater of group activity, the people who set the tone of the group so that it can move forward to attain its goals. Leaders provide the group with what is required to fulfill its maintenance and task-related needs. (Later in the chapter, we will return to the "leader as a person" as part of our discussion of the trait approach to leadership.)

Exhibit 13.4 **New York Philharmonic @ UN** The New York Philharmonic, conducted by Music Director Alan Gilbert, paid special tribute in the General Assembly Hall to UN Secretary-General Ban Ki-moon as a tribute to his 10-year term. Gilbert is the formal leader of the New York Philharmonic.

The Follower

The follower is not a passive player in the leadership process. Edwin Hollander, after many years of studying leadership, suggested that the follower is the most critical factor in any leadership event.[13] It is, after all, the follower who perceives the situation and comes to define the needs that the leader must fulfill. In addition, it is the follower who either rejects leadership or accepts acts of leadership by surrendering his power to the leader to diminish task uncertainty, to define and manage the meaning of the situation to the follower, and to orchestrate the follower's action in pursuit of goal attainment.

The follower's personality and readiness to follow determine the style of leadership that will be most effective. For example, individuals with an internal locus of control are much more responsive to participative styles of leadership than individuals with an external locus of control.[14] Individuals with an authoritarian personality are highly receptive to the effectiveness of directive acts of leadership.[15] It is the followers' expectations, as well as their performance-based needs, that determine what a leader must do in order to be effective.

The strength of the follower's self-concept has also been linked to the leadership process. High-self-esteem individuals tend to have a strong sense of self-efficacy, that is, a generalized belief they can be successful in difficult situations. They therefore tend to be strongly motivated to perform and persist in the face of adversity.[16] The high-self-esteem follower tends to be responsive to participative styles of leadership. Low-self-esteem individuals, who doubt their competence and worthiness and their ability to succeed in difficult situations, function better with supportive forms of leadership. This helps them deal with the stress, frustration, and anxiety that often emerge with difficult tasks. Followers without a readiness to follow, limited by their inability to perform and lack of motivation and commitment, usually need more directive forms of leadership.[17]

Follower behavior plays a major role in determining what behaviors leaders engage in. For example, followers who perform at high levels tend to cause their leaders to be considerate in their treatment and to play a less directive role. Followers who are poor performers, on the other hand, tend to cause their leaders to be less warm toward them and to be more directive and controlling in their leadership style.[18]

The Context

Situations make demands on a group and its members, and not all situations are the same. Context refers to the situation that surrounds the leader and the followers. Situations are multidimensional. We discuss the context as it pertains to leadership in greater detail later in this chapter, but for now let's look at it in terms of the task and task environment that confront the group. Is the task structured or unstructured? Are the goals of the group clear or ambiguous? Is there agreement or disagreement about goals? Is there a body of knowledge that can guide task performance? Is the task boring? Frustrating? Intrinsically satisfying? Is the environment complex or simple, stable or unstable? These factors create different contexts within which leadership unfolds, and each factor places a different set of needs and demands on the leader and on the followers.

The Process

The process of leadership is separate and distinct from the leader (the person who occupies a central role in the group). The process is a complex, interactive, and dynamic working relationship between leader and followers. This working relationship, built over time, is directed toward fulfilling the group's maintenance and task needs. Part of the process consists of an exchange relationship between the leader and follower. The leader provides a resource directed toward fulfilling the group's needs, and the group gives compliance, recognition, and esteem to the leader. To the extent that leadership is the exercise of influence, part of the leadership process is captured by the surrender of power by the followers and the exercise of influence over the followers by the leader.[19] Thus, the leader influences the followers and the followers influence the leader, the context influences the leader and the followers, and both leader and followers influence the context.

The Consequences

A number of outcomes or consequences of the leadership process unfold between leader, follower, and situation. At the group level, two outcomes are important:

- Have the group's maintenance needs been fulfilled? That is, do members of the group like and get along with one another, do they have a shared set of norms and values, and have they developed a good working relationship? Have individuals' needs been fulfilled as reflected in attendance, motivation, performance, satisfaction, citizenship, trust, and maintenance of the group membership?
- Have the group's task needs been met? That is, there are also important consequences of the leadership process for individuals: attendance, motivation, performance, satisfaction, citizenship, trust, and maintenance of their group membership.

The leader-member exchange (LMX) theory of the leadership process focuses attention on consequences associated with the leadership process. The theory views leadership as consisting of a number of dyadic relationships linking the leader with a follower. A leader-follower relationship tends to develop quickly and remains relatively stable over time. The quality of the relationship is reflected by the degree of mutual trust, loyalty, support, respect, and obligation. High- and low-quality relationships between a leader and each of his followers produce in and out groups among the followers. Members of the in group come to be key players, and high-quality exchange relationships tend to be associated with higher levels of performance, commitment, and satisfaction than are low-quality exchange relationships.[20] Attitudinal similarity and extroversion appear to be associated with a high-quality leader-member relationship.[21]

The nature of the leadership process varies substantially depending on the leader, the followers, and the situation and context. Thus, leadership is the function of an interaction between the leader, the follower, and the context.

The leadership context for the leader of a group of assembly line production workers differs from the context for the leader of a self-managing production team and from the context confronted by the lead scientists in a research laboratory. The leadership tactics that work in the first context might fail miserably in the latter two.

CATCHING THE ENTREPRENEURIAL SPIRIT

How a Start-Up Finds the Right Leader

Start-ups, by their very nature, require innovation to bring new products and services to market. Along with establishing a new brand or product, the leader has to develop the relationships and processes that make a company succeed, or risk its early demise. While leading an established firm has its challenges, a start-up requires even more from a leader.

How critical is leadership to a start-up? Ask the four cofounders of the now-defunct PYP (Pretty Young

Professionals), a website founded as a source of information for young professional women. What began as four young professional women working on a new start-up ended with hurt feelings and threats of legal action. In 2010, Kathryn Minshew, Amanda Pouchot, Caroline Ghosn, and Alex Cavoulacos decided to create the website and Minshew was named CEO (Cohan 2011a). Lines blurred about Minshew's authority and the ultimate look, feel, and direction of the website. Ideals about shared leadership, where the company was going, and how it was going to get there ultimately got lost in the power shuffle. By June 2011, passwords were changed and legal actions began, and in August Minshew and Cavoulacos left altogether (Cohan 2011b).

When the legal haggling from PYP was over, Alex Cavoulacos and Kathryn Minshew, joined by Melissa McCreery, tried again. But this time, rather than hoping for the best, they put a leadership plan in place. Minshew was named CEO of the new start-up, The Daily Muse, with Cavoulacos as chief operating officer and McCreery as editor in chief. Rather than trusting to luck, the three cofounders based their team positions on strengths and personalities. Cavoulacos and McCreery agreed that Minshew's outgoing personality and confidence made her the proper choice as CEO (Casserly 2013).

No single trait will guarantee that a person can lead a start-up from idea to greatness, but a survey of successful entrepreneurs does show some common traits. According to David Barbash, a partner at Boston-based law firm Posternak Blankstein & Lund LLP, personality is paramount: "You can have great technology but if you're not a great communicator it may die in the lab" (Casserly 2013 n.p.). A start-up needs a leader who is confident and willing, if not eager, to face the future. According to Michelle Randall, a principal of Enriching Leadership International, start-up CEOs have to be willing to fundraise and not be too proud to beg (Casserly 2013). Peter Shankman, an entrepreneur and angel investor, says leaders have to be willing to make the hard decisions, even risking being the bad guy (Casserly 2013).

Gary Vaynerchuk credits his success to six factors. Angel investor, social media marketer, and early social media adopter, Vaynerchuk leveraged YouTube in its early years to market wine from the family's liquor store, eventually increasing sales from $3 million to $60 million a year (Clifford 2017). Gary believes good leaders recognize that they don't dictate to the market, but rather respond to where it is going. They have respect for and believe in other people, and have a strong work ethic, what Vaynerchuk called a "lunch pail work ethic": they are willing to put in long hours because they love the work, not the perks. He also stresses that he loves technology and doesn't fear it, is obsessed with the youth of today, and is optimistic about people and the future of humanity (Vaynerchuk 2017).

Leading a startup requires more than simple management. It requires the right leader for the right company at the right time, which means matching the right management skills with the proper flexibility and drive to keep it all together and moving in the right direction.

Sources:

Casserly, Meghan. 2013. "Rocks, Paper, CEO: Finding The Best Leader For Your Startup." *Forbes*. https://www.forbes.com/sites/meghancasserly/2013/01/15/rocks-paper-ceo-finding-the-best-leader-for-your-startup/#16b520cd20a5

Clifford, Catherine. 2017. "Self-made millionaire Gary Vaynerchuk: This is the real secret to success." CNBC. https://www.cnbc.com/2017/03/13/self-made-millionaire-gary-vaynerchuk-shares-real-secret-to-success.html

Cohan, Peter. 2011a. "A Cautionary Tale: Friendship, Business Ethics, and Bad Breakups (Acts I and II). *Forbes*. August 9, 2011. https://www.forbes.com/sites/petercohan/2011/08/09/a-cautionary-tale-friendship-business-ethics-and-bad-breakups-acts-i-and-ii/#256d318b2735

Cohan, Peter. 2011b. "A Cautionary Tale: Friendship, Business Ethics, and Bad Breakups (Acts III and IV). *Forbes*. August 9, 2011. https://www.forbes.com/sites/petercohan/2011/08/09/a-cautionary-tale-friendship-business-ethics-and-bad-breakups-acts-iii-and-iv/3/#66b22dd4a4f6

Vaynerchuk, Gary. 2017. "What Makes Me a Great CEO." https://www.garyvaynerchuk.com/makes-great-ceo/

1. Why would start-up leaders need different leadership qualities than someone managing an established firm?
2. Vaynerchuk has been quoted as saying that if you live for Friday, get a different job. How does this apply to successful entrepreneurs?

CONCEPT CHECK

1. What are the processes associated with people coming to leadership positions?

13.3 | Types of Leaders and Leader Emergence

3. How do leaders influence and move their followers to action?

Leaders hold a unique position in their groups, exercising influence and providing direction. Leonard Bernstein was part of the symphony, but his role as the New York Philharmonic conductor differed dramatically from that of the other symphony members. Besides conducting the orchestra, he created a vision for the symphony. In this capacity, leadership can be seen as a differentiated role and the nucleus of group activity.

Organizations have two kinds of leaders: formal and informal. A **formal leader** is that individual who is recognized by those outside the group as the official leader of the group. Often, the formal leader is appointed by the organization to serve in a formal capacity as an agent of the organization. Jack Welch was the formal leader of General Electric, and Leonard Bernstein was the formal leader of the symphony. Practically all managers act as formal leaders as part of their assigned role. Organizations that use self-managed work teams allow members of the team to select the individual who will serve as their team leader. When this person's role is sanctioned by the formal organization, these team leaders become formal leaders. Increasingly, leaders in organizations will be those who "best sell" their ideas on how to complete a project—persuasiveness and inspiration are important ingredients in the leadership equation, especially in high-involvement organizations.[22]

Informal leaders, by contrast, are not assigned by the organization. The **informal leader** is that individual whom members of the group acknowledge as their leader. Athletic teams often have informal leaders, individuals who exert considerable influence on team members even though they hold no official, formal leadership position. In fact, most work groups contain at least one informal leader. Just like formal leaders, informal leaders can benefit or harm an organization depending on whether their influence encourages group members to behave consistently with organizational goals.

As we have noted, the terms *leader* and *manager* are not synonymous. Grace Hopper, retired U.S. Navy admiral, draws a distinction between leading and managing: "You don't manage people, you manage *things*. You lead *people*."[23] Informal leaders often have considerable leverage over their colleagues. Traditionally, the roles of informal leaders have not included the total set of management responsibilities because an informal leader does not always exercise the functions of planning, organizing, directing, and controlling. However, high-involvement organizations frequently encourage their formal and informal leaders to exercise the full set of management roles. Many consider such actions necessary for self-managing work teams to succeed. Informal leaders are acknowledged by the group, and the group willingly responds to their leadership.

Paths to Leadership

People come to leadership positions through two dynamics. In many instances, people are put into positions of leadership by forces outside the group. University-based ROTC programs and military academies (like West Point) formally groom people to be leaders. We refer to this person as the **designated leader** (in this instance the designated and formal leader are the same person). **Emergent leaders**, on the other hand, arise from the dynamics and processes that unfold within and among a group of individuals as they endeavor to achieve a collective goal.

A variety of processes help us understand how leaders emerge. Gerald Salancik and Jeffrey Pfeffer observe that power to influence others flows to those individuals who possess the critical and scarce resources (often knowledge and expertise) that a group needs to overcome a major problem.[24] They note that the dominant coalition and leadership in American corporations during the 1950s was among engineers, because organizations were engaged in competition based on product design. The power base in many organizations shifted to marketing as competition became a game of advertising aimed at differentiating products in the consumer's mind. About 10–15 years ago, power and leadership once again shifted, this time to people with finance and legal backgrounds, because the critical contingencies facing many organizations were mergers, acquisitions, hostile takeovers, and creative financing. Thus, Salancik and Pfeffer reason that power and thus leadership flow to those individuals who have the ability to help an organization or group [overcome its critical contingencies]. As the challenges facing a group change, so too may the flow of power and leadership.

Many leaders emerge out of the needs of the situation. Different situations call for different configurations of knowledge, skills, and abilities. A group often turns to the member who possesses the knowledge, skills, and abilities that the group requires to achieve its goals.[25] People surrender their power to individuals whom they believe will make meaningful contributions to attaining group goals.[26] The individual to whom power is surrendered is often a member of the group who is in good standing. As a result of this member's contributions to the group's goals, he has accumulated *idiosyncrasy credits* (a form of competency-based status). These credits give the individual a status that allows him to influence the direction that the group takes as it works to achieve its goals.[27]

It is important to recognize that the traits possessed by certain individuals contribute significantly to their emergence as leaders. Research indicates that people are unlikely to follow individuals who, for example, do not display drive, self-confidence, knowledge of the situation, honesty, and integrity.

Leadership as an Exercise of Influence

As we have noted, leadership is the exercise of influence over those who depend on one another for attaining a mutual goal in a group setting. But *how* do leaders effectively exercise this influence? *Social or (interpersonal) influence* is one's ability to effect a change in the motivation, attitudes, and/or behaviors of others. *Power*, then, essentially answers the "how" question: How do leaders influence their followers? The answer often is that a leader's social influence is the source of his power.

French and Raven provide us with a useful typology that identifies the sources and types of power that may be at the disposal of leaders:

- *Reward power*—the power a person has because people believe that he can bestow rewards or outcomes, such as money or recognition that others desire
- *Coercive power*—the power a person has because people believe that he can punish them by inflicting pain or by withholding or taking away something that they value
- *Referent power*—the power a person has because others want to associate with or be accepted by him
- *Expert power*—the power a person has because others believe that he has and is willing to share expert knowledge that they need (The concept of *resource power* extends the idea of expert power to include the power that a person has because others believe that he possesses and is willing to share resources, such as information, time, or materials that are needed.)
- *Legitimate power*—the power a person has because others believe that he possesses the "right" to influence them and that they ought to obey. This right can originate in tradition; in the charisma or appeal of the person; and in laws, institutional roles within society, moralistic appeal, and rationality (that is, logical arguments, factual evidence, reason, and internally consistent positions).[28]

Not all forms of power are equally effective (see **Exhibit 13.5**), nor is a leader's total power base the simple sum of the powers at his disposal. Different types of power elicit different forms of compliance: Leaders who rely on coercive power often alienate followers who resist their influence attempts. Leaders who rely on reward power develop followers who are very measured in their responses to [what?]; the use of rewards often leads people to think in terms of "How much am I getting?" or "How much should I give?" or "Am I breaking even?" The use of referent power produces identification with the leader and his cause. The use of rationality, expert power, and/or moralistic appeal generally elicits commitment and the internalization of the leader's goals.[29]

Exhibit 13.5   The Leader-Follower Power Relationship

Leaders who use referent and expert power commonly experience a favorable response in terms of follower satisfaction and performance. Research suggests that rationality is the most effective influence tactic in terms of its impact on follower commitment, motivation, performance, satisfaction, and group effectiveness.[30]

Reward and legitimate power (that is, relying on one's position to influence others) produce inconsistent results. Sometimes these powers lead to follower performance and satisfaction, yet they also sometimes fail. Coercive power can result in favorable performance, yet follower and resistance dissatisfaction are not uncommon.

Good leaders, whether formal or informal, develop many sources of power. Leaders who rely solely on their legitimate power and authority seldom generate the influence necessary to help their organization and its members succeed. In the process of building their power base, effective leaders have discovered that the use of coercive power tends to dilute the effectiveness of other powers, while the development and use of referent power tends to magnify the effectiveness of other forms of power. A compliment or reward from a person we like generally has greater value than one from someone we dislike, and punishment from someone we love (such as "tough love" from a parent) is less offensive than the pain inflicted by someone we dislike.[31]

In sum, one key to effective leadership, especially as it pertains to the exercise of social and interpersonal influence, relates to the type of power employed by the leader. Overall leader effectiveness will be higher when people follow because they want to follow. This is much more likely to happen when the leader's influence flows out of intrinsic such as rationality, expertise, moralistic appeal, and/or referent power.

Leadership is also about having a vision and communicating that vision to others in such a way that it provides meaning for the follower.[32] Language, ritual, drama, myths, symbolic constructions, and stories are some of the tools leaders use to capture the attention of their "followers to be" to evoke emotion and to manage the meaning "of the task (challenges) facing the group."[33] These tools help the leader influence the attitudes, motivation, and behavior of their followers.

Influence-Based Leadership Styles

Many writers and researchers have explored how leaders can use power to address the needs of various situations. One view holds that in traditional organizations members expect to be told what to do and are willing to follow highly structured directions. Individuals attracted to high-involvement organizations, however, want to make their own decisions, expect their leaders to allow them to do so, and are willing to accept and act on this responsibility. This suggests that a leader may use and employ power in a variety of ways.

The Tannenbaum and Schmidt Continuum

In the 1950s, Tannenbaum and Schmidt created a continuum (see **Exhibit 13.6**) along which leadership styles range from authoritarian to extremely high levels of worker freedom.[34] Subsequent to Tannenbaum and Schmidt's work, researchers adapted the continuum by categorizing leader power styles as *autocratic* (boss-centered), *participative* (workers are consulted and involved), or *free-rein* (members are assigned the work and decide on their own how to do it; the leader relinquishes the active assumption of the role of leadership).[35]

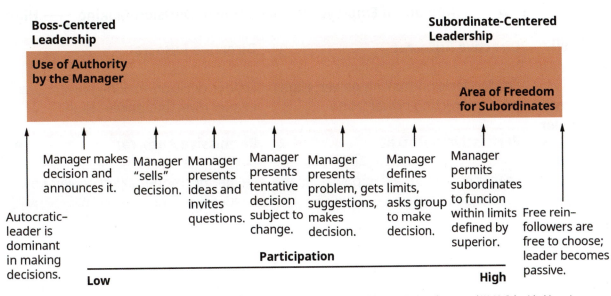

Exhibit 13.6   Tannenbaum and Schmidt's Leadership Continuum   *Source:* Modified from R. Tannenbaum and W. H. Schmidt. May—June 1971. How to choose a leadership pattern. *Harvard Business Review*, 167.

Theory X and Theory Y Leaders

McGregor's Theory X and Theory Y posits two different sets of attitudes about the individual as an organizational member.[36] Theory X and Y thinking gives rise to two different styles of leadership. The *Theory X leader* assumes that the average individual dislikes work and is incapable of exercising adequate self-direction and self-control. As a consequence, they exert a highly controlling leadership style. In contrast, *Theory Y leaders* believe that people have creative capacities, as well as both the ability and desire to exercise self-direction and self-control. They typically allow organizational members significant amounts of discretion in their jobs and encourage them to participate in departmental and organizational decision-making. Theory Y leaders are much more likely to adopt involvement-oriented approaches to leadership and organically designed organizations for their leadership group.

Theory X and Theory Y thinking and leadership are not strictly an American phenomenon. Evidence suggests that managers from different parts of the global community commonly hold the same view. A study of 3,600 managers from 14 countries reveals that most of them held assumptions about human nature that could best be classified as Theory X.[37] Even though managers might publicly endorse the merits of participatory management, most of them doubted their workers' capacities to exercise self-direction and self-control and to contribute creatively.[38]

Directive/Permissive Leadership Styles

Contemplating the central role of problem-solving in management and leadership, Jan P. Muczyk and Bernard C. Reimann of Cleveland State University offer an interesting perspective on four different leadership styles (see **Exhibit 13.7**) that revolve around decision-making and implementation processes.[39]

Exhibit 13.7   Leadership Behavior and the Uses of Power *Source:* Modified from J. P. Muczyk and B. C. Reimann. 1987. The case for directive leadership. *Academy of Management Executive*, 1:304.

A *directive autocrat* retains power, makes unilateral decisions, and closely supervises workers' activities. This style of leadership is seen as appropriate when circumstances require quick decisions and organizational members are new, inexperienced, or underqualified. A doctor in charge of a hastily constructed shelter for victims of a tornado may use this style to command nonmedical volunteers.

The *permissive autocrat* mixes his or her use of power by retaining decision-making power but permitting organizational members to exercise discretion when executing those decisions. This leader behavior is recommended when decision-making time is limited, when tasks are routine, or when organizational members have sufficient expertise to determine appropriate role behaviors.

Also sharing power is the *directive democrat,* who encourages participative decision-making but retains the power to direct team members in the execution of their roles. This style is appropriate when followers have valuable opinions and ideas, but one person needs to coordinate the execution of the ideas. A surgeon might allow the entire surgical team to participate in developing a plan for a surgical procedure. Once surgery begins, however, the surgeon is completely in charge.

Finally, the *permissive democrat* shares power with group members, soliciting involvement in both decision-making and execution. This style is appropriate when participation has both informational and motivational value, when time permits group decision-making, when group members are capable of improving decision quality, and when followers are capable of exercising self-management in their performance of work.

The permissive democratic approach to leadership is characteristic of leadership in high-involvement organizations. Here, leaders act as facilitators, process consultants, network builders, conflict managers, inspirationalists, coaches, teachers/mentors, and cheerleaders.[40] Such is the role of Ralph Stayer, founder, owner, and CEO of Johnsonville Foods. He defines himself as his company's philosopher. At Quad/Graphics, president Harry V. Quadracci is a permissive democrat because he encourages all Quad employees to play a major role in decision-making and execution as they manage their teams as independent profit centers.

Exhibit 13.8   Jeff Bezos Jeff Bezos, founder and CEO of Amazon, used to bring an empty chair to meetings to signal and remind participants of the most important people that did not have a seat at the table: the customers. He has now replaced the empty chair with Amazon employees with the job title Customer Experience Bar Raisers.

CONCEPT CHECK

1. What is the role of the leader and follower in the leadership process?
2. How do the theories of Tannenbaum and Schmidt's leadership continuum and McGregor's Theory X and Theory Y attempt to define leadership?

13.4 | The Trait Approach to Leadership

4. What are the trait perspectives on leadership?

Ancient Greek, Roman, Egyptian, and Chinese scholars were keenly interested in leaders and leadership. Their writings portray leaders as heroes. Homer, in his poem *The Odyssey*, portrays Odysseus during and after the Trojan War as a great leader who had vision and self-confidence. His son Telemachus, under the tutelage of Mentor, developed his father's courage and leadership skills.[41] Out of such stories there emerged the "great man" theory of leadership, and a starting point for the contemporary study of leadership.

The **great man theory of leadership** states that some people are born with the necessary attributes to be great leaders. Alexander the Great, Julius Caesar, Joan of Arc, Catherine the Great, Napoleon, and Mahatma Gandhi are cited as naturally great leaders, born with a set of personal qualities that made them effective leaders. Even today, the belief that truly great leaders are born is common. For example, Kenneth Labich, writer for *Fortune* magazine, commented that "the best leaders seem to possess a God-given spark."[42]

During the early 1900s, scholars endeavored to understand leaders and leadership. They wanted to know, from an organizational perspective, what characteristics leaders hold in common in the hope that people with these characteristics could be identified, recruited, and placed in key organizational positions. This gave rise to early research efforts and to what is referred to as the *trait approach to leadership.* Prompted by the great man theory of leadership and the emerging interest in understanding what leadership is, researchers focused on the leader—Who is a leader? What are the distinguishing characteristics of the great and effective leaders? The great man theory of leadership holds that some people are born with a set of personal qualities that make truly great leaders. Mahatma Gandhi is often cited as a naturally great leader.

Leader Trait Research

Ralph Stogdill, while on the faculty at The Ohio State University, pioneered our modern (late 20th century) study of leadership.[43] Scholars taking the trait approach attempted to identify physiological (appearance, height, and weight), demographic (age, education, and socioeconomic background), personality (dominance, self-confidence, and aggressiveness), intellective (intelligence, decisiveness, judgment, and knowledge), task-related (achievement drive, initiative, and persistence), and social characteristics (sociability and cooperativeness) with leader emergence and leader effectiveness. After reviewing several hundred studies of leader traits, Stogdill in 1974 described the successful leader this way:

The [successful] leader is characterized by a strong drive for responsibility and task completion, vigor and persistence in pursuit of goals, venturesomeness and originality in problem solving, drive to exercise initiative in social situations, self-confidence and sense of personal identity, willingness to accept consequences of decision and action, readiness to absorb interpersonal stress, willingness to tolerate frustration and delay, ability to influence other person's behavior, and capacity to structure social interaction systems to the purpose at hand.[44]

The last three decades of the 20th century witnessed continued exploration of the relationship between traits and both leader emergence and leader effectiveness. Edwin Locke from the University of Maryland and a number of his research associates, in their recent review of the trait research, observed that successful leaders possess a set of core characteristics that are different from those of other people.[45] Although these core traits do not solely determine whether a person will be a leader—or a successful leader—they are seen as preconditions that endow people with leadership potential. Among the core traits identified are:

- *Drive*—a high level of effort, including a strong desire for achievement as well as high levels of ambition, energy, tenacity, and initiative
- *Leadership motivation*—an intense desire to lead others
- *Honesty and integrity*—a commitment to the truth (nondeceit), where word and deed correspond
- *Self-confidence*—an assurance in one's self, one's ideas, and one's ability
- *Cognitive ability*—conceptually skilled, capable of exercising good judgment, having strong analytical abilities, possessing the capacity to think strategically and multidimensionally
- *Knowledge of the business*—a high degree of understanding of the company, industry, and technical matters
- *Other traits*—charisma, creativity/originality, and flexibility/adaptiveness[46]

While leaders may be "people with the right stuff," effective leadership requires more than simply possessing the correct set of motives and traits. Knowledge, skills, ability, vision, strategy, and effective vision implementation are all necessary for the person who has the "right stuff" to realize their leadership potential.[47] According to Locke, people endowed with these traits engage in behaviors that are associated with leadership. As followers, people are attracted to and inclined to follow individuals who display, for example, honesty and integrity, self-confidence, and the motivation to lead.

Personality psychologists remind us that behavior is a result of an interaction between the person and the situation—that is, Behavior = f [(Person) (Situation)]. To this, psychologist Walter Mischel adds the important observation that personality tends to get expressed through an individual's behavior in "weak" situations and to be suppressed in "strong" situations.[48] A strong situation is one with strong behavioral norms and rules, strong incentives, clear expectations, and rewards for a particular behavior. Our characterization of the mechanistic organization with its well-defined hierarchy of authority, jobs, and standard operating procedures exemplifies a strong situation. The organic social system exemplifies a weak situation. From a leadership perspective, a person's traits play a stronger role in their leader behavior and ultimately leader effectiveness when the situation permits the expression of their disposition. Thus, personality traits prominently shape leader behavior in weak situations.

Finally, about the validity of the "great person approach to leadership": Evidence accumulated to date does not provide a strong base of support for the notion that leaders are born. Yet, the study of twins at the University of Minnesota leaves open the possibility that part of the answer might be found in our genes. Many personality traits and vocational interests (which might be related to one's interest in assuming responsibility for others and the motivation to lead) have been found to be related to our "genetic dispositions" as well as to our life experiences.[49] Each core trait recently identified by Locke and his associates traces a significant part of its existence to life experiences. Thus, a person is not born with self-confidence. Self-confidence is developed, honesty and integrity are a matter of personal choice, motivation to lead comes from within the individual and is within his control, and knowledge of the business can be acquired. While cognitive ability does in part find its origin in the genes, it still needs to be developed. Finally, drive, as a dispositional trait, may also have a genetic component, but it too can be self- and other-encouraged. It goes without saying that none of these ingredients are acquired overnight.

Other Leader Traits

Sex and gender, disposition, and self-monitoring also play an important role in leader emergence and leader style.

Sex and Gender Role

Much research has gone into understanding the role of sex and gender in leadership.[50] Two major avenues have been explored: sex and gender roles in relation to leader emergence, and whether style differences exist across the sexes.

Evidence supports the observation that men emerge as leaders more frequently than women.[51] Throughout history, few women have been in positions where they could develop or exercise leadership behaviors. In contemporary society, being perceived as experts appears to play an important role in the emergence of women as leaders. Yet, gender role is more predictive than sex. Individuals with "masculine" (for example, assertive, aggressive, competitive, willing to take a stand) as opposed to "feminine" (cheerful, affectionate, sympathetic, gentle) characteristics are more likely to emerge in leadership roles.[52] In our society males are frequently socialized to possess the masculine characteristics, while females are more frequently socialized to possess the feminine characteristics.

Recent evidence, however, suggests that individuals who are androgynous (that is, who simultaneously possess both masculine and feminine characteristics) are as likely to emerge in leadership roles as individuals with only masculine characteristics. This suggests that possessing feminine qualities does not distract from the attractiveness of the individual as a leader.[53]

With regard to leadership style, researchers have looked to see if male-female differences exist in task and interpersonal styles, and whether or not differences exist in how autocratic or democratic men and women are. The answer is, when it comes to interpersonal versus task orientation, differences between men and women appear to be marginal. Women are somewhat more concerned with meeting the group's interpersonal needs, while men are somewhat more concerned with meeting the group's task needs. Big differences emerge in terms of democratic versus autocratic leadership styles. Men tend to be more autocratic or directive, while women are more likely to adopt a more democratic/participative leadership style.[54] In fact, it may be because men are more directive that they are seen as key to goal attainment and they are turned to more often as leaders.[55]

Dispositional Trait

Psychologists often use the terms *disposition* and *mood* to describe and differentiate people. Individuals characterized by a positive affective state exhibit a mood that is active, strong, excited, enthusiastic, peppy, and elated. A leader with this mood state exudes an air of confidence and optimism and is seen as enjoying work-related activities.

Recent work conducted at the University of California-Berkeley demonstrates that leaders (managers) with positive affectivity (a positive mood state) tend to be more competent interpersonally, to contribute more to group activities, and to be able to function more effectively in their leadership role.[56] Their enthusiasm and high energy levels appear to be infectious, transferring from leader to followers. Thus, such leaders promote group cohesiveness and productivity. This mood state is also associated with low levels of group turnover and is positively associated with followers who engage in acts of good group citizenship.[57]

Self-Monitoring

Self-monitoring as a personality trait refers to the strength of an individual's ability and willingness to read verbal and nonverbal cues and to alter one's behavior so as to manage the presentation of the self and the images that others form of the individual. "High self-monitors" are particularly astute at reading social cues and regulating their self-presentation to fit a particular situation. "Low self-monitors" are less sensitive to social cues; they may either lack motivation or lack the ability to manage how they come across to others.

Some evidence supports the position that high self-monitors emerge more often as leaders. In addition, they appear to exert more influence on group decisions and initiate more structure than low self-monitors. Perhaps high self-monitors emerge as leaders because in group interaction they are the individuals who attempt to organize the group and provide it with the structure needed to move the group toward goal attainment.[58]

CONCEPT CHECK

1. What are the trait perspectives on leadership?

13.5 | Behavioral Approaches to Leadership

5. What are the behavioral perspectives on leadership?

The nearly four decades of research that focused on identifying the personal traits associated with the emergence of leaders and leader effectiveness resulted in two observations. First, leader traits are important—people who are endowed with the "right stuff" (drive, self-confidence, honesty, and integrity) are more likely to emerge as leaders and to be effective leaders than individuals who do not possess these characteristics. Second, traits are only a part of the story. Traits only account for part of why someone becomes a leader and why they are (or are not) effective leaders.

Still under the influence of the great man theory of leadership, researchers continued to focus on the leader in an effort to understand leadership—who emerges and what constitutes effective leadership. Researchers then began to reason that maybe the rest of the story could be understood by looking at what it is that leaders *do*. Thus, we now turn our attention to leader behaviors and the behavioral approaches to leadership.

It is now common to think of effective leadership in terms of what leaders do. CEOs and management consultants agree that effective leaders display trust in their employees, develop a vision, keep their cool, encourage risk, bring expertise into the work setting, invite dissent, and focus everyone's attention on that which is important.[59] William Arruda, in a *Fortune* article, noted that "organizations with strong coaching cultures report their revenue to be above average, compared to their peer group." Sixty-five percent of employees "from strong coaching cultures rated themselves as highly engaged," compared to 13 percent of employees worldwide."[60] Jonathan Anthony calls himself an intrapreneur and corporate disorganizer, because same-old, same-old comms practices are dying in front of our eyes.[61] Apple founder Steve Jobs believed that the best leaders are coaches and team cheerleaders. Similar views have been frequently echoed by management consultant Tom Peters.

During the late 1940s, two major research programs—The Ohio State University and the University of Michigan leadership studies—were launched to explore leadership from a behavioral perspective.

The Ohio State University Studies

A group of Ohio State University researchers, under the direction of Ralph Stogdill, began an extensive and systematic series of studies to identify leader behaviors associated with effective group performance. Their results identified two major sets of leader behaviors: consideration and initiating structure.

Consideration is the "relationship-oriented" behavior of a leader. It is instrumental in creating and maintaining good relationships (that is, addressing the group's maintenance needs) with organizational members. Consideration behaviors include being supportive and friendly, representing people's interests, communicating openly with group members, recognizing them, respecting their ideas, and sharing concern for their feelings.

Initiating structure involves "task-oriented" leader behaviors. It is instrumental in the efficient use of resources to attain organizational goals, thereby addressing the group's task needs. Initiating structure behaviors include scheduling work, deciding what is to be done (and how and when to do it), providing direction to organizational members, planning, coordinating, problem-solving, maintaining standards of performance, and encouraging the use of uniform procedures.

After consideration and initiating structure behaviors were first identified, many leaders believed that they had to behave one way or the other. If they initiated structure, they could not be considerate, and vice versa. It did not take long, however, to recognize that leaders can simultaneously display any combination of both behaviors.

The Ohio State studies are important because they identified two critical categories of behavior that distinguish one leader from another. Both consideration and initiating structure behavior can significantly impact work attitudes and behaviors. Unfortunately, the effects of consideration and initiating structure are not consistent from situation to situation.[62] In some of the organizations studied, for example, high levels of initiating structure increased performance. In other organizations, the amount of initiating structure seemed to make little difference. Although most organizational members reported greater satisfaction when leaders acted considerately, consideration behavior appeared to have no clear effect on performance.

Initially, these mixed findings were disappointing to researchers and managers alike. It had been hoped that a profile of the most effective leader behaviors could be identified so that leaders could be trained in the best ways to behave. Research made clear, however, that there is no one best style of leader behavior for all situations.

The University of Michigan Studies

At about the same time that the Ohio State studies were underway, researchers at the University of Michigan also began to investigate leader behaviors. As at Ohio State, the Michigan researchers attempted to identify behavioral elements that differentiated effective from ineffective leaders.[63]

The two types of leader behavior that stand out in these studies are job centered and organizational member centered. *Job-centered behaviors* are devoted to supervisory functions, such as planning, scheduling, coordinating work activities, and providing the resources needed for task performance. *Employee-member-centered* behaviors include consideration and support for organizational members. These dimensions of behavior, of course, correspond closely to the dimensions of initiating structure and consideration identified at Ohio State. The similarity of the findings from two independent groups of researchers added to their credibility. As the Ohio State researchers had done, the Michigan researchers also found that any combination of the two behaviors was possible.

The studies at Michigan are significant because they reinforce the importance of leader behavior. They also provide the basis for later theories that identify specific, effective matches of work situations and leader behaviors. Subsequent research at Michigan and elsewhere has found additional behaviors associated with effective leadership: support, work facilitation, goal emphasis, and interaction facilitation.[64]

These four behaviors are important to the successful functioning of the group in that support and interaction facilitation contribute to the group's maintenance needs, and goal emphasis and work facilitation contribute to the group's task needs. The Michigan researchers also found that these four behaviors do not need to be brought to the group by the leader. In essence, the leader's real job is to set the tone and create the climate that ensure these critical behaviors are present.[65]

The Leadership Grid®

Much of the credit for disseminating knowledge about important leader behaviors must go to Robert R. Blake and Jane S. Mouton, who developed a method for classifying styles of leadership compatible with many of the ideas from the Ohio State and Michigan studies.[66] In their classification scheme, *concern for results* (production) emphasizes output, cost effectiveness, and (in for-profit organizations) a concern for profits. *Concern for people* involves promoting working relationships and paying attention to issues of importance to group members. As shown in **Exhibit 13.9**, the Leadership Grid® demonstrates that any combination of these two leader concerns is possible, and five styles of leadership are highlighted here.

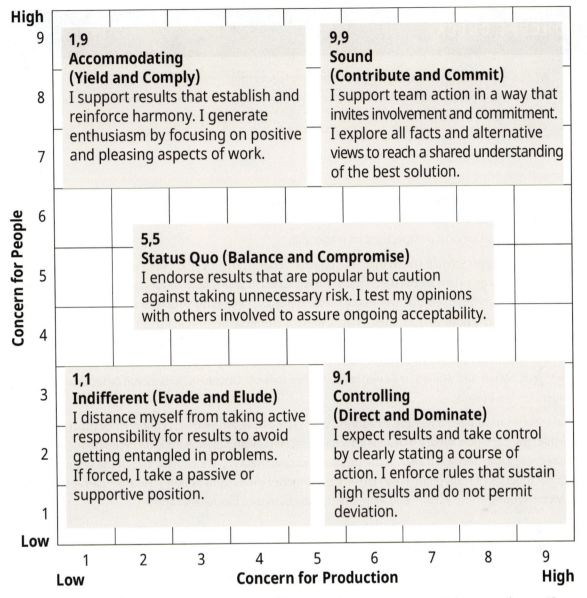

High
9

1,9
Accommodating
(Yield and Comply)
I support results that establish and reinforce harmony. I generate enthusiasm by focusing on positive and pleasing aspects of work.

9,9
Sound
(Contribute and Commit)
I support team action in a way that invites involvement and commitment. I explore all facts and alternative views to reach a shared understanding of the best solution.

5,5
Status Quo (Balance and Compromise)
I endorse results that are popular but caution against taking unnecessary risk. I test my opinions with others involved to assure ongoing acceptability.

1,1
Indifferent (Evade and Elude)
I distance myself from taking active responsibility for results to avoid getting entangled in problems. If forced, I take a passive or supportive position.

9,1
Controlling
(Direct and Dominate)
I expect results and take control by clearly stating a course of action. I enforce rules that sustain high results and do not permit deviation.

Concern for People

Low

Low   1   2   3   4   5   6   7   8   9   High

Concern for Production

Exhibit 13.9   Blake and Mouton's Managerial Grid® *Source:* Adapted from R. McKee and B. Carlson. 1999. *The Power to Change*, p.16.

Blake and Mouton contend that the sound (contribute and commit) leader (a high concern for results and people, or 9,9) style is universally the most effective.[67] While the Leadership Grid® is appealing and well structured, research to date suggests that there is no universally effective style of leadership (9,9 or otherwise).[68] There are, however, well-identified situations in which a 9,9 style is unlikely to be effective. Organizational members of high-involvement organizations who have mastered their job duties require little production-oriented leader behavior. Likewise, there is little time for people-oriented behavior during an emergency. Finally, evidence suggests that the "high-high" style may be effective when the situation calls for high levels of initiating structure. Under these conditions, the initiation of structure is more acceptable, favorably affecting follower satisfaction and performance, when the leader is also experienced as warm, supportive, and considerate.[69]

13.6 Situational (Contingency) Approaches to Leadership

6. What are the situational perspectives on leadership?

As early as 1948, Ralph Stogdill stated that "the qualities, characteristics, and skills required in a leader are determined to a large extent by the demands of the situation in which he is to function as a leader."[70] In addition, it had been observed that two major leader behaviors, initiating structure and consideration, didn't always lead to equally positive outcomes. That is, there are times when initiating structure results in performance increases and follower satisfaction, and there are times when the results are just the opposite. Contradictory findings such as this lead researchers to ask "Under what conditions are the results positive in nature?" and "When and why are they negative at other times?" Obviously, situational differences and key contingencies are at work.

Several theories have been advanced to address this issue. These are Fiedler's contingency theory of leadership, the path-goal theory of leader effectiveness, Hersey and Blanchard's life cycle theory, cognitive resource theory, the decision tree, and the decision process theory.[71] We explore two of the better-known situational theories of leadership, Fred Fiedler's contingency model and Robert J. House's path-goal theory, here. Victor Vroom, Phillip Yetton, and Arthur Jago's decision tree model also applies.

Fiedler's Contingency Model

One of the earliest, best-known, and most controversial situation-contingent leadership theories was set forth by Fred E. Fiedler from the University of Washington.[72] This theory is known as the **contingency theory of leadership.** According to Fiedler, organizations attempting to achieve group effectiveness through leadership must assess the leader according to an underlying trait, assess the situation faced by the leader, and construct a proper match between the two.

The Leader's Trait

Leaders are asked about their **least-preferred coworker (LPC),** the person with whom they *least* like to work. The most popular interpretation of the LPC score is that it reflects a leader's underlying disposition toward others—for example: pleasant/unpleasant, cold/warm, friendly/unfriendly, and untrustworthy/trustworthy. (You can examine your own LPC score by completing the LPC self-assessment on the following page.)

Fiedler states that leaders with high LPC scores are *relationship oriented*—they need to develop and maintain close interpersonal relationships. They tend to evaluate their least-preferred coworkers in fairly favorable terms. Task accomplishment is a secondary need to this type of leader and becomes important only after the need for relationships is reasonably well satisfied. In contrast, leaders with low LPC scores tend to evaluate the individuals with whom they least like to work fairly negatively. They are *task-oriented* people, and only after tasks have been accomplished are low-LPC leaders likely to work on establishing good social and interpersonal relations.

The Situational Factor

Some situations favor leaders more than others do. To Fiedler, *situational favorableness* is the degree to which leaders have control and influence and therefore feel that they can determine the outcomes of a group interaction.[73] Several years later, Fiedler changed his situational factor from situational favorability to situational control—where situational control essentially refers to the degree to which a leader can influence the group process.[74] Three factors work together to determine how favorable a situation is to a leader. In order of importance, they are (1) *leader-member relations*—the degree of the group's acceptance of the leader, their ability to work well together, and members' level of loyalty to the leader; (2) *task structure*—the degree to which the task specifies a detailed, unambiguous goal and how to achieve it; and (3) *position power*—a leader's direct ability to influence group members. The situation is most favorable for a leader when the relationship between the leader and group members is good, when the task is highly structured, and when the leader's position power is strong (cell 1 in **Exhibit 13.10**). The least-favorable situation occurs under poor leader-member relations, an unstructured task, and weak position power (cell 8).

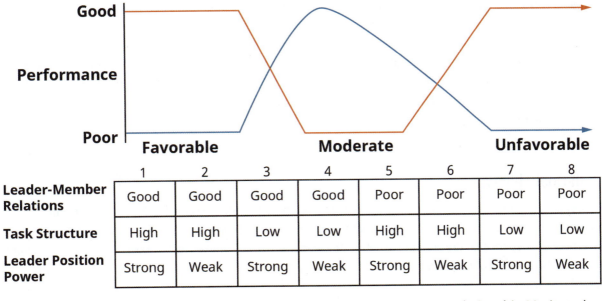

	1	2	3	4	5	6	7	8
Leader-Member Relations	Good	Good	Good	Good	Poor	Poor	Poor	Poor
Task Structure	High	High	Low	Low	High	High	Low	Low
Leader Position Power	Strong	Weak	Strong	Weak	Strong	Weak	Strong	Weak

————Task Motivated ————Relationship Motivated

Exhibit 13.10   Fiedler's Contingency Model of Leader-Situation Matches *Source:* Adapted from F. E. Fiedler and M. M. Chemers. 1974. *Leadership and effective management.* Glenview, IL: Scott, Foresman.

Leader-Situation Matches

Some combinations of leaders and situations work well; others do not. In search of the best combinations, Fiedler examined a large number of leadership situations. He argued that most leaders have a relatively unchangeable or dominant style, so organizations need to design job situations to fit the leader.[75]

While the model has not been fully tested and tests have often produced mixed or contradictory findings,[76] Fiedler's research indicates that relationship-oriented (high-LPC) leaders are much more effective under conditions of intermediate favorability than under either highly favorable or highly unfavorable situations. Fiedler attributes the success of relationship-oriented leaders in situations with intermediate favorability to the leader's nondirective, permissive attitude; a more directive attitude could lead to anxiety in followers, conflict in the group, and a lack of cooperation.

For highly favorable and unfavorable situations, task-oriented leaders (those with a low LPC) are very effective. As tasks are accomplished, a task-oriented leader allows the group to perform its highly structured tasks without imposing more task-directed behavior. The job gets done without the need for the leader's direction. Under unfavorable conditions, task-oriented behaviors, such as setting goals, detailing work methods, and guiding and controlling work behaviors, move the group toward task accomplishment.

As might be expected, leaders with mid-range LPC scores can be more effective in a wider range of situations than high- or low-LPC leaders.[77] Under conditions of low favorability, for example, a middle-LPC leader can be task oriented to achieve performance, but show consideration for and allow organizational members to proceed on their own under conditions of high situational favorability.

Controversy over the Theory

Although Fiedler's theory often identifies appropriate leader-situation matches and has received broad support, it is not without critics. Some note that it characterizes leaders through reference to their attitudes or personality traits (LPC) while it explains the leader's effectiveness through their behaviors—those with a particular trait will behave in a particular fashion. The theory fails to make the connection between the least-preferred coworker attitude and subsequent behaviors. In addition, some tests of the model have produced mixed or contradictory findings.[78] Finally, what is the true meaning of the LPC score—exactly what is being revealed by a person who sees their least-preferred coworker in positive or negative terms? Robert J. House and Ram N. Aditya recently noted that, in spite of the criticisms, there has been substantial support for Fiedler's theory.[79]

Path-Goal Theory

Robert J. House and Martin Evans, while on the faculty at the University of Toronto, developed a useful leadership theory. Like Fiedler's, it asserts that the type of leadership needed to enhance organizational effectiveness depends on the situation in which the leader is placed. Unlike Fiedler, however, House and Evans focus on the leader's observable behavior. Thus, managers can either match the situation to the leader or modify the leader's behavior to fit the situation.

The model of leadership advanced by House and Evans is called the **path-goal theory of leadership** because it suggests that an effective leader provides organizational members with a *path* to a valued *goal*. According to House, the motivational function of the leader consists of increasing personal payoffs to organizational members for work-goal attainment, and making the path to these payoffs easier to travel by clarifying it, reducing roadblocks and pitfalls, and increasing the opportunities for personal satisfaction en route.[80]

Effective leaders therefore provide rewards that are valued by organizational members. These rewards may be pay, recognition, promotions, or any other item that gives members an incentive to work hard to achieve goals. Effective leaders also give clear instructions so that ambiguities about work are reduced and followers understand how to do their jobs effectively. They provide coaching, guidance, and training so that followers can perform the task expected of them. They also remove barriers to task accomplishment, correcting shortages of materials, inoperative machinery, or interfering policies.

An Appropriate Match

According to the path-goal theory, the challenge facing leaders is basically twofold. First, they must analyze situations and identify the most appropriate leadership style. For example, experienced employees who work on a highly structured assembly line don't need a leader to spend much time telling them how to do their jobs—they already know this. The leader of an archeological expedition, though, may need to spend a great deal of time telling inexperienced laborers how to excavate and care for the relics they uncover.

Second, leaders must be flexible enough to use different leadership styles as appropriate. To be effective, leaders must engage in a wide variety of behaviors. Without an extensive repertoire of behaviors at their disposal, a leader's effectiveness is limited.[81] All team members will not, for example, have the same need for autonomy. The leadership style that motivates organizational members with strong needs for autonomy (participative leadership) is different from that which motivates and satisfies members with weaker autonomy needs (directive leadership). The degree to which leadership behavior matches situational factors will determine members' motivation, satisfaction, and performance (see **Exhibit 13.11**).[82]

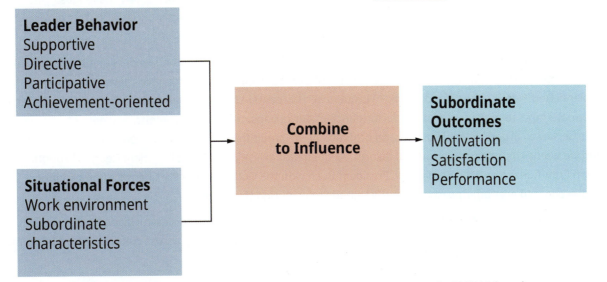

Exhibit 13.11   The Path-Goal Leadership Model (Attribution: Copyright Rice University, OpenStax, under CC-BY 4.0 license)

Behavior Dimensions

According to path-goal theory, there are four important dimensions of leader behavior, each of which is suited to a particular set of situational demands.[83]

- *Supportive leadership*—At times, effective leaders demonstrate concern for the well-being and personal needs of organizational members. Supportive leaders are friendly, approachable, and considerate to individuals in the workplace. Supportive leadership is especially effective when an organizational member is performing a boring, stressful, frustrating, tedious, or unpleasant task. If a task is difficult and a group member has low self-esteem, supportive leadership can reduce some of the person's anxiety, increase his confidence, and increase satisfaction and determination as well.
- *Directive leadership*—At times, effective leaders set goals and performance expectations, let organizational members know what is expected, provide guidance, establish rules and procedures to guide work, and schedule and coordinate the activities of members. Directive leadership is called for when role ambiguity is high. Removing uncertainty and providing needed guidance can increase members' effort, job satisfaction, and job performance.

- *Participative leadership*—At times, effective leaders consult with group members about job-related activities and consider their opinions and suggestions when making decisions. Participative leadership is effective when tasks are unstructured. Participative leadership is used to great effect when leaders need help in identifying work procedures and where followers have the expertise to provide this help.
- *Achievement-oriented leadership*—At times, effective leaders set challenging goals, seek improvement in performance, emphasize excellence, and demonstrate confidence in organizational members' ability to attain high standards. Achievement-oriented leaders thus capitalize on members' needs for achievement and use goal-setting theory to great advantage.

Cross-Cultural Context

Gabriel Bristol, the CEO of Intelifluence Live, a full-service customer contact center offering affordable inbound customer service, outbound sales, lead generation and consulting services for small to mid-sized businesses, notes "diversity breeds innovation, which helps businesses achieve goals and tackle new challenges."[84] *Multiculturalism* is a new reality as today's society and workforce become increasingly diverse. This naturally leads to the question "Is there a need for a new and different style of leadership?"

The vast majority of the contemporary scholarship directed toward understanding leaders and the leadership process has been conducted in North America and Western Europe. Westerners have "developed a highly romanticized, heroic view of leadership."[85] Leaders occupy center stage in organizational life. We use leaders in our attempts to make sense of the performance of our groups, clubs, organizations, and nations. We see them as key to organizational success and profitability, we credit them with organizational competitiveness, and we blame them for organizational failures. At the national level, recall that President Reagan brought down Communism and the Berlin Wall, President Bush won the Gulf War, and President Clinton brought unprecedented economic prosperity to the United States during the 1990s.

This larger-than-life role ascribed to leaders and the Western romance with successful leaders raise the question "How representative is our understanding of leaders and leadership across cultures?" That is, do the results that we have examined in this chapter generalize to other cultures?

Geert Hofstede points out that significant value differences (individualism-collectivism, power distance, uncertainty avoidance, masculinity-femininity, and time orientation) cut across societies. Thus, leaders of culturally diverse groups will encounter belief and value differences among their followers, as well as in their own leader-member exchanges.

There appears to be consensus that a universal approach to leadership and leader effectiveness does not exist. Cultural differences work to enhance and diminish the impact of leadership styles on group effectiveness. For example, when leaders empower their followers, the effect for job satisfaction in India has been found to be negative, while in the United States, Poland, and Mexico, the effect is positive.[86] The existing evidence suggests similarities as well as differences in such areas as the effects of leadership styles, the acceptability of influence attempts, and the closeness and formality of relationships. The distinction between task and relationship-oriented leader behavior, however, does appear to be meaningful across cultures.[87] Leaders whose behaviors reflect support, kindness, and concern for their followers are valued and effective in Western and Asian cultures. Yet it is also clear that democratic, participative, directive, and contingent-based rewards and punishment do not produce the same results across cultures. The United States is very different from Brazil, Korea, New Zealand, and Nigeria. The effective practice of leadership necessitates a careful look at, and understanding of, the individual differences brought to the leader-follower relationship by cross-cultural contexts.[88]

CONCEPT CHECK

1. Identify and describe the variables presented in Fiedler's theory of leadership.
2. What are the leadership behaviors in the path-goal theory of leadership?
3. What role does culture have in how leadership is viewed?
4. What are the differences between the trait, behavioral, and situational approaches to defining leadership?

13.7 | Substitutes for and Neutralizers of Leadership

7. What does the concept "substitute for leadership" mean?

Several factors have been discovered that can substitute for or neutralize the effects of leader behavior (see **Table 13.1**).[89] *Substitutes* for leadership behavior can clarify role expectations, motivate organizational members, or satisfy members (making it unnecessary for the leader to attempt to do so). In some cases, these substitutes supplement the behavior of a leader. Sometimes it is a group member's characteristics that make leadership less necessary, as when a master craftsperson or highly skilled worker performs up to his or her own high standards without needing outside prompting. Sometimes the task's characteristics take over, as when the work itself—solving an interesting problem or working on a familiar job—is intrinsically satisfying. Sometimes the characteristics of the organization make leadership less necessary, as when work rules are so clear and specific that workers know exactly what they must do without help from the leader (see *An Inside Look* at flat management structure and the orchestra with no leader).

Substitutes for and Neutralizers of Leader Behavior		
	Leader Behavior Influenced	
Supportive or Neutralizer	Substitute Leadership	Instrumental Leadership
A. Subordinate Characteristics:		
1. Experience, ability, training		Substitute
2. "Professional" orientation	Substitute	Substitute
3. Indifference toward rewards offered by organization	Neutralizer	Neutralizer
B. Task Characteristics:		
1. Structured, routine, unambiguous task		Substitute
2. Feedback provided by task		Substitute
3. Intrinsically satisfying task	Substitute	

Table 13.1

Substitutes for and Neutralizers of Leader Behavior		
	Leader Behavior Influenced	
Supportive or Neutralizer	Substitute Leadership	Instrumental Leadership
C. Organization Characteristics:		
1. Cohesive work group	Substitute	Substitute
2. Low position power (leader lacks control over organizational rewards)	Neutralizer	Neutralizer
3. Formalization (explicit plans, goals, areas of responsibility)		Substitute
4. Inflexibility (rigid, unyielding rules and procedures)		Neutralizer
5. Leader located apart from subordinates with only limited communication possible	Neutralizer	Neutralizer

Source: Adapted from *Leadership in organizations* by G. A. Yukl.

Table 13.1

Neutralizers of leadership, on the other hand, are not helpful; they prevent leaders from acting as they wish. A computer-paced assembly line, for example, prevents a leader from using initiating structure behavior to pace the line. A union contract that specifies that workers be paid according to seniority prevents a leader from dispensing merit-based pay. Sometimes, of course, neutralizers can be beneficial. Union contracts, for example, clarify disciplinary proceedings and identify the responsibilities of both management and labor. Leaders must be aware of the presence of neutralizers and their effects so that they can eliminate troublesome neutralizers or take advantage of any potential benefits that accompany them (such as the clarity of responsibilities provided by a union contract). If a leader's effectiveness is being neutralized by a poor communication system, for example, the leader might try to remove the neutralizer by developing (or convincing the organization to develop) a more effective system.

Followers differ considerably in their *focus of attention* while at work, thereby affecting the effectiveness of the act of leadership. Focus of attention is an employee's cognitive orientation while at work. It reflects what and how strongly an individual thinks about various objects, events, or phenomena while physically present at work. Focus of attention reflects an individual difference in that not all individuals have the same cognitive orientation while at work—some think a great deal about their job, their coworkers, their leader, or off-the-job factors, while others daydream.[90] An employee's focus of attention has both "trait" and "state" qualities. For example, there is a significant amount of minute-by-minute variation in an employee's focus of attention (the "state" component), and there is reasonable consistency in the categories of events that employees think about while they are at work (the "trait" component).

Research suggests that the more followers focus on off-job (nonleader) factors, the less they will react to the leader's behaviors. Thus, a strong focus on one's life "away from work" (for example, time with family and friends) tends to neutralize the motivational, attitudinal, and/or behavioral effects associated with any particular leader behavior. It has also been observed, however, that a strong focus on the leader, either positive or negative, enhances the impact that the leader's behaviors have on followers.[91]

MANAGERIAL LEADERSHIP

You Are Now the Leader

Leading and managing are two very different things. Being a manager means something more than gaining authority or charge over former colleagues. With the title does come the power to affect company outcomes, but it also comes with something more: the power to shape the careers and personal growth of subordinates.

According to Steve Keating, a senior manager at the Toro Company, it is important not to assume that being made a manager automatically makes you a leader. Rather, being a manager means having the *opportunity* to lead. Enterprises need managers to guide processes, but the employees—the people—need a leader. Keating believes that leaders need a mindset that emphasizes people, and the leader's job is to help the people in the organization to be successful. According to Keating, "If you don't care for people, you can't lead them" (Hakim 2017 n.p.).

For someone who has been promoted over his peers, ground rules are essential. "Promotion doesn't mean the end of friendship but it does change it," according to Keating. If a *peer* has been promoted, rather than grouse and give in to envy, it is important to step back and look at the new manager; take a hard look at why the peer was promoted and what skill or characteristic made you a less appealing fit for the position (Hakim 2017).

Carol Walker, president of Prepared to Lead, a management consulting firm, advises new managers to develop a job philosophy. She urges new managers to develop a core philosophy that provides a guide to the day-to-day job of leading. She urges managers to build up the people they are leading and work as a "servant leader." The manager's perspective should be on employee growth and success. Leaders must bear in mind that employees don't work for the manager; they work for the organization—and for themselves. Managers coordinate this relationship; they are not the center of it. Work should not be assigned haphazardly, but with the employee's skills and growth in mind. "An employee who understands why she has been asked to do something is far more likely to assume true ownership for the assignment," Walker says (Yakowicz 2015 n.p.). A leader's agenda should be on employee success, not personal glory. Employees are more receptive when they recognize that their leader is working not for their own success, but for the employee's success.

A survey from HighGround revealed one important item that most new managers and even many seasoned managers overlook: asking for feedback. Everyone has room for growth, even managers. Traditional management dictates a top-down style in which managers review subordinates. But many companies have found it beneficial to turn things around and ask employees, "How can I be a better manager?" Of course, this upward review only works if employees believe that their opinion will be heard. Managers need to carefully cultivate a rapport where employees don't fear reprisals for negative feedback. Listening to criticism from those you are leading builds trust and helps ensure that as a manager, you are providing the sort of leadership that employees need to be successful (Kauflin 2017). Showing respect and caring for employees by asking this simple question is *inspiring*—an important aspect of leadership itself. Whether asking for feedback or focusing on an employee's fit with a particular job description, a leader helps guide employees through the day-to-day, builds a positive culture, and helps employees improve their skills.

Sources

Hakim, Amy C. 2017. "When a Manager Becomes a Leader." *Psychology Today.* https://www.psychologytoday.com/blog/working-difficult-people/201706/when-manager-becomes-leader

Yakowicz, Will. 2015. "How to Help a New Manager Become a Great Leader." *Inc.* https://www.inc.com/will-yakowicz/how-new-managers-become-great-leaders.html

Kauflin, Jeff. 2017. "Every Manager Can Become A Better Leader By Asking This One Question." *Forbes.* https://www.forbes.com/sites/jeffkauflin/2017/04/21/every-manager-can-become-a-better-leader-by-asking-this-one-question/#3ca1eaff4ac1

Questions

1. What do you think are the most important qualities in a leader? In a manager? Are your two lists mutually exclusive? Why?

2. How do you think a leader can use feedback to model the growth process for employees?

CONCEPT CHECK

1. Identify and describe substitutes of leadership.

13.8 | Transformational, Visionary, and Charismatic Leadership

8. What are the characteristics of transactional, transformational, and charismatic leadership?

Many organizations struggling with the need to manage chaos, to undergo a culture change, to empower organizational members, and to restructure have looked for answers in "hiring the right leader." Many have come to believe that the transformational, visionary, and charismatic leader represents the style of leadership needed to move organizations through chaos.

The Transformational and Visionary Leader

Leaders who subscribe to the notion that "if it ain't broke, don't fix it" are often described as *transactional leaders.* They are extremely task oriented and instrumental in their approach, frequently looking for incentives that will induce their followers into a desired course of action.[92] These reciprocal exchanges take place in the context of a mutually interdependent relationship between the leader and the follower, frequently resulting in interpersonal bonding.[93] The transactional leader moves a group toward task accomplishment by initiating structure and by offering an incentive in exchange for desired behaviors. The **transformational leader**, on the other hand, moves and changes (fixes) things "in a big way"! Unlike transactional leaders, they don't cause change by offering inducements. Instead, they inspire others to action through their personal values, vision, passion, and belief in and commitment to the mission.[94] Through charisma (idealized influence), individualized consideration (a focus on the development of the follower), intellectual stimulation (questioning assumptions and challenging the status quo), and/or inspirational motivation (articulating an appealing vision), transformational leaders move others to follow.

The transformational leader is also referred to as a visionary leader. **Visionary leaders** are those who influence others through an emotional and/or intellectual attraction to the leader's dreams of what "can be." Vision links a present and future state, energizes and generates commitment, provides meaning for action, and serves as a standard against which to assess performance.[95] Evidence indicates that vision is positively related to follower attitudes and performance.[96] As pointed out by Warren Bennis, a vision is effective only to the extent that the leader can communicate it in such a way that others come to internalize it as their own.[97]

As people, transformational leaders are engaging. They are characterized by extroversion, agreeableness, and openness to experience.[98] They energize others. They increase followers' awareness of the importance of the designated outcome.[99] They motivate individuals to transcend their own self-interest for the benefit of the team and inspire organizational members to self-manage (become self-leaders).[100] Transformational leaders move people to focus on higher-order needs (self-esteem and self-actualization). When organizations face a turbulent environment, intense competition, products that may die early, and the need to move fast, managers cannot rely solely on organizational structure to guide organizational activity. In these situations, transformational leadership can motivate followers to be fully engaged and inspired, to internalize the goals and values of the organization, and to move forward with dogged determination!

Transformational leadership is positively related to follower satisfaction, performance, and acts of citizenship. These effects result from the fact that transformational leader behaviors elicit trust and perceptions of procedural justice, which in turn favorably impact follower satisfaction and performance.[101] As R. Pillai, C. Schriesheim, and E. Williams note, "when followers perceive that they can influence the outcomes of decisions that are important to them and that they are participants in an equitable relationship with their leader, their perceptions of procedural justice [and trust] are likely to be enhanced."[102] Trust and experiences of organizational justice promote leader effectiveness, follower satisfaction, motivation, performance, and citizenship behaviors.

Charismatic Leadership

Ronald Reagan, Jesse Jackson, and Queen Elizabeth I have something in common with Martin Luther King Jr., Indira Gandhi, and Winston Churchill. The effectiveness of these leaders originates in part in their **charisma**, a special magnetic charm and appeal that arouses loyalty and enthusiasm. Each exerted considerable personal influence to bring about major events.

It is difficult to differentiate the charismatic and the transformational leader. True transformational leaders may achieve their results through the magnetism of their personality. In this case, the two types of leaders are essentially one and the same, yet it is important to note that not all transformational leaders have a personal "aura."

Sociologist Max Weber evidenced an interest in charismatic leadership in the 1920s, calling **charismatic leaders** people who possess legitimate power that arises from "exceptional sanctity, heroism, or exemplary character."[103] Charismatic leaders "single-handedly" effect changes even in very large organizations. Their personality is a powerful force, and the relationship that they forge with their followers is extremely strong.

Exhibit 13.12   Travis Kalanick Travis Kalanick was a praised CEO of Uber who managed to increase the value of the company to over $60 billion. He was forced to resign after taking a leave of absence and having several key executives resign due to allegations of creating a hostile and unethical workplace.

The charismatic leadership phenomenon involves a complex interplay between the attributes of the leader and followers' needs, values, beliefs, and perceptions.[104] At its extreme, leader-follower relationships are characterized by followers' unquestioning acceptance; trust in the leader's beliefs; affection; willing obedience to, emulation of, and identification with the leader; emotional involvement with his mission; and feelings of self-efficacy directed toward the leader's mission.[105] This can work to better the welfare of individuals, such as when Lee Iacocca saved thousands of jobs through his dramatic turnaround of a failing corporate giant, the Chrysler Corporation. It also can be disastrous, as when David Koresh led dozens and dozens of men, women, and children to their fiery death in Waco, Texas. Individuals working for charismatic leaders often have higher task performance, greater task satisfaction, and lower levels of role conflict than those working for leaders with considerate or structuring behaviors.[106] What are the characteristics of these people who can exert such a strong influence over their followers? Charismatic leaders have a strong need for power and the tendency to rely heavily on referent power as their primary power base.[107] Charismatic leaders also are extremely self-confident and convinced of the rightness of their own beliefs and ideals. This self-confidence and strength of conviction make people trust the charismatic leader's judgment, unconditionally following the leader's mission and directives for action.[108] The result is a strong bond between leader and followers, a bond built primarily around the leader's personality.

Although there have been many effective charismatic leaders, those who succeed the most have coupled their charismatic capabilities with behaviors consistent with the same leadership principles followed by other effective leaders. Those who do not add these other dimensions still attract followers but do not meet organizational goals as effectively as they could. They are (at least for a time) the pied pipers of the business world, with lots of followers but no constructive direction.

ETHICS IN PRACTICE

Uber's Need for an Ethical Leader

Almost since its initial founding in 2009 as a luxury car service for the San Francisco area, controversy has followed Uber. Many complaints are against the tactics employed by the company's founder and former CEO, Travis Kalanick, but the effects are found throughout the business and its operations.

In 2009, UberBlack was a "black car" service, a high-end driving service that cost more than a taxi but less than hiring a private driver for the night. It wasn't until 2012 that the company launched UberX, the taxi-esque service most people think of today when they say "Uber." The UberX service contracted with private drivers who provided rides in their personal vehicles. A customer would use Uber's smartphone app to request the ride, and a private driver would show up. Originally launched in San Francisco, the service spread quickly, and by 2017, Uber was in 633 cities. The service was hailed by many as innovative and the free market's answer to high-priced and sometimes unreliable taxi services. But Uber has not been without its critics, both inside and outside of the company.

In 2013, as the UberX service spread, some UberBlack drivers protested at the company's headquarters complaining about poor company benefits and pay. They also claimed that competition from the newly launched UberX service was cutting into their sales and undermining job security. Kalanick rebuffed the protests, basically calling the complaints sour grapes: most of the protestors had been laid off earlier for poor service (Lawler 2013). Controversy also arose over the use of contract drivers rather than full-time employees. Contractors complained about a lack of benefits and low wages. Competitors, especially taxi services, complained that they were being unfairly undercut because Uber didn't have to abide by the same screening process and costs that traditional yellow taxi companies did. Some municipalities agreed, arguing further than Uber's lack of or insufficient screening of drivers put passengers at risk.

Uber quickly generated a reputation as a bully and Kalanick as an unethical leader (Ann 2016). The company has been accused of covering up cases of sexual assault, and Kalanick himself has been quoted as calling the service "Boob-er," a reference to using the service to pick up women (Ann 2016). Uber has been criticized for its recruiting practices; in particular, it has been accused of bribing drivers working for competitors to switch over and drive for Uber (Ann 2016).The company was also caught making false driver requests for competing companies and then canceling the order. The effect was to waste the other driver's time and make it more difficult for customers to secure rides on the competing service (D'Orazio 2014). Susan J. Fowler, former site reliability engineer at Uber, went public with cases of outright sexual harassment within Uber (Fowler 2017). Former employees described Uber's corporate culture as an "a**hole culture" and a "'Hobbesian jungle' where you can never get ahead unless someone else dies." (Wong 2017) One employee described a leadership that encouraged a company practice of developing incomplete solutions for the purpose of beating the competitor to market. Fowler went so far as to compare the experience to Game of Thrones, and other former employees even consider "making it" at Uber a black mark on a resume (Wong 2017).

In terms of social acrimony and PR disasters, arguably caused or even encouraged by leadership, Uber's rise to notoriety has arguably been more bad than good. In June 2017, Kalanick made one too many headlines and agreed to step down as the company's CEO.

Sources

Ann, Carrie. 2016. "Uber Is In Dire Need of Ethical Leadership." Industry Leaders. https://www.industryleadersmagazine.com/uber-dire-need-ethical-leadership/

D'Orazio, Dante. 2014. "Uber employees spammed competing car service with fake orders." *The Verge.* https://www.theverge.com/2014/1/24/5342582/uber-employees-spammed-competing-car-service-with-fake-orders

Fowler, Susan J. 2017. "Reflecting on One Very, Very Strange Year at Uber." https://www.susanjfowler.com/blog/2017/2/19/reflecting-on-one-very-strange-year-at-uber

Lawler, Ryan. 2013. "See, Uber — This Is What Happens When You Cannibalize Yourself." TechCruch.com. https://techcrunch.com/2013/03/15/see-uber-this-is-what-happens-when-you-cannibalize-yourself/

Wong, Julia. 2017. "Uber's 'hustle-oriented' culture becomes a black mark on employees' résumés" *The Guardian.* https://www.theguardian.com/technology/2017/mar/07/uber-work-culture-travis-kalanick-susan-fowler-controversy

Questions

1. In the summer of 2017, Transport of London (TfL) began proceedings to revoke Uber's permit to operate in London. How do think Uber's poor corporate reputation may have been a factor in TfL's thinking?

2. What steps do you think Uber's new CEO, Dara Khosrowshahi, needs to take to repair Uber's reputation?

3. Despite Uber's apparent success in launching in multiple markets, it continues to post quarterly losses in the millions and shareholders effectively subsidize 59 percent of every ride (https://www.reuters.com/article/us-uber-profitability/true-price-of-an-uber-ride-in-question-as-investors-assess-firms-value-idUSKCN1B3103). How is this an outworking of Uber's overall corporate culture?

CONCEPT CHECK

1. What are the defining characteristics of transformational and charismatic leaders?

13.9 | Leadership Needs in the 21st Century

9. How do different approaches and styles of leadership impact what is needed now?

Frequent headlines in popular business magazines like *Fortune* and *Business Week* call our attention to a major movement going on in the world of business. Organizations are being reengineered and restructured, and network, virtual, and modular corporations are emerging. People talk about the transnational organization, the boundaryless company, the post-hierarchical organization. By the end of the decade, the organizations that we will be living in, working with, and competing against are likely to be vastly different from what we know today.

The transition will not be easy; uncertainty tends to breed resistance. We are driven by linear and rational thinking, which leads us to believe that "we can get there from here" by making some incremental changes in who we are and what we are currently doing. Existing paradigms frame our perceptions and guide our thinking. Throwing away paradigms that have served us well in the past does not come easily.

A look back tells most observers that the past decade has been characterized by rapid change, intense competition, an explosion of new technologies, chaos, turbulence, and high levels of uncertainty. A quick scan of today's business landscape suggests that this trend is not going away anytime soon. According to Professor Jay A. Conger from Canada's McGill University, "In times of great transition, leadership becomes critically important. Leaders, in essence, offer us a pathway of confidence and direction as we move through seeming chaos. The magnitude of today's changes will demand not only *more* leadership, but *newer forms* of leadership."[109]

According to Conger, two major forces are defining for us the genius of the next generation of leaders. The first force is the organization's external environment. Global competitiveness is creating some unique leadership demands. The second force is the growing diversity in organizations' internal environments. Diversity will significantly change the relationship between organizational members, work, and the organization in challenging, difficult, and also very positive ways.

What will the leaders of tomorrow be like? Professor Conger suggests that the effective leaders of the 21st century will have to be many things.[110] They will have to be *strategic opportunists;* only organizational visionaries will find strategic opportunities before competitors. They will have to be *globally aware;* with 80 percent of today's organizations facing significant foreign competition, knowledge of foreign markets, global economics, and geopolitics is crucial. They will have to be *capable of managing a highly decentralized organization;* movement toward the high-involvement organization will accelerate as the environmental demands for organizational speed, flexibility, learning, and leanness increase. They will have be *sensitive to diversity;* during the first few years of the 21st century, fewer than 10 percent of those entering the workforce in North America will be white, Anglo-Saxon males, and the incoming women, minorities, and immigrants will bring with them a very different set of needs and concerns. They will have to be *interpersonally competent;* a highly diverse workforce will necessitate a leader who is extremely aware of and sensitive to multicultural expectations and needs. They will have to be *builders of an organizational community;* work and organizations will serve as a major source of need fulfillment, and in the process leaders will be called on to help build this community in such a way that organizational members develop a sense of ownership for the organization and its mission.

Finally, it is important to note that leadership theory construction and empirical inquiry are an ongoing endeavor. While the study of traits, behavior, and contingency models of leadership provide us with a great deal of insight into leadership, the mosaic is far from complete. During the past 15 years, several new theories of leadership have emerged; among them are leader-member exchange theory, implicit leadership theory, neocharismatic theory, value-based theory of leadership, and visionary leadership,[111] each of which over time will add to our bank of knowledge about leaders and the leadership process.

Leaders of the 21st-century organization have a monumental challenge awaiting them and a wealth of self-enriching and fulfilling opportunities. The challenge and rewards awaiting effective leaders are awesome!

CONCEPT CHECK

1. What is the role of leadership in the 21st century?

🔑 Key Terms

charisma A special personal magnetic charm or appeal that arouses loyalty and enthusiasm in a leader-follower relationship.

charismatic leader A person who possesses legitimate power that arises from "exceptional sanctity, heroism, or exemplary character."

consideration A "relationship-oriented" leader behavior that is supportive, friendly, and focused on personal needs and interpersonal relationships.

contingency theory of leadership A theory advanced by Dr. Fred E. Fiedler that suggests that different leadership styles are effective as a function of the favorableness of the leadership situation least preferred.

designated leader The person placed in the leadership position by forces outside the group.

emergent leader The person who becomes a group's leader by virtue of processes and dynamics internal to the group.

formal leader That individual who is recognized by those outside the group as the official leader of the group.

great man theory of leadership The belief that some people are born to be leaders and others are not.

informal leader That individual whom members of the group acknowledge as their leader.

initiating structure A "task-oriented" leader behavior that is focused on goal attainment, organizing and scheduling work, solving problems, and maintaining work processes.

leadership A social (interpersonal) influence relationship between two or more persons who depend on each other to attain certain mutual goals in a group situation.

Least-preferred coworker (LPC) The person with whom the leader least likes to work.

path-goal theory of leadership A theory that posits that leadership is path- and goal-oriented, suggesting that different leadership styles are effective as a function of the task confronting the group.

transformational leader A leader who moves and changes things "in a big way" by inspiring others to perform the extraordinary.

visionary leader A leader who influences others through an emotional and/or intellectual attraction to the leader's dreams of what "can be."

📑 Summary of Learning Outcomes

13.1 The Nature of Leadership

1. What is the nature of leadership and the leadership process?

Leadership is a primary vehicle for fulfilling the directing function of management. Because of its importance, theorists, researchers, and practitioners have devoted a tremendous amount of attention and energy to unlocking the secrets of effective leadership. They have kept at this search for perhaps a greater period of time than for any other single issue related to management.

13.2 The Leadership Process

2. What are the processes associated with people coming to leadership positions?

Organizations typically have both formal and informal leaders. Their leadership is effective for virtually identical reasons. Leadership and management are not the same. Although effective leadership is a necessary part of effective management, the overall management role is much larger than leadership alone. Managers plan, organize, direct, and control. As leaders, they are engaged primarily in the directing function.

13.3 Types of Leaders and Leader Emergence

3. How do leaders influence and move their followers to action?

There are many diverse perspectives on leadership. Some managers treat leadership primarily as an exercise of power. Others believe that a particular belief and attitude structure makes for effective leaders. Still others believe it is possible to identify a collection of leader traits that produces a leader who should be universally effective in any leadership situation. Even today, many believe that a profile of behaviors can universally guarantee successful leadership. Unfortunately, such simple solutions fall short of the reality.

13.4 The Trait Approach to Leadership

4. What are the trait perspectives on leadership?

13.5 Behavioral Approaches to Leadership

5. What are the behavioral perspectives on leadership?

It is clear that effective leaders are endowed with the "right stuff," yet this "stuff" is only a precondition to effective leadership. Leaders need to connect with their followers and bring the right configuration of knowledge, skills, ability, vision, and strategy to the situational demands confronting the group.

13.6 Situational (Contingency) Approaches to Leadership

6. What are the situational perspectives on leadership?

We now know that there is no one best way to be an effective leader in all circumstances. Leaders need to recognize that how they choose to lead will affect the nature of their followers' compliance with their influence tactics, and ultimately impacts motivation, satisfaction, performance, and group effectiveness. In addition, the nature of the situation—contextual demands and characteristics of the follower—dictates the type of leadership that is likely to be effective. Fiedler focuses on leader traits and argues that the favorableness of the leadership situation dictates the type of leadership approach needed. He recommends selecting leaders to match the situation or changing the situation to match the leader. Path-goal theory focuses on leader behavior that can be adapted to the demands of a particular work environment and organizational members' characteristics. Path-goal theorists believe both that leaders can be matched with the situation and that the situation can be changed to match leaders. Together, these theories make clear that leadership is effective when the characteristics and behavior of the leader match the demands of the situation.

13.7 Substitutes for and Neutralizers of Leadership

7. What does the concept of "substitute for leadership" mean?

Characteristics of followers, tasks, and organizations can substitute for or neutralize many leader behaviors. Leaders must remain aware of these factors, no matter which perspective on leadership they adopt. Such awareness allows managers to use substitutes for, and neutralizers of, leadership to their benefit, rather than be stymied by their presence.

13.8 Transformational, Visionary, and Charismatic Leadership

8. What are the characteristics of transactional, transformational, and charismatic leadership?

In recent years, there has been a renewed interest in key leader traits and behaviors. As organizations face increasing amounts of chaos in their external environments, searches for "the right leader" who can bring about major organizational transformations has intensified. This search once again focuses our attention on a set of "key" motives, knowledge, skills, and personality attributes. Emerging from this search has been the identification of the charismatic and transformational leader.

13.9 Leadership Needs in the 21st Century

9. How do different approaches and styles of leadership impact what is needed now?

Leadership in the high-involvement organization differs dramatically from that in the traditional and control-oriented organization. Leaders external to the team have as one of their primary roles empowering group members and the teams themselves to self-lead and self-manage. Leaders internal to the team are peers; they work alongside and simultaneously facilitate planning, organizing, directing, controlling, and the execution of the team's work.

Although we know a great deal about the determinants of effective leadership, we have much to learn. Each theory presented in this chapter is put into practice by managers every day. None provides the complete answer to what makes leaders effective, but each has something important to offer.

Finally, our understanding of leadership has many shortcomings and limitations. The existing literature is largely based on observations from a Western industrialized context. The extent to which our theories of leadership are bound by our culture, limiting generalization to other cultures, is largely unknown. Cross-cultural leadership research will no doubt intensify as the global economy becomes an ever more dominant force in the world.

Chapter Review Questions

1. Define leadership and distinguish between leadership and management.
2. Discuss the processes associated with people coming to positions of leadership.
3. Discuss the different forms of power available to leaders and the effects associated with each.
4. It has been observed that effective leaders have the "right stuff." What traits are commonly associated with leader emergence and effective leaders?
5. Both the Ohio State University and University of Michigan leadership studies identified central leader behaviors. What are these behaviors, and how are they different from one another?
6. Blake and Mouton's work with the Leadership Grid® identified several leadership types. What are they, and how does this leadership model look from the perspective of situation theories of leadership?
7. Identify and describe the three situational variables presented in Fiedler's contingency theory of leadership.
8. What are the four leadership behaviors in the path-goal theory of leadership?
9. Discuss the differences between the internal and external leadership roles surrounding self-managed work teams.
10. What are substitutes for leadership? What are neutralizers? Give an example of each.
11. What are the distinguishing features of the transformational and the charismatic leader?

Management Skills Application Exercises

1. Identify a charismatic leader and a leader with little charisma. What are the traits and skills that allow them to succeed in their roles? How can you incorporate the traits that allow them to be successful in their roles into the skills you will need to have in a leadership position?
2. You have just taken a leadership position where 40 percent of the workforce telecommutes. You want to encourage teamwork and want to ensure that telecommuting is not hurting teamwork. What is your plan to discover how things are working and how to communicate your desire to have effective teamwork?
3. You are at a meeting, and during the meeting someone on the team addresses their manager and points out a crucial mistake that could doom the project. The person says that their manager should have

caught it and because of that should resign. As a leader of the group, how would you deal with the subordinate, the manager, and communication with the entire team?

Managerial Decision Exercises

1. You are the newly appointed commissioner of a major sports league that is currently in a very public game three of a best-of-seven-game playoff. After an emotional opening ceremony that recognizes a tragic event in the community that is widely praised, you settle in to enjoy the game. Early in the game, a player on one team is seen celebrating a scoring play by acting out a racially insensitive behavior after the play. How would you act in a leadership position? Read the ESPN article [**http://www.espn.com/mlb/story/_/id/21199462/rob-manfred-leadership-was-tested-yuli-gurriel-racially-insensitive-behavior-passed**] and comment on how this commissioner acted in this instance.

2. One of the challenges for a new manager in a leadership position is managing stress. Reflect on a time in your life where you have taken a leadership role in a summer job, as a member of a team, or in a study group for this or another course. Develop a stress management plan that includes how you can recognize stress, how you will notice the stress, how you will manage changes to address stress, and how you will seek outside counsel and help, including a mentor to help you manage stress.

3. Few people would want to hire a skilled manager with no leadership skills, and you would not want to hire an inspirational leader who can't manage planning, delegating, or keeping things organized. Draw two "T accounts" with positive attributes on the left and negative attributes on the right for managerial skills and leadership skills that you would look for as a hiring manager for a crucial managerial and leadership position in your organization.

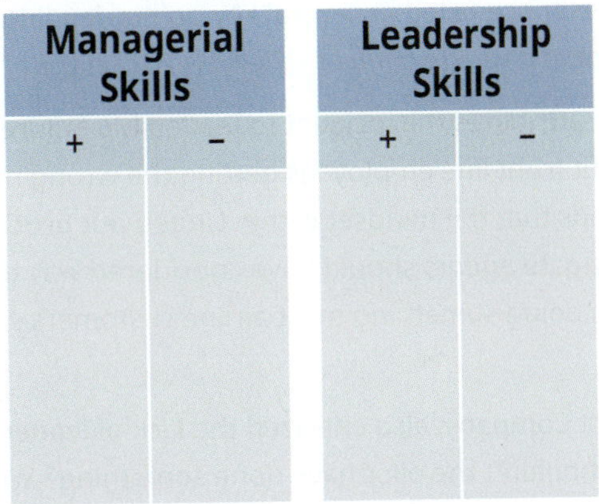

Managerial Skills		Leadership Skills	
+	−	+	−

Exhibit 13.13   (Attribution: Copyright Rice University, OpenStax, under CC-BY 4.0 license)

Critical Thinking Case

The Leadership Challenge at United

Anyone who has traveled even a little has at least one airline horror story: being stranded at an airport, obnoxious passengers, missed connections, flight delays, or just bad in-flight food. Even the most seasoned travelers would be hard-pressed to match Dr. David Dao's experience of being forcibly removed, kicking and screaming, from a United Airlines flight. Most airline horror stories don't end in a concussion, missing teeth, and a broken nose.

United Airlines CEO Oscar Munoz's strangely detached response only made things worse. The incident was caught on video, and that video went viral almost immediately. Munoz issued a response that mischaracterized what plainly happened in the video and termed the violent assault as a passenger "re-accommodation" (Taylor 2017). Social media erupted with condemnation, which was echoed by late-night monologues. United was left with a damaged reputation, and its management was left wondering why their processes failed, what to do to mitigate the damage, and how to both restore their reputation and ensure that company values are followed in the future.

William Taylor (2017), in a commentary in *Fortune*, attributes United's "re-accommodation" disaster as the product of company policy, airport security procedures, pilot protocols, and the "wisdom of crowds." At each step, the gate agent, pilot, airport security, and the passengers themselves could have intervened but didn't.

Brian Fielkow, business leader, author, and keynote speaker, writing at Entrepreneur.com, outlined some points that apply to Munoz's response and the first reactions by United. Citing United's core values, Fielkow points to Munoz's failure to address the incident in light of the company's values, take the blame, or even accurately describe what happened on the plane. Any *one* of these lapses in leadership would have caused confusion or stymied the recovery process. As a leader, Munoz was setting the tone for thousands of people. Seemingly abandoning United's core values likely caused a rift in trust or just simple confusion company-wide. Miscasting the situation in a world of smartphones and social media reach only multiplied the effect. As a leader, Munoz was duty-bound to take responsibility for what literally the entire world saw—a breach of social ethics, let alone United's core values. Failing to do this immediately created a problem larger than poorly planned company policy or just a perfect storm of contributing outside factors. Fielkow is keen to point out another crucial part of a company response— "You can't walk it back" (2017 n.p.). Before responding, leadership should take time to gather the facts and thoroughly consider the possibilities of how the message will be received. Again, Munoz's response failed at several key points, leading to the perception that Munoz's second statement was "an attempt at damage control" (Fielkow 2017 n.p.).

Al Bolea, a leadership trainer, also attributes the incident to leadership failure. In a piece written for *Applied Leadership*, Bolea writes, "It's about front line employees getting the wrong messages from the most senior levels of the company." He contends that the mindset within United put procedures above context in the minds of the employees. What the gate agents should have considered was the company's reputation, which should have prevented them from doing something most airline customers see as "profoundly immoral" (Bolea 2017 n.p.)

William C. Taylor, cofounder of Fast Company, also criticized the lack of leadership across United. As the presumptive leader of the flight, shouldn't the pilot have done something? Why didn't the gate agent think outside the box to solve the problem of getting the crew members from Chicago to Louisville, Kentucky? Why didn't—or couldn't—the gate agent use what Taylor refers to as a "common sense and a little bit of creativity" and prevent a highly embarrassing (and ultimately expensive) fiasco? Taylor muses that he would like to think he would have done more than shoot video, but the passengers on the flight remained quiet and submissive, expressing no group outrage. Finally, Taylor questions the weak initial response from United's CEO, Oscar Munoz, writing, "If CEO Oscar Munoz's goal was to make a disastrous situation even worse, well, he gets credit as a leader for succeeding at that" (2017 n.p.). And of the board, he questions their response, and says that response will be a "make or break test" of the company's character (Taylor 2017).

So what will it take to lead United out of such a public mistake?

According to Brian Fielkow, the incident flew in the face of United's core values, values which should never be sacrificed. United should have acknowledged this and addressed that failure. United should have held itself accountable for the incident rather than try to deflect blame. Fielkow contends that Munoz's first response was to blame the passenger when Munoz should have accepted responsibility instead. Further, Fielkow writes that companies should anticipate what "can" go wrong, something the gate agents at United failed to do. Increasing passenger compensation to even three times the normal ticket price would have been cheaper than the PR nightmare (and stock price drop) that followed. After Munoz's tepid response failed to quell general complaints about United's handling of the passenger, he tried to issue a second "more appropriate" statement, but by then the damage had been done. Fielkow recommends waiting before issuing a response if need be. It's better to prepared and issue a suitable response than to try to walk back a bad response. Above all, Fielkow recommends leaders "be human." The first response Munoz gave had little empathy and made him, and United, appear insensitive and callous. A company's first response should be to empathize with the customer, even if the customer is wrong. He writes, "When triaging a difficult problem, above all recognize the human factor" (Fielkow 2017 n.p.).

Writing in *Forbes*, Glenn Llopis emphasizes that how managers react to failure shapes their futures as leaders. Not only how leaders respond, but what is learned from a failure, will affect how future decisions are approached. Remember, you have to be doing something to fail, and if you never fail, then you aren't stretching yourself. Venturing into the unknown and unfamiliar always risks failure (Llopis 2012).

Sources:

Fielkow, Brian. 2017. "5 Leadership Failures that Contributed to the United Fiasco." *Entrepreneur.* https://www.entrepreneur.com/article/292820

Bolea, Al. 2017. "United Airlines: A System Failure?" *Applied Leadership.* http://appliedleadership.co/leadership/united-airlines-system-failure/

Taylor, William C. 2017. "Where was the Pilot on That United Airlines Flight?" *Fortune.* http://fortune.com/2017/04/11/united-airlines-video/

Llopis, Glenn. 2012. "5 Things Failure Teaches You About Leadership." *Forbes.* https://www.forbes.com/sites/glennllopis/2012/08/20/5-things-failure-teaches-you-about-leadership/2/#2f44c3873e70

Questions:
1. How have other airlines handled similar situations?
2. How much was in United Airlines's control, and how much was actually outside their control? What social or company factors caused a seemingly common practice to escalate to this level?
3. How did the other airlines or the industry respond to the United Airlines incident?

✎ Introduction

Learning Outcomes

After reading this chapter, you should be able to answer these questions:

1. Define motivation, and distinguish direction and intensity of motivation.
2. Describe a content theory of motivation, and compare and contrast the main content theories of motivation: manifest needs theory, learned needs theory, Maslow's hierarchy of needs, Alderfer's ERG theory, Herzberg's motivator-hygiene theory, and self-determination theory.
3. Describe the process theories of motivation, and compare and contrast the main process theories of motivation: operant conditioning theory, equity theory, goal theory, and expectancy theory.
4. Describe the modern advancements in the study of human motivation.

EXPLORING MANAGERIAL CAREERS

Bridget Anderson

Bridget Anderson thought life would be perfect out in the "real world." After earning her degree in computer science, she landed a well-paying job as a programmer for a large nonprofit organization whose mission she strongly believed in. And—initially—she was happy with her job.

Lately however, Bridget gets a sick feeling in her stomach every morning when her alarm goes off. Why this feeling of misery? After all, she's working in her chosen field in an environment that matches her values. What else could she want? She's more puzzled than anyone.

It's the end of her second year with the organization, and Bridget apprehensively schedules her annual performance evaluation. She knows she's a competent programmer, but she also knows that lately she's been motivated to do only the minimum required to get by. Her heart is just not in her work with this organization. Not exactly how she thought things would turn out, that's for sure.

Bridget's manager Kyle Jacobs surprises her when he begins the evaluation by inquiring about her professional goals. She admits that she hasn't thought much about her future. Kyle asks if she's content in her current position and if she feels that anything is missing. Suddenly, Bridget realizes that she *does* want more professionally.

Question: Are Bridget's motivational problems intrinsic or extrinsic? Which of her needs are currently not being met? What steps should she and her manager take to improve her motivation and ultimately her performance?

Outcome: Once Bridget admits that she's unhappy with her position as a computer programmer, she's ready to explore other possibilities. She and Kyle brainstorm for tasks that will motivate her and bring her greater job satisfaction. Bridget tells Kyle that while she enjoys programming, she feels isolated and misses interacting with other groups in the organization. She also realizes that once she had mastered the initial learning curve, she felt bored. Bridget is ready for a challenge.

Kyle recommends that Bridget move to an information systems team as their technical representative. The team can use Bridget's knowledge of programming, and Bridget will be able to collaborate more frequently with others in the organization.

Bridget and Kyle set specific goals to satisfy her needs to achieve and to work collaboratively. One of Bridget's goals is to take graduate classes in management and information systems. She hopes that this will lead to an MBA and, eventually, to a position as a team leader. Suddenly the prospect of going to work doesn't seem so grim—and lately, Bridget's been beating her alarm!

If you've ever worked with a group of people, and we all have, you have no doubt noticed differences in their performance. Researchers have pondered these differences for many years. Indeed, John B. Watson first studied this issue in the early 1900s. Performance is, of course, an extremely important issue to employers because organizations with high-performing employees will almost always be more effective.

To better understand why people perform at different levels, researchers consider the major determinants of performance: ability, effort (motivation), accurate role perceptions, and environmental factors (see **Exhibit 14.2**). Each performance determinant is important, and a deficit in one can seriously affect the others. People who don't understand what is expected of them will be constrained by their own inaccurate role perceptions, even if they have strong abilities and motivation and the necessary resources to perform their job. None of the performance determinants can compensate for a deficiency in any of the other determinants. Thus, a manager cannot compensate for an employee's lack of skills and ability by strengthening their motivation.

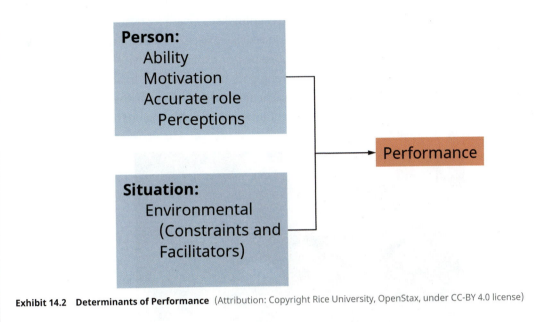

Exhibit 14.2 **Determinants of Performance** (Attribution: Copyright Rice University, OpenStax, under CC-BY 4.0 license)

14.1 | Motivation: Direction and Intensity

1. Define motivation and distinguish direction and intensity of motivation.

Ability refers to the knowledge, skills, and receptiveness to learning that a person brings to a task or job. Knowledge is what a person knows. Skill is their capacity to perform some particular activity (like welding or accounting), including knowing what is expected of them (called accurate role perceptions). Receptiveness to learning is a function of how quickly a person acquires new knowledge. Some people have more ability than others, and high-ability people generally perform better than low-ability people (although we will see that this is not always the case).[1]

Accurate **role perceptions** refer to how well an individual understands their organizational role. This includes the goals (outcomes) the person is expected to achieve and the process by which the goals will be achieved. An employee who has accurate role perceptions knows both their expected outcomes *and* how to go about making those outcomes a reality. Incomplete or inaccurate role perceptions limit employees' capacity to meet expectations, regardless of their abilities and motivation.

The **performance environment** refers to those factors that impact employees' performance but are essentially out of their control. Many environmental factors influence performance. Some factors facilitate performance, while others constrain it. A word processor who has to work with a defective personal computer is certainly not going to perform at peak levels, regardless of ability or desire. Students who are working full time and carrying a full load of classes may not do as well on an exam as they would if they could cut back on their work hours, despite the fact that they have high ability and high motivation.

Motivation is the fourth major factor that determines whether a person will perform a task well. **Motivation** is a force within or outside of the body that energizes, directs, and sustains human behavior. Within the body, examples might be needs, personal values, and goals, while an incentive might be seen as a force outside of the body. The word stems from its Latin root *movere*, which means "to move." Generally speaking, motivation arises as a consequence of a person's desire to (1) fulfill unmet needs or (2) resolve conflicting thoughts that produce anxiety (an unpleasant experience). There are many ways in which we describe and categorize human needs, as we will see later in this chapter. Certain needs are fundamental to our existence, like the need for food and water. When we are hungry, we are energized to satisfy that need by securing and ingesting food.

Our other needs operate in a similar manner. When a need is unfulfilled, we are motivated to engage in behaviors that will satisfy it. The same is true for situations in which we experience conflicting thoughts. When we find ourselves in situations inconsistent with our beliefs, values, or expectations, we endeavor to eliminate the inconsistency. We either change the situation, or we change our perception of it. In both cases, motivation arises out of our interaction with and perception of a particular situation. We perceive the situation as satisfying our needs, or not. Motivation is thus a result of our interacting with situations to satisfy unmet needs or to resolve cognitive dissonance.

Exhibit 14.3   Tom Brady   At the University of Michigan, Tom Brady was always a backup to high-potential quarterbacks and was a sixth-round draft pick after his college career. He commented, "A lot of people don't believe in you. It's obvious by now, six other quarterbacks taken and 198 other picks. And I always thought 'you know what, once I get my shot, I'm gonna be ready. I'm gonna really take advantage of that.'" Rather than give up, he hired a sports psychologist to help him deal with constant frustrations. Brady would eventually become an elite quarterback and is now considered one of the greatest players ever. "I guess in a sense I've always had a chip on my shoulder. If you were the 199th pick, you were the 199th pick for a reason: because someone didn't think you were good enough." His passion and motivation helped him achieve that status. (Credit: Brook Ward/ flickr/ Attribution 2.0 Generic (CC BY 2.0))

Simply stated, **work motivation** is the amount of effort a person exerts to achieve a certain level of job performance. Some people try very hard to perform their jobs well. They work long hours, even if it interferes with their family life. Highly motivated people go the "extra mile." High scorers on an exam make sure they know the examination material to the best of their ability, no matter how much midnight oil they have to burn. Other students who don't do as well may just want to get by—football games and parties are a lot more fun, after all.

Motivation is of great interest to employers: *All* employers want their people to perform to the best of their abilities. They take great pains to screen applicants to make sure they have the necessary abilities and motivation to perform well. They endeavor to supply all the necessary resources and a good work environment. Yet motivation remains a difficult factor to manage. As a result, it receives the most attention from organizations and researchers alike, who ask the perennial question "What motivates people to perform well?"

In this chapter we look at current answers to this question. What work conditions foster motivation? How can theories of motivation help us understand the general principles that guide organizational behavior? Rather than analyze why a particular student studies hard for a test, we'll look at the underlying principles of our general behavior in a variety of situations (including test taking). We also discuss the major theories of motivation, along with their implications for management and organizational behavior. By the end of this chapter you should have a better understanding of why some people are more motivated than others. Successful employees know what they want to achieve (direction), and they persist until they achieve their goals (intensity).

Our discussion thus far implies that motivation is a matter of effort. This is only partially true. Motivation has two major components: direction and intensity. **Direction** is *what* a person wants to achieve, what they intend to do. It implies a target that motivated people try to "hit." That target may be to do well on a test. Or it may be to perform better than anyone else in a work group. **Intensity** is *how hard* people try to achieve their targets. Intensity is what we think of as effort. It represents the energy we expend to accomplish something. If our efforts are getting nowhere, will we try different strategies to succeed? (High-intensity-motivated people are persistent!)

It is important to distinguish the direction and intensity aspects of motivation. If *either* is lacking, performance will suffer. A person who knows what they want to accomplish (direction) but doesn't exert much effort (intensity) will not succeed. (Scoring 100 percent on an exam—your target—won't happen unless you study!) Conversely, people who don't have a direction (what they want to accomplish) probably won't succeed either. (At some point you have to decide on a major if you want to graduate, even if you do have straight As.)

Employees' targets don't always match with what their employers want. Absenteeism (some employees call this "calling in well") is a major example.[2] Pursuing your favorite hobby (your target) on a workday (your employer's target) is a conflict in direction; below, we'll examine some theories about why this conflict occurs.

There is another reason why employees' targets are sometimes contrary to their employers'—sometimes employers do not ensure that employees understand what the employer wants. Employees can have great intensity but poor direction. It is management's job to provide direction: Should we stress quality as well as quantity? Work independently or as a team? Meet deadlines at the expense of costs? Employees flounder without direction. Clarifying direction results in accurate *role perceptions,* the behaviors employees think they are expected to perform as members of an organization. Employees with accurate role perceptions understand their purpose in the organization and how the performance of their job duties contributes to organizational objectives. Some motivation theorists assume that employees know the correct direction for their jobs. Others do not. These differences are highlighted in the discussion of motivation theories below.

At this point, as we begin our discussion of the various motivation theories, it is reasonable to ask "Why isn't there just one motivation theory?" The answer is that the different theories are driven by different philosophies of motivation. Some theorists assume that humans are propelled more by needs and instincts than by reasoned actions. Their **content motivation theories** focus on *the content of what* motivates people. Other theorists focus on the process by which people are motivated. **Process motivation theories** address *how* people become motivated—that is, how people perceive and think about a situation. Content and process theories endeavor to predict motivation in a variety of situations. However, none of these theories can predict what will motivate an individual in a given situation 100 percent of the time. Given the complexity of human behavior, a "grand theory" of motivation will probably never be developed.

A second reasonable question at this point is "Which theory is best?" If that question could be easily answered, this chapter would be quite short. The simple answer is that there is no "one best theory." All have been supported by organizational behavior research. All have strengths and weaknesses. However, understanding something about each theory is a major step toward effective management practices.

CONCEPT CHECK

1. Explain the two drivers of motivation: direction and intensity.
2. What are the differences between content and process theories of motivation?
3. Will there ever be a grand theory of motivation?

14.2 | Content Theories of Motivation

2. Describe a content theory of motivation.

The theories presented in this section focus on the importance of human needs. A common thread through all of them is that people have a variety of needs. A **need** is a human condition that becomes "energized" when people feel deficient in some respect. When we are hungry, for example, our need for food has been energized. Two features of needs are key to understanding motivation. First, when a need has been energized, we are motivated to satisfy it. We strive to make the need disappear. **Hedonism,** one of the first motivation theories, assumes that people are motivated to satisfy mainly their own needs (seek pleasure, avoid pain). Long since displaced by more refined theories, hedonism clarifies the idea that needs provide direction for motivation. Second, once we have satisfied a need, it ceases to motivate us. When we've eaten to satiation, we are no longer motivated to eat. Other needs take over and we endeavor to satisfy them. A **manifest need** is whatever need is motivating us at a given time. Manifest needs dominate our other needs.

Instincts are our natural, fundamental needs, basic to our survival. Our needs for food and water are instinctive. Many needs are learned. We are not born with a high (or low) need for achievement—we learn to need success (or failure). The distinction between instinctive and learned needs sometimes blurs; for example, is our need to socialize with other people instinctive or learned?

Manifest Needs Theory

One major problem with the need approach to motivation is that we can make up a need for every human behavior. Do we "need" to talk or be silent? The possibilities are endless. In fact, around the 1920s, some 6,000 human needs had been identified by behavioral scientists!

Henry A. Murray recognized this problem and condensed the list into a few instinctive and learned needs.[3] Instincts, which Murray called **primary needs**, include physiological needs for food, water, sex (procreation), urination, and so on. Learned needs, which Murray called **secondary needs**, are learned throughout one's life and are basically psychological in nature. They include such needs as the need for achievement, for love, and for affiliation (see **Table 14.1**).[4]

Sample Items from Murray's List of Needs	
Social Motive	Brief Definition
Abasement	To submit passively to external force. To accept injury, blame, criticism, punishment. To surrender.
Achievement	To accomplish something difficult. To master, manipulate, or organize physical objects, human beings, or ideas.
Affiliation	To draw near and enjoyably cooperate or reciprocate with an allied other (an other who resembles the subject or who likes the subject). To please and win affection of a coveted object. To adhere and remain loyal to a friend.
Aggression	To overcome opposition forcefully. To fight. To revenge an injury. To attack, injure, or kill another. To oppose forcefully or punish another.
Autonomy	To get free, shake off restraint, break out of confinement.
Counteraction	To master or make up for a failure by restriving.
Defendance	To defend the self against assault, criticism, and blame. To conceal or justify a misdeed, failure, or humiliation. To vindicate the ego.
Deference	To admire and support a superior. To praise, honor, or eulogize.
Dominance	To control one's human environment. To influence or direct the behavior of others by suggestion, seduction, persuasion, or command.
Exhibition	To make an impression. To be seen and heard. To excite, amaze, fascinate, entertain, shock, intrigue, amuse, or entice others.
Harm avoidance	To avoid pain, physical injury, illness, and death. To escape from a dangerous situation. To take precautionary measures.
Infavoidance	To avoid humiliation. To quit embarrassing situations or to avoid conditions that may lead to belittlement or the scorn or indifference of others.
Nurturance	To give sympathy and gratify the needs of a helpless object: an infant or any object that is weak, disabled, tired, inexperienced, infirm, defeated, humiliated, lonely, dejected, sick, or mentally confused. To assist an object in danger. To feed, help, support, console, protect, comfort, nurse, heal.
Order	To put things in order. To achieve cleanliness, arrangement, organization, balance, neatness, tidiness, and precision.

Table 14.1

Sample Items from Murray's List of Needs	
Social Motive	Brief Definition
Play	To act for "fun" without further purpose. To like to laugh and make jokes. To seek enjoyable relaxation from stress.
Rejection	To separate oneself from a negatively valued object. To exclude, abandon, expel, or remain indifferent to an inferior object. To snub or jilt an object.
Sentience	To seek and enjoy sensuous impressions.
Sex	To form and further an erotic relationship. To have sexual intercourse.
Succorance	To have one's needs gratified by the sympathetic aid of an allied object.
Understanding	To ask or answer general questions. To be interested in theory. To speculate, formulate, analyze, and generalize.

Source: Adapted from C. S. Hall and G. Lindzey, *Theories of Personality.* Sample items from Murray's List of Needs. Copyright 1957 by John Wiley & Sons, New York.

Table 14.1

Murray's main premise was that people have a variety of needs, but only a few are expressed at a given time. When a person is behaving in a way that satisfies some need, Murray called the need manifest. **Manifest needs theory** assumes that human behavior is driven by the desire to satisfy needs. Lucretia's chattiness probably indicates her need for affiliation. This is a manifest need. But what if Lucretia also has a need to dominate others? Could we detect that need from her current behavior? If not, Murray calls this a latent need. A **latent need** cannot be inferred from a person's behavior at a given time, yet the person may still possess that need. The person may not have had the opportunity to express the need. Or she may not be in the proper environment to solicit behaviors to satisfy the need. Lucretia's need to dominate may not be motivating her current behavior because she is with friends instead of coworkers.

Manifest needs theory laid the groundwork for later theories, most notably McClelland's learned needs theory, that have greatly influenced the study of organizational behavior. The major implication for management is that some employee needs are latent. Managers often assume that employees do not have certain needs because the employees never try to satisfy them at work. Such needs may exist (latent needs); the work environment is simply not conducive to their manifestation (manifest needs). A reclusive accountant may not have been given the opportunity to demonstrate his need for achievement because he never received challenging assignments.

Learned Needs Theory

David C. McClelland and his associates (especially John W. Atkinson) built on the work of Murray for over 50 years. Murray studied many different needs, but very few in any detail. McClelland's research differs from Murray's in that McClelland studied three needs in depth: the need for achievement, the need for affiliation, and the need for power (often abbreviated, in turn, as nAch, nAff, and nPow).[5] McClelland believes that these three needs are learned, primarily in childhood. But he also believes that each need can be taught, especially nAch. McClelland's research is important because much of current thinking about organizational behavior is based on it.

Need for Achievement

The **need for achievement (nAch)** is how much people are motivated to excel at the tasks they are performing, especially tasks that are difficult. Of the three needs studied by McClelland, nAch has the greatest impact. The need for achievement varies in intensity across individuals. This makes nAch a personality trait as well as a statement about motivation. When nAch is being expressed, making it a manifest need, people try hard to succeed at whatever task they're doing. We say these people have a high achievement motive. A **motive** is a source of motivation; it is the need that a person is attempting to satisfy. Achievement needs become manifest when individuals experience certain types of situations.

To better understand the nAch motive, it's helpful to describe high-nAch people. You probably know a few of them. They're constantly trying to accomplish something. One of your authors has a father-in-law who would much rather spend his weekends digging holes (for various home projects) than going fishing. Why? Because when he digs a hole, he gets results. In contrast, he can exert a lot of effort and still not catch a fish. A lot of fishing, no fish, and no results equal failure!

McClelland describes three major characteristics of high-nAch people:

1. They feel personally responsible for completing whatever tasks they are assigned. They accept credit for success and blame for failure.
2. They like situations where the probability of success is moderate. High-nAch people are not motivated by tasks that are too easy or extremely difficult. Instead, they prefer situations where the outcome is uncertain, but in which they believe they can succeed if they exert enough effort. They avoid both simple and impossible situations.
3. They have very strong desires for feedback about how well they are doing. They actively seek out performance feedback. It doesn't matter whether the information implies success or failure. They want to know whether they have achieved or not. They constantly ask how they are doing, sometimes to the point of being a nuisance.

Why is nAch important to organizational behavior? The answer is, the success of many organizations is dependent on the nAch levels of their employees.[6] This is especially true for jobs that require self-motivation and managing others. Employees who continuously have to be told how to do their jobs require an overly large management team, and too many layers of management spell trouble in the current marketplace. Today's flexible, cost-conscious organizations have no room for top-heavy structures; their high-nAch employees perform their jobs well with minimal supervision.

Many organizations manage the achievement needs of their employees poorly. A common perception about people who perform unskilled jobs is that they are unmotivated and content doing what they are doing. But, if they have achievement needs, the job itself creates little motivation to perform. It is too easy. There are not enough workers who feel personal satisfaction for having the cleanest floors in a building. Designing jobs that are neither too challenging nor too boring is key to managing motivation. Job enrichment is one effective strategy; this frequently entails training and rotating employees through different jobs, or adding new challenges.

Exhibit 14.4   New York Metro workers carrying a sign   The New York City Metropolitan Transit Authority undertook a new approach to how they perform critical inspection and maintenance of subway components that are necessary to providing reliable service. Rather than schedule these inspections during regular hours, they consulted with the maintenance workers, who suggested doing the inspections while sections of the subway were closed to trains for seven consecutive hours. This process was adopted and provided a safer and more efficient way to maintain and clean New York City's sprawling subway. With no trains running, MTA employees are able to inspect signals, replace rails and crossties, scrape track floors, clean stations, and paint areas that are not reachable during normal train operation. Workers also took the opportunity to clean lighting fixtures, change bulbs, and repair platform edges while performing high-intensity station cleaning. (Credit: Patrick Cashin/ flickr/ Attribution 2.0 Generic (CC BY 2.0))

Need for Affiliation

This need is the second of McClelland's learned needs. The **need for affiliation (nAff)** reflects a desire to establish and maintain warm and friendly relationships with other people. As with nAch, nAff varies in intensity across individuals. As you would expect, high-nAff people are very sociable. They're more likely to go bowling with friends after work than to go home and watch television. Other people have lower affiliation needs. This doesn't mean that they avoid other people, or that they dislike others. They simply don't exert as much effort in this area as high-nAff people do.

The nAff has important implications for organizational behavior. High-nAff people like to be around other people, including other people at work. As a result, they perform better in jobs that require teamwork. Maintaining good relationships with their coworkers is important to them, so they go to great lengths to make the work group succeed because they fear rejection. So, high-nAff employees will be especially motivated to perform well if others depend on them. In contrast, if high-nAff people perform jobs in isolation from other people, they will be less motivated to perform well. Performing well on this job won't satisfy their need to be around other people.

Effective managers carefully assess the degree to which people have high or low nAff. Employees high in nAff should be placed in jobs that require or allow interactions with other employees. Jobs that are best performed alone are more appropriate for low-nAff employees, who are less likely to be frustrated.

Need for Power

The third of McClelland's learned needs, the **need for power (nPow)**, is the need to control things, especially other people. It reflects a motivation to influence and be responsible for other people. An employee who is often talkative, gives orders, and argues a lot is motivated by the need for power over others.

Employees with high nPow can be beneficial to organizations. High-nPow people do have effective employee behaviors, but at times they're disruptive. A high-nPow person may try to convince others to do things that are detrimental to the organization. So, when is this need good, and when is it bad? Again, there are no easy answers. McClelland calls this the "two faces of power."[7] A *personal power seeker* endeavors to control others mostly for the sake of dominating them. They want others to respond to their wishes whether or not it is good for the organization. They "build empires," and they protect them.

McClelland's other power seeker is the *social power seeker.* A high social power seeker satisfies needs for power by influencing others, like the personal power seeker. They differ in that they feel best when they have influenced a work group to achieve the group's goals, and not some personal agenda. High social power seekers are concerned with goals that a work group has set for itself, and they are motivated to influence others to achieve the goal. This need is oriented toward fulfilling responsibilities to the employer, not to the self.

McClelland has argued that the high need for social power is the most important motivator for successful managers. Successful managers tend to be high in this type of nPow. High need for achievement can also be important, but it sometimes results in too much concern for personal success and not enough for the employer's success. The need for affiliation contributes to managerial success only in those situations where the maintenance of warm group relations is as important as getting others to work toward group goals.

The implication of McClelland's research is that organizations should try to place people with high needs for social power in managerial jobs. It is critical, however, that those managerial jobs allow the employee to satisfy the nPow through social power acquisition. Otherwise, a manager high in nPow may satisfy this need through acquisition of personal power, to the detriment of the organization.

ETHICS IN PRACTICE

Corporate Social Responsibility as a Motivating Force

Whatever their perspective, most people have a cause that they are passionate about. Bitcoin or net neutrality, sea levels or factory farming—social causes bind us to a larger context or assume a higher purpose for living better.

So what motivates employees to give their all, work creatively, and be fully engaged? According to CB Bhattacharya, the Pietro Ferrero Chair in Sustainability at ESMT European School of Management and Technology in Berlin, Germany, employment engagement, or how positive employees feel about their current job, was at an all-time low globally in 2016: 13 percent. But not all companies battle such low engagement rates. Unilever employees more than 170,000 workers globally and has an employ engagement level around 80 percent. How? Bhattacharya credits the success of Unilever, and other companies with similar engagement levels, to an emphasis on a "sustainable business model." He outlines eight steps that companies take to move sustainability and social responsibility from buzzwords to a company mission capable of motivating employees (Knowledge @ Wharton 2016).

According to Bhattacharya, a company needs to first define what it does and its long-term purpose, and then reconcile its sustainability goals with its economic goals. With its purpose and goals defined, it can then educate the workforce on sustainable methods to create knowledge and competence. Champions for the effort must be found throughout the organization, not just at the top. Competition should be encouraged among employees to find and embrace new goals. Sustainability should be visible both within and outside the company. Sustainability should be tied to a higher purpose and foster a sense of unity not simply among employees, but even with competition at a societal level (Knowledge @ Wharton 2016).

Other companies have made social responsibility an everyday part of what they do. Launched in 2013, Bombas is the brain child of Randy Goldberg and David Heath. Goldberg and Heath discovered that socks are the most-requested clothing at homeless shelters. In response, the two entrepreneurs launched a line of socks that not only "reinvents" the sock (they claim), but also helps those in need. For each pair of socks purchased, the company donates a pair of socks to someone in need (Mulvey 2017). According to the company website, "Bombas exists to help solve this problem, to support the homeless community, and to bring awareness to an under-publicized problem in the United States" (n.p.). Although the New York–based company is still growing, as of October 2017 Bombas had donated more than four million pairs of socks (Bombas 2017).

In 2016, the Royal Bank of Scotland (RBS) launched a pilot program called Jump in which employees participated in challenges on ways to save water and electricity, as well as other sustainability issues. At the end of the pilot, 95 percent of the employees reported that they felt the program had contributed to employee engagement, team building, and environmental stability. Given the success of the program, in 2017 it was expanded to all RBS sites and a smartphone app was added to help employees participate in the challenges (Barton 2017).

Placing a *company* in a larger context and adding a second, higher purpose than the established company goals motivates employees to police the company itself to be a better global citizen. Companies benefit from reduced waste and increased employee engagement. Many companies are successfully motivating their staff, and working toward more sustainable practices, while improving lives directly.

Sources:

Barton, Tynan. 2017. "RBS boosts employee motivation and engagement through its CSR approach." *employee benefits.* https://www.employeebenefits.co.uk/issues/april-2017/rbs-boosts-employee-motivation-engagement-csr-approach/

Bombas. 2017. "Giving Back." https://bombas.com/pages/giving-back

Knowledge @ Wharton. 2016. "How Companies Can Tap Sustainability to Motivate Staff." http://knowledge.wharton.upenn.edu/article/how-companies-tap-sustainability-to-motivate-staff/

Mulvey, Kelsey. 2017. "This company spent two years perfecting gym socks, and it paid off." *Business*

Insider. http://www.businessinsider.com/bombas-athletic-sock-review-2017-1

1. Do you think social responsibility to promote sustainable practices? Why or why not?
2. Do you think most companies' CSR programs are essentially PR gimmicks? Why or why not? Give examples.

Maslow's Hierarchy of Needs

Any discussion of needs that motivate performance would be incomplete without considering Abraham Maslow.[8] Thousands of managers in the 1960s were exposed to Maslow's theory through the popular writings of Douglas McGregor.[9] Today, many of them still talk about employee motivation in terms of Maslow's theory.

Maslow was a psychologist who, based on his early research with primates (monkeys), observations of patients, and discussions with employees in organizations, theorized that human needs are arranged hierarchically. That is, before one type of need can manifest itself, other needs must be satisfied. For example, our need for water takes precedence over our need for social interaction (this is also called *prepotency*). We will always satisfy our need for water before we satisfy our social needs; water needs have prepotency over social needs. Maslow's theory differs from others that preceded it because of this hierarchical, prepotency concept.

Maslow went on to propose five basic types of human needs. This is in contrast to the thousands of needs that earlier researchers had identified, and also fewer than Murray identified in his theory. Maslow condensed human needs into a manageable set. Those five human needs, in the order of prepotency in which they direct human behavior, are:

1. *Physiological and survival needs.* These are the most basic of human needs, and include the needs for water, food, sex, sleep, activity, stimulation, and oxygen.
2. *Safety and security needs.* These needs invoke behaviors that assure freedom from danger. This set of needs involves meeting threats to our existence, including extremes in environmental conditions (heat, dust, and so on), assault from other humans, tyranny, and murder. In other words, satisfaction of these needs prevents fear and anxiety while adding stability and predictability to life.
3. *Social needs.* These needs reflect human desires to be the target of affection and love from others. They are especially satisfied by the presence of spouses, children, parents, friends, relatives, and others to whom we feel close. Feelings of loneliness and rejection are symptoms that this need has not been satisfied.
4. *Ego and esteem.* Esteem needs go beyond social needs. They reflect our need to be respected by others, and to have esteem for ourselves. It is one thing to be liked by others. It is another thing to be respected for our talents and abilities. Ego and esteem needs have internal (self) and external (others) focuses. An internal focus includes desires for achievement, strength, competence, confidence, and independence. An external focus includes desires to have prestige, recognition, appreciation, attention, and respect from others. Satisfaction of external esteem needs can lead to satisfaction of internal esteem needs.
5. *Self-actualization.* Self-actualization needs are the most difficult to describe. Unlike the other needs, the need for self-actualization is never completely satisfied. Self-actualization involves a desire for self-fulfillment, "to become more and more what one is, to become everything that one is capable of becoming."[10] Because people are so different in their strengths and weaknesses, in capacities and limitations, the meaning of self-actualization varies greatly. Satisfying self-actualization needs means developing all of our special abilities to their fullest degree.

Exhibit 14.5   Seattle protester with sign   (Credit: Adrenalin Tim /flickr/ Attribution 2.0 Generic (CC BY 2.0))

Exhibit 14.5 A protester at an anti-war demonstration in Seattle held up this sign. Where would you place that on Maslow's hierarchy of needs?

Exhibit 14.6 illustrates Maslow's proposed hierarchy of needs. According to his theory, people first direct their attention to satisfying their lower-order needs. Those are the needs at the bottom of the pyramid (physiological, safety, and security). Once those needs have been satisfied, the next level, social needs, become energized. Once satisfied, we focus on our ego and esteem needs. Maslow believed that most people become fixated at this level. That is, most people spend much of their lives developing self-esteem and the esteem of others. But, once those esteem needs are satisfied, Maslow predicted that self-actualization needs would dominate. There are no higher levels in the pyramid, because self-actualization needs can never be fully satisfied. They represent a continuing process of self-development and self-improvement that, once satisfied on one dimension (painting), create motivation to continue on other dimensions (sculpting). One wonders if athletes like Tim Tebow are self-actualizing when they participate in multiple sporting endeavors at the professional level.

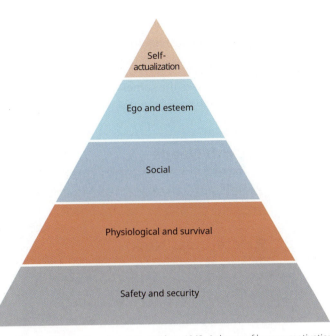

Exhibit 14.6   Maslow's Hierarchy of Needs *Source:* Based on A. H. Maslow. 1943. A theory of human motivation. *Psychological Bulletin* 50:370–396.

An overriding principle in this theory is that a person's attention (direction) and energy (intensity) will focus on satisfying the lowest-level need that is not currently satisfied. Needs can also be satisfied at some point but become active (dissatisfied) again. Needs must be "maintained" (we must continue to eat occasionally). According to Maslow, when lower-level needs are reactivated, we once again concentrate on that need. That is, we lose interest in the higher-level needs when lower-order needs are energized.

The implications of Maslow's theory for organizational behavior are as much conceptual as they are practical. The theory posits that to maximize employee motivation, employers must try to guide workers to the upper parts of the hierarchy. That means that the employer should help employees satisfy lower-order needs like safety and security and social needs. Once satisfied, employees will be motivated to build esteem and respect through their work achievements. **Exhibit 14.6** shows how Maslow's theory relates to factors that organizations can influence. For example, by providing adequate pay, safe working conditions, and cohesive work groups, employers help employees satisfy their lower-order needs. Once satisfied, challenging jobs, additional responsibilities, and prestigious job titles can help employees satisfy higher-order esteem needs.

Maslow's theory is still popular among practicing managers. Organizational behavior researchers, however, are not as enamored with it because research results don't support Maslow's hierarchical notion. Apparently, people don't go through the five levels in a fixed fashion. On the other hand, there is some evidence that people satisfy the lower-order needs before they attempt to satisfy higher-order needs. Refinements of Maslow's theory in recent years reflect this more limited hierarchy.[11] The self-assessment below will allow you to evaluate the strength of your five needs.

Alderfer's ERG Theory

Clayton Alderfer observed that very few attempts had been made to test Maslow's full theory. Further, the evidence accumulated provided only partial support. During the process of refining and extending Maslow's theory, Alderfer provided another need-based theory and a somewhat more useful perspective on motivation.[12] Alderfer's **ERG theory** compresses Maslow's five need categories into three: existence, relatedness, and growth.[13] In addition, ERG theory details the dynamics of an individual's movement between the need categories in a somewhat more detailed fashion than typically characterizes interpretations of Maslow's work.

As shown in **Exhibit 14.7**, the ERG model addresses the same needs as those identified in Maslow's work:

Growth Needs
1. Internal self-esteem needs
2. Self-actualization needs

Relatedness Needs
1. Social needs
2. Social esteem needs
3. Interpersonal safety needs

Existence Needs
1. Physiological needs
2. Material safety needs

Exhibit 14.7   Alderfer's ERG Theory (Attribution: Copyright Rice University, OpenStax, under CC-BY 4.0 license)

- *Existence needs* include physiological and material safety needs. These needs are satisfied by material conditions and not through interpersonal relations or personal involvement in the work setting.
- *Relatedness needs* include all of Maslow's social needs, plus social safety and social esteem needs. These needs are satisfied through the exchange of thoughts and feelings with other people.
- *Growth needs* include self-esteem and self-actualization needs. These needs tend to be satisfied through one's full involvement in work and the work setting.

Exhibit 14.8 identifies a number of ways in which organizations can help their members satisfy these three needs.

Growth Opportunities
- Challenging job
- Creativity
- Organizational advancement
- Responsibility
- Autonomy
- Interesting work
- Achievement
- Participation

Relatedness Opportunities
- Friendship
- Interpersonal security
- Athletic teams
- Social recognition
- Quality supervision
- Work teams
- Social events
- Merit pay

Existence Opportunities
- Heat
- Lighting
- Base salary
- Insurance
- Retirement
- Air conditioning
- Restrooms
- Cafeteria
- Job security
- Health programs
- Clean air
- Drinking water
- Safe conditions
- No layoffs
- Time off

Exhibit 14.8 **Satisfying Existence, Relatedness, and Growth Needs** (Attribution: Copyright Rice University, OpenStax, under CC-BY 4.0 license)

Four components—satisfaction progression, frustration, frustration regression, and aspiration—are key to understanding Alderfer's ERG theory. The first of these, *satisfaction progression,* is in basic agreement with Maslow's process of moving through the needs. As we increasingly satisfy our existence needs, we direct energy toward relatedness needs. As these needs are satisfied, our growth needs become more active. The second component, *frustration,* occurs when we attempt but fail to satisfy a particular need. The resulting frustration may make satisfying the unmet need even more important to us—unless we repeatedly fail to satisfy that need. In this case, Alderfer's third component, *frustration regression,* can cause us to shift our attention to a previously satisfied, more concrete, and verifiable need. Lastly, the *aspiration* component of the ERG model notes that, by its very nature, growth is intrinsically satisfying. The more we grow, the more we want to grow. Therefore, the more we satisfy our growth need, the more important it becomes and the more strongly we are motivated to satisfy it.

Exhibit 14.9   Jamie Dimon Jamie Dimon, CEO at JP Morgan Chase, is reported to make $27 million dollars per year, and as CEO has an interesting and intrinsically rewarding job. Starting tellers at a Chase Bank make a reported $36,100 per year and are in a position that has repeated tasks and may not be the most rewarding from a motivational point of view. How does this pay structure relate to self-determination theory (SDT)? (Credit: Stefan Chow/ flickr/ Attribution 2.0 Generic (CC BY 2.0))

Alderfer's model is potentially more useful than Maslow's in that it doesn't create false motivational categories. For example, it is difficult for researchers to ascertain when interaction with others satisfies our need for acceptance and when it satisfies our need for recognition. ERG also focuses attention explicitly on movement through the set of needs in both directions. Further, evidence in support of the three need categories and their order tends to be stronger than evidence for Maslow's five need categories and their relative order.

Herzberg's Motivator-Hygiene Theory

Clearly one of the most influential motivation theories throughout the 1950s and 1960s was Frederick Herzberg's motivator-hygiene theory.[14] This theory is a further refinement of Maslow's theory. Herzberg argued that there are two sets of needs, instead of the five sets theorized by Maslow. He called the first set "motivators" (or growth needs). **Motivators**, which relate to the jobs we perform and our ability to feel a sense of achievement as a result of performing them, are rooted in our need to experience growth and self-actualization. The second set of needs he termed "hygienes." **Hygienes** relate to the work environment and are based in the basic human need to "avoid pain." According to Herzberg, growth needs motivate us to perform well and, when these needs are met, lead to the experience of satisfaction. Hygiene needs, on the other hand, must be met to avoid dissatisfaction (but do not necessarily provide satisfaction or motivation).[15]

Hygiene factors are not directly related to the work itself (job content). Rather, hygienes refer to job context factors (pay, working conditions, supervision, and security). Herzberg also refers to these factors as "dissatisfiers" because they are frequently associated with dissatisfied employees. These factors are so frequently associated with dissatisfaction that Herzberg claims they never really provide satisfaction. When they're present in sufficient quantities, we avoid dissatisfaction, but they do not contribute to satisfaction. Furthermore, since meeting these needs does not provide satisfaction, Herzberg concludes that they do not motivate workers.

Motivator factors involve our long-term need to pursue psychological growth (much like Maslow's esteem and self-actualization needs). Motivators relate to *job content.* Job content is what we actually *do* when we perform our job duties. Herzberg considered job duties that lead to feelings of achievement and recognition to be motivators. He refers to these factors as "satisfiers" to reflect their ability to provide satisfying experiences. When these needs are met, we experience satisfaction. Because meeting these needs provides satisfaction, they motivate workers. More specifically, Herzberg believes these motivators lead to high performance (achievement), and the high performance itself leads to satisfaction.

The unique feature of Herzberg's theory is that job conditions that prevent dissatisfaction do not cause satisfaction. Satisfaction and dissatisfaction are on different "scales" in his view. Hygienes can cause dissatisfaction if they are not present in sufficient levels. Thus, an employee can be dissatisfied with low pay. But paying him more will not cause long-term satisfaction *unless* motivators are present. Good pay *by itself* will only make the employee neutral toward work; to attain satisfaction, employees need challenging job duties that result in a sense of achievement. Employees can be dissatisfied, neutral, or satisfied with their jobs, depending on their levels of hygienes and motivators. Herzberg's theory even allows for the possibility that an employee can be satisfied and dissatisfied at the same time—the "I love my job but I hate the pay" situation!

Herzberg's theory has made lasting contributions to organizational research and managerial practice. Researchers have used it to identify the wide range of factors that influence worker reactions. Previously, most organizations attended primarily to hygiene factors. Because of Herzberg's work, organizations today realize the potential of motivators. Job enrichment programs are among the many direct results of his research.

Herzberg's work suggests a two-stage process for managing employee motivation and satisfaction. First, managers should address the hygiene factors. Intense forms of dissatisfaction distract employees from important work-related activities and tend to be demotivating.[16] Thus, managers should make sure that such basic needs as adequate pay, safe and clean working conditions, and opportunities for social interaction are met. They should then address the much more powerful motivator needs, in which workers experience recognition, responsibility, achievement, and growth. If motivator needs are ignored, neither long-term satisfaction nor high motivation is likely. When motivator needs are met, however, employees feel satisfied and are motivated to perform well.

Self-Determination Theory

One major implication of Herzberg's motivator-hygiene theory is the somewhat counterintuitive idea that managers should focus more on motivators than on hygienes. (After all, doesn't everyone want to be paid well? Organizations have held this out as a chief motivator for decades!) Why might concentrating on motivators give better results? To answer this question, we must examine *types* of motivation. Organizational behavior researchers often classify motivation in terms of what stimulates it. In the case of **extrinsic motivation**, we endeavor to acquire something that satisfies a lower-order need. Jobs that pay well and that are performed in safe, clean working conditions with adequate supervision and resources directly or indirectly satisfy these lower-order needs. These "outside the person" factors are *extrinsic rewards*.

Factors "inside" the person that cause people to perform tasks, **intrinsic motivation**, arise out of performing a task in and of itself, because it is interesting or "fun" to do. The task is enjoyable, so we continue to do it *even in the absence* of extrinsic rewards. That is, we are motivated by *intrinsic rewards,* rewards that we more or less give ourselves. Intrinsic rewards satisfy higher-order needs like relatedness and growth in ERG theory. When we sense that we are valuable contributors, are achieving something important, or are getting better at some skill, we like this feeling and strive to maintain it.

Self-determination theory (SDT) seeks to explain not only what causes motivation, but also how extrinsic rewards affect intrinsic motivation.[17] In SDT, extrinsic motivation refers to the performance of an activity in order to attain some valued outcome, while intrinsic motivation refers to performing an activity for the inherent satisfaction of the activity itself. SDT specifies when an activity will be intrinsically motivating and when it will not. Considerable numbers of studies have demonstrated that tasks are intrinsically motivating when they satisfy at least one of three higher-order needs: competence, autonomy, and relatedness. These precepts from SDT are entirely consistent with earlier discussions of theories by McClelland, Maslow, Alderfer, and Herzberg.

SDT takes the concepts of extrinsic rewards and intrinsic motivation further than the other need theories. SDT researchers have consistently found that as the level of extrinsic rewards increases, the amount of intrinsic motivation *decreases.* That is, SDT posits that extrinsic rewards not only do not provide intrinsic motivation, they diminish it. Think of this in terms of hobbies. Some people like to knit, others like to carve wood. They do it because it is intrinsically motivating; the hobby satisfies needs for competence, autonomy, and relatedness. But what happens if these hobbyists start getting paid well for their sweaters and carvings? Over time the hobby becomes less fun and is done in order to receive extrinsic rewards (money). Extrinsic motivation increases as intrinsic motivation decreases! When extrinsic rewards are present, people do not feel like what they do builds competence, is self-determined, or enhances relationships with others.

SDT theory has interesting implications for the management of organizational behavior. Some jobs are by their very nature uninteresting and unlikely to be made interesting. Automation has eliminated many such jobs, but they are still numerous. SDT would suggest that the primary way to motivate high performance for such jobs is to make performance contingent on extrinsic rewards. Relatively high pay is necessary to sustain performance on certain low-skill jobs. On the other hand, SDT would suggest that to enhance intrinsic motivation on jobs that are interesting, don't focus only on increasing extrinsic rewards (like large pay bonuses). Instead, create even more opportunities for employees to satisfy their needs for competence, autonomy, and relatedness. That means giving them opportunities to learn new skills, to perform their jobs without interference, and to develop meaningful relationships with other customers and employees in other departments. Such actions enhance intrinsic rewards.

You may have noticed that content theories are somewhat quiet about what determines the intensity of motivation. For example, some people steal to satisfy their lower-order needs (they have high intensity). But most of us don't steal. Why is this? Process theories of motivation attempt to explain this aspect of motivation by focusing on the intensity of motivation as well as its direction. According to self-determination theory, skilled workers who are given a chance to hone their skills and the freedom to practice their craft will be intrinsically motivated.

1. Understand the content theories of motivation.
2. Understand the contributions that Murray, McClelland, Maslow, Alderfer, and Herzberg made toward an understanding of human motivation.

14.3 | Process Theories of Motivation

3. Describe the process theories of motivation, and compare and contrast the main process theories of motivation: operant conditioning theory, equity theory, goal theory, and expectancy theory.

Process theories of motivation try to explain *why* behaviors are initiated. These theories focus on the mechanism by which we choose a target, and the effort that we exert to "hit" the target. There are four major process theories: (1) operant conditioning, (2) equity, (3) goal, and (4) expectancy.

Operant Conditioning Theory

Operant conditioning theory is the simplest of the motivation theories. It basically states that people will do those things for which they are rewarded and will avoid doing things for which they are punished. This premise is sometimes called the "law of effect." However, if this were the sum total of conditioning theory, we would not be discussing it here. Operant conditioning theory does offer greater insights than "reward what you want and punish what you don't," and knowledge of its principles can lead to effective management practices.

Operant conditioning focuses on the learning of voluntary behaviors.[18] The term **operant conditioning** indicates that learning results from our "operating on" the environment. After we "operate on the environment" (that is, behave in a certain fashion), consequences result. These consequences determine the likelihood of similar behavior in the future. Learning occurs because we do something to the environment. The environment then reacts to our action, and our subsequent behavior is influenced by this reaction.

The Basic Operant Model

According to **operant conditioning theory**, we learn to behave in a particular fashion because of consequences that resulted from our past behaviors.[19] The learning process involves three distinct steps (see **Table 14.2**). The first step involves a *stimulus* (S). The stimulus is any situation or event we perceive that we then respond to. A homework assignment is a stimulus. The second step involves a *response* (R), that is, any behavior or action we take in reaction to the stimulus. Staying up late to get your homework assignment in on time is a response. (We use the words response and behavior interchangeably here.) Finally, a *consequence* (C) is any event that follows our response and that makes the response more or less likely to occur in the future. If Colleen Sullivan receives praise from her superior for working hard, and if getting that praise is a pleasurable event, then it is likely that Colleen will work hard again in the future. If, on the other hand, the superior ignores or criticizes Colleen's response (working hard), this consequence is likely to make Colleen avoid working hard in the future. It is the experienced consequence (positive or negative) that influences whether a response will be repeated the next time the stimulus is presented.

Process Theories of Motivation	
General Operant Model: S → R → C	
Ways to Strengthen the S → R Link	
1. S → R → C+	(Positive Reinforcement)
2. S → R → C–	(Negative Reinforcement)
3. S → R → (no C–)	(Avoidance Learning)
Ways to Weaken the S → R Link	
1. S → R → (no C)	(Nonreinforcement)
2. S → R → C–	(Punishment)

Table 14.2 (Attribution: Copyright Rice University, OpenStax, under CC-BY 4.0 license)

Reinforcement occurs when a consequence makes it more likely the response/behavior will be repeated in the future. In the previous example, praise from Colleen's superior is a reinforcer. **Extinction** occurs when a consequence makes it less likely the response/behavior will be repeated in the future. Criticism from Colleen's supervisor could cause her to stop working hard on any assignment.

There are three ways to make a response more likely to recur: positive reinforcement, negative reinforcement, and avoidance learning. In addition, there are two ways to make the response less likely to recur: nonreinforcement and punishment.

Making a Response More Likely

According to reinforcement theorists, managers can encourage employees to repeat a behavior if they provide a desirable consequence, or reward, after the behavior is performed. A **positive reinforcement** is a desirable consequence that satisfies an active need or that removes a barrier to need satisfaction. It can be as simple as a kind word or as major as a promotion. Companies that provide "dinners for two" as awards to those employees who go the extra mile are utilizing positive reinforcement. It is important to note that there are wide variations in what people consider to be a positive reinforcer. Praise from a supervisor may be a powerful reinforcer for some workers (like high-nAch individuals) but not others.

Another technique for making a desired response more likely to be repeated is known as **negative reinforcement**. When a behavior causes something undesirable to be taken away, the behavior is more likely to be repeated in the future. Managers use negative reinforcement when they remove something unpleasant from an employee's work environment in the hope that this will encourage the desired behavior. Ted doesn't like being continually reminded by Philip to work faster (Ted thinks Philip is nagging him), so he works faster at stocking shelves to avoid being criticized. Philip's reminders are a negative reinforcement for Ted.

Approach using negative reinforcement with extreme caution. Negative reinforcement is often confused with punishment. Punishment, unlike reinforcement (negative or positive), is intended to make a particular behavior go away (not be repeated). Negative reinforcement, like positive reinforcement, is intended to make a behavior more likely to be repeated in the future. In the previous example, Philip's reminders simultaneously punished one behavior (slow stocking) and reinforced another (faster stocking). The difference is often a fine one, but it becomes clearer when we identify the behaviors we are trying to encourage (reinforcement) or discourage (punishment).

Exhibit 14.10   Workers stacking eggs A worker stacks eggs on the shelves at a supermarket. Consider the interchange between Ted and Philip regarding speeding up the shelf restocking process. What could go wrong? (Credit: Alex Barth/ flickr/ Attribution 2.0 Generic (CC BY 2.0))

A third method of making a response more likely to occur involves a process known as avoidance learning. **Avoidance learning** occurs when we learn to behave in a certain way to avoid encountering an undesired or unpleasant consequence. We may learn to wake up a minute or so before our alarm clock rings so we can turn it off and not hear the irritating buzzer. Some workers learn to get to work on time to avoid the harsh words or punitive actions of their supervisors. Many organizational discipline systems rely heavily on avoidance learning by using the threat of negative consequences to encourage desired behavior. When managers warn an employee not to be late again, when they threaten to fire a careless worker, or when they transfer someone to an undesirable position, they are relying on the power of avoidance learning.

Making a Response Less Likely

At times it is necessary to discourage a worker from repeating an undesirable behavior. The techniques managers use to make a behavior less likely to occur involve doing something that frustrates the individual's need satisfaction or that removes a currently satisfying circumstance. **Punishment** is an aversive consequence that follows a behavior and makes it less likely to reoccur.

Note that managers have another alternative, known as **nonreinforcement**, in which they provide no consequence at all following a worker's response. Nonreinforcement eventually reduces the likelihood of that response reoccurring, which means that managers who fail to reinforce a worker's desirable behavior are also likely to see that desirable behavior less often. If Philip never rewards Ted when he finishes stocking on time, for instance, Ted will probably stop trying to beat the clock. Nonreinforcement can also reduce the likelihood that employees will repeat undesirable behaviors, although it doesn't produce results as quickly as punishment does. Furthermore, if other reinforcing consequences are present, nonreinforcement is unlikely to be effective.

While punishment clearly works more quickly than does nonreinforcement, it has some potentially undesirable side effects. Although punishment effectively tells a person what *not* to do and stops the undesired behavior, it does not tell them what they *should* do. In addition, even when punishment works as intended, the worker being punished often develops negative feelings toward the person who does the punishing. Although sometimes it is very difficult for managers to avoid using punishment, it works best when reinforcement is also used. An experiment conducted by two researchers at the University of Kansas found that using nonmonetary reinforcement in addition to punitive disciplinary measures was an effective way to decrease absenteeism in an industrial setting.[20]

Schedules of Reinforcement

When a person is learning a new behavior, like how to perform a new job, it is desirable to reinforce effective behaviors every time they are demonstrated (this is called *shaping*). But in organizations it is not usually possible to reinforce desired behaviors every time they are performed, for obvious reasons. Moreover, research indicates that constantly reinforcing desired behaviors, termed *continuous reinforcement,* can be detrimental in the long run. Behaviors that are learned under continuous reinforcement are quickly extinguished (cease to be demonstrated). This is because people will expect a reward (the reinforcement) every time they display the behavior. When they don't receive it after just a few times, they quickly presume that the behavior will no longer be rewarded, and they quit doing it. Any employer can change employees' behavior by simply not paying them!

If behaviors cannot (and should not) be reinforced every time they are exhibited, how often should they be reinforced? This is a question about **schedules of reinforcement**, or the frequency at which effective employee behaviors should be reinforced. Much of the early research on operant conditioning focused on the best way to maintain the performance of desired behaviors. That is, it attempted to determine how frequently behaviors need to be rewarded so that they are not extinguished. Research zeroed in on four types of reinforcement schedules:

Fixed Ratio. With this schedule, a fixed number of responses (let's say five) must be exhibited before any of the responses are reinforced. If the desired response is coming to work on time, then giving employees a $25 bonus for being punctual every day from Monday through Friday would be a fixed ratio of reinforcement.

Variable Ratio. A variable-ratio schedule reinforces behaviors, *on average,* a fixed number of times (again let's say five). Sometimes the tenth behavior is reinforced, other times the first, but on average every fifth response is reinforced. People who perform under such variable-ratio schedules like this don't know *when* they will be rewarded, but they do know that they *will* be rewarded.

Fixed Interval. In a fixed-interval schedule, a certain amount of time must pass before a behavior is reinforced. With a one-hour fixed-interval schedule, for example, a supervisor visits an employee's workstation and reinforces the first desired behavior she sees. She returns one hour later and reinforces the next desirable behavior. This schedule doesn't imply that reinforcement will be received automatically after the passage of the time period. The time must pass *and* an appropriate response must be made.

Variable Interval. The variable interval differs from fixed-interval schedules in that the specified time interval passes *on average* before another appropriate response is reinforced. Sometimes the time period is shorter than the average; sometimes it is longer.

Which type of reinforcement schedule is best? In general, continuous reinforcement is best while employees are learning their jobs or new duties. After that, variable-ratio reinforcement schedules are superior. In most situations the fixed-interval schedule produces the least effective results, with fixed ratio and variable interval falling in between the two extremes. But remember that effective behaviors must be reinforced with some type of schedule, or they may become extinguished.

Equity Theory

Suppose you have worked for a company for several years. Your performance has been excellent, you have received regular pay increases, and you get along with your boss and coworkers. One day you come to work to find that a new person has been hired to work at the same job that you do. You are pleased to have the extra help. Then, you find out the new person is making $100 more per week than you, despite your longer service and greater experience. How do you feel? If you're like most of us, you're quite unhappy. Your satisfaction has just evaporated. Nothing about your job has changed—you receive the same pay, do the same job, and work for the same supervisor. Yet, the addition of one new employee has transformed you from a happy to an unhappy employee. This feeling of unfairness is the basis for equity theory.

Equity theory states that motivation is affected by the outcomes we receive for our inputs compared to the outcomes and inputs of other people.[21] This theory is concerned with the reactions people have to outcomes they receive as part of a "social exchange." According to equity theory, our reactions to the outcomes we receive from others (an employer) depend both on how we value those outcomes in an absolute sense *and* on the circumstances surrounding their receipt. Equity theory suggests that our reactions will be influenced by our perceptions of the "inputs" provided in order to receive these outcomes ("Did I get as much out of this as I put into it?"). Even more important is our comparison of our inputs to what we believe others received for their inputs ("Did I get as much for my inputs as my coworkers got for theirs?").

The Basic Equity Model

The fundamental premise of equity theory is that we continuously monitor the degree to which our work environment is "fair." In determining the degree of fairness, we consider two sets of factors, inputs and outcomes (see **Exhibit 14.11**). **Inputs** are any factors we contribute to the organization that we feel have value and are relevant to the organization. Note that the value attached to an input is based on *our* perception of its relevance and value. Whether or not anyone else agrees that the input is relevant or valuable is unimportant to us. Common inputs in organizations include time, effort, performance level, education level, skill levels, and bypassed opportunities. Since any factor we consider relevant is included in our evaluation of equity, it is not uncommon for factors to be included that the organization (or even the law) might argue are inappropriate (such as age, sex, ethnic background, or social status).

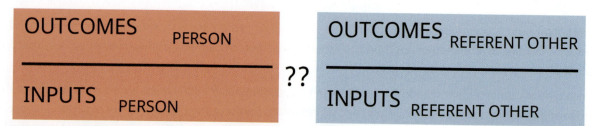

Exhibit 14.11   The Equity Theory Comparison (Attribution: Copyright Rice University, OpenStax, under CC-BY 4.0 license)

Outcomes are anything we perceive as getting back from the organization in exchange for our inputs. Again, the value attached to an outcome is based on our perceptions and not necessarily on objective reality. Common outcomes from organizations include pay, working conditions, job status, feelings of achievement, and friendship opportunities. Both positive and negative outcomes influence our evaluation of equity. Stress, headaches, and fatigue are also potential outcomes. Since any outcome we consider relevant to the exchange influences our equity perception, we frequently include unintended factors (peer disapproval, family reactions).

Equity theory predicts that we will compare our outcomes to our inputs in the form of a ratio. On the basis of this ratio we make an initial determination of whether or not the situation is equitable. If we perceive that the outcomes we receive are commensurate with our inputs, we are satisfied. If we believe that the outcomes are not commensurate with our inputs, we are dissatisfied. This dissatisfaction can lead to ineffective behaviors for the organization if they continue. The key feature of equity theory is that it predicts that we will compare our ratios to the ratios of other people. It is this comparison of the two ratios that has the strongest effect on our equity perceptions. These other people are called referent others because we "refer to" them when we judge equity. Usually, referent others are people we work with who perform work of a similar nature. That is, **referent others** perform jobs that are similar in difficulty and complexity to the employee making the equity determination (see **Exhibit 14.11**).

Three conditions can result from this comparison. Our outcome-to-input ratio could equal the referent other's. This is a **state of equity**. A second result could be that our ratio is greater than the referent other's. This is a state of **overreward inequity**. The third result could be that we perceive our ratio to be less than that of the referent other. This is a state of **underreward inequity**.

Equity theory has a lot to say about basic human tendencies. The motivation to compare our situation to that of others is strong. For example, what is the first thing you do when you get an exam back in class? Probably look at your score and make an initial judgment as to its fairness. For a lot of people, the very next thing they do is look at the scores received by fellow students who sit close to them. A 75 percent score doesn't look so bad if everyone else scored lower! This is equity theory in action.

Most workers in the United States are at least partially dissatisfied with their pay.[22] Equity theory helps explain this. Two human tendencies create feelings of inequity that are not based in reality. One is that we tend to overrate our performance levels. For example, one study conducted by your authors asked more than 600 employees to anonymously rate their performance on a 7-point scale (1 = poor, 7 = excellent). The average was 6.2, meaning the *average* employee rated his or her performance as *very good to excellent.* This implies that the average employee also expects excellent pay increases, a policy most employers cannot afford if they are to remain competitive. Another study found that the average employee (one whose performance is better than half of the other employees and worse than the other half) rated her performance at the 80th percentile (better than 80 percent of the other employees, worse than 20 percent).[23] Again it would be impossible for most organizations to reward the average employee at the 80th percentile. In other words, most employees inaccurately overrate the inputs they provide to an organization. This leads to perceptions of inequity that are not justified.

The second human tendency that leads to unwarranted perceptions of inequity is our tendency to *overrate* the outcomes of others.[24] Many employers keep the pay levels of employees a "secret." Still other employers actually forbid employees to talk about their pay. This means that many employees don't know for certain how much their colleagues are paid. And, because most of us overestimate the pay of others, we tend to think that they're paid more than they actually are, and the unjustified perceptions of inequity are perpetuated.

The bottom line for employers is that they need to be sensitive to employees' need for equity. Employers need to do everything they can to prevent feelings of inequity because employees engage in effective behaviors when they perceive equity and ineffective behaviors when they perceive inequity.

Perceived Overreward Inequity

When we perceive that overreward inequity exists (that is, we unfairly make more than others), it is rare that we are so dissatisfied, guilty, or sufficiently motivated that we make changes to produce a state of perceived equity (or we leave the situation). Indeed, feelings of overreward, when they occur, are quite transient. Very few of us go to our employers and complain that we're overpaid! Most people are less sensitive to overreward inequities than they are to underreward inequities.[25] However infrequently they are used for overreward, the same types of actions are available for dealing with both types of inequity.

Perceived Underreward Inequity

When we perceive that underreward inequity exists (that is, others unfairly make more than we do), we will likely be dissatisfied, angered, and motivated to change the situation (or escape the situation) in order to produce a state of perceived equity. As we discuss shortly, people can take many actions to deal with underreward inequity.

Reducing Underreward Inequity

A simple situation helps explain the consequences of inequity. Two automobile workers in Detroit, John and Mary, fasten lug nuts to wheels on cars as they come down the assembly line, John on the left side and Mary on the right. Their inputs are equal (both fasten the same number of lug nuts at the same pace), but John makes $500 per week and Mary makes $600. Their equity ratios are thus:

$500	$600
John:	<Mary:
10 lug nuts/car	10 lug nuts/car

As you can see, their ratios are not equal; that is, Mary receives greater outcome for equal input. Who is experiencing inequity? According to equity theory, both John *and* Mary—underreward inequity for John, and overreward inequity for Mary. Mary's inequity won't last long (in real organizations), but in our hypothetical example, what might John do to resolve this?

Adams identified a number of things people do to reduce the tension produced by a perceived state of inequity. They change their own outcomes or inputs, *or* they change those of the referent other. They distort their own perceptions of the outcomes or inputs of either party by using a different referent other, or they leave the situation in which the inequity is occurring.

1. Alter inputs of the person. The perceived state of equity can be altered by changing our own inputs, that is, by decreasing the quantity or quality of our performance. John can effect his own mini slowdown and install only nine lug nuts on each car as it comes down the production line. This, of course, might cause him to lose his job, so he probably won't choose this alternative.

2. Alter outcomes of the person. We could attempt to increase outcomes to achieve a state of equity, like ask for a raise, a nicer office, a promotion, or other positively valued outcomes. So John will likely ask for a raise. Unfortunately, many people enhance their outcomes by stealing from their employers.

3. Alter inputs of the referent other. When underrewarded, we may try to achieve a state of perceived equity by encouraging the referent other to increase their inputs. We may demand, for example, that the referent other "start pulling their weight," or perhaps help the referent other to become a better performer. It doesn't matter that the referent other is already pulling their weight—remember, this is all about perception. In our example, John could ask Mary to put on two of his ten lug nuts as each car comes down the assembly line. This would not likely happen, however, so John would be motivated to try another alternative to reduce his inequity.

4. Alter outcomes of the referent other. We can "correct" a state of underreward by directly or indirectly reducing the value of the other's outcomes. In our example, John could try to get Mary's pay lowered to reduce his inequity. This too would probably not occur in the situation described.

5. Distort perceptions of inputs or outcomes. It *is* possible to reduce a perceived state of inequity without changing input or outcome. We simply distort our own perceptions of our inputs or outcomes, *or* we distort our perception of those of the referent other. Thus, John may tell himself that "Mary does better work than I thought" or "she enjoys her work much less than I do" or "she gets paid less than I realized."

6. Choose a different referent other. We can also deal with both over- and underreward inequities by changing the referent other ("my situation is really more like Ahmed's"). This is the simplest and most powerful way to deal with perceived inequity: it requires neither actual nor perceptual changes in anybody's input or outcome, and it causes us to look around and assess our situation more carefully. For example, John might choose as a referent other Bill, who installs dashboards but makes less money than John.

7. Leave the situation. A final technique for dealing with a perceived state of inequity involves removing ourselves from the situation. We can choose to accomplish this through absenteeism, transfer, or termination. This approach is usually not selected unless the perceived inequity is quite high or other attempts at achieving equity are not readily available. Most automobile workers are paid quite well for their work. John is unlikely to find an equivalent job, so it is also unlikely that he will choose this option.

Implications of Equity Theory

Equity theory is widely used, and its implications are clear. In the vast majority of cases, employees experience (or perceive) underreward inequity rather than overreward. As discussed above, few of the behaviors that result from underreward inequity are good for employers. Thus, employers try to prevent unnecessary perceptions of inequity. They do this in a number of ways. They try to be as fair as possible in allocating pay. That is, they measure performance levels as accurately as possible, then give the highest performers the highest pay increases. Second, most employers are no longer secretive about their pay schedules. People are naturally curious about how much they are paid relative to others in the organization. This doesn't mean that employers don't practice discretion—they usually don't reveal specific employees' exact pay. But they do tell employees the minimum and maximum pay levels for their jobs and the pay scales for the jobs of others in the organization. Such practices give employees a factual basis for judging equity.

Supervisors play a key role in creating perceptions of equity. "Playing favorites" ensures perceptions of inequity. Employees want to be rewarded on their merits, not the whims of their supervisors. In addition, supervisors need to recognize differences in employees in their reactions to inequity. Some employees are highly sensitive to inequity, and a supervisor needs to be especially cautious around them.[26] Everyone is sensitive to reward allocation.[27] But "equity sensitives" are even more sensitive. A major principle for supervisors, then, is simply to implement fairness. Never base punishment or reward on whether or not you like an employee. Reward behaviors that contribute to the organization, and discipline those that do not. Make sure employees understand what is expected of them, and praise them when they do it. These practices make everyone happier and your job easier.

Goal Theory

No theory is perfect. If it was, it wouldn't be a theory. It would be a set of facts. Theories are sets of propositions that are right more often than they are wrong, but they are not infallible. However, the basic propositions of goal theory* come close to being infallible. Indeed, it is one of the strongest theories in organizational behavior.

The Basic Goal-Setting Model

Goal theory states that people will perform better if they have difficult, specific, accepted performance goals or objectives.[28],[29] The first and most basic premise of goal theory is that people will attempt to achieve those goals that they *intend* to achieve. Thus, if we intend to do something (like get an A on an exam), we will exert effort to accomplish it. Without such goals, our effort at the task (studying) required to achieve the goal is less. Students whose goals are to get As study harder than students who don't have this goal—we all know this. This doesn't mean that people without goals are unmotivated. It simply means that people with goals are more motivated. The intensity of their motivation is greater, and they are more directed.

The second basic premise is that *difficult* goals result in better performance than easy goals. This does not mean that difficult goals are always achieved, but our performance will usually be better when we intend to achieve harder goals. Your goal of an A in Classical Mechanics at Cal Tech may not get you your A, but it may earn you a B+, which you wouldn't have gotten otherwise. Difficult goals cause us to exert more effort, and this almost always results in better performance.

Another premise of goal theory is that *specific* goals are better than vague goals. We often wonder what we need to do to be successful. Have you ever asked a professor "What do I need to do to get an A in this course?" If she responded "Do well on the exams," you weren't much better off for having asked. This is a vague response. Goal theory says that we perform better when we have specific goals. Had your professor told you the key thrust of the course, to turn in *all* the problem sets, to pay close attention to the essay questions on exams, and to aim for scores in the 90s, you would have something concrete on which to build a strategy.

A key premise of goal theory is that people must *accept* the goal. Usually we set our own goals. But sometimes others set goals for us. Your professor telling you your goal is to "score at least a 90 percent on your exams" doesn't mean that you'll accept this goal. Maybe you don't feel you can achieve scores in the 90s. Or, you've heard that 90 isn't good enough for an A in this class. This happens in work organizations quite often. Supervisors give orders that something must be done by a certain time. The employees may fully understand what is wanted, yet if they feel the order is unreasonable or impossible, they may not exert much effort to accomplish it. Thus, it is important for people to accept the goal. They need to feel that it is also their goal. If they do not, goal theory predicts that they won't try as hard to achieve it.

Goal theory also states that people need to *commit* to a goal in addition to accepting it. **Goal commitment** is the degree to which we dedicate ourselves to achieving a goal. Goal commitment is about setting priorities. We can accept many goals (go to all classes, stay awake during classes, take lecture notes), but we often end up doing only some of them. In other words, some goals are more important than others. And we exert more effort for certain goals. This also happens frequently at work. A software analyst's major goal may be to write a new program. Her minor goal may be to maintain previously written programs. It is minor because maintaining old programs is boring, while writing new ones is fun. Goal theory predicts that her commitment, and thus her intensity, to the major goal will be greater.

Allowing people to participate in the goal-setting process often results in higher goal commitment. This has to do with ownership. And when people participate in the process, they tend to incorporate factors they think will make the goal more interesting, challenging, and attainable. Thus, it is advisable to allow people some input into the goal-setting process. Imposing goals on them from the outside usually results in less commitment (and acceptance).

The basic goal-setting model is shown in **Exhibit 14.12**. The process starts with our values. Values are our beliefs about how the world should be or act, and often include words like "should" or "ought." We compare our present conditions against these values. For example, Randi holds the value that everyone should be a hard worker. After measuring her current work against this value, Randi concludes that she doesn't measure up to her own value. Following this, her goal-setting process begins. Randi will set a goal that affirms her status as a hard worker. **Exhibit 14.12** lists the four types of goals. Some goals are self-set. (Randi decides to word process at least 70 pages per day.) Participative goals are jointly set. (Randi goes to her supervisor, and together they set some appropriate goals for her.) In still other cases, goals are assigned. (Her boss tells her that she must word process at least 60 pages per day.) The fourth type of goal, which can be self-set, jointly determined, or assigned, is a "do your best" goal. But note this goal is vague, so it usually doesn't result in the best performance.

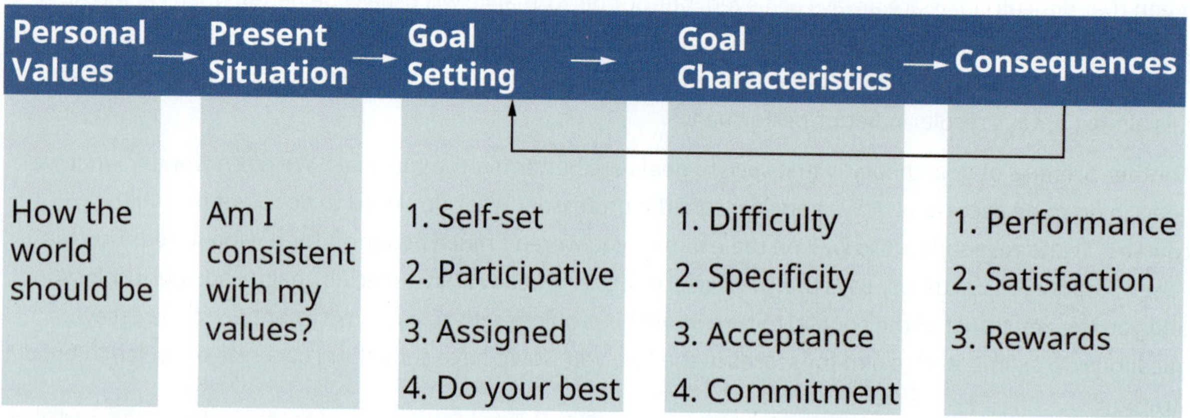

Personal Values	Present Situation	Goal Setting	Goal Characteristics	Consequences
How the world should be	Am I consistent with my values?	1. Self-set 2. Participative 3. Assigned 4. Do your best	1. Difficulty 2. Specificity 3. Acceptance 4. Commitment	1. Performance 2. Satisfaction 3. Rewards

Exhibit 14.12   The Goal-Setting Process (Attribution: Copyright Rice University, OpenStax, under CC-BY 4.0 license)

Depending on the characteristics of Randi's goals, she may or may not exert a lot of effort. For maximum effort to result, her goals should be difficult, specific, accepted, and committed to. Then, if she has sufficient ability and lack of constraints, maximum performance should occur. Examples of constraints could be that her old computer frequently breaks down or her supervisor constantly interferes.

The consequence of endeavoring to reach her goal will be that Randi will be satisfied with herself. Her behavior is consistent with her values. She'll be even more satisfied if her supervisor praises her performance and gives her a pay increase!

In Randi's case, her goal achievement resulted in several benefits. However, this doesn't always happen. If goals are not achieved, people may be unhappy with themselves, and their employer may be dissatisfied as well. Such an experience can make a person reluctant to accept goals in the future. Thus, setting difficult yet attainable goals cannot be stressed enough.

Goal theory can be a tremendous motivational tool. In fact, many organizations practice effective management by using a technique called "management by objectives" (MBO). MBO is based on goal theory and is quite effective when implemented consistently with goal theory's basic premises.

Despite its many strengths, several cautions about goal theory are appropriate. Locke has identified most of them.[30] First, setting goals in one area can lead people to neglect other areas. (Randi may word process 70 pages per day, but neglect her proofreading responsibilities.) It is important that goals be set for most major duties. Second, goal setting sometimes has unintended consequences. For example, employees set easy goals so that they look good when they achieve them. Or it causes unhealthy competition between employees. Or an employee sabotages the work of others so that only she has goal achievement.

Some managers use goal setting in unethical ways. They may manipulate employees by setting impossible goals. This enables them to criticize employees even when the employees are doing superior work and, of course, causes much stress. Goal setting should never be abused. Perhaps the key caution about goal setting is that it often results in too much focus on quantified measures of performance. Qualitative aspects of a job or task may be neglected because they aren't easily measured. Managers must keep employees focused on the qualitative aspects of their jobs as well as the quantitative ones. Finally, setting individual goals in a teamwork environment can be counterproductive.[31] Where possible, it is preferable to have group goals in situations where employees depend on one another in the performance of their jobs.

The cautions noted here are not intended to deter you from using goal theory. We note them so that you can avoid the pitfalls. Remember, employees have a right to reasonable performance expectations and the rewards that result from performance, and organizations have a right to expect high performance levels from employees. Goal theory should be used to optimize the employment relationship. Goal theory holds that people will exert effort to accomplish goals if those goals are difficult to achieve, accepted by the individual, and specific in nature.

Expectancy Theory

Expectancy theory posits that we will exert much effort to perform at high levels so that we can obtain valued outcomes. It is the motivation theory that many organizational behavior researchers find most intriguing, in no small part because it is currently also the most comprehensive theory. Expectancy theory ties together many of the concepts and hypotheses from the theories discussed earlier in this chapter. In addition, it points to factors that other theories miss. Expectancy theory has much to offer the student of management and organizational behavior.

Expectancy theory is sufficiently general that it is useful in a wide variety of situations. Choices between job offers, between working hard or not so hard, between going to work or not—virtually any set of possibilities can be addressed by expectancy theory. Basically, the theory focuses on two related issues:

1. When faced with two or more alternatives, which will we select?
2. Once an alternative is chosen, how motivated will we be to pursue that choice?

Expectancy theory thus focuses on the two major aspects of motivation, *direction* (which alternative?) and *intensity* (how much effort to implement the alternative?). The attractiveness of an alternative is determined by our "expectations" of what is likely to happen if we choose it. The more we believe that the alternative chosen will lead to positively valued outcomes, the greater its attractiveness to us.

Expectancy theory states that, when faced with two or more alternatives, we will select the most attractive one. And, the greater the attractiveness of the chosen alternative, the more motivated we will be to pursue it. Our natural hedonism, discussed earlier in this chapter, plays a role in this process. We are motivated to maximize desirable outcomes (a pay raise) and minimize undesirable ones (discipline). Expectancy theory goes on to state that we are also logical in our decisions about alternatives. It considers people to be *rational*. People evaluate alternatives in terms of their "pros and cons," and then choose the one with the most "pros" and fewest "cons."

The Basic Expectancy Model

The three major components of expectancy theory reflect its assumptions of hedonism and rationality: effort-performance expectancy, performance-outcome expectancy, and valences.

The **effort-performance expectancy**, abbreviated E1, is the perceived probability that effort will lead to performance (or E ➡ P). Performance here means anything from doing well on an exam to assembling 100 toasters a day at work. Sometimes people believe that no matter how much effort they exert, they won't perform at a high level. They have weak E1s. Other people have strong E1s and believe the opposite—that is, that they can perform at a high level if they exert high effort. You all know students with different E1s—those who believe that if they study hard they'll do well, and those who believe that no matter how much they study they'll do poorly. People develop these perceptions from prior experiences with the task at hand, and from self-perceptions of their abilities. The core of the E1 concept is that people don't always perceive a direct relationship between effort level and performance level.

The **performance-outcome expectancy**, E2, is the perceived relationship between performance and outcomes (or P ➡ O).[1] Many things in life happen as a function of how well we perform various tasks. E2 addresses the question "What will happen if I perform well?" Let's say you get an A in your Classical Mechanics course at Cal Tech. You'll be elated, your classmates may envy you, and you are now assured of that plum job at NASA. But let's say you got a D. Whoops, that was the last straw for the dean. Now you've flunked out, and you're reduced to going home to live with your parents (perish the thought!). Likewise, E2 perceptions develop in organizations, although hopefully not as drastically as your beleaguered career at Cal Tech. People with strong E2s believe that if they perform their jobs well, they'll receive desirable outcomes—good pay increases, praise from their supervisor, and a feeling that they're really contributing. In the same situation, people with weak E2s will have the opposite perceptions—that high performance levels don't result in desirable outcomes and that it doesn't really matter how well they perform their jobs as long as they don't get fired.

---

1   Sometimes E2s are called *instrumentalities,* because they are the perception that performance is instrumental in getting some desired outcome.

Valences are the easiest of the expectancy theory concepts to describe. Valences are simply the degree to which we perceive an outcome as desirable, neutral, or undesirable. Highly desirable outcomes (a 25 percent pay increase) are positively valent. Undesirable outcomes (being disciplined) are negatively valent. Outcomes that we're indifferent to (where you must park your car) have neutral valences. Positively and negatively valent outcomes abound in the workplace—pay increases and freezes, praise and criticism, recognition and rejection, promotions and demotions. And as you would expect, people differ dramatically in how they value these outcomes. Our needs, values, goals, and life situations affect what valence we give an outcome. Equity is another consideration we use in assigning valences. We may consider a 10 percent pay increase desirable until we find out that it was the lowest raise given in our work group.

Exhibit 14.13 summarizes the three core concepts of expectancy theory. The theory states that our perceptions about our surroundings are essentially predictions about "what leads to what." We perceive that certain effort levels result in certain performance levels. We perceive that certain performance levels result in certain outcomes. Outcomes can be **extrinsic**, in that others (our supervisor) determine whether we receive them, or **intrinsic**, in that we determine if they are received (our sense of achievement). Each outcome has an associated valence (outcome A's valence is V_a). Expectancy theory predicts that we will exert effort that results in the maximum amount of positive-valence outcomes.[2] If our E1 or E2 is weak, or if the outcomes are not sufficiently desirable, our motivation to exert effort will be low. Stated differently, an individual will be motivated to try to achieve the level of performance that results in the most rewards.

2

It can also be expressed as an equation:

$$\textit{Force to Choose A level of Effort} = E1 \times \sum (E2_o \times V_o)$$

Where V_o is the valence of a given outcome (o), and $E2_o$ is the perceived probability that a certain level of performance (e.g., Excellent, average, poor) will result in that outcome. So, for multiple outcomes, and different performance levels, the valence of the outcome and its associated performance→outcome expectancy (E2) are multiplied and added to the analogous value for the other outcomes. Combined with the E1 (the amount of effort required to produce a level of performance), the effort level with the greatest *force* associated with it will be chosen by the individual.

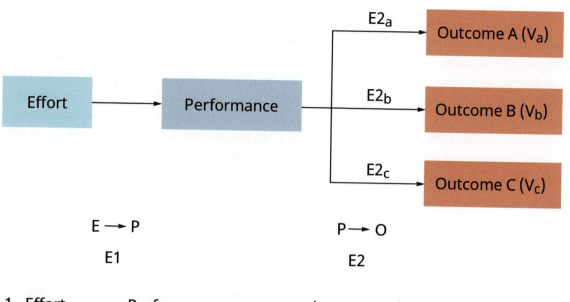

1. Effort ⟶ Performance expectancy (E ⟶ P; E1)
2. Performance ⟶ Outcome expectancy (P ⟶ O; E2)
3. Valences (V) of Outcomes (V_o)

Exhibit 14.13 The Expectancy Theory of Motivation (Attribution: Copyright Rice University, OpenStax, under CC-BY 4.0 license)

V_o is the valence of the outcome. The effort level with the greatest force associated with it will be chosen by the individual.

Implications of Expectancy Theory

Expectancy theory has major implications for the workplace. Basically, expectancy theory predicts that employees will be motivated to perform well on their jobs under two conditions. The first is when employees believe that a reasonable amount of effort will result in good performance. The second is when good performance is associated with positive outcomes and low performance is associated with negative outcomes. If neither of these conditions exists in the perceptions of employees, their motivation to perform will be low.

Why might an employee perceive that positive outcomes are not associated with high performance? Or that negative outcomes are not associated with low performance? That is, why would employees develop weak E2s? This happens for a number of reasons. The main one is that many organizations subscribe too strongly to a principle of equality (not to be confused with equity). They give all of their employees equal salaries for equal work, equal pay increases every year (these are known as across-the-board pay raises), and equal treatment wherever possible. Equality-focused organizations reason that some employees "getting more" than others leads to disruptive competition and feelings of inequity.

In time employees in equality-focused organizations develop weak E2s because no distinctions are made for differential outcomes. If the best and the worst salespeople are paid the same, in time they will both decide that it isn't worth the extra effort to be a high performer. Needless to say, this is not the goal of competitive organizations and can cause the demise of the organization as it competes with other firms in today's global marketplace.

Expectancy theory states that to maximize motivation, organizations must make outcomes contingent on performance. This is the main contribution of expectancy theory: it makes us think about *how* organizations should distribute outcomes. If an organization, or a supervisor, believes that treating everyone "the same" will result in satisfied and motivated employees, they will be wrong more times than not. From equity theory we know that some employees, usually the better-performing ones, will experience underreward inequity. From expectancy theory we know that employees will see no difference in outcomes for good and poor performance, so they will not have as much incentive to be good performers. Effective organizations need to actively encourage the perception that good performance leads to positive outcomes (bonuses, promotions) and that poor performance leads to negative ones (discipline, termination). Remember, there is a big difference between treating employees equally and treating them equitably.

What if an organization ties positive outcomes to high performance and negative outcomes to low performance? Employees will develop strong E2s. But will this result in highly motivated employees? The answer is maybe. We have yet to address employees' E1s. If employees have weak E1s, they will perceive that high (or low) effort does *not* result in high performance and thus will not exert much effort. It is important for managers to understand that this can happen despite rewards for high performance.

Task-related abilities are probably the single biggest reason why some employees have weak E1s. **Self-efficacy** is our belief about whether we can successfully execute some future action or task, or achieve some result. High self-efficacy employees believe that they are likely to succeed at most or all of their job duties and responsibilities. And as you would expect, low self-efficacy employees believe the opposite. Specific self-efficacy reflects our belief in our capability to perform a specific task at a specific level of performance. If we believe that the probability of our selling $30,000 of jackrabbit slippers in one month is .90, our self-efficacy for this task is high. Specific self-efficacy is our judgment about the likelihood of successful task performance measured immediately before we expend effort on the task. As a result, specific self-efficacy is much more variable than more enduring notions of personality. Still, there is little doubt that our state-based beliefs are some of the most powerful motivators of behavior. Our efficacy expectations at a given point in time determine not only our initial decision to perform (or not) a task, but also the amount of effort we will expend and whether we will persist in the face of adversity.[32] Self-efficacy has a strong impact on the E1 factor. As a result, self-efficacy is one of the strongest determinants of performance in any particular task situation.[33]

Employees develop weak E1s for two reasons. First, they don't have sufficient resources to perform their jobs. Resources can be internal or external. Internal resources include what employees bring to the job (such as prior training, work experience, education, ability, and aptitude) and their understanding of what they need to do to be considered good performers. The second resource is called role perceptions—how employees believe their jobs are done and how they fit into the broader organization. If employees don't know *how* to become good performers, they will have weak E1s. External resources include the tools, equipment, and labor necessary to perform a job. The lack of good external resources can also cause E1s to be weak.

The second reason for weak E1s is an organization's failure to measure performance accurately. That is, performance *ratings* don't correlate well with actual performance *levels*. How does this happen? Have you ever gotten a grade that you felt didn't reflect how much you learned? This also happens in organizations. Why are ratings sometimes inaccurate? Supervisors, who typically give out ratings, well, they're human. Perhaps they're operating under the mistaken notion that similar ratings for everyone will keep the team happy. Perhaps they're unconsciously playing favorites. Perhaps they don't know what good and poor performance levels are. Perhaps the measurements they're expected to use don't fit their product/team/people. Choose one or all of these. Rating people is rarely easy.

Whatever the cause of rating errors, some employees may come to believe that no matter what they do they will never receive a high performance rating. They may in fact believe that they are excellent performers but that the performance rating system is flawed. Expectancy theory differs from most motivation theories because it highlights the need for accurate performance measurement. Organizations cannot motivate employees to perform at a high level if they cannot identify high performers.

Organizations exert tremendous influence over employee choices in their performance levels and how much effort to exert on their jobs. That is, organizations can have a major impact on the direction and intensity of employees' motivation levels. Practical applications of expectancy theory include:

1. Strengthening the effort ➧ performance expectancy by selecting employees who have the necessary abilities, providing proper training, providing experiences of success, clarifying job responsibilities, etc.

2. Strengthening the performance ➧ outcome expectancy with policies that specify that desirable behavior leads to desirable outcomes and undesirable behavior leads to neutral or undesirable outcomes. Consistent enforcement of these policies is key—workers must believe in the contingencies.

3. Systematically evaluating which outcomes employees value. The greater the valence of outcomes offered for a behavior, the more likely employees will commit to that alternative. By recognizing that different employees have different values and that values change over time, organizations can provide the most highly valued outcomes.

4. Ensuring that effort actually translates into performance by clarifying what actions lead to performance and by appropriate training.

5. Ensuring appropriate worker outcomes for performance through reward schedules (extrinsic outcomes) and appropriate job design (so the work experience itself provides intrinsic outcomes).

6. Examining the level of outcomes provided to workers. Are they equitable, given the worker's inputs? Are they equitable in comparison to the way other workers are treated?

7. Measuring performance levels as accurately as possible, making sure that workers are capable of being high performers.

MANAGING CHANGE

Differences in Motivation across Cultures

The disgruntled employee is hardly a culturally isolated feature of business, and quitting before leaving takes the same forms, regardless of country. Cross-cultural signaling, social norms, and simple language barriers can make the task of motivation for the global manager confusing and counterintuitive. Communicating a passion for a common vision, coaching employees to see themselves as accountable and as owning their work, or attempting to create a "motivational ecosystem" can all fall flat with simple missed cues, bad translations, or tone-deaf approaches to a thousand-year-old culture.

Keeping employees motivated by making them feel valued and appreciated is not just a "Western" idea. The Ghanaian blog site Starrfmonline emphasizes that employee motivation and associated work quality improve when employees feel "valued, trusted, challenged, and supported in their work." Conversely, when employees feel like a tool rather than a person, or feel unengaged with their work, then productivity suffers. A vicious cycle can then begin when the manager treats an employee as unmotivated and incapable, which then demotivates the employee and elicits the predicted response.

The blogger cites an example from Eastern Europe where a manager sidelined an employee as inefficient and incompetent. After management coaching, the manager revisited his assessment and began working with the employee. As he worked to facilitate the employee's efficiency and motivation, the employee went from being the lowest performer to a valuable team player. In the end, the blog says, "The very phrase 'human resources' frames employees as material to be deployed for organizational objectives. While the essential nature of employment contracts involves trading labour for remuneration, if we fail to see and appreciate our employees as whole people, efforts to motivate them will meet with limited success" (Starrfmonline 2017 n.p.).

Pavel Vosk, a business and management consultant based in Puyallup, Washington, says that too often, overachieving employees turn into unmotivated ones. In looking for the answer, he found that the most common source was a lack of recognition for the employee's effort or exceptional performance. In fact, Vosk found that most employees go the extra mile only three times before they give up. Vosk's advice is to show gratitude for employees' effort, especially when it goes above and beyond. He says the recognition doesn't have to be over the top, just anything that the employees will perceive as gratitude, from a catered lunch for a team working extra hours to fulfill a deadline to a simple face-to-face thank you (Huhman 2017).

Richard Frazao, president of Quaketek, based in Montreal, Quebec, stresses talking to the employees and making certain they are engaged in their jobs, citing boredom with one's job as a major demotivating factor (Huhman 2017).

But motivating employees is not "one size fits all" globally. Rewarding and recognizing individuals and their achievements works fine in Western cultures but is undesirable in Asian cultures, which value teamwork and the collective over the individual. Whether to reward effort with a pay raise or with a job title or larger office is influenced by culture. Demoting an employee for poor performance is an effective motivator in Asian countries but is likely to result in losing an employee altogether in Western cultures. According to Matthew MacLachlan at Communicaid, "Making the assumption that your international workforce will be motivated by the same incentives can be dangerous and have a real impact on talent retention" (2016 n.p.).

Huhman, Heather R. 2017. "Employee Motivation Has to Be More Than 'a Pat on the Back.'" *Entrepreneur.* https://www.entrepreneur.com/article/287770

MacLachlan, Matthew. 2016. "Management Tips: How To Motivate Your International Workforce." *Communicaid.* https://www.communicaid.com/cross-cultural-training/blog/motivating-international-workforce/

Starrfmonline. 2017. "HR Today: Motivating People Starts With Right Attitude."

http://starrfmonline.com/2017/03/30/hr-today-motivating-people-starts-with-right-attitude/#

1. As a Western manager working in the Middle East or sub-Saharan Africa, what motivational issues might you face?
2. What problems would you expect a manager from a Confucian culture to encounter managing employees in America? In Europe?
3. What regional, cultural, or ethnic issues do you think managers have to navigate within the United States?

Expectancy Theory: An Integrative Theory of Motivation

More so than any other motivation theory, expectancy theory can be tied into most concepts of what and how people become motivated. Consider the following examples.

1. *Need theories* state that we are motivated to satisfy our needs. We positively value outcomes that satisfy unmet needs, negatively value outcomes that thwart the satisfaction of unmet needs, and assign neutral values to outcomes that do neither. In effect, the need theories explain how valences are formed.

2. *Operant conditioning theories* state that we will probably repeat a response (behavior) in the future that was reinforced in the past (that is, followed by a positively valued consequence or the removal of a negatively valued consequence). This is the basic process involved in forming performance ➡ outcome expectancies. Both operant theories and expectancy theory argue that our interactions with our environment influence our future behavior. The primary difference is that expectancy theory explains this process in cognitive (rational) terms.

3. *Equity theories* state that our satisfaction with a set of outcomes depends not only on how we value them but also on the circumstances surrounding their receipt. Equity theory, therefore, explains part of the process shown in **Exhibit 14.11**. If we don't feel that the outcomes we receive are equitable compared to a referent other, we will associate a lower or even negative valence with those outcomes.

4. *Goal theory* can be integrated with the expanded expectancy model in several ways. Locke has noted that expectancy theory explains how we go about choosing a particular goal.[34] A reexamination of **Exhibit 14.11** reveals other similarities between goal theory and expectancy theory. Locke's use of the term "goal acceptance" to identify the personal adoption of a goal is similar to the "choice of an alternative" in the expectancy model. Locke's "goal commitment," the degree to which we commit to reaching our accepted (chosen) goal, is very much like the expectancy description of choice of effort level. Locke argues that the difficulty and specificity of a goal are major determinants of the level of performance attempted (goal-directed effort), and expectancy theory appears to be consistent with this argument (even though expectancy theory is not as explicit on this point). We can reasonably conclude that the major underlying processes explored by the two models are very similar and will seldom lead to inconsistent recommendations.

CONCEPT CHECK ✓

1. Understand the process theories of motivation: operant conditioning, equity, goal, and expectancy theories.
2. Describe the managerial factors managers must consider when applying motivational approaches.

14.4 | Recent Research on Motivation Theories

4. Describe the modern advancements in the study of human motivation.

Employee motivation continues to be a major focus in organizational behavior.[35] We briefly summarize current motivation research here.

Content Theories

There is some interest in testing content theories (including Herzberg's two-factor theory), especially in international research. Need theories are still generally supported, with most people identifying such workplace factors as recognition, advancement, and opportunities to learn as the chief motivators for them. This is consistent with need satisfaction theories. However, most of this research does not include actual measures of employee performance. Thus, questions remain about whether the factors that employees *say* motivate them to perform actually do.

Operant Conditioning Theory

There is considerable interest in operant conditioning theory, especially within the context of what has been called organizational behavior modification. Oddly enough, there has not been much research using operant conditioning theory in designing reward systems, even though there are obvious applications. Instead, much of the recent research on operant conditioning focuses on punishment and extinction. These studies seek to determine how to use punishment appropriately. Recent results still confirm that punishment should be used sparingly, should be used only after extinction does not work, and should not be excessive or destructive.

Equity Theory

Equity theory continues to receive strong research support. The major criticism of equity theory, that the inputs and outcomes people use to evaluate equity are ill-defined, still holds. Because each person defines inputs and outcomes, researchers are not in a position to know them all. Nevertheless, for the major inputs (performance) and outcomes (pay), the theory is a strong one. Major applications of equity theory in recent years incorporate and extend the theory into the area called *organizational justice.* When employees receive rewards (or punishments), they evaluate them in terms of their fairness (as discussed earlier). This is *distributive justice.* Employees also assess rewards in terms of how fair the processes used to distribute them are. This is *procedural justice.* Thus during organizational downsizing, when employees lose their jobs, people ask whether the loss of work is fair (distributive justice). But they also assess the fairness of the process used to decide *who* is laid off (procedural justice). For example, layoffs based on seniority may be perceived as more fair than layoffs based on supervisors' opinions.

Goal Theory

It remains true that difficult, specific goals result in better performance than easy and vague goals, assuming they are accepted. Recent research highlights the positive effects of performance feedback and goal commitment in the goal-setting process. Monetary incentives enhance motivation when they are tied to goal achievement, by increasing the level of goal commitment. There are negative sides to goal theory as well. If goals conflict, employees may sacrifice performance on important job duties. For example, if both quantitative and qualitative goals are set for performance, employees may emphasize quantity because this goal achievement is more visible.

Expectancy Theory

The original formulation of expectancy theory specifies that the motivational force for choosing a level of effort is a function of the multiplication of expectancies and valences. Recent research demonstrates that the individual components predict performance just as well, without being multiplied. This does not diminish the value of expectancy theory. Recent research also suggests that high performance results not only when the valence is high, but also when employees set difficult goals for themselves.

One last comment on motivation: As the world of work changes, so will the methods organizations use to motivate employees. New rewards—time off instead of bonuses; stock options; on-site gyms, cleaners, and dental services; opportunities to telecommute; and others—will need to be created in order to motivate employees in the future. One useful path that modern researchers can undertake is to analyze the previous studies and aggregate the findings into more conclusive understanding of the topic through meta-analysis studies.[36]

CATCHING THE ENTREPRENEURIAL SPIRIT

Entrepreneurs and Motivation

Motivation can be difficult to elicit in employees. So what drives entrepreneurs, who by definition have to motivate themselves as well as others? While everyone from Greek philosophers to football coaches warn about undirected passion, a lack of passion will likely kill any start-up. An argument could be made that motivation is simply *part* of the discipline, or the *outcome* of remaining fixed on a purpose to mentally remind yourself of why you get up in the morning.

Working from her home in Egypt, at age 30 Yasmine El-Mehairy launched Supermama.me, a start-up aimed at providing information to mothers throughout the Arab world. When the company began, El-Mehairy worked full time at her day job and 60 hours a week after that getting the site established. She left her full-time job to manage the site full time in January 2011, and the site went live that October. El-Mehairy is motivated to keep moving forward, saying that if she stops, she might not get going again (Knowledge @ Wharton 2012).

For El-Mehairy, the motivation didn't come from a desire to work for a big company or travel the world and secure a master's degree from abroad. She had already done that. Rather, she said she was motivated to "do something that is useful and I want to do something on my own" (Knowledge @ Wharton 2012 n.p.).

Lauren Lipcon, who founded a company called Injury Funds Now, attributes her ability to stay motivated to three factors: purpose, giving back, and having fun outside of work. Lipcon believes that most entrepreneurs are not motivated by money, but by a sense of purpose. Personally, she left a job with Arthur Andersen to begin her own firm out of a desire to help people. She also thinks it is important for people to give back to their communities because the change the entrepreneur sees in the community loops back, increasing motivation and making the business more successful. Lipcon believes that having a life outside of work helps keep the entrepreneur motivated. She particularly advocates for physical activity, which not only helps the body physically, but also helps keep the mind sharp and able to focus (Rashid 2017).

But do all entrepreneurs agree on what motivates them? A July 17, 2017 survey on the hearpreneur blog site asked 23 different entrepreneurs what motivated them. Seven of the 23 referred to some sense of purpose in what they were doing as a motivating factor, with one response stressing the importance of discovering one's "personal why." Of the remaining entrepreneurs, answers varied from keeping a positive attitude (three responses) and finding external sources (three responses) to meditation and prayer (two responses). One entrepreneur said his greatest motivator was fear: the fear of being in the same place financially one year in the future "causes me to take action and also alleviates my fear of risk" (Hear from Entrepreneurs 2017 n.p.). Only one of the 23 actually cited money and material success as a motivating factor to keep working.

However it is described, entrepreneurs seem to agree that passion and determination are key factors that carry them through the grind of the day-to-day.

Sources:

Hear from Entrepreneurs. 2017. "23 Entrepreneurs Explain Their Motivation or if 'Motivation is Garbage.'" https://hear.ceoblognation.com/2017/07/17/23-entrepreneurs-explain-motivation-motivation-garbage/

Knowledge @ Wharton. 2012. "The Super-motivated Entrepreneur Behind Egypt's SuperMama." http://knowledge.wharton.upenn.edu/article/the-super-motivated-entrepreneur-behind-egypts-supermama/

Rashid, Brian. 2017. "How This Entrepreneur Sustains High Levels of Energy and Motivation." *Forbes.* https://www.forbes.com/sites/brianrashid/2017/05/26/how-this-entrepreneur-sustains-high-levels-of-energy-and-motivation/2/#2a8ec5591111

Questions:
1. In the article from Hear from Entrepreneurs, one respondent called motivation "garbage"? Would you agree or disagree, and why?
2. How is staying motivated as an entrepreneur similar to being motivated to pursue a college degree? Do you think the two are related? How?
3. How would you expect motivation to vary across cultures?[/BOX]

CONCEPT CHECK

1. Understand the modern approaches to motivation theory.

🔑 Key Terms

ability The knowledge, skills, and receptiveness to learning that an individual brings to a task or job.

avoidance learning Occurs when people learn to behave in a certain way to avoid encountering an undesired or unpleasant consequence.

content motivation theories Theories that focus on what motivates people.

direction What a person is motivated to achieve.

effort-performance expectancy E1, the perceived probability that effort will lead to performance (or E ➡ P).

equity theory States that human motivation is affected by the outcomes people receive for their inputs, compared to the outcomes and inputs of other people.

ERG theory Compresses Maslow's five need categories into three: existence, relatedness, and growth.

expectancy theory Posits that people will exert high effort levels to perform at high levels so that they can obtain valued outcomes.

extinction Occurs when a consequence or lack of a consequence makes it less likely that a behavior will be repeated in the future.

extrinsic motivation Occurs when a person performs a given behavior to acquire something that will satisfy a lower-order need.

extrinsic outcomes Are awarded or given by other people (like a supervisor).

goal commitment The degree to which people dedicate themselves to achieving a goal.

goal theory States that people will perform better if they have difficult, specific, accepted performance goals or objectives.

hedonism Assumes that people are motivated to satisfy mainly their own needs (seek pleasure, avoid pain).

hygienes Factors in the work environment that are based on the basic human need to "avoid pain."

input Any personal qualities that a person views as having value and that are relevant to the organization.

instincts Our natural, fundamental needs, basic to our survival.

intensity (1) The degree to which people try to achieve their targets; (2) the forcefulness that enhances the likelihood that a stimulus will be selected for perceptual processing.

intrinsic motivation Arises out of performing a behavior in and of itself, because it is interesting or "fun" to do.

intrinsic outcomes Are awarded or given by people to themselves (such as a sense of achievement).

latent needs Cannot be inferred from a person's behavior at a given time, yet the person may still possess those needs.

manifest needs Are needs motivating a person at a given time.

manifest needs theory Assumes that human behavior is driven by the desire to satisfy needs.

motivation A force within or outside of the body that energizes, directs, and sustains human behavior. Within the body, examples might be needs, personal values, and goals, while an incentive might be seen as a force outside of the body. The word stems from its Latin root *movere*, which means "to move."

motivators Relate to the jobs that people perform and people's ability to feel a sense of achievement as a result of performing them.

motive A source of motivation; the need that a person is attempting to satisfy.

need A human condition that becomes energized when people feel deficient in some respect.

need for achievement (nAch) The need to excel at tasks, especially tasks that are difficult.

need for affiliation (nAff) The need to establish and maintain warm and friendly relationships with other people.

need for power (nPow) The need to control things, especially other people; reflects a motivation to influence and be responsible for other people.

negative reinforcement Occurs when a behavior causes something undesirable to be removed, increasing the likelihood of the behavior reoccurring.

nonreinforcement Occurs when no consequence follows a worker's behavior.

operant conditioning A learning process based on the results produced by a person "operating on" the environment.

operant conditioning theory Posits that people learn to behave in a particular fashion as a result of the consequences that followed their past behaviors.

outcome Anything a person perceives as getting back from an organization in exchange for the person's inputs.

overreward inequity Occurs when people perceive their outcome/input ratio to be greater than that of their referent other.

performance environment Refers to those factors that impact employees' performance but are essentially out of their control.

performance-outcome expectancy E2, the perceived relationship between performance and outcomes (or $P \rightarrow O$).

positive reinforcement Occurs when a desirable consequence that satisfies an active need or removes a barrier to need satisfaction increases the likelihood of a behavior reoccurring.

primary needs Are instinctual in nature and include physiological needs for food, water, and sex (procreation).

process motivation theories Theories that focus on the how and why of motivation.

punishment An aversive consequence that follows a behavior and makes it less likely to reoccur.

referent others Workers that a person uses to compare inputs and outcomes, and who perform jobs similar in difficulty and complexity to the employee making an equity determination.

reinforcement Occurs when a consequence makes it more likely a behavior will be repeated in the future.

role perceptions The set of behaviors employees think they are expected to perform as members of an organization.

schedules of reinforcement The frequency at which effective employee behaviors are reinforced.

secondary needs Are learned throughout one's life span and are psychological in nature.

self-determination theory (SDT) Seeks to explain not only what causes motivation, but also the effects of extrinsic rewards on intrinsic motivation.

self-efficacy A belief about the probability that one can successfully execute some future action or task, or achieve some result.

state of equity Occurs when people perceive their outcome/input ratio to be equal to that of their referent other.

underreward inequity Occurs when people perceive their outcome/input ratio to be less than that of their referent other.

valences The degree to which a person perceives an outcome as being desirable, neutral, or undesirable.

work motivation The amount of effort a person exerts to achieve a level of job performance

Summary of Learning Outcomes

14.1 Motivation: Direction and Intensity

1. Define motivation, and distinguish direction and intensity of motivation.

This chapter has covered the major motivation theories in organizational behavior. Motivation theories endeavor to explain how people become motivated. Motivation has two major components: direction and intensity. Direction is what a person is trying to achieve. Intensity is the degree of effort a person expends to achieve the target. All motivation theories address the ways in which people develop direction and intensity.

14.2 Content Theories of Motivation

2. Describe a content theory of motivation, and compare and contrast the main content theories of motivation: manifest needs theory, learned needs theory, Maslow's hierarchy of needs, Alderfer's ERG theory, Herzberg's motivator-hygiene theory, and self-determination theory.

Motivation theories are classified as either content or process theories. Content theories focus on what motivates behavior. The basic premise of content theories is that humans have needs. When these needs are not satisfied, humans are motivated to satisfy the need. The need provides direction for motivation. Murray's manifest needs theory, McClelland's learned needs theory, Maslow's hierarchy of needs, and Herzberg's motivator-hygiene theory are all content theories. Each has something to say about the needs that motivate humans in the workplace.

14.3 Process Theories of Motivation

3. Describe the process theories of motivation, and compare and contrast the main process theories of motivation: operant conditioning theory, equity theory, goal theory, and expectancy theory.

Process theories focus on how people become motivated. Operant conditioning theory states that people will be motivated to engage in behaviors for which they have been reinforced (rewarded). It also states that people will avoid behaviors that are punished. The rate at which behaviors are rewarded also affects how often they will be displayed. Equity theory's main premise is that people compare their situations to those of other people. If a person feels that they are being treated unfairly relative to a referent other, the person may engage in behaviors that are counterproductive for the organization. Employers should try to develop feelings of fairness in employees. Goal theory is a strong theory. It states that difficult, specific goals will result in high performance if employees accept the goals and are committed to achieving them.

14.4 Recent Research on Motivation Theories

4. Describe the modern advancements in the study of human motivation.

Expectancy theory is a process theory. It also is the broadest of the motivation theories. Expectancy theory predicts that employees will be motivated to be high performers if they perceive that high performance leads to valued outcomes. Employees will be motivated to avoid being low performers if they perceive that it leads to negative outcomes. Employees must perceive that they are capable of achieving high performance, and they must have the appropriate abilities and high self-efficacy. Organizations need to provide adequate resources and to measure performance accurately. Inaccurate performance ratings discourage high performance. Overall, expectancy theory draws attention to how organizations structure the work environment and distribute rewards.

🗐 Chapter Review Questions

1. Discuss the benefits that accrue when an organization has a good understanding of employee needs.
2. How might Maslow explain why organizational rewards that motivate workers today may not motivate the same workers in 5 or 10 years?
3. Describe the process by which needs motivate workers.
4. Discuss the importance of Herzberg's motivators and hygienes.
5. Describe a work situation in which it would be appropriate to use a continuous reinforcement schedule.

6. Discuss the potential effectiveness and limitations of punishment in organizations.
7. How can equity theory explain why a person who receives a high salary might be dissatisfied with their pay?
8. Equity theory specifies a number of possible alternatives for reducing perceived inequity. How could an organization influence which of these alternatives a person will pursue?
9. What goals would be most likely to improve your learning and performance in an organizational behavior class?
10. Identify two reasons why a formal goal-setting program might be dysfunctional for an organization.
11. What steps can an organization take to increase the motivational force for high levels of performance?
12. Discuss how supervisors sometimes unintentionally weaken employees E ➡ P and P ➡ O expectancies.
13. How can an employee attach high valence to high levels of performance, yet not be motivated to be a high performer?
14. Is there "one best" motivation theory? Explain your answer.

Management Skills Application Exercises

1. Many companies strive to design jobs that are intrinsically motivating. Visit several small and large company websites and search their career section. What job features related to motivation are highlighted? What type of employees do you think the companies will attract with these jobs?
2. You will be paired with another student in this class. Each of you will take one side of the issue and debate:
   a. Student A: All members of the organization should be given the same specific, difficult-to-achieve goals.
   b. Student B: Specific, difficult-to-achieve goals should only be given to certain members of the organization.
3. Assume the role of sales manager, and write a memo to two of your reports that have the following situations and job performance.
   a. Employee 1: Shawn is a onetime stellar performer. They were twice the top performing salesperson in the company in the past decade. In the past year, Shawn has missed goal by 4 percent. Shawn recently became the parent to twins and says that the reason for missing goal this year was due to the territory being saturated with product from previous years.
   b. Employee 2: Soo Kim is an energetic salesperson who is putting in long hours and producing detailed sales reports, but their performance on the sales side has not met expectations. When you examine the customer feedback page on your website, you notice that they have five times as many positive reviews and glowing comments about Soo Kim.

Managerial Decision Exercises

1. You are a manager and it's performance appraisal time, which is a yearly exercise to provide feedback to your direct reports that is often stressful for both the employee and the manager. You feel that the feedback process should be more of an ongoing process than the yearly formal process. What are the benefits of this yearly process, and what, if any, are the drawbacks of providing both positive and remediation feedback to your direct reports?
2. You have been told by a worker on another team that one of your direct reports made an inappropriate

comment to a coworker. What do you do to investigate the matter, and what actions would you take with your report, the person that the comment was directed to, and other people in the organization?

3. You learn that an employee who doesn't report to you has made an inappropriate comment to one of your direct reports. What do you do to investigate the matter, and what actions would you take with your report, the person that made the comment, their manager, and other people in the organization?

4. Your company is considering implementing a 360° appraisal system where up to 10 people in the organization provide feedback on every employee as part of the annual performance appraisal process. This feedback will come from subordinates, peers, and senior managers as well as individuals in other departments. You have been asked to prepare a memo to the director of human resources about the positive and negative effects this could have on the motivation of employees. Note that not all of the employees are on a bonus plan that will be impacted by this feedback.

Critical Thinking Case

Motivating Employees at JCPenney, Walmart, and Amazon in the Age of Online Shopping

In the 1980s, Walmart had killed (or was killing) the mom-and-pop store. "Buy local" signs were seen, urging consumers to buy from their local retailers rather than from the low-cost behemoth. Markets have continued to shift and the "buy local" signs are still around, but now the battleground has shifted with the disruptive growth of e-commerce. Even mighty Walmart is feeling some growing pains.

Census Bureau data for 2017 shows that e-commerce, or online shopping, accounted for 8.9 percent of all retail sales in the United States, accounting for $111.5 billion (U.S. Census Bureau 2017). Feeling the pinch, many malls across the country are closing their doors, and their empty retail spaces are being repurposed. Credit Suisse predicts that due to competition from online shopping, 20 to 25 percent of American malls will close within the next five years (Dying Malls Make Room for New Condos Apartment 2017). Furthermore, according to a 2017 study, 23 percent of Americans already purchase their groceries online (Embrace the Internet, Skip the Checkout 2017).

Whether face-to-face with customers or filling orders in a warehouse, motivated employees are essential to business success. And company culture helps drive that motivation. As a 2015 *Harvard Business Review* article put it, "Why we work determines how well we work" (McGregor & Doshi 2015). Adapting earlier research for the modern workplace, the study found six reasons that people work: play, purpose, potential, emotional pressure, economic pressure, and inertia. The first three are positive motives while that later three are negative. The researchers found that role design, more than any other factor, had the highest impact on employee motivation.

Anecdotally, using role design to motivate employees can be seen across industries. Toyota allows factory workers to innovate new processes on the factory floor. Southwest Airlines encourages a sense of "play" among crewmembers who interact directly with passengers (which has resulted in some humorous viral videos). A sense of the organization's identity (and a desire to be part of it) and how the career ladder within the company is perceived are second and third in their impact on employee motivation. Unhealthy competition for advancement can do more harm than good to employee motivation, and as a result many large companies are restructuring their performance review and advancement systems (McGregor & Doshi 2015). Conversely, costs from unmotivated employees can be high. In August 2017, retailer JCPenney had an employee arrested who had allegedly cost the company more than $10,000 in stolen cash and under-rung merchandise at a mall store. Another employee had stolen more than $1,000 of clothes from the store less than a month earlier.

Brick-and-mortar retail outlets from Macy's to Walmart have come under pressure by increased online shopping, particularly at Amazon.com. Walmart has responded by both trying to improve the shopping experience in its stores and creating an online presence of its own. A recent study funded by Walmart found that 60 percent of retails workers lack proficiency in reading and 70 percent have difficulty with math (Class is in session at Walmart Academy 2017). Increasing math and team skills for the employees would increase efficiency and certainly help improve employee self-image and motivation. With this in mind, Walmart has created one of the largest employer training programs in the country, Walmart Academy (McGregor & Doshi 2015). The company expects to graduate more than 225,000 of its supervisors and managers from a program that covers topics such as merchandising and employee motivation. In another program, Pathways, Walmart has created a course that covers topics such as merchandising, communication, and retail math (Walmart 2016 Global Responsibility Report 2016). The Pathways program was expected to see 500,000 entry-level workers take part in 2016 (Walmart 2016). All employees who complete the course receive a dollar an hour pay increase. Educating employees pays off by recognizing that the effort put in pays off with better-motivated and better-educated employees. In the case of Walmart, "upskilling" has become a priority.

Walmart has gone beyond education to motivate or empower employees. In 2016, pay raises for 1.2 million employees took effect as part of a new minimum-wage policy, and it streamlined its paid time off program that same year (Schmid 2017). In its 2016 Global Responsibility Report, Walmart points out that over the course of two years, the company has invested $2.7 billion in wages, benefits, and training in the United States (Staley 2017).

Sources:

Ciubotariu, Nick. 2015. "An Amazonian's response to "Inside Amazon: Wrestling Big Ideas in a Bruising Workplace." *LinkedIn.* https://www.linkedin.com/pulse/amazonians-response-inside-amazon-wrestling-big-ideas-nick-ciubotariu/?redirectFromSplash=true

Class is in session at Walmart Academy. 2017. Bend Bulletin. http://www.bendbulletin.com/home/5507742-151/class-is-in-session-at-walmart-academy

Cook, John. 2015. "Full memo: Jeff Bezos responds to brutal NYT story, says it doesn't represent the Amazon he leads." *GeekWire.* https://www.geekwire.com/2015/full-memo-jeff-bezos-responds-to-cutting-nyt-expose-says-tolerance-for-lack-of-empathy-needs-to-be-zero/

"Dying Malls Make Room for New Condos Apartment." 2017. Bend Bulletin. http://www.bendbulletin.com/business/5654908-151/dying-malls-make-room-for-new-condos-apartments

"Embrace the Internet, Skip the Checkout." 2017. Bend Bulletin. http://www.bendbulletin.com/business/5635713-151/embrace-the-internet-skip-the-checkout

McGregor, Lindsay and Doshi, Neel. 2015. "How Company Culture Shapes Employee Motivation." Boston, MA: Harvard Business Review. https://hbr.org/2015/11/how-company-culture-shapes-employee-motivation

Schmid, Emily. 2017. "Work That Matters: Looking Back on 2 Years of Investing in People." *Walmart Today.* Bentonville, AR: Walmart Digital Communications. https://blog.walmart.com/opportunity/20170223/work-that-matters-looking-back-on-2-years-of-investing-in-people

Staley, Oliver. 2017. " Walmart—yes, Walmart—is making changes that could help solve America's wealth inequality problem." *Yahoo! Finance.* https://finance.yahoo.com/news/walmart-yes-walmart-making-changes-100102778.html

U.S. Census Bureau. 2017. *Quarterly Retail E-Commerce Sales, 2nd Quarter 2017.* Washington, DC: U.S. Department of Commerce. https://www.census.gov/retail/mrts/www/data/pdf/ec_current.pdf

WalMart 2016 Global Responsibility Report. 2016. Bentonville, AR: Walmart. https://corporate.walmart.com/2016grr

Walmart. 2016. "Pathways program infographic. Bentonville, AR: Walmart. https://corporate.walmart.com/photos/pathways-program-infographic

Questions:

1. A 2015 *New York Times* article described Amazon as "a soulless, dystopian workplace where no fun is had and no laughter heard" (Cook 2015 n.p.). Employees themselves came to the company's defense (Ciubotariu 2015). Does this reputation continue to haunt Amazon, or has it been addressed?

2. How do employees differ between a Walmart retail location and an Amazon order fulfillment center? How many white-collar or skilled jobs does Amazon have compared to Walmart?

3. With Amazon moving into the retail market with the purchase of Whole Foods, and with Walmart expanding its e-commerce, how are employee motivation challenges going to shift?

Exhibit 15.1 (Credit: MabelAmber/ Pixabay/ (CC BY 0))

Introduction

Learning Outcomes

After reading this chapter, you should be able to answer these questions:

1. What is the benefit of working in teams, and what makes teams effective?
2. How do teams develop over time?
3. What are some key considerations in managing teams?
4. What are the benefits of conflict for a team?
5. How does team diversity enhance decision-making and problem-solving?
6. What are some challenges and best practices for managing and working with multicultural teams?

EXPLORING MANAGERIAL CAREERS

Eva Hartmann, Trellis LLC

Eva Hartmann has nearly 20 years of experience as a strategic, results-driven, innovative leader with significant expertise in human resources strategy, talent and leadership development, and organizational effectiveness. She has worked in a variety of industries, from manufacturing to Fortune 500 consulting. Eva is a transformational change agent who has developed and led strategic human capital programs and talent initiatives in multiple challenging environments globally. Eva is passionate about enhancing both individual and organizational performance.

Eva began her career in one of the large "Big 6" management consulting firms at the time, and she happily returned several years ago to consulting. She is the founder and president of Trellis LLC, a human capital consulting and staffing firm in Richmond, Virginia.

Prior to Trellis, Eva was the global human resources leader for a large global manufacturer of plastic film products and was responsible for the HR strategy and operations of a $600 million global division. In this role, Eva led a global team of HR managers in North and South America, Europe, and Asia to support global HR initiatives to drive business results and build human capital and performance across the division.

Eva has also held a variety of leadership and managerial roles in both human resources and quality functions at several nationally and globally recognized companies, including Wachovia Securities, Genworth Financial, Sun Microsystems, and Andersen Consulting (now Accenture).

Eva holds an MBA from the College of William and Mary in Williamsburg, Virginia, and a BA in anthropology from the University of Virginia in Charlottesville, Virginia. She is also an adjunct faculty member with the University of Richmond Robins School of Business. Eva currently serves on the board of the Society of Human Resource Management (SHRM) of Richmond, Virginia.

Much of the work that is performed today in organizations requires a focus on teamwork. The ability to work successfully as a team member, as well as the ability to lead teams, is an ultimate advantage within the workforce. Teams themselves must be managed, in addition to managing just the individuals, to be successful. We've all heard the quote originally coined by Aristotle that states that "the whole is greater than the sum of its parts." This captures the nature of the team perfectly—there is such a synergy that comes from a team that the individuals alone are not able to create. This chapter details the importance of and benefits that you may derive from working as a team, as well as some of the ways we can make our teams more successful.

15.1 | Teamwork in the Workplace

1. What is a team, and what makes a team effective?

Teamwork has never been more important in organizations than it is today. Whether you work in a manufacturing environment and utilize self-directed work teams, or if you work in the "**knowledge economy**" and derive benefits from collaboration within a team structure, you are harnessing the power of a team.

A team, according to Katzenbach and Smith in their *Harvard Business Review* (HBR) article "The Discipline of Teams," is defined as "people organized to function cooperatively as a group".[1] The five elements that make teams function are:

- Common commitment and purpose
- Specific performance goals
- Complementary skills
- Commitment to how the work gets done
- Mutual accountability

A team has a specific purpose that it delivers on, has shared leadership roles, and has both individual and mutual accountabilities. Teams discuss, make decisions, and perform real work together, and they measure their performance by assessing their collective work products. Wisdom of Teams reference. This is very different from the classic **working group** in an organization (usually organized by functional area) in which there is a focused leader, individual accountabilities and work products, and a group purpose that is the same as the broader organizational mission. Think of the finance organization or a particular business unit in your company—these are, in effect, larger working groups that take on a piece of the broader organizational mission. They are organized under a leader, and their effectiveness is measured by its influence on others within the business (e.g., financial performance of the business.)

Exhibit 15.2   Finance Working Group Smart managers understand that not all of a company's influential relationships appear as part of the organization chart. Consider a publishing company that might have a lead finance head for each group, such as adult fiction, nonfiction, young adult, and children's book divisions. A finance team working group would help spread best practices and lead to more cohesive operations for the entire organization. (Credit: thetaxhaven /flickr / Attribution 2.0 Generic (CC BY 2.0))

So, what makes a team truly effective? According to Katzenbach and Smith's "Discipline of Teams," there are several practices that the authors have observed in successful teams. These practices include:

Establish urgency, demanding performance standards, and direction. Teams work best when they have a compelling reason for being, and it is thus more likely that the teams will be successful and live up to performance expectations. We've all seen the teams that are brought together to address an "important initiative" for the company, but without clear direction and a truly compelling reason to exist, the team will lose momentum and wither.

Select members for their skill and skill potential, not for their personality. This is not always as easy as it sounds for several reasons. First, most people would prefer to have those with good personalities and positive attitudes on their team in order to promote a pleasant work environment. This is fine, but make sure that those individuals have the skill sets needed (or the potential to acquire/learn) for their piece of the project. The second caveat here is that you don't always know what skills you need on a project until you really dig in and see what's going on. Spend some time up front thinking about the purpose of the project and the anticipated deliverables you will be producing, and think through the specific types of skills you'll need on the team.

Pay particular attention to first meetings and actions. This is one way of saying that first impressions mean a lot—and it is just as important for teams as for individuals. Teams will interact with everyone from functional subject-matter experts all the way to senior leadership, and the team must look competent and be perceived as competent. Keeping an eye on your team's level of **emotional intelligence** is very important and will enhance your team's reputation and ability to navigate stakeholders within the organization.

Set some clear rules of behavior. I have been through many meetings and team situations in which we have rushed through "**ground rules**" because it felt like they were obvious—and everyone always came up with the same list. It is so critical that the team takes the time up front to capture their own rules of the road in order to keep the team in check. Rules that address areas such as attendance, discussion, confidentiality, project approach, and conflict are key to keeping team members aligned and engaged appropriately.

Set and seize upon a few immediate performance-oriented tasks and goals. What does this mean? Have some quick wins that make the team feel that they're really accomplishing something and working together well. This is very important to the team's confidence, as well as just getting into the practices of working as a team. Success in the larger tasks will come soon enough, as the larger tasks are really just a group of smaller tasks that fit together to produce a larger deliverable.

Challenge the group regularly with fresh facts and information. That is, continue to research and gather information to confirm or challenge what you know about your project. Don't assume that all the facts are static and that you received them at the beginning of the project. Often, you don't know what you don't know until you dig in. I think that the pace of change is so great in the world today that new information is always presenting itself and must be considered in the overall context of the project.

Spend lots of time together. Here's an obvious one that is often overlooked. People are so busy that they forget that an important part of the team process is to spend time together, think together, and bond. Time in person, time on the phone, time in meetings—all of it counts and helps to build camaraderie and trust.

Exploit the power of positive feedback, recognition, and reward. Positive reinforcement is a motivator that will help the members of the team feel more comfortable contributing. It will also reinforce the behaviors and expectations that you're driving within the team. Although there are many extrinsic rewards that can serve as motivators, a successful team begins to feel that its own success and performance is the most rewarding.

Collaboration is another key concept and method by which teams can work together very successfully. Bringing together a team of experts from across the business would seem to be a best practice in any situation. However, Gratton and Erickson, in their article Eight Ways to Build Collaborative Teams, found that collaboration seems to decrease sharply when a team is working on complex project initiatives. In their study, they examined 55 larger teams and identified those with strong collaboration skills, despite the level of complexity. There were eight success factors for having strong collaboration skills:

- "Signature" relationship practices
- Role models of collaboration among executives
- Establishment of "gift" culture, in which managers mentor employees
- Training in relationship skills
- A sense of community
- Ambidextrous leaders—good at task and people leadership
- Good use of heritage relationships
- Role clarity and talk ambiguity[2]

As teams grow in size and complexity, the standard practices that worked well with small teams don't work anymore. Organizations need to think about how to make collaboration work, and they should leverage the above best practices to build relationships and trust.

CONCEPT CHECK

1. What is the definition of a team?
2. Name some practices that can make a team more successful.

15.2 Team Development Over Time

2. How do teams develop over time?

If you have been a part of a team—as most of us have—then you intuitively have felt that there are different "stages" of team development. Teams and team members often start from a position of friendliness and excitement about a project or endeavor, but the mood can sour and the team dynamics can go south very quickly once the real work begins. In 1965, educational psychologist Bruce Tuckman at Ohio State University developed a four-stage model to explain the complexities that he had witnessed in team development. The original model was called Tuckman's Stages of Group Development, and he added the fifth stage of "Adjourning" in 1977 to explain the disbanding of a team at the end of a project. The four stages of the Tuckman model are:[3]

- Forming
- Storming
- Norming
- Performing
- Adjourning

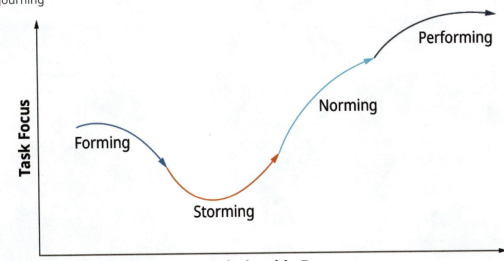

Exhibit 15.3   Tuckman's Model of Team Development Attribution: Copyright Rice University, OpenStax, under CC BY-NC-SA 4.0 license

The **Forming** stage begins with the introduction of team members. This is known as the "polite stage" in which the team is mainly focused on similarities and the group looks to the leader for structure and direction. The team members at this point are enthusiastic, and issues are still being discussed on a global, ambiguous level. This is when the informal pecking order begins to develop, but the team is still friendly.

The **Storming** stage begins as team members begin vying for leadership and testing the group processes. This is known as the "win-lose" stage, as members clash for control of the group and people begin to choose sides. The attitude about the team and the project begins to shift to negative, and there is frustration around goals, tasks, and progress.

Exhibit 15.4   The Storming Stage In the storming stage, protracted competition vying for leadership of the group can hinder progress. You are likely to encounter this in your coursework when a group assignment requires forming a team. (Credit: Gerald R. Ford School of Public Policy/ flickr/ Attribution 2.0 Generic (CC BY 2.0))

After what can be a very long and painful Storming process for the team, slowly the **Norming** stage may start to take root. During Norming, the team is starting to work well together, and buy-in to group goals occurs. The team is establishing and maintaining ground rules and boundaries, and there is willingness to share responsibility and control. At this point in the team formation, members begin to value and respect each other and their contributions.

Finally, as the team builds momentum and starts to get results, it is entering the **Performing** stage. The team is completely self-directed and requires little management direction. The team has confidence, pride, and enthusiasm, and there is a congruence of vision, team, and self. As the team continues to perform, it may even succeed in becoming a high-performing team. High-performing teams have optimized both task and people relationships—they are maximizing performance and team effectiveness. Katzenberg and Smith, in their study of teams, have created a "team performance curve" that graphs the journey of a team from a working group to a high-performing team. The team performance curve is illustrated in **Exhibit 15.5**.

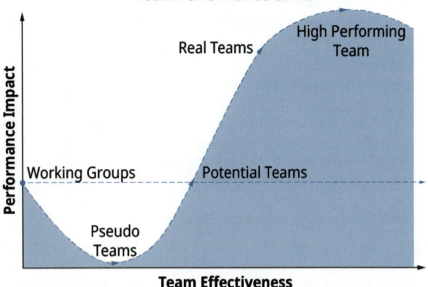

Exhibit 15.5   Team Performance Curve (Attribution: Copyright Rice University, OpenStax, under CC-BY 4.0 license)

The process of becoming a high-performance team is not a linear process. Similarly, the four stages of team development in the Tuckman model are not linear, and there are also factors that may cause the team to regress to an earlier stage of development. When a team member is added to the group, this may change the dynamic enough and be disruptive enough to cause a backwards slide to an earlier stage. Similarly, if a new project task is introduced that causes confusion or anxiety for the group, then this may also cause a backwards slide to an earlier stage of development. Think of your own experiences with project teams and the backslide that the group may have taken when another team member was introduced. You may have personally found the same to be true when a leader or project sponsor changes the scope or adds a new project task. The team has to re-group and will likely re-Storm and re-Form before getting back to Performing as a team.

CATCHING THE ENTREPRENEURIAL SPIRIT

Starting the Startup Team

Nothing is more exciting than a startup business. The enthusiasm is high, and people are excited about the new venture and the prospects that await. Depending on the situation, there may be funding that the startup has received from investors, or the startup could be growing and powering itself organically. Either way, the startup faces many different questions in the beginning, which will have a tremendous impact on its growth potential and performance down the road. One of the most critical questions that faces a startup —or any business for that matter—is the question of who should be on the team. Human capital is the greatest asset that any company can have, and it is an especially critical decision in a startup environment when you have limited resources and those resources will be responsible for building the company from ground up.

In Noam Wasserman's January 2012 HBSP article "Assembling the Startup Team," Wasserman asserts:

"Nothing can bedevil a high-potential startup more than its people problems. In research on startup performance, venture capitalists attributed 65% of portfolio company failures to problems within the startup's

management team. Another study asked investors to identify problems that might occur at their portfolio companies; 61% of the problems involved team issues. These problems typically result from choices that founders make as they add team members..."

These statistics are based on people problems in startups, and it isn't quite clear what percent of larger company failures could be directly or indirectly attributed to people and team issues. I would imagine that the percentage is also significant. The impact of people problems and team issues in a startup organization that is just getting its footing and trying to make the right connections and decisions can be very significant. If you know anyone who has a company in startup mode, you may have noticed that some of the early team members who are selected to join the team are trusted family members, friends, or former colleagues. Once a startup company grows to a certain level, then it may acquire an experienced CEO to take the helm. In any case, the startup is faced early on with important questions on how to build the team in a way that will maximize the chance of success.

In "Assembling the Startup Team," the author refers to the three Rs: relationships, roles, and rewards as being key elements that must be managed effectively in order to avoid problems in the long term. Relationships refers to the actual team members that are chosen, and there are several caveats to keep in mind. Hiring relatives or close friends because they are trusted may seem like the right idea in the beginning, but the long-term hazards (per current research) outweigh the benefits. Family and friends may think too similarly, and the team misses the benefit of other perspectives and connections. Roles are important because you have to think about the division of labor and skills, as well as who is in the right roles for decision-making. The startup team needs to think through the implications of assigning people to specific roles, as that may dictate their decision power and status. Finally, defining the rewards can be difficult for the startup team because it essentially means that they are splitting the pie—i.e., both short-term and long-term compensation. For startup founders, this can be a very difficult decision when they have to weigh the balance of giving something away versus gaining human capital that may ultimately help the business to succeed. Thinking through the tradeoffs and keeping alignment between the "three Rs" is important because it challenges the startup team to think of the long-term consequences of some of their early decisions. It is easy to bring family and friends into the startup equation due to trust factors, but a careful analysis of the "three Rs" will help a startup leadership team make decisions that will pay off in the long term.

Discussion Questions

1. Why might it be a bad decision to hire someone for a key startup role based only on the fact that the person is close family or a friend? What are the potential tradeoffs to the business?
2. What does it mean for the "three Rs" to be in alignment? What is the potential risk of these not being in alignment? What could go wrong?

CONCEPT CHECK

1. What are the four stages of team development?
2. What can cause a team to regress in its development?

15.3 | Things to Consider When Managing Teams

3. What are some key considerations in managing teams?

For those of us who have had the pleasure of managing or leading a team, we know that it can feel like a dubious distinction. Leading a team is fulfilling—especially if the task or organizational mandate at hand is so critical to the organization that people are happy to be a part of the team that drives things forward. It can also be an exercise in frustration, as the charge is to lead a group composed of various individuals, which at various times will act both like a group and like a bunch of individuals. Managing teams is no small feat, and the most experience managers truly understand that success ultimately depends on their ability to build a strong and well-functioning team. In J.J. Gabarro's *The Dynamics of Taking Charge* (HBS Press, 1987, pp. 85–87), he quotes a manager who had successfully worked to turn around a number of organizations:[4]

"People have to want to work together; they have to see how to do it. There has to be an environment for it and that takes time. It's my highest priority right now but I don't write it down anywhere because it's not like other priorities. If I told corporate that building a team was my prime goal they'd tell me, so what? They'd expect that as part of making things better."

I love this quotation because it's so indicative of the state of most organizations today. The focus is on corporate goals and priorities—very task-driven and outcome-driven—but it is the people dynamics and how people work together in the company and in TEAMS that can make a real difference to the goals and outcome.

MANAGERIAL LEADERSHIP

Who Am I Managing?

Making the jump from individual contributor to manager is never easy, and it doesn't take long for a new manager to realize that what got him there is much different than what is needed to be successful in the future. Individual contributors that have been recently promoted would probably say that they have strong technical skills in their area, and that they were very good at doing what they were doing. In a more savvy organization that recognizes leadership competencies, individual contributors would probably say that they have strong technical skills AND that they showed some behaviors and potential to lead others. When new managers enter their new roles, they expect that they will be managing people—that is, the people on their teams. Few new managers fully realize that the challenge ahead is not just in managing their people, but in managing all the other stakeholders and constituencies that want to and need to weigh in.

One of the key challenges that faces new managers is figuring out to balance all of the multiple demands from both the team and the stakeholders and constituencies external to the team. Linda A. Hill, the Wallace Brett Donham Professor of Business Administration at Harvard Business School, states that "among all the challenges facing new managers, the need to reconcile different constituencies' expectations and interests is probably the most difficult." She asserts that the demands that the new manager's direct reports, his peers, his boss, and the company's customers place on the new manager will cause conflict at times. Having teams of their own, new managers may think that managing their direct reports is the most important role to play, even at the exclusion of managing other stakeholders. This is incorrect. A new manager needs to "manage his other consistencies just as carefully." ("Helping New Managers Succeed," Lauren Keller Johnson, *HBR* 2008).

Whenever I started a new role, I always created a quick stakeholder checklist for myself. This document is essentially a list of all the stakeholders (beyond the team I am managing) with whom I need to build a relationship in order to be successful. I listed the names of my boss, my boss's boss, my peers, and any other key influencers or internal customers from the business. This is a quick checklist of the people that

I need to immediately have a "meet and greet" with and then possibly even set up a regular meeting with at a certain cadence. I have learned over the years that each of these stakeholders will have some input and impact on my success, and the quicker and more effectively I engage them in the work my team is performing, the better the chance of my team's success. Some of the questions I will ask myself when figuring out my stakeholder list include:

- Whose support will I need?
- Who needs my support? What do they need from me or my team?
- Who can keep me and my team from being successful?
- What is my ongoing influencing strategy?

Some new managers will feel that these strategies for building stakeholder support are too "political" and they don't feel right. Trust me when I tell you that this is a necessary part of the new manager role, because now the role and the work call for greater interdependence and relation building in order to be successful. It is no longer just about individual technical skills, but more about building and managing relationships with people who will support you and your team to get your work done. So, if you are a new manager asking "Who am I managing?" ... the answer is EVERYONE.

Discussion Questions

1. Do you agree with the statement that "what got you there isn't what will make you successful in the future"? Why or why not?

2. Who would be on your stakeholder checklist? Which stakeholders are you already engaging and building relationships with?

In Linda A. Hill's *Harvard Business Review* article "Managing Your Team"[5] (HBR 1995), she discusses that managing a team means managing paradox. **Paradox** exists in the fact that teams have both individual and collective identities and goals. Each individual has goals and ideas as to what he wants to accomplish—on the project, in one's career, and in life. The team itself, of course, has goals and success metrics that it needs to meet in order to be successful. Sometimes these can be in conflict with each other. Competition may arise among team members, and a win-loss attitude may take place over a collaborative and problem-solving team dynamic. The team manager may need to step in to help integrate all of the individual differences to enable them to productively pursue the team goal. Therein lies the primary paradox—balancing individual differences and goals AND the collective identity and goals. Other paradoxes include:

- Fostering support AND confrontation among team members
- Focusing on performance AND learning and development
- Balancing managerial authority AND team member discretion and autonomy
- Balancing the Triangle of Relationships—manager, team, and individual

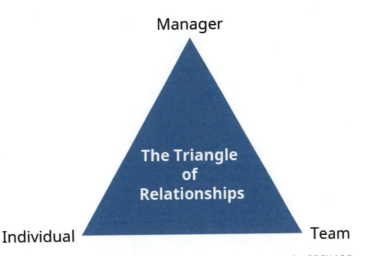

Exhibit 15.6 **The Triangle of Relationships** (Attribution: Copyright Rice University, OpenStax, under CC-BY 4.0 license)

Managing a team also means managing its boundaries. Managing the team's **boundaries**—or space between the team and its external forces, stakeholders, and pressures—is a delicate balance of strategy, stakeholder management, and organizational behavior. The team manager must serve, in part, as a buffer to these external factors so that they don't derail or distract the team from its goals. However, the manager must also understand enough about the external environment and have enough emotional intelligence to understand which forces, players, or situations must be synthesized within the team for its own benefit. Think about any medium or large-scale change initiative that you have been a part of in your career. Ideally, there is generally a vision for change and a level of sponsorship at the senior levels of the organization that is supposed to pave the way for that change to take root. The project team is officially "blessed" to kick off the team, create a charter, and identify the needed actions to drive the initiative to successful completion.

The dynamic that ensues after the kickoff is really what will determine the success of the team. There are numerous stakeholders in any organization, and many will be pro–change initiative, but others may be against the initiative—either due to lack of understanding or concerns about losing power, territory, etc. The external environment and business strategy may not be particularly well suited for a change initiative to take place, and so there may be the feeling of forces opposing the project team efforts. A strong team manager needs manage these "boundaries" with the organization to help the team navigate through and with the organizational complexities, goals, nuances, and egos that are a part of any organization. In Linda A. Hill's *Harvard Business Review* article "Exercising Influence," she states that "managers also need to manage relationships with those who are outside their team but inside their organizations.[6] To do so, they must understand the power dynamics of the larger organization and invest time and energy in building and maintaining relationship with those on who the team is dependent." It is also, in her view, "the manager's job, at a minimum, to educate other about organizational structures, systems, or politics that interfere with the team's performance." With all of the potential external influences on a team, managing a team's boundaries can truly mean the difference between success and failure.

The final element of managing a team is to manage the team itself—both the people elements and the process elements, or task at hand. The process-focused elements include managing the work plan to reach the overall goal, as well as the incremental meetings and milestones that are a part of the team's journey to reach the longer-term goal. Keeping the team focused on its objectives—beginning with setting agendas all the way to managing project tasks and celebrating milestones—assures that the team will stay on track. Projects and initiatives vary in size, scope, and complexity, and so the project management tools shouldn't be prescribed in a general sense. The important takeaway here is to choose an approach and a tool that works for the culture of the team and the organization, and that helps the team understand where they are, where they need to go, and what resources are a part of that process.

In managing the team members and interpersonal dynamics, there is the important element of selecting the right team members, shaping the team's norms and culture (how are decisions made, what are our rules, how do we manage conflict, etc.), and coaching the team. Defining the right skill sets, functions, perspectives, and expertise of the members will ensure a solid foundation. Helping the team to identify and formalize the ground rules for team engagement will help manage in the face of adversity or team conflict in the future. Finally, playing a role as a supportive coach will help both the individual team members and the group entity think through issues and make progress towards goals. A coach doesn't solve the individual/team problem, but helps the team think through a solution and move forward. Teams may need guidance on how to work things out within the team, and the manager must provide feedback and hold team members accountable for their behavior and contribution. Continuous improvement is the name of the game. A team may not start out as high performing, but they can certainly achieve that goal if everyone is focused on incremental improvements to communication, collaboration, and performance.

CONCEPT CHECK

1. Discuss the paradox(es) of a team.
2. How can a leader manage team boundaries?

15.4 | Opportunities and Challenges to Team Building

4. What are the benefits of conflict for a team?

There are many sources of **conflict** for a team, whether it is due to a communication breakdown, competing views or goals, power struggles, or conflicts between different personalities. The perception is that conflict is generally bad for a team and that it will inevitably bring the team down and cause them to spiral out of control and off track. Conflict does have some potential costs. If handled poorly, it can create distrust within a group, it can be disruptive to group progress and moral, and it could be detrimental to building lasting relationships. It is generally seen as a negative, even though constructive conflicts and constructive responses to conflicts can be an important developmental milestone for a team. Some potential benefits of conflict are that it encourages a greater diversity of ideas and perspectives and helps people to better understand opposing points of view. It can also enhance a team's problem-solving capability and can highlight critical points of discussion and contention that need to be given more thought.

Another key benefit or outcome of conflict is that a team that trusts each other—its members and members' intentions—will arise from conflict being a stronger and higher-performing team. Patrick Lencioni, in his bestselling book *The Five Dysfunctions of a Team* (2002, p. 188), writes:[7]

"The first dysfunction is an absence of trust among team members. Essentially, this stems from their unwillingness to be vulnerable within the group. Team members who are not genuinely open with one another about their mistakes and weaknesses make it impossible to build a foundation for trust. This failure to build trust is damaging because it sets the tone for the second dysfunction: fear of conflict. Teams that lack trust are incapable of engaging in unfiltered and passionate debate of ideas. Instead, they resort to veiled discussions and guarded comments."

Lencioni also asserts that if a team doesn't work through its conflict and air its opinions through debate, team members will never really be able to buy in and commit to decisions. (This lack of commitment is Lencioni's third dysfunction.) Teams often have a fear of conflict so as not to hurt any team members' feelings. The downside of this avoidance is that conflicts still exist under the surface and may resurface in more insidious and back-channel ways that can derail a team. How can a team overcome its fear of conflict and move the team forward? Lencioni names a few strategies that teams can use to make conflict more common and productive. **Mining** is a technique that can be used in teams that tend to avoid conflict. This technique requires that one team member "assume the role of a 'miner of conflict'—someone who extracts buried disagreements within the team and sheds the light of day on them. They must have the courage and confidence to call out sensitive issues and force team members to work through them." **Real-time permission** is another technique to "recognize when the people engaged in conflict are becoming uncomfortable with the level of discord, and then interrupt to remind them that what they are doing is necessary." This technique can help the group to focus on the points of conflict by coaching the team not to sweep things under the rug.

The team leader plays a very important role in the team's ability to address and navigate successfully through conflicts. Sometime a leader will have the attitude that conflict is a derailer and will try to stymie it at any cost. This ultimately leads to a team culture in which conflict is avoided and the underlying feelings are allowed to accumulate below the surface of the discussion. The leader should, by contrast, model the appropriate behavior by constructively addressing conflict and bringing issues to the surface to be addressed and resolved by the team. This is key to building a successful and effective team.

There are a variety of individual responses to conflict that you may see as a team member. Some people take the constructive and thoughtful path when conflicts arise, while others may jump immediately to destructive behaviors. In *Managing Conflict Dynamics: A Practical Approach*, Capobianco, Davis, and Kraus (2005) recognized that there are both constructive and destructive responses to conflict, as well as active and passive responses that we need to recognize. In the event of team conflict, the goal is to have a constructive response in order to encourage dialogue, learning, and resolution.[8] Responses such as perspective taking, creating solutions, expressing emotions, and reaching out are considered active and constructive responses to conflict. Reflective thinking, delay responding, and adapting are considered passive and constructive responses to conflict. See **Exhibit 15.7** for a visual of the constructive responses, as well as the destructive responses, to conflict.

	Constructive	**Destructive**
Active	• Perspective taking • Creating solutions • Expressing emotions • Reaching out	• Winning • Displaying anger • Demeaning others • Retaliating
Passive	• Reflective thinking • Delay responding • Adapting	• Avoiding • Yielding • Hiding emotions • Self-criticizing

Exhibit 15.7   Responses to Conflict (Attribution: Copyright Rice University, OpenStax, under CC-BY 4.0 license)

In summary, conflict is never easy for an individual or a team to navigate through, but it can and should be done. Illuminating the team about areas of conflict and differing perspectives can have a very positive impact on the growth and future performance of the team, and it should be managed constructively.

CONCEPT CHECK

1. What are some techniques to make conflict more productive?
2. What are some destructive responses to conflict?

| 15.5 | **Team Diversity** |

5. How does team diversity enhance decision-making and problem-solving?

Decision-making and problem-solving can be much more dynamic and successful when performed in a diverse team environment. The multiple diverse perspectives can enhance both the understanding of the problem and the quality of the solution. As I reflect on some of the leadership development work that I have done in my career, I can say from experience that the team activities and projects that intentionally brought diverse individuals together created the best environments for problem-solving. Diverse leaders from a variety of functions, from across the globe, at varying stages of their careers and experiences with and outside of the company had the most robust discussions and perspectives. **Diversity** is a word that is very commonly used today, but the importance of diversity and building diverse teams can sometimes get lost in the normal processes of doing business. Let's discuss why we need to keep these principles front of mind.

In the *Harvard Business Review* article "Why Diverse Teams are Smarter" (Nov. 2016), David Rock and Heidi Grant support the idea that increasing workplace diversity is a good business decision.[9] A 2015 McKinsey report on 366 public companies found that those in the top quartile for ethnic and racial diversity in management were 35% more likely to have financial returns above their industry mean, and those in the top quartile for gender diversity were 15% more likely to have returns above the industry mean. Similarly, in a global analysis conducted by Credit Suisse, organizations with at least one female board member yielded a higher return on equity and higher net income growth than those that did not have any women on the board.

Exhibit 15.8   The Benefits of Diversity for Teams Teams made up of diverse members tend to perform better than teams of similar backgrounds. Here, the Women of Color in Technology work on a project. The tech industry has been criticized for the lack of diversity among its ranks, and groups like the Women of Color in Technology are looking to change that. (Credit: WOCin Tech Chat/ flickr/ Attribution 2.0 Generic (CC BY 2.0))

Additional research on diversity has shown that diverse teams are better at decision-making and problem-solving because they tend to focus more on facts, per the Rock and Grant article.[10] A study published in the *Journal of Personality and Social Psychology* showed that people from diverse backgrounds "might actually alter the behavior of a group's social majority in ways that lead to improved and more accurate group thinking." It turned out that in the study, the diverse panels raised more facts related to the case than homogenous panels and made fewer factual errors while discussing available evidence. Another study noted in the article showed that diverse teams are "more likely to constantly reexamine facts and remain objective. They may also encourage greater scrutiny of each member's actions, keeping their joint cognitive resources sharp and vigilant. By breaking up workforce homogeneity, you can allow your employees to become more aware of their own potential biases—entrenched ways of thinking that can otherwise blind them to key information and even lead them to make errors in decision-making processes." In other words, when people are among homogeneous and like-minded (nondiverse) teammates, the team is susceptible to groupthink and may be reticent to think about opposing viewpoints since all team members are in alignment. In a more diverse team with a variety of backgrounds and experiences, the opposing viewpoints are more likely to come out and the team members feel obligated to research and address the questions that have been raised. Again, this enables a richer discussion and a more in-depth fact-finding and exploration of opposing ideas and viewpoints in order to solve problems.

Diversity in teams also leads to greater innovation. A Boston Consulting Group article entitled "The Mix that Matters: Innovation through Diversity" explains a study in which BCG and the Technical University of Munich conducted an empirical analysis to understand the relationship between diversity in managers (all management levels) and innovation. The key findings of this study show that:[11]

- The positive relationship between management diversity and innovation is statistically significant—and thus companies with higher levels of diversity derive more revenue from new products and services.
- The innovation boost isn't limited to a single type of diversity. The presence of managers who are either female or are from other countries, industries, or companies can cause an increase in innovation.
- Management diversity seems to have a particularly positive effect on innovation at complex companies—those that have multiple product lines or that operate in multiple industry segments.
- To reach its potential, gender diversity needs to go beyond tokenism. In the study, innovation performance only increased significantly when the workforce included more than 20% women in management positions. Having a high percentage of female employees doesn't increase innovation if only a small number of women are managers.
- At companies with diverse management teams, openness to contributions from lower-level workers and an environment in which employees feel free to speak their minds are crucial for fostering innovation.

When you consider the impact that diverse teams have on decision-making and problem-solving—through the discussion and incorporation of new perspectives, ideas, and data—it is no wonder that the BCG study shows greater innovation. Team leaders need to reflect upon these findings during the early stages of team selection so that they can reap the benefits of having diverse voices and backgrounds.

CONCEPT CHECK

1. Why do diverse teams focus more on data than homogeneous teams?
2. How are diversity and innovation related?

15.6 | Multicultural Teams

6. What are some challenges and best practices for managing and working with multicultural teams?

As globalization has increased over the last decades, workplaces have felt the impact of working within multicultural teams. The earlier section on team diversity outlined some of the highlights and benefits of working on diverse teams, and a multicultural group certainly qualifies as diverse. However, there are some key practices that are recommended to those who are leading multicultural teams so that they can parlay the diversity into an advantage and not be derailed by it.

People may assume that communication is the key factor that can derail multicultural teams, as participants may have different languages and communication styles. In the *Harvard Business Review* article "Managing Multicultural Teams," the authors point out four key cultural differences that can cause destructive conflicts in a team.[12] The first difference is *direct versus indirect communication*. Some cultures are very direct and explicit in their communication, while others are more indirect and ask questions rather than pointing our problems. This difference can cause conflict because, at the extreme, the direct style may be considered offensive by some, while the indirect style may be perceived as unproductive and passive-aggressive in team interactions.

The second difference that multicultural teams may face is *trouble with accents and fluency*. When team members don't speak the same language, there may be one language that dominates the group interaction—and those who don't speak it may feel left out. The speakers of the primary language may feel that those members don't contribute as much or are less competent. The next challenge is when there are *differing attitudes toward hierarchy*. Some cultures are very respectful of the hierarchy and will treat team members based on that hierarchy. Other cultures are more egalitarian and don't observe hierarchical differences to the same degree. This may lead to clashes if some people feel that they are being disrespected and not treated according to their status. The final difference that may challenge multicultural teams is *conflicting decision-making norms*. Different cultures make decisions differently, and some will apply a great deal of analysis and preparation beforehand. Those cultures that make decisions more quickly (and need just enough information to make a decision) may be frustrated with the slow response and relatively longer thought process.

These cultural differences are good examples of how everyday team activities (decision-making, communication, interaction among team members) may become points of contention for a multicultural team if there isn't adequate understanding of everyone's culture. The authors propose that there are several potential interventions to try if these conflicts arise. One simple intervention is **adaptation**, which is working with or around differences. This is best used when team members are willing to acknowledge the cultural differences and learn how to work with them. The next intervention technique is **structural intervention**, or reorganizing to reduce friction on the team. This technique is best used if there are unproductive subgroups or cliques within the team that need to be moved around. **Managerial intervention** is the technique of making decisions by management and without team involvement. This technique is one that should be used sparingly, as it essentially shows that the team needs guidance and can't move forward without management getting involved. Finally, **exit** is an intervention of last resort, and is the voluntary or involuntary removal of a team member. If the differences and challenges have proven to be so great that an individual on the team can no longer work with the team productively, then it may be necessary to remove the team member in question.

There are some people who seem to be innately aware of and able to work with cultural differences on teams and in their organizations. These individuals might be said to have **cultural intelligence**. Cultural intelligence is a competency and a skill that enables individuals to function effectively in cross-cultural environments. It develops as people become more aware of the influence of culture and more capable of adapting their behavior to the norms of other cultures. In the *IESE Insight* article entitled "Cultural Competence: Why It Matters and How You Can Acquire It" (Lee and Liao, 2015), the authors assert that "multicultural leaders may relate better to team members from different cultures and resolve conflicts more easily.[13] Their multiple talents can also be put to good use in international negotiations." Multicultural leaders don't have a lot of "baggage" from any one culture, and so are sometimes perceived as being culturally neutral. They are very good at handling diversity, which gives them a great advantage in their relationships with teammates.

In order to help employees become better team members in a world that is increasingly multicultural, there are a few best practices that the authors recommend for honing cross-cultural skills. The first is to "broaden your mind"—expand your own cultural channels (travel, movies, books) and surround yourself with people from other cultures. This helps to raise your own awareness of the cultural differences and norms that you may encounter. Another best practice is to "develop your cross-cultural skills through practice" and experiential learning. You may have the opportunity to work or travel abroad—but if you don't, then getting to know some of your company's cross-cultural colleagues or foreign visitors will help you to practice your skills. Serving on a cross-cultural project team and taking the time to get to know and bond with your global colleagues is an excellent way to develop skills. In my own "past life," I led a global human resources organization, and my team included employees from China, India, Brazil, Hungary, the Netherlands, and the United States. We would have annual meetings as a global HR team, and it was so rewarding to share and learn about each other's cultures. We would initiate the week with a gift exchange in a "show and tell" format from our various countries, so that everyone would learn a little bit more about the cultures in which our fellow colleagues were working. This type of interaction within a global team is a great way to facilitate cross-cultural understanding and communication, and to sharpen everyone's cultural intelligence.

MANAGING CHANGE

Understanding Our Global Colleagues

If you are a part of a global team, there are so many challenges that confront you even before you talk about people dynamics and cultural differences. You first may have to juggle time zone differences to find an adequate meeting time that suits all team members. (I used to have a team call with my Chinese colleagues at 8 p.m. my time, so that I could catch them at 8 a.m. in China the next day!) Language challenges can also pose a problem. In many countries, people are beginning to learn English as one of the main business languages. However, as I have experienced, people don't always speak their language the same way that you might learn their language in a book. There are colloquialisms, terms, and abbreviations of words that you can't learn in a classroom—you need to experience how people speak in their native countries.

You also need to be open-minded and look at situations from the perspective of your colleagues' cultures, just as you hope they will be open-minded about yours. This is referred to as cultural intelligence. Whenever I would travel globally to visit my colleagues in other countries, I would see foods, traditions, situations, and behaviors that were very "foreign" to me. Although my first response to experiencing these might be to think "wow, that's strange," I would try to think about what some of my global colleagues find "foreign" when they come to visit me in the United States. For example, my travel to China would put me in contact with chicken feet, a very popular food in China and one that I dislike immensely. Whenever I was offered chicken feet, I would turn them down in the most polite way possible and would take another food that was offered instead. I started to wonder about what my Chinese colleagues thought about the food when they'd come to visit me in the United States. Every year, I would host a global HR meeting in the United States, and a bit part of that meeting was the camaraderie and the sharing of various meals together. When I asked my Chinese colleagues what foods they thought were unpleasant, they mentioned cheese and meat. I was surprised about the meat, and when I asked, they said that it wasn't the meat itself necessarily, but it was the giant portions of meat that Americans will eat that, to them, is pretty unappetizing. Again, it is so important to check yourself and your own culture every so often, and to think about those elements that we take for granted (e.g., gigantic meat portions) and try to look at them from the eyes of another culture. It really makes us smarter and better partners to our global colleagues around the world.

In the *HBR* article "Getting Cross-Cultural Teamwork Right," the author states that three key factors—mutual learning, mutual understanding, and mutual teaching—build trust with cross-cultural colleagues as you try to bridge cultural gaps. With mutual learning, global colleagues learn from each other and absorb the new culture and behaviors through listening and observation. In mutual understanding, you try to understand the logic and cultural behaviors of the new culture to understand why people are doing what they do. This, of course, requires suspending judgment and trying to understand and embrace the differences. Finally, mutual teaching involves instructing and facilitating. This means trying to bridge the gap between the two cultures and helping yourself and others see where different cultures are coming from in order to resolve misunderstandings.

Understanding and finding common ground with your global colleagues isn't easy, and it takes patience and continuous improvement. In the end, however, I think that you will find it one of the most rewarding and enlightening things you can do. The more we work to close the multicultural "gap" and make it a multicultural advantage, the better off we will be as professionals and as people.

Once you have a sense of the different cultures and have started to work on developing your cross-cultural skills, another good practice is to "boost your cultural metacognition" and monitor your own behavior in multicultural situations. When you are in a situation in which you are interacting with multicultural individuals, you should test yourself and be aware of how you act and feel. Observe both your positive and negative interactions with people, and learn from them. Developing "**cognitive complexity**" is the final best practice for boosting multicultural skills. This is the most advanced, and it requires being able to view situations from more than one cultural framework. In order to see things from another perspective, you need to have a strong sense of emotional intelligence, empathy, and sympathy, and be willing to engage in honest communications.

In the *Harvard Business Review* article "Cultural Intelligence," the authors describe three sources of cultural intelligence that teams should consider if they are serious about becoming more adept in their cross-cultural skills and understanding. These sources, very simply, are **head, body,** and **heart**. One first learns about the beliefs, customs, and taboos of foreign cultures via the **head**. Training programs are based on providing this type of overview information—which is helpful, but obviously isn't experiential. This is the cognitive component of cultural intelligence. The second source, the **body**, involves more commitment and experimentation with the new culture. It is this physical component (demeanor, eye contact, posture, accent) that shows a deeper level of understanding of the new culture and its physical manifestations. The final source, the **heart**, deals with a person's own confidence in their ability to adapt to and deal well with cultures outside of their own. Heart really speaks to one's own level of emotional commitment and motivation to understand the new culture.

The authors have created a quick assessment to diagnose cultural intelligence, based on these cognitive, physical, and emotional/motivational measures (i.e., head, body, heart).

Please refer to **Table 15.1** for a short diagnostic that allows you to assess your cultural intelligence.

Assessing Your Cultural Intelligence
Give your responses using a 1 to 5 scale where 1 means that you strongly disagree and 5 means that you strongly agree with the statement.
Before I interact with people from a new culture, I wonder to myself what I hope to achieve.
If I encounter something unexpected while working in a new culture, I use that experience to build new ways to approach other cultures in the future.
I plan on how I am going to relate to people from a different culture before I meet with them.
When I come into a new cultural situation, I can immediately sense whether things are going well or if things are going wrong.
Add your total from the four questions above.

Table 15.1

Assessing Your Cultural Intelligence
Divide the total by 4. This is your *Cognitive Cultural Quotient*.
It is easy for me to change my body language (posture or facial expression) to suit people from a different culture.
I can alter my expressions when a cultural encounter requires it.
I can modify my speech style by changing my accent or pitch of voice to suit people from different cultures.
I can easily change the way I act when a cross-cultural encounter seems to require it.
Add your total from the four questions above.
Divide the total by 4. This is your *Cognitive Physical Quotient*.
I have confidence in my ability to deal well with people from different cultures than mine.
I am certain that I can befriend people of different cultural backgrounds than mine.
I can adapt to the lifestyle of a different culture with relative ease.
I am confident in my ability to deal with an unfamiliar cultural situation or encounter.
Add your total from the four questions above.
Divide the total by 4. This is your *Emotional/Motivational Cognitive Quotient*.
Generally, scoring below 3 in any one of the three measures signals an area requiring improvement. Averaging over 4 displays strength in cultural intelligence.
Adapted from "Cultural Intelligence," Earley and Mosakowski, *Harvard Business Review*, October 2004

Table 15.1

Cultural intelligence is an extension of emotional intelligence. An individual must have a level of awareness and understanding of the new culture so that he can adapt to the style, pace, language, nonverbal communication, etc. and work together successfully with the new culture. A multicultural team can only find success if its members take the time to understand each other and ensure that everyone feels included. Multiculturalism and cultural intelligence are traits that are taking on increasing importance in the business world today.[14] By following best practices and avoiding the challenges and pitfalls that can derail a multicultural team, a team can find great success and personal fulfillment well beyond the boundaries of the project or work engagement.

CONCEPT CHECK

1. What are some of the challenges of a multicultural team?
2. Explain the cultural intelligence techniques of head, body, and heart.

🔑 Key Terms

adaptation Technique of working with or around differences

boundaries Lines that make the limits of an area; team boundaries separate the team from its external stakeholders

cognitive complexity The ability to view situations from more than one cultural framework

collaboration The action of working with someone to produce or create something

cultural intelligence A skill that enables individuals to function effectively in cross-cultural environments

emotional intelligence The capability of individuals to recognize their own emotions and others' emotions

exit Technique of last resort—removal of a team member

Forming The first stage of team development—the positive and polite stage

ground rules Basic rules or principles of conduct that govern a situation or endeavor

head, body, and heart Techniques for becoming more adept in cross-cultural skills—learning about cultures (head), physical manifestations of culture (body), and emotional commitment to new culture (heart)

knowledge economy The information society, using knowledge to generate tangible and intangible values

managerial intervention Technique of making decisions by management and without team involvement

mining To delve in to extract something of value; a technique for generating discussion instead of burying it

Norming The third stage of team development—when team resolves its differences and begins making progress

paradox A self-contradictory statement or situation

Performing The fourth stage of team development—when hard work leads to the achievement of the team's goal

real-time permission A technique for recognizing when conflict is uncomfortable, and giving permission to continue

Storming The second stage of team development—when people are pushing against the boundaries

structural intervention Technique of reorganizing to reduce friction on a team

working group Group of experts working together to achieve specific goals; performance is made up of the individual results of all members

📑 Summary of Learning Outcomes

15.1 Teamwork in the Workplace
1. What is a team, and what makes teams effective?

A team is defined as "people organized to function cooperatively as a group." Some of the characteristics of a team are that it has a common commitment and purpose, specific performance goals, complementary skills, commitment to how the work gets done, and mutual accountability.

Some of the practices that make a team effective are that they have a sense of urgency and direction; they set clear rules of behavior; they spend lots of time together; and they utilize feedback, recognition, and reward.

15.2 Team Development Over Time
2. How do teams develop over time?

Teams go through different stages of team development, which were coined in 1977 as Tuckman's Stages of Group Development by educational psychologist Bruce Tuckman. Tuckman's model includes these four stages: Forming, Storming, Norming, and Performing. A fifth stage, Adjourning, was added later to explain the disbanding and closure of a team at the end of a project.

Forming begins with team members being happy and polite as they get to know each other and understand the work they'll do together. Storming starts once the work is underway and the team is getting to know each other, and conflicts and project stress begins to seep in. During Norming, the team starts to set rules of the road and define how they want to work together. Performing means that the team is underway and is having some successes and gaining traction. This is definitely not a linear process. Teams can regress to earlier stages if there are changes in team members or work orders that cause disruption and loss of momentum and clarity.

15.3 Things to Consider When Managing Teams
3. What are some key considerations in managing teams?

Managing a team is often more complex than people would admit. Although a team and the team leader may be focused on the task or project work, it is actually the people dynamics and how the team works together that will make a real difference to the goals and outcomes. Managers need to remember that most of their time will be spent managing the people dynamics—not the tasks.

Managing teams also means a certain amount of paradox. A team has both individual and collective goals that need to be managed effectively. A manager needs to foster both team supportiveness and the ability to engage in conflict and confrontation. A team manager also needs to help the team with its boundaries and act as a buffer, a stakeholder manager, or a strategist when the situation calls for each. Exercising influence with key stakeholder groups external to the project group is one of the most critical functions in managing a team.

15.4 Opportunities and Challenges to Team Building
4. What are the benefits of conflict for a team?

Conflict during team interactions can feel like it derails progress, but it is one of the most important experiences that a team can have together. A team that can productively work through conflict will end up stronger, building more trust and being more open to sharing opinions. Team members will feel safe buying in and committing to decision-making as a team.

One of the other key benefits of conflict is that it encourages a greater diversity of ideas and perspectives, and it helps people to better understand opposing points of view. If a team doesn't work through conflict well and doesn't feel comfortable with the sharing and debating of ideas, it loses the opportunity to effectively vet ideas and potential solutions. The result is that the decision or solution will be limited, as team members haven't fully shared their concerns and perspectives.

15.5 Team Diversity
5. How does team diversity enhance team decision-making and problem-solving?

Decision-making and problem-solving is so much more dynamic and successful when performed in a diverse team environment. Much like the benefits of conflict, diversity can bring forward opposing points of view and different perspectives and information that might not have been considered if the team were more homogeneous. Diverse teams are thus made "smarter" by bringing together an array of information, sources, and experiences for decision-making.

Other research on diversity indicates that diverse teams excel at decision-making and problem-solving because they tend to focus more on facts. Studies indicate that diverse team members may actually sway the team's behavior to focus more on proven data—possibly because of the prospect of having to explain and back up one's perspectives if a conflict should erupt on the team. In a more homogenous team, there is more risk of "groupthink" and the lack of challenging of ideas.

15.6 Multicultural Teams

6. What are some challenges and best practices for managing and working with multicultural teams?

With the increase in globalization over the years, teams have seen the addition of multicultural individuals on their teams, who bring with them their own diverse backgrounds and perspectives. There are very positive aspects that result from the added diversity, as discussed in the previous questions. There are also challenges that we need to be aware of when we are managing these teams.

Challenges can arise from communication styles and accents, but can also appear in the form of decision-making norms and attitudes toward hierarchy. There are some team manager interventions that are best practices for addressing these challenges. There are also some best practices for building the cultural intelligence that will make the team more adept at understanding and dealing with differences among cultures.

Chapter Review Questions

1. What are the key differences between a team and a working group?
2. At what stage of team development does the team finally start to see results?
3. What can cause a team to digress to an earlier stage of team development?
4. What can a team leader do to manage the team's boundaries?
5. How does managing conflict help a team learn and grow?
6. What are some strategies to make conflict more productive?
7. Why are diverse teams better at decision-making and problem-solving?
8. Why do diverse teams utilize data more often than homogeneous teams?
9. What are some of the challenges that multicultural teams face?
10. What are the key sources of cultural intelligence?

Management Skills Application Exercises

1. Do you agree with Katzenbach and Smith's key practices that make teams effective? Why or why not? Which of these practices have you personally experienced? Are there any additional practices that you would add?
2. Have you ever been part of a team that made it through all four stages of team development? In which stage did the team remain the longest? In which stage did the team remain the shortest amount of time? What did you learn?
3. Why do you think it is so important to manage a team's boundaries? How can external stakeholders impact the function and performance of the team? Why is emotional intelligence such an important skill to have when managing a team?
4. In your experience, have you ever been in a situation in which conflict became a negative thing for a team? How was the conflict handled? How can a team manager ensure that conflict is handled constructively?
5. What is the difference between cultural intelligence and emotional intelligence? How can the cultural intelligence of a team improve performance? Have you ever been on a multicultural team that was high on cultural intelligence? How about a team that was low on cultural intelligence? What were the impacts?

⅄ Managerial Decision Exercises

1. You are a manager of a team that is taking a long time to move through the Storming stage. There are two individuals on the team that seem to be unproductive when dealing with conflict and are holding the team back. What would you do to help the team move through conflict management and begin Norming and Performing?

2. One of your direct reports on your team is very focused on his own personal development. He is a strong employee individually, but hasn't had as much experience working in a team environment on a project. He wants to do well, but isn't exactly sure how to work within this context. How would you instruct him?

3. You are leading a team responsible for a very important strategic initiative at your company. You have launched the project, and your team is very motivated and excited to move forward. You have the sense, however, that your sponsor and some other stakeholders are not fully engaged. What do you do to engage them?

4. You are the project manager of a cross-functional team project that was just approved. You have been given several good team members who are from different functions, but many of them think similarly and are unlikely to question each other on team decisions. You have the choice of keeping a homogeneous team that will probably have few team issues or building a diverse team that may well engage in conflict and take much longer to come to decisions. What choice would you make? What other information would you want to know to make the decision?

5. You are the director of a multicultural team with employees across the globe. Your team rarely has the opportunity to meet in person, but you have been given the budget to bring everyone together for a week-long global team meeting and team building. How would you structure the time together? What are some of the activities you would suggest to build stronger relationships among team members?

💡 Critical Thinking Case

Diverse Teams Hold Court

Diverse teams have been proven to be better at problem-solving and decision-making for a number of reasons. First, they bring many different perspectives to the table. Second, they rely more on facts and use those facts to substantiate their positions. What is even more interesting is that, according to the *Scientific American* article "How Diversity Makes Us Smarter," simply "being around people who are different from us makes more creative, diligent, and harder-working."

One case in point is the example of jury decision-making, where fact-finding and logical decision-making are of utmost importance. A 2006 study of jury decision-making, led by social psychologist Samuel Sommers of Tufts University, showed that racially diverse groups exchanged a wider range of information during deliberation of a case than all-white groups did. The researcher also conducted mock jury trials with a group of real jurors to show the impact of diversity on jury decision-making.

Interestingly enough, it was the mere presence of diversity on the jury that made jurors consider the facts more, and they had fewer errors recalling the relevant information. The groups even became more willing to discuss the role of race case, when they hadn't before with an all-white jury. This wasn't the case because the diverse jury members brought new information to the group—it happened because, according to the author, the mere presence of diversity made people more open-minded and diligent. Given what we discussed on the benefits of diversity, it makes sense. People are more likely to be prepared, to be diligent, and to think logically about something if they know that they will be pushed or tested on it. And who else would push you or test you on something, if not someone who is different from you in perspective, experience, or thinking. "Diversity jolts us into cognitive action in ways that homogeneity simply does not."

So, the next time you are called for jury duty, or to serve on a board committee, or to make an important decision as part of a team, remember that one way to generate a great discussion and come up with a strong solution is to pull together a diverse team.

Critical Thinking Questions
1. If you don't have a diverse group of people on your team, how can you ensure that you will have robust discussions and decision-making? What techniques can you use to generate conversations from different perspectives?
2. Evaluate your own team at work. Is it a diverse team? How would you rate the quality of decisions generated from that group?

Sources: Adapted from Katherine W. Phillips, "How Diversity Makes Us Smarter," *Scientific American*, October 2014, p. 7–8.

Exhibit 16.1 (Credit: UC Davis College of Engineering/ flickr/ Attribution 2.0 Generic (CC BY 2.0))

 Introduction

Learning Outcomes

After reading this chapter, you should be able to answer these questions:

1. Understand and describe the communication process.
2. Know the types of communications that occur in organizations.
3. Understand how power, status, purpose, and interpersonal skills affect communications in organizations.
4. Describe how corporate reputations are defined by how an organization communicates to all of its stakeholders.
5. Know why talking, listening, reading, and writing are vital to managing effectively.

EXPLORING MANAGERIAL CAREERS

John Legere, T-Mobile

The chief executive officer is often the face of the company. He or she is often the North Star of the company, providing guidance and direction for the entire organization. With other stakeholders, such as shareholders, suppliers, regulatory agencies, and customers, CEOs often take more reserved and structured approaches. One CEO who definitely stands out is John Legere, the CEO of T-Mobile. The unconventional CEO of the self-proclaimed "un-carrier" hosts a Sunday morning podcast called "Slow Cooker Sunday" on Facebook Live, and where most CEOs appear on television interviews in standard business attire, Legere appears with shoulder-length hair dressed in a magenta T-shirt, black jacket, and pink sneakers. Whereas most CEOs use well-scripted language to address business issues and competitors, Legere refers to T-Mobile's largest competitors, AT&T and Verizon, as "dumb and dumber."

In the mobile phone market, T-Mobile is the number-three player competing with giants AT&T and Verizon and recently came to an agreement to merge with Sprint. Of all the consolidation sweeping through the media and telecommunications arena, T-Mobile and Sprint are the most direct of competitors. Their merger would reduce the number of national wireless carriers from four to three, a move the Federal Communications Commission has firmly opposed in the past. Then again, the wireless market looks a bit different now, as does the administration in power.

John Legere and other CEOs such as Mark Cuban, Elon Musk, and Richard Branson have a more public profile than executives at other companies that keep a lower profile and are more guarded in their public comments, often restricting their public statements to quarterly investor and analyst meetings. It is likely that the personality and communication style that the executives reveal in public is also the way that they relate to their employees. The outgoing personality of someone such as John Legere will motivate some employees, but he might be seen as too much of a cheerleader by other employees.

Sometimes the unscripted comments and colorful language that Legere uses can cause issues with employees and the public. For instance, some T-Mobile employees in their call center admonished Legere for comments at a press event where he said Verizon and AT&T were "raping" customers for every penny they have. Legere's comments caused lengthy discussions in online forums such as Reddit about his choice of words. Legere is known for speaking his mind in public and often uses profanity, but many thought this comment crossed the line. While frank, open communication is often appreciated and leads to a clarity of message, senders of communication, be it in a public forum, an internal memo, or even a text message, should always think through the consequences of their words.

Sources: Tara Lachapelle, "T-Mobile's Argument for Sprint Deal is as Loud as CEO John Legere's Style," *The Seattle Times*, July 9, 2018, https://www.seattletimes.com/business/t-mobiles-argument-for-sprint-deal-is-as-loud-as-ceo-john-legeres-style/; Janko Roettgers, "T-Mobile CEO John Legere Pokes Fun at Verizon's Go90 Closure," *Variety*, June 29, 2018, https://variety.com/2018/digital/news/john-legere-go90-1202862397/; Rachel Lerman, "T-Mobile's Loud, Outspoken John Legere is Not Your Typical CEO," *The Chicago Tribune*, April 30, 2018, www.chicagotribune.com/business/sns-tns-bc-tmobile-legere-20180430-story.html; Steve Kovach, T-Mobile Employees Speak Out and Call CEO's Recent Rape Comments "Violent" and "Traumatizing"," *Business Insider*, June 27, 2014, https://www.businessinsider.com/t-mobile-employees-speak-out-legere-rape-comment-2014-6; Brian X. Chen, One on One: John Legere, the Hip New Chief of T-Mobile USA," *New York Times*, January 9, 2013, https://bits.blogs.nytimes.com/2013/01/09/one-on-one-john-legere-the-hip-new-chief-of-t-mobile-usa/.

We will distinguish between communication between two individuals and communication amongst several individuals (groups) and communication outside the organization. We will show that managers spend a majority of their time in communication with others. We will examine the reasons for communication and discuss the basic model of interpersonal communication, the types of interpersonal communication, and major influences on the communication process. We will also discuss how organizational reputation is defined by communication with stakeholders.

16.1 | The Process of Managerial Communication

1. Understand and describe the communication process.

Interpersonal communication is an important part of being an effective manager:

- It influences the opinions, attitude, motivation, and behaviors of others.
- It expresses our feelings, emotions, and intentions to others.
- It is the vehicle for providing, receiving, and exchanging information regarding events or issues that concern us.
- It reinforces the formal structure of the organization by such means as making use of formal channels of communication.

Interpersonal communication allows employees at all levels of an organization to interact with others, to secure desired results, to request or extend assistance, and to make use of and reinforce the formal design of the organization. These purposes serve not only the individuals involved, but the larger goal of improving the quality of organizational effectiveness.

The model that we present here is an oversimplification of what really happens in communication, but this model will be useful in creating a diagram to be used to discuss the topic. **Exhibit 16.2** illustrates a simple communication episode where a **communicator** encodes a message and a **receiver** decodes the message.[1]

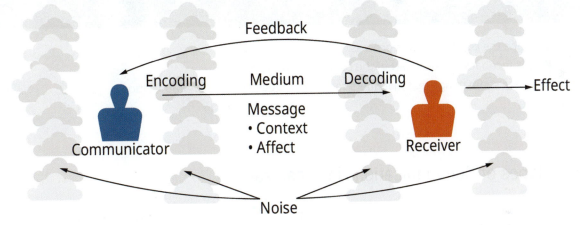

Exhibit 16.2   The Basic Communication Model (Attribution: Copyright Rice University, OpenStax, under CC-BY 4.0 license)

Encoding and Decoding

Two important aspects of this model are **encoding** and **decoding**. Encoding is the process by which individuals initiating the communication translate their ideas into a systematic set of symbols (language), either written or spoken. Encoding is influenced by the sender's previous experiences with the topic or issue, her emotional state at the time of the message, the importance of the message, and the people involved. Decoding is the process by which the recipient of the message interprets it. The receiver attaches meaning to the message and tries to uncover its underlying intent. Decoding is also influenced by the receiver's previous experiences and frame of reference at the time of receiving the message.

Feedback

Several types of feedback can occur after a message is sent from the communicator to the receiver. Feedback can be viewed as the last step in completing a communication episode and may take several forms, such as a verbal response, a nod of the head, a response asking for more information, or no response at all. As with the initial message, the response also involves encoding, medium, and decoding.

There are three basic types of feedback that occur in communication.[2] These are informational, corrective, and reinforcing. In informational feedback, the receiver provides nonevaluative information to the communicator. An example is the level of inventory at the end of the month. In corrective feedback, the receiver responds by challenging the original message. The receiver might respond that it is not her responsibility to monitor inventory. In reinforcing feedback, the receiver communicated that she has clearly received the message and its intentions. For instance, the grade that you receive on a term paper (either positive or negative) is reinforcing feedback on your term paper (your original communication).

Noise

There is, however, a variety of ways that the intended message can get distorted. Factors that distort message clarity are **noise**. Noise can occur at any point along the model shown in **Exhibit 16.2**, including the decoding process. For example, a manager might be under pressure and issue a directive, "I want this job completed today, and I don't care what it costs," when the manager does care what it costs.

CONCEPT CHECK

1. Describe the communication process.
2. Why is feedback a critical part of the communication process?
3. What are some things that managers can do to reduce noise in communication?

16.2 Types of Communications in Organizations

2. Know the types of communications that occur in organizations.

In the communication model described above, three types of communication can be used by either the communicator in the initial transmission phase or the receiver in the feedback phase. These three types are discussed next.

Oral Communication

This consists of all messages or exchanges of information that are spoken, and it's the most prevalent type of communication.

Written Communication

This includes e-mail, texts, letters, reports, manuals, and annotations on sticky notes. Although managers prefer oral communication for its efficiency and immediacy, the increase in electronic communication is undeniable. As well, some managers prefer written communication for important messages, such as a change in a company policy, where precision of language and documentation of the message are important.

MANAGERIAL LEADERSHIP

Dealing with Information Overload

One of the challenges in many organizations is dealing with a deluge of emails, texts, voicemails, and other communication. Organizations have become flatter, outsourced many functions, and layered technology to speed communication with an integrated communication programs such as Slack, which allows users to manage all their communication and access shared resources in one place. This can lead to information overload, and crucial messages may be drowned out by the volume in your inbox.

Add the practice of "reply to all," which can add to the volume of communication, that many coworkers use, and that means that you may get five or six versions of an initial e-mail and need to understand all of the responses as well as the initial communication before responding or deciding that the issue is resolved and no response is needed. Here are suggestions to dealing with e-mail overload upward, horizontally, and downward within your organization and externally to stakeholders and customers.

One way to reduce the volume and the time you spend on e-mail is to turn off the spigot of incoming messages. There are obvious practices that help, such as unsubscribing to e-newsletters or turning off notifications from social media accounts such as Facebook and Twitter. Also consider whether your colleagues or direct reports are copying you on too many emails as an FYI. If yes, explain that you only need to be updated at certain times or when a final decision is made.

You will also want to set up a system that will organize your inbox into "folders" that will allow you to manage the flow of messages into groups that will allow you to address them appropriately. Your system might look something like this:

1. **Inbox**: Treat this as a holding pen. E-mails shouldn't stay here any longer than it takes for you to file them into another folder. The exception is when you respond immediately and are waiting for an immediate response.
2. **Today**: This is for items that need a response today.
3. **This week**: This is for messages that require a response before the end of the week.
4. **This month/quarter**: This is for everything that needs a longer-term response. Depending on your role, you may need a monthly or quarterly folder.
5. **FYI**: This is for any items that are for information only and that you may want to refer back to in the future.

This system prioritizes e-mails based on timescales rather than the e-mails' senders, enabling you to better schedule work and set deadlines.

Another thing to consider is your outgoing e-mail. If your outgoing messages are not specific, too long, unclear, or are copied too widely, your colleagues are likely to follow the same practice when communicating with you. Keep your communication clear and to the point, and managing your outbox will help make your inbound e-mails manageable.

Critical Thinking Questions
1. How are you managing your e-mails now? Are you mixing personal and school and work-related e-mails in the same account?
2. How would you communicate to a colleague that is sending too many FYI e-mails, sending too may unclear e-mails, or copying too many people on her messages?

Sources: Amy Gallo, Stop Email Overload, *Harvard Business Review*, February 21, 2012, https://hbr.org/ 2012/02/stop-email-overload-1; Barry Chingel, "How to beat email Overload in 2018", *CIPHER*, January 16, 2018, https://www.ciphr.com/advice/email-overload/; Monica Seely, "At the Mercy of Your Inbox? How to Cope With Email Overload", *The Guardian*, November 6, 2017, https://www.theguardian.com/small-business-network/2017/nov/06/at-the-mercy-of-your-inbox-how-to-cope-with-email-overload.

Nonverbal Communication

There is also the transformation of information without speaking or writing. Some examples of this are things such as traffic lights and sirens as well as things such as office size and placement, which connote something or someone of importance. As well, things such as body language and facial expression can convey either conscious or unconscious messages to others.

Exhibit 16.3   Body Language at a Meeting Your body language can send messages during a meeting. (Credit: Amtec Photos/ Flickr/ Attribution 2.0 Generic (CC BY 2.0))

Major Influences on Interpersonal Communication

Regardless of the type of communication involved, the nature, direction, and quality of interpersonal communication processes can be influenced by several factors.[3]

Social Influences

Communication is a social process, as it takes at least two people to have a communication episode. There is a variety of social influences that can affect the accuracy of the intended message. For examples, status barriers between employees at different levels of the organization can influence things such as addressing a colleague as at a director level as "Ms. Jones" or a coworker at the same level as "Mike." Prevailing norms and roles can dictate who speaks to whom and how someone responds. **Exhibit 16.4** illustrates a variety of communications that illustrate social influences in the workplace.

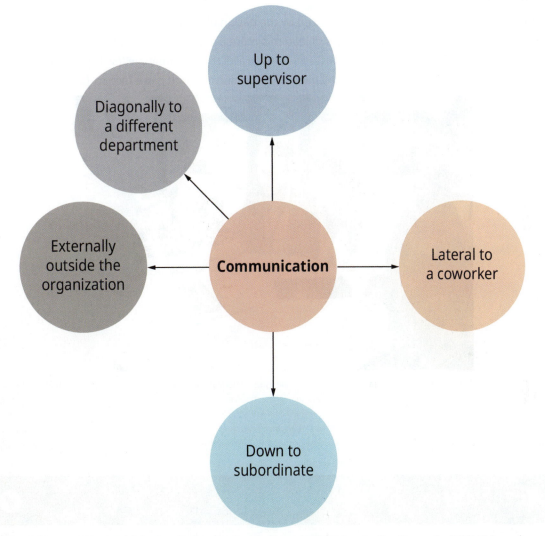

Exhibit 16.4   Patterns of Managerial Communication (Attribution: Copyright Rice University, OpenStax, under CC-BY 4.0 license)

Perception

In addition, the communication process is heavily influenced by perceptual processes. The extent to which an employee accurately receives job instructions from a manager may be influences by her perception of the manager, especially if the job instructions conflict with her interest in the job or if they are controversial. If an employee has stereotyped the manager as incompetent, chances are that little that the manager says will be taken seriously. If the boss is well regarded or seen as influential in the company, everything that she says may be interpreted as important.

Interaction Involvement

Communication effectiveness can be influenced by the extent to which one or both parties are involved in conversation. This attentiveness is called **interaction attentiveness** or **interaction involvement**.[4] If the intended receiver of the message is preoccupied with other issues, the effectiveness of the message may be diminished. Interaction involvement consists of three interrelated dimensions: responsiveness, perceptiveness, and attentiveness.

Organizational Design

The communication process can also be influenced by the design of the organization. It has often been argued to decentralize an organization because that will lead to a more participative structure and lead to improved communication in the organization. When messages must travel through multiple levels of an organization, the possibility of distortion can also occur, which would be diminished with more face-to-face communication.

Exhibit 16.5   Informal Communication in Organizations Smart managers understand that not all of a company's influential relationships appear as part of the organization chart. A web of informal, personal connections exists between workers, and vital information and knowledge pass through this web constantly. Using social media analysis software and other tracking tools, managers can map and quantify the normally invisible relationships that form between employees at all levels of an organization. How might identifying a company's informal organization help managers foster teamwork, motivate employees, and boost productivity? (Credit: Exeter/ flickr/ Attribution 2.0 Generic (CC BY 2.0))

CONCEPT CHECK

1. What are the three major types of communication?
2. How can you manage the inflow of electronic communication?
3. What are the major influences on organizational communication, and how can organizational design affect communication?

16.3 | Factors Affecting Communications and the Roles of Managers

3. Understand how power, status, purpose, and interpersonal skills affect communications in organizations.

The Roles Managers Play

In Mintzberg's seminal study of managers and their jobs, he found the majority of them clustered around three core management roles.[5]

Interpersonal Roles

Managers are required to interact with a substantial number of people during a workweek. They host receptions; take clients and customers to dinner; meet with business prospects and partners; conduct hiring and performance interviews; and form alliances, friendships, and personal relationships with many others. Numerous studies have shown that such relationships are the richest source of information for managers because of their immediate and personal nature.[6]

Three of a manager's roles arise directly from formal authority and involve basic interpersonal relationships. First is the **figurehead role**. As the head of an organizational unit, every manager must perform some ceremonial duties. In Mintzberg's study, chief executives spent 12% of their contact time on ceremonial duties; 17% of their incoming mail dealt with acknowledgments and requests related to their status. One example is a company president who requested free merchandise for a handicapped schoolchild.[7]

Managers are also responsible for the work of the people in their unit, and their actions in this regard are directly related to their role as a leader. The influence of managers is most clearly seen, according to Mintzberg, in the leader role. Formal authority vests them with great potential power. Leadership determines, in large part, how much power they will realize.

Does the leader's role matter? Ask the employees of Chrysler Corporation (now Fiat Chrysler). When Sergio Marchionne, who passed away in 2018, took over the company in the wake of the financial crisis, the once-great auto manufacturer was in bankruptcy, teetering on the verge of extinction. He formed new relationships with the United Auto Workers, reorganized the senior management of the company, and—perhaps, most importantly—convinced the U.S. federal government to guarantee a series of bank loans that would make the company solvent again. The loan guarantees, the union response, and the reaction of the marketplace, especially for the Jeep brand, were due in large measure to Marchionne's leadership style and personal charisma. More recent examples include the return of Starbucks founder Howard Schultz to reenergize and steer his company and Amazon CEO Jeff Bezos and his ability to innovate during a downturn in the economy.[8]

Popular management literature has had little to say about the liaison role until recently. This role, in which managers establish and maintain contacts outside the vertical chain of command, becomes especially important in view of the finding of virtually every study of managerial work that managers spend as much time with peers and other people outside of their units as they do with their own subordinates. Surprisingly, they spend little time with their own superiors. In Rosemary Stewart's (1967) study, 160 British middle and top managers spent 47% of their time with peers, 41% of their time with people inside their unit, and only 12% of their time with superiors. Guest's (1956) study of U.S. manufacturing supervisors revealed similar findings.

Informational Roles

Managers are required to gather, collate, analyze, store, and disseminate many kinds of information. In doing so, they become information resource centers, often storing huge amounts of information in their own heads, moving quickly from the role of gatherer to the role of disseminator in minutes. Although many business organizations install large, expensive management information systems to perform many of those functions, nothing can match the speed and intuitive power of a well-trained manager's brain for information processing. Not surprisingly, most managers prefer it that way.

As monitors, managers are constantly scanning the environment for information, talking with liaison contacts and subordinates, and receiving unsolicited information, much of it because of their network of personal contacts. A good portion of this information arrives in verbal form, often as gossip, hearsay, and speculation.[9]

In the disseminator role, managers pass privileged information directly to subordinates, who might otherwise have no access to it. Managers must decide not only who should receive such information, but how much of it, how often, and in what form. Increasingly, managers are being asked to decide whether subordinates, peers, customers, business partners, and others should have direct access to information 24 hours a day without having to contact the manager directly.[10]

In the spokesperson role, managers send information to people outside of their organizations: an executive makes a speech to lobby for an organizational cause, or a supervisor suggests a product modification to a supplier. Increasingly, managers are also being asked to deal with representatives of the news media, providing both factual and opinion-based responses that will be printed or broadcast to vast unseen audiences, often directly or with little editing. The risks in such circumstances are enormous, but so too are the potential rewards in terms of brand recognition, public image, and organizational visibility.[11]

Decisional Roles

Ultimately, managers are charged with the responsibility of making decisions on behalf of both the organization and the stakeholders with an interest in it. Such decisions are often made under circumstances of high ambiguity and with inadequate information. Often, the other two managerial roles—interpersonal and informational—will assist a manager in making difficult decisions in which outcomes are not clear and interests are often conflicting.

In the role of entrepreneur, managers seek to improve their businesses, adapt to changing market conditions, and react to opportunities as they present themselves. Managers who take a longer-term view of their responsibilities are among the first to realize that they will need to reinvent themselves, their product and service lines, their marketing strategies, and their ways of doing business as older methods become obsolete and competitors gain advantage.

While the entrepreneur role describes managers who initiate change, the disturbance or crisis handler role depicts managers who must involuntarily react to conditions. Crises can arise because bad managers let circumstances deteriorate or spin out of control, but just as often good managers find themselves in the midst of a crisis that they could not have anticipated but must react to just the same.[12]

The third decisional role of resource allocator involves managers making decisions about who gets what, how much, when, and why. Resources, including funding, equipment, human labor, office or production space, and even the boss's time, are all limited, and demand inevitably outstrips supply. Managers must make sensible decisions about such matters while still retaining, motivating, and developing the best of their employees.

The final decisional role is that of negotiator. Managers spend considerable amounts of time in negotiations: over budget allocations, labor and collective bargaining agreements, and other formal dispute resolutions. During a week, managers will often make dozens of decisions that are the result of brief but important negotiations between and among employees, customers and clients, suppliers, and others with whom managers must deal.[13]

CONCEPT CHECK

1. What are the major roles that managers play in communicating with employees?
2. Why are negotiations often brought in to communications by managers?

16.4 | Managerial Communication and Corporate Reputation

4. Describe how corporate reputations are defined by how an organization communicates to its stakeholders.

Management communication is a central discipline in the study of communication and corporate reputation. An understanding of language and its inherent powers, combined with the skill to speak, write, listen, and form interpersonal relationships, will determine whether companies succeed or fail and whether they are rewarded or penalized for their reputations.

At the midpoint of the twentieth century, Peter Drucker wrote, "Managers have to learn to know language, to understand what words are and what they mean. Perhaps most important, they have to acquire respect for language as [our] most precious gift and heritage. The manager must understand the meaning of the old definition of rhetoric as 'the art which draws men's hearts to the love of true knowledge.'"[14]

Later, Eccles and Nohria reframed Drucker's view to offer a perspective of management that few others have seen: "To see management in its proper light, managers need first to take language seriously."[15] In particular, they argue, a coherent view of management must focus on three issues: the use of rhetoric to achieve a manager's goals, the shaping of a managerial identity, and taking action to achieve the goals of the organizations that employ us. Above all, they say, "the essence of what management is all about [is] the effective use of language to get things done."[16] One of the things managers get done is the creation, management, and monitoring of corporate reputation.

The job of becoming a competent, effective manager thus becomes one of understanding language and action. It also involves finding ways to shape how others see and think of *you* in *your* role as a manager. Many noted researchers have examined the important relationship between communication and action within large and complex organizations and conclude that the two are inseparable. Without the right words, used in the right way, it is unlikely that the right reputations develop. "Words do matter," write Eccles and Nohria. "They matter very much. Without words we have no way of expressing strategic concepts, structural forms, or designs for performance measurement systems." Language, they conclude, "is too important to managers to be taken for granted or, even worse, abused."[17]

So, if language is a manager's key to corporate reputation management, the next question is obvious: How good are managers at using language? Managers' ability to act—to hire a talented workforce, to change an organization's reputation, to launch a new product line—depends entirely on how effectively they use management communication, both as a speaker and as a listener. Managers' effectiveness as a speaker and writer will determine how well they are able to manage the firm's reputation. And their effectiveness as listeners will determine how well they understand and respond to others and can change the organization in response to their feedback.

We will now examine the role management communication plays in corporate reputation formation, management, and change and the position occupied by rhetoric in the life of business organizations. Though, this chapter will focus on the skills, abilities, and competencies for using language, attempting to influence others, and responding to the requirements of peers, superiors, stakeholders, and the organization in which managers and employees work.

Management communication is about the movement of information and the skills that facilitate it—speaking, writing, listening, and processes of critical thinking. It's also about understanding who your organization is (identity), who others think your organization is (reputation), and the contributions individuals can make to the success of their business considering their organization's existing reputation. It is also about confidence—the knowledge that one can speak and write well, listen with great skill as others speak, and both seek out and provide the feedback essential to creating, managing, or changing their organization's reputation.

At the heart of this chapter, though, is the notion that communication, in many ways, is the work of managers. We will now examine the roles of writing and speaking in the role of management, as well as other specific applications and challenges managers face as they play their role in the creation, maintenance, and change of corporate reputation.

CONCEPT CHECK

1. How are corporate reputations affected by the communication of managers and public statements?
2. Why is corporate reputation important?

16.5 | The Major Channels of Management Communication Are Talking, Listening, Reading, and Writing

5. Know why talking, listening, reading, and writing are vital to managing effectively.

The major channels of managerial communication displayed in **Exhibit 16.6** are talking, listening, reading, and writing. Among these, talking is the predominant method of communicating, but as e-mail and texting increase, reading and writing are increasing. Managers across industries, according to Deirdre Borden, spend about 75% of their time in verbal interaction. Those daily interactions include the following.

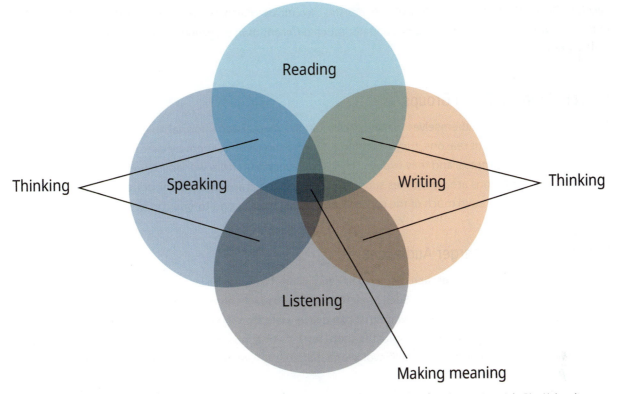

Exhibit 16.6 Reading, Writing, Speaking, and Listening: How They Help in Creating Meaning (Attribution: Copyright Rice University, OpenStax, under CC-BY 4.0 license)

One-on-One Conversations

Increasingly, managers find that information is passed orally, often face-to-face in offices, hallways, conference rooms, cafeterias, restrooms, athletic facilities, parking lots, and literally dozens of other venues. An enormous amount of information is exchanged, validated, confirmed, and passed back and forth under highly informal circumstances.

Telephone Conversations

Managers spend an astounding amount of time on the telephone these days. Curiously, the amount of time per telephone call is decreasing, but the number of calls per day is increasing. With the nearly universal availability of cellular and satellite telephone service, very few people are out of reach of the office for very long. The decision to switch off a cellular telephone, in fact, is now considered a decision in favor of work-life balance.

Video Teleconferencing

Bridging time zones as well as cultures, videoconferencing facilities make direct conversations with employees, colleagues, customers, and business partners across the nation or around the world a simple matter. Carrier Corporation, the air-conditioning manufacturer, is now typical of firms using desktop videoconferencing to conduct everything from staff meetings to technical training. Engineers at Carrier's Farmington, Connecticut, headquarters can hook up with service managers in branch offices thousands of miles away to explain new product developments, demonstrate repair techniques, and update field staff on matters that would, just recently, have required extensive travel or expensive, broadcast-quality television programming. Their exchanges are informal, conversational, and not much different than they would be if the people were in the same room.[18]

Presentations to Small Groups

Managers frequently find themselves making presentations, formal and informal, to groups of three to eight people for many different reasons: they pass along information given to them by executives, they review the status of projects in process, and they explain changes in everything from working schedules to organizational goals. Such presentations are sometimes supported by overhead transparencies or printed outlines, but they are oral in nature and retain much of the conversational character of one-to-one conversations.

Public Speaking to Larger Audiences

Most managers are unable to escape the periodic requirement to speak to larger audiences of several dozen or, perhaps, several hundred people. Such presentations are usually more formal in structure and are often supported by PowerPoint or Prezi software that can deliver data from text files, graphics, photos, and even motion clips from streaming video. Despite the more formal atmosphere and sophisticated audio-visual support systems, such presentations still involve one manager talking to others, framing, shaping, and passing information to an audience.

A series of scientific studies, beginning with Rankin, Nichols and Stevens, and Wolvin and Coakley, confirm: most managers spend the largest portion of their day talking and listening.[19] Werner's thesis, in fact, found that North American adults spend more than 78% of their communication time either talking or listening to others who are talking.

According to Werner and others who study the communication habits of postmodern business organizations, managers are involved in more than just speeches and presentations from the dais or teleconference podium. They spend their days in meetings, on the telephone, conducting interviews, giving tours, supervising informal visits to their facilities, and at a wide variety of social events.[20]

Exhibit 16.7   Public speaking   Public speaking is often a terrifying but crucial skill for managers. (Credit: Mike Mozart/ flickr/ Attribution 2.0 Generic (CC BY 2.0))

Each of these activities may look to some managers like an obligation imposed by the job. Shrewd managers see them as opportunities to hear what others are thinking, to gather information informally from the grapevine, to listen in on office gossip, to pass along viewpoints that haven't yet made their way to the more formal channels of communication, or to catch up with a colleague or friend in a more relaxed setting. No matter what the intention of each manager who engages in these activities, the information they produce and the insight that follows from them can be put to work the same day to achieve organizational and personal objectives. "To understand why effective managers behave as they do," writes Kotter, "it is essential first to recognize two fundamental challenges and dilemmas found in most of their jobs." Managers must first figure out what to do, despite an enormous amount of potentially relevant information (along with much that is not), and then they must get things done "through a large and diverse group of people despite having little direct control over most of them."[21]

The Role of Writing

Writing plays an important role in the life of any organization. In some organizations, it becomes more important than in others. At Procter & Gamble, for example, brand managers cannot raise a work-related issue in a team meeting unless the ideas are first circulated in writing. For P&G managers, this approach means explaining their ideas in explicit detail in a standard one-to-three-page memo, complete with background, financial discussion, implementation details, and justification for the ideas proposed.

Other organizations are more oral in their traditions—3M Canada is a "spoken" organization—but the fact remains: the most important projects, decisions, and ideas end up in writing. Writing also provides analysis, justification, documentation, and analytic discipline, particularly as managers approach important decisions that will affect the profitability and strategic direction of the company.

Writing is a career sifter. If managers demonstrate their inability to put ideas on paper in a clear, unambiguous fashion, they're not likely to last. Stories of bad writers who've been shown the door early in their careers are legion. Managers' principal objective, at least during the first few years of their career, is to keep their name out of such stories. Remember: those who are most likely to notice the quality and skill in managers' written documents are the very people most likely to matter to managers' future.

Managers do most of their own writing and editing. The days when managers could lean back and thoughtfully dictate a letter or memo to a skilled secretarial assistant are mostly gone. Some senior executives know how efficient dictation can be, especially with a top-notch administrative assistant taking shorthand, but how many managers have that advantage today? Very few, mostly because buying a computer and printer is substantially cheaper than hiring another employee. Managers at all levels of most organizations draft, review, edit, and dispatch their own correspondence, reports, and proposals.

Documents take on lives of their own. Once it's gone from the manager's desk, it isn't theirs anymore. When they sign a letter and put it in the mail, it's no longer their letter—it's the property of the person or organization it was sent to. As a result, the recipient is free to do as she sees fit with the writing, including using it against the sender. If the ideas are ill-considered or not well expressed, others in the organization who are not especially sympathetic to the manager's views may head for the copy machine with the manager's work in hand. The advice for managers is simple: do not mail the first draft, and do not ever sign your name to a document you are not proud of.

Communication Is Invention

Without question, communication is a process of invention. Managers literally create meaning through communication. A company, for example, is not in default until a team of auditors sits down to examine the books and review the matter. Only after extended discussion do the accountants conclude that the company is, in fact, in default. It is their discussion that creates the outcome. Until that point, default was simply one of many possibilities.

The fact is managers create meaning through communication. It is largely through discussion and verbal exchange—often heated and passionate—that managers decide who they wish to be: market leaders, takeover artists, innovators, or defenders of the economy. It is only through communication that meaning is created for shareholders, employees, customers, and others. Those long, detailed, and intense discussions determine how much the company will declare in dividends this year, whether the company is willing to risk a strike or labor action, and how soon to roll out the new product line customers are asking for. Additionally, it is important to note that managers usually figure things out by talking about them as much as they talk about the things they have already figured out. Talk serves as a wonderful palliative: justifying, analyzing, dissecting, reassuring, and analyzing the events that confront managers each day.

Information Is Socially Constructed

If we are to understand just how important human discourse is in the life of a business, several points seem especially important.

Information is created, shared, and interpreted by people. Meaning is a truly human phenomenon. An issue is only important if people think it is. Facts are facts only if we can agree upon their definition. Perceptions and assumptions are as important as truth itself in a discussion about what a manager should do next.[22] Information never speaks for itself. It is not uncommon for a manager to rise to address a group of her colleagues and say, "The numbers speak for themselves." Frankly, the numbers never speak for themselves. They almost always require some sort of interpretation, some sort of explanation or context. Do not assume that others see the facts in the same way managers do, and never assume that what is seen is the truth. Others may see the same set of facts or evidence but may not reach the same conclusions. Few things in life are self-explanatory.

Context always drives meaning. The backdrop to a message is always of paramount importance to the listener, viewer, or reader in reaching a reasonable, rational conclusion about what she sees and hears. What's in the news these days as we take up this subject? What moment in history do we occupy? What related or relevant information is under consideration as this new message arrives? We cannot possibly derive meaning from one message without considering everything else that surrounds it.

A messenger always accompanies a message. It is difficult to separate a message from its messenger. We often want to react more to the source of the information than we do to the information itself. That's natural and entirely normal. People speak for a reason, and we often judge their reasons for speaking before analyzing what they have to say. Keep in mind that, in every organization, message recipients will judge the value, power, purpose, intent, and outcomes of the messages they receive by the source of those messages as much as by the content and intent of the messages themselves. If the messages managers send are to have the impact hoped for, they must come from a source the receiver knows, respects, and understands.

Managers' Greatest Challenge

Every manager knows communication is vital, but every manager also seems to "know" that she is great at it. Managers' greatest challenge is to admit to flaws in their skill set and work tirelessly to improve them. First, managers must admit to the flaws.

Larkin and Larkin write, "Deep down, managers believe they are communicating effectively. In ten years of management consulting, we have never had a manager say to us that he or she was a poor communicator. They admit to the occasional screw-up, but overall, everyone, without exception, believes he or she is basically a good communicator."[23]

Managers' Task as Professionals

As a professional manager, the first task is to recognize and understand one's strengths and weaknesses as a communicator. Until these communication tasks at which one is most and least skilled are identified, there will be little opportunity for improvement and advancement.

Foremost among managers' goals should be to improve existing skills. Improve one's ability to do what is done best. Be alert to opportunities, however, to develop new skills. Managers should add to their inventory of abilities to keep themselves employable and promotable.

Two other suggestions come to mind for improving managers' professional standing. First, acquire a knowledge base that will work for the years ahead. That means speaking with and listening to other professionals in their company, industry, and community. They should be alert to trends that could affect their company's products and services, as well as their own future.

It also means reading. Managers should read at least one national newspaper each day, including the *Wall Street Journal*, the *New York Times*, or the *Financial Times*, as well as a local newspaper. Their reading should include weekly news magazines, such as *U.S. News & World Report, Bloomberg's Business Week*, and the *Economist*. Subscribe to monthly magazines such as *Fast Company* and *Fortune*. And they should read at least one new hardcover title a month. A dozen books each year is the bare minimum on which one should depend for new ideas, insights, and managerial guidance.

Managers' final challenge is to develop the confidence needed to succeed as a manager, particularly under conditions of uncertainty, change, and challenge.

ETHICS IN PRACTICE

Disney and H-1B Visas

On January 30, 2015, The Walt Disney Company laid off 250 of its IT workers. In a letter to the laid-off workers, Disney outlined the conditions for receipt of a "stay bonus," which would entitle each worker to a lump-sum payment of 10% of her annual salary.

Of course, there was a catch. Only those workers who trained their replacements over a 90-day period would receive the bonus. One American worker in his 40s who agreed to Disney's severance terms explained how it worked in action:

> "The first 30 days was all capturing what I did. The next 30 days, they worked side by side with me, and the last 30 days, they took over my job completely. I had to make sure they were doing my job correctly."

To outside observers, this added insult to injury. It was bad enough to replace U.S. workers with cheaper, foreign labor. But to ask, let alone strong-arm, the laid-off workers into training their replacements seemed a bit much.

However unfortunate, layoffs are commonplace. But this was different. From the timing to the apparent neglect of employee pride, the sequence of events struck a nerve. For many, the issue was simple, and Disney's actions seemed wrong at a visceral level. As criticism mounted, it became clear that this story would develop legs. Disney had a problem.

For David Powers and Leo Perrero, each a 10-year information technology (IT) veteran at Disney, the invitation came from a vice president of the company. It had to be good news, the men thought. After all, they were not far removed from strong performance reviews—perhaps they would be awarded performance bonuses. Well, not exactly. Leo Perrero, one of the summoned workers, explains what happened next.

"I'm in the room with about two-dozen people, and very shortly thereafter an executive delivers the news that all of our jobs are ending in 90 days, and that we have 90 days to train our replacements or we won't get a bonus that we've been offered."

Powers explained the deflating effect of the news: "When a guillotine falls down on you, in that moment you're dead . . . and I was dead."

These layoffs and the hiring of foreign workers under the H-1B program lay at the center of this issue. Initially introduced by the Immigration and Nationality Act of 1965, subsequent modifications produced the current iteration of the H-1B visa program in 1990. Importantly, at that time, the United States faced a shortage of skilled workers necessary to fill highly technical jobs. Enter the H-1B visa program as the solution. This program permits U.S. employers to temporarily employ foreign workers in highly specialized occupations. "Specialty occupations" are defined as those in the fields of architecture, engineering, mathematics, science, medicine, and others that require technical and skilled expertise.

Congress limited the number of H-1B visas issued to 85,000 per year. That total is divided into two subcategories: "65,000 new H-1B visas issued for overseas workers in professional or specialty occupation positions, and an additional 20,000 visas available for those with an advanced degree from a U.S. academic institution." Further, foreign workers are not able to apply for an H-1B visa. Instead, a U.S. employer must petition on their behalf no earlier than six months before the starting date of employment.

In order to be eligible for an employer to apply a foreign worker for an H-1B visa, the worker needed to meet certain requirements, such as an employee-employer relationship with the petitioning U.S. employer and a position in a specialty occupation related to the employee's field of study, where the employee must meet one of the following criteria: a bachelor's degree or the foreign equivalent of a bachelor's degree, a degree that is standard for the position, or previous qualified experience within the specialty occupation.

If approved, the initial term of the visa is three years, which may be extended an additional three years. While residing in the United States on an H-1B visa, a worker may apply to become a permanent resident and receive a green card, which would entitle the worker to remain indefinitely.

U.S. employers are required to file a Labor Condition Application (LCA) on behalf of each foreign worker they seek to employ. That application must be approved by the U.S. Department of Labor. The LCA requires the employer to assure that the foreign worker will be paid a wage and be provided working conditions and benefits that meet or exceed the local prevailing market and to assure that the foreign worker will not displace a U.S. worker in the employer's workforce.

Given these representations, U.S. employers have increasingly been criticized for abuse of the H-1B program. Most significantly, there is rising sentiment that U.S. employers are displacing domestic workers in favor of cheaper foreign labor. Research indicates that a U.S. worker's salary for these specialty occupations often exceeds $100,000, while that of a foreign worker is roughly $62,000 for the very same job. The latter figure is telling, since $60,000 is the threshold below which a salary would trigger a penalty.

Disney faced huge backlash and negative press because of the layoffs and hiring of foreign workers. Because of this, Disney had communication challenges, both internally and externally.

Disney executives framed the layoffs as part of a larger plan of reorganization intended to enable its IT division to focus on driving innovation. Walt Disney World spokesperson Jacquee Wahler gave the following explanation:

"We have restructured our global technology organization *to significantly increase our cast member focus on future innovation and new capabilities*, and are continuing to work with leading technical firms to maintain our existing systems as needed." (Italics added for emphasis.)

That statement is consistent with a leaked memo drafted by Disney Parks and Resort CIO Tilak Mandadi, which he sent to select employees on November 10, 2014 (not including those who would be laid off), to explain the rationale for the impending layoffs. The memo read, in part, as follows:

"To enable a majority of our team to *shift focus to new capabilities*, we have executed five new managed services agreements to support testing services and application maintenance. Last week, we began working with both our internal subject matter experts and the suppliers to start transition planning for these agreements. We expect knowledge transfer to start later this month and last through January. Those Cast Members who are involved will be contacted in the next several weeks."

Responding to the critical *New York Times* article, Disney represented that when all was said and done, the company had in fact produced a net jobs increase. According to Disney spokesperson Kim Prunty:

"Disney has created almost 30,000 new jobs in the U.S. over the past decade, and the recent changes to our parks' IT team resulted in a larger organization with 70 additional in-house positions in the U.S. External support firms are responsible for complying with all applicable employment laws for their employees."

New jobs were promised due to the restructuring, Disney officials said, and employees targeted for termination were pushed to apply for those positions. According to a confidential Disney source, of the approximately 250 laid-off employees, 120 found new jobs within Disney, 40 took early retirement, and 90 were unable to secure new jobs with Disney.

On June 11, 2015, Senator Richard Durbin of Illinois and Senator Jeffrey Sessions of Alabama released a statement regarding a bipartisan letter issued to the attorney general, the Department Homeland Security, and the Department of Labor.

"A number of U.S. employers, including some large, well-known, publicly-traded corporations, have laid off thousands of American workers and replaced them with H-1B visa holders . . . . To add insult to injury, many of the replaced American employees report that they have been forced to train the foreign workers who are taking their jobs. That's just plain wrong and we'll continue to press the Administration to help solve this problem."

On July 7, 2015, *The Daily Caller* reported that the Department of Labor had commenced investigations of Disney after having received several formal complaints from laid-off workers. According to the report, Department of Labor personnel reached out to the former Disney workers to conduct phone interviews regarding names of displaced employees as well as typical salaries for the positions. Disney declined to comment on the report.

In response to request for comment on the communications issues raised by the Disney layoffs and aftermath, *New York Times* columnist Julia Preston shared the following exclusive analysis:

"I would say Disney's handling of those lay-offs is a case study in how not to do things. But in the end it's not about the communications, it's about the company. Those layoffs showed a company that was not living up to its core vaunted family values and no amount of shouting by their communications folks could change the facts of what happened."

Questions for Discussion
1. Is it ethical for U.S. companies to lay off workers and hire foreign workers under the H-1B program? Should foreign countries restrict the hiring of foreign workers that meet their workforce requirements?
2. Discuss the internal and external communications that Disney employed in this situation. The examples here are of the formal written communications. What should Disney have been

communicating verbally to their employees and externally?

Sources: Preston, Julia, *Pink Slips at Disney. But First, Training Foreign Replacements*, <u>The New York Times</u> June 3, 2015, http://www.nytimes.com/2015/06/04/us/last-task-after-layoff-at-disney-train-foreign-replacements.html; Vargas, Rebecca, *EXCLUSIVE: Former Employees Speak Out About Disney's Outsourcing of High-Tech Jobs*, WWSB ABC 7 (Oct. 28, 2015), http://www.mysuncoast.com/news/local/exclusive-former-employees-speak-out-about-disney-s-outsourcing-of/ article_d8867148-7d8c-11e5-ae40-fb05081380c1.html; Boyle, Mathew, *Ahead of GOP Debate, Two Ex-Disney Workers Displaced by H1B Foreigners Speak Out for First Time,* Breitbart.com, October 28, 2015, http://www.breitbart.com/big-government/2015/10/28/ahead-of-gop-debate-two-ex-disney-workers-displaced-by-h1b-foreigners-speak-out-for-first-time; Sandra Pedicini, *Tech Workers File Lawsuits Against Disney Over H-1B Visas*, *Orlando Sentinel*, published January 25, 2016, accessed February 6, 2016, available at http://www.orlandosentinel.com/business/os-disney-h1b-visa-lawsuit-20160125-story.html; U.S. Citizenship and Immigration Services, Understanding H-1B Requirements, accessed February 6, 2016, available at https://www.uscis.gov/eir/visa-guide/h-1b-specialty-occupation/understanding-h-1b-requirements; May, Caroline, Sessions, Durbin: Department Of Labor Has Launched Investigation Into H-1B Abuses, Breitbart.com (June 11, 2015), http://www.breitbart.com/big-government/2015/06/11/ sessions-durbin-department-of-labor-has-launched-investigation-into-h-1b-abuses/; Stoltzfoos, Rachel, Feds Investigate Disney, HCL America Over January Layoffs, The Daily Caller (July 7, 2015), http://dailycaller.com/2015/07/07/feds-investigate-disney-hcl-america-over-january-layoffs/#ixzz41DY4x8Dy; Email from Julia Preston, National Immigration Correspondent, The New York Times, to Bryan Shannon, co-author of this case study, dated February 10, 2016.

CONCEPT CHECK

1. What are the four components of communication discussed in this section?
2. Why is it important to understand your limitations in communicating to others and in larger groups?
3. Why should managers always strive to improve their skills?

🔑 Key Terms

communicator The individual, group, or organization that needs or wants to share information with another individual, group, or organization.

decoding Interpreting and understanding and making sense of a message.

encoding Translating a message into symbols or language that a receiver can understand.

figurehead role A necessary **role** for a manager who wants to inspire people within the organization to feel connected to each other and to the institution, to support the policies and decisions made on behalf of the organization, and to work harder for the good of the institution.

interaction attentiveness/ interaction involvement A measure of how the receiver of a message is paying close attention and is alert or observant.

noise Anything that interferes with the communication process.

receiver The individual, group, or organization for which information is intended.

📑 Summary of Learning Outcomes

16.1 The Process of Managerial Communication

1. Understand and describe the communication process.

The basic model of interpersonal communication consists of an encoded message, a decoded message, feedback, and noise. Noise refers to the distortions that inhibit message clarity.

16.2 Types of Communications in Organizations

2. Know the types of communications that occur in organizations.

Interpersonal communication can be oral, written, or nonverbal. Body language refers to conveying messages to others through such techniques as facial expressions, posture, and eye movements.

16.3 Factors Affecting Communications and the Roles of Managers

3. Understand how power, status, purpose, and interpersonal skills affect communications in organizations.

Interpersonal communication is influenced by social situations, perception, interaction involvement, and organizational design. Organizational communication can travel upward, downward, or horizontally. Each direction of information flow has specific challenges.

16.4 Managerial Communication and Corporate Reputation

4. Describe how corporate reputations are defined by how an organization communicates to all of its stakeholders.

It is important for managers to understand what your organization stands for (identity), what others think your organization is (reputation), and the contributions individuals can make to the success of the business considering their organization's existing reputation. It is also about confidence—the knowledge that one can speak and write well, listen with great skill as others speak, and both seek out and provide the feedback essential to creating, managing, or changing their organization's reputation.

16.5 The Major Channels of Management Communication Are Talking, Listening, Reading, and Writing

5. Describe the roles that managers perform in organizations.

There are special communication roles that can be identified. Managers may serve as gatekeepers, liaisons, or opinion leaders. They can also assume some combination of these roles. It is important to recognize that communication processes involve people in different functions and that all functions need to operate effectively to achieve organizational objectives.

Chapter Review Questions

1. Describe the communication process.
2. Why is feedback a critical part of the communication process?
3. What are some things that managers can do to reduce noise in communication?
4. Compare and contrast the three primary forms of interpersonal communication.
5. Describe the various individual communication roles in organizations.
6. How can managers better manage their effectiveness by managing e-mail communication?
7. Which communication roles are most important in facilitating managerial effectiveness?
8. Identify barriers to effective communication.
9. How can barriers to effective communication be overcome by managers?

Management Skills Application Exercises

1. The e-mails below are not written as clearly or concisely as they could be. In addition, they may have problems in organization or tone or mechanical errors. Rewrite them so they are appropriate for the audience and their purpose. Correct grammatical and mechanical errors. Finally, add a subject line to each.

E-Mail 1

To: Employees of The Enormously Successful Corporation

From: CEO of The Enormously Successful Corporation

Subject:

Stop bringing bottled soft drinks, juices and plastic straws to work. Its an environment problem that increases our waste and the quality of our water is great. People don't realize how much wasted energy goes into shipping all that stuff around, and plastic bottles, aluminum cans and straws are ruining our oceans and filling land fills. Have you seen the floating island of waste in the Pacific Ocean? Some of this stuff comes from other countries like Canada Dry I think is from canada and we are taking there water and Canadians will be thirsty. Fancy drinks isn't as good as the water we have and tastes better anyway.

E-Mail 2

To: All Employees

From: Management

Subject:

Our Committee to Improve Inter-Office Communication has decided that there needs to be an update and revision of our policy on emailing messages to and from those who work with us as employees of this company. The following are the results of the committee's decisions, and constitute recommendations for the improvement of every aspect of email communication.

1. Too much wordiness means people have to read the same thing over and over repeatedly, time after time. Eliminating unnecessary words, emails can be made to be shorter and more to the point, making them concise and taking less time to read.

2. You are only allowed to send and receive messages between 8:30AM east coat time and 4:30PM east coast time. You are also not allowed to read e-mails outside of these times. We know that for those of you on the west coast or travelling internationally it will reduce the time that you are allowed to attend to e-mail, but we need this to get it under control.

3. You are only allowed to have up to 3 recipients on each e-mail. If more people need to be informed it is up to the people to inform them.

2. Write a self-evaluation that focuses specifically on your class participation in this course. Making comments during class allows you to improve your ability to speak extemporaneously, which is exactly what you will have to do in all kinds of business situations (e.g., meetings, asking questions at presentations, one-on-one conversations). Thus, write a short memo (two or three paragraphs) in which you describe the frequency with which you make comments in class, the nature of those comments, and what is easy and difficult for you when it comes to speaking up in class.

   If you have made few (or no) comments during class, this is a time for us to come up with a plan to help you overcome your shyness. Our experience is that as soon as a person talks in front of a group once or twice, it becomes much easier—so we need to come up with a way to help you break the ice.

   Finally, please comment on what you see as the strengths and weaknesses of your discussions and presentations in this class.

3. Refer to the photo in **Exhibit 16.3**. Comment on the body language exhibited by each person at the meeting and how engaged they are in the communication.

4. In the movie *The Martian*, astronaut Mark Watney (played by Matt Damon) is stranded on Mars with limited ability to communicate with mission control. Watney holds up questions to a camera that can transmit photographs of his questions, and mission control could respond by pointing the camera at a "yes" or "no" card with the camera. Eventually, they are able to exchange "text" messages but no voice exchanges. Also, there is a significant time delay between the sending and receipt of the messages. Which part of the communication process would have to be addressed to ensure that the encoding of the messages, the decoding of the messages, and that noise is minimized by Watney and mission control?

Managerial Decision Exercises

1. Ginni Rometty is the CEO of IBM. Shortly after taking on the role of CEO and being frustrated by the progress and sales performance, Rometty released a five-minute video to all 400,000 plus IBM employees criticizing the lack of securing deals to competitors and lashed out at the sales organization for poor sales in the preceding quarter. Six months later, Rometty sent another critical message, this time via e-mail. How effective will the video and e-mail be in communicating with employees? How should she follow up to these messages?

2. Social media, such as Facebook, is now widespread. Place yourself as a manager that has just received a "friend" request from one of your direct reports. Do you accept, reject, or ignore the request? Why, and what additional communication would you have regarding this with the employee?

3. During a cross-functional meeting, one of the attendees who reports to a manager who is also at the meeting accuses one of your reports of not being fit for the position she is in. You disagree and feel that your report is a good fit for her role. How do you handle this?

🔆 Critical Thinking Case

Facebook, Inc.

Facebook has been in the news with criticism of its privacy policies, sharing customer information with Fusion GPS, and criticism regarding the attempts to influence the 2016 election. In March 2014, Facebook released a study entitled "Experimental evidence of massive-scale emotional contagion through social networks." It was published in the *Proceedings of the National Academy of Sciences (PNAS)*, a prestigious, peer-reviewed scientific journal. The paper explains how social media can readily transfer emotional states from person to person through Facebook's News Feed platform. Facebook conducted an experiment on members to see how people would respond to changes in a percentage of both positive and negative posts. The results suggest that emotional contagion does occur online and that users' positive expressions can generate positive reaction, while, in turn, negative expression can generate negative reaction.

Facebook has two separate value propositions aimed at two different markets with entirely different goals.

Originally, Facebook's main market was its end users—people looking to connect with family and friends. At first, it was aimed only at college students at a handful of elite schools. The site is now open to anyone with an Internet connection. Users can share status updates and photographs with friends and family. And all of this comes at no cost to the users.

Facebook's other major market is advertisers, who buy information about Facebook's users. The company regularly gathers data about page views and browsing behavior of users in order to display targeted advertisements to users for the benefit of its advertising partners.

The value proposition of the Facebook News Feed experiment was to determine whether emotional manipulation would be possible through the use of social networks. This clearly could be of great value to one of Facebook's target audiences—its advertisers.

The results suggest that the emotions of friends on social networks influence our own emotions, thereby demonstrating emotional contagion via social networks. Emotional contagion is the tendency to feel and express emotions similar to and influenced by those of others. Originally, it was studied by psychologists as the transference of emotions between two people.

According to Sandra Collins, a social psychologist and University of Notre Dame professor of management, it is clearly unethical to conduct psychological experiments without the informed consent of the test subjects. While tests do not always measure what the people conducting the tests claim, the subjects need to at least know that they are, indeed, part of a test. The subjects of this test on Facebook were not explicitly informed that they were participating in an emotional contagion experiment. Facebook did not obtain informed consent as it is generally defined by researchers, nor did it allow participants to opt out.

When information about the experiment was released, the media response was overwhelmingly critical. Tech blogs, newspapers, and media reports reacted quickly.

Josh Constine of TechCrunch wrote:

> " . . . there is some material danger to experiments that depress people. Some people who are at risk of depression were almost surely part of Facebook's study group that were shown a more depressing feed, which could be considered dangerous. Facebook will endure a whole new level of backlash if any of those participants were found to have committed suicide or had other depression-related outcomes after the study."

The *New York Times* quoted Brian Blau, a technology analyst with the research firm Gartner, "Facebook didn't do anything illegal, but they didn't do right by their customers. Doing psychological testing on people crosses the line." Facebook should have informed its users, he said. "They keep on pushing the boundaries, and this is one of the reasons people are upset."

While some of the researchers have since expressed some regret about the experiment, Facebook as a company was unapologetic about the experiment. The company maintained that it received consent from its users through its terms of service. A Facebook spokesperson defended the research, saying, "We do research to improve our services and make the content people see on Facebook as relevant and engaging as possible. . . . We carefully consider what research we do and have a strong internal review process."

With the more recent events, Facebook is changing the privacy settings but still collects an enormous amount of information about its users and can use that information to manipulate what users see. Additionally, these items are not listed on Facebook's main terms of service page. Users must click on a link inside a different set of terms to arrive at the data policy page, making these terms onerous to find. This positioning raises questions about how Facebook will employ its users' behaviors in the future.

Critical Thinking Questions

1. How should Facebook respond to the 2014 research situation? How could an earlier response have helped the company avoid the 2018 controversies and keep the trust of its users?

2. Should the company promise to never again conduct a survey of this sort? Should it go even further and explicitly ban research intended to manipulate the responses of its users?

3. How can Facebook balance the concerns of its users with the necessity of generating revenue through advertising?

4. What processes or structures should Facebook establish to make sure it does not encounter these issues again?

5. Respond in writing to the issues presented in this case by preparing two documents: a communication strategy memo and a professional business letter to advertisers.

Sources: Kramer, Adam; Guillory, Jamie; and Hancock, Jeffrey, "Experimental evidence of massive scale emotional contagion through social networks," *PNAS (Proceedings of the National Academy of Sciences of the United States of America)*. March 25, 2014 http://www.pnas.org/content/111/24/8788.full; Laja, Peep. "Useful Value Proposition Examples (and How to Create a Good One), *ConversionXL*, 2015 http://conversionxl.com/value-proposition-examples-how-to-create/; Yadav, Sid. "Facebook - The Complete Biography," Mashable, Aug. 25, 2006. http://mashable.com/2006/08/25/facebook-profile/#orb9TmeYHiqK; Felix, Samantha, "This Is How Facebook Is Tracking Your Internet Activity," *Business Insider*, Sept. 9, 2012 http://www.businessinsider.com/this-is-how-facebook-is-tracking-your-internet-activity-2012-9;

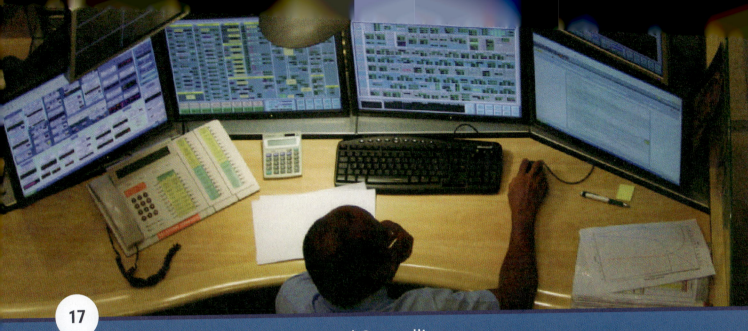

Exhibit 17.1 (Credit: marcusrg/ flickr/ Attribution 2.0 Generic (CC BY 2.0))

Introduction

Learning Outcomes

After reading this chapter, you should be able to answer these questions:

1. Understand the importance of planning and why organizations need to plan and control.
2. Outline the planning and controlling processes.
3. Identify different types of plans and control systems employed by organizations.
4. Explain the individual and organizational effects associated with goal setting and planning.
5. Understand how planning occurs in today's organizations.
6. Discuss the impact that control has on organizational members.
7. Describe management by objectives as a philosophy and as a management tool/technique; describe its effects.
8. Differentiate between the execution of the planning and controlling activities under control- and involvement-oriented management practices.

EXPLORING MANAGERIAL CAREERS

Elizabeth Charbonnier: ChezPastis.com

ChezPastis.com, the brainchild of Elisabeth Charbonnier, specializes in selling French and other gourmet foods online. Before starting ChezPastis.com, Elisabeth and her partners were professional chefs, and their goal for their company is to make gourmet products available to the world. ChezPastis.com began with a bang, and before long Elisabeth and her partners were too busy to plan for the future and were just trying to survive. After six months, ChezPastis.com experienced growing pains similar to other Internet start-ups.

One of the partners, Zack Fortuna, was online one day trying to order some books for his daughter's birthday. The message he got after attempting to place his order was frustrating: "Sorry! The items you have requested are currently on back order and will not be available for two months." Zack needed the books in two weeks, not two months. He decided to drive to the bookstore and buy books that were in stock rather than waste time online searching for items that might not be in stock. Suddenly, Zack realized that ChezPastis.com frequently runs out of items as well and this delays customer orders. Perhaps ChezPastis.com's growing pains have something to do with their supply problems.

Question: Are ChezPastis.com's inventory problem attributable to poor planning, poor control, or both? How can Elisabeth, Zack, and the other partners improve the situation?

"If you are good enough, it isn't necessary to set aside time for formal planning. After all, 'planning time' takes away from 'doing time.'" Managers often make such statements, possibly as a way of rationalizing their lack of a formal planning program. These claims are simply not valid—planning *does* influence the effectiveness of the entire organization.

Some years ago, the Calico Candy Company developed and produced a highly successful saltwater taffy Santa Claus. Buoyed by this success, the company planned and manufactured a saltwater taffy Easter Bunny and produced the Santa at Christmas again. This time, however, Calico got stuck with its taffy through faulty planning. Market research clearly showed that consumer preferences had shifted from taffy to chocolate. Rather than plan its products to meet this new preference, the company stayed with what had worked in the past and lost a "ton of money." Yes, planning is important.

Outcome: Zack comes to work the next day excited about his insight. The partners know that inventory has been an ongoing trouble spot but hadn't realized the effect it could be having on potential customers who get frustrated with delayed orders and go elsewhere. After collecting data on customer requests and back orders, the partners discover that they fill customer orders immediately only 50 percent of the time! Jolted by this thunderbolt, the partners decide to hold regular strategic planning meetings where they will view the big picture and plan for the future. The first things they decide to do are install better control systems over their inventory process and collect data on customer online experiences with ChezPastis.com.

Elisabeth proposes setting a goal of never having to tell a customer that requested items are on back order. Zack agrees that this is an admirable goal; however, he thinks they should set a daring but reachable goal of immediately filling customer orders 80 percent of the time. After all, they are a small business in an unpredictable environment, and they don't want to frustrate employees with a potentially impossible goal.

The essence of planning is to see opportunities and threats in the future and, respectively, exploit or combat them as the case may be. . . . Planning is a philosophy, not so much in the literal sense of that word but as an attitude, a way of life.[1]

17.1 | Is Planning Important

1. Understand the importance of planning and why organizations need to plan and control.

Planning is the process by which managers establish goals and specify how these goals are to be attained.

Plans have two basic components: outcome or goal statements and action statements. **Outcome** or **goal statements** represent the *end* state—the targets and outcomes managers hope to attain. **Action statements** reflect the *means* by which organizations move forward to attain their goals. British prime minister Theresa May is determined to change the way that public companies' boards are comprised by advocating that employees be part of every board. As a part of her action statement, she advocated putting an employee representative in every boardroom, just like Mick Barker, a railway worker since the 1970s, has been quietly helping to shape decision-making as a member of the board of directors at the top of transport giant First Group.[2]

Planning is an intellectual activity.[3] It is difficult to see managers plan, because most of this activity unfolds in the mind of those doing the planning. While planning, managers have to think about what has to be done, who is going to do it, and how and when they will do it. Planners think both retrospectively (about past events) and prospectively (about future opportunities and impending threats). Planning involves thinking about organizational strengths and weaknesses, as well as making decisions about desired states and ways to achieve them.[4]

Planning for organizational events, whether in the internal or external environment, should be an ongoing process—part of a manager's daily, weekly, and monthly duties and a routine task for all members of high-involvement organizations. Plans should be continually monitored. Managers and other organizational members should check to see if their plans need to be modified to accommodate changing conditions, new information, or new situations that will affect the organization's future. Plans need to be administered with flexibility, as organizations learn about new and changing conditions. Clearly, the Calico Candy Company failed to monitor its plans in this way. By thinking of planning as a continuous activity, methods can be formulated for handling emerging and unforeseen opportunities and threats. Planning is one process through which organizational activity can be given meaning and direction.

Why Should Managers Plan?

Managers have several reasons for formulating plans for themselves, their employees, and various organizational units: (1) to offset uncertainty and change; (2) to focus organizational activity on a set of objectives; (3) to provide a coordinated, systematic road map for future activities; (4) to increase economic efficiency; and (5) to facilitate control by establishing a standard for later activity.

Several forces contribute to the necessity for organizational planning. First, in the internal environment, as organizations become larger and more complex, the task of managing becomes increasingly complex. Planning maps out future activities in relation to other activities in the organization. Second, as the external environment becomes increasingly complex and turbulent, the amount of uncertainty faced by a manager increases. Planning enables organizations to approach their environment systematically.

A study out of Cornell University and Indiana University found that absenteeism cost companies $40 billion per year; the absence of planning was one of the biggest problems businesses face. Firms that follow a clearly defined plan in their day-to-day operations will be more successful than those that do not. The authors state, "organizational controlled consequences that would tend to deter absenteeism." Interestingly, this may be as simple as inspecting the organizational policies that provide the "rules" for employee absenteeism.[5]

Do Managers Really Plan?

Managers should plan formally, but do they? Some observers contend that managers typically are too busy to engage in a regular form of systematic planning. McGill University management professor Henry Mintzberg notes:

> When managers plan, they do so implicitly in the context of daily actions, not in some abstract process reserved for two weeks in the organization's mountain retreat. The plans of the chief executives I have studied seemed to exist only in their heads—as flexible, but often specific, intentions. . . . The job of managing does not breed reflective planners; the manager is a real-time responder to stimuli.[6]

Others disagree. After reviewing a number of studies focused on the degree to which planning and other managerial activities are inherent parts of managing, management professors J. Carroll and J. Gillen state that "the classical management functions of Fayol, Urwick, and others are not folklore as claimed by some contemporary management writers but represent valid abstractions of what managers actually do and what managers should do."[7] Barbara Allen, president of Sunbelt Research Associates, notes that she did a considerable amount of planning before launching her new business. Now that she is operating successfully, she reviews and updates her plans periodically.[8]

Managers often are very busy people. Some act without a systematic plan of action; however, many managers do plan systematically.[9] For example, many managers develop systematic plans for how their organization will react to a crisis. United Airlines, for example, created a crisis planning group. The group developed United's crisis contingency plan book, which specifies what the airline's crisis management team should do in the event of a crisis. Keri Calagna, principal, Deloitte Risk and Financial Advisory, Deloitte & Touche LLP, comments that up to 20.7% of a firm's value resides in reputation but that CEOs and 77% of board of directors members identified reputation risk as the area about which they felt most vulnerable and that only 39% had a plan to address it.[10]

The question about whether managers really plan and the observation that many times they are simply too busy to retreat to the mountaintop and reflect on where the organization should be going and how it should get there miss the point: there are different types of planning.

Exhibit 17.2   Theresa May The United Kingdom may have voted to leave the European Union (EU), a move known as "Brexit," but if Prime Minister Theresa May gets her way, British companies might look a little more like those in EU countries such as Germany and France. Theresa May favors an overhaul of corporate governance, including appointing employee representatives to boards of directors. (Credit: Arno Mikkor/ flickr/ Attribution 2.0 Generic (CC BY 2.0))

CONCEPT CHECK

1. What is the process where managers establish goals and outline how these goals will be met called?.
2. How do the internal and external environments of the organization and its strengths and weaknesses impact the planning process?
3. Why should managers plan?

17.2 The Planning Process

2. Outline the planning and controlling processes.

Planning is a process. Ideally it is future oriented, comprehensive, systematic, integrated, and negotiated.[11] It involves an extensive search for alternatives and analyzes relevant information, is systematic in nature, and is commonly participative.[12] The planning model described in this section breaks the managerial function of planning into several steps, as shown in **Exhibit 17.3**. Following this step-by-step procedure helps ensure that organizational planning meets these requirements.

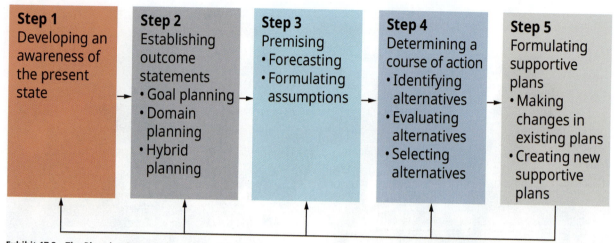

Exhibit 17.3   **The Planning Process** *Source:* Adapted from H. Koontz and C. O'Donnell, 1972. *Principles of management: An analysis of managerial functions.* New York: McGraw-Hill, 113.

Step 1: Developing an Awareness of the Present State

According to management scholars Harold Koontz and Cyril O'Donnell, the first step in the planning process is awareness.[13] It is at this step that managers build the foundation on which they will develop their plans. This foundation specifies an organization's current status, pinpoints its commitments, recognizes its strengths and weaknesses, and sets forth a vision of the future. Because the past is instrumental in determining where an organization expects to go in the future, managers at this point must understand their organization and its history. It has been said—"The further you look back, the further you can see ahead."[14]

Step 2: Establishing Outcome Statements

The second step in the planning process consists of deciding "where the organization is headed, or is going to end up." Ideally, this involves establishing goals. Just as your goal in this course might be to get a certain grade, managers at various levels in an organization's hierarchy set goals. For example, plans established by a university's marketing department curriculum committee must fit with and support the plans of the department, which contribute to the goals of the business school, whose plans must, in turn, support the goals of the university. Managers therefore develop an elaborate network of organizational plans, such as that shown in **Exhibit 17.4**, to achieve the overall goals of their organization.

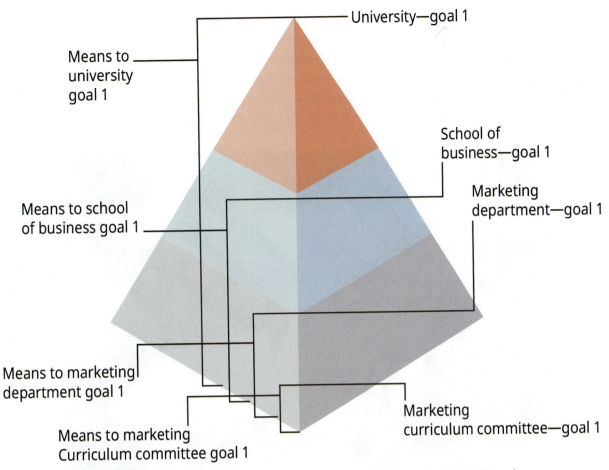

Exhibit 17.4 **Network of Organization Plans** (Attribution: Copyright Rice University, OpenStax, under CC-BY 4.0 license)

Goal vs. Domain Planning

Outcome statements can be constructed around specific goals or framed in terms of moving in a particular direction toward a viable set of outcomes. In **goal planning**, people set specific goals and then create action statements.[15] For example, freshman Kristin Rude decides that she wants a bachelor of science degree in biochemistry (the goal). She then constructs a four-year academic plan that will help her achieve this goal. Kristin is engaging in goal planning. She first identifies a goal and then develops a course of action to realize her goal.

Another approach to planning is **domain/directional planning**, in which managers develop a course of action that moves an organization toward one identified domain (and therefore away from other domains).[16] Within the chosen domain may lie a number of acceptable and specific goals. For example, high-school senior Neil Marquardt decides that he wants to major in a business-related discipline in college. During the next four years, he will select a variety of courses from the business school curriculum yet never select a major. After selecting courses based on availability and interest, he earns a sufficient number of credits within this chosen domain that enables him to graduate with a major in marketing. Neil never engaged in goal planning, but in the end he will realize one of many acceptable goals within an accepted domain.

The development of the Post-it® product by the 3M Corporation demonstrates how domain planning works. In the research laboratories at 3M, efforts were being made to develop new forms and strengths of cohesive substances. One result was cohesive material with no known value because of its extremely low cohesive level.

A 3M division specialist, Arthur L. Fry, frustrated by page markers falling from his hymn book in church, realized that this material, recently developed by Spencer F. Silver, would stick to paper for long periods and could be removed without destroying the paper. Fry experimented with the material as page markers and note pads—out of this came the highly popular and extremely profitable 3M product Scotch Post-it®. Geoff Nicholson, the driving force behind the Post-it® product, comments that rather than get bogged down in the planning process, innovations must be fast-tracked and decisions made whether to continue or move on early during the product development process.[17]

Exhibit 17.5   Post It Notes Post-it® notes, a 3M product, are often used to create and edit shared documents, such as a company strategic plan. How might technology that allows multiple people to share and edit documents such as Word or PowerPoint files affect the sales of Post-it® products? (Credit: Kevin Wen/ flickr/ Attribution 2.0 Generic (CC BY 2.0))

Situations in which managers are likely to engage in domain planning include (1) when there is a recognized need for flexibility, (2) when people cannot agree on goals, (3) when an organization's external environment is unstable and highly uncertain, and (4) when an organization is starting up or is in a transitional period. In addition, domain planning is likely to prevail at upper levels in an organization, where managers are responsible for dealing with the external environment and when task uncertainty is high. Goal planning (formulating goals compatible with the chosen domain) is likely to prevail in the technical core, where there is less uncertainty.

Hybrid Planning

Occasionally, coupling of domain and goal planning occurs, creating a third approach, called **hybrid planning**. In this approach, managers begin with the more general domain planning and commit to moving in a particular direction. As time passes, learning occurs, uncertainty is reduced, preferences sharpen, and managers are able to make the transition to goal planning as they identify increasingly specific targets in the selected domain. Movement from domain planning to goal planning occurs as knowledge accumulates, preferences for a particular goal emerge, and action statements are created.

Consequences of Goal, Domain, and Hybrid Planning

Setting goals not only affects performance directly, but also encourages managers to plan more extensively. That is, once goals are set, people are more likely to think systematically about how they should proceed to realize the goals.[18] When people have vague goals, as in domain planning, they find it difficult to draw up detailed action plans and are therefore less likely to perform effectively. When studying the topic of motivation, you will learn about goal theory. Research suggests that goal planning results in higher levels of performance than does domain planning alone.[19]

Step 3: Premising

In this step of the planning process, managers establish the premises, or assumptions, on which they will build their action statements. The quality and success of any plan depends on the quality of its underlying assumptions. Throughout the planning process, assumptions about future events must be brought to the surface, monitored, and updated.[20]

Managers collect information by scanning their organization's internal and external environments. They use this information to make assumptions about the likelihood of future events. As Kristin considers her four-year pursuit of her biochemistry major, she anticipates that in addition to her savings and funds supplied by her parents, she will need a full-time summer job for two summers in order to cover the cost of her undergraduate education. Thus, she includes finding full-time summer employment between her senior year of high school and her freshman year and between her freshman and sophomore years of college as part of her plan. The other two summers she will devote to an internship and finding postgraduate employment—much to mom and dad's delight! Effective planning skills can be used throughout your life. The plan you develop to pay for and complete your education is an especially important one.

Step 4: Determining a Course of Action (Action Statements)

In this stage of the planning process, managers decide how to move from their current position toward their goal (or toward their domain). They develop an action statement that details what needs to be done, when, how, and by whom. The course of action determines how an organization will get from its current position to its desired future position. Choosing a course of action involves determining alternatives by drawing on research, experimentation, and experience; evaluating alternatives in light of how well each would help the organization reach its goals or approach its desired domain; and selecting a course of action after identifying and carefully considering the merits of each alternative.

Step 5: Formulating Supportive Plans

The planning process seldom stops with the adoption of a general plan. Managers often need to develop one or more supportive or derivative plans to bolster and explain their basic plan. Suppose an organization decides to switch from a 5-day, 40-hour workweek (5/40) to a 4-day, 40-hour workweek (4/40) in an attempt to reduce employee turnover. This major plan requires the creation of a number of supportive plans. Managers might need to develop personnel policies dealing with payment of daily overtime. New administrative plans will be needed for scheduling meetings, handling phone calls, and dealing with customers and suppliers.

Planning, Implementation, and Controlling

After managers have moved through the five steps of the planning process and have drawn up and implemented specific plans, they must monitor and maintain their plans. Through the controlling function (to be discussed in greater detail later in this chapter), managers observe ongoing human behavior and organizational activity, compare it to the outcome and action statements formulated during the planning process, and take corrective action if they observe unexpected and unwanted deviations. Thus, planning and controlling activities are closely interrelated (planning ➡ controlling ➡ planning . . .). Planning feeds controlling by establishing the standards against which behavior will be evaluated during the controlling process. Monitoring organizational behavior (the control activity) provides managers with input that helps them prepare for the upcoming planning period—it adds meaning to the awareness step of the planning process.

Influenced by total quality management (TQM) and the importance of achieving continuous improvement in the processes used, as well as the goods and services produced, organizations such as IBM-Rochester have linked their planning and controlling activities by adopting the Deming cycle (also known as the Shewhart cycle).

It has been noted on numerous occasions that many organizations that do plan fail to recognize the importance of continuous learning. Their plans are either placed on the shelf and collect dust or are created, implemented, and adhered to without a systematic review and modification process. Frequently, plans are implemented without first measuring where the organization currently stands so that future comparisons and evaluations of the plan's effectiveness cannot be determined. The **Deming cycle**, shown in **Exhibit 17.6**, helps managers assess the effects of planned action by integrating organizational learning into the planning process. The cycle consists of four key stages: (1) Plan—create the plan using the model discussed earlier. (2) Do—implement the plan. (3) Check—monitor the results of the planned course of action; organizational learning about the effectiveness of the plan occurs at this stage. (4) Act—act on what was learned, modify the plan, and return to the first stage in the cycle, and the cycle begins again as the organization strives for continuous learning and improvement.

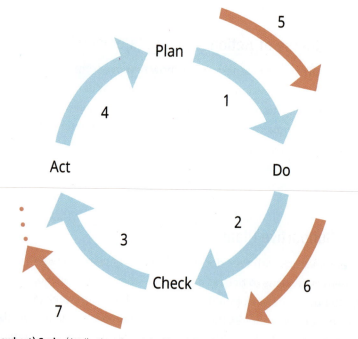

Exhibit 17.6 The Deming (Shewhart) Cycle (Attribution: Copyright Rice University, OpenStax, under CC-BY 4.0 license)

1. What are the five steps in the planning process?
2. What is the difference between goal, domain, and hybrid planning?
3. How are planning, implementation, and controlling related?

17.3 | Types of Plans

3. Identify different types of plans and control systems employed by organizations.

From an activity perspective, organizations are relatively complex systems, as they are involved in numerous activities. Many of these activities require management's attention from both a planning and controlling perspective. Managers therefore create different types of plans to guide operations and to monitor and control organizational activities. In this section, we introduce several commonly used plans. The major categories are hierarchical, frequency-of-use (repetitiveness), time-frame, organizational scope, and contingency. **Table 17.1** provides a closer look at many types of plans that fall in each of these categories.

Hierarchical Plans

Organizations can be viewed as a three-layer cake, with its three levels of organizational needs. Each of the three levels—institutional, administrative, and technical core—is associated with a particular type of plan. As revealed in **Table 17.1**, the three types of hierarchical plans are strategic, administrative, and operating (technical core). The three hierarchical plans are interdependent, as they support the fulfillment of the three organizational needs. In the organization's hierarchy, the technical core plans day-to-day operations.

Organizational Plans
Hierarchical Plans
• Strategic plans (institutional)—define the organization's long-term vision; articulate the organization's mission and value statements; define what business the organization is in or hopes to be in; articulate how the organization will integrate itself into its general and task environments.   • Administrative plans—specify the allocation of organizational resources to internal units of the organization; address the integration of the institutional level of the organization (for example, vision formulation) with the technical core (vision implementation); address the integration of the diverse units of the organization.   • Operating plans (technical core)—cover the day-to-day operations of the organization.
Frequency-of-Use Plans
Standing Plans

Table 17.1 (Attribution: Copyright Rice University, OpenStax, under CC-BY 4.0 license)

Organizational Plans
• Policies—general statements of understanding or intent; guide decision-making, permitting the exercise of some discretion; guide behavior (for example, no employee shall accept favors and/or entertainment from an outside organization that are substantial enough in value to cause undue influence over one's decisions on behalf of the organization). • Rules—guides to action that do not permit discretion in interpretation; specify what is permissible and what is not permissible. • Procedures—like rules, they guide action; specify a series of steps that must be taken in the performance of a particular task.

Single-Use Plans

• Programs—a complex set of policies, rules, and procedures necessary to carry out a course of action. • Projects—specific action plans often created to complete various aspects of a program. • Budgets—plans expressed in numerical terms.

Time-Frame Plans

• Short-, medium-, and long-range plans—differ in the distance into the future projected:
   ◦ Short-range—several hours to a year
   ◦ Medium-range—one to five years
   ◦ Long-range—more than five years

Organizational Scope Plans

• Business/divisional-level plans—focus on one of the organization's businesses (or divisions) and its competitive position. • Unit/functional-level plans—focus on the day-to-day operations of lower-level organization units; marketing, human resources, accounting, and operations plans (production). • Tactical plans—division-level or unit-level plans designed to help an organization accomplish its strategic plans.

Contingency Plans

• Plans created to deal with events that might come to confront the organization (e.g., natural disasters, terrorist threats); alternative courses of action that are to be implemented if events disrupt a planned course of action.

Table 17.1 (Attribution: Copyright Rice University, OpenStax, under CC-BY 4.0 license)

Strategic Plans

Strategic management is that part of the management process concerned with the overall integration of an organization's internal divisions while simultaneously integrating the organization with its external environment. Strategic management formulates and implements tactics that try to match an organization as closely as possible to its task environment for the purpose of meeting its objectives.

Strategic plans address the organization's institutional-level needs. Strategic plans outline a long-term vision for the organization. They specify the organization's reason for being, its strategic objectives, and its operational strategies—the action statements that specify how the organization's strategic goals are to be achieved.

Part of strategic planning involves creating the organization's mission, a statement that specifies an organization's reason for being and answers the question "What business(es) should we undertake?" The mission and the strategic plan are major guiding documents for activities that the organization pursues. Strategic plans have several defining characteristics: They are long-term and position an organization within its task environment; they are pervasive and cover many organizational activities; they integrate, guide, and control activities for the immediate and the long term; and they establish boundaries for managerial decision-making.

Operating plans provide direction and action statements for activities in the organization's technical core. **Administrative plans** work to integrate institutional-level plans with the operating plans and tie together all of the plans created for the organization's technical core.

Frequency-of-Use Plans

Another category of plans is frequency-of-use plans. Some plans are used repeatedly; others are used for a single purpose. **Standing plans**, such as rules, policies, and procedures, are designed to cover issues that managers face repeatedly. For example, managers may be concerned about tardiness, a problem that may occur often in the entire work force. These managers might decide to develop a standing policy to be implemented automatically each time an employee is late for work. The procedure invoked under such a standing plan is called a standard operating procedure (SOP).

Single-use plans are developed for unique situations or problems and are usually replaced after one use. Managers generally use three types of single-use plans: programs, projects, and budgets. See **Table 17.1** for a brief description of standing and single-use plans.

Time-Frame Plans

The organization's need to address the future is captured by its time-frame plans. This need to address the future through planning is reflected in short-, medium-, and long-range plans. Given the uniqueness of industries and the different time orientations of societies—study Hofstede's differentiation of cultures around the world in terms of their orientation toward the future—the times captured by short, medium, and long range vary tremendously across organizations of the world. Konosuke Matsushita's 250-year plan, which he developed for the company that bears his name, is not exactly typical of the long-range plans of U.S. companies!

Short-, medium-, and long-range plans differ in more ways than the time they cover. Typically, the further a plan projects into the future, the more uncertainty planners encounter. As a consequence, long-range plans are usually less specific than shorter-range plans. Also, long-range plans are usually less formal, less detailed, and more flexible than short-range plans in order to accommodate such uncertainty. Long-range plans also tend to be more directional in nature.

Exhibit 17.7   Tower with digital clock Digital clocks were installed on the Sapporo TV tower, which was donated by Matsushita Electric Industrial Company, a Japanese electronics manufacturer. This installation was suggested by the founder of the company, Konosuke Matsushita, who thought these digital clocks would draw great attention to the tower. Matsushita is revered as a management thought leader in Japan and favored long-term planning, including 250-year plans. (Credit: Arjan Richerter/ flickr/ Attribution 2.0 Generic (CC BY 2.0))

Organizational Scope Plans

Plans vary in scope. Some plans focus on an entire organization. For example, the president of the University of Minnesota advanced a plan to make the university one of the top five educational institutions in the United States. This strategic plan focuses on the entire institution. Other plans are narrower in scope and concentrate on a subset of organizational activities or operating units, such as the food services unit of the university. For further insight into organizational scope plans, see **Table 17.1**.

Contingency Plans

Organizations often engage in contingency planning (also referred to as scenario or "what if" planning). You will recall that the planning process is based on certain premises about what is likely to happen in an organization's environment. **Contingency plans** are created to deal with what might happen if these assumptions turn out to be wrong. Contingency planning is thus the development of alternative courses of action to be implemented if events disrupt a planned course of action. A contingency plan allows management to act immediately if an unplanned occurrence, such as a strike, boycott, natural disaster, or major economic shift, renders existing plans inoperable or inappropriate. For example, airlines develop contingency plans to deal with terrorism and air tragedies. Most contingency plans are never implemented, but when needed, they are of crucial importance.

CONCEPT CHECK

1. Define and describe the different types of plans defined in Table 17.1 and how organizations use them.

17.4 Goals or Outcome Statements

4. Explain the individual and organizational effects associated with goal setting and planning.

Creating goals is an inherent part of effective managerial planning. There are two types of organizational goals that are interrelated—official and operational goals.[21] **Official goals** are an organization's general aims as expressed in public statements, in its annual report, and in its charter. One official goal of a university, for example, might be to be "the school of first choice." Official goals are usually ambiguous and oriented toward achieving acceptance by an organization's constituencies. **Operational goals** reflect management's specific intentions. These are the concrete goals that organization members are to pursue.[22] For example, an operational goal for a hospital might be to increase the number of patients treated by 5 percent or to reduce readmission.

The importance of goals is apparent from the purposes they serve. Successful goals (1) guide and direct the efforts of individuals and groups; (2) motivate individuals and groups, thereby affecting their efficiency and effectiveness; (3) influence the nature and content of the planning process; and (4) provide a standard by which to judge and control organizational activity. In short, goals define organizational purpose, motivate accomplishment, and provide a yardstick against which progress can be measured.

Goal Formulation—Where Do Organizational Goals Come From?

There are two different views about how organizational goals are formulated. The first view focuses on an organization and its external environment. You will recall that there are many stakeholders (e.g., owners, employees, managers) who have a vested interest in the organization. Organizational goals emerge as managers try to maintain the delicate balance between their organization's needs and those of its external environment.[23] The second view concentrates on the set of dynamics in the organization's internal environment. Internally, an organization is made up of many individuals, coalitions, and groups who continually interact to meet their own interests and needs.[24] They bargain, trade, and negotiate, and through these political processes, organizational goals eventually emerge.

Neither approach to goal formulation can alone provide for long-term organizational success. Goals must fit an organization into its external environment while satisfying the needs of external constituencies. In addition, goals must enable an organization's internal components to work in harmony. For example, the goals of its marketing department need to mesh with those of its production and finance departments. The challenge for managers is to balance these forces and preserve the organization.

Multiple Goals and the Goal Hierarchy

Consistent with the two views of goal emergence, Peter Drucker offers the perspective that organizations must simultaneously pursue multiple goals. A well-known management scholar, consultant, and writer, Drucker believes that to achieve organizational success, managers must try to achieve multiple goals simultaneously—namely, market standing, innovation, productivity, profitability; physical and financial resources, manager performance and development, employee performance and attitude, and public responsibility.[25] Reflecting his concerns, the Hewlett-Packard Corporation has established the seven corporate goals listed in **Table 17.2**. Sometimes units within organizations may pursue goals that actually conflict with the goals of other internal units. The innovation goal of a research and development department, for example, might conflict with the production department's goal of efficiency.[26] Managers must strive to integrate the network of goals and resolve internal conflicts when they arise.

Hewlett-Packard's Corporate Goals
Profit. To achieve sufficient profit to finance our company growth and to provide the resources we need to achieve our other corporate objectives.
Customers. To provide products and services of the greatest possible value to our customers, thereby gaining and holding their respect and loyalty.
Field of Interest. To enter new fields only when the ideas we have, together with our technical, manufacturing and marketing skills, assure that we can make a needed and profitable contribution to the field.
Growth. To let our growth be limited only by our profits and our ability to develop and produce technical products that satisfy real customer needs.
People. To help our own people share in the company's success, which they make possible: to provide job security based on their performance, to recognize their individual achievements, and to help them gain a sense of satisfaction and accomplishment from their work.
Management. To foster initiative and creativity by allowing the individual great freedom of action in attaining well-defined objectives.
Citizenship. To honor our obligations to society by being an economic, intellectual and social asset to each nation and each community in which we operate.
Source: Adapted from Y. K. Shetty. 1979. New look at corporate goals. *California Management Review* 22(2): 71–79.

Table 17.2

Broad organizational goals, such as productivity, innovation, and profitability, are likely to be broken into subgoals at various organizational levels. The complexities posed by many interrelated systems of goals and major plans can be illustrated by a **goal hierarchy**.[27] Thus, an organization sets organizational-level, divisional-level, departmental-level, and job-related goals. In the process, managers must make sure that lower-level goals combine to achieve higher-level goals.

CONCEPT CHECK

1. What is the difference between official and operational goals?
2. How do multiple goals fit into a goal hierarchy?

17.5   Formal Organizational Planning in Practice

5. Understand how planning occurs in today's organizations.

Studies indicate that, in the 1950s, approximately 8.3 percent of all major U.S. firms (1 out of every 12) employed a full-time long-range planner. By the late 1960s, 83 percent of major U.S. firms used long-range planning. Today it is estimated that nearly all U.S. corporations with sales over $100 million prepare formal long-range plans.[28] Most formal plans extend five years into the future, and about 20 percent extend at least ten years.

Encouraging Planning

In spite of the advantages to be gained by planning, many managers resist it. Some feel that there is not enough time to plan or that it is too complicated and costs too much. Others worry about the possible consequences of failing to reach the goals they set. Instead of preplanning, sometimes referred to as blueprint planning (that is, formulating outcome and action statements before moving forward), many managers simply fail to plan or at best engage in in-process planning (they read events and think about the next step just before acting). In-process planning works extremely well when individuals have a sense of what it is that they want to achieve and can improvise as they move forward in a sea of uncertainty and turbulence. This is much like skilled hockey players relying on their instincts, reading the defense, and improvising as they move up the ice and toward the opponent's net. This process often works better than attempting to implement a detailed preplan, as often characterizes plays in football.

In situations where we want to encourage preplanning, certain techniques facilitate the process:

- Develop an organizational climate that encourages planning.
- Top managers support lower-level managers' planning activities—for example, by providing such resources as personnel, computers, and funds—and serve as role models through their own planning activities.
- Train people in planning.
- Create a reward system that encourages and supports planning activity and carefully avoids punishment for failure to achieve newly set goals.
- Use plans once they are created.

In order for managers to invest the time and energy needed to overcome resistance to planning, they must be convinced that planning does in fact pay off.

Does Planning Really Pay Off?

Managers of organizations in complex and unstable environments may find it difficult to develop meaningful plans, yet it is precisely conditions of environmental complexity and instability that produce the greatest need for a good set of organizational plans. Yet the question remains, does planning really pay off?

We know from our earlier discussion that setting goals is an important part of the planning process. Today, much is known about what characterizes effective individual goals. (We discuss this issue in greater detail later in this chapter.) Although group and organizational goals have been studied less, it is probably safe to assume that most of our knowledge about individual goals also applies to group and organizational goals. The research suggests that effective organizational goals should (1) be difficult but reachable with effort, (2) be specific and clearly identify what is desired, (3) be accepted by and have the commitment of those who will help achieve them, (4) be developed by employees if such participation will improve the quality of the goals and their acceptance, and (5) be monitored for progress regularly.

While the evidence is not abundant, studies suggest that firms that engage in planning are more financially successful than those that do not.[29] For example, one study reports that the median return on investment for a five-year period is 17.1 percent for organizations engaged in strategic planning, versus 5.9 percent for those that do not.[30] Similarly, of 70 large commercial banks, those that had strategic planning systems outperformed those that did not.[31]

Although planning clearly has observable benefits, it can be expensive. The financial commitment can be large for organizations with a formal planning staff. Even so, research suggests that planning is warranted.

The Location of the Planning Activity

Classical management thinking advocates a separation of "planning" and "doing." According to this school of thought, managers plan for technical core employees and formulate most of the plans for the upper levels of the organization, with little participation from lower-level managers and workers. In contrast, behavioral management theorists suggest involving organization members in drawing up plans that affect them. Implementation of a management-by-objectives program (to be discussed later in this chapter), for example, is one means by which this participative planning can be realized. Researchers at the Tavistock Institute in England promote the idea of self-managed work groups as a means of expanding the level of employee involvement. According to their socio-technical model, work groups assume a major role in planning (as well as in organizing, directing, and controlling) the work assigned to them. Many organizations—for example, the John Lewis Partnership, Volvo, and Motorola—have had successful experiences with employee involvement in planning and controlling activities.[32]

Planning Specialists

To keep pace with organizational complexity, technological sophistication, and environmental uncertainty, many organizations use planning specialists. Professional planners develop organizational plans and help managers plan. Boeing and Ford are among the many organizations with professional planning staffs. Planning specialists at United Airlines developed United's crisis management plan.

Organizations have planning specialists and planning departments in place for a variety of reasons. These specialized roles have emerged because planning is time-consuming and complex and requires more attention than line managers can provide. In rapidly changing environments, planning becomes even more complex and often necessitates the development of contingency plans, once again demanding time for research and special planning skills. At times, effective planning requires an objectivity that managers and employees with vested interests in a particular set of organizational activities cannot provide.

A planning staff's goals are varied. Their primary responsibility is to serve as planning advisors to top management and to assist lower-level line managers in developing plans for achieving their many and varied organizational objectives. Frequently, they coordinate the complex array of plans created for the various levels within an organization. Finally, a planning staff provides encouragement, support, and skill for developing formal organizational plans.

MANAGING CHANGE

Using Technology for a More Efficient Business

The need to control costs has been around since trade, buying and selling, began. Each new technology creates new possibilities in production and cost reduction. Recent technology isn't any different. Leaps in connectivity and data management are creating as many start-ups and new ways of identifying and solving problems.

Innovu uses new technology to help small and start-up business control the costs of their health benefits. Most small companies and start-ups are self-insured; that is, the company pays any covered employee medical bills or finances any wellness programs directly. According to Diane Hess, the executive director of the Central Penn Business Group on Health, employers account for 30 percent of the $2.9 trillion in health care spending in the United States, and workers' compensation cost employers $91 billion in 2014. These costs included $31.4 billion for medical and $30.9 in cash payments (Hess 2016). Innovu mines employee claims to find trends and also provides data on costs due to absenteeism, disability, and workers' compensation (Mamula 2017). As employers move to wellness programs to improve productivity and reduce medical costs, Innovu helps employers "make sure there are improvements to justify the expenses"(Hess 2016 n.p.).

In a similar vein, Marsh & McLennan Agency Michigan LLC is moving from simply providing insurance and generic "wellness programs" to helping companies focus on improving employees' overall well-being. While traditional wellness programs focus on physical health to improve productivity, the emerging trend is to help employees with family, social, and financial issues as well. The most comprehensive program from Marsh & McLennan is its MMA Michigan's Wellbeing University, which works to expand traditional wellness programs into nontraditional support services. The comprehensive approach of the program helps midsize employers "attract and retain talent, encourage employee satisfaction and reduce absenteeism." The move beyond simple wellness is a move toward investing in employees. Bret Jackson, president of Economic Alliance for Michigan, said, "If you have a happy and healthy employee, productivity increases" (Greene 2017 n.p.).

Branch Messenger is a novel idea to solve employee scheduling. Employees are able to view schedules, cover shifts, and ask for time off, all from an app on their phone. It integrates with existing company systems to allow data analysis, but perhaps more importantly, it allows employees to connect. The start-up's program has been adopted by large companies, such as Target, McDonald's, and Walgreens, to allow employees to swap shifts simply by using an app on their cell phones. This process streamlines the process of swapping shifts by allowing employees to handle most of the leg work, "bridg[ing] the communication gap between workers and the companies that employ them." The application is free to employees and runs on both iOS and Android devices. It can also generate digital schedules from paper schedules and create messaging channels that are workplace specific. Moving past simple shift flexibility, the application allows businesses to tap into an "on-demand" workforce that is more elastic. It also allows enterprises to "extend the value of existing workforce management systems without the need to switch costs" (Takahasi 2017 n.p.).

Allison Harden, a shift manager for a Pizza Hut in Tampa, Florida, likes the added connectivity of the program. "The messaging feature and the ability to share pictures and posts makes it really easy to stay connected with them," Allison says. "It's a way that I can do it outside a social network. Not everyone has Facebook and stuff like that—so it's good and work-friendly, safe for work" (Branch Messenger 2017 n.p.).

"Safe for work" can carry connotations of "oversharing" on social media, but during Hurricane Irma, Allison and her crew relied on Branch Messenger for storm preparation, allowing the manager to post a safety checklist and update shifts. Then during the storm itself and after, drivers were able to tell each other which gas stations actually had gas, who still had electricity, and who was safe (Branch Messenger 2017).

Sources:

Branch Messenger. 2017. "A Branch Customer Story: How A Tampa Pizza Hut Stayed in Contact During Hurricane Irma." http://blog.branchmessenger.com/a-branch-customer-story-how-a-tampa-pizza-hut-stayed-in-contact-during-hurricane-irma/

Greene, Jay. 2017. "New course for Marsh & McLennan Agency as clients seek well-being." *Crain's Detroit Business.* http://www.crainsdetroit.com/article/20170806/news/635676/new-course-for-marsh-mclennan-agency-as-clients-seek-well-being

Hess, Diane. 2016. "Column: Using data to make business more efficient, employees more healthy." *Lancaster Online,* November 8, 2016. http://lancasteronline.com/business/local_business/column-using-data-to-make-business-more-efficient-employees-more/article_c5887508-a529-11e6-98ae-4be5cc57a478.html

Mamula, Kris B. 2017. "Station Square data analytics company to use $6.5 million to grow." *Post-Gazette,* August 10, 2017. http://www.post-gazette.com/business/tech-news/2017/08/10/innovu-ex...-pittsburgh-employee-benefits-health-insurance/stories/201708100025

Takahasi, Dean. 2017. "Branch Manager helps hourly workers swap shifts on mobile." venturebeat.com. https://venturebeat.com/2017/08/02/branch-messenger-helps-hourly-shift-workers-schedule-their-lives-on-mobile/

Questions:
1. What ethical problems could surface with data mining as it applies to employee health records?
2. What security risks would a company need to consider when utilizing smartphone apps for work?

Exhibit 17.8   Shelf of tide pods   Procter & Gamble, the maker of Tide Pods, has faced two issues with its popular new laundry product. Early after its introduction, reports came in that 180 children had visited hospitals after ingesting the colorful pods thinking that they were candy. P&G quickly reacted by making tamper-proof packaging making it more difficult for children to access, adding a nontoxic flavor that would dissuade children from swallowing the pods, and initiating a product information campaign aimed at informing parents about the dangers—overall, a well-orchestrated contingency plan. In 2017, however, P&G began receiving reports about teenagers intentionally swallowing the product in a "pods challenge" that went viral on social media. Whenever notified, P&G decided to contact the teens directly and contact tech companies such as Facebook and YouTube to remove these posts and videos but did not publicize this, fearing that it would only cause more teens to accept the challenge or challenge others. (Credit: Mike Mozart/ flickr/ Attribution 2.0 Generic (CC BY 2.0))

CONCEPT CHECK

1. How do today's organizations approach planning?
2. Does planning pay off for today's organizations?
3. Which people in the organization should be involved in planning, and what are their roles?

17.6 Employees' Responses to Planning

6. Discuss the impact that control has on organizational members.

Managers, of course, want their employees to work hard. However, effort alone is not enough; it must be directed toward the appropriate target and executed in a proper manner. The question we explore here is, do planning, goal setting, and the development of action statements have a favorable impact on employee motivation, performance, and job satisfaction?

We turn to goal theory for our answer. Research provides us with a clear and unequivocal picture of the effects of setting goals for organizational members. Goal theory specifies that certain types of goals motivate employee behavior and thereby contribute to the level of employee performance. Goal theory, while somewhat narrow in scope, is the most completely supported theory of motivation.[33] You have learned or will learn about the implications of goal setting as a fundamental part of the planning process and as a standard for the exercise of control when studying motivation. For goals to be effective, they must be difficult, specific, and accepted by the employee, and they must be met with feedback from management. Manufacturers often use production goals to motivate employees.

Characteristics of Goals That Motivate Performance

Goal theory (and the research related to it) highlights several important goal attributes—goal difficulty, goal specificity, goal acceptance and commitment, and goal feedback. As **Exhibit 17.9** shows, workers who have a goal, even if it is quite general, usually perform better than those with no goals. Yet certain types of goals are more effective than others. Two primary characteristics of goals that enhance their motivating potential are goal specificity and goal difficulty.[34] With regard to goal specificity, a goal that states "improve your performance" or "do your best" is generally not very effective because it is too general. Weyerhaeuser, for example, observed that its truck drivers hauling logs significantly increased their performance level when they were instructed to load their trucks to 94 percent of legal weight capacity, as opposed to simply "doing their best." The drivers found the specific goal to be motivating, and they often competed with one another to achieve the prescribed goal. In the first nine months following the introduction of the 94 percent target, Weyerhaeuser estimated its savings to be approximately $250,000.

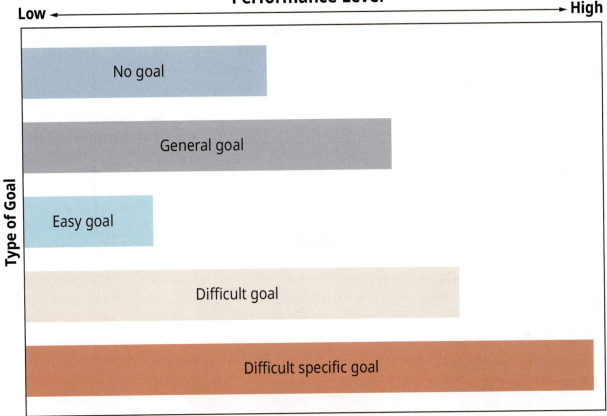

Exhibit 17.9   The Effects of Goals on Performance (Attribution: Copyright Rice University, OpenStax, under CC-BY 4.0 license)

The second component of an effective goal is goal difficulty. People with difficult goals perform better than those with easy goals (note the third and fourth bars in **Exhibit 17.9**). If goals are perceived as too difficult or impossible, however, they lose their motivating effectiveness. Ideally, goals will be both specific and difficult. Thus, setting specific and challenging goals contributes more to planning effectiveness and organizational performance than does working under "no-goal" or "do your best" goal conditions.[35]

Even a goal that is both difficult and specific, however, is not going to be effective unless it is accepted by the person who is expected to achieve it.[36] Goal acceptance is the degree to which people accept a goal as their own ("I agree that this report must be finished by 5 p.m.").[37] Goal commitment is more inclusive, referring to our level of attachment to or determination to reach a goal ("I *want* to get that report done on time").[38] Goals sometimes fail to motivate people when managers assign them without making sure that workers have accepted or committed to the goals. **Exhibit 17.10** summarizes the conditions necessary to maximize goal-directed effort (motivation 5 direction 1 intensity), a major contributor to subsequent performance, while **Exhibit 17.11** summarizes the three sets of factors that facilitate goal commitment.[39]

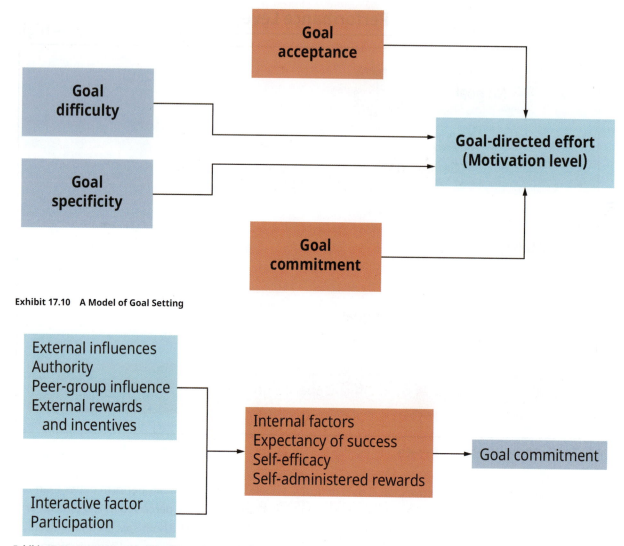

Exhibit 17.10   A Model of Goal Setting

Exhibit 17.11   Determinants of Goal Commitment Source: Adapted from E. A. Locke, G. P. Latham, and M. Erez. 1988. The determinants of goal commitment. *Academy of Management Review* 13:28. Copyright 1998 by Academy of Management. Reproduced with permission of Academy of Management in the format Textbook via Copyright Clearance Center; an from E. Erez and P. C. Earley. 1987. Comparative analysis of goal setting across cultures. *Journal of Applied Psychology* 72:658–665.

Goal feedback is the last important goal attribute. Goal feedback provides us with knowledge about the results of our efforts. This information can come from a variety of sources, such as supervisors, peers, subordinates, customers, inanimate performance monitoring systems, and self-assessment. Regardless of the source, the right kind of feedback serves two important functions: directional and effort. Directionally, good feedback tells employees whether they are on the right path and on target or suggests the need for redirection. In addition, it should provide information that suggests the adequacy or inadequacy of the employee's level of effort. Thus, feedback is of critical importance!

The Negative Side of Goals

There is, however, a negative side to goal setting. Total quality management (TQM) pioneer W. Edwards Deming fears that goals tend to narrow the performer's vision and invite people to slack off once the goal is achieved. TQM is also oriented more toward process (means) than toward success (goals, outcomes).

Organizational learning and continuous improvement, a central component of TQM, is oriented toward continually finding problems in the production process that when eliminated will result in performance increases.[40] Performance goals, on the other hand, generally focus the performer's attention on successfully achieving a specified level of accomplishment at some future point.

Evidence also reveals a negative side to an employee's commitment to difficult goals. When organizational members are strongly committed to achieving difficult goals, their involvement in acts of good organizational citizenship is likely to decline.[41] This negative relationship is unfortunate because organizations operating in highly turbulent, competitive, and uncertain environments are extremely fragile social systems. They need the commitment and the sense of ownership that propel organizational members to spontaneously engage in behaviors that are not specified in their job descriptions but that are important to the organization's success and well-being.

There are several other negative effects associated with goals: The methods and means created to accomplish organizational goals may themselves become the goal (means-ends inversion). Organizational goals may be in conflict with personal or societal goals. Goals that are too specific may inhibit creativity and innovation. Ambiguous goals may fail to provide adequate direction, and goals and reward systems are often incompatible. For example, universities commonly encourage faculty members to be better teachers, but their reward systems primarily encourage good research.[42]

Goal Setting and Employee Job Satisfaction

The statement "goal setting enhances job satisfaction" is not exactly accurate.[43] The relationship between goal setting and planning and job satisfaction is somewhat more complex. Goal setting, and therefore planning, impacts job satisfaction by working through the employee's level of performance and level of aspiration. Job satisfaction (or dissatisfaction) is most likely determined by the level of performance and not by the goals that have been set.

An employee's affective reaction to performance is determined not by the performance level itself but by the level of performance in relation to his aspiration level.[44] Job satisfaction, therefore, stems from the employee's evaluation of his actual performance in comparison to his aspiration level (or performance goal). In cases (see **Exhibit 17.12**) where performance reaches or passes the level aspired to, a positive emotion (job satisfaction) is likely to be produced. Performance that fails to reach aspirations causes a negative emotion (job dissatisfaction). In addition, if performance is valued by the employee because of the extrinsic rewards tied to it, high performance will create job satisfaction only if achieving the performance goal leads to the receipt of these valued extrinsic rewards.[45] Thus, goal setting is indirectly and contingently related to job satisfaction. If goal setting contributes to employees reaching their performance aspirations and/or the outcomes that are associated with that performance, job satisfaction is a likely by-product.

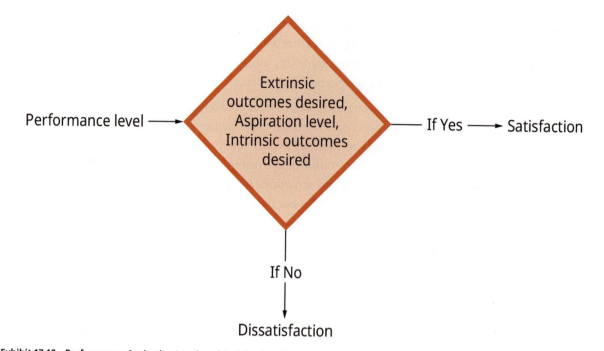

Performance level $\longrightarrow$ Extrinsic outcomes desired, Aspiration level, Intrinsic outcomes desired $\longrightarrow$ If Yes $\longrightarrow$ Satisfaction

If No

Dissatisfaction

Exhibit 17.12   Performance, Aspiration Level, and Satisfaction (Attribution: Copyright Rice University, OpenStax, under CC-BY 4.0 license)

Managing through Goal Setting

What can managers do to motivate employees through goal setting? First, it is important to encourage goal acceptance and commitment. This can be accomplished by working with organizational members to set difficult, specific, and reasonable goals and to make certain that members perceive them as reasonable. If necessary, provide training and other support needed to make the goals attainable. Offer feedback that lets people know when they are approaching the goal. Avoid using threats. Feedback that criticizes without providing insight into ways to contribute to performance improvements is both frustrating and unlikely to be effective. One of Deming's concerns about goal setting is that it creates fear in employees—fear of the failure to reach the goal. He sees fear as a serious disease that contributes to poor organizational performance.[46] Instead, a positive, success-oriented approach is almost always more effective. If and when negative feedback is needed to correct errors, a manager's criticisms of an employee should be credible, constructive, and objective. In addition, it is important to recall that feedback that simply criticizes, without providing insight into how to make the needed corrections, will produce few if any positive results. Finally, keep in mind that, whereas goal acceptance occurs before people work on a task and can be encouraged through promises of reward, goal commitment can be nurtured throughout the performance period as workers receive rewards for progress.

Encourage the development of work-group norms that contribute to goal commitment. Use legitimate authority to encourage the setting of specific and difficult goals. Stimulate workers to develop a sense of ownership in goals, thus producing goal acceptance and commitment. There are those who believe goal acceptance and commitment can be nurtured when workers come together as members of a family working toward the common goal of proving their worth.[47]

Controlling as an Organizational Activity

A few years ago, the Duluth Police Department found itself struggling with employee morale. The summer had passed, and the department discovered that it had allowed too much vacation time given the volume of summer activity facing the department. As it developed its staffing plans for the upcoming summer, it would have to grant fewer requests for summer vacations. Management soon learned that there would actually be more requests for summer vacation than the previous summer. A conflict between management and the police union appeared inevitable.

The department turned to creative problem solving. In the process, it came up with the idea of moving from a seven-day week to an eight-day week. Under the old schedule, a police officer worked a traditional five days a week, eight hours a day, 40 hours, with two days off each week. Under the new schedule, officers would work 12 hours a day and 48 hours a week. In addition, officers would work four days and then have four days off. This would in effect give officers half the upcoming summer off without taking a single day of vacation. The plan was endorsed by both the police union and the city council. Following the endorsement of the new staffing plan, the department developed a plan for monitoring the effectiveness of this new schedule and collected baseline data so that subsequent assessment of the schedule could be compared to previous work schedules.[48]

In January, the new compressed work schedule was implemented. This was accompanied by a control system that would monitor the effectiveness of the new schedule. The department was particularly concerned about the impact of the schedule on stress levels, job satisfaction, and the overall effectiveness of its policing function. That is, would the 12-hour workday negatively affect performance? Periodically during the next couple of years, the department monitored the consequences of its new work schedule. There were several positive results. The level of stress appeared to decline along with the increases in hours worked and leisure time satisfaction, without any negative performance effects. Now, several years later, there is virtually no desire to return to the old, more traditional work schedule.

In effective organizations, the activities of planning and controlling are intricately interwoven. For each plan deemed important to the functioning of the organization, a system to monitor the plan's effectiveness must be designed and implemented. In the remainder of this chapter, we explore the nature of control, the control process, and its effects on the organization and its members.

Controlling and the Control Process

Controlling is a managing activity. **Controlling** is defined as the process of monitoring and evaluating organizational effectiveness and initiating the actions needed to maintain or improve effectiveness. Thus, managers who engage in the controlling activity watch, evaluate, and when needed, suggest corrective action.

Like the managerial functions of planning, organizing, and directing, controlling is a complex activity that is performed at many organizational levels. Upper-level managers, for example, monitor their organization's overall strategic plans, which can be implemented only if middle-level managers control the organization's divisional and departmental plans, which, in turn, rely on lower-level managers' control of groups and individual employees (see our earlier discussion of the goal hierarchy).

The Need for Control

Although there is a continual and universal need for control in organizations, the importance, amount, and type of control vary across organizational situations. Probably the most important influence on the nature of an organization's control systems is the amount of environmental change and complexity it faces.

Organizations that operate with relatively stable external environments usually need to change very little, so managers eventually are able to control their organizations by using a set of routine procedures. With greater levels of environmental change and the accompanying uncertainty, however, controlling requires continual attention from managers. Routines and rigid control systems are simply not adequate for such conditions.

Environmental complexity also affects the nature of control systems. Simple environments contain a limited number of highly similar components that are relatively easy to control through common sets of rules and procedures. The same bureaucratic control system, for example, can be used at most branch offices of a large bank. As complexity increases through organizational growth, product diversification, and so on, managers' needs for up-to-date information and coordination among organizational activities intensify. The complexity that calls for increased control, however, also requires open, organic systems that can respond quickly and effectively to complex environments. In such complicated situations, organizations often specify the development of flexible systems as a means goal: "To allow us to manage the complexities of our organization, we must remain flexible and open." Other control activities shift to ends goals, such as "We want to increase market share 10 percent in each of our divisions." Flexibility allows substantial choice as to how ends goals will be met: "Each division may decide how to achieve its 10 percent increase in market share." **Exhibit 17.13** shows the level of control organizations need under different environmental conditions.

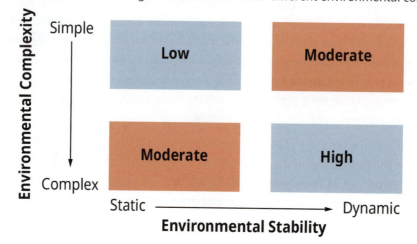

Exhibit 17.13   Need for Control (Attribution: Copyright Rice University, OpenStax, under CC-BY 4.0 license)

A Control Model

In essence, control affects every part of an organization. Among some of the major targets of the organization's control efforts are the resources it receives, the output it generates, its environmental relationships, its organizational processes, and all managerial activities. Especially important targets of control include the functional areas of operations, accounting, marketing, finance, and human resources.

Traditional control models (see **Exhibit 17.14**) suggest that controlling is a four-step process.

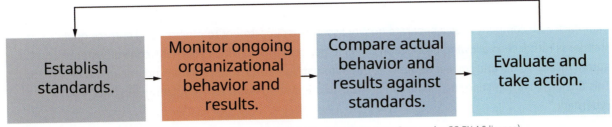

Exhibit 17.14   The Traditional Control Model (Attribution: Copyright Rice University, OpenStax, under CC-BY 4.0 license)

1. *Establish standards.* Standards are the ends and means goals established during the planning process; thus, planning and controlling are intricately interwoven. Planning provides the basis for the control process by providing the standards of performance against which managers compare organizational activities. Subsequently, the information generated as a part of the control process (see the subsequent steps in the control model) provides important input into the next planning cycle.

2. *Monitor ongoing organizational behavior and results.* After determining what should be measured, by whom, when, and how, an assessment of what has actually taken place is made.

3. *Compare actual behavior and results against standards.* Ongoing behavior is compared to standards. This assessment involves comparing actual organizational accomplishments relative to planned ends (what an organization is trying to accomplish) and means (how an organization intended for actions to unfold). The outcome of this comparison provides managers with the information they will evaluate in the final step.

4. *Evaluate and take action.* Using their comparative information, managers form conclusions about the relationships found between expectations and reality and then decide whether to maintain the status quo, change the standard, or take corrective action.

Variations in Control Systems

Although all good control systems follow the process described above, this doesn't mean that all control systems are identical. Control systems differ in terms of the degree to which they are self-managing, as opposed to externally managed, and by the point in the process at which control is exercised.

Cybernetic and Noncybernetic Systems

Control systems differ in the amount of outside attention required for them to operate effectively. Systems using **cybernetic control** are based on self-regulating procedures that automatically detect and correct deviations from planned activities and effectiveness levels. Few organizational control systems are totally cybernetic, but some come close. The control system for a coal-fired electrical generating station at Detroit Edison, for example, uses computers to monitor the flow of pulverized coal into the burning chamber. The computers speed up or reduce the flow as necessary to maintain adequate fuel supplies.

Merely automating a work system does not necessarily mean that the control system is cybernetic. The drone submarine sent to explore and photograph the sunken *Titanic* was fully automated, but humans on the surface monitored the effectiveness of the sub's operations and its adherence to the planned mission. To be classified as a cybernetic system, a work system must have built-in automatic control capabilities, although the built-in control need not be machine-based. A group of workers who control their own activities without outside assistance constitute a cybernetic system.

Control systems that are operated completely independently from the work system itself involve **noncybernetic control**. They rely on external monitoring systems in much the same way that a manufacturing company uses a separate quality assurance department to monitor and enforce quality standards rather than allowing production crews to perform this activity. Cybernetic control systems automatically detect and correct deviations, but automating a control system does not mean it is cybernetic. This technician is adjusting the mixture in the vat, so this system is not self-regulating and thus is not cybernetic.

Time Perspectives

Organizations can introduce the control activity at three stages in the work process: prior to, during, or after the performance of a work activity.[49] In practice, most managers use a **hybrid control system** that incorporates control at each of these intervals so that managers can prepare for a job, guide its progress, and assess its results.

Managers use **precontrols** (or preaction controls) to prevent deviation from a desired plan of action before work actually begins. For example, Butch Ledworowski, owner of Lil' America Building Contractors, inspects all construction materials to see that they meet industry standards. Managers can use two types of **concurrent controls** (steering and screening control) to prevent deviation from the planned course of action while work is in progress. Steering controls are reactive concurrent controls; they occur after work has begun but before it is completed. At Lil' America, for instance, Butch visits each construction site and watches his carpenters, offering advice and instruction as they work. Screening controls (also referred to as yes/no, go/no-go controls) are preventive concurrent controls. As activity at a critical stage is completed, managers use screening controls to assess work performed to that point and to judge whether progress is adequate. If it is, a yes decision is made to proceed to the next stage. At Lil' America, for example, Butch always inspects carpentry work after walls have been framed. Unless he approves the work, electricians cannot begin wiring the structure.

Managers use **postaction controls** after the product or service is complete to examine the output. After each remodeling job, Butch assesses the work to determine whether it meets specifications, was completed on time, and came in at or under budget. Postaction controls play an important role in future planning, but their primary function is to provide feedback by describing the degree to which previous activities have succeeded.

Characteristics of Effective Control Systems

Successful control systems have certain common characteristics. First, a good control system follows the prescriptions in the control model (see **Exhibit 17.14**) and adequately addresses each organizational target. Next, to the extent possible, an effective control system takes a hybrid approach so that precontrol, concurrent, and postaction control systems can be used to monitor and correct activities at all points in an organization's operations. Other characteristics of a good control system include its treatment of information, its appropriateness, and its practicality.[50]

The control process itself and, certainly, all effective control systems are based on information. Without good information, managers cannot assess whether ends and means goals are met. They cannot determine the relationship between them or provide feedback to planners. To be effective, information must be accurate, objective, timely, and distributed to organization members who need it. High-involvement organizations work to make sure that virtually all organizational information is accessible by any employee who needs it in order to make quality decisions. Oticon, a Danish manufacturer of hearing aids, for example, scans all company communications and places them in its information system that all employees can access.

Exhibit 17.15 Oticon building As a management control procedure, Oticon, the Danish manufacturer of hearing aids, scans all company communications and places them in its information system that all employees can access. (Credit: News Oresund/ flickr/ Attribution 2.0 Generic (CC BY 2.0))

Another characteristic of a good control system is its focus on issues of importance to the organization. Managers who develop control procedures for virtually all work activities and outcomes waste resources and, as will be discussed later in this chapter, risk creating a control system that produces negative feelings and reactions.

A final characteristic of a good control system is its practicality. Something that works well for another organization or looks wonderful in print still has to fit *your* organization to work well there. Some practical considerations to look for in a control system include feasibility, flexibility, the likelihood that organization members will accept it, and the ease with which the system can be integrated with planning activities.

The Impact of Control on Organizational Members

Thus far, you have been learning about the importance of the controlling function. Consider now what the controlling function does for—or to—the organization's members. If designed well, control systems have many positive effects both for organizations and for the people who work in them (see **Table 17.3**).[51] Unfortunately, sometimes control systems can produce a number of negative effects.

The Impact of Control on Organization Members
Potential Positive Effects of Control
Clarifies expectations

Table 17.3 (Attribution: Copyright Rice University, OpenStax, under CC-BY 4.0 license)

The Impact of Control on Organization Members
Reduces ambiguity
Provides feedback
Facilitates goal setting
Enhances satisfaction
Enhances performance
Potential Negative Effects of Control
Consumes resources
Creates feelings of frustration and helplessness
Creates red tape
Creates inappropriate goals
Fosters inappropriate behavior
Decreases satisfaction
Increases absenteeism
Increases turnover
Creates stress

Table 17.3 (Attribution: Copyright Rice University, OpenStax, under CC-BY 4.0 license)

Positive Effects

Organizational control systems can provide many positive effects for organization members in terms of motivation, performance, and satisfaction. This occurs by providing adequate structure, appropriate feedback, and effective goal-setting programs.

When workers want clarification of what they are expected to do, a leader can improve both their performance and satisfaction by providing structure. The guidance provided by both precontrol and concurrent control systems can likewise be received favorably. Another potential and related benefit for employees with an uncertainty avoidance or low tolerance for ambiguity personality is that the structure of a good control system reduces the uncertainty of a work situation.

A good control system also provides constructive feedback. Most employees react quite favorably to the timely provision of accurate feedback about their effectiveness.[52] Feedback helps workers correct ineffective behaviors. Perhaps more importantly, feedback can be very rewarding. People who have a need to succeed (individuals with a high need for achievement) are gratified when feedback tells them that they are, in fact, succeeding. Feedback can improve job performance if workers use it to adjust their goals, approach, or effort levels appropriately. Both concurrent and postaction controls provide employees with feedback about the appropriateness of their behavior and the degree to which their work is producing successful results.

You have already seen that goal setting can be an important contributor to effective management. A good control system is very useful for identifying appropriate goals. Consider the control system used by the sales company where Maria Castro works. It specifies an expected sales approach (means goal) that helps her work toward a specific, difficult sales goal (ends goal). Precontrols help her understand how to achieve the desired sales level by providing such means goals as specific sales calls to make and promotional specials to offer. Concurrent controls and postcontrols provide feedback that helps Maria monitor her progress. The combined effects of goal setting and feedback about goal progress are particularly powerful.

Negative Effects

Unfortunately, control systems don't always function well. Excessive controls are a waste of money and energy. Donald Pemble, for example, needs a larger travel budget because he must personally inspect bridges under his new control system. His inspectors spend the time they could have used to inspect bridges in logging entries, painting numbers, and griping about the unfairness of the situation. Not only do excessive controls waste money because they fail to enhance effectiveness, but they can also create additional problems. For example, Shannon and her coworkers have changed from good corporate citizens who kept accurate records and conducted comprehensive inspections into harried workers who falsify log entries. Worse, unsuspecting motorists travel over what might be unsafe bridges.

The vast amount of paperwork and documentation called for by an excessive control system can also cause frustration and helplessness. The red tape created by many universities' control systems, for example, wastes students' time. Standing in lines for hours, they wait to pay dorm fees, purchase meal tickets, rent parking spaces, pay tuition, and register for classes. Their frustration and dissatisfaction are mirrored by many university employees who question the competence, the reasonableness, and perhaps even the intelligence of supervisors who insist on maintaining excessive control.

Another dysfunctional result of poor control systems can be seen in their effect on goal-setting programs. Whereas a good control system can help design and monitor valuable goal-setting programs, a poor control system can accomplish quite the opposite. A control system focused on unreasonable ends and means goals can motivate workers to establish inappropriate individual goals. For instance, the ends goal Donald Pemble established of having all bridges inspected within two years was unreachable, and his monthly inspection quotas (means goals) were unobtainable. Donald's insistence on maintaining these inappropriate goals was evident in his reactions when the inspectors failed to meet them. Consequently, Shannon and her coworkers focused on preserving their jobs as a primary goal, rather than on conducting quality inspections.

In addition to encouraging the formation of inappropriate goals, poor control systems emphasize and reward behaviors that, although not necessarily inappropriate, may hinder more productive behavior. Managers who concentrate on workers' attendance, for example, may not promote such desirable behaviors as creativity, cooperation, and team building.[53] Although there is nothing wrong with encouraging attendance, a control system that fosters attendance (by punishing tardiness) because it is easier to measure than creativity encourages rigid, uncreative behavior (on the part of employees who are almost always at work). An advertising agency that controls attendance but not creativity, for example, would soon be in serious trouble.

Even when control systems help identify appropriate goals and encourage appropriate behavior, rigid adherence to narrow goals can create problems. A large number of specific, concrete goals, for example, can inhibit creativity. The vast amount of time organization members must spend tending to concrete goals leaves them little time or energy to create. It is not only creativity that suffers, however. Every minute used taking attendance in a classroom is one less minute available for teaching. Every hour a police officer spends completing paperwork is one less hour available for public service. Managers should use only the goals they need, no more.

The Need for Personal Control

Organizations clearly have a need to control their members and operations, but individuals also have a need for personal control, a need to believe that they have the "ability to effect a change, in a desired direction, on the environment."[54] Sometimes organizations, through their structures and management processes, make people feel they have too little control. For example, managers can execute the control function by designing and demanding strict adherence to organizational rules and standard operating procedures. Colleges and universities, for example, tell students which classes they are allowed to take and when, what grades they have to maintain, how to behave outside the classroom, and so on. Companies tell employees when to come to work, how many hours to work, what to wear, when to take breaks, how to perform their jobs, and many other things. The challenge facing managers is to strike a balance between the amount of control their organization needs and the amount of personal control needed by its members. Studies suggests that, when this balance is reached, both the satisfaction and performance of organization members can be enhanced.[55] In addition, evidence reveals that a number of other organizationally undesirable consequences can result from low or less than desired levels of personal control, such as withdrawal and health-related effects (stress, frustration, and depression).[56]

Finding the optimal balance between organizational and personal control is not an easy task, however, because most employees desire more personal control than their organizations allow. People will strive to gain greater control "in spite of (and frequently because of) the barriers and constraints the organization places on the attainment of personal control."[57] Repeated failures to gain personal control may cause workers to develop what has been called learned helplessness.[58] People who learn that they are helpless to influence their work environment are likely to be the source of low productivity, low quality, high absenteeism, dissatisfaction, and turnover. They tend to react with depression, anxiety, stress, frustration, hostility, anger, and alienation. Furthermore, once helplessness has been learned, people often continue to behave helplessly, even if the environment changes to permit them greater control. Managers must thus prevent employees from developing learned helplessness because reversing it is very difficult. They should allow workers to control the aspects of their work lives that they can adequately control and use only the necessary amount of organizational control.

In Search of Balance

At this point, it might seem that managers should just accede to workers' persistent demands for greater control. Research shows, however, that indiscriminately giving employees larger amounts of control actually causes performance to suffer if such control exceeds their capacity to use it.[59]

If a control system that is too excessive does not work, and if giving workers all of the personal control they desire is not effective, what do managers do to achieve the proper balance? First, people need to possess personal control; therefore, give them the amount of control they are able to handle. Second, make certain that workers given control believe they can use it effectively. Help them translate their effort into successful performance. Third, recognize that organizational control systems influence the personal control perceptions of organizational members. These, in turn, change behavior and attitudes.

By interviewing and/or surveying employees, managers can learn more about employees' needs for control. Through organizational scans, managers can determine the amount and location of control already existing in the organization, as well as the areas needing control. The objective then becomes one of achieving the best possible match between employees and their work environment.

17.7 | Management by Objectives: A Planning and Control Technique

7. Describe management by objectives as a philosophy and as a management tool/technique; describe its effects.

When people are personally committed to their organization's plans, those plans are more likely to be accomplished. This truism is the philosophy underlying management by objectives.

Management by objectives (MBO) is a philosophy of management, a planning and controlling technique, and an employee-involvement program.[60] As a management philosophy, MBO stems from the human resource model and Theory Y's assumption that employees are capable of self-direction and self- control. MBO also is anchored in Maslow's need theory. The reasoning is that employee involvement in the planning and control processes provides opportunities for the employee to immerse the self in work-related activities, to experience work as more meaningful, and to satisfy higher-order needs (such as self-esteem), which leads to increased motivation and job performance (see **Exhibit 17.16**). It is hypothesized that, through involvement, employee commitment to a planned course of action will be enhanced and job satisfaction will be increased.

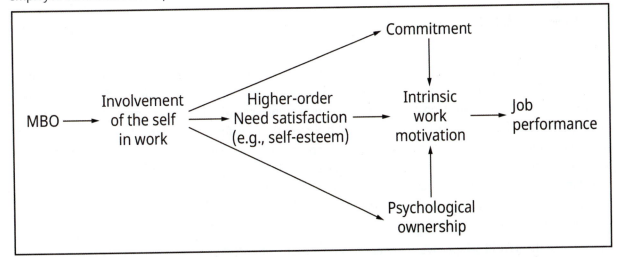

Exhibit 17.16 MBO and Its Effect on Employees (Attribution: Copyright Rice University, OpenStax, under CC-BY 4.0 license)

Although there are many variations in the practice of MBO, it is basically a process by which an organization's goals, plans, and control systems are defined through collaboration between managers and their employees. Together they identify common goals, define the results expected from each individual, and use these measurements to guide the operation of their unit and to assess individual contributions.[61] In this process, the knowledge and skills of many organizational members are used. Rather than managers telling workers "These are your goals"—the approach of classical management philosophy—managers ask workers to join them in deciding what their goals should be.

After an acceptable set of goals has been established for each employee through a give-and-take, collaborative process, employees play a major role in developing an action plan for achieving these goals. In the final stage in the MBO process, employees develop control processes, monitor their own performance, and recommend corrections if unplanned deviations occur. At this stage, the entire process begins again. **Exhibit 17.17** depicts the major stages of the MBO process.

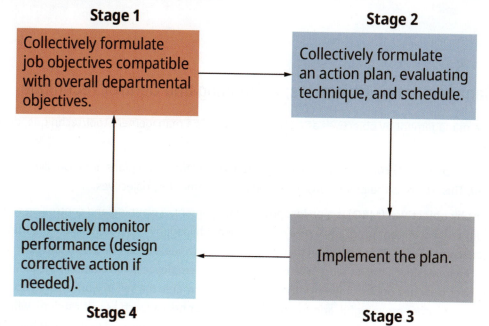

Exhibit 17.17   The Management by Objective (MBO) Process (Attribution: Copyright Rice University, OpenStax, under CC-BY 4.0 license)

The Theory of MBO

MBO has the potential to enhance organizational effectiveness. The following four major components of the MBO process are believed to contribute to its effectiveness: (1) setting specific goals; (2) setting realistic and acceptable goals; (3) joint participation in goal setting, planning, and controlling; and (4) feedback.[62] First, as we saw earlier, employees working with goals outperform employees working without goals. Second, it is assumed that participation contributes to the setting of realistic goals for which there is likely to be goal acceptance and commitment. Setting realistic and acceptable goals is an important precondition for successful outcomes, especially if the goals are difficult and challenging in nature. Finally, feedback plays an important role. It is only through feedback that employees learn whether they should sustain or redirect their efforts in order to reach their goal, and it is only through feedback that they learn whether or not they are investing sufficient effort.

Thus, from a theoretical perspective, there are several reasons why MBO should produce a positive impact on employee performance, motivation, commitment, and job satisfaction. In the next section, we briefly look at what the research tells us about the effectiveness of MBO programs.

The Evidence

In both the public and private sectors, MBO is a widely employed management tool. A recent review of the research on MBO provides us with a clear and consistent view of the effects of these programs. In the 70 cases studied by Robert Rodgers and John Hunter, 68 showed increased productivity gains, and only 2 showed losses.[63] In addition, the increases in performance were significant. Rodgers and Hunter report that the mean increase exceeded 40 percent.

While the results are generally positive in nature, differences in performance effects appear to be associated with the level of top management commitment. In those cases where top management is emotionally, intellectually (that is, top management espouses the value and importance of MBO), and behaviorally (top management actually uses MBO themselves) committed, the performance effects tend to be the strongest. The weakest MBO effects appear when top management does very little to "talk the value/importance of MBO" and they don't use the system themselves, even as they implement it for others.[64] This evidence tells us that "the processes" used to implement MBO may render a potentially effective program ineffective. Thus, not only should managers pay attention to the strategies used to facilitate planning and controlling (like MBO), they should also be concerned with how they go about implementing the plans. MBO requires top management commitment, and it should be initiated from the top down.[65]

Research shows that an MBO program can play a meaningful role in achieving commitment to a course of action and improving performance. In fact, research clearly documents instances where MBO programs have increased organizational effectiveness. Still, there have been failures. After reviewing 185 studies of MBO programs, one researcher concluded that they are effective under some circumstances but not all.[66] For example, MBO tends to be more effective in the short term (less than two years), in the private sector, and in organizations removed from direct contact with customers. These factors also affect the success of an MBO program:

- The intensity of upper-level managers' commitment: Half-hearted commitment to an MBO system is associated with a higher failure rate.
- The time element: Is there enough time for employees to learn how to participate in an MBO process, that is, to learn how to set meaningful goals, develop good action statements, and develop effective monitoring systems? Is there enough time for employees to learn how to assume responsibility in a new context? Is there enough time for employees and managers to collaborate in a joint planning and controlling process?
- The legitimacy of the system: Is it integrated into an overall philosophy of management? Or does it seem like a gimmick to seduce employees into being more productive?
- The integration of employees' goals: Are goals for each employee integrated well enough into the goals of their larger work unit?

To be truly effective over the long haul, MBO programs probably need to be coupled with some type of gainsharing program (that is, programs whereby organizations share some of the financial gains accrued from the ideas, productivity improvements, and cost savings that stem from employee participation). Based on his extensive observation of involvement-oriented organizations, Edward E. Lawler III notes that information, knowledge, power, and rewards are four key components of an effective and sustained high involvement.[67] Typically, MBO systems don't provide mechanisms through which employees share in the economic gains that may accrue to the organization as a result of their expanded role and responsibility. In light of the conditions that influence the effectiveness of MBO programs, management is challenged to provide an appropriate context for the design and maintenance of an effective MBO system.

CONCEPT CHECK

1. What is management by objectives?

17.8 | The Control- and Involvement-Oriented Approaches to Planning and Controlling

8. Differentiate between the execution of the planning and controlling activities under control- and involvement-oriented management practices.

Planning and controlling are approached with distinctive differences under control-oriented and involvement-oriented approaches to management. In the mechanistic organization, both activities tend to be lodged with management in the organizational hierarchy, often above the point in the organization where the plans are being carried out. The hierarchy plays an active role in both the planning and controlling process, and the employee is often a passive player carrying out the planning directives and the target of the control activity.

The organic organization, with its involvement-oriented management practices, places the employee as an active player in both the planning and controlling activity. Management's role becomes one of a consultant, facilitator, enabler, philosopher, teacher, coach, and resource provider as employees take on active roles in planning and controlling and in assuming responsibility for the execution of both activities.

Upper-level managers assume responsibility for planning and controlling their units while employees assume the right and responsibility for planning and controlling at their job level. As upper-level managers carry out their planning and controlling activities, they do so by soliciting input from those below them in the organizational hierarchy.

Systems such as MBO are much more likely to characterize the planning and controlling process in involvement-oriented organizations than in control-oriented organizations. Control in high-involvement organizations is diffused through many groups and is commonly focused on task accomplishment and overcoming obstacles, with a de-emphasis on fixing blame with a particular individual for performance failures. In many control-oriented management systems, the reins of control are firmly held by the hierarchy, and the activities of individuals are carefully controlled. Performance failures, therefore, tend to become focused on the individual who fails to perform.

Finally, mechanistic organizations are more likely to create large planning departments and to centralize the planning function with specialists. As organizations confront increasing environmental or technology-induced uncertainty, rapid environmental change, and turbulence, planning and controlling move closer to the point in the organization where the plans are implemented and carried out on a day-to-day basis. In place of hierarchy-based control, organizations rely more on professional employees and groups of employees to control their own actions as they execute organizational plans.

Exhibit 17.18   Maersk Line ship A new blockchain solution from IBM and Maersk will help manage and track the paper trail of tens of millions of shipping containers across the world by digitizing the supply chain process. (Credit: Kees Torn/ flickr/ Attribution 2.0 Generic (CC BY 2.0))

MANAGING CHANGE

Blockchain and Managing Currency Fluctuations

When a business goes from being local, even if local is defined as a whole country, to being a global business, a whole new set of constraints is presented and must be controlled and planned. Traditionally, currency fluctuations can be one of the more interesting if not daunting elements of global business. Modern technology, however, has taken that challenge one step further.

The impact of currency fluctuations on profitability is discussed in economics, finance, and various accounting texts. What currency should be used to buy inventory? To sell inventory? How do puts and calls mitigate currency fluctuations? Is the added expense worth covering the potential loss? These are all questions businesses must consider when moving into a global market. When Tata Consultancy Services, India's largest software services exporter, reported first quarter results that were below expectations in the first quarter of 2017, much of the blame was laid on currency fluctuations, which accounted for 80 basis points of the drop in profitability (Alawadhi 2017).

But starting in 2009, financial transactions, including global financial transactions, became a little more complicated. Or did they? Bitcoin emerged in 2009 from an unknown source only known as Satoshi Nakamoto (The Economist Explains 2015). Built on what is called blockchain technology, Bitcoin and other cryptocurrencies (jargon for digital assets that are secured by cryptography) are a technological unknown in the future of exchange and financing. The technology behind blockchain and the resulting assets is complicated but not necessary to understand the potential effects of the technology. Effectively, Bitcoin is a "peer-to-peer electronic cash system that uses a distributed ledger to bypass central control systems for transactions" (Pepijn 2017). As peer-to-peer transactions, cryptocurrencies bypass the normal channels, such as banks and credit card processors. Theoretically, this lowers transaction costs for both the buyer and the seller. Blockchain, which can include assets beyond currency, also allows firms to raise funds directly from investors, bypassing investment bankers and venture capitalists. According to the *Financial Post*, "High levels of encryption protect the transaction by validating the parties involved and by preventing hacking, erasure or amendments" (Francis 2017).

Bitcoin uses blockchain technology to maintain a record of its currency ecosystem. The viability of blockchain technology as a thing in itself should not be confused with Bitcoin's price volatility, which has seen its price increase (and decrease) by several orders of magnitude. Shady bitcoin exchanges and a shifting regulatory landscape, a result of governments attempting to regulate the very concept of a means of exchange, have produced enormous swings up and down (Crypto Investor 2017).

But however volatile the new currencies, blockchain technology is seeing other, relatively sane applications. Isabel Cooke at Barclays has already used "distributed ledger technology," or blockchain technology, to process a trade finance transaction in the real world: "Our pilot trade brought the sign-off time from ten days to four hours. It reduced costs, added transparency, decreased risk and looked to improve the customer experience" (Why blockchain is 'difficult and exciting' 2017). With an immutable, public ledger to work from, "Creating a really clear audit trail across organisations provides real value – whether that's with land registration or trade finance. If we have a shared view of data on ledgers, we can then build business logic on top of that, and that can apply to interest rates swaps or smart contracts within the investment bank" (Crypto Investor 2017).

So are blockchains and cryptocurrencies the wave of the future or just a modern financial bubble or threat to global financial security? Some industry writers say that the decentralization and lower costs of the technology are necessary and will launch even more industries (Pepijn 2017). Even governments and central banks are looking at the potential benefits and costs savings of an electronic currency. According to investment banker Alex Tapscott, if the Bank of England replaced 30 percent of the traditional British currency with digital money, he thinks it would add 3 percent to British GDP. The expectation is that digital currency would lower consumer prices and increase sellers' profits. And the encryption technology would prevent counterfeiting, fraud, or tampering (Francis 2017).

In a perfect world, exchanges in a global currency, such as the blockchain-based crypotocurrencies, could sidestep currency fluctuations. In the real world, however, the wild value fluctuations of cryptocurrencies mean blockchain technology has a way to go before delivering on that possibility, if it ever does.

Sources:

Alawadhi, Neha. 2017. "Currency fluctuations and BFSI, retail sluggishness hurt TCS's Q1 show." Moneycontrol.com. http://www.moneycontrol.com/news/business/earnings-business/currency-fluctuations-and-bfsi-retail-sluggishness-hurt-tcss-q1-show-2325575.html

Crypto Investor. 2017. "Bitcoin: Three Ways the Bubble Could Pop." *Medium.com,* September 15, 2017. https://medium.com/@Truth_Investor/bitcoin-three-ways-the-bubble-will-pop-40678ce11698

Economist Explains, The. 2015. "Who is Satoshi Nakamoto?" *The Economist,* November 2, 1015. https://www.economist.com/blogs/economist-explains/2015/11/economist-explains-1

Francis, Diane. 2017. "Why the smart money is betting on blockchain." *Financial Post.* http://business.financialpost.com/diane-francis/why-the-smart-money-is-betting-on-blockchain

Pepijn, Daan. 2017. "With smart controls and contracts, blockchain tech is bridging the real and virtual worlds." *The Next Web.* https://thenextweb.com/contributors/2017/07/31/smart-controls-contracts-blockchain-tech-bridging-real-virtual-worlds/#.tnw_oDCnSKF2

"Why blockchain is 'difficult and exciting.'" 2017. *Barclays,* May 16, 2017. https://www.home.barclays/news/2017/05/Isabel-Cooke-on-blockchain.html

Questions

1. What other applications can you see for blockchain technology? Would they reduce costs?
2. What drawbacks or potentials risks do you see in blockchain technology?
3. Do you think blockchain technology could be used to offset currency fluctuations? Would this likely increase or decrease the risk?
4. Why would governments be suspicious of cryptocurrencies and consider regulating or outlawing them? Have any governments done so to date?

CONCEPT CHECK

1. Describe the execution of the planning and controlling activities under control- and involvement-oriented management practices.

🔑 Key Terms

action statements The means by which an organization moves forward to attain its goals.

administrative plans Plans that work to integrate institutional-level plans with the operating plans and tie together all of the plans created for the organization's technical core.

concurrent controls Controls intended to prevent deviation from a planned course of action while work is in progress.

contingency plans Plans that deal with alternative courses of action.

controlling Monitoring the behavior of organizational members and the effectiveness of the organization itself to determine whether organizational goals are being achieved and taking corrective action if necessary.

cybernetic control Self-regulating control procedures.

Deming cycle A planning model directed toward attaining continuous improvement by integrating organizational learning into the planning process (plan, do, check, act).

domain/directional planning The development of a course of action that moves an organization toward one domain or direction (and, therefore, away from other domains or directions).

goal hierarchy The interrelationship among an organization's job-, department-, divisional-, and organizational-level goals.

goal planning Development of action statements to move toward the attainment of a specific goal.

hybrid control system Control system that exercises control prior to, during, and after the performance of a work activity.

hybrid planning The coupling of domain and goal planning.

management by objectives (MBO) A philosophy of management, a planning and controlling technique, and an employee involvement program.

noncybernetic control Control systems that operate independently from the work system that is being monitored; a monitoring system that is external to the target of control.

official goals The aims of an organization that are expressed in highly abstract and general terms, generally employed for the organization's external constituents.

operating plans Direction and action statements for activities in the organization's technical core.

operational goals The aims of an organization that reflect management's specific intentions.

outcome or goal statements End states—the targets and outcomes that managers hope to attain.

planning The process by which managers establish goals and specify how these goals are to be attained.

postaction controls Controls employed after a product or service is complete.

precontrols Controls designed to prevent deviation from a desired plan of action before work actually begins.

single-use plans Plans developed for unique situations or problems and one-time use.

standing plans Rules, policies, and procedures about how to deal with issues that managers face repeatedly.

strategic plans Hierarchical plans that address an organization's institutional-level needs and attempt to position it advantageously within its task environment.

📑 Summary of Learning Outcomes

17.1 Is Planning Important

1. Understand the importance of planning and why organizations need to plan and control.

Planning is the process through which managers establish goals and detail how these goals will be attained.

17.2 The Planning Process

2. Outline the planning and controlling processes.

There are five major stages in the planning process. First, an organization establishes its preplanning foundation, which reviews past events and describes the current situation. In the second step, the organization sets forth goals based on the preplanning foundation. In the third step, managers forecast what is likely to happen in the organization's internal and external environments in order to develop alternative courses of action. Then, managers identify possible courses of action for meeting their objectives, evaluate each alternative, and select a course of action. Finally, planners develop the supportive plans necessary to accomplish the organization's major plan of action. Once implemented, that plan is monitored and controlled so that it meets the goals established in the second step.

17.3 Types of Plans

3. Identify different types of plans and control systems employed by organizations.

Managers create many types of plans based on hierarchical level, frequency of use, time frame, and organizational scope. Contingency plans to be used in case of unexpected events or wrong assumptions are critical for effective management in highly turbulent environments.

17.4 Goals or Outcome Statements

4. Explain the individual and organizational effects associated with goal setting and planning.

Goal development is an important part of the planning process. Goals developed for employees, for departments, and for entire organizations greatly enhance organizational effectiveness. Evidence reveals that performance is higher when organizations, as well as individuals, operate under difficult (but attainable), specific goals.

17.5 Formal Organizational Planning in Practice

5. Understand how planning occurs in today's organizations.

Plans reduce uncertainty and risk, focus attention on goals, and enhance understanding of the external environment. Although most major organizations engage in formal planning, many managers fail to plan appropriately. Lack of time, uncertainty about the future, and fear of failure are among the reasons given by managers for their failure to plan.

17.6 Employees' Responses to Planning

6. Discuss the impact that control has on organizational members.

The primary purposes of the controlling function are to monitor the extent to which an organization's plans are being followed and their effectiveness and to identify when and where it is necessary to take corrective action. To accomplish these ambitious tasks, managers construct control systems that touch most aspects of an organization's functional areas, its relationship with the external and internal environments, and its relationships across different hierarchical levels.

The control process consists of four steps. In Steps 1 and 2, managers create standards and monitor ongoing organizational behavior. In Step 3, they examine the degree to which ongoing activity is consistent with their goals and means objectives and the relationship between the two. In Step 4, managers develop prescriptions to correct problems, to maintain strengths, and to provide feedback to an organization's planners.

Whereas all control systems have the same general purposes, they differ in their specifics. Some are self-managing cybernetic systems; noncybernetic systems require regular external supervision to be effective. Other variations in control systems include the point at which control activities are applied: before the work has begun (precontrols), while work is in progress (concurrent controls), and after work has been completed (postaction controls). A hybrid control system engages a variety of control activities at many points in time.

Although there are variations in control systems, all good systems have characteristics that enable them to work well in a given organization. Managers evaluating a control system might thus gauge its adequacy in providing accurate, timely, objective information to appropriate people in the organization. They also should examine whether the system focuses on the most critical aspects of their organization's conditions in a feasible, flexible manner that will be accepted by organizational members. Because of the importance of the information it provides, a good control system should also be integrated with planning activities.

Any control system can produce both positive and negative effects. If it is well designed, a control system provides needed structure and feedback and facilitates the development and execution of effective goal-setting programs. The result can be a satisfied, motivated, and productive workforce. Inappropriate control systems, however, can cause frustration, dissatisfaction, and poor performance. Being aware of a control system's potential effects on organization members helps managers capitalize on its positive aspects, reduce the impact of negative effects, and promote workers' acceptance of the system.

The effort to maintain control is not restricted to managers. All employees have a need for personal control, a need that sometimes conflicts with their organization's need to maintain control. To achieve effectiveness, managers must balance the control needs of both the organization and its members.

17.7 Management by Objectives: A Planning and Control Technique

7. Describe management by objectives as a philosophy and as a management tool/technique; describe its effects.

Management by objectives (MBO), with its emphasis on goal setting, participation, and feedback, frequently contributes to increased employee goal commitment, motivation, and performance. If performance matches the employee's aspirations, job satisfaction is likely to be an important by-product of the organization's planning and controlling activities.

17.8 The Control- and Involvement-Oriented Approaches to Planning and Controlling

8. Differentiate between the execution of the planning and controlling activities under control- and involvement-oriented management practices.

Planning and controlling are approached with distinctive differences under control-oriented and involvement-oriented approaches to management. In the mechanistic organization, both activities tend to be lodged with management in the organizational hierarchy, often above the point in the organization where the plans are being carried out. The hierarchy plays an active role in both the planning and controlling process, and the employee is often a passive player carrying out the planning directives and the target of the control activity.

Chapter Review Questions

1. Define managerial planning and controlling.
2. Discuss the relationship between the two managerial functions of planning and controlling.
3. Identify and briefly describe each stage in the planning and controlling processes.
4. Compare and contrast three different types of planning.
5. What are multiple goals? What is a goal hierarchy? How are these concepts related?
6. Briefly describe the two views of the goal formulation process, and explain how they differ.
7. Describe the MBO process, the philosophy behind it, and its relationship with performance.
8. Distinguish between cybernetic and noncybernetic control and between pre, concurrent, and postaction

control systems.

9.   Identify and discuss three positive and three negative effects often associated with control systems.

10.   How does the desire for personal control affect managers, and how can they balance it with organizational control systems?

Management Skills Application Exercises

1.   Use the tools described in this chapter to write a plan that will help you set goals, plans on how to achieve them (e.g., achieve an A average in all of my core concentration courses and A– in all courses I am taking). Also account for personal time and other activities you are involved in and goals that you have for these, such as keeping physically fit, etc.

2.   You are managing a small manufacturing operation that involved the final assembly of Children sippy cups. There are two components to the sippy cup: the cup, a lid, and a straw as well as the box that will hold the product. You have 2 direct reports who you can assign to assemble the product. You also have a dotted-line report with the purchasing agent for the company that procures the components of the product (a dotted-line report is where one employee must work for and report to more than one manager) as well as the boxes and material needed (e.g., plastic that is used on the shrink-wrapping machine) to complete the product for sale. You have been given the following metrics.

     a.   You have been given a goal of producing 2,300 units per week.

     b.   It takes 1 minute to assemble the sippy cup.

     c.   It takes 45 seconds to place the sippy cup in the box and shrink-wrap the product.

     d.   It takes 15 seconds to examine the product for meeting quality, and you expect that 99.5% of the products will meet or exceed expectations.

     e.   The employees work for 8 hours per day.

     Write up a plan that has achievable goals for your two direct reports and your dotted-line report. Also prepare a memo to your supervisor about how you plan on achieving your goal.

3.   You and another student will engage in a role-play exercise. One will be the manager, and one will be an employee who is not happy with the aggressive goals that he has been given. After a 10-minute discussion, you both report on what was resolved, what was not, and how this would affect job satisfaction and performance for the employee.

Managerial Decision Exercises

1.   You are a manager, and your direct report is complaining about not being involved in the planning process. How do you respond?

2.   You are a sales manager and have reviewed the monthly sales goals and conclude that the targets can't be achieved without additional hires or paying employees overtime to secure additional orders. Also, you think that the product could have an 8% price increase without hindering sales units. You review the operational plans and want to provide an alteration of the plans to your boss. What should you do to plan that discussion?

Critical Thinking Case

How Do Amazon, UPS, and FedEx Manage Peak Seasons?

Typically, the day after Thanksgiving (Black Friday) marks the beginning of the holiday shopping season in the United States. Holiday sales, typically defined as sales occurring in November and December, account for roughly 30 percent of annual sales for U.S. retailers (Holiday Forecasts and Historical Sales 2015). For 2016, total online sales from November 10 to December 31 amounted to 91.7 billion dollars. And the top retailers for this period were eBay, Amazon, Walmart, and Target (Tasker 2016). The growth in online sales appears inevitable, but how do the top shippers, UPS and FedEx, manage the sudden upsurge?

Not always so well. In 2013, both FedEx and UPS underestimated holiday demand, and with bad weather conditions as well, struggled to deliver packages as promised. Since then, both carriers have worked hard to keep adequate resources available to handle the end-of-year upsurge. But in 2014, UPS overcompensated and had too much capacity, once again damaging profitability (Livengood 2017).

Matching retailer expectations to reality is a challenge, and not just for the shipping companies. Although retailers would prefer to know how much to expect in sales, forecasts will be inaccurate, sometimes wildly so. In preparing its forecast for the 2017 peak season, Logistics Management examined economic factors, such as GDP, job growth, retail sales, and inventory levels. It also looked at imports. An informal survey of logistical professionals found that 93.5 percent expect the 2017 season to be the same as 2016 (35.5 percent) or more active (58 percent) (Berman 2017).

In June 2017, UPS announced that it would be adding a surcharge to some peak season rates. According to the UPS website, "During the 2016 holiday season, the company's average daily volume exceeded 30 million packages on more than half of the available shipping days. In contrast, on an average nonpeak day, the company ships more than 19 million packages" (UPS Establishes New Peak Shipping Charge 2017). The rate for the 2017 peak season would apply to select services and to oversize shipments, primarily (UPS Establishes New Peak Shipping Charge 2017). Analysts see the surcharge as a signal that UPS is the rate setter in parcel delivery. Such an assessment is not surprising given that the increase in parcel delivery as an outcome of increased e-commerce is seen as a core driver of earnings for UPS (Franck 2017).

Second-ranked FedEx, in contrast, announced that it would not follow suit but instead would "forgo most holiday surcharges on home deliveries this year" (Schlangenstein 2017). The surcharges levied by UPS are aimed primarily at small shippers, not the larger contract shippers. By not adding a seasonal surcharge, FedEx might hope to capture sales from individuals and small businesses that are deterred by the UPS surcharge (Schlangenstein 2017).

Kevin Sterling, a Seaport Global Holdings analyst, believes that FedEx has the existing capacity to absorb additional ground shipments. "[FedEx is] going to let UPS be Scrooge at Christmas" (Schlangenstein 2017). UPS already has a contract with Amazon, the de facto behemoth of online shopping, for normal shipping, leaving room for FedEx to pick up the slack during the holiday rush (Schlangenstein 2017).

In contrast, UPS reports that the additional charge is needed to offset the costs of additional resources necessary to achieve expected upsurges in capacity. UPS spokesperson Glenn Zaccara commented, "UPS's peak season pricing positions the company to be appropriately compensated for the high value we provide at a time when the company must double daily delivery volume for six to seven consecutive weeks to meet customer demands" (Schlangenstein 2017).

With or without surcharges, price structures at both companies strive to discourage shipment of heavy, odd-sized, or oversized packages because such packages won't flow through either company's sorting systems and require special handling. All the same, FedEx has seen a 240 percent increase in such shipments over the last 10 years, which make up roughly 10 percent of all packages shipped using its ground services. And although

FedEx is not adding a holiday surcharge, per se, it has added charges for packages that require extra handling, particularly shipments between November 20 through December 24 (Schlangenstein 2017).

Sources:

Berman, Jeff. 2017. "Prospects for Peak Season appear to be cautiously optimistic." *Logistics Management.* http://www.logisticsmgmt.com/article/prospects_for_peak_season_appear_to_be_cautiously_optimistic

Franck, Thomas. 2017. "UPS set to make a boatload on its new surcharges during holiday season, Citi predicts." CNBC. https://www.cnbc.com/2017/08/08/ups-set-to-make-a-boatload-on-its-new-surcharges-during-holiday-season-citi-predicts.html

Holiday Forecasts and Historical Sales. 2015. National Retail Federation. https://nrf.com/resources/holiday-headquarters/holiday-forecasts-and-historical-sales

Livengood, Anna. 2017. "UPS' Peak Season Surprise." Veriship Resource Center. https://veriship.com/resources/ups-peak-season-surprise/

Schlangenstein, Mary. 2017. "FedEx Will Shun Most Home Holiday Fees, Unlike UPS." *Transport Topics.* http://www.ttnews.com/articles/fedex-will-shun-most-home-holiday-fees-unlike-ups

Tasker, Becky. 2016. "2016 Holiday Shopping: Up-To-The-Minute Data From ADI." CMO.com. http://www.cmo.com/adobe-digital-insights/articles/2016/11/8/2016-holiday-shopping-up-to-the-minute-data-from-adi.html

UPS Establishes New Peak Shipping Charge." 2017. UPS Pressroom. https://www.pressroom.ups.com/pressroom/ContentDetailsViewer.page?ConceptType=PressReleases&id=1497873904827-900

1. What do you think are some of the difficulties of adding 25 percent more employees for the holiday season? What kind of planning do you think would be needed?
2. China effectively shuts down for two weeks each year and celebrates the lunar new year. How does that resemble (or not) peak season in Western countries?
3. The case focuses on U.S. markets. How are European markets affected by holiday shopping?
4. Have your own shopping habits changed with the ease of online shopping? If so, how? Do you expect them to change when you graduate and have more disposable income?

18 Management of Technology and Innovation

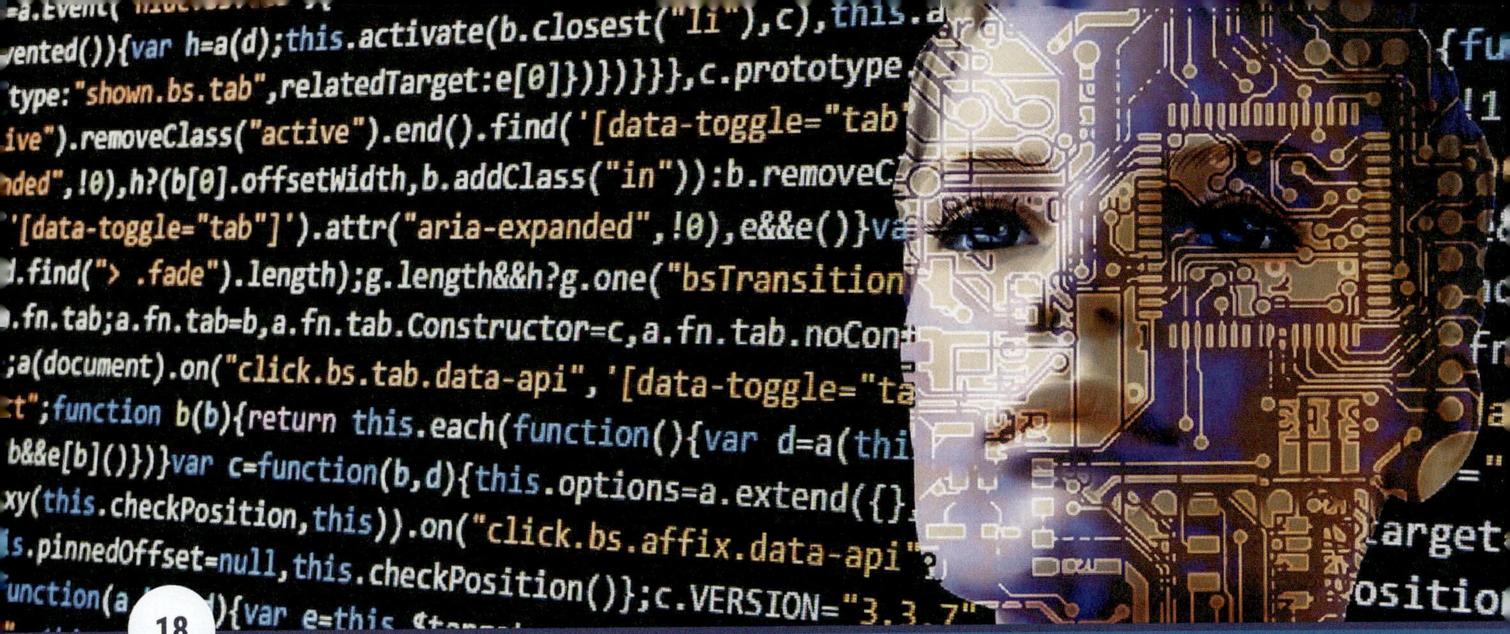

Exhibit 18.1 (Credit: 6eo tech/ flickr/ Attribution 2.0 Generic (CC BY 2.0))

Introduction

Learning Outcome

After reading this chapter, you should be able to answer these questions:

1. What do we mean by management of technology and innovation (MTI), and why is it crucial?
2. How do organizations develop technology and innovation?
3. What are external sources of technology and innovation development, and when are they best used?
4. What are internal sources of technology and innovation development, and when are they best used?
5. How and why do entrepreneurs develop MTI skills?
6. No matter what method is used, what skills do you need to successfully manage technology and innovation?
7. How do you look into the future to keep pace?

EXPLORING MANAGERIAL CAREERS

Acer Group—Becoming a Hardware + Software + Services Global Competitor

Do you think that you would be interested in a career in the technology space? Here is an overview of the history of Acer Corporation that will provide a glimpse into this industry. Acer Group was established in 1976. The Acer Group's family of brands includes Acer, Gateway, Packard Bell, and eMachines. The multibrand strategy of Acer allows each brand to target different customer needs in the worldwide personal computer market. Acer was the third-largest maker of personal computers (second largest in notebooks) in 2008 and had revenues exceeding $16 billion. In 2017, Acer is sixth in the personal computer industry with revenues exceeding $70 billion. This Taiwanese firm has established itself as a global player in the PC market and has expanded into gaming and other related businesses. How it got there is through innovative use of alliances and acquisitions as well as forward-looking development within the firm.

The Firm's History

Acer was founded in 1976 as Multitech. The focus of Multitech was on trade and product design (internal innovation). Just three years later, Multitech designed Taiwan's first mass-produced computer product. The focus from the start was on a product for export—Taiwan is such a small market the firm knew it needed to make a global footprint in the computer market. Multitech, which became Acer in 1987, developed a long-term mission to allow anyone to use and benefit from technology. They have built their reputation on development and manufacturing of sophisticated, intuitive, easy-to-use products.

Early Innovations

When Multitech first started, the PC market was young and the founders saw many opportunities. Acer holds more patents than any other Taiwanese-based corporation, and Taiwan accounts for 70 percent of global computer hardware manufacturing. When Acer beat IBM to the market with 32-bit PCs in 1986, it signaled the beginning of the end for IBM's PC business. Until 1990, Acer was more internally innovative than it was externally oriented for alliances and acquisitions.

External Technology Development

In 1990, Altos Peripherals was acquired. This marked the beginning of two decades of multiple alliances and acquisitions by Acer. Because of Acer's success in developing innovations, other companies were willing and eager to development different types of alliances. Some of the early alliances allowed Acer to partner with some of the biggest players in the computer technology industry. For example:

- 1996—Acer signed a reciprocal patent licensing agreement with IBM, Intel, and Texas Instruments allowing use of one other's patented technology.
- 1999—Acer Group and IBM formed a seven-year procurement and technology alliance.

This strategy has continued:

- 2010—Acer and Founder Technology signed a memorandum of mutual understanding to strengthen their long-term PC business cooperation.
- 2016—Acer's board of directors approved the establishment of a joint venture with Starbreeze AB to design, manufacture, promote, market, and serve StarVR Virtual Reality Head-Mounted Displays.

As Acer grew in strength in the marketplace, it began to make acquisitions. These acquisitions were aimed at multibranding as well as obtaining technological innovations. For example:

- 1998—Acer acquired Texas Instruments' TI-Acer interest and renamed the company Acer Semiconductor Manufacturing Inc.
- 2007—Acer merged with Gateway Inc.
- 2008—Acer merged with Packard Bell Inc.
- 2008—Acer acquired E-TEN.
- 2015—Acer acquired GPS cycling computer brand Xplova.
- 2016—Acer acquired wireless pet camera maker Pawbo.

To illustrate the usefulness of this strategy, in 2011 Acer Inc. bought iGware Inc. for $320 million to try to enter the potentially lucrative cloud market. Then in 2012, Acer created cloud software and infrastructure tools for devices.

Acer also developed equity-based partnerships. Examples of this strategy include:

- 2009—Acer acquired 29.9% of Olidata.
- 2015—Acer invested in robotics start-up company Jibo.
- 2016—Acer made an equity investment in grandPad, a provider of technology solutions specifically designed for senior citizens.
- 2017—Acer became largest corporate shareholder of AOPEN Inc.

Becoming a Global Competitor

While Acer was changing its business model from internal innovations as well as evolving from a manufacturing company to a development and marketing firm, it continued to spread its global footprint. It did this through various partnerships and by developing innovative products with its partners and within its own R&D areas. For example, in 2003 Acer launched the Empowering Technology Platform to meld hardware, software, and service to provide end-to-end technologies to customers. In 2008, the Aspire One was launched as the company's first mobile Internet device. In addition, Acer made a strong move into the high-end gaming market with the Aspire Predator series.

These steps were designed to enhance and strengthen Acer's global position. Acer's product range includes PC notebooks and netbooks, desktop computers, storage systems, peripheral devices, LCD televisions, and e-business solutions. The firm is number one in a number of markets with various products. The Europe, Middle East, and Africa (EMEA) market is a stronghold for Acer's mobile computing solutions. Acer is the largest supplier of LCD televisions in Western Europe. Acer is first in the notebook market in Italy, Spain, Austria, Holland, Switzerland, Russia, Belgium, Denmark, Hungary, Poland, and the Slovakian Republic.

In the United States and Canada, Acer is making its mark through its Channel Business Model (CBM). It developed this model as it expanded beyond Taiwan and continued to improve it as it divested its manufacturing facilities. This model allows Acer to be flexible in adapting to global IT market trends. CBM involves collaboration with partners and suppliers to develop and market top-tier products and services. In 2003, they used this model to co-brand a notebook computer with Ferrari, the Italian carmaker.

In 2009, Acer unveiled the Acer F900 and M900 smartphones at the Mobile World Congress. They began by shipping to channel partners in EMEA and Asia. These products have a relatively large 3.8-inch-wide VGA display and a 3.75G HSPA connectivity for high-speed data transfer, and they are the introductory products with Acer's new widget-based user interface that provides easy navigation with vivid 3D animation. The acquisition of Packard Bell was key to Acer's entrance into this market with this advanced product.

From 2008 to 2013, Acer's strategy was to enhance worldwide presence with a new multibrand strategy. With the successful completion of the mergers of Gateway and Packard Bell, Acer then heavily emphasized its goal to further strengthen its global footprint with a multibrand strategy and solid partnerships. Since 2014, the Acer Group has been transforming into a hardware + software + services company.

To accomplish this shift, Acer needed to spin off or divest certain units. This accomplished two things: 1) it made cash available for acquisitions and other new business development, and 2) it refocused the strategy of Acer.

Examples of the spin-offs and divestments included:

- 2000—Acer spun off its manufacturing operation to focus on developing technologically advanced, user-friendly solutions.
- 2000—Acer split off its OEM (Original Equipment Manufacturing) business unit to create Wistron Corp., an independent design and IT manufacturing company.

Acer continues to lead in notebook technology while extending its product lines to enhance people's lives through technology. In notebook technology, Acer was the leader in branding notebooks (Ferrari 4000 carbon-fiber notebook—2005), green notebooks (2010), and lightest notebook with the longest battery life (Aspire line—2012), as well as the Chromebook launch in 2015 with a 15.6-inch screen. However, its product lines have multiplied into cloud technology, gaming, and other technologies that "add value to customers' lives" (Acer annual report).

Acer has used a variety of strategic moves to continue to be competitive in the changing world of computer-related technology. Early on, they used internal innovation as a primary growth strategy to build reputation and establish a footprint in the industry. Then they used external methods of acquiring technology and markets—mergers, acquisitions, alliances, joint ventures, equity positions, etc. Acer continues to nurture its strengths in research and development while continuing to look for new opportunities for acquisition and alliances.

Sources: Anonymous. 2009. Acer website , "Showcases Multi-brand Products at Computex 2009 including Aspire Timeline Notebook, Aspire One Netbook, Aspire All-In-One PC." *JCN Newswire- Japan Corporate News Network*. Tokyo, June 3, 2018; www.acer-group.com; Acer Group 10-K reports.

18.1 | MTI—Its Importance Now and In the Future

1. What do we mean by management of technology and innovation (MTI), and why is it crucial?

Management of technology and innovation is critical to the organization. Because of innovations and new technologies, we have historically seen the emergence of innovative organizational structures and new ways of performing work. For example, the Industrial Revolution ushered in the functional structure for organizations. As business moved from small craft businesses like blacksmiths to railroads, there was a need to introduce a more complex business structure. Today, we see the innovations in information technology changing structures to more network based with people being able to work remotely. The changes in structure are innovations in the technology of how work is accomplished; the innovations brought on by the invention of new products influence the technology we use and how we use it.

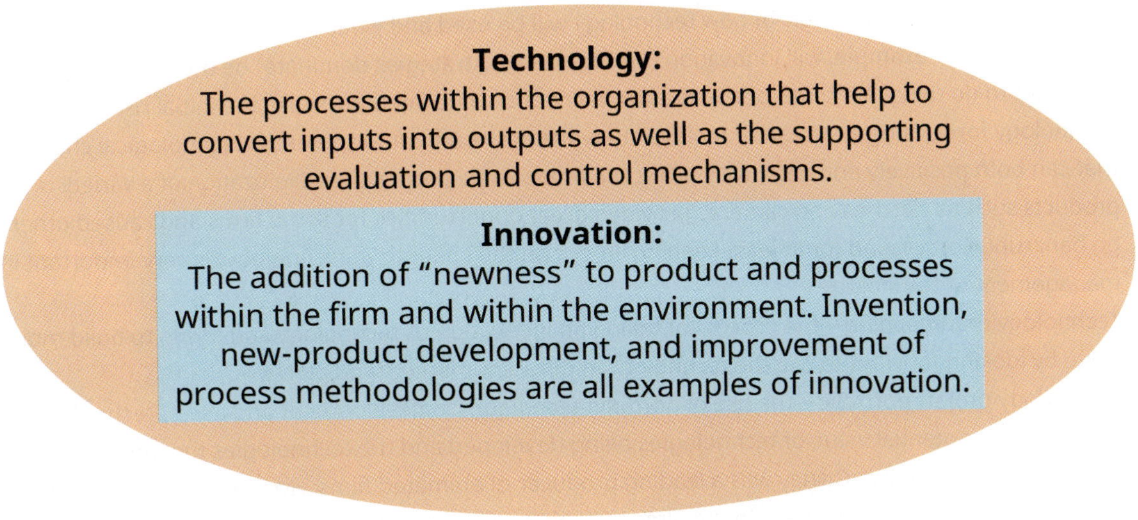

Technology:
The processes within the organization that help to convert inputs into outputs as well as the supporting evaluation and control mechanisms.

Innovation:
The addition of "newness" to product and processes within the firm and within the environment. Invention, new-product development, and improvement of process methodologies are all examples of innovation.

Exhibit 18.2   Technology and Innovation Defined (Attribution: Copyright Rice University, OpenStax, under CC-BY 4.0 license)

Technology can be defined in a number of ways. The basic purpose of a system (such as an organization) is to convert inputs into outputs. Therefore, we will define organizational technology as the processes within the organization that help to convert inputs into outputs as well as the supporting evaluation and control mechanisms. The **management of technology** involves the planning, implementation, evaluation, and control of the organization's resources and capabilities in order to create value and competitive advantage. This involves managing:

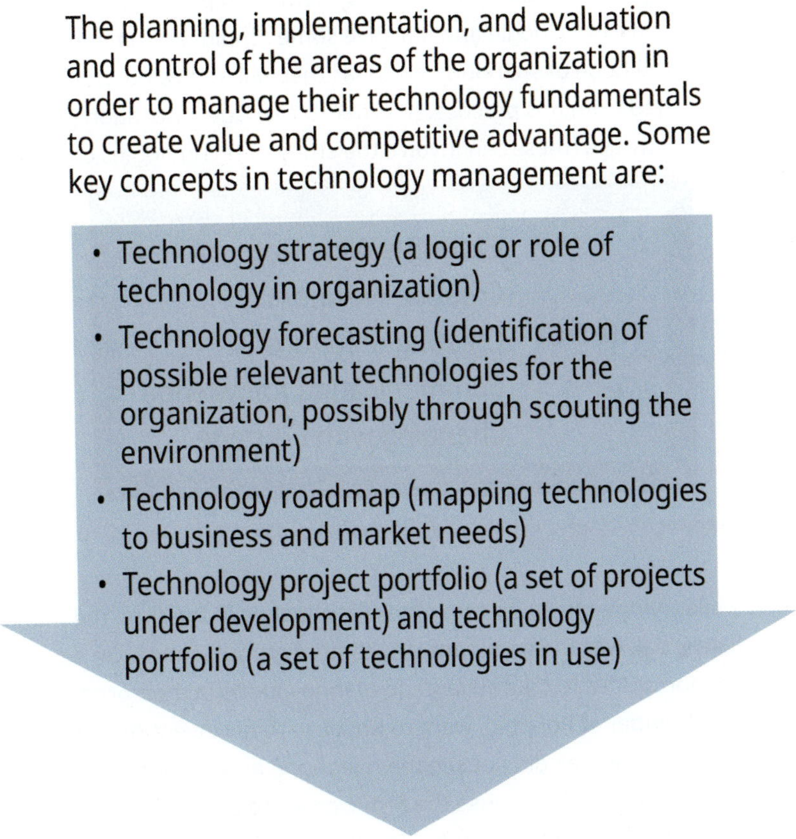

The planning, implementation, and evaluation and control of the areas of the organization in order to manage their technology fundamentals to create value and competitive advantage. Some key concepts in technology management are:

- Technology strategy (a logic or role of technology in organization)
- Technology forecasting (identification of possible relevant technologies for the organization, possibly through scouting the environment)
- Technology roadmap (mapping technologies to business and market needs)
- Technology project portfolio (a set of projects under development) and technology portfolio (a set of technologies in use)

Exhibit 18.3   Management of Technology (Attribution: Copyright Rice University, OpenStax, under CC-BY 4.0 license)

1. Technology strategy—the logic of how technology will be used and what role technology will have in the organization. For example, will innovation (first-to-market strategies dominate) be the focus, or will the firm want to do things better to obtain market share and value (let others take the initial risks)?

2. Technology forecasting—the use of tools to study the environment for potential technological changes that can both positively and negatively affect the firm's value proposition. Digitization of a variety of products such as watches and cameras provided great opportunities for some firms and caused others to go bankrupt. Forecasting (or at least keeping an eye on the changes in technology) is very important in management of technology.

3. Technology roadmapping—the process of taking an innovation or technology and trying to build more value by looking for ways to use the technology in different markets and places.

4. Technology project portfolio—the use of portfolio techniques in development and use of technology enhances the potential value of technologies being developed and the technologies that are currently part of a firm's portfolio. Disney was a leading producer of animated films. However, Disney did not stop there—the portfolio of characters in the films are now marketed as products and displayed in Disney theme parks, and Disney very carefully manages the availability of the animated films.

Innovation activities are an important subset of technology activities. Innovation includes "newness" in the development and used of products and/or processes within a firm and within an industry. Invention, new product development, and process-improvement methods are all examples of innovation. **Management of innovation** includes both change management and managing organizational processes that encourage innovation. The management of innovation is more than just planning new products, services, brand extensions, or technology inventions—it is about imagining, mobilizing, and competing in new ways. For the organization, innovation management involves setting up systems and processes that allow newness that adds value to emerge. Some firms, like Google and 3M, give some employees time during the workweek to work on their own ideas with the hope of sparking new ideas that will add value. Google News and 3M Post-it Notes are products that emerged from this practice. In order to manage innovation processes successfully, the firm must undertake several activities (these can involve the study of technologies currently in use).

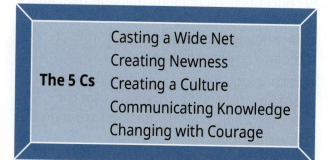

Exhibit 18.4   Innovation Management (Attribution: Copyright Rice University, OpenStax, under CC-BY 4.0 license)

1. Casting a wide net while trying to keep up with potential changes in the firm, the market, the competition, etc. is crucial. Eastman Kodak was the dominant U.S. camera manufacturer. On several occasions in their history they missed opportunities to take advantage of innovations in their product line—they did not cast their net out. Land, the founder of Polaroid, went to Kodak with his invention of instant photographs—Kodak said no. Kodak did not see the telephone as a potential competitor until it was too late. Kodak was especially vulnerable because the firm was a late entrant into the digital camera market. As a result of failure to cast a wide net in keeping up with trends and innovations, Kodak went bankrupt.

2. Creating newness with existing products can expand the portfolio of value of a product. 3M has done this with all kinds of tape and with different formats and forms of Post-it Notes. Asking "how else can the

product be altered or used?" is critical to developing platforms of products.

3. Creating a culture open to newness is critical to cultivating ideas. If the leadership of the firm is open to ideas from all over the organization, then the firm will be more innovative. Some large firms such as Texas Instruments encourage employees to start new businesses if TI does not want to keep a product in house. Often, TI is the first investor and customer of these small firms.

4. Communicating knowledge throughout the firm is important. This knowledge can be positive and negative at first glance. For Post-it Notes, the glue used emerged from the laboratory efforts to create a stronger glue to compete with Elmer's Super Glue. Obviously, the outcome did not meet the original goal, but the communication of the new formula's characteristics—tacky and leaves no residue—triggered other usage.

5. Changing with courage is necessary if a firm is going to manage innovation and stay competitive. Too often firms get comfortable with where they are, narrow their focus in studying the environment, and focus on building strength in their current market. This leads to **strategic inertia**—not innovating and losing customers and market share to more innovative companies. Just as Kodak failed to change, so did IBM—famously, the CEO of IBM was quoted as saying "who wants a computer on their desk?" as IBM continued manufacturing mainframes while desktops and then laptops were emerging.

MANAGING CHANGE

E-Hubs Integrate Global Commerce

Thanks to the wonders of technological advancement, global electronic trading now goes far beyond the Internet retailing and trading that we are all familiar with. Special websites known as trading hubs, or eMarketplaces, facilitate electronic commerce between businesses in specific industries such as automotive manufacturing, retailing, telecom provisioning, aerospace, financial products and services, and more. Virtually all Forex (foreign exchange) is done via trading hubs that provide an open market for trading of a variety of currencies. Because there are a large number of trades involving currencies, the price is discoverable and there is transparency in the market. By contrast, Bitcoin is mainly traded in smaller quantities, and there are often large discrepancies between prices for the cryptocurrency in different exchanges.

The trading hub functions as a means of integrating the electronic collaboration of business services. Each hub provides standard formats for the electronic trading of documents used in a particular industry, as well as an array of services to sustain e-commerce between businesses in that industry. Services include demand forecasting, inventory management, partner directories, and transaction-settlement services. And the payoff is significant—lowered costs, decreased inventory levels, and shorter time to market—resulting in bigger profits and enhanced competitiveness. For example, large-scale manufacturing procurement can amount to billions of dollars. Changing to "just-in-time purchasing" on the e-hub can save a considerable percentage of these costs.

Electronic trading across a hub can range from the collaborative integration of individual business processes to auctions and exchanges of goods (electronic barter). Global content management is an essential factor in promoting electronic trading agreements on the hub. A globally consistent view of the "content" of the hub must be available to all. Each participating company handles its own content, and applications such as *content managers* keep a continuously updated master catalog of the inventories of all members of the hub. The *transaction manager* application automates trading arrangements between companies, allowing the hub to provide aggregation and settlement services.

Ultimately, trading hubs for numerous industries could be linked together in a global e-commerce web—an inclusive "hub of all hubs ." One creative thinker puts it this way: "The traditional linear, one step at a time, supply chain is dead. It will be replaced by parallel, asynchronous, real-time marketplace decision-making. Take manufacturing capacity as an example. Enterprises can bid their excess production capacity on the world e-commerce hub. Offers to buy capacity trigger requests from the seller for parts bids to suppliers who in turn put out requests to other suppliers, and this whole process will all converge in a matter of minutes."

Sources: "Asian Companies Count Losses—Hatch Ways to Cope with Weak Dollar," *Reuters*, https://www.reuters.com, January 24, 2018; Rob Verger, "This Is What Determines the Price of Bitcoin," *Popular Science*, https://www.popsci.com, January 22, 2018; Bhavan Jaipragas, "Alibaba's Electronic Trading Hub to Help Small and Medium-sized Enterprises Goes Live in Malaysia," *This Week in Asia*, http://www.scmp.com, November 3, 2017.

Critical Thinking Questions
1. How do companies benefit from participating in an electronic trading hub?
2. What impact does electronic trading have on the global economy?

There are six critical areas that affect society and business and thus require firms to practice good management of technology and innovation. Each of these must be managed for value to be created and captured:[1]

1. Management of Human Resources. Work environment (tools and structures) are much different today than they were at the turn of the millennium. For example, the iPhone was first introduced in 2007. Cell phone technology in the year 2000 was not for everyone—most people still had landline telephones. The introduction of cell phone technology and its use in business has made many employees feel like they are on 24-hour call. Because workers tend to carry their phones everywhere, they are available to be called, texted, or e-mailed.

   Providing learning opportunities (whether online or traditional training and development) has become a more important part of human resources management—employees need to be given time to adjust to the introduction of new ways of working, new software, etc. For example, it is the rare 45-year-old manager today that owned or used a laptop computer before graduating college.
2. Cooperative Model Expansion. The more rapidly innovation occurs, the more rapidly technology occurs within firms, within industries, and within economies. These changes require that cooperatives be developed. These cooperatives can take a variety of forms, both internal and external to the firm. We will discuss internal and external MTI as well entrepreneurial MTI.
3. Internationalization. There is much more internationalization of products and markets. Sometimes, the innovations spread in ways that were not predicted. For example, GE wanted to develop a portable MRI machine to be used in less-developed countries. The machine would be portable and would use a laptop interface to send images for diagnoses. It was successful developed and a plant was built overseas, and then GE discovered there were markets in more-developed economies that they had not considered. For example, large-animal veterinarians wanted to use the machines on farms and ranches. Finding the best markets and the best production options has become an important part of MTI.
4. Issues around Environmental Concerns. Environmental concerns can be important throughout the whole life cycle of a product. From development to manufacturing to usage to disposal, are all concerns for MTI. For example, energy production is a cause of great concern. The use of fossil fuels such as coal, oil, and

natural gas have impacted carbon levels in the atmosphere. Nuclear power does not have that impact, but accidents at such facilities can be catastrophic. Use of wind, water, waves, and sunlight to produce energy does not lead to carbon emissions, but there are other environmental concerns. Building large dams such as Hoover Dam in the United States is much more difficult now because society is much more aware of the changes in the ecosystem such large projects cause.

5. Growth of Service Industries. As economies become more knowledge and information based, service industries will continue to grow. The services provided by Internet suppliers, specialists in network security, etc. will influence how business will grow for the foreseeable future—especially in developing economies. The emergence of a more knowledge- and information-based global economy means that services will become more critical and service industries will continue to grow at a faster pace than product-based industries.[2]

6. Use of Intellectual Property Rights (IPR) as a Strategic Resource. Because many new products and processes are based on intellectual property rights (patents, copyrights, and trademarks), it is crucial that organizations manage their IPR as a valuable asset. This requires value articulation through value transference, translation, and transportation.[3] For example, Dolby Laboratories patented innovative noise-reduction technology that was translated to a stereo film sound technique that was patent protected to transportation to new patents protecting "analog world." As a result, Dolby enjoyed long-term growth from its innovation and over 80 percent of its revenues came from licensing the technology rather than producing competing products.

Exhibit 18.5   Ideo   To demonstrate the process for innovation for a 1999 episode of ABC's late-night news show *Nightline*, IDEO created a new shopping cart concept, considering issues such as maneuverability, shopping behavior, child safety, and maintenance cost. The show concentrated on IDEO's design process, recording as a multidisciplinary team brainstormed, researched, prototyped, and gathered user feedback on a design that went from idea to a working appearance model in four days. (Credit: David Armano/ flickr/ Attribution 2.0 Generic (CC BY 2.0))

Organizations have to be flexible in the management of technology and innovation. Acer, in the opening case, has used a variety of methods to acquire new technology and to innovate and expand its platforms. When Acer started out, the management realized that being a domestic company in Taiwan was very limiting, so they cast their net widely. They originally used internal R&D to grow. Then they expanded their markets and their product lines through mergers and acquisitions. They have increased their product offerings as the laptop market has matured. They are now using services platforms to continue their expansion and growth.

18.2 | Developing Technology and Innovation

2. How do organizations develop technology and innovation?

There are a number of ways that organizations can develop and manage technology and innovation. We will focus on organization-level activities and the three strategic processes in this section of the chapter.

In order for a firm to develop a successful management of technology and innovation strategy, it is imperative that the organization be readied for the effort. This requires agility because changes and adjustments to products and processes are filled with risk and uncertainty. However, agility is inherently less efficiency if it is to be effective. Therefore, the management of technology and innovation must balance short-term efficiency with long-term effectiveness in the market if the firm is to add value and thrive in a changing environment. Strong dynamic capabilities are needed if the organization is going to be able to address the challenges of innovation and dynamic competition.[4] There are four things the firm should do to balance the conflicting demands of being agile in a dynamic environment. These are:

1. Design systems and processes that can identify, assess, and develop technology based opportunities (or protect from new technology threats). The systems and processes should be able to sense what is coming.
2. Identify communication needs and efficiently turn data into information so that the right information can be available to make the best decision in a timely fashion. The current interest in big data and what it can tell firms is tied to the notion that we have a lot of bytes of data available because of computer technology that are not being used effectively or efficiently.
3. Develop employees through training and learning opportunities. This becomes more critical as the competitive environment for the organization becomes more dynamic. The management of technology and innovation requires that all levels of the organization are involved and that efforts are made to ensure that employees are allowed to enhance their skills for themselves and the organization. The more dynamic the environment, the more important skill enhancement is for the firm and the individual.
4. Use good change management processes to help the firm succeed in introducing newness into the organization. Many firms learned expensive lessons when desktop computers were introduced into the workplace. First, most managers did not type, so they did not adopt the new technology. Second, younger staff members were more likely to be comfortable with the new computers (even elated because the computer was better than they could afford at home), so knowledge power was turned upside down from the hierarchy and seniority. Third, many firms installed desktops with little or no training (because they were "upgraded typewriters") while leaving the typewriters easily accessible. The result was that some companies deemed desktops a failure and sold the equipment at a loss. Obviously, desktop computers are now a vital tool in the workplace, but this just illustrates what happens when a good change management process that includes proper support systems, communication, and training is not implemented.

1. Designing systems and processes
2. Identifying communication needs
3. Implementing training and development to address change
4. Using excellent change management processes

Exhibit 18.6   Key Management Activities (Attribution: Copyright Rice University, OpenStax, under CC-BY 4.0 license)

There are three basic organizational processes—buying and partnering, developing newness within the firm, and entrepreneurially exploiting a space in the environment. Exhibit 18.6 delineates the three types. Buying and partnering includes mergers and acquisitions, joint ventures, contractual agreements, and other forms of acquiring technology/innovation from external sources. Internal sources of new technology/innovation for the organization include research and development of new products as well as reconfiguring or developing new processes—ways of doing things. This can be organization structure or redesigning an assembly line. Adding robotics to a manufacturing process may be an internally driven process, or a firm may buy a robotics manufacturer to acquire the capability to add robotics to the assembly process.

Exhibit 18.7   Three Methods of Creating New Technologies/Innovations (Attribution: Copyright Rice University, OpenStax, under CC-BY 4.0 license)

The third type of creating new technologies/innovations involves exploiting a space in the environment through entrepreneurial or new-business development activities. Michael Dell started Dell in his dormitory room at University of Texas. He wanted a better computer than he could buy, so he bought parts and assembled his own. Friends asked him to build one for them. He realized there was an innovative process of customizing computers and delivering directly from the manufacturer to the customer. Michael Dell's exploitation of the custom-built, direct manufacturer-to-customer delivery led to a multibillion dollar business. Table 18.1 lists the advantages and disadvantages of each of the technology/innovation creation methods.

Advantages and Disadvantages of Creation Methods		
Method	Advantages	Disadvantages
External Processes: M&A, joint ventures, contractual relationships, cross-organizational projects, informal relationships	a. Quicker b. Blending rather than discovering c. Often less costly	a. Requires bringing different firm cultures together b. Often leads to perception of winners and losers c. Not-invented-here syndrome
Internal Processes: R&D	a. Clear ownership of the technology/ innovation b. Legal protections may be stronger	a. Often takes longer b. Key personnel may leave at a critical time c. Can be very costly
New Business/Entrepreneurship	a. Usually more agile and flexible in the marketplace b. Dedicated leadership—it is their "baby"	a. Highest risk factor b. Lack of skills within the firm to do things besides innovation c. Usually have very little slack

Table 18.1 (Attribution: Copyright Rice University, OpenStax, under CC-BY 4.0 license)

CONCEPT CHECK

1. How do managers develop technology and innovation?
2. What are the advantages and disadvantages of each creation method?

18.3 | External Sources of Technology and Innovation

3. What are external sources of technology and innovation development, and when are they best used?

The external processes for developing and acquiring technology and innovation include a variety of options. They are most successfully used under the following circumstances:

1. The product line or the processes of the firm have fallen behind those of its competitors.

2. A new entrant into the market of the industry has changed the competitive dynamics.

3. A firm believes that its product mix or way of doing things is not going to be successful in the long run.

The major advantage of using an external process is speed—for the focal firm, the time needed to blend an acquired technology or innovation is usually much shorter than the time required to try to make a discovery and bring it to market or implement it within the firm. Often, the external processes are less costly. The disadvantages are tied to the need to blend different firms or bring "others" into the activities of the firm. For example, there may be cultural conflicts in an acquisition or there may be resistance to acceptance of the newness that is brought into the firm.

The most common types of external processes used to enhance technology and innovation in a firm include:

1. **Mergers/acquisitions (M&A)**, which involve ownership changes within the firms. For an acquisition, one firm buys another; for a merger, the two firms come together and form a new firm. The essence of both of these approaches is that a new, larger organizational entity is formed. The new firm should have more market power (be larger) and should gain knowledge about a technology or domain of activity. The blending of two cultures, two sets of processes, and two structures are all potential disadvantages of M&A activity.

2. **Joint ventures** are long-term alliances that involve the creation of a new entity to specifically carry out a product/process innovation. The entity is usually governed by a contractual relationship that specifies the contributions and obligations of the partners in the joint venture. There are potential culture clashes as well as the potential for **strategic drift**—losing strategic focus on the reasons for the joint venture.

3. **Franchise agreements** are usually long-term agreements that involve long payoffs for the sharing of known technology. Fast food restaurants, such as McDonald's, use franchise agreements with store owners. McDonald's provides R&D for new processes and new products. The store owners (franchisees) pay a fee for the use of the name and the marketing of the product. The contract and monitoring costs associated with franchise agreements are the big disadvantage of this type of alliance.

4. **Licensing agreements** involve technology acquisition without R&D. For example, Dolby contracts with producers of various type of sound equipment to allow them to use their technology to have better sound quality. Licensing agreements are quite common in high-tech industries. The contract costs and constraints are the disadvantages of licensing agreements.

5. **Formal and informal contracts** are used to allow firms to share technology between them. For formal contracts, the length of time the contract is enforceable is a defining characteristic. The more formal a contract, usually the longer it is, and it usually includes more details about the usage and limitations of the technology. For the informal contract, the advantage is that if the activity is no longer beneficial, it is much easier to disband.

All of the methods are of use to firms large and small. In the opening case, Acer used a number of methods to externally acquire technology.

CONCEPT CHECK

Look at the Acer case at the beginning of the chapter and respond to the following items.

1. Identify the times Acer used external methods of acquiring newness for their organization.

2. What goals did they accomplish?

18.4 | Internal Sources of Technology and Innovation

4. What are internal sources of technology and innovation development, and when are they best used?

The most common type of internal process for technology and innovation in the organization is **research and development (R&D)**. R&D involves the seeking and developing of new technologies, products, and/or processes through creative efforts within the firm. The benefits of internal processes include ownership of the technology/innovation that provide legal protections (i.e., patents and trademarks). In addition, the understanding and the knowledge gained from the process of R&D can give the firm a head start on the next generation of technology. Apple's place as a first mover in the technology of laptops and telephones allowed it to maintain a creative advantage for a number of years. The disadvantages of R&D are that it is usually slower and more costly and can be disrupted by the departure of key personnel. The death of Steve Jobs has slowed the innovation of Apple in the eyes of many consumers.

ETHICS IN PRACTICE

Unearthing Your Secrets

Cybercrimes in our technologically driven world are on the increase—identity theft, pornography, and sexual predator victim access, to name a few. The FBI's computer analysis response team confirms their caseload includes 800 cases reported *per day* in 2017. To keep up with the changing world we live in, law enforcement, corporations, and government agencies have turned to new crime-fighting tools, one of the most effective being digital forensics.

The leader in this technology is Guidance Software, founded in 1997 to develop solutions that search, identify, recover, and deliver digital information in a forensically sound and cost-effective manner. Headquartered in Pasadena, California, the company employs 391 people at offices and training facilities in Chicago, Illinois; Washington, DC; San Francisco, California; Houston, Texas; New York City; and Brazil, England, and Singapore. The company's more than 20,000 high-profile clients include leading police agencies, government investigation and law enforcement agencies, and Fortune 1000 corporations in the financial service, insurance, high-tech and consulting, health care, and utility industries.

Guidance Software's suite of EnCase® solutions is the first computer forensics tool able to provide world-class electronic investigative capabilities for large-scale complex investigations. Law enforcement officers, government/corporate investigators, and consultants around the world can now benefit from computer forensics that exceed anything previously available. The software offers an investigative infrastructure that provides network-enabled investigations, enterprise-wide integration with other security technologies, and powerful search and collection tools. With EnCase, clients can conduct digital investigations, handle large-scale data collection needs, and respond to external attacks.

Notably, the company's software was used by law enforcement in the Casey Anthony murder case and the Sony PlayStation security breach, and was used to examine data retrieved by U.S. special forces in the Osama bin Laden raid.

Guidance Software also helps reduce corporate and personal liability when investigating computer-related fraud, intellectual property theft, and employee misconduct. It protects against network threats such as hackers, worms, and viruses and hidden threats such as malicious code.

In response to increases in the number and scope of discovery requests, Guidance Software developed its eDiscovery Suite. The software package dramatically improves the practice of large-scale discovery—the identification, collection, cataloging, and saving of evidence—required in almost every major legal case these days. eDiscovery integrates with other litigation-support software to significantly decrease the time for corporations to accomplish these tasks. At the same time, it improves regulatory compliance and reduces disruption. The result is many millions of dollars in cost savings. In late 2017, Guidance Software was acquired by OpenText, an enterprise information management company that employs more than 10,000 people worldwide.

Sources: FBI website, https://www.fbi.gov, accessed January 15, 2018; Guidance Software website, https://www.guidancesoftware.com, accessed January 15, 2018; OpenText website, https://www.opentext.com, accessed January 15, 2018; "Casey Anthony: The Computer Forensics," *The State v Casey Anthony website*, https://statevcasey.wordpress.com, July 18, 2011; Declan McCullagh, "Finding Treasures in Bin Laden Computers," *CBS News*, https://www.cbsnews.com, May 6, 2011; Evan Narcisse, " Who's Cleaning Up the PSN Debacle for Sony?" *Time*, http://techland.time.com, May 4, 2011.

Critical Thinking Questions

1. How is Guidance Software responding to and helping to manage changes in our technology-driven world?
2. What other types of forensics software do you foresee a need for in the future? Do you think there are ethical issues in using forensics software, and why or why not?
3. What are the benefits and risks of Guidance Software being acquired by a larger company?

CONCEPT CHECK

1. Look at the Acer case at the beginning of the chapter. Identify the times they used internal methods of acquiring newness for their organization.
2. What goals did they accomplish?

18.5 Management Entrepreneurship Skills for Technology and Innovation

5. How and why do entrepreneurs need to develop MTI skills?

Entrepreneurial activities in the marketplace often signal newness in a product or process. For an entrepreneurial firm, the value proposition is a key factor. The **value proposition** answers the follow two questions:

1. How will the firm make money on the product and/or services offered?
2. How will the firm be positioned in the marketplace?

New business entities (a type of entrepreneurial activity) are usually more flexible and agile in the marketplace. The entrepreneur is very dedicated to the success of the firm because the new business is the "baby" of the entrepreneur. The starting of a new business is the riskiest approach for introducing new products and processes. The failure rate for entrepreneurs is high. Because the firm is new, there is usually very little slack in resources available—money is tight, labor is limited, and time is fleeting. Therefore, entrepreneurial activities are most successful when the **lean start-up** process can be used. It is applicable where development costs are low and revisions are not very costly. One reason there are many startups in the development of applications for mobile phones is that the costs are low and improvement of the product (once successful) is relatively easy. Entrepreneurs have the ability to adapt their plans incrementally, especially when using lean start-up methods.[5] For entrepreneurs, the capabilities to sense, seize, and transform can be an advantage if they stay agile and avoid overcommitting to a course of action.[6] Entrepreneurs, by definition, are more agile than the more-established organizations.

This agility is true within large firms that want to continue to be entrepreneurial in their activities. Firms such as Google and 3M allow their employees to work on innovative projects during their working hours. Google modeled their policy of allowing employees time to explore other potential products and processes after 3M's longtime policy. Both of these firms are known as innovative firms because they encourage employees to look for and test innovative and valuable propositions. The flexibility allowed employees gives both Google and 3M the agility to find new ways of doing things.

CONCEPT CHECK

1. In the beginning, Acer was very entrepreneurial. However, the firm realized that if it was to continue to grow, it needed to develop some structures and processes. What adjustments did Acer make to become a global firm?

18.6 | Skills Needed for MTI

6. No matter what method is used, what skills do you need to successfully manage technology and innovation?

There are a number of skills needed to successfully manage technology and innovation in the organization. No matter what organization you are a part of, there are two skills the organization must develop to be successful—the ability to manage learning and knowledge processes, and the ability to analyze and forecast future trends. Individual skills that are critical to the organization's success include leadership/followership and creative thinking.

Organizational skills involve how the firm puts people and resources together to create value—building capabilities. With the right capabilities, the organization can develop a competitive advantage. In the world of technology and innovation, the management of learning and knowledge processes is critical. The organization needs to have systems in place that allow it to collect data that can be analyzed to form information. The information needs to be used to gain knowledge and insight. At each step, learning takes place. **Organizational learning** is the acquisition of knowledge through the collection of data that is analyzed to gather information, which is then transferred and shared through communication among members of the organization. This communication process provides the foundation for knowledge acquisition and enhancement within the firm. There are two types of knowledge that must be managed: **explicit knowledge** (codified or written down as rules or guidelines) and **tacit knowledge** (which emerges from experience of an individual). Tacit knowledge can become explicit at some point if the expert is able to codify the knowledge for others. However, it is not always possible to codify tacit knowledge. For example, Henry Bessemer was sued by the patent purchasers who could not get his steel-making process to work. In the end Bessemer set up his own steel company because he knew how to gauge when to add and subtract heat based on the impurities in the iron ore, even though he could not convey it to his patent users. Bessemer's company became one of the largest in the world and changed the face of steelmaking. After the introduction of the Bessemer process, steel and wrought iron became similarly priced, and some users, primarily railroads, turned to steel.[7] The insights and experiences that are gained from the gathering of data and converting that data into information are key to successful MTI. Organizational knowledge is the sharing and utilization of the learning that takes place in the firm.

Exhibit 18.8 Ben Fried In today's high-tech world, CIOs must possess not only the technical smarts to implement global IT infrastructures, integrate communications systems with partners, and protect customer data from insidious hackers, but they must also have strong business acumen. Google's acclaimed tech chief Ben Fried manages the technology necessary to deliver more than nine billion searches daily, with an eye towards greater business efficiency, growth, and profits. *Why is it important for CIOs to possess both technological and business expertise?* (Credit: Enterprise 2.0 Conference/ flickr/ Attribution 2.0 Generic (CC BY 2.0))

The ability to forecast the future is another key organizational skill in the management of technology and innovation. This involves scanning the environment for trends and possible areas of value-creation opportunities. It also involves understanding the risk involved with newness in the firm and the risk involved in not seeking newness—both can cause the firm to lose value. Any method of forecasting comes with limitations. These include:

1. Forecasting methods, by definition, are uncertain in their outcomes. Usually the firm is trying to develop scenarios concerning best, worst, and most likely outcomes. With this information, risk can be assessed.
2. Forecasts are imperfect—the firm cannot predict all potential influences in the competitive marketplace. Bessemer knew he had a better process, but he did not predict the problems he had licensing his patent.
3. Forecasts are at best an educated guess. Many forecast techniques rely on statistical analysis, but the numbers used in the analysis are forecasts themselves or rely on patterns of behavior continuing in the marketplace.
4. With all the issues with forecasting, a company that produces excellent forecasts will most likely formulate better strategy and capture more value.

The knowledge-management system of the firm can help the ability of the firm to forecast. Experience and learning about industry and general environment trends can help individuals and teams forecast more accurately.

Individuals within the firm also need to have certain skills to enhance the management of technology and innovation processes. These skills include a balance of leadership and followship and the ability to think creatively.

- Organizational
  - Knowledge management
  - Forecasting
- Individual
  - Leadership
  - Followship

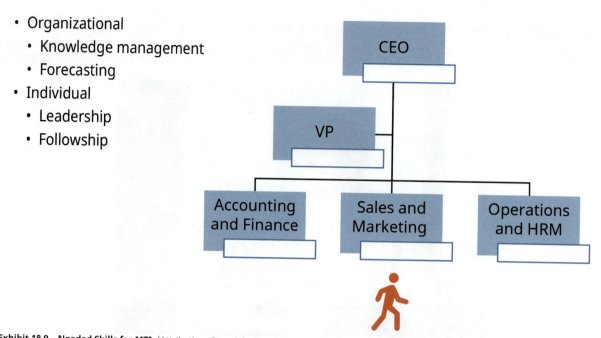

Exhibit 18.9   Needed Skills for MTI (Attribution: Copyright Rice University, OpenStax, under CC-BY 4.0 license)

Most individuals in the organization understand what **leadership** is. For MTI, it is important that the right person be in the leadership position when needed. For example, in new product development, the leader during the design phase is likely to be an engineer, the leader in the prototype development phase may be an engineer or a production person, and as the product is introduced to the marketplace the leader may be a marketing person. It is necessary for these individuals to communicate, and they may all be on a project team that is under the direction/coordination of a dedicated project manager. However, the leadership on the project shifts within the creation-to-market process. While leadership is critical, so is **followship**. Followship is the mirror image of leadership. Most will never have taken a class in followship. You cannot have leaders without followers. There is a skill set for leadership and a skill set for followship. It is the actions of followers that determine the success of a leader. The success of organizations is more the result of good followship than of great leadership. Leadership is influencing others, and followship is seeking or accepting influence. In the case of new product development outlined above, each of the individuals were leaders during some point in the project and each were followers during the project. Individuals spend a lot of time seeking and learning about leadership, but followship is also critical to organizational success. Innovative companies are often lead by a combination of two individuals who lead and follow each other. For example, Microsoft was founded by Bill Gates and Paul Allen. The names of firms started or built by two people are common: Sears & Roebuck, Proctor & Gamble, Marks and Spencer. The characteristics of a good follower include:

1. They are truthful. Followers who tell the truth and leaders who listen are an unbeatable combination.
2. They are supportive. Don't blame your boss for an unpopular decision or policy. "I know this is an unpopular decision, but..." Absent person example of trust. [I call it confessing the sins of the boss in the hallway after the meeting.]
3. They give the boss the benefit of their knowledge and experience. Your job is to make the organization successful.
4. They take the Initiative to solve problems by providing solutions, not just issues.
5. They keep the leader Informed. The higher a manager is in an organization, the more people are less inclined to talk openly with them. Great followers provide the good, the bad, and the ugly of information, knowledge, and experience.

CONCEPT CHECK

1. What is organizational learning?
2. What are the differences between leadership and followship?
3. What forecasting techniques are used in the management of technology and innovation?

18.7 | Managing Now for Future Technology and Innovation

7. How do you look into the future to keep pace?

To keep pace with changes in technology and to keep up with needed innovation processes, individuals within the firm must keep track of what competitors are doing as well as what inventions or discoveries may usurp an industry's place in the market. This is an external process, and that involves scanning the environment. The information gathered during scanning should inform the firm about the general trends and opportunities to create new value. Internally, the firm wants to understand the task and processes as well as understand the skills that currently exist in the organization. By identifying potential future scenarios in the external environment and understanding what resources and capabilities the firm has, the task for those managing technology and innovation becomes answering the key questions:

1. Where are we now?
2. Where do we want to be?
3. What do we need to move from here to there?

CONCEPT CHECK

1. How do you keep up with a constantly evolving environment of technology and innovation?

🔑 Key Terms

entrepreneurial activities The implementation of new ventures and idea generation in organizations.

explicit knowledge Information codified or written down as rules or guidelines.

followship The process of seeking or accepting influence.

formal and informal contracts Used to allow firms to share technology between each other.

franchise agreements Long-term agreements that involve long payoffs for the sharing of known technology.

innovation Invention, new product development, and process-improvement methods are all examples of innovation.

joint ventures Long-term alliances that involve the creation of a new entity to specifically carry out a product/process innovation.

leadership The action of leading a group of people or an organization.

licensing agreements Involve technology acquisition without R&D.

management of innovation Includes both change management and managing organizational processes that encourage innovation.

management of technology The planning, implementation, evaluation, and control of the organization's resources and capabilities in order to create value and competitive advantage.

mergers/acquisitions (M&A) For an acquisition, one firm buys another; for a merger, the two firms come together and form a new firm.

organizational learning The acquisition of knowledge through the collection of data that is analyzed to gather information, which is then transferred and shared through communication among members of the organization.

research and development (R&D) Involves the seeking and developing of new technologies, products, and/ or processes through creative efforts within the firm.

strategic drift Occurs when a joint venture loses strategic focus on the reasons for the joint venture.

strategic inertia The tendency of organizations to continue on their current trajectory.

tacit knowledge Emerges from experience of an individual.

technology The branch of knowledge that deals with the creation and use of technical means and the application of this knowledge for practical ends.

value proposition A promise by a company to a customer or market segment.

📖 Summary of Learning Outcomes

18.1 MTI—Its Importance Now and In the Future

1. What do we mean by management of technology and innovation (MTI), and why is it crucial?

Management of technology and innovation is critical to the organization. Because of innovations and new technologies, we have historically seen the emergence of innovative organizational structures and new ways of performing work. The management of technology involves the planning, implementation, evaluation, and control of the organization's resources and capabilities in order to create value and competitive advantage. Management of innovation includes both change management and managing organizational processes that encourage innovation.

18.2 Developing Technology and Innovation

2. How do organizations develop technology and innovation?

There are four things the firm should do to balance the conflicting demands of being agile in a dynamic environment. These are: design systems and processes, identify communication needs and efficiently turn data into information, develop employees through training and learning, and use good change management processes. There are three basic organizational processes—buying and partnering, developing newness within the firm, and entrepreneurially exploiting a space in the environment.

18.3 External Sources of Technology and Innovation

3. What are external sources of technology and innovation development, and when are they best used?

The external processes for developing and acquiring technology and innovation include a variety of options. They are most successfully used under the following circumstances:

1. The product line or the processes of the firm have fallen behind those of its competitors.
2. A new entrant into the market of the industry has changed the competitive dynamics.
3. A firm believes that its product mix or way of doing things is not going to be successful in the long run.

The most common types of external processes used to enhance technology and innovation in a firm include: mergers/acquisitions (M&A), joint ventures, franchise agreements, licensing agreements, and formal and informal contracts.

18.4 Internal Sources of Technology and Innovation

4. What are internal sources of technology and innovation development, and when are they best used?

The most common type of internal process for technology and innovation in the organization is research and development (R&D). R&D involves the seeking and developing of new technologies, products, and/or processes through creative efforts within the firm. The disadvantages of R&D are that it is usually slower and more costly and can be disrupted by the departure of key personnel.

18.5 Management Entrepreneurship Skills for Technology and Innovation

5. How and why do entrepreneurs develop MTI skills?

For an entrepreneurial firm, the value proposition is a key factor. New business entities (a type of entrepreneurial activity) are usually more flexible and agile in the marketplace; however, the failure rate for new entrepreneurial firms is high. Entrepreneurs, by definition, are more agile than the more-established organizations. Agility is crucial within large firms that want to continue to be entrepreneurial in their activities.

18.6 Skills Needed for MTI

6. No matter what method is used, what skills do you need to successfully manage technology and innovation?

There are two skills the organization must develop to be successful—the ability to manage learning and knowledge processes, and the ability to analyze and forecast future trends. Individual skills that are critical to the organization's success include leadership/followship and creative thinking. There are two types of knowledge that must be managed: explicit knowledge and tacit knowledge.

18.7 Managing Now for Future Technology and Innovation

7. How do you look into the future to keep pace?

To keep pace with changes in technology and to keep up with needed innovation processes, individuals within the firm must keep track of what competitors are doing as well as what inventions or discoveries may usurp an industry's place in the market. This is an external process, and that involves scanning the environment.

Chapter Review Questions

1. How do we define technology and innovation, and how are they related?
2. What are the four areas that need to be managed by the firm if it is going to take advantage of the technology it has and the technology it needs to create?
3. What are the five Cs of managing innovation, and how do they help direct a firm's innovation activities?
4. How does an organization enhance its agility? When is more agility needed in the firm?
5. Compare and contrast the advantages and disadvantages of the three approaches for technology and innovation development.
6. What circumstances indicate a firm should consider an external process for developing/acquiring technology?
7. How does a firm determine the type of external process for developing/acquiring technology it should pursue?
8. What are the benefits of using internal sources for developing new technologies, products, and/or processes? What are the potential disadvantages?
9. How does an entrepreneurial firm identify and utilize a value proposition?
10. How does knowledge management impact the management of technology and innovation?
11. Followship is critical to MTI—how does the quality of followship in the organization impact the ability of leadership to create value?
12. How does the management of technology and innovation help a firm create value? Why should the firm strive to have a unique value proposition?

Management Skills Application Exercises

1. Assess the education that you have received from grade school up to this course. What technology has been used to provide education to you? What technology and innovation would improve the "product" of education?
2. Come up with 50 alternative uses for the following products: day-old newspapers, old television sets, ballpoint pens, used Dixie cups. Share your results with other students as see if that develops new ideas.
3. Think of the best experience you have had using a smartphone app (e.g., banking, rideshare, etc.) and a bad experience that could be improved through an app. Describe the features and functionality and the benefits for both the customers and organization that would use the app.

Managerial Decision Exercises

1. You are a manager at a traditional automobile manufacturer (Ford, GM, Daimler-Chrysler). You know that Tesla is an up-and-coming competitor, and you're also working on electric cars for your company. An article in the *Wall Street Journal* about electric cars and the future of gas stations has caught your interest.[8] One sentence has caught your eye: "Until you drive an EV, you are colored by 135 years of going to the gas station. Under that scenario, you say 'Where is the new company that's doing EV charging on street corners or in my highway entrance?,' but that isn't really how this works." What innovations regarding recharging or other aspects of traditional "driving" could be incorporated into the electric vehicles you are developing?
2. You are a sales manager and know that technologies like automation, robotics, artificial intelligence, and

the Internet of things are changing the way that you use and interact with the products that you use. You sense that your customers might be a good source for forecasting future product innovations. You decide to ask your salespeople to interview their toughest customers to generate ideas. Write up eight questions that your sales representatives can use to gather the information.

3. In October 2015, Google restructured into Alphabet, a holding company, which analysts said would facilitate innovation among its diverse subsidiaries. What are the benefits and risks of this decision, and would you have made a similar or alternative decision?

Critical Thinking Case

Novartis's Prescription for Invoice Processing

What do you do when you have more than 600 business units operating through 360 independent affiliates in 140 countries around the world—processing complex invoices in various languages and currencies? You seek out the best technology solution to make the job easier.

At global pharmaceutical giant Novartis, the IT department is a strategic resource, a community of 2,000 people serving 63,000 customers in 200 locations and 25 data centers. Because most of the company's invoices come from international suppliers, they have differences in design, language, taxes, and currency. Consequently, many ended up as "query items" requiring manual resolution by Novartis accounting staff—which delayed payments and made those invoices extremely costly to process. In fact, finance personnel spent so much of their time resolving queried invoices that other work suffered. A solution was badly needed.

To maximize its investment, Novartis needed a flexible solution that would meet its current and future needs and function in other business departments in a variety of geographic locations. It should provide fast, accurate document capture and multilanguage support, and should extend to other types of information—such as faxes and electronic data—in addition to paper documents. Finally, in order to obtain financing for the project, return on investment (ROI) was required within nine months of project implementation.

Input *Accel* for Invoices from EMC/Captiva was the answer. The software extracts data from paper documents, applies intelligent document recognition (IDR) technology to convert them to digital images, and sends relevant data to enterprise resource planning, accounts payable (A/P), and other back-end management systems. The specialized Input *Accel* server manages output by recognizing and avoiding holdups in the workflow process. It also ensures if a server goes offline, others will carry on functioning, thus avoiding downtime.

Now Novartis scans incoming invoices at a centrally located site, and the images are transmitted to the Input *Accel* for Invoices server for image improvement. Invoice data is then extracted and validated against supplier information. Most invoices are transferred directly for payment, with relatively few invoices requiring transfer to one of three accounts payable clerks who deal with queries manually. Novartis is a global leader in research and development of products that improve health issues. Input *Accel* was selected by Novartis to be part of its accounting system.

Thanks to IT, overall efficiency has increased, processing errors are reduced, and accounting personnel can use their time and expert knowledge for more meaningful tasks than resolving invoice errors. For Novartis, it is "mission accomplished."

Critical Thinking Questions

1. What factors contributed to Novartis's invoice processing being so complex?
2. How did IT help the company solve that problem?
3. What other uses and functions does Input *Accel* serve, and how will this be useful to Novartis over the long term? (You may want to visit the EMC/Captiva website, **https://www.emc.com**, for more information on Input *Accel*'s capabilities.)

Sources: "OpenText Acquires EMC Enterprise Division," *MetaSource*, http://www.metasource.com, September 20, 2016; Novartis corporate website, http://www.novartis.com, March 20, 2006; "Processing Invoices From Around the World," *ECM Connection*, https://www.ecmconnection, February 2, 2006; Kathryn Balint, "Captiva's Paper Chase Paying Off," *San Diego Union-Tribune,* December 9, 2005, pp. C1, C5.

References

Introduction

1. Hannaway, J. (1989*). Managers Managing: The Workings of an Administrative System*. New York: Oxford University Press, P. 39.

2. Eccles, R. G. & Nohria, N. (1992). *Beyond the Hype: Rediscovering the Essence of Management*. Boston: The Harvard Business School Press, p. 47.

What Do Managers Do?

3. Hannaway, J. (1989*). Managers Managing: The Workings of an Administrative System*. New York: Oxford University Press, P. 39; and Kotter, J. P. (1982). *The General Managers*. New York: The Free Press.

4. Mintzberg, H. (1973). *The Nature of Managerial Work*. New York: Harper & Row. P. 37.

5. Kotter, J. P. (1999). "What Effective General Managers Really Do," *Harvard Business Review*, March–April 1999, pp. 145–159.

6. Kotter, J. P. (1999). "What Effective General Managers Really Do," *Harvard Business Review*, March–April 1999, pp. 145–159.

7. Sproull, L. S. (1984)."The Nature of Managerial Attention," in L. S. Sproull (ed.), *Advances in Information Processing in Organizations*. Greenwich, CT: JAI Press.

8. Stewart, R. (1967). *Managers and Their Jobs*. London: Macmillan.

9. Eccles, R. G. & Nohria, N. (1992). *Beyond the Hype: Rediscovering the Essence of Management*. Boston: The Harvard Business School Press, p. 47.

10. Mintzberg, H. (1973). *The Nature of Managerial Work*. New York: Harper & Row. P. 37.

11. Pondy, L. R. (1978). "Leadership Is a Language Game," in M. W. McCall, Jr. and M. M. Lombardo (eds.), *Leadership: Where Else Can We Go?* Durham, NC: Duke University Press.

12. Mintzberg, H. (2009). *Managing*. San Francisco, Berrett-Kohler Publishers. P. 26-28.

13. Eccles, R. G. & Nohria, N. (1992). *Beyond the Hype: Rediscovering the Essence of Management*. Boston: The Harvard Business School Press, pp. 47-48.

The Roles Managers Play

14. Mintzberg, H. (1990). "The Manager's Job: Folklore and Fact." *Harvard Business Review*, March–April 1990, pp. 166–167.

15. Mintzberg, H. (1990). "The Manager's Job: Folklore and Fact." *Harvard Business Review*, March–April 1990, p. 167.

16. Mintzberg, H. (1990). "The Manager's Job: Folklore and Fact." *Harvard Business Review*, March–April 1990, p. 168.

17. McGregor, J. (2008). "Bezos: How Frugality Drives Innovation," *BusinessWeek*, April 28, 2008, pp. 64–66.

18. Stewart, R. (1967). *Managers and Their Jobs*. London: Macmillan.

19. Mintzberg, H. (1990). "The Manager's Job: Folklore and Fact." *Harvard Business Review*, March–April 1990.

Major Characteristics of the Manager's Job

20. Mintzberg, H. (1990). "The Manager's Job: Folklore and Fact." *Harvard Business Review*, March–April 1990, p. 167.

21. Katz, Robert L., (1974). "Skills of an Effective Administrator." Harvard Business Review, September-October 1974.

Overview of Managerial Decision-Making

1. Lynn Stout. 2012. The Shareholder Value Myth: How Putting Shareholders First Harms Investors, Corporations, and the Public. San Francisco, CA: Berrett-Koehler Publishers.

How the Brain Processes Information to Make Decisions: Reflective and Reactive Systems

2. Peter A. Facione & Noreen C. Facione. 2007. Thinking and Reasoning in Human Decision Making: The Method of Argument and Heuristic Analysis, Millbrae, CA: The California Academic Press.

3. Matthew D. Lieberman. 2003. "Reflexive and reflective judgment processes: A social cognitive neuroscience approach." In (Eds.) Joseph P. Forgas, Kipling D. Williams, & William von Hippel's: Social judgments: Implicit and explicit processes, 44-67. Cambridge, UK: Cambridge University Press.

4. Adam L. Darlow & Steven A. Sloman. 2010. "Two systems of reasoning: Architecture and relation to emotion," *WIREs Cognitive Science*, 1: 382-392.

5. Malcolm Gladwell. 2005. Blink: The Power of Thinking Without Thinking. New York: Back Bay Books.

6. Jennifer M. George. 2000. "Emotions and leadership: The role of emotional intelligence." *Human Relations*, 53, 1027-1055.

Barriers to Effective Decision-Making

7. Christopher L. Aberson, Michael Healy, & Victoria Romero. 2000. Ingroup Bias and Self-Esteem: A Meta-Analysis. *Personality and Social Psychology Review*, 4: 157-173.

8. Elizabeth Kolbert. 2017. Why Facts Don't Change our Minds. *The New Yorker*, February 27, 2017.

9. Karen A. Jehn & Elizabeth A. Mannix. 2001. The Dynamic Nature of Conflict: A Longitudinal Study of Intragroup Conflict and Group Performance. *Academy of Management Journal*, 44: 238-251.

Improving the Quality of Decision-Making

10. Linda K. Trevino & Michael E. Brown. 2004. Managing to be ethical: Debunking five business ethics myths. *Academy of Management Executive*, 18: 69-81.

11. James R. Rest. 1986. *Moral development: Advances in research and theory*. Praeger Publishers.

Introduction

1. Jackson, Eric, "Sun Tzu's 31 Best Pieces Of Leadership Advice", Forbes, May 23, 2014. https://www.forbes.com/sites/ryanholiday/2012/05/07/9-lessons-on-leadership-from-genghis-khan-yes-genghis-khan/; https://www.forbes.com/sites/ericjackson/2014/05/23/sun-tzus-33-best-pieces-of-leadership-advice/#124ac8a05e5e

2. https://www.newyorker.com/magazine/2010/09/20/the-face-of-facebook

The Early Origins of Management

3. George, Claude S. (1972). History of Management Thought. Prentice Hall, Englewood Cliffs New Jersey.

4. Wren, D. A., & Bedeian, A. G. 2009. The evolution of management thought. (6th ed.), New York: Wiley.

5. Wren, D. A., & Bedeian, A. G. 2009. The evolution of management thought. (6th ed.), New York: Wiley.

6. Wren, D. A., & Bedeian, A. G. 2009. The evolution of management thought. (6th ed.), New York: Wiley.

7. Fairbank, J.K. (1991). *China: a New History*. Harvard University Press. Cambridge.

The Italian Renaissance

8. Ruggiero, Guido. The Renaissance in Italy: A Social and Cultural History of the Rinascimento (Cambridge University Press, 2015).

9. Muldoon, J., & Marin, D. B. (2012). John Florio and the introduction of management into the English vocabulary. Journal of Management History, 18(2), 129-136.

10. Haynes, M.S. (1991), The Italian Renaissance and Its Influence on Western Civilization, University Press of America, New York, NY.

The Industrial Revolution

11. Bridgen, S. (2001), New Worlds, Lost Worlds: The Rule of the Tudors, 1485-1603, Viking Penguin, New York, NY.

12. Muldoon, J., & Marin, D. B. (2012). John Florio and the introduction of management into the English vocabulary. Journal of Management History, 18(2), 129-136.

13. Bryce, George (1968). The Remarkable History of Hudson's Bay Company. New York: B. Franklin.

14. Williams, Roger (2015). London's Lost Global Giant: In Search of the East India Company. London: Bristol Book Publishing.

15. Ross, Ian Simpson (2010). The Life of Adam Smith (2 ed.). Oxford University Press.

16. Smith, Adam (1977) [1776]. An Inquiry into the Nature and Causes of the Wealth of Nations. University of Chicago Press

17. Ashton, Thomas S. (1948). "The Industrial Revolution (1760–1830)". Oxford University Press.

18. Landes, David (1999). The Wealth and Poverty of Nations. W. W. Norton & Company.

19. Wren, D. A., & Bedeian, A. G. 2009. The evolution of management thought. (6th ed.), New York: Wiley

20. Lacey, Robert. Ford: The Men and the Machine Little, Brown, 1986.

21. Hassard, J. S. (2012). Rethinking the Hawthorne Studies: The Western Electric research in its social, political and historical context. Human Relations, 65(11), 1431-1461.

22. Howe, D. W. (2008). What God Hath Wrought. New York Oxford University Press.

23. Bendickson, J., Muldoon, J., Liguori, E., & Davis, P. E. (2016). Agency theory: the times, they are a-changin'. Management Decision, 54(1), 174-193.

24. Bendickson, J., Muldoon, J., Ligouri, E.W. and Davis, P.E. (2016), "Agency theory: background and epistemology", Journal of Management History, Vol. 22 No. 4, pp. 437-449

25. Bendickson, J., Muldoon, J., Ligouri, E.W. and Davis, P.E. (2016), "Agency theory: background and epistemology", Journal of Management History, Vol. 22 No. 4, pp. 437-449

26. Wren, D. A., & Bedeian, A. G. 2009. The evolution of management thought. (6th ed.), New York: Wiley.

27. Wren, D.A. (2005), The History of Management Thought, 5th ed., John Wiley and Sons, Hoboken, NJ

Taylor-Made Management

28. McGerr, Michael. A Fierce Discontent: The Rise and Fall of the Progressive Movement in America, 1870–1920 (2003

29. Wiebe, Robert. The Search For Order, 1877–1920 (1967)

30. Kanigel, Robert (1997) The one best way : Frederick Winslow Taylor and the enigma of efficiency (London : Little, Brown)

31. Kanigel, Robert (1997) The one best way : Frederick Winslow Taylor and the enigma of efficiency (London : Little, Brown)

32. Wren, D. A., & Bedeian, A. G. 2009. The evolution of management thought. (6th ed.), New York: Wiley.

33. Wren, D. A., & Bedeian, A. G. 2009. The evolution of management thought. (6th ed.), New York: Wiley.

34. Drucker, P.F. 1954: The Practice of Management (New York: Harper & Brothers)

35. Kakar, Sudhir (1970). Frederick Taylor: a study in personality and innovation. Cambridge: University of Wisconsin Press.

36. Spencer Klaw, "Frederick Winslow Taylor: The Messiah of Time and Motion." American Heritage, 1979, 30(5), 26-39.

37. Charles D. Wrege and Ronald G. Greenwood, Frederick W. Taylor: The Father of Scientific Management (Homewood, IL: Business One Irwin, 1991), 253-260.

38. The Principles of Scientific Management. New York and London, Harper & brothers

39. Wren, D. A., & Bedeian, A. G. 2009. The evolution of management thought. (6th ed.), New York: Wiley.

40. Krenn, M. (2011). From Scientific Management to homemaking: Lillian M. Gilbreth's contributions to the development of management thought. Management & Organizational History, 6(2), 145-161.

41. Charles D. Wrege and Ronald G. Greenwood, Frederick W. Taylor: The Father of Scientific Management (Homewood, IL: Business One Irwin, 1991), 253-260.

42. Edwin A. Locke, "The Ideas of Frederick W. Taylor: An Evaluation." Academy of Management Review, 1982, 7, 14-24

Administrative and Bureaucratic Management

43. Pryor, J.L.; Guthrie, C. (2010). "The private life of Henri Fayol and his motivation to build a management science". Journal of Management History.

44. Daniel A. Wren, Arthur G. Bedeian, John D. Breeze, (2002) "The foundations of Henri Fayol's administrative theory", Management Decision, Vol. 40 Iss: 9, pp.906 - 918

45. Industrial and General Administration. Translated by J.A. Coubrough, London: Sir Isaac Pitman & Sons.

46. Max Weber, "Ideal Bureaucracy" in The Theory of Social and Economic Organizations (ed. & trans. Talcott Parsons & Alexander H. Henderson). (New York: Oxford University Press, 1922/1947)

47. Robert K. Merton, "Bureaucratic Structure and Personality." Social Forces, 1940, 18, 500-508.

Human Relations Movement

48. Jeffrey A. Sonnenfeld, "Shedding Light on the Hawthorne Studies." Journalof Occupational Behavior, 1985, 6, 111-130.

49. Wren, D. A., & Bedeian, A. G. 2009. The evolution of management thought. (6th ed.), New York: Wiley.

50. Wren, D. A., & Bedeian, A. G. 2009. The evolution of management thought. (6th ed.), New York: Wiley.

51. Gehani, R. Ray (2002) "Chester Barnard's "executive" and the knowledge-based firm", Management Decision 40(10): 980 - 991.

52. Chester I. Barnard, *The Functions of the Executive* (Cambridge: Harvard University Press, 1938),

53. Wren, D. A., & Bedeian, A. G. 2009. The evolution of management thought. (6th ed.), New York: Wiley.

54. Mary P. Follett: Creating Democracy, Transforming Management, Tonn, Joan C., New Haven: Yale University Press, 2003

55. Mary P. Follett: Creating Democracy, Transforming Management, Tonn, Joan C., New Haven: Yale University Press, 2003

56. Follett, M. P. (1926). The psychological foundations: Constructive conflict in Henry metcalf. Scientific Foundations of Business administration, Baltimore, MD, The Williams & Wilkins Company pg. 116.

Contingency and System Management

57. Kenneth E. Boulding, "General Systems Theory C The Skeleton of Science."Management Science, 1956, 2, 197-208.

58. Woodward, J. 1970. Industrial organization: Behavior and control. London: Oxford University Press.

59. Sutton, R., & Staw, B. (1995). What theory is not. Administrative Science Quarterly, 40, 371-384.

60. Pfeffer, J. and Sutton, R.I. (2006). Harvard Business Review, 84 (1) 62-74.; and Pfeffer, J. and Sutton, R.I. (2006). Hard Facts, Dangerous Half-Truths and Total Nonsense: Profiting From Evidence-Based Management. Cambridge: Harvard Business School Press.

Introduction

1. Panetta, Kasey, "Gartner Top 10 Strategic Technology Trends for 2018", *Gartner*, October 3, 2017. https://www.gartner.com/smarterwithgartner/gartner-top-10-strategic-technology-trends-for-2018/

2. Mearian, Lucas, "What is blockchain? The most disruptive technology in decades", *Computerworld*, May 31, 2018. https://www.computerworld.com/article/3191077/security/what-is-blockchain-the-most-disruptive-tech-in-decades.html; https://www.forbes.com/sites/theyec/2018/01/10/23-trends-that-will-shake-the-business-world-in-2018/#6b6c3524583f

3. Young Entrepreneurship Council, "23 Trends That Will Shake the Business World in 2018", *Forbes*, January 10, 2018. https://www.forbes.com/sites/theyec/2018/01/10/23-trends-that-will-shake-the-business-world-in-2018/#6b6c3524583f

The Organization's External Environment

4. This is a broad definition which has been used in different forms. The source here is "What is an External Environment in Business" Chapter 5, *study.com*, Accessed October 15, 2018. https://study.com/academy/

lesson/what-is-an-external-environment-in-business-definition-types-factors.html

5. Jamrisko, Michelle, "China's Economy to Overtake Euro Zone This Year", *Bloomberg*, March 6, 2018. https://www.bloomberg.com/news/articles/2018-03-06/china-s-economy-is-set-to-overtake-combined-euro-area-this-year

6. China Owns US Debt, but How Much? | *Investopedia*, April 6, 2018. https://www.investopedia.com/articles/investing/080615/china-owns-us-debt-how-much.asp#ixzz5DcHG4d7k

7. Rawlinson, Paul, "A prediction for globalization in 2018", *World Economic Forum*, January 22, 2018. https://www.weforum.org/agenda/2018/01/prediction-globalization-2018/

8. Bersin, Josh and Mazor, Art, "Culture Engagement and Beyond", *Deloitte Insights*, February 28, 2017. https://www2.deloitte.com/insights/us/en/focus/human-capital-trends/2017/improving-the-employee-experience-culture-engagement.html?id=us:2ps:3gl:confidence:eng:cons:::na:LIxmKVLK:1079836504:244787795449:b:RLSA_Human_Capital_Trends::nb

9. Cilluffo, Anthony and Cohen, D'Vera, "10 demographic trends shaping the U. S. and the World in 2017", *Pew Research Center*, April 27, 2017. http://www.pewresearch.org/fact-tank/2017/04/27/10-demographic-trends-shaping-the-u-s-and-the-world-in-2017/

10. Graf, Nikki, Sexual Harassment at work in the Era of #MeToo", *Pew Research Center*, April 4, 2018. http://www.pewsocialtrends.org/2018/04/04/sexual-harassment-at-work-in-the-era-of-metoo/

11. The Global Risks Report 2018 13th Edition. (2018). *The World Economic Forum*, http://www3.weforum.org/docs/WEF_GRR18_Report.pdf, p. 6. Also see http://reports.weforum.org/global-risks-2018/global-risks-landscape-2018/

12. Fry, Richard, "It's becoming more common for young adults to live at home for longer stretches", *Pew Research Center*, May 5, 2017. http://www.pewresearch.org/fact-tank/2017/05/05/its-becoming-more-common-for-young-adults-to-live-at-home-and-for-longer-stretches/

13. DeSilver, Drew, "Women scarce at the top of U.S. business- and in the job that lead there", *Pew Research Center*, April 30, 2018. http://www.pewresearch.org/fact-tank/2018/04/30/women-scarce-at-top-of-u-s-business-and-in-the-jobs-that-lead-there/

14. Hunt, Vivian et al, "Delivering Through Diversity", *McKinsey*, January 2018. https://www.mckinsey.com/~/media/McKinsey/Business%20Functions/Organization/Our%20Insights/Delivering%20through%20diversity/Delivering-through-diversity_full-report.ashx

15. The Global Economic Report, 13th Edition, *World Economic Forum*, 2018. http://www3.weforum.org/docs/WEF_GRR18_Report.pdf

16. Rice, Doyle, "Thousands of low-lying islands may become 'uninhabitable' within decades as seas rise", *USA Today*, April 25, 2018. https://www.usatoday.com/story/news/world/2018/04/25/thousands-low-lying-islands-may-become-uninhabitable-within-decades-seas-rise/550659002/

External Environments and Industries

17. Felice De Toni, A. and G. De Zan. (2016), The complexity dilemma, Three tips for dealing with complexity in organizations, *Practitioner*, Dec. 31, https://journal.emergentpublications.com/article/the-complexity-dilemma/

18. Eisenhardt, K. M., & Sull, D. N. (2001). "Strategy as simple rules", *Harvard Business Review*, 79(1): 106-119

19. Ibid.

Organizational Designs and Structures

20. Bersin, Josh, et al, "2017 Global Human Capital trends", *Deloitte Insights*, February 28, 2017. https://www2.deloitte.com/insights/us/en/focus/human-capital-trends/2017/organization-of-the-future.html

21. Ibid.

22. Burns, T. & Stalker, G. M. (1961), The Management of Innovation, Tavistock, London; Mintzberg, H. 1979. The structuring of organizations. Englewood Cliffs, NJ: *Prentice-Hall*; Emery, Fred E. and Eric L. Trist, (1965), "The

Causal Texture of Organizational Environments", pp 21-32 in *Human Relations*, February 1965

23. Anand, N. and R. Daft. (2007). What is the Right Organization Design? *Organizational Dynamics*, Vol. 36, No. 4, pp. 329–344.

24. Ibid.

25. This section draws on a number of scholarly and practitioner sources, including the following: R. Daft. (2016). Organization Theory & Design, 12th ed. *Cengage Learning*, Boston, MA; https://blog.hubspot.com/marketing/team-structure-diagrams; Burton and Obel. (2018). *Journal of Organization Design* Vol. 7, Issue 5, Devaney, Erik, "7 types of organizational Structure & Whom They're Suited For [Diagrams], *Hubspot*, accessed November 18, 2018. https://doi.org/10.1186/s41469-018-0029-2; "Matrix Teams", *Global Integration*, accessed November 18, 2018. http://www.global-integration.com/glossary/matrix-teams/; and Bersin, josh, "The organization of the Future: Arriving Now', 2017 Global Human Capital Trends, *Deloitte Insights*, February 28, 2017. https://www2.deloitte.com/insights/us/en/focus/human-capital-trends/2017/organization-of-the-future.html

26. Brent Durbin. Matrix organization, *Encyclopedia Britannica*, https://www.britannica.com/topic/matrix-organization

27. "Matrix Teams", *Global Integration*, accessed November 18, 2018. http://www.global-integration.com/glossary/matrix-teams/

28. ibid.

29. G. Satell. (June 8, 2015). What Makes an Organization "Networked", *Harvard Business Review*, https://hbr.org/2015/06/what-makes-an-organization-networked

30. Satell, Greg, "The Story of Networks", *Digital Tonto*, September 26, 2010. https://www.digitaltonto.com/2010/the-story-of-networks/; and "Networked Organizations", *Global Integration*, accessed November 18, 2018. http://www.global-integration.com/glossary/matrix-teams/ http://www.global-integration.com/glossary/networked-organization/

31. J. Bersin, T. McDowell, A. Rahnema, and Yves Van Durme. (February 28, 2017), "The organization of the future: Arriving now, 2017" Global Human Capital Trends, *Deloitte*. https://www2.deloitte.com/insights/us/en/focus/human-capital-trends/2017/organization-of-the-future.html

32. Lister, Jonathan, "The Disadvantages of Network-based organizational Structure", *Chron*, accessed November 18, 2018. http://smallbusiness.chron.com/disadvantages-networkbased-organization-structure-35988.html

33. Sources in this section include the following: C. Handy. (May–June 1995). Trust and the Virtual Organization, *Harvard Business Review*, https://hbr.org/1995/05/trust-and-the-virtual-organization; M. Ahuja and K. Carley. (1999), Network Structure in Virtual Organizations, *Organization Science*, Volume 10, Issue 6, June, pp. 741 – 757; http://www.yourarticlelibrary.com/organization/what-is-virtual-organisation-definition-characteristics-and-types/35533

34. D. Onley. (Apr 29, 2015), *Environment*, https://www.shrm.org/ResourcesAndTools/hr-topics/technology/Pages/How-Telecommuting-Helps-the-Environment.aspx

35. I. McCarthy, T. Lawrence, B. Wixted, and B. Gordon. (2010). A Multidimensional Conceptualization of Environmental Velocity, *Academy of Management Review* 34, no. 4, pp. 604-626

The Internal Organization and External Environments
36. Katz, D. & Kahn R. L. (1966). The social psychology of organizations, *John Wiley*, New York, N.Y.

37. Bertalanffy, L. (1968). General System Theory, *George Braziller*, publisher, New York.

38. Adapted from Arie Y. Lewin and Carroll U. Stephens, "CEO Attributes as Determinants of Organization Design: An integrated Model," *Organization Studies* 15, no. 2 (1994): 183-212

39. J. Trevor and B. Varcoe. (2017). How Aligned Is Your Organization? Harvard Business Review, February, https://hbr.org/2017/02/how-aligned-is-your-organization

40. Dalavagas, Iason, "McDonald's Corp: A Short SWOT Analysis, *Value line*, May 11, 2015. http://www.valueline.com/Stocks/Highlights/McDonalds_Corp__A_Short_SWOT_Analysis.aspx#.WyqOj1VKiig

41. "Amazon accounts for 43% of US online retail sales" *Business Insider*, February 3, 2017. http://www.businessinsider.com/amazon-accounts-for-43-of-us-online-retail-sales-2017-2

42. Dudovskiy, John, "Amazon Organizational Structure", *Research Methodology*, August 1, 2018 https://research-methodology.net/amazon-organizational-structure-2/

43. Meyer, Pauline, "Amazon.com Inc.'s Organizational Structure Characteristics (An Analysis)", *Panmore Institute*, September 8, 2018 http://panmore.com/amazon-com-inc-organizational-structure-characteristics-analysis

44. Ibid.

45. Cohan, Peter, "3 Reasons Amazon Is the World's Best Business", *Forbes*, February 2, 2018. https://www.forbes.com/sites/petercohan/2018/02/02/3-reasons-amazon-is-the-worlds-best-business/#563e86e63565

Corporate Cultures

46. Hyken, Shep, "Drucker said Culture Eats Strategy for Breakfast", *Forbes*, December 5, 2015. https://www.forbes.com/sites/shephyken/2015/12/05/drucker-said-culture-eats-strategy-for-breakfast-and-enterprise-rent-a-car-proves-it/#7a7572822749

47. Ed Schein. (2010). Organizational Culture and Leadership, 4th ed., San Francisco, CA: *Jossey-Bass*; J.W. Weiss. (2014). An Introduction to Leadership, 2nd ed., Bridgepoint Education, Inc.C

48. This discussion of the CVF is based on these sources: K. Cameron, R. Quinn, J. Degraff, and A. Thakor, (2014). Competing Values Leadership, 2nd ed., *New Horizons in Management*, Northampton, MA; K. Cameron and R. Quinn (2006). Diagnosing and Changing Organizational Culture: Based on the Competing Values Framework, San Francisco, CA: *Jossey-Bass*; and https://www.ocai-online.com/blog/2016/09/Organizational-culture-Create-Collaborate-Control-Compete

49. T. Yu and N. Wu. (2009). "A Review of Study on the Competing Values Framework", *International Journal of Business Management*, Vol.4, No. 7, July, pp. 47-42.

50. Nocera, Joe, "Jeff Bezos and The Amazon way", *The New York Times*, August 21, 2015. https://www.nytimes.com/2015/08/22/opinion/joe-nocera-jeff-bezos-and-the-amazon-way.html

51. Farber, Madeline, "Amazon Employee Attempts Suicide After Sending Email to Colleagues", *Fortune*, November 29, 2016. http://fortune.com/2016/11/29/amazon-employee-suicide-attempt/

Organizing for Change in the 21st Century

52. The Global Economic Report, 13th Edition, *World Economic Forum*, 2018. http://www3.weforum.org/docs/WEF_GRR18_Report.pdf, p. 8 and pp. 54-57.

53. Agarwal, Dimple, "Introduction: The Rise of the Social Enterprise", *Deloitte Insights*, March 28, 2018.? https://www2.deloitte.com/insights/us/en/focus/human-capital-trends/2018/introduction.html

54. Ibid.

55. Ibid.

Ethics and Business Ethics Defined

1. Hartman, L., J. DesJardins and MacDonald, C. (2018). Business Ethics: Decision Making for Personal Integrity and Social Responsibility, 4th ed., McGraw-Hill, New York, New York; and Weiss, J.W. (2014). Business Ethics, A Stakeholder and Issues Management Approach, 6th ed. Oakland, CA: Berrett-Koehler Publishers.

2. Eleazar Melendez. (2013). Financial Crisis Cost Tops $22 Trillion. https://www.huffingtonpost.co/2013/02/14/financial-crisis-cost-gao_n_2687553.html

3. James Flanigan. (2002). Enron Is Proving Costly to Economy, http://articles.latimes.com/2002/jan/20/news/mn-23790

4. David Auerbach. (2015). The Programs That Become the Programmers, http://www.slate.com/articles/technology/bitwise/2015/09/

pedro_domingos_master_algorithm_how_machine_learning_is_reshaping_how_we.html

5. Julia Angwin, Jeff Larson, Surya Mattu and Lauren Kirchner. (2016). Machine Bias. ProPublica analysis of data from Broward County, Fla., https://www.propublica.org/article/machine-bias-risk-assessments-in-criminal-sentencing

6. Hern, A. "Growth of AI Could Boost Cybercrime and Security Threats, Report Warns", The Guardian, February 21, 2018. https://www.theguardian.com/technology/2018/feb/21/ai-security-threats-cybercrime-political-disruption-physical-attacks-report

7. Nevejans, N. (2016). European Civil Law Rules in Robotics, http://www.europarl.europa.eu/RegData/etudes/STUD/2016/571379/IPOL_STU(2016)571379_EN.pdf

8. Ripple, W., World Scientists' Warning to Humanity: A Second Warning", XXXX / Vol. XX No. X • *BioScience*, 2017, http://scientists.forestry.oregonstate.edu/sites/sw/files/Ripple_et_al_warning_2017.pdf.

9. Samuel Chiu. (2017). Climate experts release latest science on sea level rise projections, https://phys.org/news/2017-04-climate-experts-latest-science-sea.html

10. Friedman, Z. (2018). Trump Administration Requests $0 In Funding For Consumer Protection Agency, https://www.forbes.com/sites/zackfriedman/2018/01/19/cfpb-funding-trump/#61dd837c1826

11. AACSB, *A Collective Vision for Business Education*, AACSB International, 2016, https://www.aacsb.edu/-/media/aacsb/publications/research-reports/collective-vision/collective-vision-for-business-education.ashx

Dimensions of Ethics: The Individual Level

12. ECI Connects. (2016). https://connects.ethics.org/search?executeSearch=true&SearchTerm=22+percent&l=1

13. Rokeach, M., *The Nature of Human Values*, Free Press, 1973, p. 56.

14. Ibid.

15. Comrie, H. (2017). Wells Fargo Fake Accounts Scandal, https://sevenpillarsinstitute.org/wells-fargo-fake-accounts-scandal/

16. Carouchi, R. (2016). Why Ethical People Make Unethical Choices, https://hbr.org/2016/12/why-ethical-people-make-unethical-choices

Ethical Principles and Responsible Decision-Making

17. This section is based on and taken from J.W. Weiss, (2014), Business Ethics, A Stakeholder and Issues Management Approach, 6th edition, Barrett-Koehler Publishers, Oakland, CA.

18. Covey, S. R. (2004). *The 7 habits of highly effective people: Restoring the character ethic*. New York: Free Press.

19. Sarros, J., Cooper, B.K., and Santora, J.C., "Building a Climate for Innovation Through Transformational Leadership and Organizational Culture", Journal of Leadership and Organizational Studies, June 30, 2008.

20. Velasquez, M., Andre, C., Shanks, T., & Meyer, M. (2014). Can Ethics Be Taught? http://www.scu.edu/ethics-center/aboutcenter

21. Sisodia, R., Wolfe, D., and Sheth, J. (2007). Firms of endearment: How world- class companies profit from passion and purpose, 137. Upper Saddle River, NJ: Wharton School Publishing.

Leadership: Ethics at the Organizational Level

22. Collins, J. (2001). Good to great, 21. New York: HarperCollins; and parts of this section are based on J.W.Weiss (2015), Introduction to Leadership, 2nd edition, *Bridgepoint Education, Inc.*

23. Barnard, C. (1939). The functions of the executive, 259. Cambridge, MA: *Harvard University Press*.

24. Rost, J. C., and Barker, R.A., "Leadership Education in Colleges: Toward a 21st Century Paradigm", *Journal of Organizational Studies*, January 1, 2000.

25. Kauflin,J. (2017). The World's Most Ethical Companies, https://www.forbes.com/sites/jeffkauflin/2017/03/

14/the-worlds-most-ethical-companies-2017/#1a0f42e07bc3

26. Ephisphsere, (2017). Worlds Most Ethical Companies. http://worldsmostethicalcompanies.com/honorees/

27. Beauchamp, T. L., & Bowie, N. F. (1988). Ethical theory and business (3rd ed.). Englewood Cliffs, NJ: *Prentice Hall*.

28. Lelyveld, J. *Great Soul: Mahatma Gandhi and His Struggle with India* , Knopf, 2011.

29. The Guardian. (2014). Corporate transparency: why honesty is the best policy, https://www.theguardian.com/sustainable-business/corporate-transparency-honesty-best-policy

30. Cialdini, Petia, Petrova, and Goldstein, "The Hidden Costs of Organizational Dishonesty", MIT Sloan Review, Spring, 2004.

31. Oates, D., "Young Dallas philanthropist impacts the world from her Deep Ellum shop", *Culture Map*, October 30, 2014, http://dallas.culturemap.com/news/fashion/10-30-14-akola-project-flagship-store-deep-ellum-brittany-underwood/#slide=0.

32. Xavier University News and Events, "Former Malden Mills CEO Aaron Feuerstein speaking at Heroes of Professional Ethics event March 30", March 24, 2009, https://www2.xavier.edu/campusuite25/modules/news.cfm?seo_file=Former-Malden-Mills-CEO-Aaron-Feuerstein-speaking-at-Heroes-of-Professional-Ethics-event-March-30&grp_id=1#.W6FLZPZFyUk

33. Lussier, R. and Achua, C., Leadership: Theory, Application, and Skill Development, Thomson/South-Western, 2006.

34. Greenleaf, R.K., Servant Leadership: A Journey Into the Nature of Legitimate Power and Greatness, *Paulist Press*, 1977.

35. DeGraaf, D., Tilley C., & Neal, L. (2004). Servant-leadership characteristics in organizational life.

36. Driscoll, D. M., and Hoffman, W. (2000). Ethics matters, 68. Waltham, MA: Center for Business Ethics.

37. Fortune editors. (2016). The World's 19 Most Disappointing Leaders, http://fortune.com/2016/03/30/most-disappointing-leaders/

Ethics, Corporate Culture, and Compliance

38. Schein, E. (2017). Organizational culture and leadership, 5th ed., Hoboken, N.J.: John Wiley & Sons.

39. Cameron, K. and R. Quinn. (2011). Diagnosing and Changing Organization Culture, 3rd ed. San Francisco, CA: John Wiley & Sons publishers.

40. Schein, E. (2017). Organizational culture and leadership, 5th ed., Hoboken, N.J.: John Wiley & Sons.

41. Coleman, J. (2013). Six Components of a Great Corporate Culture, https://hbr.org/2013/05/six-components-of-culture

42. This section is based on and extrapolates from Ephisphere's Erica Salmon Byrnes' 2017 article " Culture Matters: The Advantages of a Strong Ethical Culture are Manifold," found at https://insights.ethisphere.com/culture-matters/:

43. Killingsworth, S. (2012), Modeling the Message: Communicating Compliance through Organizational Values and Culture. The Georgetown Journal of Legal Ethics,Vol. 25:961-987. file:///C:/Users/jweiss/Downloads/SSRN-id2161076.pdf

44. This section is based on and extrapolates from Ephisphere's Erica Salmon Byrnes' 2017 article " Culture Matters: The Advantages of a Strong Ethical Culture are Manifold," found at https://insights.ethisphere.com/culture-matters/

45. Weller, A. (2017). Exploring Practitioners' Meaning of "Ethics," "Compliance," and "Corporate Social Responsibility" Practices: A Communities of Practice Perspective, Business & Society, pp. 1-27, http://journals.sagepub.com/doi/pdf/10.1177/0007650317719263

46. The Sarbanes-Oxley Act of 2002. (March 2003). PricewaterhouseCoopers. http://www.pwc.com/en_US/us/sarbanes-oxley/assets/so_overview_final.pdf, accessed February 13, 2012.

47. Carroll, A. B. (2008). A History of Corporate Social Responsibility: Concepts and Practices, in The Oxford

Handbook of Corporate Social Responsibility, Chapter: Chapter 2, Publisher: Oxford University Press, pp.19 - 46

Corporate Social Responsibility (CSR)

48. Freeman, R. E. and Gilbert, D. R., Jr. (1988). Corporate strategy and the search for ethics. Englewood Cliffs, NJ: Prentice-Hall.

49. Rudominer, R. (2017). Corporate Social Responsibility Matters: Ignore Millennials at Your Peril. https://www.huffingtonpost.com/ryan-rudominer/corporate-social-responsi_9_b_9155670.html

50. Ibid.

51. Elkington, J., Cannibals with Forks, Oxford University Press, 1999.

52. Villas, N. (2017). Top 20 Corporate Social Responsibility Initiatives for 2017, https://www.smartrecruiters.com/blog/top-20-corporate-social-responsibility-initiatives-for-2017/

53. Friedman, Z. (2018). Trump Administration Requests $0 In Funding For Consumer Protection Agency, https://www.forbes.com/sites/zackfriedman/2018/01/19/cfpb-funding-trump/#61dd837c1826

54. Teng, D. and R. Yazdanifard. (2014). Does Corporate Social Responsibility make any differences when it comes to "Un-substitutable" Product from Customer Point of View, Journal of Research in Marketing Volume 2 No.2 April, pp. 167-171.

55. Menichini, T. and Rosati, F., "The Strategic Impact of CSR Consumer-Company Alignment", Procedia-Behavioral and Social Sciences, 109 (2014) 360 – 364, and Becker-Olsen and Hill, "The impact of perceived corporate social responsibility on consumer behavior", Journal of Business Research, 59 (1) (2006), pp. 46-53.

56. Orlitzky, O, F. Schmidt and S.Rynes. (2003). Corporate Social and Financial Performance: A Meta-Analysis, Organization Studies, 24:3 pp.403-441.

57. Robbins, R. (2015, May 5). Does Corporate Social Responsibility Increase Profits?, http://business-ethics.com/2015/05/05/does-corporate-social-responsibility-increase-profits/

58. Berman, S., Wicks, A., Kotha, S., and Jones, T. (1999). Does stakeholder orientation matter? The relationship between stakeholder management models and firm financial performance. Academy of Management Journal, 42, No. 5,October, pp. 488–506.

59. Freeman, R. E. (1999). Divergent stakeholder theory. Academy of Management Review, 24, 233–236.

60. Weiss, J.W. (2014). Business Ethics, A Stakeholder and Issues Management Approach, 6th ed. Oakland, CA: Berrett-Koehler Publishers; and Bowie, N., and Duska, R. (1991). Business ethics, 2nd ed. Englewood Cliffs, NJ:Prentice Hall.

61. Freeman, R. E. and Gilbert, D. R., Jr. (1988). Corporate strategy and the search for ethics. Englewood Cliffs, NJ: Prentice-Hall.

62. Donaldson T. and L. Preston. (1995), The Stakeholder Theory of the Corporation: Concepts, Evidence, and Implications Academy of Manage Review, January 1,Vol. 20 no. 1, pp. 65-91 ; and Weiss, J.W. (2014). Business Ethics, A Stakeholder and Issues Management Approach, 6th ed. Oakland, CA: Berrett-Koehler Publishers.

63. Falck, O. and S. Heblich, ". (2007). Corporate Social Responsibility: Doing Well By Doing Good, Business Horizons 50 (2007): 247–254.

64. Curtis C. Verschoor and Elizabeth A. Murphy, "The Financial Performance of Large U.S. Firms and Those with Global Prominence: How Do the Best Corporate Citizen Rate?" Business and Society Review 107, no. 2 (Fall 2002), 371–381.

65. Dvorak, P. (2007). Theory & Practice: Finding the Best Measure of 'Corporate Citizenship, The Wall Street Journal, July 2, B3 ; and Greening, D. and D.Turban. (2000). Corporate Social Performance as a Competitive Advantage in Attracting a Quality Workforce, Business and Society 39, no. 3, September, 254.

Ethics around the Globe

66. Daft, R. (2016). Organizational Theory & Design, 12th ed. Boston, MA: Cengage Learning.

67. Weiss, J.W. (2014). Business Ethics, A Stakeholder and Issues Management Approach, 6th ed. Oakland, CA:

Berrett-Koehler Publishers.

68. Cassin, R. (2017). Halliburton pays $29 million to settle Angola FCPA offenses, http://www.fcpablog.com/blog/2017/7/27/halliburton-pays-29-million-to-settle-angola-fcpa-offenses.html

69. Weiss, J.W. (2014). Business Ethics, A Stakeholder and Issues Management Approach, 6th ed. Oakland, CA: Berrett-Koehler Publishers.

70. Vijay Govindarajan, reported in Gail Dutton, "Building a Global Brain," Management Review (May 1999), 34–38.

71. United nations Global Compact, "The Ten principles of the united Nations Global Compact", https://www.unglobalcompact.org/what-is-gc/mission/principles.

72. Donaldson, T. and T. Dunfee(2000). A Review of Donaldson and Dunfee's Ties That Bind: A Social Contracts Approach to Business Ethics, Journal of Business Ethics, December, volume 28, issue 4, pp 383–387.

73. Hanna, D. (2016). Where can corporate culture and national cultures meet? https://www.insidehr.com.au/where-can-corporate-culture-and-national-cultures-meet/

74. Wittenberg-Cox, A. (2017). How Royal DSM Is Improving Its Geographic and Gender Diversity, https://hbr.org/2017/07/how-royal-dsm-is-improving-its-geographic-and-gender-diversity.

75. Ibid.

76. Vijay Govindarajan, reported in Gail Dutton, "Building a Global Brain," Management Review (May 1999), 34–38.

77. Homer H. Johnson, "Does It Pay to Be Good? Social Responsibility and Financial Performance," Business Horizons (November–December 2003), 34–40

78. Ethisphere, " Advancing Business Integrity for Compatitive Advantage", https://ethisphere.com/?gclid=EAIaIQobChMI_JSz4IOS2QIVzQOGCh2cXwXFEAAYASAAEgIaAfD_BwE.

Emerging Trends in Ethics, CSR, and Compliance

79. The Wall Street Journal/CFO Journal Deloitte, 2018, https://deloitte.wsj.com/riskandcompliance/2018/06/04/whistleblower-programs-who-should-be-in-charge-3/

80. Kaptein, M. (2017). The Moral Entrepreneur: A New Component of Ethical Leadership, Journal of Business Ethics. May, Pp. 1-16.

81. Brown, M and Trevino L., "Ethical leadership: A review and future directions", *The Leadership Quarterly*, December 2006, Pages 595-616.

82. Ibid.

83. Kaptein, M. (2017). The Moral Entrepreneur: A New Component of Ethical Leadership, Journal of Business Ethics. May, Pp. 1-16.

84. Brown, M and Trevino L., "Ethical leadership: A review and future directions", *The Leadership Quarterly*, December 2006, Pages 595-616.

85. Gregory, T., "Small Catholic University, Big Muslim Enrollment Try To Build Bridges", *The Chicago Tribune*, January 14, 2017, http://www.chicagotribune.com/news/ct-benedictine-university-muslims-met-20170115-story.html.

86. Smith, "Could Your Leadership Style be Influencing Bad Behavior?", *INSEAD Knowledge*, October 14, 2014, https://knowledge.insead.edu/leadership-organisations/could-your-leadership-style-be-influencing-bad-behaviour-3638.

87. van Prooijen, A.M. and Ellemers, N, "Does it pay to be moral? How indicators of morality and competence enhance organizational and work team attractiveness", *British Journal of Management* 26 (2), 225-236

Introduction

1. Pankaj Ghemawat, "Globalization in the age of Trump," *Harvard Business Review,* July-August, 2017, pp. 712-716.

Importance of International Management

2. Divesh Kaul, "Eliminating trade barriers through preferential trade agreements: perspectives from South Asia," *Tulane Journal of International and Comparative Law,* Vol 25, pp. 355-402.

3. https://www.wto.org/

4. Bloomberg BusinessWeek,"Now on EBay: Russian micro-multinationals," 3-20-17, businessweek.com

Hofstede's Cultural Framework

5. Geert Hofstede, "*Culture's consequences: Comparing values, behaviors and institutions across nations,*" 2nd edition, 2001, Thousand Oaks, CA: Sage Publications.

6. Geert Hofstede, "*Culture's consequences: Comparing values, behaviors and institutions across nations,*" 2nd edition, 2001, Thousand Oaks, CA: Sage Publications.

7. Bradley L. Kirkman, Kevin B. Lowe and Cristina B. Gibson, "A quarter century of culture's consequences: A review of empirical research incorporating Hofstede's cultural values framework," *Journal of International Business Studies,* Vol 37 , pp. 285-320.

The GLOBE Framework

8. R.J. House, P.J. Hanges, M. Javidan, P.W. Dorfman and V. Gupta (eds), 2004, *Culture, Leadership and Organizations: The GLOBE Study of 62 Societies*, Thousand Oaks, CA: Sage.

9. Mansour Javidan, Peter W. Dorfman, Mary Sully de Luque, and Robert J. House, 2006, "In the eye of the beholder: Cross-cultural lessons in leadership for project GLOBE," *The Academy of Management Perspectives*, February, *20*(1), pp. 67–90

Cultural Stereotyping and Social Institutions

10. Erin Meyer, "Being the boss in Brussels, Boston and Beijing," *Harvard Business Review,* July-August, 2017, pp. 70-77.

11. Joyce S. Osland and Allan Bird, "Beyond sophisticated stereotyping: Cultural sensemaking in context," *Academy of Management Executive,* Vol 14, 2000, pp. 65-77.

12. Vas Taras, Piers Steel and Bradley L. Kirkman, "Does country equate with culture? Beyond geography in the search for cultural boundaries," *Management International Review,* 2016, Vol. 56, pp. 455-487.

13. Turner, J. H. 1997. *The Institutional Order.* New York: Addison-Wesley, 6.

14. M.E. Olsen, "*Societal dynamics: Exploring macrosociology,*" pp. 375, Englewood Cliffs, NJ: Prentice Hall.

15. K. Praveen Parboteeah and John B. Cullen, "Social institutions and work centrality: Explorations beyond national culture," *Organization Science, 2003,* Vol 14, pp. 137-148.

16. K. Praveen Parboteeah, John B. Cullen and Martin Hoegl, "Managers' gender role attitudes: A country institutional approach," *Journal of International Business Studies,* 2008, Vol. 39, pp. 795-813.

17. Fisher, Mary P. 1999. *Living Religions,* 7th ed. Upper Saddle River, NJ: Prentice Hall 273.

18. Pew Research: http://www.pewresearch.org/fact-tank/2017/04/05/christians-remain-worlds-largest-religious-group-but-they-are-declining-in-europe/

19. Fisher, Mary P. 1999. *Living Religions,* 7th ed. Upper Saddle River, NJ: Prentice Hall.

20. Parboteeeah, K.P, Walter, S., Block, J. 2015. When faith meets innovation: Religion, entrepreneurial opportunities, and entrepreneurial activity. *Journal of Business Ethics*, 130, 447-465.

Cross-Cultural Assignments

21. Jacob Eisenberg, Hyun-Jung Lee, Frank Bruck, Barbara Brenner, Marie-Therese Claes, Jacek Mironski and Roger Bell, "Can business schools make students culturally competent? Effects of cross-cultural management courses on cultural intelligence," *Academy of Management Learning and Education,* 2013, Vol. 12, pp. 603-621.

22. Jase R. Ramsey and Melanie Lorenz, "Exploring the impact of cross-cultural management on cultural intelligence, student satisfaction, and commitment," *Academy of Management Learning and Education, 2016, Vol. 15, pp. 79-99.*

23. Tomasz Lenartowicz, James P. Johnson and Robert Konopaske, "The application of learning theories to improve cross-cultural training programs in MNCs," *International Journal of Human Resource Management,* 2014, Vol. 25, pp. 1697-1719.

24. Tomasz Lenartowicz, James P. Johnson and Robert Konopaske, "The application of learning theories to improve cross-cultural training programs in MNCs," *International Journal of Human Resource Management,* 2014, Vol. 25, pp. 1697-1719.

25. Tomasz Lenartowicz, James P. Johnson and Robert Konopaske, "The application of learning theories to improve cross-cultural training programs in MNCs," *International Journal of Human Resource Management,* 2014, Vol. 25, pp. 1697-1719.

26. Shira Mor, Michael Morris and Johann Joh, "Identifying and training adaptive cross-cultural management skilss: The crucial role of cultural metacognition," *Academy of Management Learning and Education,* 2013, Vol. 12, pp. 453-475.

27. Rita Bennett, Anne Aston and Tracy Colquhoun, "Cross-cultural training: A critical step in ensuring the success of international assignments," *Human Resource Management,* Summer/Fall 2000, Vol. 39, pp. 239-250.

28. Yu-lin Wang and Emma Tran, "Effects of cross-cultural and language training on expatriates' adjustment and job performance in Vietnam," *Asia Pacific Journal of Human Resources,* 2012, Vol. 50, pp. 327-350.

29. Molinsky, A, "The mistakes most managers make with cross-cultural training," *Harvard Business Review,* January 15, 2015, pp. 2-4.

Strategies for Expanding Globally

30. Alain Verbeke and Christian G. Asmussen, "Global, local, or regional? The locus of MNE strategies," *Journal of Management Studies,* 2016, Vol. 53, pp. 1051-1075.

31. Ellen Hughes Cromwick, "Ford Motor company's global electrification strategy," *Business Economics,* 2011, Vol. 46, pp. 167-170.

32. http://www.mcdonaldsindia.net/

33. https://www.bayer.com/en/crop-science-division.aspx

34. Maya Townsend, Lisa Coen and Kittie Watson, "From regional to global: Using a network strategy to align a multinational organization," *People+Strategy,* Spring 2017, Vol. 40, pp. 32-38.

The Necessity of Global Markets

35. https://www.bcgperspectives.com/content/articles/globalization_growth_time_reengage_retreat_emerging_markets/

36. U.S Department of Commerce, "A basic guide to exporting," 11th edition, 2015, https://www.export.gov/article?id=Why-Companies-should-export

37. U.S Department of Commerce, "A basic guide to exporting," 11th edition, 2015, https://www.export.gov/article?id=Why-Companies-should-export

38. https://www.export.gov/welcome

39. Daniel Simonet, "Entry modes of European firms in Vietnam," *Emerging Markets Journal,* 2012, Vol 2, pp. 10-29.

40. Priya S. Lakshmi, BB Mani Latha, H. Chiathra, T. Kavya and Roopika Ashwanth, "Study on food franchise in India: With special reference to Bangalore," *International Journal of Research in Commerce and Management,* 2015, Vol. 6, pp. 80-83.

41. Priya S. Lakshmi, BB Mani Latha, H. Chiathra, T. Kavya and Roopika Ashwanth, "Study on food franchise in India: With special reference to Bangalore," *International Journal of Research in Commerce and Management,* 2015, Vol. 6, pp. 80-83.

42. Rajesh Kumar, "Managing ambiguity in strategic alliances," *California Management Review,* Summer 2014, Vol. 56, pp. 82-102.

43. PWC, 2015, "Courting China Inc: Expectations, pitfalls, and success factors of Sino-foreign business

partnerships in China," https://www.pwc.com.au/asia-practice/assets/courting-china-aug15.pdf

44. Minjung Kim, "The effects of strategic alliances on firm productivity in South Korea," *Applied Economics,* 2015, Vol. 47, pp. 5034-5044.

45. Economist, "Not lovin' it," 2017, September 30, pp. 60.

46. Sylvie Chetty and Colin Campbell-Hunt, "A strategic approach to internationalization: A traditional versus a "born-global" approach," *Journal of International Marketing,* 2004, Vol 12, pp. 57-81.

47. Sylvie Chetty and Colin Campbell-Hunt, "A strategic approach to internationalization: A traditional versus a "born-global" approach," *Journal of International Marketing,* 2004, Vol 12, pp. 57-81.

48. Economist, "Why does Kenya lead the world in mobile money," 2015, March 2nd, Online Edition.

49. Kieran Monks, "M-PESA: Kenya's mobile money success story turns 10," *CNN,* February 24, http://www.cnn.com/2017/02/21/africa/mpesa-10th-anniversary/index.html

50. Eliane Choquette, Morten Rask, Davide Sala and Phillipp Schroder, "Born globals - is there fire behind the smoke," *International Business Review,* Vol. 26, pp. 448-460.

51. Sylvie Chetty and Colin Campbell-Hunt, "A strategic approach to internationalization: A traditional versus a "born-global" approach," *Journal of International Marketing,* 2004, Vol 12, pp. 57-81.

52. Lidia Danik and Izabela Kowalik, "Success factors and development barriers perceived by the Polish born global companies. Empirical study results," *Journal for East European Management Studies,* 2015, Vol. 20, pp. 360-390.

53. Andreas P. Petrou, "Foreign market entry strategies in retail banking: Choosing an entry mode in a landscape of constraints," *Long Range Planning,* 2009, Vol. 42, pp. 614-632.

54. Lidia Danik and Izabela Kowalik, "Success factors and development barriers perceived by the Polish born global companies. Empirical study results," *Journal for East European Management Studies,* 2015, Vol. 20, pp. 360-390.

Entrepreneurship

1. Shannon McMahon, "Stepping into a Fortune," *San Diego Union-Tribune,* April 5, 2005, p. C4.

2. Dashel Pierson, "10 Things You Should Know about Surfing in the Olympics," *Surfline,* http://www.surfline.com, August 5, 2016.

3. Steve Chapple, "Reef Brand's Co-founder Eyes the Horizon," *San Diego Union Tribune,* https://www.sandiegouniontribune.com, December 13, 2013.

4. Andrew Morse, "An Entrepreneur Finds Tokyo Shares Her Passion for Bagels," *The Wall Street Journal,* October 18, 2005, p. B1.

5. Barbara Farfan, "Amazon.com's Mission Statement", *The Balance.* April 15, 2018, https://www.thebalance.com/amazon-mission-statement-4068548.

6. "About StartupNation," https://startupnation.com, accessed February 1, 2018; Jim Morrison, "Entrepreneurs," *American Way Magazine,* October 15, 2005, p. 94.

Characteristics of Successful Entrepreneurs

7. Martha Irvine, "More 20-Somethings Are Blazing Own Paths in Business," *San Diego Union-Tribune,* November 22, 2004, p. C6.

8. Keith McFarland, "What Makes Them Tick," *Inc. 500,* October 19, 2005, http://www.inc.com.

9. Ibid.

Small Business

10. U.S. Small Business Administration, "Make Sure You Meet SBA Size Standards," https://www.sba.gov, accessed February 1, 2018.

11. "Who We Are," http://www.kauffman.org, accessed February 1, 2018; "Ewing Marion Kauffman Foundation," http://en.wikipedia.org, accessed February 1, 2018.

12. "Annual Survey of Entrepreneurs," https://www.census.gov, accessed February 1, 2018.

13. "The Kauffman Index," http://www.kauffman.org, accessed February 2, 2018.

Start Your Own Business

14. Adapted from "They've Founded Million Dollar Companies and They're not Even 30,"https://www.inc.com/30-under-30.

15. McFarland, "What Makes Them Tick."

16. "The Kauffman Index," http://www.kauffman.org, accessed February 2, 2018.

17. Andrew Blackman, "Know When to Give Up," *The Wall Street Journal,* May 9, 2005, p. R9.

Managing a Small Business

18. Michelle Prather, "Talk of the Town," *Entrepreneur Magazine,* February 2003, http://www.entrepreneur.com.

The Large Impact of Small Business

19. Forbes, "Ten Best Cities for Entrepreneurs" https://www.forbes.com/pictures/feki45igde/10-best-cities-for-young-entrepreneurs/#5bc189726058.

20. Don Debelak, "Rookie Rules," *Business Start-Ups Magazine,* http://www.entrepreneur.com, March 2, 2006.

21. McFarland, "What Makes Them Tick."

The Small Business Administration

22. Much of the statistical information for the SBA section is from the Small Business Administration website at http://www.sba.gov.

23. "SBA Lending Activity in FY 2017 Shows Consistent Growth," https://www.sba.gov, October 13, 2017.

Trends in Entrepreneurship and Small-Business Ownership

24. "Small Business Profile: 2016," https://www.sba.gov, accessed February 2, 2018.

25. "The State of Women-Owned Businesses: 2017," http://about.americanexpress.com, accessed February 2, 2018.

26. Ibid.

27. Steve Strauss, "Boomers' Role in Entrepreneurship Is, Well, Booming," *USA Today,* https://www.usatoday.com, August 25, 2017.

28. Scott Hanson, "Baby Boomers Are Rewriting Retirement History," *Kiplinger,* https://www.kiplinger.com, January 3, 2018.

29. "SBA Lending Activity in FY 2017 Shows Consistent Growth."

30. SBA Office of Advocacy, "Annual Report of the Office of Economic Research: 2016," https://www.sba.gov, accessed February 2, 2018.

31. Lora Kolodny, "This Start-up Fled the High Cost of Silicon Valley to Help Non-Tech Workers Get an Education," *CNBC,* https://www.cnbc.com, September 6, 2017.

32. Tamara Chuang, "4 Silicon Valley Venture Firms Invest $21 Million in Denver's Guild Education," *The Denver Post,* https://www.denverpost.com, September 6, 2017.

33. PwC/CB Insights, "MoneyTree Report Q3 2017," https://www.pwc.com, accessed February 2, 2018.

34. Ibid.

Introduction

1. PDR (2016). Lauri Goodman Lampson, President + CEO. http://www.pdrcorp.com/lauri-goodman-lampson/ Accessed July 28, 2017.

2. Steelcase, (n.d.). Accenture Relocation Aids Collaboration. https://www.steelcase.com/research/articles/topics/real-estate-optimization/accenture/ Accessed July 28, 2017.

3. PDR (2016). Lauri Goodman Lampson President + CEO. http://www.pdrcorp.com/lauri-goodman-lampson/

Accessed July 28, 2017.

4. Steelcase (2011). Accenture Case Study. https://www.youtube.com/watch?v=y4oIlY3HJfo&t=219s Accessed July 28, 2017.

Using SWOT for Strategic Analysis

5. Paychex (2017). Company History. https://www.paychex.com/corporate/history.aspx Accessed July 28, 2017.

A Firm's External Macro Environment: PESTEL

6. Chris Mooney (January 10, 2017). "America's first 'clean coal' plant is now operational — and another is on the way." *The Washington Post*. https://www.washingtonpost.com/news/energy-environment/wp/2017/01/10/americas-first-clean-coal-plant-is-now-operational-and-another-is-on-the-way/?utm_term=.0020d0987631 Accessed July 28, 2017.

7. Smith, Geoffrey (2017). "Paris Wants to Ban the Combustion Engine by 2030." *Fortune*. Oct. 12, 2017. *http://fortune.com/2017/10/12/paris-combustion-engine-ban/*

8. Trangbæk, Roar Rude (2016). "LEGO Group to invest 1 Billion DKK Boosting Search for Sustainable Materials." https://www.lego.com/en-us/aboutus/news-room/2015/june/sustainable-materials-centre. Accessed July 29, 2017.

9. Brand Finance (2017). "Toys 25 2016." http://brandfinance.com/images/upload/brand_finance_toys_25_2017_report_locked.pdf Accessed July 29, 2017.

10. Holodny, Elena (2016). TIMELINE: The tumultuous 155-year history of oil prices. *Business Insider*. http://www.businessinsider.com/timeline-155-year-history-of-oil-prices-2016-12 Accessed July 29, 2017.

11. Peters, Adele (2015). "Why LEGO is Spending Millions to Ditch Oil-Based Plastic." *Fast Company*. https://www.fastcompany.com/3048017/why-lego-is-spending-millions-to-ditch-oil-based-plastic Accessed July 29, 2017.

The Internal Environment

12. Ridester (2017). "How Much do Uber Drivers Actually Make? The Inside Scoop." *Ridester.com*. https://www.ridester.com/how-much-do-uber-drivers-make/ Accessed July 29, 2017.

13. Bensinger, Greg (2017). "Lyft Shifts Gears With New Driverless-Car Division; San Francisco company to hire hundreds of engineers and open new Silicon Valley office." *The Wall Street Journal*. July 21, 2017.

14. Edelstein, Stephen (2017). "Lyft Finally Launches Its Boston Self-Driving Car Pilot Program." *The Drive*. Dec. 17, 2017. http://www.thedrive.com/tech/16779/lyft-finally-launches-its-boston-self-driving-car-pilot-program

15. O'Kane, Sean (2018). "I took a gamble by riding in a self-driving Lyft in Las Vegas." *The Verge*. January 8, 2018. https://www.theverge.com/2018/1/8/16860590/self-driving-lyft-las-vegas-ces-2018

16. Korosec, Kristen (2018). "Uber self-driving cars back on public roads, but in manual mode/" *Tech Crunch*. July 24, 2018. https://techcrunch.com/2018/07/24/uber-self-driving-cars-back-on-public-roads-but-in-manual-mode/

Introduction

1. Feldman, Amy (2016). "Costco For Millennials: How Chieh Huang Built Boxed, A Mobile Juggernaut With $100M+ In Revenue." *Forbes*. https://www.forbes.com/sites/forbestreptalks/2016/10/19/costco-for-millennials-how-chieh-huang-built-boxed-a-mobile-juggernaut-with-100m-in-revenue/#7870fb552adb Accessed September 4, 2017.

2. Mccausland, Christianna (2016). "Boxed founder Chieh Huang shares lessons in entrepreneurship." *Johns Hopkins Magazine*. https://hub.jhu.edu/magazine/2016/summer/boxed-chieh-huang-interview/. Accessed September 4, 2017.

3. Huang, Chieh (2016). Interview on Mad Money, MSNBC. Available on Youtube: https://www.youtube.com/watch?v=3ANAe1vLAIw

Firm Vision and Mission
4. The Marketing Blender (2017). "Best Examples of Company Vision and Mission Statements."
http://www.themarketingblender.com/vision-mission-statements/
5. Ibid.

Strategic Objectives and Levels of Strategy
6. CBInsights (2018). "Walmart's Been On A Buying Spree. Which Company Could It Acquire Next?."
CBInsights.com. https://www.cbinsights.com/research/walmart-acquisition-targets/. Jan. 5, 2018.

Planning Firm Actions to Implement Strategies
7. Tesla (2017). "Tesla Gigafactory." Tesla.com. https://www.tesla.com/gigafactory. Accessed September 4, 2017.

Organizational Structures and Design
1. For an in-depth exploration of the field of organizational development and change, see Cummings, Thomas G. and Worley, Christopher G., *Organization Development and Change*, 11th edition, Cengage Learning, 2019.
2. Katz, D. and Kahn, R. L., *The Social Psychology of Organizations*, 2nd edition, John Wiley and Sons, 1978; and Schein, Edgar, *Organizational Psychology*, 3rd edition, Prentice Hall, 1980.
3. Weber, Max, *From Max Weber: Essays in Sociology*, Oxford University Press, 1958.

Organizational Change
4. Brown, K. and Eisenhardt, M., "The Art of Continuous Change: Linking Complexity Theory and Time-Paced Evolution in Relentlessly Shifting Organizations", *Administrative Science Quarterly*, 42, 1997, pp 1-34.
5. Kotter, J. and Schlesinger, L., "Choosing Strategies for Change", *Harvard Business Review*, 57, 1979, pp. 106-114.
6. Setter, Craig Joseph and The Council for Six Sigma Certification, *Six Sigma: A Complete Step-by-Step Guide*, The Council for Six Sigma Certification, 2018.
7. Eisenbach, R., Watson, K., and Pillai, R., "Transformational Leadership in the Context of Organizational Change", *Journal of Organizational Change Management*, 12, 1999, pp. 80-89.

Managing Change
8. Cummings, Thomas G. and Worley, Christopher G., *Organization Development and Change*, 11th edition, Cengage Learning, 2019.
9. Quinn, R. E. (2015). *The Positive Organization: Breaking Free from Conventional Cultures, Constraints, and Beliefs* (1 edition). Oakland: Berrett-Koehler Publishers.
10. Lewin, K., *Field Theory in Social Science*, Harper & Row, 1951; and Kotter, J., *Leading Change*, Harvard Business School Press, 2012.
11. Cooperrider, David L., *The Appreciative Inquiry Handbook: For Leaders of Change*, Berrett-Kohler, 2008.
12. Olson, Edwin E. and Eoyang, Glenda H., *Facilitating Organizational Change: Lessons from Complexity Science*, Pfeiffer, 2001.
13. Bright, D. S. (2009). Appreciative Inquiry and Positive Organizational Scholarship: A Philosophy of Practice for Turbulent Times. *OD Practitioner, 41*(3), 2–7.
14. Whitney, D., & Trosten-Bloom, A. (2010). *The Power of Appreciative Inquiry: A Practical Guide to Positive Change* (Second Edition). Berrett-Koehler Publishers.
15. Burnes, B. (2005). Complexity theories and organizational change. *International Journal of Management Reviews, 7*(2), 73–90.
16. Owen, H. (2008). *Open Space Technology: A User's Guide* (Third Edition). Berrett-Koehler Publishers.
17. Olson, E. E., & Eoyang, G. H. (2001). *Facilitating Organization Change: Lessons From Complexity Science* (1st ed.). Pfeiffer.
18. ibid.

An Introduction to Human Resource Management

1. Ulrich, Younger, Brockbank, Younger, HR From the Outside In, 2012. SHRM.org

Performance Management

2. "The Performance Management Revolution", Harvard Business Review, October 2016).

3. Buckingham and Goodall, "Reinventing Performance Management", Harvard Business Review, 2015.

4. Goler, Gale and Grant, "Let's Not Kill Performance Evaluations Yet", Harvard Business Review, Nov 2016.

5. Capelli and Tavis, "The Performance Management Revolution", Harvard Business Review, 2016, p. 9-11.

Influencing Employee Performance and Motivation

6. Stephen Miller, "Study: Pay for Performance Pays Off", Society for Human Resource Management, 2011.

7. 2015 World at Work "Compensation Programs and Practices Report"

8. Nohria, Groysberg, Lee, "Employee, Motivation: A Powerful New Model" Harvard Business Review, August 2008.

Building an Organization for the Future

9. Fernandez-Araoz, Groysberg, Nohria, "The Definitive Guide to Recruiting in Good Times and Bad", Harvard Business Review, 2009.

10. Ibid.

Talent Development and Succession Planning

11. Effron and Ort, One Page Talent Management, Harvard Business School Press, 2010.

An Introduction to Workplace Diversity

1. McGrath, J. E., Berdahl, J.L., & Arrow, H. (1995). Traits, expectations, culture, and clout: The dynamics of diversity in work groups. In S.E. Jackson & M.N. Ruderman (Eds.), Diversity in Work Teams, 17-45. Washington, D.C.: American Psychological Association.

2. Thomas, R. R. 1991. Beyond race and gender. New York, NY: AMACOM.

3. Cox, Taylor H., and Stacy Blake. "Managing cultural diversity: Implications for organizational competitiveness." The Executive (1991): 45-56.

4. Pelled, L. H., Ledford, G. E., Jr., & Mohrman, S. A. (1999). Demographic dissimilarity and workplace inclusion. Journal of Management Studies, 36, 1013-1031.

5. Lambert, J.R., & Bell, M.P. (2013). Diverse forms of difference. In Q. Roberson (Ed.) Oxford Handbook of Diversity and Work (pp. 13 – 31). New York: Oxford University Press.

6. Harrison, D.A., Price, K.H., & Bell, M.P. (1998). Beyond relational demography: time and the effects of surface- and deep-level diversity on work group cohesion. Academy of Management Journal, 41(1), 96-107.

7. Lambert, J.R., & Bell, M.P. (2013). Diverse forms of difference. In Q. Roberson (Ed.) Oxford Handbook of Diversity and Work (pp. 13 – 31). New York: Oxford University Press.

8. Clair, J.A., Beatty, J.E., & Maclean, T.L. (2005). Out of sight but not out of mind: Managing invisible social identities in the workplace. Academy of Management Review, 30 (1), 78-95.

9. Philips, K.W., Rothbard, N.P., & Dumas, T.L. (2009). To disclose or not to disclose? Status distance and self-disclosure in diverse environments. Academy of Management Review, 34(4), 710-732.

Diversity and the Workforce

10. Judy, R.W., D'Amico, C., & Geipel, G.L.(1997). Workforce 2020: Work and Workers in the 21st Century. Indianapolis, Ind: Hudson Institute.

11. U.S. Bureau of Labor Statistics. (2017). Labor force characteristics by race and ethnicity, 2016. Retrieved from https://www.bls.gov/opub/reports/race-and-ethnicity/2016/home.htm

12. U.S. Department of Labor, Bureau of Labor Statistics. (2017). Table A-1. Employment status of the civilian population by sex and age. Retrieved from https://www.bls.gov/news.release/empsit.t01.htm; DeWolf, M. (Mar 1 2017). 12 stats about working women. Retrieved from https://blog.dol.gov/2017/03/01/12-stats-about-working-women

13. Toosi, Mitra,"Labor force projections to 2024: the labor force is growing, but slowly," Monthly Labor Review, U.S. Bureau of Labor Statistics, December 2015, https://doi.org/10.21916/mlr.2015.48.

14. U.S. Bureau of Labor Statistics. (2017). Labor force characteristics by race and ethnicity, 2016. Retrieved from https://www.bls.gov/opub/reports/race-and-ethnicity/2016/home.htm

15. U.S. Department of Labor, Bureau of Labor Statistics. (2017). Table 2: Employment status of the civilian noninstitutional population 16 years and over by sex, 1977 to date 11. Retrieved from https://www.bls.gov/cps/cpsaat02.pdf.

16. Toosi, Mitra,"Labor force projections to 2024: the labor force is growing, but slowly," Monthly Labor Review, U.S. Bureau of Labor Statistics, December 2015, https://doi.org/10.21916/mlr.2015.48.

17. U.S. Department of Labor, Bureau of Labor Statistics. (2017). Table 2: Employment status of the civilian noninstitutional population 16 years and over by sex, 1977 to date 11. Retrieved from https://www.bls.gov/cps/cpsaat02.pdf.

18. DeWolf, M. (2017). 12 stats about working women. U.S. Department of Labor Blog.

19. Eagly, A.H., & Karau, S.J.(2002). Role congruity theory of prejudice toward female leaders. Psychological Review, 109 (3): 573-598.

20. EEOC, "Facts About Sexual Harassment." Retrieved from https://www.eeoc.gov/eeoc/publications/fs-sex.cfm

21. Ibid.

22. EEOC, "Sexual Harassment." Retrieved from https://www.eeoc.gov/laws/types/sexual_harassment.cfm

23. Feldblum, C.R., & Lipnic, V.A. (2016).Report of the Co-Chairs of the EEOC Select Task Force on the Study of Harassment in the Workplace. Retrieved from https://www.eeoc.gov/eeoc/task_force/harassment/report.cfm

24. Hernandez, T.K. (2000). Sexual Harassment and Racial Disparity: The Mutual Construction of Gender and Race. Gender, Race and Justice (4J): 183 -224. Retrieved from http://ir.lawnet.fordham.edu/faculty_scholarship/12

25. Fitzgerald, L.F., Drasgow, R., Hulin, C.L., Gelfand, M.J., & Magley, V.J. (1997). Antecedents and consequences of sexual harassment in organizations: A test of an integrated model. Journal of Applied Psychology, 82: 578-589; Shaffer, M.A., Joplin, J.R.W., Bell, M.P., Lau, T., & Oguz, C. (2000). Gender discrimination and job-related outcomes: A cross-cultural comparison of working women in the United States and China. Journal of Vocational Behavior, 57(4): 395-427.

26. Toosi, Mitra,"Labor force projections to 2024: the labor force is growing, but slowly," Monthly Labor Review, U.S. Bureau of Labor Statistics, December 2015, https://doi.org/10.21916/mlr.2015.48.

27. Ibid.

28. Ibid.

29. U.S. Equal Employment Opportunity Commission. African-Americans in the American Workforce. Retrieved from https://www1.eeoc.gov/eeoc/statistics/reports/american_experiences/african_americans.cfm?renderforprint=1

30. Quilian, L., Pager, D., Midtboen, A.H., & Hexel, O. (Oct 2017). Hiring discrimination against Black Americans hasn't declined in 25 years. Harvard Business Review.

31. https://www.theguardian.com/technology/2016/sep/08/airbnb-discrimination-policy-changes-racial-discrimination

32. U.S. Department of Labor, Bureau of Labor Statistics. (2017). Table 11: Employed persons by detailed occupation, sex, race, and Hispanic or Latino ethnicity. Retrieved from https://www.bls.gov/cps/tables.htm#charemp.

33. Ibid

34. Adams, S. (June 2014). White high school drop-outs are as likely to land jobs as black college students. Forbes. Retrieved from https://www.forbes.com/sites/susanadams/2014/06/27/white-high-school-drop-outs-are-as-likely-to-land-jobs-as-black-college-students/#51715c547b8f

35. Pager, D. (2003). The mark of a criminal record. *American Journal of Sociology, 108* (5): 937-975.

36. Bertrand, M. & Mullainathan, S. (2004). Are Emily and Greg more employable than Lakisha and Jamal? A field experiment on labor market discrimination. *American Economic Review, 94* (4): 991-1013

37. Robinson, C. L., Taylor, T., Tomaskovic-Devey, D., Zimmer, C. & Irwin Jr., M.W. (2005). "Studying race or ethnic and sex segregation at the establishment level: Methodological issues and substantive opportunities using EEO-1 reports." *Work and Occupations 32*(1): 5–38.

38. Kraiger, K., & Ford, J. K. (1985). A Meta-Analysis of Ratee Race Effects in Performance Ratings. *Journal of Applied Psychology, 70*(1), 56-65.

39. Mays, V. M., Coleman, L. M., & Jackson, J. S. (1996). Perceived Race-Based Discrimination, Employment Status, and Job Stress in a National Sample of Black Women: Implications for Health Outcomes. Journal of Occupational Health Psychology, 1(3), 319–329.

40. Lopez, G., Ruiz, N.G., & Patten, E. (2017). Key facts about Asian Americans, a diverse and growing population. Pew Research Center. Retrieved from http://www.pewresearch.org/fact-tank/2017/09/08/key-facts-about-asian-americans/; Flores, A. (Sep 18 2017). How the U.S. Hispanic population is changing. Pew Research Center. Retrieved from http://www.pewresearch.org/fact-tank/2017/09/18/how-the-u-s-hispanic-population-is-changing/ft_17-09-18_hispanics_ushispanicpop/

41. U.S. Bureau of Labor Statistics. (2017). Labor force characteristics by race and ethnicity, 2016. Retrieved from https://www.bls.gov/opub/reports/race-and-ethnicity/2016/home.htm

42. Tafoya, S. (2004). Shades of belonging. Pew Hispanic Center. Retrieved from http://www.pewhispanic.org/2004/12/06/shades-of-belonging/

43. Ibid.

44. Hispanics in the U.S. fast facts. (Mar 31 2017). CNN. Retrieved from https://www.cnn.com/2013/09/20/us/hispanics-in-the-u-s-/index.html

45. Ibid.

46. Liu, E. (May 30 2014). Why are Hispanics identifying as white? CNN.

47. Ibid.

48. Tafoya, S. (2004). Shades of Belonging. Washington D.C.: Pew Hispanic Center. Retrieved from http://pewhispanic.org/files/reports/35.pdf.

49. Taylor, P., Lopex, M.H., Martinez, J., & Velasco. G. (2012). When labels don't fit: Hispanics and their views of identity. Retrieved from http://www.pewhispanic.org/2012/04/04/when-labels-dont-fit-hispanics-and-their-views-of-identity/

50. Flores, A. (Sep 18 2017). How the U.S. Hispanic population is changing. Pew Research Center. Retrieved from http://www.pewresearch.org/fact-tank/2017/09/18/how-the-u-s-hispanic-population-is-changing/ft_17-09-18_hispanics_ushispanicpop/

51. Avery, D.R., McKay, P.F., Wilson, D.C., Tonidandel, S. (2007). Unequal attendance: The relationships between race, organizational diversity cues, and absenteeism. Personnel Psychology, 60: 875-902.

52. Lopez, G., Ruiz, N.G., & Patten, E. (2017). Key facts about Asian Americans, a diverse and growing population. Pew Research Center. Retrieved from http://www.pewresearch.org/fact-tank/2017/09/08/key-facts-about-asian-americans/

53. Ibid.

54. Ibid.

55. Ono, K. A., & Pham, V. N. (2009). Asian Americans and the Media. Cambridge, England: Polity.; Paek, H.J., & Shah, H. (2003). Racial ideology, model minorities, and the 'not so silent partner:" Stereotyping of Asian Americans in U.S. magazine advertising. Howard Journal of Communications, 14(4): 225-244.

56. Hernandez, T.K. (2000). Sexual Harassment and Racial Disparity: The Mutual Construction of Gender and Race. Gender, Race and Justice (4J): 183 -224. Retrieved from http://ir.lawnet.fordham.edu/faculty_scholarship/

12

57. Ibid.

58. Committee of 100: American attitudes toward Chinese Americans and Asian Americans. (2004, Summer). The Diversity Factor, 12(3): 38-44. Retrieved from http://www.committee100.org/publications/survey/ C100survey.pdf

59. Hernandez, T.K. (2000). Sexual Harassment and Racial Disparity: The Mutual Construction of Gender and Race. Gender, Race and Justice (4J): 183 -224. Retrieved from http://ir.lawnet.fordham.edu/faculty_scholarship/ 12

60. Committee of 100: American attitudes toward Chinese Americans and Asian Americans. (2004, Summer). The Diversity Factor, 12(3): 38-44. Retrieved from http://www.committee100.org/publications/survey/ C100survey.pdf

61. Multiracial in America. (June 11 2015) Pew Research Center. Retrieved from http://www.pewsocialtrends.org/2015/06/11/multiracial-in-america/

62. Ibid.

63. Ibid.

64. U.S. Bureau of Labor Statistics. (2017). Labor force characteristics by race and ethnicity, 2016. Retrieved from https://www.bls.gov/opub/reports/race-and-ethnicity/2016/home.htm

65. Ibid.

66. Ibid.

67. Philips, K.W., Rothbard, N.P., & Dumas, T.L. (2009). To disclose or not to disclose? Status distance and self-disclosure in diverse environments. Academy of Management Review, 34(4), 710-732.

68. U.S. Bureau of Labor Statistics. (2017). Labor force characteristics by race and ethnicity, 2016. Retrieved from https://www.bls.gov/opub/reports/race-and-ethnicity/2016/home.htm

69. Alley, D., & Crimmins, E. 2007. The demography of aging and work. In K. S. Shultz & G. A. Adams (Eds.), Aging and work in the 21st century: 7-23. New York: Psychology Press.

70. Cuddy, A. J. C., & Fiske, S. T. (2002). Doddering but dear: Process, content, and function in stereotyping of older persons. In T. D. Nelson (Ed.), Ageism: Stereotyping and prejudice against older persons (pp. 3–26). Cambridge, MA: MIT Press.; Cuddy, A. J. C., Norton, M. I., & Fiske, S. T. (2005). This old stereotype: The pervasiveness and persistence of the elderly stereotype. Journal of Social Issues, 61, 267–285.

71. Desmette, D., & Gaillard, M. (2008). When a "worker" becomes an "older worker": The effects of age-related social identity on attitudes towards retirement and work. Career Development International, 13, 168–185.

72. Ng, T. W., & Feldman, D. C. (2008). The relationship of age to ten dimensions of job performance. Journal of Applied Psychology, 93, 392–423.

73. Bell, M.P., Ozbilgin, M.F., Beauregard, T.A. and Surgevil, O. (2011), "Voice, silence, and diversity in 21st century organizations: strategies for inclusion of gay, lesbian, bisexual, and transgender employees", Human Resource Management, Vol. 50 No. 1, pp. 131-146.

74. Human Rights Campaign. (2018). State maps of laws and policies. Retrieved from http://www.hrc.org/ state-maps/employment

75. Ragins, B.R., Cornwell, J.M. and Miller, J.S. (2003), "Heterosexism in the workplace: do race and gender matter?", Group & Organization Management, Vol. 28, pp. 45-74.

76. Button, S.B. (2001), "Organizational efforts to affirm sexual diversity: a cross-level examination", Journal of Applied Psychology, Vol. 86 No. 1, pp. 17-28.

77. Human Rights Campaign Foundation (2018), "Corporate equality index 2018 ", available at:https://assets2.hrc.org/files/assets/resources/ CEI-2018-FullReport.pdf?_ga=2.120762824.1791108882.1521675202-2105331900.1521675202

78. GLAAD media reference guide (10th ed.). 2016. Los Angeles, CA: Gay and Lesbian Alliance Against

Defamation. Retrieved from http://www.glaad.org/sites/default/files/GLAAD-Media-Reference-Guide-Tenth-Edition.pdf

79. Lamber, J. (2015). The impact of gay-friendly recruitment statements and due process employment on a firm's attractiveness as an employer. Equality, Diversity, and Inclusion: An International Journal, 34 (6): 510-526.

80. Black, D., Gates, G., Sanders, S., & Taylor, L. 2000. Demographics of the gay and lesbian population in the United States: Evidence from available systematic data sources. Demography, 37(2): 139-154.

81. Ragins, B.R., Cornwell, J.M., & Miller, J.S. 2003. Heterosexism in the workplace: Do race and gender matter? Group & Organization Management, 28: 45-74.;Tilcsik, A. (2011), "Pride and prejudice: employment discrimination against openly gay men in the United States", American Journal of Sociology, Vol. 117 No. 2, pp. 586-626.

82. Clair, J.A., Beatty, J.E., & Maclean, T.L. (2005). Out of sight but not out of mind: Managing invisible social identities in the workplace. Academy of Management Review, 30 (1), 78-95.

83. Ibid.

84. Barron, G.L. and Hebl, M. (2013), "The force of law: The effects of sexual orientation anti-discrimination legislation on interpersonal discrimination in employment", Psychology, Public Policy, and Law, Vol. 19 No. 2, pp. 191-205.

85. Button, S.B. (2001), "Organizational efforts to affirm sexual diversity: a cross-level examination", Journal of Applied Psychology, Vol. 86 No. 1, pp. 17-28.

86. Trautwein, C. Apr 7 2017. H-1B Visa applications just hit their limit for the year in less than a week. Time. Retrieved 4/21/2017 from http://time.com/4731665/h1b-visa-application-cap/; U.S. Citizenship and Immigration Services. (2017, Apr 7). USCIS reaches FY 2018 H-1B Cap. Retrieved on 4/21/2017 at https://www.uscis.gov/news/news-releases/uscis-reaches-fy-2018-h-1b-cap

87. U.S. Citizenship and Immigration Services. (2013). Working in the U.S. Retrieved from http://www.uscis.gov/working-united-states/working-us; U.S. Department of State, Bureau of Consular Affairs. (2014). Directory of Visa Categories. Retrieved from http://travel.state.gov/content/visas/english/general/all-visa-categories.html#iv

88. Bureau of Labor Statistics, U.S. Department of Labor. (2016, May 19). Labor force characteristics of foreign-born workers summary. Economic News Release. Retrieved online at https://www.bls.gov/news.release/forbrn.nr0.htm

89. Kandel, W. A. (2011). The US foreign-born population: Trends and selected characteristics. Congressional Research Service Report. Retrieved from http://www.fas.org/sgp/crs/misc/R41592.pdf

90. Bound, J., Demirci, M., Khanna, G., & Turner, S. (2014). Finishing degrees and finding jobs: U.S. higher education and the flow of foreign IT workers (NBER Working Paper No. 20505). Retrieved January 4, 2015, from http://www.nber.org/papers/w20505

91. Avery, D. R., Tonidandel, S., Volpone, S. D., & Raghuram, A. (2010). Overworked in America?: How work hours, immigrant status, and interpersonal justice affect perceived work overload. Journal of Managerial Psychology, 25(2), 133–147.; Bloomekatz, R. (2007). Rethinking immigration status discrimination and exploitation in the low-wage workplace. UCLA Law Review, 54, 1963-2010.

92. Lambert, J.R., Basuil, D.A., Bell, M.P., & Marquardt, D. (2017).Coming to America: Work Visas, International Diversity, and Organizational Attractiveness among Highly Skilled Asian Immigrants. International Journal of Human Resource Management, 1-27.

93. Jamieson, D. (2011). Student guest workers at Hershey plant allege exploitative conditions.Huffington Post. Retrieved from http://www.huffingtonpost.com/2011/08/17/student-guestworkers-at-hershey-plant_n_930014.html.

94. Wigglesworth, V. (2013). Tech giant Infosys settles allegation of visa fraud in Plano office for $34 million. Dallas News. Retrieved from http://www.dallasnews.com/news/community-news/plano/headlines/

20131030-tech-giant-infosys-settles-allegations-of-visa-fraud-in-plano-office-for-34-million.ece?nclick_check=1

95. U.S. Department of Labor. (2012). Key points on Disability and Occupational Projections Tables. Retrieved from https://www.dol.gov/odep/pdf/20141022-KeyPoints.pdf

96. Ibid.

97. U.S. Census Bureau. (2008). Table 75. Self-Described Religious Identification of Adult Population: 1990, 2001 and 2008. Retrieved from https://www2.census.gov/library/publications/2010/compendia/statab/130ed/tables/11s0075.pdf

Diversity and Its Impact on Companies

98. Cox, T.H. & Blake, S. (1991). Managing cultural diversity: Implications for organizational competitiveness. Academy of Management Executive, 5(3): 45-56.

99. Williams, K., & O'Reilly, CA. 1998. Demography and diversity: A review of 40 years of research.In B. Staw and R. Sutton (Eds.), Research in organizational behavior, 20: 77-140. Greenwich, CT: JAI Press.

100. Tsui, A.S., Egan, T. D., & O'Reilly, C.A. 1992. Being different: relational demography and organizational attachment. Administrative Science Quarterly, 37: 549-579.

101. Kim, S.S. & Gelfand, M. J. (2003).The influence of ethnic identity on perceptions of organizational recruitment. Journal of Vocational Behavior, 63: 396- 416.

102. Perkins, L. A., Thomas, K. M., & Taylor, G. A. 2000. Advertising and recruitment: Marketing tominorities. Psychology and Marketing, 17: 235-255.; Thomas, K.M., & Wise, P.G. 1999. Organizational attractiveness and individual differences: Are diverse applicants attracted by different factors? Journal of Business and Psychology,13: 375-390.

103. Janis, I.L. (1972). Victims of groupthink: A psychological study of foreign policy decisions and fiascoes. Boston: Houghton Mifflin Company.

104. Richard, O.C., Barnett, T., Dwyer, S., Chadwick, K. (2004). Cultural diversity in management, firmperformance, and the moderating role of entrepreneurial orientation dimensions. Academy of Management Journal, 47 (2): 255-266.

105. McMahan, G.C., Bell, M.P., & Virick, M. (1998). Strategic human resource management: Employee involvement, diversity, and international issues. Human Resource Management Review, 8 (3): 193-214.

106. Barney, J. (1991). Firm resources and sustained competitive advantage. Journal of Management, 17(1): 99-120.

107. Kauflin, J. (Jan 23 2018). America's best employers for diversity. Forbes. Retrieved from https://www.forbes.com/sites/jeffkauflin/2018/01/23/americas-best-employers-for-diversity/#84f151c71647

108. Graduate Management Admission Council. (Oct 6 2016Where are women in graduate business school? Retrieved from https://www.gmac.com/market-intelligence-and-research/research-insights/application-trends/where-are-women-in-graduate-business-school.aspx

109. Cox, T. H., Lobel, S. A., & McLeod, P. L. (1991). Effects of ethnic group cultural differences on cooperative and competitive behavior on a group task. Academy of management journal, 34(4), 827-847.

110. Richard, O.C., Barnett, T., Dwyer, S., Chadwick, K. (2004). Cultural diversity in management, firm performance, and the moderating role of entrepreneurial orientation dimensions. Academy of Management Journal, 47 (2): 255-266.

111. Dezso, C.L., & Ross, D.G. (2012). Does female representation in top management improve firm performance? A panel data investigation. Strategic Management Journal, 33: 1072-1089.

Challenges of Diversity

112. Tsui, A.S., Egan, T. D., & O'Reilly, C.A. 1992. Being different: relational demography and organizational attachment. Administrative Science Quarterly, 37: 549-579.

113. New York Times. (March 31, 1995). Reverse discrimination complaints rare, labor study reports. Retrieved from https://www.nytimes.com/1995/03/31/us/reverse-discrimination-complaints-rare-labor-study-reports.html

114. Mosbergen, D. (Oct 25 2017). Majority of White Americans believe White people face discrimination. Huff Post. Retrieved from https://www.huffingtonpost.com/entry/white-americans-discrimination-poll-npr_us_59f03071e4b04917c594209a

115. U.S. Equal Employment Opportunity Commission. (2018). About EEOC. Retrieved from https://www.eeoc.gov/eeoc/

116. Discrimination by Type. https://www.eeoc.gov/laws/types/index.cfm (Accessed February 15, 2018); Equal Pay and Compensation Discrimination. https://www.eeoc.gov/laws/types/equalcompensation.cfm (Accessed February 15, 2018)

117. Institute for Women's Policy Research. https://www.iwpr.org (Accessed February 22, 2018)

118. U.S. Equal Employment Opportunity Commission. https://www.eeoc.gov (Accessed February 22, 2018)

119. Harassment. https://www.eeoc.gov/laws/types/harassment.cfm (Accessed February 22, 2018)

120. Age Discrimination. https://www.eeoc.gov/laws/types/age.cfm(Accessed February 22, 2018)

121. ADA at 25. The Law. https://www.eeoc.gov/eeoc/history/ada25th/thelaw.cfm (Accessed November 26, 2017).

122. Disability Discrimination. https://www.eeoc.gov/laws/types/disability.cfm (Accessed February 27, 2018)

123. National Origin Discrimination. https://www.eeoc.gov/laws/types/nationalorigin.cfm (Accessed February 27, 2018)

124. Pregnancy Discrimination. https://www.eeoc.gov/laws/types/pregnancy.cfm (Accessed February 27, 2018)

125. Race/Color Discrimination. https://www.eeoc.gov/laws/types/race_color.cfm (Accessed February 27, 2018)

126. Religious Discrimination. https://www.eeoc.gov/laws/types/religion.cfm (Accessed February 27, 2018)

127. Sex-Based Discrimination. https://www.eeoc.gov/laws/types/sex.cfm (Accessed February 27, 2018)

128. Bell, Myrtle P. Diversity in organizations. Cengage Learning, 2011.

129. King, Eden B., et al. "The stigma of obesity in customer service: A mechanism for remediation and bottom-line consequences of interpersonal discrimination." Journal of Applied Psychology 91.3 (2006): 579.

Key Diversity Theories

130. Miller, C. C., Burke, L. M., & Glick, W. H. 1998. Cognitive diversity among upper-echelon executives: Implications for strategic decision processes. Strategic Management Journal, 19: 39-58.

131. Horwitz, S.K., & Horwitz, I.B. (2007). The effects of team diversity on team outcomes: A meta-analytic review of team demography. Journal of Management, 33 (6): 987-1015.

132. Watson, W.E., Kumar, K., & Michaelsen, L.K. (1993). Cultural diversity's impact on interaction process and performance: Comparing homogeneous and diverse task groups. Academy of Management Journal, 36(3): 590-602.

133. Tsui, A.S., Egan, T. D., & O'Reilly, C.A. 1992. Being different: relational demography and organizational attachment. Administrative Science Quarterly, 37: 549-579.

134. Byrne, D. (1971). The attraction paradigm. New York: Academic Press.

135. Perkins, L. A., Thomas, K. M., & Taylor, G. A. 2000. Advertising and recruitment: Marketing to minorities. Psychology and Marketing, 17: 235-255.; Thomas, K.M., & Wise, P.G. 1999. Organizational attractiveness and individual differences: Are diverse applicants attracted by different factors? Journal of Business and Psychology, 13: 375-390.

136. Lambert, J. R. (2015). The impact of gay-friendly recruitment statements and due process employment on a firm's attractiveness as an employer. Equality, Diversity and Inclusion: An International Journal, 34, 510–526.

137. Lambert, J.R., Basuil, D.A., Bell, M.P., & Marquardt, D. J. (2017). Coming to America: Work visas, international diversity, and organizational attractiveness among highly skilled Asian immigrants. The

International Journal of Human Resource Management, 0, 1-27.

138. Bertrand, Marianne, and Sendhil Mullainathan. "Are Emily and Greg more employable than Lakisha and Jamal? A field experiment on labor market discrimination." *The American Economic Review* 94, no. 4 (2004): 991-1013.

139. Tajfel, H. 1974. Social identity and intergroup behavior. Social Science Information, 15: 1010-118.; Tajfel H, Turner JC. (1985). The social identity theory of intergroup behavior. In S. Worchel, and W.G. Austin (Eds.), Psychology of Intergroup Relations (2nd ed., pp. 7–24). Chicago:Nelson-Hall.

140. Goldberg, Caren B. "Relational demography and similarity-attraction in interview assessments and subsequent offer decisions: are we missing something?." *Group & Organization Management* 30, no. 6 (2005): 597-624.

141. Fiske ST, Taylor SE. (1991). Social cognition (2nd ed.). New York: McGraw-Hill.

142. Crandall, Christian S., and Amy Eshleman. "A justification-suppression model of the expression and experience of prejudice." Psychological bulletin 129.3 (2003): 414.

Benefits and Challenges of Workplace Diversity

143. Ely, Robin J., and David A. Thomas. "Cultural diversity at work: The effects of diversity perspectives on work group processes and outcomes." Administrative science quarterly. 46.2 (2001): 229-273.

144. Ely, Robin J., and David A. Thomas. "Cultural diversity at work: The effects of diversity perspectives on work group processes and outcomes." *Administrative science quarterly.* 46.2 (2001): 229-273.

145. Ely, Robin J., and David A. Thomas. "Cultural diversity at work: The effects of diversity perspectives on work group processes and outcomes." *Administrative science quarterly.* 46.2 (2001): 229-273.

Recommendations for Managing Diversity

146. McCarthy, J.M, Van Iddekinge, C.H., & Campion, M.(2010). Are highly structured job interviews resistant to demographic similarity effects?: *Personnel Psychology, 63*: 325-359.

147. McCarthy, J.M, Van Iddekinge, C.H., & Campion, M.(2010). Are highly structured job interviews resistant to demographic similarity effects?: *Personnel Psychology, 63*: 325-359, p.333.; Campion M.A., Palmer D.K., Campion J.E. (1997). A review of structure in the selection interview. *Personnel Psychology, 50*, 655–702.

148. Young, Cheri A., Badiah Haffejee, and David L. Corsun. "Developing Cultural Intelligence and Empathy Through Diversified Mentoring Relationships." *Journal of Management Education* (2017): 1052562917710687.

149. Thoms, D.A., & Ely, R.J. (Sep 1996). Making differences matter: A new paradigm for managing diversity. Harvard Business Review.

Introduction

1. Louise Axon, Elisa Friedman, and Kathy Jordan. 2015 (July). Leading Now: Critical Capabilities for a Complex World. *Harvard Business Publishing,* (Accessed July 25, 2017) http://www.harvardbusiness.org/leading-now-critical-capabilities-complex-world.

2. K. Labich. 1988 (Oct. 24). The seven keys to business leadership. *Fortune,* 58.

3. W. Bennis. 1989. *Why leaders can't lead.* San Francisco: Jossey-Bass.

The Nature of Leadership

4. B.M. Bass. 1990. *Bass & Stogdill's handbook of leadership: Theory, research, and managerial applications.* New York: The Free Press.

5. W. Bennis. 1989. *Why leaders can't lead.* San Francisco: Jossey-Bass; W. Bennis, & B. Nanus. 1985. *Leaders: The strategies for taking charge.* New York: Harper & Row.

6. T.B. Pickens, Jr. 1992 (Fall/Winter). Pickens on leadership. *Hyatt Magazine,* 21.

7. E.P. Hollander & J.W. Julian. 1969. Contemporary trends in the analysis of leadership process. *Psychological Bulletin* 7(5): 387–397.

8. E.P. Hollander. 1964. Emergent leadership and social influence. In E.P. Hollander (ed.), *Leaders, groups, &*

influence. New York: Oxford University Press.

9. F.E. Fiedler. 1996. Research on leadership selection and training: One view of the future. *Administrative Science Quarterly* 41:241–250.

The Leadership Process
10. Hollander & Julian, 1969.

11. R.M. Stogdill. 1948. Personal factors associated with leadership: A survey of the literature. *Journal of Psychology* 28: 35–71.

12. A.J. Murphy. 1941. A study of the leadership process. *American Sociological Review* 6:674–687.

13. Hollander, 1964.

14. R.J. House & T.R. Mitchell. 1974 (Autumn). Path-goal theory of leadership. *Journal of Contemporary Business* 81–97.

15. G. Yukl. 1971. Toward a behavioral theory of leadership. *Organizational Behavior and Human Performance* 6:414–440.

16. D.G. Gardner & J.L. Pierce. 1998. Self-esteem and self-efficacy within the organizational context. *Group & Organization Management* 23(1):48–70.

17. P. Hersey & K.H. Blanchard. 1988. *Management of organizational behavior utilizing human resources.* Englewood Cliffs, NJ: Prentice-Hall.

18. C.N. Greene. 1975. The reciprocal nature of influence between leader and subordinate. *Journal of Applied Psychology* 60: 187–193.

19. Hollander & Julian, 1969.

20. B.B. Graen & M. Wakabayashi. 1994. Cross-cultural leadership-making: Bridging American and Japanese diversity for team advantage. In M. D. Dunnette (ed.), *Handbook of industrial and organizational psychology,* 4 (2nd ed.): 415–446. Palo Alto: Consulting Psychologists Press.

21. C.A. Schriesheim, S.L. Castro, & F.J. Yammarino. 2000. Investigating contingencies: An examination of the impact of span of supervision and upward controlling on leader-member exchange using traditional and multivariate within- and between-entities analysis. *Journal of Applied Psychology* 85:659–677; A.S. Phillips & A.G. Bedeian. 1994. Leader-follower exchange quality: The role of personality and interpersonal attributes. *Academy of Management Journal* 37:990–1001.

Types of Leaders and Leader Emergence
22. J.A. Conger. 1993. The brave new world of leadership training. *Organizational Dynamics* 21(3):46–59.

23. Pickens, 1992, 21.

24. G.R. Salancik & J. Pfeffer. 1977 (Winter). Who gets power and how they hold on to it: A strategic contingency model of power. *Organizational Dynamics,* 3–21.

25. A.J. Murphy. 1941. A study of the leadership process. *American Sociological Review* 6:674–687.

26. L. Smircich & G. Morgan. 1982. Leadership: The management of meaning. *Journal of Applied Behavioral Science* 18(3): 257–273; Stogdill, 1948.

27. Hollander, 1964.

28. J. R. P. French, Jr. & B. Raven. 1959. The bases of social power. In D. Cartwright (ed.), *Studies in social power.* Ann Arbor, MI: Institute for Social Research, University of Michigan, 150– 167.

29. A. Etzioni. 1961. *A comparative analysis of complex organizations, on power, involvement, and their correlates.* New York: Free Press of Glenco; H. C. Kelman. 1958. Compliance, identification, and internalization: Three processes of attitude change. *Journal of Conflict Resolution,* 51–61.

30. G. Yukl & J. B. Tracey. 1992. Consequences of influence tactics used with subordinates, peers, and the boss. *Journal of Applied Psychology* 77:525–535; T.R. Hinkin & CA. Schriesheim. 1990. Relationships between subordinate perceptions of supervisor influence tactics and attributed bases of supervisory power. *Human Relations* 43:221–237; P.M. Podsakoff & C.A. Schriesheim. 1985. Field studies of French and Raven's bases of power: Critique, reanalysis, and suggestions for future research. *Psychological Bulletin* 97:398–411.

31. T.R. Hinkin & C.A. Schriesheim. 1990. Relationships between subordinate perceptions of supervisor influence tactics and attributed based of supervisory power. *Human Relations* 43:221–237.

32. Bennis, 1989.

33. L. Smircich & G. Morgan. 1982. Leadership: The management of meaning. *Journal of Applied Behavioral Sciences* 18(3): 257–273.

34. R. Tannenbaum & W.H. Schmidt. 1958 (Mar.–Apr.). How to choose a leadership pattern. *Harvard Business Review,* 95–101; R. Tannenbaum & W.H. Schmidt. 1973 (May–June). How to choose a leadership pattern. *Harvard Business Review,* 162–175.

35. K. Davis & J.W. Newstrom. 1985. *Human behavior at work: Organization behavior.* New York: McGraw-Hill.

36. D. McGregor. 1957. The human side of enterprise, *Management Review* 46:22–28, 88–92; D. McGregor. 1960. *The human side of enterprise.* New York: McGraw-Hill.

37. M. Haire, E.E. Ghiselli, & L.W. Porter. 1966. *Managerial thinking: An international study.* New York: Wiley.

38. R.E. Miles. 1975. *Theories of management: Implications for organizational behavior and development.* New York: McGraw-Hill.

39. J.P. Muczyk & B.C. Reimann. 1987. The case for directive leadership. *The Academy of Management Executive* 1:301–311.

40. W. A. Pasmore. 1988. *Designing effective organizations: The sociotechnical systems perspective.* New York: Wiley; T. J. Peters & R.H. Waterman, Jr. 1982. *In search of excellence: Lessons from America's best-run companies.* New York: Harper & Row.

The Trait Approach to Leadership

41. F. A. Kramer. 1992 (Summer). Perspectives on leadership from Homer's Odyssey. *Business and the Contemporary World* 168–173.

42. K. Labich. 1988 (Oct. 24). The seven keys to business leadership. *Fortune,* 58.

43. Stogdill, 1948; R. M. Stogdill. 1974. *Handbook of leadership: A survey of theory and research.* New York: Free Press.

44. Ibid., 81. See also Stogdill, 1948.

45. S.A. Kirkpatrick & E.A. Locke. 1991. Leadership: Do traits matter? *The Executive* 5(2):48–60. E.A. Locke, S. Kirkpatrick, J.K. Wheeler, J. Schneider, K. Niles, H. Goldstein, K. Welsh, & D.-O. Chad. 1991. *The essence of leadership: The four keys to leading successfully.* New York: Lexington.

46. Kirkpatrick & Locke. 1991. The best managers: What it takes. 2000 (Jan. 10). *Business Week,* 158.

47. Locke et al., 1991; T.A. Stewart. 1999 (Oct. 11). Have you got what it takes? *Fortune* 140(7):318–322.

48. W. Mischel. 1973. Toward a cognitive social learning reconceptualization of personality. *Psychological Review* 80:252– 283.

49. R.J. House & R.N. Aditya. 1997. The social scientific study of leadership: Quo vadis? *Journal of Management* 23:409– 473; T.J. Bouchard, Jr., D.T. Lykken, M. McGue, N.L. Segal, & A. Tellegen. 1990. Sources of human psychological differences: The Minnesota study of twins reared apart. *Science* 250:223–228.

50. S. Helgesen. 1990. *The female advantage.* New York: Doubleday/Currency; J. Fierman. 1990 (Dec. 17). Do women manage differently? *Fortune* 122:115–120; J.B. Rosener. 1990 (Nov.–Dec.). Ways women lead. *Harvard Business Review* 68(6): 119–125.

51. J.B. Chapman. 1975. Comparison of male and female leadership styles. *Academy of Management Journal* 18:645–650; E.A. Fagenson 1990. Perceived masculine and feminine attributes examined as a function of individual's sex and level in the organizational power hierarchy: A test of four theoretical perspectives. *Journal of Applied Psychology* 75:204–211.

52. R.L. Kent & S.E. Moss. 1994. Effects of sex and gender role on leader emergence. *Academy of Management Journal* 37: 1335–1346.

53. Ibid.

54. A.H. Early & B.T. Johnson. 1990. Gender and leadership style: A meta-analysis. *Psychological Bulletin* 108:233–256.

55. G.H. Dobbins, W.S. Long, E. Dedrick, & T.C. Clemons. 1990. The role of self-monitoring and gender on leader emergence: A laboratory and field study. *Journal of Management* 16:609–618.

56. B.M. Staw & S.G. Barsade. 1993. Affect and managerial performance: A test of the sadder-but-wiser vs happier-and-smarter hypothesis. *Administrative Science Quarterly* 38:304–331.

57. J.M. George & K. Bellenhausen. 1990. Understanding prosocial behavior, sales performance, and turnover: A group-level analysis in a service context. *Journal of Applied Psychology* 75:698–709.

58. Dobbins et al., 1990.

Behavioral Approaches to Leadership

59. K. Labich, 1988, 58–66.

60. C. Williams. 2017 (June 23). Leadership: Coaching has a Role to Play in Business. *Central Penn Business Journal*. http://www.cpbj.com/article/20170623/CPBJ01/170629935/leadership-coaching-has-role-to-play-in-business

61. J. Anthony. 2017. *This Much We Know.* (Accessed August 4, 2017). https://thismuchweknow.net/2016/09/21/10-ideas-and-concepts-that-describe-me-really-well/

62. E.A. Fleishman. 1953. The description of supervisory behavior. *Personnel Psychology* 37:1–6; E.A. Fleishman & E.F. Harris. 1962. Patterns of leadership behavior related to employee grievances and turnover. *Personnel Psychology* 15:43–56; A. W. Halpin & B. J. Winer. 1957. A factorial study of the leader behavior descriptions. In R.M. Stogdill & A.C. Coons (eds.), *Leader behavior: Its description and measurement.* Columbus: Bureau of Business Research, Ohio State University; J.K. Hemphill & A.E. Coons. 1975. Development of the leader behavior description questionnaire. In R. M. Stogdill & A. E. Coons (eds.), *Leader behavior*; S. Kerr & C. Schriesheim. 1974. Consideration, initiating structure, and organizational criteria—an update of Korman's 1966 review. *Personnel Psychology* 27:555–568.

63. D. Katz & R.L. Kahn. 1952. Some recent findings in human relations research. In E. Swanson, T. Newcomb, & E. Hartley (eds.), *Readings in social psychology,* New York: Holt, Rinehart, & Winston; D. Katz, N. Macoby, & N. Morse. 1950. *Productivity, supervision, and morale in an office situation,* Ann Arbor, MI: Institute for Social Research; F.C. Mann & J. Dent. 1954. The supervisor: Member of two organizational families. *Harvard Business Review* 32:103–112.

64. D. G. Bowers & S. C. Seashore. 1966. Pretesting organizational effectiveness with a four-factor theory of leadership. *Administrative Science Quarterly* 11:238–262; Yukl, 1971; D.A. Nadler, G.D. Jenkins, Jr., C. Cammonn, and E.E. Lawler, III. 1975. *The Michigan organizational assessment package progress report.* Ann Arbor: Institute for Social Research, University of Michigan.

65. Bowers & Seashore, 1966.

66. R.R. Blake & J.S. Mouton. 1964. *The managerial grid.* Houston: Gulf; R.R. Blake & J.S. Mouton. 1981. *The versatile manager: A grid profile,* Homewood, IL: Dow Jones-Irwin; R.R. Blake & J.S. Mouton. 1984. *The new managerial grid III.* Houston: Gulf.

67. R.R. Blake & J.S. Mouton. 1981. Management by grid® principles or situationalism: Which? *Group and Organization Studies* 6:439–455.

68. L. L. Larson, J. G. Hunt, & R. N. Osborn. 1976. The great hi-hi leader behavior myth: A lesson from Occam's razor. *Academy of Management Journal* 19:628–641.

69. D. Tjosvold. 1984. Effects of warmth and directiveness on subordinate performance on a subsequent task. *Journal of Applied Psychology* 69:422–427; A.W. Halpin. 1957. The leader behavior and effectiveness of aircraft commanders. In R.M. Stogdill & A. E. Coons (eds.). *Leader Behavior: Its description and measurement.* Columbus, OH: The Ohio State University, Bureau of Business Research.; E.A. Fleishman & J. Simmons. 1970. Relationship between leadership patterns and effectiveness ratings among Israeli foremen. *Personnel Psychology* 23:169–172.

Situational (Contingency) Approaches to Leadership

70. Stogdill, 1948, 63.

71. House & Aditya, 1997.

72. F.E. Fiedler & M.M. Chemers. 1974. *Leadership and effective management.* Glenview, IL: Scott, Foresman.

73. F.E. Fiedler. 1976. The leadership game: Matching the men to the situation. *Organizational Dynamics,* 4, 9.

74. Personal conversation between Robert J. House and Fred Fiedler in September 1996, as reported in House & Aditya, 1997.

75. F.E. Fiedler. Sept.–Oct. 1965. Engineering the job to fit the manager. *Harvard Business Review,* 115–122.

76. See, for example, the supporting results of M.M. Chemers & G.J. Skrzypek. 1972. Experimental test of the contingency model of leadership effectiveness. *Journal of Personality and Social Psychology* 24:172–177; and the contradictory results of R.P. Vecchio. 1977. An empirical examination of the validity of Fiedler's model of leadership effectiveness. *Organizational Behavior and Human Performance* 19:180–206.

77. R.B. Dunham. 1984. [Interview with Fred E. Fiedler.] *Organizational behavior: People and processes in management.* Homewood, IL: Irwin, 368; J. L. Kennedy, Jr. 1982. Middle LPC leaders and the contingency model of leadership effectiveness. *Organizational Behavior and Human Performance* 30:1–14.

78. Chemens & Skrzpek, 1972; Vecchio, 1977.

79. House & Aditya. 1997; L.H. Peters, D.D. Hartke, & J.T. Pohlman. 1985. Fiedler's contingency model of leadership: An application of the meta-analysis procedure of Schmidt and Hunter. *Psychological Bulletin* 97:274–285.

80. R.J. House. 1971. A path goal theory of leader effectiveness. *Administrative Science Quarterly* 16:324.

81. R. Hoojiberg. 1996. A multidimensional approach toward leadership: An extension of the concept of behavioral complexity. *Human Relations* 49(7):917–946.

82. R.J. House & T.R. Mitchell. 1974 (Autumn). Path-goal theory of leadership, *Journal of Contemporary Business,* 86; R.J. House & G. Dessler. 1974. The path-goal theory of leadership: Some post hoc and a priori tests. In J. Hunt & L. Larson (eds.). *Contingency approaches to leadership.* Carbondale, IL: Southern Illinois University Press.

83. House & Mitchell, 1974; House & Dessler, 1974; R.T. Keller. 1989. A test of the path-goal theory of leadership with need for clarity as a moderator in research and development organizations. *Journal of Applied Psychology* 74:208–212.

84. G. Bristol. 2016. Why Diversity in the Workplace is Imperative. *Entrepreneur,* March 25. (Accessed august 4, 2017) https://www.entrepreneur.com/article/270110

85. J.R. Meindl, S.B. Ehrlich, & J.M. Dukerich. 1985. The romance of leadership. *Administrative Science Quarterly* 30:78–102.

86. C. Robert, T. M. Probst, J. J. Martocchion, F. Drasgow, & J. J. Lawler. 2000. Empowerment and continuous improvement in the United States, Mexico, Poland, and India: Predicting fit on the basis of the dimensions of power distance and individualism. *Journal of Applied Psychology* 85:643–658.

87. P.W. Dorfman & S. Roonen. 1991. *The universality of leadership theories: Challenges and paradoxes.* Paper presented at the Academy of Management Meetings, Miami.

88. P.W. Dorfman, J.P. Howell, S. Hiblino, J.K. Lee, U. Tate, & A. Bautista. 1997. Leadership in Western and Asian countries: Commonalities and differences in effective leadership processes across cultures. *Leadership Quarterly* 8(3):233–274.

Substitutes for and Neutralizers of Leadership

89. P.M. Podsakoff, B.P. Niehoff, S.B. MacKenzie, & M.L. Williams. 1993. Do substitutes for leadership really substitute for leadership: An empirical examination of Kerr and Jermier's situational leadership model.

Organizational Behavior and Human Decision Processes 54:1–44; S. Kerr. 1977. Substitutes for leadership: Some implications for organizational design. *Organization and Administrative Sciences* 8:135–146; S. Kerr & J.M. Jermier. 1978. Substitutes for leadership: Their meaning and measurement. *Organizational Behavior and Human Performance* 22:375– 403; J. P. Howell & P. W. Dorfman. 1981. Substitutes for leadership: Test of a construct. *Academy of Management Journal* 24:714– 728; J.L. Pierce, R.B. Dunham, & L.L. Cummings. 1984. Sources of environmental structuring and participant responses. *Organizational Behavior and Human Performance* 33:214–242.

90. D.G. Gardner, R.B. Dunham, L.L. Cummings, & J.L. Pierce. 1989. Focus of attention at work: Construct definition and empirical validation. *Journal of Occupational Psychology* 62:61–77.

91. D.G. Gardner, R.B. Dunham, L.L. Cummings, & J.L. Pierce. 1987. Focus of attention at work and leader-follower relationships. *Journal of Occupational Behaviour* 8:277–294.

Transformational, Visionary, and Charismatic Leadership

92. G.A. Yukl. 1981. *Leadership in organizations.* Englewood Cliffs, NJ: Prentice-Hall.

93. B. Kellerman. 1984. *Leadership: Multidisciplinary perspectives.* Englewood Cliffs, NJ: Prentice-Hall; F. L. Landy. 1985. *Psychology of work behavior.* Homewood, IL: Dorsey Press.

94. J.M. Burns. 1978. *Leadership.* New York: Harper & Row; B. M. Bass. 1985. *Leadership and performance beyond expectations.* New York: Free Press.

95. R.L. Daft. 2018. *The Leadership Experience* 7th edition. Mason, OH: Cengage Learning.

96. J. R. Baum, E. A. Locke, & S. A. Kirkpatrick. 1998. A longitudinal study of the relation of vision and vision communication to venture growth in entrepreneurial firms. *Journal of Applied Psychology* 83:43–54; J.M. Howell & P.J. Frost. 1989. A laboratory study of charismatic leadership. *Organizational Behavior and Human Decision Processes* 43:243–269.

97. Bennis, 1989.

98. T. A. Judge & J.E. Bono. 2000. Five-factor model of personality and transformational leadership. *Journal of Applied Psychology* 85:751–765.

99. R. Pillai, C.A. Schriesheim, & E.S. Williams. 1999. Fairness perceptions and trust as mediators for transformational and transactional leadership: A two-sample study. *Journal of Management* 25:897–933.

100. C.C. Manz & H.P. Sims, Jr. 1987. Leading workers to lead themselves: The external leadership of self-managed work teams. *Administrative Science Quarterly* 32:106–129.

101. Pillai, Schriesheim, & Williams, 1999.

102. Ibid., 901.

103. S.N. Eisenstadt. 1968. *Max Weber: On charisma and institution building.* Chicago: University of Chicago Press, 46.

104. J.A. Conger & R.N. Kanungo. 1987. Toward a behavioral theory of charismatic leadership in organizational settings. *Academy of Management Review* 12:637–647; Howell & Frost, 1989.

105. R.J. House & M.L. Baetz. 1979. Leadership: Some empirical generalizations and new research directions. *Research in Organizational Behavior* 1:341–423; Conger and Kanungo, 1987.

106. Howell & Frost, 1989.

107. R. J. House. 1977. A 1976 theory of charismatic leadership. In J. G. Hunt & L. L. Larson (eds.). *Leadership: The cutting edge.* Carbondale, IL: Southern Illinois University Press.

108. A. R. Willner. 1984. *The spellbinders: Charismatic political leadership.* New Haven, CT: Yale University Press.

Leadership Needs in the 21st Century

109. Conger, 1993.

110. Ibid.

111. House & Aditya, 1997.

Motivation: Direction and Intensity

1. J.E. Hunter & R.E. Hunter. 1984. Validity and utility of alternative predictors of job performance. *Psychological Bulletin* 96: 72–98.

2. Statistics on the prevalence of this choice are available. "Calling in Well: A Look at leave Time Tracking Trends," *actiTIME* website, June 2016, https://www.actitime.com/human-resources/leave-time-tracking-trends.php.

Content Theories of Motivation

3. H. A. Murray. 1938. *Explorations in personality.* New York: Oxford University Press.

4. Murray also hypothesized that people would differ in the degree to which they felt these needs. His list of secondary needs became a basis for his theory of personality.

5. Representative references include J.W. Atkinson & D.C. McClelland. 1948. The projective expression of needs. II. The effect of different intensities of the hunger drive on thematic apperception. *Journal of Experimental Psychology* 38:643–658; D.C. McClelland, J.W. Atkinson, R.A. Clark, & E.L. Lowell. 1953. *The achievement motive.* New York: Appleton-Century-Crofts; R.C. DeCharms. 1957. Affiliation motivation and productivity in small groups. *Journal of Abnormal Psychology* 55:222– 276; D.C. McClelland. 1961. *The achieving society.* Princeton, NJ: Van Nostrand; and D.C. McClelland. 1975. *Power: The inner experience.* New York: Irvington.

6. In fact, McClelland argued that the success of entire societies is dependent on its achievement needs.

7. D. C. McClelland. 1970. The two faces of power. *Journal of International Affairs* 24:29–47.

8. A.H. Maslow. 1943. A theory of human motivation. *Psychological Bulletin* 50:370–396; A.H. Maslow. 1954. *Motivation and personality.* New York: Harper & Row; A. H. Maslow. 1965. *Eupsychian management.* Homewood, IL: Irwin.

9. D. McGregor. 1960. *The human side of enterprise.* New York: McGraw-Hill; D. McGregor. 1967. *The professional manager.* New York: McGraw-Hill.

10. Maslow, 1943, 382.

11. C.P. Alderfer. 1972. *Existence, relatedness, and growth: Human needs in organizational settings.* New York: Free Press.

12. D.T. Hall & K.E. Nougaim. 1968. An examination of Maslow's need hierarchy in an organizational setting. *Organizational Behavior and Human Performance* 3:12–35; E.E. Lawler, III & J.L. Suttle. 1972. A causal correlational test of the need hierarchy concept. *Organizational Behavior and Human Performance* 7:265–287; M.A. Wahba & L.G. Bridwell. 1973. Maslow reconsidered: A review of research on the need hierarchy theory. *Proceedings of the thirty-third annual meeting of the Academy of Management,* 514–520.

13. C.P. Alderfer. 1972. *Existence, relatedness, and growth: Human needs and organizational settings.* New York: Free Press.

14. Note that Herzberg's theory has often been labeled the "two-factor theory" because it focuses on two continua. This name, however, implies that only two factors are involved, which is not correct. Herzberg prefers not to use the term "two-factor theory" because his two *sets* of needs identify a much larger *number* of needs.

15. F. Herzberg, B. Mausner, & B. Snyderman. 1959. *The motivation to work.* New York: Wiley; F. Herzberg. 1966. *Work and the nature of man.* New York: Crowell; F. Herzberg. 1968. One more time: How do you motivate employees? *Harvard Business Review* 46:54–62.

16. R.B. Dunham, J.L. Pierce, & J.W. Newstrom. 1983. Job context and job content: A conceptual perspective. *Journal of Management* 9:187–202.

17. R.M. Ryan & E.L. Deci. 2000. Self-determination theory and the facilitation of intrinsic motivation, social development, and well-being. *American Psychologist* 55:68–78.

Process Theories of Motivation

18. B.F. Skinner. 1953. *Science and human behavior.* New York: Free Press; B.F. Skinner. 1969. *Contingencies of* *reinforcement.* East Norwalk, CT: Appleton Century-Crofts; B.F. Skinner. 1971. *Beyond freedom and dignity.* New York: Bantam Books.

19. Ibid.

20. R. W. Kempen & R. V. Hall. 1977. Reduction of industrial absenteeism: Results of a behavioral approach. *Journal of Organizational Behavior Management* 20:1–21.

21. J.S. Adams. 1965. Inequity in social exchange. In L. Berkowitz (ed.), *Advances in experimental social psychology* (Vol. 2). New York: Academic Press; G.C. Homans. 1961. *Social behavior: Its elementary forms.* New York: Harcourt, Brace, & World.

22. Ibid.

23. J. Kane & E.E. Lawler, III. 1979. Performance appraisal effectiveness. In B. Staw (ed.), *Research in organizational behavior* (Vol. 1). Greenwood, CT: JAI Press.

24. E.E. Lawler, III. 1972. Secrecy and the need to know. In M. Dunnette, R. House, & H. Tosi (eds.), *Readings in managerial motivation and compensation.* East Lansing: Michigan State University Press.

25. I.R. Andrews. 1967. Wage inequity and job performance: An experimental study. *Journal of Applied Psychology* 51:39–45; J.S. Adams. 1963a. Towards an understanding of inequity. *Journal of Abnormal Social Psychology* 67:422–436; J.S. Adams. 1963b. Wage inequities, productivity and work quality. *Industrial Relations* 3:9–16.

26. R.C. Huseman., J.D. Hatfield, & E.W. Miles. 1987. A new perspective on equity theory: The equity sensitivity construct. *Academy of Management Review* 12:222–234; E.W. Miles, J.D. Hatfield, & R.C. Huseman. 1989. The equity sensitivity construct: Potential implications for worker performance. *Journal of Management* 15:581–588.

27. R.J. Bies. 1987. The predicament of justice: The management of moral outrage. In B.M. Staw & L.L. Cummings (eds.), *Research in organizational behavior* (Vol. 9). Greenwich, CT: JAI Press, 289–319; J. Greenberg. 1987. A taxonomy of organizational justice theories. *Academy of Management Review* 12:9–22.

28. E.L. Locke. 1978. The ubiquity of the technique of goal setting in theories of and approaches to employee motivation. *Academy of Management Review* 3:594–601; F.W. Taylor. 1911. *The principles of scientific management.* New York: Norton; K. Lewin. 1935. *A dynamic theory of personality.* New York: McGraw-Hill; K. Lewin. 1938. *The conceptual representation and the measurement of psychological forces.* Durham, NC: Duke University Press; K. Lewin, T. Dembo, L. Festinger, & P.S. Sears. 1944. Level of aspiration. In J. McVicker Hunt (ed.), *Personality and behavior disorders.* New York: Ronald Press, 333–378; P. Drucker. 1954. *The practice of management.* New York: Wiley; D. McGregor. 1957. An uneasy look at performance appraisal. *Harvard Business Review* 35:89–94; E.A. Locke. 1968. Toward a theory of task motivation and incentives. *Organizational Behavior and Human Performance* 3:157–189; E.A. Locke, K.N. Shaw, L.M. Saari, & G.P. Latham. 1981. Goal setting and task performance: 1969– 1980. *Psychological Bulletin* 90:125–152; G. P. Latham & E.A. Locke. 1984. *Goal setting: A motivational technique that works!* Englewood Cliffs, NJ: Prentice Hall.

29. C.C. Pinder. 1984. *Work motivation: Theory, issues, and applications.* Glenview, IL: Scott, Foresman.

30. Locke, 1979.

31. T.R. Mitchell & W.S. Silver. 1990. Individual and group goals when workers are interdependent: Effects on task strategies and performance. *Journal of Applied Psychology* 75:185–193.

32. A. Bandura. 1977. Self-efficacy: Toward a unifying theory of behavioral change. *Psychological Review* 84:191–215; A. Bandura. 1986b. The explanatory and predictive scope of self- efficacy theory. *Journal of Social and Clinical Psychology* 4:359– 373; A. Bandura. 1997. *Self-efficacy: The exercise of control.* New York: Freeman.

33. D.G. Gardner & J.L. Pierce. 1998. Self-esteem and self-efficacy within the organizational context: An empirical comparison. *Group and Organization Management* 23:48–70.

34. Locke, 1978.

Recent Research on Motivation Theories

35. M.L. Ambrose & C.T. Kulik. 1999. Old friends, new faces: Motivation research in the 1990s. *Journal of Management* 25: 231–292.

36. Chad H. Iddekinge, Herman Aguinis, Jeremy D. Mackey, Philip S. DeOrtentiis, "A Meta-Analysis of the Interactive, additive, and Relative Effects of Cognitive Ability and Motivation on Performance," *Journal of Management*, Vol. 44, No. 1, January, 2018.

Teamwork in the Workplace
1. Katzenbach and Smith, "*The Discipline of Teams*", *Harvard Business Review, July 2005*.
2. Gratton and Erickson, "*Eight Ways to Build Collaborative Teams*", Harvard Business Review, Nov 2007.

Team Development Over Time
3. Bruce Tuckman, "Development Sequence in Small Groups", 1965.

Things to Consider When Managing Teams
4. J.J. Gabarro, The Dynamics of Taking Charge, Harvard Business School Press, 1987, pp. 85-87.
5. Linda A. Hill, "Managing Your Team", Harvard Business Review, 1995.
6. Linda A. Hill, "Exercising Influence", Harvard Business Review, 1994.

Opportunities and Challenges to Team Building
7. Patrick Lencioni, The Five Dysfunctions of a Team, *2002, p. 188.*
8. Capobianco, Davis and Kraus, Managing Conflict Dynamics: A Practical Approach, (2005)

Team Diversity
9. David Rock and Heidi Grant, "*Why Diverse Teams are Smarter*", Harvard Business Review, Nov 2016.
10. Ibid.
11. Lorenzo, Yoigt, Schetelig, Zawadzki, Welpe, Brosi, "The Mix that Matters: Innovation Through Diversity", Boston Consulting Group, April 2017.

Multicultural Teams
12. Brett, Behfar, Kern, "*Managing Multicultural Teams*", Harvard Business Review, 2007.
13. Li and Liao, "*Cultural Competence: Why it Matters and How You Can Acquire It*", IESE Insight, 2015.
14. Earley and Mosakowski, "*Cultural Intelligence*", Harvard Business Review article 2004.

The Process of Managerial Communication
1. C. Shannon and W. Weaver, *The Mathematical Theory of Communication*, University of Illinois Press, 1948.
2. R. E. Quinn, S. R. Faerman, M. P. Thompson, M.R. McGrath, and D. S. Bright, *Becoming a Master Manager*, Sixth edition, Wiley, 2015, Page 48.

Types of Communications in Organizations
3. F. M. Jablin and Linda L. Putnam, *The New Handbook of Organizational Communication*, Sage, 2005.
4. D. L. Worthington and G. D. Bodie, *The Sourcebook of Listening Research: Methodology and Measures*, Wiley, 2018.

Factors Affecting Communications and the Roles of Managers
5. Mintzberg, H. (1973). *The Nature of Managerial Work*. New York: Harper & Row, p. 31.
6. Ibid, p. 166-167.
7. Ibid, p. 167.
8. McGregor, J. (2008). "Bezos: How Frugality Drives Innovation," *BusinessWeek*, April 28, 2008, pp. 64–66.
9. Mintzberg, H. (1990). "The Manager's Job: Folklore and Fact." *Harvard Business Review*, March–April 1990, pp. 166–167.
10. Ibid.
11. Ibid

12. H. Mintzberg, *Mintzberg on Management: Inside our Strange World of Organizations*, Free Press, 2007.

13. Mintzberg, H. (1990). "The Manager's Job: Folklore and Fact." *Harvard Business Review*, March–April 1990, pp. 166–167.

Managerial Communication and Corporate Reputation

14. Drucker, P. F. (1954). *The Practice of Management*. New York: Harper & Row.

15. Eccles, R. G. & Noria, N. (1992). *Beyond the Hype: Rediscovering the Essence of Management*. Boston: The Harvard Business School Press, p. 205.

16. Ibid, p. 211.

17. Ibid, p. 209.

The Major Channels of Management Communication Are Talking, Listening, Reading, and Writing

18. Ziegler, B. (1994). "Video Conference Calls Change Business," *Wall Street Journal*, October 13, 1994, pp. B1, B12.

19. Rankin, P. T. (1952). *The Measurement of the Ability to Understand Spoken Language.* (unpublished Ph.D. dissertation, University of Michigan, 1926). Dissertation Abstracts 12, No. 6 (1952), pp. 847–848; Nichols, R. G. & Stevens, L. (1957). *Are You Listening?* New York: McGraw-Hill; and Wolvin, A. D. & Coakley, C. G. (1982). *Listening.* Dubuque, IA: Wm. C. Brown and Co.; and Werner, E. K. (1975). *A Study of Communication Time.* (M.S. thesis, University of Maryland, College Park)

20. Kotter, J. P. (1999). "What Effective General Managers Really Do," *Harvard Business Review*, March–April 1999, pp. 145–159

21. Berger, P. L. & Luckmann, T. (1966). *The Social Construction of Reality*. New York: Doubleday; and Searle, J. R. (1967). *The Construction of Social Reality*. New York: The Free Press, 1995.

22. Larkin, T. J. & Larkin, S. (1994). *Communicating Change: Winning Employee Support for New Business Goals*. New York: McGraw-Hill.

23. Ibid.

Introduction

1. G.A. Steiner. 1969. *Top management planning.* London: Macmillan, 6–7.

Is Planning Important

2. Prepare for Employees in the Boardroom. 2016 (September 10). *The Telegraph,* http://www.telegraph.co.uk/business/2016/09/10/prepare-for-employee-directors-in-the-boardroom/.

3. H. Koontz & C. O'Donnell. 1972. *Principles of management: An analysis of managerial functions.* New York: McGraw-Hill, 113–114.

4. B.E. Goetz. 1949. *Management planning and control.* New York: McGraw-Hill.

5. Dalton, D. R., Enz, C. A. (1987). Absenteeism in remission: Planning, policy, culture [Electronic version].Human Resource Planning, 10(2), 81-91. Retrieved July 24, 2017, from Cornell University School of Hotel Administration site: http://scholarship.sha.cornell.edu/articles/506.

6. H. Mintzberg. 1975 (July–Aug.). The manager's job: Folklore and fact. *Harvard Business Review,* 51.

7. S.J. Carroll & D.J. Gillen. 1984. The classical management functions: Are they really outdated? *Academy of Management Proceedings* 44:132–136.

8. Williams, 1993.

9. T.A. Mahoney, T.H. Jerdee, & S.J. Carroll, Jr. 1963. *Development of managerial performance: A research approach.* Cincinnati: Southwestern; T.A. Mahoney, T.H. Jerdee, & S.J. Carroll, Jr. 1965. The jobs of management. *California Management Review* 4:97–110; J. A. Hass, A. M. Porat, & J. A. Vaughan. 1969. Actual vs. ideal time allocations reported by managers: A study of managerial behavior. *Personnel Psychology* 22:61–75; R.V. Penfield. 1975. Time allocation patterns and effectiveness of managers. *Personnel Psychology* 27:245–255.

10. Keri Calcagna, "Strong Reputations Help Companies Withstand Crises," *The Wall Street Journal,* January 16,

2018, deloitte.wsj.com/cmo/2018/01/16/strong-reputations-help-companies-withstand-crises/.

The Planning Process
11. P. Lorange & R.V. Vancil. 1977. *Strategic planning systems.* Englewood Cliffs, NJ: Prentice-Hall; Steiner, 1969.

12. K.G. Smith, E.A. Locke, & D. Barry. 1986. *Goal setting, planning effectiveness and organizational performance: An experimental simulation.* Unpublished manuscript, University of Maryland, College of Business and Management, College Park, Maryland.

13. Koontz & O'Donnell, 1972, 124–128.

14. Amy Edmondson, "Strategies for learning from Failure," *Harvard Business Review,* April 2011 Issue, https://hbr.org/2011/04/strategies-for-learning-from-failure.

15. Steiner, 1969, 7; M.B. McCaskey. 1974. A contingency approach to planning: Planning with goals and planning without goals. *Academy of Management Journal* 17:281–291.

16. McCaskey, 1974.

17. Ryan Huang, "Six Sigma Killed Innovation in 3M," *ZD net,* March 14, 2013, www.zdnet.com/article/six-sigma-killed-innovation-in-3m/; and T. J. Peters & R. J. Waterman, Jr. 1982. *In search of excellence: Lessons from America's best-run companies.* New York: Harper & Row.

18. P.C. Earley, P. Wojnarock, & W. Prest. 1987. Task planning and energy expended: An exploration of how goals influence performance. *Journal of Applied Psychology* 47:107–104; P. C. Earley & B. Perry. 1987. Work plan availability and performance: An assessment of task strategy priming on subsequent task completion. *Organizational Behavior and Human Decision Processes,* 39:279–302.

19. Smith, Locke, & Barry, 1986.

20. R.H. Kilman. 1984. *Beyond the quick fix.* San Francisco: Jossey-Bass, 50–51.

Goals or Outcome Statements
21. C. Perrow. 1961. The analysis of goals in complex organizations. *American Sociological Review* 26:854.

22. Richard L. Daft, *Organization Theory and Design,* Boston, MA, Cengage Learning, 2016, P. 54-56.

23. J.D. Thompson & W.J. McEwen. 1958. Organizational goals and environment. *American Sociological Review* 23:23–30.

24. Richard L. Daft, *Organization Theory and Design,* Boston, MA, Cengage Learning, 2016, P. 142-146.

25. P. F. Drucker. 1954. *The practice of management.* New York: Harper.

26. J. Hage. 1965. An axiomatic theory of organizations. *Administrative Science Quarterly* 10:289–320.

27. M.R. Richards. 1978. *Organizational goal structures.* St. Paul, MN: West, 27.

Formal Organizational Planning in Practice
28. J.J. Reitz & L.N. Jewell. 1985. *Managing,* Glenview, IL.: Scott, Foresman, 66.

29. "U.S. Businesses Restructuring Operations to Reap Future Financial Success, Says Intelenet Global Services". *Broadwayworld.com,* July 10, 2017; http://www.broadwayworld.com/bwwgeeks/article/US-Businesses-Restructuring-Operations-to-Reap-Future-Financial-Success-Says-Intelenet-Global-Services-20170710; H. Mintzberg, et al, *Strategy Safari,* Free Press, New York, N.Y., 2013; W. Lindsay & L. Rue. 1980. Impact of the organization environment on the long-range planning process: A contingency view. *Academy of Management Journal* 23:385–404; D. Herold. 1972. Long-range planning and organizational performance: A cross-validation study. *Academy of Management Journal* 15:91–102; C. Saunders & F.D. Tuggle. 1977. *Toward a contingency theory of planning.* Presented at the 37th Annual Meeting of the Academy of Management, Orlando, FL; S.S. Thune & R.J. House. 1970. Where long-range planning pays off. *Business Horizons* 13:81–87.

30. E.H. Bowman. 1976. Strategy and the weather. *Sloan Management Review* 17:53.

31. D.R. Wood & R.L. LaForge. 1979. The impact of comprehensive planning on financial performance. *Academy of Management Journal* 22:516–526.

32. Bill Taylor, "Companies That Do Right by Their Workers Start by Elevating Their Definition of Success," *Harvard Business Review*, January 18, 2018, https://hbr.org/2018/01/companies-that-do-right-by-their-workers-start-by-elevating-their-definition-of-success.

Employees' Responses to Planning

33. E.A. Locke & G.P. Latham. 1990. *A theory of goal setting and task performance.* Englewood Cliffs, NJ: Prentice-Hall; E.A. Locke & G.P. Latham. 1984. *Goal setting: A motivational technique that works!* Englewood Cliffs, NJ: Prentice-Hall.

34. E.A. Locke. 1982. Relation of goal performance with a short work period and multiple goal levels. *Journal of Applied Psychology* 67:512–514; G.P. Latham & J.J. Baaldes. 1975. The practical significance of Locke's theory of goal setting. *Journal of Applied Psychology* 60:187–90; G.P. Latham & E.A. Locke. 1979. Goal setting—A motivational technique that works. *Organizational Dynamics,* 68–80.

35. E.A. Locke, K.N. Shaw, L.M. Saari, & G.P. Latham. 1981. Goal setting and task performance: 1969–1980. *Psychological Bulletin* 90:125–152.

36. Locke, 1982; H. Garland. 1983. Influence of ability-assigned goals, and normative information of personal goals and performance: A challenge to the goal attainability assumption. *Journal of Applied Psychology* 68:20–30; J. R. Hollenbeck & H.J. Klein. 1987. Goal commitment and the goal setting process: Problems, prospects, and proposals for future research. *Journal of Applied Psychology* 72:212–20.

37. Locke, Shaw, Saari, & Latham, 1981.

38. E.A. Locke, G.P. Latham, & M. Erez. 1988. The determinants of goal commitment. *Academy of Management Review* 13: 23–39.

39. Ibid.

40. R.R. Hackman & R. Wageman. 1995. Total quality management: Empirical, conceptual, and practical issues. *Administrative Science Quarterly* 40:309–342; W.E. Deming. 1993. *The new economics for industry, government, education.* Cambridge, MA: MIT Center for Advanced Engineering Study; W.E. Deming. 1986. *Out of the crises.* Cambridge, MA: MIT Center for Advanced Engineering Study.

41. P.W. Wright, J.M. George, S.R. Farnsworth, & G.C. McMahan. 1993. Productivity and extra-role behavior: The effects of goals and incentives on spontaneous helping. *Journal of Applied Psychology* 78:374–381.

42. R.M. Steers. 1977. *Organizational effectiveness: A behavioral view.* Santa Monica, CA: Goodyear, 20–23.

43. Locke & Latham, 1990.

44. K. Lewin. 1958. Psychology of success and failure. In C.L. Stacey and M. F. Demartino, *Understanding human motivation.* Cleveland: Allen.

45. Locke & Latham, 1990.

46. Deming, 1986.

47. Jay A. Conger. 1991 (Feb.). Inspiring others: The language of leadership. *Academy of Management Executive* 5(1):31–45.

48. See the following article for the findings from this work schedule change: J.L. Pierce & R.B. Dunham. 1992. The 12-hour work day: A 48-hour, 8-day week. *Academy of Management Journal* 35:1086–1098.

49. W.H. Newman. 1975. *Constructive control.* Englewood Cliffs, N. J.: Prentice Hall, 6.

50. W.H. Newman. 1984. Managerial control. In J.E. Rosenzweig & F. E. Kast (eds.), *Modules in management series.* Chicago: Science Research Associates, 1-42; W.H. Newman, J.R. Logan, & W.H. Hegarty. 1985. *Strategy, policy, and central management.* Cincinnati: Southwestern; W.H. Sihler. 1979. Toward better management control systems. *California Management Review,* 14:33–39; E.P. Strong & R.D. Smith. 1968. *Management control models.* New York: Holt, Rinehart & Winston.

51. M.S. Taylor, C.D. Fisher, & D.R. Ilgen. 1984. Individuals' reactions to performance feedback in organizations: A control theory perspective. In K. M. Rowland & G. R. Ferris (eds.), *Research in Personnel and Human Resources Management.* Greenwich, CT: JAI Press, 81–124.

52. E.A. Locke & G.P. Latham. 1984. *Goal setting: A motivational technique that works.* Englewood Cliffs, NJ: Prentice-Hall.

53. Interview with Steven Kerr appearing in R.D. Dunham 1984. *Organizational behavior: People and processes in management.* Homewood, IL: Irwin, 147; S. Kerr. 1987. On the folly of rewarding A, while hoping for B. *Academy of Management Journal* 18: 769–783.

54. D.B. Greenberger, S. Strasser, L.L. Cummings, & R.B. Dunham. 1989. The impact of personal control on performance and satisfaction. *Organizational Behavior and Human Decision Processes* 43:31; D.B. Greenberger & S. Strasser. 1986. Development and application of a model of personal control in organizations. *Academy of Management Review* 11:164.

55. Greenberger, Strasser, Cummings, & Dunham, 1989.

56. S.M. Miller. 1977. Controllability and human stress: Method, evidence and behavior. *Research and Therapy,* 171, 287– 304; M.E.P. Seligman. 1975. *Helplessness: On depression, development and death.* New York: Freeman.

57. Greenberger & Strasser, 1986, 174.

58. Floyd Brown and Mary Beth Brown, "Learned helplessness and the problems of American business: The Browns," *The Jersey Journal,* August 11, 2012, www.nj.com/hudson/voices/index.ssf/2012/08/ learned_helplessness_and_the_p.html; J.B. Ovmier & M.E.P. Seligman. 1967. Effects of inescapable shock upon subsequent escape and avoidance learning. *Journal of Comparative and Physiological Psychology* 63:28–33; M.J. Martinko & W. L. Gardner. 1982. Learned helplessness: An alternate explanation for performance deficits. *Academy of Management Journal* 7:195–204.

59. M.H. Bazerman. 1982. Impact of personal control on performance: Is added control always beneficial? *Journal of Applied Psychology* 67:472–479.

Management by Objectives: A Planning and Control Technique

60. P. Drucker, 1954; A.P. Raia. 1974. *Managing by objectives.* Glenview, IL: Scott, Foresman; R.G. Greenwood. 1981. Management by objectives: As developed by Peter Drucker, assisted by Harold Smiddy. *Academy of Management Review* 6:225–230.

61. G.S. Odiorne. 1979. *M.B.O. II.* Belmont, CA: Fearon.

62. R. Rodgers & J.E. Hunter. 1991. Impact of management by objectives on organizational productivity. *Journal of Applied Psychology Monograph* 76:322–336.

63. Ibid.

64. R.W. Hollmann. 1976. Applying MBO research to practice. *Human Resource Management* 15(4):28–36; J.M. Ivancevich, J.H. Donnelly, & J.M. Gibson. 1976. Evaluating MBO: The challenge ahead.

65. J.C. Aplin & P. P. Schoderbek. 1976. MBO: Requisites for success in the public sector. *Human Resource Management* 15(2): 30–36.

66. J.N. Kondrasuk. 1981. Studies in MBO effectiveness. *Academy of Management Review* 6:419–30.

67. E.E. Lawler, III. 1986. *High-involvement management.* San Francisco: Jossey-Bass; E. E. Lawler, III. 1992. *The ultimate advantage: Creating high involvement organizations.* San Francisco: Jossey-Bass.

MTI—Its Importance Now and In the Future

1. Brockhoff, K (2017). "The emergence of technology and innovation." *Technology and Innovation* Vol 19. Pp. 461-480.

2. United Nations Commission for Europe, editors. Promoting innovation in the service sector: Review of experiences and policies. New York: United Nations; 2011.

3. Conley, JG, Bican PM, Ernst H. (2013) "Value articulation: A framework for the strategic management of intellectual property." *California Management Review.* 55(4). Pp. 102-120.

Developing Technology and Innovation

4. Teece D., Peterar M., Leih, S. (2016) "Dynamic capabilities and organizational agility: Risk, uncertainty, and strategy in the innovation economy" *California Management Review*. 58(4). Pp. 13-35.

Management Entrepreneurship Skills for Technology and Innovation

5. Ries, E (2011). *The Lean Startup: How Today's Entrepreneurs Use Continuous Innovation to Create Radically Successful Businesses* (New York, NY: Crown Business).

6. Teece, D et al. (2016) *op cit.*

Skills Needed for MTI

7. Misa, Thomas J. (1999) *A Nation of Steel: The Making of Modern America, 1865–1925*. Johns Hopkins studies in the history of technology. (Baltimore, Md.: The Johns Hopkins University Press).

Managing Now for Future Technology and Innovation

8. Stoll, John D., "Why the Gas Station Isn't a Model for Electric Cars,' Wall Street Journal, August 13, 2017, http://www.businessinnovationbrief.com/exercises/technology/?open-article-id=7217183&article-title=4-strategic-thinking-exercises-to-envision-future-strategy&blog-domain=brainzooming.com&blog-title=brainzooming.

Index